THE VILLAGE OF BERNADETTE

THE IRISH CONNECTION

LOURDES
STORIES, MIRACLES & CURES

COLM KEANE & UNA O'HAGAN

CAPEL
ISLAND

First published in Ireland in 2019

by

CAPEL ISLAND PRESS
Baile na nGall,
Ring, Dungarvan,
County Waterford,
Ireland

ISBN 978-1-9995920-1-1

Printed and bound in Great Britain by Clays Ltd, Elcograf S.p.A.
Typesetting and cover design by Typeform Ltd

For Seán

Colm Keane has published 28 books, including eight No.1 bestsellers, among them *The Little Flower: St. Thérèse of Lisieux, Padre Pio: Irish Encounters with the Saint, Going Home, We'll Meet Again* and *Heading for the Light.* He is a graduate of Trinity College, Dublin, and Georgetown University, Washington DC. As a broadcaster, he won a Jacob's Award and a Glaxo Fellowship for European Science Writers.

Una O'Hagan is a No.1 bestselling author and former news-reader with Radio Telefís Éireann. A DIT journalism graduate, she has interviewed Nelson Mandela, accompanied President Mary Robinson on a state visit to Australia and hosted live programmes on the deaths of former Taoisigh Jack Lynch and Garret FitzGerald and the state visit of Queen Elizabeth II to Ireland. This is her third book.

CONTENTS

When you have seen her once, you would willingly die to see her again.

Bernadette of Lourdes (1844 – 1879)

INTRODUCTION

In August 1968, a Dublin woman named Annie emerged from the baths at Lourdes and walked for the first time in two years. Just days earlier, she was dying from cancer and had arrived at the shrine on a stretcher. The disease had first attacked her thyroid gland and then spread to her right arm, which required amputation. When the cancer travelled to her spine, she received the Last Sacraments. In desperation, she went to Lourdes in search of a cure.

A few days prior to her departure, a doctor had stated: "She will go to Lourdes, but she will hardly come back." He had good reason to say so. The 25-year-old woman was in severe pain, her left leg was paralysed, and she was confined to bed. She had to be ferried by ambulance to the airport and lifted on board the plane. On the journey home, things were different. Following immersion in the baths, she could walk perfectly well. In short, she was cured. Her consultant "couldn't believe it," she said, "and he was the doctor who had no hope for me at all."

At the heart of Annie's story is a town in south-west France which, in itself, is of no great significance or importance. The population of Lourdes is small; its industrial profile negligible; its geographic location remote. "Prior to its one great awakening it was even off the highways of France, hidden under the shadows of the Pyrenees, grouped straggly about its little swift-flowing, glacier-fed Gave, and the home of the very poor, simple and good," Msgr. John Walsh, an Irish cleric and author, wrote in 1918.

Extraordinary events in 1858 changed all that. On a cold, dark February day, a 14-year-old girl, named Bernadette Soubirous, left her home in search of firewood. Accompanied by her sister and her sister's friend, she headed for a rocky outcrop known as Massabielle. There, she became separated from her companions. Attracted by the sound of rushing wind, she looked towards a niche in the Massabielle grotto, where she saw a soft light and a white figure. Bernadette later described the figure as a beautiful lady who would, in time, proclaim herself to be the Immaculate Conception.

A total of 18 visions took place, spread over more than five months. Details of the conversations between Bernadette and the lady spread like wildfire and captured the public's imagination. It was revealed that the lady had smiled at Bernadette, prayed with her, taught her a special prayer, disclosed secrets – which were never publicly divulged – helped identify a previously-unknown spring, asked that a chapel be built at the site, and declared who she was. She also told Bernadette that she did not promise to make her happy in this world, but in the next.

Huge crowds arrived to witness the events. The author Rose Lynch, from Cork, who lived for six months in Lourdes and who met many witnesses, described one such scene: "The lower space in front of the grotto was one mass of people. On the ledges of the rock, hundreds of feet from the ground, groups of men were to be seen risking their lives without a thought of danger. The trees along the river bank swayed beneath the living freight of human beings, while, on the other side of the river, the fields were black with people."

Within weeks of the initial vision, miracles were being reported – the first involving the restoration of power to a woman's hand, another involving the revival of a young boy who was dying.

Both of them followed immersion in the newly-located spring. Thousands of miracles ensued. Within 50 years, almost 4,000 cures were recorded, involving recoveries from tuberculosis (TB), paralysis, tumours, abscesses, necrosis, blindness, stomach ulcers, lupus and many other illnesses and diseases. Although only 70 cures would, in time, be formally recognised by the Catholic Church, the reputation of Lourdes as a source of miraculous revivals was copper-fastened.

None of this would have happened without the little peasant girl, from a poverty-stricken background, named Bernadette Soubirous. She was sweet, pleasing and attractive, according to the French author Henri Lasserre who, during Bernadette's lifetime, became her unofficial biographer. Lasserre particularly noted her brown eyes. They possessed "a calm and profound beauty," he said. Her hair was "black and soft." Her childish features were tanned by the sun. Physically, she was short for her age and cut a sad sight in her worn-out, patched black dress.

She hadn't always been poor. Her father had once run a mill, where the family lived surrounded by the sound of millstones grinding grain. Bernadette grew up there in relative prosperity. Unfortunately, her happy childhood was curtailed when the business failed. A combination of mismanagement and too much generosity in business dealings led to the mill's rapid decline. Her parents ended up on the scrapheap, taking any casual work they could find and living in a hovel with their four starving children.

Due to a lack of schooling, caused by circumstances at home, Bernadette initially could not read or write. This changed following the apparitions, when she attended school. "Though never an intellectual, her standard of education was well above the average, her spelling quite good, her penmanship finally elegant," her

Irish biographer Msgr. Joseph Deery wrote in 1958. As she got older, he said, she was also noted for her "soundness of judgement and for common-sense, allied to a practical turn of mind and a well-balanced sense of order."

Away from the grotto, while still only 14 years old, Bernadette became famous, a bit like a modern-day superstar. Although she detested the limelight, thousands came to visit her. They included senior churchmen, writers, lawyers, townsfolk, and even a relative of the Pope. Queues formed outside her house. "You would think," the police commissioner remarked, "that no one wants to leave Lourdes without having had a close view of her."

Everyone wanted to touch her, embrace her, ask her for an autograph or have their rosaries blessed. "I am not a priest!" she would say when asked for a blessing. Instead, she would touch their beads with the ones she used during the apparitions, and that made them happy. One bishop asked for her priceless beads, offering his in exchange, but she refused. The Pope's relative requested her rosary for the Pontiff, but again she refused. He settled on an autograph instead.

Her face was known everywhere due to the recent introduction of photography. She hated posing for the camera, calling it a "trial." "No, that's not right! That's not the expression you had when the Virgin was there," her first photographer exclaimed, trying to capture the mood. "Well, it's because she isn't here!" Bernadette replied, in her direct way. She disapproved of the sale of the images, which sold far and wide. The downside was that, just like a modern celebrity, she couldn't go anywhere without being recognised.

She was also proud. When she became famous, well-wishers would offer her money. The offers were always turned down, no matter how kind the intention. One gentleman placed a small fortune on the household table, pointing out that he was rich and wanted to help. Bernadette refused, saying, "I desire nothing, Monsieur, take that back." He persisted, arguing, "It is not for you, my child, it is for your parents." Both parents, who were watching, interrupted and said: "Neither Bernadette nor we desire anything." The offer was graciously declined.

She always appeared to be telling the truth. No amount of interrogations or investigations – and there were many – could break her. She was quizzed at length by the imperial prosecutor, the inspector of police, members of an ecclesiastical commission of inquiry, bishops, judges, doctors, lawyers and journalists, yet she never changed her story. Even when threatened with prison or "hell fire," she remained resolute and unmoved.

Her facts were consistent, her details unwavering, her sincerity recognised even by sceptics and detractors. "No one could see her or hear her speak without being convinced of her good faith," Henri Lasserre remarked. "All those who saw her and conversed with her were entirely convinced of her veracity, and fully persuaded that something very extraordinary had taken place at the Rocks of Massabielle."

The last apparition at the Massabielle grotto took place on 16 July, after which the significance of Bernadette in the story of Lourdes faded away. Her work was done; the shrine and devotion to Our Lady took over. She continued to live in the town for the next eight years, where most of her time was spent as a boarder with the local Sisters of Charity, who protected her from unwanted visitors and sightseers. Eventually, at the age of 22, she moved to the motherhouse of the Sisters of Charity, in Nevers, and became a nun. She never saw Lourdes again.

Meanwhile, the number of pilgrims journeying to Lourdes grew exponentially. They were drawn there out of curiosity, as an act of faith or in search of cures through the intercession of Our Lady. The Irish were quick to join them. One of the earliest Irish pilgrims was a County Waterford-born priest, who met Bernadette on many occasions. He was soon followed by other Irish Catholics, acting on their own or as part of organised pilgrimages. Their journeys were long, tiring and arduous, given the travel conditions of the time.

"Leaving Clonmel, I took a steamer at Waterford, for Milford, and thence went by train through London, to Newhaven," an Irish pilgrim reported in 1877. "Arriving by steamer at Dieppe, I went by train to Paris, and, after some hours delay in the capital, I started for Toulouse, where I arrived, after a journey of twenty-six hours. I was now on my direct route to Lourdes, which is some twelve hours' drive from Toulouse. Knowing only two words – *Anglais, Irlandais* – of French, I was rather un-easy."

That sense of unease diminished after 1947, when the first Irish charter flight took off for Lourdes from Dublin. It wasn't the first formal pilgrimage from Ireland by air – that would take place a few years later. Instead, it consisted of a party of five people from Waterford – one of them an invalid – who had chartered a small Aer Rianta Consul aircraft for a visit to the shrine. Soon, fleets of DC-3s, Viscounts and, eventually, Jumbo jets – all in the colours of Aer Lingus – were ferrying thousands of Irish people each year to the little town in south-west France.

"Going to Lourdes is no longer a penitential exercise," an Irish visitor remarked in the 1970s. "Arrival by night is normal so that you wake up in the morning without the gradual easing into a new environment which the train offered to the last generation.

6

Not only that, but couriers await you at the airport, eliminating any difficulties which might arise." There were more changes, though – the storytelling associated with long journeys was gone; fasting was gone, too, as airline meals were provided *en route*; while duty-free goods could be bought "when one should be thinking of other things," the pilgrim drily remarked.

In the following decades, Lourdes became one of the most visited shrines on earth. The statistics are breathtaking. One million pilgrims arrived in 1908 for the 50th anniversary of the apparitions; that number rose to nine million for the 150th anniversary in 2008. Lourdes now attracts more pilgrims than Mecca; the town is second only to Paris in its stock of hotels; more candles are consumed there than in any other town in the world. Pro rata, greater Dublin would need to attract more than a billion tourists each year to match the annual number of visitors to Lourdes.

Yet, statistics tell only the tiniest part of the Lourdes story. They miss the heart of what it's about. The well-regarded Irish novelist and short story writer, John D. Sheridan, put it well in the 1950s: "The most moving experience of all is the blessing of the sick when they are lined up in their wheelchairs and wait for the Blessed Sacrament to pass. It is like an investiture, a bestowing of awards. The sick are seen in their real stature, and the rest of us are merely spectators. For these are the chosen ones who have been singled out to carry the world's burdens and they are very dear to God."

Lourdes is also a place of intense kindness. "I keep seeing all sorts of little things that moved me so much," the eminent English journalist, Malcolm Muggeridge, commented after making a TV documentary at the shrine. "You see a woman with a hopelessly sick child, and she's trying to steer that child to the front so that, as the procession of the host goes by, he would be near. You may say it's hopeless, it's not going to make him any better, and I don't suppose it did. But the eagerness with which she did it, the tenderness with which she did it, in itself was a sort of miracle."

The shrine, furthermore, is a source of great serenity. Almost all visitors comment on it. "Immediately you enter the place a sense of peace descends upon you," an Irish pilgrim remarked in the 1940s. "You feel as if you were in an entirely new world. You never want to leave the place, nor do you feel in any way lonely for your friends and relations..... you are happy and want for nothing in the sense of fulfilment."

Perhaps the final words should be left to Cork author, Rose Lynch, who visited the shrine on numerous occasions, including as part of the famous 1913 Irish National Pilgrimage. "I never met a man, woman, or child who did not love Lourdes, who did not want to prolong his or her visit there," she wrote. "I have seen strong men's lips quiver, their eyes fill with tears, as they took their last look at Lourdes; one and all hope on leaving they may live to come again." Those comments, if nothing more, illustrate the enduring power of Lourdes.

BERNADETTE

Bernadette was an unflappable, headstrong young girl. She could battle with her toughest interrogators. On one occasion, she was interviewed by a Jesuit who clearly disbelieved her account of the apparitions. Tiring of the man's line of questioning, she turned to her companion and said, "He doesn't wish to believe. Let's get out of here." And she did!

On another occasion, at school, she was ridiculed by a nun about the ongoing apparitions. "Ah! You have not yet finished with your carnival?" the nun said. "No, my dear Sister, not yet," the 14-year-old curtly replied. Her response astonished the other schoolchildren. "We were very pleased," one of them later said, "for we heartily detested Sr. Anastasie."

All those characteristics – confidence, self-belief, obstinacy, impatience and an unwillingness to be pushed around – allied to honesty, kindness, humility and a sense of fun, stood to Bernadette during her teenage years, starting at the age of 13.

When she was aged 13, Bernadette and her family were forced to live in a foul, squalid hovel in Lourdes. Their fall from grace followed the collapse of her father's business.

Bernadette's family home at 15 Rue des Petits Fossés was the nastiest slum dwelling in Lourdes. In truth, it wasn't really a dwelling – it was a hovel. A one-roomed cesspit, it was dark, dank and infested with lice. The walls sweated condensation. There was mildew in the corners and in the cracks. It smelled of manure. This wretched basement, measuring roughly four yards by five, became home to Bernadette, her parents, sister and two brothers in 1857.

The property – if it could be called that – was known as "le cachot", which translates from the French as "the dungeon". A former gaol, it was owned by a cousin of Bernadette's mother, who was renting it to them for free. In winter, it was freezing cold. In summer, it was boiling hot. There was a dung heap in the backyard. No one wanted to rent it. In retrospect, it is hard to believe that Bernadette's parents had begged the cousin to allow them to live there; the alternative was the streets.

The family possessed almost nothing when they moved in. They were destitute. Most of their belongings had either been seized or sold off to buy food. They had some bedding, a few old chairs, a broken-legged table and a trunk for their linen. Their wedding wardrobe – a cherished possession – had been pawned. At one time, they had lived in the Boly Mill, where life had been good and times had been different, but their dreams had long since collapsed and they were now reduced to this.

The family were desperate for money. The father took odd jobs as a labourer. Bernadette and her sister supplemented the family's meagre income by collecting rags, scrap metal and old bones, which they exchanged for money. The family foraged in the nearby forest for firewood, which would lead to a strange meeting with a most mysterious lady later on. Matters weren't helped by Bernadette's asthma, which she had suffered from since childhood. She wheezed and had a bad chest, which was exacerbated by her living conditions.

The family were constantly hungry. How bad the problem was is evident in the following story. Although Bernadette kept an eye on her six-year-old brother, Jean-Marie, he would sometimes disappear. No one knew where he went. It later emerged that he was searching for food. A woman, Mademoiselle Estrade, spotted him one day in the parish church, where she was praying. She noticed how emaciated he was, how undernourished he looked. Having returned to her prayers, he continued to make noise behind her.

She turned around. "I watched him closely and noticed that he was bending down and scraping the flagstones and then putting his hand to his mouth," the woman recalled. "He was actually eating the wax which had fallen from the candles during a funeral service." She brought him to her home and, from then on, she fed him. He refused to go inside her apartment, instead sitting on the staircase, which he used as a table and where he would devour his food.

The hapless Jean-Marie was also too young and too innocent to understand the family's rules about accepting money from strangers or, indeed, from anyone. One day, he thought he had got lucky. He rushed home with two francs in his hand, saying he had brought some wealthy people to the grotto, drawn water for them, and this was his reward. He was clearly delighted. Bernadette was outraged and ordered him to give back the money. He did so, and she searched him on his return, just to be sure.

Given her role as second mother in the family, Bernadette's schooling suffered and she received little or no education. Matters weren't helped by her parents' dire circumstances and the chaos that reigned at home. She learned to knit, sew and do patchwork, and she had a talent for dressmaking. But when it came to the skills of the classroom, she was out of her depth.

She had one ambition, and that was to receive her First Holy Communion. It was not only an important landmark of her Catholic faith, but it was seen as a rite of passage in her day – the moment when you finally left childhood and became an adult. Now that she was 13 years of age, the time had come to pursue her goal. There was a ceremony planned for the following summer – the summer of 1858 – and that was her target. Unfortunately, there was a long road to travel before that would take place.

In the autumn of 1857, Bernadette was forced to work as a shepherdess and domestic help. She was obliged to do so as her parents could no longer afford to feed her.

The road from Lourdes to Bartrès winds its way through the countryside along the foothills of the Pyrenees. It was once a lonely, narrow country road, lined by trees and fields. The most you could expect to meet was a farm worker walking home, shepherds with their sheep, or a farmer's wife bringing produce into town. Otherwise, you were on your own, left with your thoughts, listening to the silent whispers of God.

It was along this quiet country road that Bernadette walked in September 1857. At the age of 13, she was heading to her first job, the lowly unpaid position of shepherdess and domestic help. Her destination was the village of Bartrès, nestled in the hills, little more than two miles from the town of Lourdes. There, her mistress would be Marie Lagües, who had wet-nursed Bernadette as a little child. A devout woman, she was known to be cold and mean. The prospects of working for her hardly warmed the young girl's heart.

The deal was simple – the Lagües needed someone to care for their sheep and five children, especially their two-year-old son, while Bernadette's parents could no longer afford to feed their growing child. Bernadette would live with the family in their home located at the village edge. There would be no wages, just food and keep, and the promise of catechism lessons in preparation for the girl's First Holy Communion the following summer back in Lourdes.

Each morning, Bernadette looked after the children, helped clean the house, and then departed for the nearby stable to collect her lambs. Delighted by her arrival, they would rush to her and gather around. Together, they would head for the fields and rolling hills. There, in the company of her Pyrenean sheepdog, Pigou, she cared for them and made sure they were safe.

On warm days, the sun blazed down. On frosty days, her breath froze. In stormy weather, clouds swept down from the Pyrenees, driving her into the little thatched shelter where she and her flock would hide from the weather. Loud, frightening peals of thunder rolled along the hills, while brilliant flashes of lightning illuminated the sky. Rain poured down in torrents, emptying the clouds into the exposed fields.

Bernadette loved her little lambs. There was one she liked most of all – small, beautiful, pure white, perhaps the youngest in the flock. "Why do you like that one more than the others?" a friend asked. "Because it's the smallest," she answered. "I love everything that's small." The lamb liked Bernadette, too, and would come to her looking to be caressed.

The little lamb pestered Bernadette and loved playing tricks. When she turned her back on him, he would butt her from behind. Her knees would bend and she would fall. She loved to build little altars, as many shepherds did back then. The lamb would butt them, too, and knock them over. The more he did so, the more she liked him. The memory of that adorable lamb stayed with her up to the time she died.

She also worried about her sheep and cared for them dearly. "Why are you so upset?" her father once asked, having come to visit. "It's my sheep," she said, pointing to their backs. Her father looked and noticed large green marks printed on their curly coats. Although knowing it was a dealer's marks, and obviously applied the night before, he jokingly replied: "They are green because they have eaten too much grass." "Could they die?" Bernadette asked, deeply worried. "They could," he answered, sending the child into floods of tears.

"Don't be worried," her father reassured her, "it's merely a dealer's marks." In time, Bernadette told this story to a friend, who said: "How could you have been so innocent? Why did you believe him?" "I have never lied," Bernadette replied, "so why should I believe my father would tell me anything but the truth!"

The months passed by – five long, lonely months stretching from the autumn through the short, dark, lamp-lit days of winter. Bernadette yearned for home. Her food was poor, the work tough, the hours long; the promise of proper catechism lessons sadly forgotten. Marie Lagües tried her best at tuition, but she was no teacher and Bernadette was always tired. She made up her mind – she was going home.

She sent messages to her parents, asking them to collect her. She sent one message through her godmother, who had come to see her. She passed on another through a woman she met while working in the fields. She tried again through a servant girl, who was travelling into town. Her parents never replied. Tired, weary, lonely, and worried about her forthcoming First

Holy Communion, she finally retraced the steps she had taken the previous September and, on 21 January 1858, she headed home alone.

Just three weeks after arriving home, Bernadette saw her first apparition at the grotto in Lourdes. The event took place on 11 February 1858.

It was the sound of the wind that first captured the attention of Bernadette. It was coming from somewhere close by. The sudden gust stood out, at odds with the weather that day. She looked towards the trees near the river, but they weren't moving. She heard the sound again. It was like a rushing wind. This time, she looked the other way, towards a niche in the rocky outcrop situated nearby. The niche was like a small cave.

It was close to midday and Bernadette was alone. As she stared at the cave, she noticed a wild rose bush set in its opening. A branch of the rose bush was moving. There was a soft light behind it, neither dazzling nor blinding. Something else was there, too. In the alcove was a white figure, with the appearance of a lady. The story of that "beautiful" lady, as Bernadette later described her, would transform Marian devotion and the lives of millions in the years ahead.

Another busy day had dawned at Bernadette's home earlier that morning. The weather was cold, as it often is in Lourdes at that time of year. The family urgently needed firewood. Three children set out to collect it – Bernadette, her sister Toinette, and a classmate of Toinette named Jeanne Abadie. Because of her asthma and the weather, Bernadette's mother didn't want her to go. After agreeing to wear a cape and stockings with her sabots

– shoes carved from blocks of wood – her mother eventually gave her the go-ahead.

The three girls arrived at a location known as the grotto of Massabielle. Half a mile west of Lourdes, it was unknown to the three foragers arriving that day. Confronted by a stream, Toinette and Jeanne took off their sabots and waded through the water, which was bitterly cold. Bernadette wavered, trying to think of a better way to cross. Eventually, she gave up and began removing her stockings. By this stage, her two companions were out of sight. She was all alone. That's when she heard the wind and gazed at the grotto.

Standing there was a "lady in white," Bernadette later said. She was wearing a long, white gown which extended to her feet. She also wore a blue sash, which was tied around her waist and hung down below her knees. On her head was a white veil. Her feet were bare. On each foot was a yellow rose. On her right arm hung a rosary made of white beads, joined together by a chain of brightest gold. The gold of the chain shone like the roses on her feet.

Bernadette was afraid. She stepped back. She wanted to call the others but was too frightened to do so. "I rubbed my eyes again and again. I thought I must be mistaken," she said. Raising her eyes, she saw the lady was smiling and seemed to be inviting her to come nearer. She was still frightened although, as she put it, she "would have stayed there forever looking at her."

The best thing to do, she thought, was to pray. Taking her rosary from her pocket, she fell to her knees and tried to make the sign of the cross. Feeling as if she was paralysed, she couldn't lift her hand to her forehead. It was then that the lady stepped to one side and turned towards Bernadette. "She was holding the large beads in her hand," Bernadette recalled. "She crossed herself as though to pray. My hand was trembling. I tried again to make the sign of the cross, and this time I could. After that I was not afraid."

Bernadette recited the rosary. The lady accompanied her, her beads slipping through her fingers, although her lips never moved. Once they finished, the white lady bowed smilingly. She then "retired within the niche and disappeared all of a sudden," the young girl recalled. The whole event had lasted little more than the space of a rosary.

Soon, the two other girls returned and were shocked by the appearance of Bernadette. "She was white, as though she were dead," Toinette later remarked. Bernadette told them her story on their way home. Word quickly got out. First, Bernadette's mother was informed. The details were then revealed to two priests. Lourdes was small and news travelled fast. It wasn't long before the apparition was being talked about all over town.

Further appearances followed. Crowds waited for Bernadette at the grotto. At first, they amounted to a handful. Numbers eventually grew into the tens of thousands. People started to come from far away. Like them, Bernadette was drawn to the cave; drawn there to see her beautiful lady. Later, when she was dying, she was asked by a five-year-old girl who visited her if the lady really was lovely. "Oh, yes," Bernadette responded, "so lovely that, when you have seen her once, you would willingly die to see her again."

Bernadette saw the white lady consistently over the following weeks. We are fortunate to have an eyewitness account of her during one of the apparitions. The account provides us with a rare insight to her actions and demeanour.

One day, a senior government official, Jean Baptiste Estrade, had a visit from his sister in Lourdes. She entered his office and asked: "Have you heard the rumours which are going about? It is said that a little girl of the town has been favoured with an appearance of the Virgin in a grotto near the Gave." Estrade wasn't impressed. Like many of his fellow professionals, he had known of the apparitions and regarded them as "silly, childish and absurd." Despite his reservations, he agreed with his sister that they should visit the grotto the following day.

True to their word, they arrived at the grotto at about six o'clock the next morning, as dawn was breaking. "A hundred and fifty or two hundred persons were already there before us," he later recalled. "Many women were on their knees praying and I had great difficulty to keep myself from laughing on seeing the childish belief of these simple Christians." Among them were three or four men from Lourdes who, like himself, had come out of curiosity or to oblige their friends. The sight of them made him feel better.

Bernadette arrived soon afterwards. A murmur went through the crowd. They parted to let her pass. The men, including Estrade, used their elbows and pushed their way up to her side. "From this moment she was under our closest observation," he noted. "Our eyes were riveted upon her and did not leave her for an instant."

Bernadette knelt down, took her rosary out of her pocket, and began to pray reverentially. "She did it all without the least shade of awkwardness or self-consciousness, just as simply and naturally as if she had gone into the parish church for her ordinary devotions," the government official recalled. "Whilst she was passing the beads between her fingers she looked up towards the rock as though waiting for something.

"Suddenly, as in a flash of lightning, an expression of wonder illuminated her face and she seemed to be born into another life. A light shone in her eyes; wonderful smiles played upon her lips; an unutterable grace transfigured her whole being..... Bernadette was no longer Bernadette; she was one of those privileged beings, the face all glorious with the glory of heaven." The men – spontaneously and without a thought of how they appeared to others – took off their hats and fell to their knees.

Estrade saw nothing and heard nothing, but evidently some ethereal presence had arrived at the grotto. Initially, on seeing the vision, Bernadette was overjoyed. She then listened. After that, she began to speak. "What we could and did see and understand was that a conversation was going on between the mysterious lady and the child upon whom our gaze was fixed," Estrade remarked.

"Her movements and gestures and the play of her features quickly gave evidence of all the characteristics of a conversation. Sometimes smiling, sometimes grave, at one time the child would show her approval by an inclination of the head, at another she would appear to be asking a question.

"When the lady spoke a thrill of joy seemed to convulse the girl's body; when on the contrary Bernadette made a request she would bow herself down to the ground and be moved almost to tears. We could see that at certain moments the conversation was broken off, and then the child would return to her rosary but with her eyes still fixed upon the rock. She seemed afraid to lower her eyes lest she should lose the vision of the ravishing object which she contemplated."

Estrade made two further insightful observations. First, he remarked on Bernadette's reverence for the invisible lady: "I have been in the world, only too much perhaps, and I have met models of grace and distinction. But I have never seen anyone make a bow with such grace or such distinction as Bernadette." Second, he had never seen anyone else who made such a heartfelt sign of the cross: "On that same day, when returning from the grotto, I said that if the sign of the cross is made in heaven it must be made as Bernadette made it."

The apparition lasted for an hour. At the end of that time, Bernadette crawled on her knees from the place where she was praying to just below the wild rose tree hanging from the rock. There, while concentrating hard, she kissed the earth. She then crawled back to where she had been positioned before.

"A last glow of light lit up her face, then gradually, almost imperceptibly, the transfiguring glory of the ecstasy grew fainter and finally disappeared," Estrade recollected. Bernadette continued praying for a few moments, but "it was only the face of the little peasant child which we saw," he said. Soon, she got up, left for home, and was lost in the crowd.

The authorities weren't amused by the news of Bernadette and the apparitions. Inspector of Police, Monsieur Jacomet, decided to investigate. A battle of David versus Goliath ensued. David won.

Monsieur Dominique Jacomet, Inspector of Police, cut a most impressive figure in Lourdes. He strolled about the boulevards, dressed in his finely-tailored suits, well-cut coat and top hat.

From time to time, he bowed to passing ladies or he offered greetings to respected citizens. Even the poor seemed to admire him. He felt on top of the world, aware of his importance, and well able to impose his authority at will.

Jacomet was known as a shrewd operator, adept at pursuing the guilty, a maestro at ferreting out offenders and detecting crimes. Nothing could get in his way, especially not a humble 14-year-old child. It is said that he relished the arrival of Bernadette, who had just been arrested having left the church after Vespers. Notebook at the ready, he anticipated an easy triumph. He even had a witness to observe his pending success.

After a calm and friendly introduction, Jacomet upped the pace considerably. Question after question was directed at Bernadette. "Your name?" he snapped. "Bernadette," she quickly answered. "Bernadette what?" "Soubirous," she replied. "Your mother's name?" "Louise." "Louise what?" "Soubirous." "No, her maiden name." "Castérot," she responded. Jacomet smiled. He was on his way.

"So then, Bernadette, you see the Holy Virgin?" he queried, laying a bit of a trap. "I do not say that I have seen the Holy Virgin," came the quick reply. "Ah, good," he continued, "you haven't seen anything." "I did see something." "What did you see?" "Something white." "Some *thing* or some *one*?" "That thing has the form of a little young lady," she answered. "There were other girls with you when you saw it?" "Yes, sir." "Did they see it?" "No, sir." "How do you know?" "They told me so." "Why didn't they see it?" "I don't know."

"Well, then, this girl, this young lady, how was she dressed?" the interrogator probed. "A white dress, tied with a blue ribbon, a white veil on her head, and a yellow rose on each foot, the colour of the chain of her rosary," Bernadette said. "Was she

21

pretty?" "Oh, yes, sir, very beautiful." "Pretty like who? Like Madame Pailhasson? Like Mademoiselle Dufo?" Bernadette didn't bother being diplomatic. "They cannot compare with her," she bluntly replied.

On and on it went. Any hopes Jacomet had of an easy result were fading fast. "You are a liar," he suddenly exclaimed. "You are deceiving everybody, and unless you confess the truth at once, I will have you arrested by the gendarmes." Bernadette wasn't fazed. Nor was she agitated. Instead, she preserved her tranquillity. "Sir," she said, calmly but firmly, "you may have me arrested by the gendarmes, but I can only say what I have already said. It is the truth."

Jacomet tried a different approach, re-reading her statement, which he had been jotting down. To put it more correctly, he had jotted down *his* version of what she had allegedly said. "The Virgin smiles at me," he mentioned at one stage. "I didn't say 'the Virgin,'" Bernadette corrected him. He also referred to how she had spoken of "the girl." Bernadette admonished him again, pointing out that she had not used that phrase either. Tiring of the game, she declared: "Sir, you have altered everything on me." She added: "I'm tired of it all."

Reports have it that two people listening at the keyhole – one of whom was Jacomet's wife – heard the inspector raise his voice and state more than loudly phrases like "brazen hussy" and "you are getting everyone to run after you." They later heard him moderate his tone and plead with Bernadette to promise never to go back to the grotto. "Sir, I promised to go there," she replied. "All right, have it your way," the exasperated policeman growled. "I am going to get the policemen to take you to prison."

At that moment, Jacomet heard a knock at the front door, and that's where he headed. He was confronted by Bernadette's father, who had been told his daughter was arrested and had come to take her away. Home she went, in fine health, to the cheers of a crowd which had collected outside, leaving behind a tired, unhappy, badly dejected Inspector of Police.

It wasn't as if Bernadette was able to completely forget the experience. There were memories she retained, but they weren't of a serious nature. In fact, the main thing she could recall – and she did so with laughter – was an object on the top of Jacomet's policeman's cap. "He was trembling," she would say, "and there was a tassel on his cap which kept going ting-a-ling!"

Four days later, on 25 February 1858, Bernadette was back at the grotto, where an event of profound significance occurred. On that date, the famous Lourdes water was revealed.

Had the tabloid press existed, shock headlines would have hit newsstands after the events of Thursday, 25 February 1858. "Visionary Deranged," "Madness at Grotto" or "Bernadette Insane" they might have proclaimed. Such headlines would have been justified. On that day, Bernadette behaved strangely, seemed confused, crawled across the ground, consumed muddy water and ate grass. Some onlookers jeered; others quickly departed. Many believed she had gone mad.

On the contrary, what had happened that day, at the ninth apparition, was one of the most important events ever to occur in the town of Lourdes. It was the day when "Lourdes water" was discovered; when a young girl, under Our Lady's instructions, revealed a previously-unknown spring. In time, that spring would produce miraculous cures. Its legend would traverse the world.

In the meantime, on that Thursday, people regarded what they were seeing as utter insanity.

From early morning, a sizeable crowd had assembled at the grotto. More than 300 people were there. They had arisen in the early hours, intending to secure the best vantage points. Despite their efforts, many had difficulty finding a place to stand. Bernadette's aunts, Basile and Lucile, were present. Jean Baptiste Estrade, whose description of Bernadette we saw earlier, was there, too. His sister had arrived, as well. The innkeeper's daughter was also present. Everyone expected to see a spiritual, uplifting event. They were to be gravely disappointed.

Bernadette, on arrival, had to force her way through the crowd. Her subsequent behaviour was not as expected. As she said the rosary, instead of being in some sort of hypnotic reverie, as she normally would be, she seemed agitated and distracted. She began moving about on her knees and travelled in different directions. Eventually, she headed towards a spot under the grotto. There, she dug at the ground with her hands and seemed to smear her face with mud. Bernadette then picked up some grass and ate it. The crowd were appalled by this macabre spectacle. It was certainly not what they had come to see.

Bernadette later explained what had happened. The apparition had asked her "to go drink from the spring and wash there." Unaware of any spring, she began to head towards the River Gave. The lady spoke again. "She said that that was not the right place and she pointed to another place, showing me the spring under the grotto," Bernadette recalled. "I went to the place she showed me, but all I saw was a tiny bit of muddy water. There was so little of it that I was hardly able to get any of it in my hands.

"I tried to drink it, but it was so dirty that the first three times it came back up. On the fourth try, I was able to drink a little of it. She asked me, for the sake of sinners, would I mind eating some grass that was in the same place where I drank. She asked that only once; I do not know why. She said, 'Would you be willing to kiss the ground for the sake of sinners?' 'Would you be willing to crawl on your knees for the sake of sinners?'" It was all about "penance, penance, penance," the young Bernadette concluded.

Once Bernadette's features became properly visible to the crowd, their reaction was one of astonishment. Her face was stained with mud. To them, she looked demented. "They were surprised," an onlooker remarked. "They could not understand what it meant." Bernadette's aunts rushed forward and cleaned her face. After returning to do more praying, she eventually departed for home. Even then, despite the crowd's reaction, she seemed untroubled. There was no sense of anything being amiss; instead, she retained her normal look of calmness, tranquillity and contentment.

What happened next was remarkable. "In the afternoon, some of the people returned to the grotto. They looked at the hole that Bernadette had dug. It was as big as a soup-tureen," René Laurentin, the French theologian and world expert on Mariology, later wrote. Some people took a drink, copying Bernadette. One woman dug in the muddy pool with a stick, revealing the bubbling sound of water. Bit by bit, the flow of water increased. The faster it flowed, the clearer it became.

"Two bottles of the water went back to town that day," Laurentin noted in his book *Bernadette of Lourdes*. One was brought by a woman to her father, who was unwell. "He must drink some of this water," she thought. The other was brought home by the tobacconist's son, who wore an eye patch. It was soon noticed that he had discarded the patch. Within days of its discovery, the curative power of the water had already been established; major miracles would soon follow.

One of the first Lourdes miracles concerned a tiny little boy who was on the edge of death. His miracle was attributed to immersion in the newly-discovered spring water. It took place while the apparitions were still ongoing.

During a late afternoon in July 1858, at around five o'clock, a frantic woman was seen running towards the grotto at Lourdes. She carried a limp, seemingly-dead two-year-old baby in her arms. She moved at a fast pace, praying out loud, invoking the Blessed Virgin, and oblivious to everybody who stood in her way. People said, later on, that she looked demented, insane, as if her mind was consumed by fever or some sort of unnatural pain.

The baby boy who lay in her arms was named Justin Bouhort. He had been unwell since birth, never able to walk, suffered from a slow consumptive fever, and was rapidly approaching death. His eyes were glazed, his body motionless, and his breathing barely noticeable. Minutes earlier, his father, a day labourer, had said in the family's squalid home, "He is dead." The mother, named Croisine, replied, "He is not dead." Instead, a hurried thought crossed her mind – she was taking Justin to the grotto, where Our Lady would cure him.

Croisine snatched the motionless infant from his cradle, wrapped him in her apron, and fled from the family home. She was "plunged in despair," the nineteenth-century journalist and writer, Henri Lasserre, remarked. His testimony is reliable, as he spoke to the family, and met Justin, as part of a subsequent investigation of the case. Not content with studying official documents, correspondence and reports, he endeavoured to "see everything for myself" and to bring "freshly before my eyes" the "memory and narrative of eye-witnesses." His aim, he declared, was "the restless search after truth."

On that late afternoon, in 1858, there were some 500 – 600 people already at the grotto, praying and hoping to witness Bernadette. Croisine plunged through them, with her child clutched in her arms. At the entrance to the grotto, she prostrated herself and prayed, after which she dragged herself on her knees towards the miraculous spring. The water was freezing, and the tiny child she produced from inside her apron was in a state of undress. "What is she going to do?" people cried out in horror.

Without hesitating, Croisine thrust the child into the icy water, immersing him up to his neck. The crowd was appalled. "The woman is insane," some onlookers murmured. "You are killing your child," others said. One person touched the mother on her shoulder, but she turned around and exclaimed, "Let me alone, let me alone." "For a whole quarter of an hour, before the astonished eyes of the multitude, in the midst of the cries, reproaches, and insults heaped upon her by the crowd of bystanders, she kept her child immersed in the mysterious water," Lasserre recalled.

Justin remained motionless as a corpse, showing no sign of life. His mother once again wrapped him in her apron and hastily returned home. His body was as cold as ice. Having placed him in his cradle, she bent over him, listening, and suddenly exclaimed,

"He is breathing!" With his eyes still closed, and his tiny body immobile, the child fell into a calm, deep sleep. Every minute that night, Croisine listened to his breathing, which gradually improved. She awaited daybreak with hope but also with much apprehension.

The following morning, at break of day, Croisine saw that her little child was looking at her with a "mild ray of life sparkling in his laughing eyes." Some colour had returned to his cheeks, and his features looked rested. He started to feed again. He even showed signs of wanting to escape from his cradle, which his mother resisted as he had never walked before. The next day again, he slept as his parents went about their daily work. Later, on the mother's arrival home, she was confronted with an extraordinary sight.

When the mother opened the front door on her return, "she almost fainted at the sight presented to her view," Lasserre remarked. "The cradle was empty. Justin had risen without any assistance from where his mother had laid him; he was on his legs going to and fro, touching the different articles of furniture, and disarranging the chairs. In short, the little paralysed child was walking." His cure was complete. "You now see that he was not dead, and that the Blessed Virgin has saved him," Croisine said to her husband.

Seventy-five years later, at the age of 77, Justin Bouhort attended the canonisation of Bernadette in Rome. He lived for two more years after that, dying in 1935. His case was accredited as one of Lourdes' official miracles, having been recognised in January 1862. It was an important case, knocking on the head the idea of "autosuggestion" or "self-healing" as a cause of recovery

– after all, how could a baby of two effect its own revival in such a manner?

The medical analysis was to the point. "A bath of cold water of a quarter of an hour's duration" should have produced an "immediate death," concluded an official medical investigation of the cure, which was conducted by Prof. Henri Vergez, from the Faculty of Medicine, Montpellier. Instead, the patient had revived and soon after had begun to walk. His report concluded that the recovery was "in a manner altogether supernatural."

Arguably the most significant apparition took place on 25 March 1858. On that date, the identity of the beautiful lady was revealed.

For six weeks, the population of Lourdes had struggled with the identity of the lady at the grotto. There was wild speculation and debate. Perhaps it was the soul of a departed family relation. Maybe it was an evil spirit. Indeed, as one local newspaper speculated, it might be the Blessed Virgin. Most people agreed with this latter suggestion, but how could anyone be sure. The only person who could come up with the answer was Bernadette.

For two weeks, Bernadette had been questioning the beautiful lady. "I went every day for a fortnight, and each day I asked her who she was, and this petition always made her smile," she later reflected. Bernadette never received an answer. Things were to change on Thursday, 25 March. It was the Feast of the Annunciation and the date of the sixteenth apparition. On that day, the smiling was over, the truth was out.

Bernadette arose at five o'clock in the morning and headed to the grotto. Even at that early hour, the place was crowded.

On her approach, she noticed a soft light in the niche. The lady was waiting! "She was there, tranquil and smiling and watching the crowd just as a fond mother watches her children," Bernadette recalled. Having knelt down, she asked for the lady's forgiveness as she believed she was late. The lady indicated there was no need for an apology.

A strange thing happened that day – the lady moved from the niche into the grotto, coming closer to Bernadette. Rising to her feet, Bernadette went in closer still, narrowing the gap even further. Her parents and some friends eased in behind her. Other people who had arrived that day watched in awe. There was only one matter on Bernadette's mind – who was the lady? What was her name?

"Madame, will you kindly tell me who you are?" Bernadette asked. The response was the same as ever – a bow and a smile. She asked again, and got the same reaction. Not to be put off, she tried one more time. "I do not know why, but I felt more courageous. I begged her once more to do me the favour of telling me her name," Bernadette later said.

This time, Bernadette got her answer. The lady spread her arms. She then brought her hands together over her breast. Raising her eyes to heaven, she spoke. "I am the Immaculate Conception," she said. It was quick; it was brief; and it was all over in an instant. The lady smiled and disappeared!

At last, Bernadette had a name – or at least a title – and she could now go to the parish priest, Abbé Dominique Peyramale, and tell him her news. The abbé had persistently pressed her to ask the lady who she was. Now, she had important information to give him, although – having only recently reached the age of

14 – she had no idea what the Immaculate Conception meant, nor had she heard the phrase before.

To make sure she didn't forget the words, she repeated them all the way home. She continued to recite them *en route* to the rectory. On arrival, she was still reciting them, fearful of letting them slip from her mind. The abbé was outraged, thinking she was referring to herself. His mood changed once she told him they were the words of the lady. "I was so amazed by it that I felt myself stagger and I was on the point of falling," he later recalled.

"How could Bernadette have known unless the lady had told her?" the abbé wondered. It was only little more than three years since the dogma – proclaiming that Mary had been free from original sin from the moment of conception – had been declared by the Pope as a doctrine to be "believed by all the faithful." Not many people had heard of it; even fewer had understood it. The young 14-year-old couldn't have known about it. Great theologians struggled to explain it. From that moment on, Abbé Peyramale believed in Bernadette.

"I did not know what this meant," Bernadette later wrote to the Pope, in reference to the phrase Immaculate Conception. "I had never heard those words before. Since that time, when meditating on this, I have often said to myself: how good the Most Holy Virgin is. It seems that she came to confirm our Holy Father's words. This is what makes me believe that she must protect you in a very special way."

In many ways, the revelation on that day in March 1858 brought Bernadette's time at Lourdes to a close. The story of the shrine was about to move on. Lourdes would soon become a place of pilgrimage, a centre for great miracles, and a world-famous focal point of Marian devotion. For Bernadette, her work was done. The time was coming when she would leave the town forever and become a nun.

At the age of 22, Bernadette left Lourdes and joined the Sisters of Charity at Nevers. The name she was given as a nun was Sr. Marie-Bernard.

On Tuesday, 3 July 1866, Bernadette went to the grotto for the very last time. It was an emotional visit, as she was leaving the following day to become a nun. Falling to her knees, she began to pray. With her eyes focused on the statue of the Immaculate Conception, she wept uncontrollably. She then kissed the now-famous rock and, without looking back, she walked away.

There were further tears the next day at Lourdes railway station. Bernadette, who was 22 years of age, stood there in a new blue dress with dark blue stripes, topped off with a little striped headscarf tied at the side. Her parents, aunts and other family members had been crying all that morning. Her young brother, who was aged six, was inconsolable. "I can't stay here forever," she told them, as she held back her tears. Then, she boarded the train and was gone. She would never see Lourdes again.

Bernadette shed even more tears after becoming a novice at the motherhouse of the Sisters of Charity in Nevers. The novice mistress, Mother Marie-Thérèse Vauzou, instantly disliked her. "Now that we have you, we can knock you into shape" were her opening remarks. She applied herself to the task with relish. No humiliation was too harsh for Bernadette. She was blamed for things she had not done. It seemed she was constantly kneeling and kissing the tiled floor as punishment for her alleged misdeeds.

Mother Vauzou ridiculed her new novice's social standing. On one occasion, Bernadette won a prize of a little statue of St. Germaine Cousin, a shepherdess who had slept in a stable or on vine branches in a garret. In front of the other nuns, the mistress remarked: "A shepherd girl could only fall into the hands of a shepherd girl." Later in life, when Bernadette's canonisation was being discussed, the mistress said: "Let them wait till I am dead."

The superior of the convent didn't behave much better. One day, having encountered Bernadette in the cloister, she said, "You're good for nothing." On another occasion, on her return from Rome, she gave each novice an embrace and had a kind word for all of them. When it came to Bernadette, she weakly put her arms around her and said not a word. One of Bernadette's fellow nuns confessed that, having witnessed what was happening, she would say to herself, "How lucky not to be Bernadette!"

Sadly, things got progressively worse. On her profession day, Bernadette waited to hear what convent she was being assigned to. All the other nuns received their postings. When Bernadette's turn came, the bishop looked at the superior and asked: "What are you going to do with her?" The superior replied: "That child is good for nothing. She would only be a burden to the house we'd send her to." The bishop turned to Bernadette and said: "The occupation I give you is to pray." Bernadette later confessed she felt deeply humiliated.

There were many explanations for the harsh treatment meted out to Bernadette. To begin with, her superiors envied her, not only for her fame but for having been graced with the apparitions at Lourdes. Hers were the eyes that had stared at the Blessed Virgin. She possessed secrets beyond anything they could ever pretend to know. One nun wondered if these factors – especially the fame – "did not give umbrage" in some way.

Regarding the novice mistress, she was the daughter of a notary and was very class-conscious. To her, Bernadette was a mere peasant. It pained her that every day Bernadette received letters from marquesses and counts, asking for her prayers or thanking her for favours received. She had heard how on her way to Nevers Bernadette had to stop at Pau where she was mobbed by crowds and had to be protected by police. This information didn't please her.

The novice mistress – from whom no secrets could be kept – also decided to ask Bernadette about the three secrets revealed by Our Lady. Bernadette froze and said nothing. "The impression was unmistakable that she was completely outside Mère Vauzou's reach, that this all-powerful novice mistress would never be able to break into her inner citadel," Margaret Trouncer, a biographer of Bernadette, wrote in 1958. Mother Vauzou was outraged. She wondered why the Virgin Mary chose Bernadette. "She is quite ordinary," she was known to mutter, "quite ordinary."

Bernadette bore her suffering with dignity. In private, she would cry. In public, she would pretend there was nothing wrong. She never complained or showed signs of displeasure. She attended to her tasks – minor roles as an assistant in the infirmary or as a sacristan – and she would pray. She particularly loved praying at a remote part of the convent garden, where there was a statue of Our Lady. The figure had a lovely smile and had arms outstretched, reminding her of home.

"Those days are passed and gone," she said, thinking back on the extraordinary times she once knew at Lourdes. "My poor grotto, I wouldn't recognise it anymore," she added. Her days as a shepherdess also crossed her mind and she would sing songs of a little lamb "cloaked with white wool, and his eyes spotted with black." They were wonderful memories, comforting thoughts to help her through the hard times she was enduring. There were other compensations, too, most notably the company of her fellow nuns.

Bernadette was one of the most popular nuns in the convent, where her kindness and sense of humour stood out. She also had a great sense of fun.

One of Bernadette's companions has left us with a wonderful description of a singing test conducted at the convent in Nevers. The purpose of the test was to assess the quality of newcomers' voices. Those who might shine at delivering liturgical chants or singing the divine office would be identified. On the other hand, those with flat, broken voices, or with voices that sounded like foghorns, would be singled out, too.

Conducted in the presence of the Mother General, the test was a serious affair. There was no scope for fun or laughter; absolutely nothing humorous about it. Drastic renditions were glossed over and, as we might expect, they were in plentiful supply. One nun forgot her notes; another sang out of tune; others had voices that would shatter glass. Adding to the scene was the sound of someone choking as she struggled to contain her laughter and battled to keep a straight face. It was, of course, Bernadette, or Sr. Marie-Bernard, as she was called in the convent!

Bernadette's infectious laughter wasn't exactly welcomed by those in charge of the convent's spiritual affairs. Not only did she frequently have to confess her outbursts to her superiors, but she also got her companions into trouble. They, too, would roll around in fits of the giggles. The result was that a long file of nuns would head off to divulge their faults to the novice mistress.

One such event took place in the refectory when Bernadette was eating the hard cores of carrots. Unfortunately, she pressed too hard with her fork, causing them to roll the length of the table. At first, Bernadette uttered a stifled giggle; then produced a loud laugh. Soon, the whole table was in convulsions. The laughter was so contagious that "we couldn't eat any more," one nun remarked. "Let's go!" Bernadette said after the meal, and they all headed off to confess their faults.

Another time, she roared laughing when informed that the price of her photographs in Lourdes had been reduced to ten centimes. "That's all I'm worth," she said, highly amused. On a further occasion, when she was supposed to be praying to Our Lady, she became absent-minded and knelt at the wrong statue. "You are distracted: you are praying to the Blessed Virgin but kneeling at St. Joseph's statue," she was told. Don't worry, she replied. "The Blessed Virgin and St. Joseph are in perfect agreement. There is no jealousy in heaven."

She was also a wonderful mimic. Her target was usually the convent physician, whose habits and characteristics she could copy to a tee. "That excellent man had some little whims and mannerisms which we all knew, and Bernadette used to entertain us with imitations of him which made us laugh so much that tears came into our eyes," one of the congregation later recalled. "Her mimicry was brilliant, full of delicate touches of wit and sometimes of sly roguishness. But I must say that there was never anything unkind."

Bernadette's kindness could be seen in other ways, too. She was particularly nice to one of the kitchen maids who, at the age of 17, had come to work at the convent. After the maid caught a severe chill, Bernadette would climb the stairs to the convent eaves to pay her a visit. Given her chronic asthma, the climb was hardly an easy task. She would break the rules by humming to announce she was coming. The maid was always delighted to see her, not only because Bernadette would plump up her pillow and tidy her bed but because her company was so pleasant.

There were other nuns who she loved but who gave her a headache. One of them – Julie Garros – was from Lourdes and had known Bernadette as a child. She had been present at three of the apparitions. Regarded as an *enfant terrible* at school, she hadn't changed one bit since arriving at Nevers. "She was a real friend to me," Julie, who became Sr. Vincent, recollected. "She loved me supernaturally, otherwise she would not have put up with me in the way she did."

On one occasion, Bernadette came across Julie while she was cleaning the mother mistress's room. She found her spitting into the font, as she had forgotten to fill it with holy water. Bernadette insisted she head off and confess her fault. Another time, when Bernadette was in the infirmary, Julie brought her a cup of burnt chocolate. Knowing it tasted awful, Julie took a sip and said, "It's excellent. It's simply delicious." Bernadette then tasted it and cryptically replied: "So it is – much better than usual." Julie got the message.

At least in her early years at Nevers, Bernadette's sincerity and sense of childlike fun never left her. Those early days were her better days; her times of most joy. Soon, she would need to lean on other qualities and draw from different strengths. The truth was that she had always battled illness as a nun, and things were getting worse. People who knew her noticed the change – the weight loss, the poor pallor, the struggle with infirmity and disease. The dark nights were coming, and her life would end all too soon.

Behind the pleasant smiles and joyful laughter, Bernadette's time in the convent was blighted by illness. After much suffering, she died at 35 years of age.

Bernadette became ill within months of arriving at the convent in Nevers. Like many young people of her era, including Thérèse of Lisieux, she developed TB. In September, she haemorrhaged after a prolonged fit of coughing. Little more than a month later, she haemorrhaged again. At one stage, it seemed she was going to die, with her doctor predicting she would be gone by morning. She survived, although her problem didn't disappear. Instead, it became a long-term affliction – her "job of being ill," as she put it.

Within a year, a tumour appeared on her knee. Before long, the tumour developed a deep and painful abscess, which was crippling and debilitating. Despite performing as many duties as she could, she spent almost 13 years battling a frightful array of symptoms. These included coughing up blood, painful bone decay, deafness-inducing ear abscesses, chest pains and stomach pains, in addition to her chronic asthma. All of this, of course, was on top of the dreadful treatment she received from those in charge of the convent.

Her knee became a major problem, especially towards the end. It was "huge" and the pain "terrible," according to notes written by one of her carers. Sometimes, it took an hour to change her position in bed. "She became like a corpse," the notes reveal. Not only was she "completely vanquished by the pain" but "passed whole nights without sleep." Even when she slept, "the least movement of the leg drew a cry of anguish." Her cries stopped other patients in the infirmary from sleeping.

She suffered disturbing nightmares. One of her fellow nuns, Sr. Philomène, who cared for her, observed her gasping and moaning one night. "She had a nightmare, which woke her up," she recalled. "I rushed forward at once. Perspiration was pouring from her brow. 'My dear Sister,' I said, 'do you need anything?' She moaned a little, as if she were still under the impression of a terrifying dream. And then she said in a broken voice, 'I was far away at Massabielle.'"

Although Bernadette spat up whole basins of blood, she never sought a miracle. When the convent chaplain suggested prayers for a cure, she responded: "To pray for my cure? Not a bit of it." Another person – a nun – suggested praying to the Blessed Virgin in the hope of receiving some consolation. Bernadette replied: "No, no consolations, only strength and patience." Instead of praying for herself, she spent her time praying for others.

Her darkest hour came around Easter 1879. She found it very difficult to breathe; the skin on her back was raw; every movement she made was a form of torture. "I should never have thought that one had to suffer so much to die," she remarked. She said goodbye to one of her friends who came to visit – the best she could do being to smile with her eyes and playfully wink with one eye. "This time it is the end," she whispered.

Her final night was one of her worst. "From time to time, suffering would wrest a low moan from her, which made me start in my chair," recalled Mother Alphonse, who sat beside Bernadette all night. "She asked me quite often to help her to turn, so that she could find a little relief for her poor body, which was flayed alive. She was lying on her wounds, as it were."

The next morning, her companions moved her from the bed to an armchair in front of the fireplace. Her feet were resting on the footrest. The fire was lighting. Her fellow Sisters were passing to and fro. She tried to drink from a bowl, but her hands were trembling. It was clear the end was near.

Suddenly, she raised her left hand to her forehead. With radiant eyes, she looked upwards, fixing her gaze on a distant spot. "Her face was calm, serene, tinged with melancholy," one eyewitness said. Then, sounding surprised, she uttered a loud cry. Her body started to tremble. Her hand dropped to her heart. She said, in a voice filled with love, "My God, I love you with all my heart, with all my soul and with all my strength."

It was shortly after three o'clock. Her convent companions knelt alongside her. She joined in their prayers. "Holy Mary, Mother of God, pray for me, poor sinner," she repeated after them. She said it again. Her last words were "poor sinner."

Holding her crucifix against her heart, she died. Two large tears rolled down her cheeks as she passed away. Her head was resting to the side. A friend said that in death she was "very beautiful." The little shepherdess was on her way to meet another beautiful lady in heaven.

DESTINATION LOURDES

Bernadette's death was noted with great sorrow in Ireland. "Last Wednesday evening there died in the thriving old city of Nevers, in her convent home on the banks of the Loire, a young and holy nun, whose name and whose sanctity will long be a treasured inheritance of the Catholic Church," *The Freeman's Journal* reported.

Already, Bernadette was well-known among the Irish public. Reports of sensational happenings at Lourdes had surfaced in newspapers within weeks of the first apparition. Details of events spread by word of mouth, from pulpits, and through raging debates conducted in journals and in the broadsheet press.

People were enthralled by the wonderful miracles that came to light. Books about Lourdes went on sale, written by Irish authors. Plans were set in train for pilgrimages. The nation was on the move, spurred on by revelations that a "humble peasant girl" – as Bernadette was described in one Irish newspaper – had been visited by Our Lady at Lourdes.

News reports of events at Lourdes first appeared in an Irish newspaper four weeks after the apparitions began.

On 12 March 1858, *The Dublin Evening Mail* received a story by electric telegraph from the city of Tarbes, France. It came from the newsroom of *L'Intérêt Public*, a journal committed, as its name suggests, to "public interest" issues. The story's headline used the word "miracle," which must have caught the editor's eye in his Parliament Street office. Something must have done the trick, as the story's location – Lourdes – was barely known at the time.

On that day, in 1858, the newspaper – later renamed the *Evening Mail* – published the first account in Ireland of the apparitions at Lourdes. "A considerable agitation has been of late manifested in the neighbourhood of Lourdes," the report began. It went on to explain that "a young girl of 14" – the "daughter of a day labourer" – "prays every morning early to a grotto, in which springs forth a gush of water forming a rivulet." This girl, the newspaper added, "affirms that the Virgin Mary has appeared to her, and ordered that she should every morning, for a fortnight, pray in the grotto during the space of half an hour."

The newspaper then described Bernadette: "At first, when she kneels down, she is represented as being pale, and almost convulsed; but as her communication with the Virgin proceeds, her features become calm and radiant." The crowds were also noted: "A vast number of persons accompany her in her visits, believing fully in the truth of her assertion.....We understand that not less than 5,000 persons are present now each morning near the grotto, and that the authorities are beginning to disapprove of such assemblages."

Many Irish newspapers took a negative stance on the news emanating from Lourdes. The reactions of the established, loyalist, largely Protestant-owned Irish press were particularly hostile and cynical. One newspaper accused Bernadette of perpetrating "a swindle upon the chronic ailments of Catholicity." Another wrote of "The Lourdes Fabrication" and remarked that "solid profits" would be the only upshot of "this silly girl's" activities. A further newspaper slammed the Church, accusing it of endorsing the "impostures" of Lourdes.

The Kerry Evening Post adopted an exceptionally vitriolic line, featuring articles that were condescending and untrue. This staunchly loyalist newspaper – which was published on Wednesdays and Saturdays from its offices in Denny Street, Tralee – served a small but cohesive readership of mostly local Protestants. The proprietors at the time – Messrs. Eagar and Raymond – took a particularly dismissive view of Bernadette and Lourdes.

"An ignorant peasant girl," was how the newspaper curtly described the future saint. It also alleged – falsely – that the authorities in Lourdes had "sent her to a lunatic asylum." It further attacked the Church, in a front-page article, pointing to "the gross superstition which the French clergy have of late been endeavouring to encourage among the ignorant peasantry in the rural districts by means of pretended miracles such as those at Lourdes."

Money and miracles were the potent mix at Lourdes, the Kerry publication argued. "Infidels and Protestants" might not comprehend miraculous apparitions, but the potential profits from Lourdes water "was within the grasp of their degraded intellects," one of the newspaper's opinion columns cynically remarked. "Turning this girl's vision into permanent profit might have another advantage. It would compel the girls of other towns to examine grottoes with attention and care. It might elicit other miracles," the piece sardonically concluded.

In contrast to the surprisingly negative reaction of much of the established press, some Irish newspapers responded positively to the news. *The People*, which was published out of Wexford, was one of those titles. "Whatever explanation may be given of the facts related by the young girl – and there are many such – no one as yet doubts her good faith," the newspaper declared to its readers not long after the news broke. "She has been often offered money and objects likely to tempt her, but has constantly refused everything, and her disinterestedness is now as far removed from doubt as her sincerity."

Referring to her subsequent interrogation by the authorities concerning the truthfulness of her claims, the newspaper added: "The answers of the child seemed simple, straightforward, natural, and devoid of contradiction. She related all the circumstances of the apparition, and described in detail the figure she had seen, its air, shape, costume, and general bearing. Both menaces and caresses were made use of to induce her to vary or contradict herself, but she repeated and maintained her narrative."

It could be said that the battle between the rival newspapers – in the main, Catholic versus Protestant – reflected a greater struggle between the two faiths that was occurring in Ireland at the time. Bernadette and Mary became vibrant, threatening symbols of Catholicism; ridiculing them was a way of keeping that faith in check. This battle for supremacy between the main churches kept Lourdes in the headlines, incited people's interest and prompted them to find out more. It didn't take long before they were heading for Lourdes.

The County Waterford-born priest, Monsignor Thomas John Capel, met Bernadette Soubirous in 1859, most likely becoming the first Irishman to do so.

Bernadette was merely 15 years of age when, in 1859, Msgr. Thomas John Capel came to visit her. At the time, the priest, who had been born in Ardmore, was 23 years of age and about to take over pastoral duties in the city of Pau, about 40 km up the road from Lourdes. He met Bernadette at the Lourdes convent run by the Sisters of Charity, where the Mother Superior agreed that an interview could take place. It was a rare encounter as the nuns were protecting her from members of the public who were desperate to see and meet her.

The monsignor was smitten by Bernadette from the moment he saw her in the room. In appearance she seemed "puny and childlike," he said, noting that she wore what he called a "fish-hook" on her head – in other words "a handkerchief with a tail stuck up." He was particularly taken by her "modesty and quietness," especially when he questioned her regarding the apparitions at the grotto.

Bernadette's answers were always delivered with honesty and candour, in a clear and uncomplicated way, Msgr. Capel remarked. Over seven successive winters – the duration of time he would spend at Pau – he questioned her and not once did she deviate from her story. Everything she said had the mark of "truthfulness" and "simplicity." Not only did he believe her, but he went on to become one of her biggest advocates and defenders in the decades ahead.

At the time he met Bernadette, Msgr. Capel was starting out on a career that would see him become one of the most famous preachers in Britain and an influential figure in Vatican circles. Born in Ardmore, County Waterford, on 28 October 1836, he was the second-eldest in a family of six. His mother was a farmer's daughter; his father was a Royal Navy recruit who eventually joined the coastguard. After the family moved to Hastings, in England, he rose from schoolboy to priest, to vice-principal of a third-level college, and would later become an outstanding preacher.

First, however, he moved to Pau, in south-west France, where he became chaplain to the English-speaking Catholics who either lived there or visited on vacation. While at Pau, he travelled frequently to nearby Lourdes, where he befriended Bernadette and came to know the townspeople and pilgrims. "Soldiers, workmen, shopkeepers, railway officials, servants, and priests have, with rare exceptions, expressed a firm conviction of the truth of the vision," he later wrote. As for the pilgrims, he pointed out that they came for justifiable reasons – to "pray," to "repent of their sins," to "increase their piety" or to be "cured of bodily ailments." He asked: what is wrong with that?

He also referred to the apparitions: "After frequent and lengthened examinations of Bernadette and of some of the miracles" – and in light of the "human testimony" – he said that the apparitions at Lourdes had "every claim to be received as an undeniable fact." He additionally addressed the miracles. The truth, he argued, was that several pilgrims return home "freed from their sickness" – a conclusion, he pointed out, which was shared by Dr. Dozous, the eminent district inspector of epidemic diseases and medical assistant of the Court of Justice, who he knew.

After almost eight years in France, Msgr. Capel returned to England, where he won enormous acclaim for his preaching. "Monsignor Capel is gifted with a magnificent voice, clear as a bell, soft, sonorous, and most pleasing in tone, and so strong that every word he spoke – and he spoke without the slightest effort – was distinctly heard to the farthest limits of the extensive building. His delivery and enunciation merit all the eulogy that has been lavished on them," a leading newspaper said of a lecture he delivered in Dublin.

Following many visits to Rome, he caught the attention of Pope Pius IX, who made him his private chamberlain, with the title of monsignor. It was in London, however, that Msgr. Capel reached the height of his fame. "He is certainly the most popular priest in London," the distinguished American journalist, L. J. Jennings, wrote in *The World* in 1877. "His portrait may be seen in almost every shop window where photographs are sold, and among the large audiences which gather to hear him preach there are almost as many Protestants as Catholics. I doubt whether any living man has made so many converts to his Church."

Another well-known American journalist, Arthur Warren, from Boston, dined with the monsignor at his magnificent Kensington home. There, he would entertain the great and the good while dressed in his purple-edged cassock, with purple buttons and broad purple sash. He cut "a dignified, even an imposing figure" as he entertained in this stately home, seated by the fire, with photographs of celebrities adorning the walls. Unfortunately, he was living beyond his means and he was soon declared bankrupt.

As a result of his blighted financial affairs, in 1883, aged 47, Msgr. Capel departed for America and settled in California. He continued to preach and lecture, and became prelate of a local Catholic church. Then, in 1911, on the cusp of his 75th birthday, he died of heart failure. One of his last sermons, delivered less than 24 hours earlier, was on "Death and its Reward." No doubt the reward he hoped for was a reunion with the love of his life, a person he knew from long before – Bernadette of Lourdes.

The Kerry landowner Denis Shine Lawlor was another of the earliest Irish people to visit Lourdes. He arrived there in 1868.

Denis Shine Lawlor lost his wife Isabella in the autumn of 1867. He was devastated. "During long years" she had been "the light and honour of my existence," he reflected. A member of the gentry, he owned substantial landholdings throughout County Kerry and County Cork, together with property in Killarney. Two of his daughters had married into the family of the Liberator, Daniel O'Connell. Up to that autumn, life could not have been better. Now that his wife had died, he was depressed, distraught, and didn't know what to do.

On the advice of friends, he travelled to the continent, to the fashionable French resort of Biarritz. "Its pleasant climate, its great tranquillity during the winter season, and the society of a gifted and pious friend, contributed to render my sojourn there both useful and agreeable," he remarked. He hadn't realised it, but the upmarket resort was just a five-hour rail journey from Lourdes. He also hadn't known that the shrine was the talking point of France, due to the apparitions reported by Bernadette a decade earlier. He decided to travel to Lourdes as soon as he could.

On his arrival in 1868, Shine Lawlor was surprised by the huge number of people who, ten years after the apparitions, had congregated at the shrine, having come from near and far. At one point, he noted 1,500 people kneeling before the grotto; at another stage, he observed more than 1,000 people lined up for communion. Masses were being said from sunrise to noon; priests were constantly occupied at the confessionals. The whole town was throbbing with religious fervour.

There were peasant girls in traditional costumes; ladies of noble birth dressed in silken attire; beggars in tattered garments. It appeared as if the whole of humanity was represented at Lourdes. "Differences of rank and condition disappear in this community of faith and piety," he thought to himself. At one point, he noticed a young man standing aloof, with furrowed brow, his arms folded, and a disinterested look on his face. Yet, he stood there "in respect, if not in reverence," Shine Lawlor observed. Such was the power of Lourdes.

The Kerryman also witnessed the arrival of more than 1,000 women pilgrims from Bayonne: "I was present at the station at Lourdes, which is about two miles distant from the grotto, when this goodly caravan arrived. It was interesting to see so many women, coming from afar, immediately arrange themselves into processional order; and, after a railway journey of five hours, proceed directly to the grotto. The sun was intensely hot, and compelled them to carry parasols."

In the afternoon, the women hastened to "a street of tents" near the grotto, where accessories and souvenirs were sold. There, they bought tapers to burn at the shrine; rosary beads blessed by missionary priests; mementoes engraved with the legend of Lourdes; and images of every price and value. Also for sale were wax candles, which they bought and put under the niche where the statue of the Immaculate Conception was placed. Around the tents was the sound of busy voices and noise of commerce, as the women acquired their crucifixes, portraits of Bernadette and sepia-toned photographic images of the shrine.

Following his visit to Lourdes, Denis Shine Lawlor returned to Kerry, where he outlined his observations in an influential book, *Pilgrimages in the Pyrenees and Landes*. The book was well-received by critics, who called it "masterly," "delightful," "a literary treat" and a "most interesting work." Mr. Lawlor "happily combines the nerve and vigour of an accomplished writer with the piety of a devout Catholic," another critic declared. With readers – or, more correctly, with people at the time who could read and afford to buy books – his work certainly hit the mark, providing the first popular insights to Lourdes brought back by an Irishman.

As for Shine Lawlor, he lived on until 1887, when he died in his 79th year. He was remembered for the kindness he showed to his tenants during difficult times; for his work in Kerry business and politics; for his Catholicism, which had resulted in an audience with the Pope; and, as one commentator put it, no doubt with his tongue firmly in his cheek, for being "a strong and unflinching advocate of his own opinions."

However, the Kerryman would probably have preferred to be remembered for what he called his "humble but affectionate labour" – his book – which had realised its aim of "directing the steps of his countrymen" to the "abounding fountain of grace and mercy" – Lourdes! That, he felt, was his ultimate achievement.

Within months of its publication, Denis Shine Lawlor's book about Lourdes led to an extraordinary Irish cure. It involved a young woman from County Kerry who suffered from a life-threatening disease.

In early 1870, Denis Shine Lawlor presented a copy of his book, *Pilgrimages in the Pyrenees and Landes*, to one of his neighbours in County Kerry. The neighbours in question were the Morrogh Bernards, who lived just across Lough Leane from the author's estate, where they owned extensive landholdings amounting to 7,000 acres. Although Shine Lawlor could not have predicted it, the gift of his book would inspire what is believed to be Ireland's first Lourdes-related miraculous cure.

At that time, the Morrogh Bernards' 28-year-old daughter Agnes, who was a nun based in Dublin, suffered from alarming ill-health. To begin with, she had chronic eczema, which caused painful open sores to develop on her skin. More worryingly, the sores had become infected with streptococcal bacteria, causing a life-threatening condition known as erysipelas. In those pre-antibiotic days, erysipelas had resulted in the deaths of many people including author Charles Lamb, political philosopher John Stuart Mill, Pope Gregory XVI and John Brown, personal attendant and companion to Queen Victoria, among others.

On 2 October 1869, Agnes – whose religious name was Sr. Arsenius – had been rushed to St. Vincent's Hospital, Dublin. She was in a frightful state. Her face was swollen from the infection. Her treatment was extremely painful. "I had to keep the sores open by a very unpleasant and drastic method," her infirmarian, Sr. Canisius Cullen, stated. "What I had to do for her must have caused her excruciating pain. She humbly bowed her head in obedience. She never once complained, nor asked me to shorten the treatment."

Many treatments were resorted to, including a spell by the sea in the hope that fresh salt air might cure the wounds and relieve the pain. Nothing worked. Her condition deteriorated with the result that any noise – even a light footstep – caused the pain in her head to intensify. Six months passed by, and by mid-March a decision was taken to operate.

The prescribed surgical procedure – trepanning – was an ancient and dangerous one involving the use of a small circular saw to drill a hole in the patient's skull. Although it would hopefully relieve pressure, it was a risky form of intervention at the time. The operation was scheduled for 5 April 1870. "I offered my life to God," the patient, who was calm, remarked. So serious was the procedure, however, that she was given the Last Sacraments.

Not long before the operation, Shine Lawlor presented his book, which had recently been published, to the patient's mother. She was inspired and excited by what she read, especially about the miracles and cures. She instantly thought of her daughter in Dublin. We must get some Lourdes water, she said, and we need it urgently. Without any contacts in Lourdes, she wrote to the nuns in her daughter's order and begged them to somehow secure a sample for her ailing child.

Something fortunate – even providential – then took place. One of the patient's nurses, Sr. Otteran Kerr, had a problem with her eyesight and was in need of a cure. On the evening before Agnes's operation, a friend called to the nurse and said: "I have been given a drop of Lourdes water, and I thought it might be good for your eyes." The nurse couldn't believe it. She immediately ran into Agnes's sickroom and cried out: "I have it, I have it." She sprinkled the patient's head with the water.

The following morning, a clinician by the name of O'Leary arrived at Agnes's bedside to prepare her for the operation. He pressed softly on her head; she didn't respond. He pressed a little harder; there was no response again. He pressed harder still; once more there was no reaction. Normally, she would cry out in agony. "There is something strange here," he remarked, something "miraculous." He was mystified and perplexed. She told him about the Lourdes water. He then departed to tell the surgeon that he was no longer required. "Something beyond medical skill" has taken place, the baffled doctor declared.

For the remainder of her long life – she died aged 90 – Sr. Arsenius was convinced that it was Our Lady of Lourdes who brought about her miraculous cure. She had good cause to believe so, as not only did she recover full health but she went on to live an extraordinary life with her order, the Sisters of Charity. She was soon appointed to managerial positions and, in time, became rectress of a new convent in Ballaghaderreen, County Roscommon. There, she set up a national school, which provided meals, and an industrial school.

Greater things were yet to come. Sr. Arsenius also opened a convent in Foxford, County Mayo, in April 1891. The following year, 1892, she established the famous Foxford Woollen Mills, while additionally providing community education and even setting up a brass and reed band. Although a pioneer and visionary, she always credited the role of Providence in everything she achieved. Then again, why wouldn't she? After all, she believed that Providence brought the water from Lourdes which resulted in her miraculous cure all those years before, in 1870.

In light of the hopeful news regarding Lourdes cures, the first loosely-formed Irish pilgrimage departed Dublin for the shrine in 1876. Its purpose was to present a special gift on behalf of the people of Ireland.

In 1876, William Thompson – a wealthy wine merchant – left Dublin port by steamship and headed for Lourdes. He was a gentleman of stature, with premises in an imposing Georgian building in the capital's Lower Gardiner Street. There, this prosperous importer and retailer of fine wines ran his affairs alongside fellow professionals including surgeons, architects, solicitors and barristers.

Thompson's commercial set-up was impressive: "A visit to his extensive wine vaults and cellars, with their row upon row of hogsheads and barrels of every description of wine, must convince the most sceptical of the extent of his business," a leading newspaper remarked in the 1860s. A devout Catholic, by the 1870s he was regarded as a notable member of the merchant class in the city.

There was a purpose to Thompson's journey to Lourdes. For some time, a group of Irish Catholics had planned to present a special gift to the shrine on behalf of the people of Ireland. Knowing that other nations had made similar presentations, they believed it wrong that Catholic Ireland was not included. Wanting to make a mark, they settled on the idea of presenting a lamp – not just any old lamp, but the finest that could be manufactured in the country and, most importantly, the best that would be on display at Lourdes.

Thompson was accompanied on his journey by other esteemed gentlemen and, in a few cases, their wives. John O'Hagan, from Newry, County Down, was a noted lawyer, author and public speaker, and most of all a devout Catholic. "Anything and everything that Mr. John O'Hagan writes or says will be always sure to more than repay perusal," a Dublin newspaper remarked in the 1870s. Michael Gill ran a publishing company, concentrating on educational and primarily Catholic religious books. The grandson of Daniel O'Connell was another prominent Catholic. All three were there.

The Ardmore-born Msgr. Thomas John Capel, who we heard about earlier, also travelled, as did a number of other priests and businessmen. There was solicitor Henry V. Colclough, of Dublin's Dame Street; Fr. Cuddihy, of the diocese of Dublin, who was planning to make a short address at the ceremony; and Lady Duncan, a member of the aristocracy. The man who raised the money, Fr. Thomas Kinane, from County Tipperary, couldn't make it. They all knew each other, whether meeting at weddings, charity events or through business.

The group typified the new, confident Irish middle class, which was slowly flexing its muscles as a new sense of national pride spread through the land. They took an interest in self-rule, learned to speak their native language, were proud of the country's artistic and cultural heritage and, above all, were not afraid of being Catholic. They owned no land, as that had been expropriated by the British centuries before. They were also not barons of industry, as Ireland had little industry of note. Instead, they had risen to prominence in commerce, in the professions and through the Church. Their time in the sunshine was arriving, and they knew it.

It wasn't as if this new stratum of self-assured Catholics was respected by their Anglo-Irish or English counterparts; on the contrary, they were seen as a threat. So real was the hostility that one newspaper – *The Dundalk Democrat* – wrote in the mid-1870s of how the departing pilgrims might be in danger: "If the pilgrims land at Liverpool and proceed to London and Dover, they will be stared at by thousands, and insulted, perhaps, by hundreds; for the average Great Britain is a coarse animal, and he does not admire Irish Papists. But Irish Catholics can afford to smile at insults of this kind. Their forefathers have borne more serious assaults for the faith."

No doubt fortified by such reassurances, the party of Irish pilgrims set out for Lourdes in early September 1876. They brought with them the lamp, which had been manufactured at Patrick Donegan's jewellery establishment in Dublin's prestigious Dame Street. His business, which he had inherited from his late father, John, was a great success. Anything crafted by him – which included "timekeepers" and "snuff-boxes" – was guaranteed to be "well done," a newspaper from the period commented. Not only was he "respected and patriotic," as the broadsheet pointed out, but he was also, of course, Catholic.

The octagonal lamp, which was made of solid silver and weighed 400 ounces, was a beautiful piece of craftsmanship, a genuine work of art. The main body of the lamp was divided into eight panels, with each one containing representations of scriptural scenes or scenes of Irish interest. The vase for oil was made of coloured glass, encased in pierced Gothic silverwork.

The lamp's crown – of Gothic design – hung from ornate chains. The work was valued at £260, a lot of money for its time.

The lamp was "the latest evidence of the skill and genius of our Irish workmen in the silver trade manufacture for ecclesiastical purposes," remarked a commentary in *The Nation*, the prominent nationalist newspaper published out of Dublin. "High commendation is due for producing such a magnificent piece of work in our city," the commentary added. Not only did Patrick Donegan manufacture it for one-half the price that a similar imported model would cost but, exactly as was hoped, the lamp was "about the most valuable as yet presented by any nation to Lourdes."

On 8 September 1876, the Irish lamp was formally handed over to the authorities at Lourdes by the Dublin wine merchant, William Thompson. He had carried it to the church, at the head of a formal procession. "In a few moments the lamp was lifted to its position, and we had the joy of seeing it in the place of honour in the church, suspended in the very front of the tabernacle of the great altar, and right in the midst of a glittering array of lamps from nearly every Catholic country in the world," one of the Irish pilgrims later recalled.

Everyone was overjoyed, including American and European visitors who had dropped by to the event. "We all of us, priests as well as laics, felt somewhat – we hope pardonably – vain as we listened to the comments of admiration at our offering," an Irish pilgrim said. They had a right to be happy, as they had achieved what they had set out to do – imprint the mark of Catholic Ireland at the shrine in Lourdes. But they had done more than that – together they had formed the first informal Irish pilgrimage to the shrine of Our Lady and set in train a tradition that would be sustained by hundreds of thousands of Irish people in the years ahead.

It hadn't gone unnoticed by William Thompson and his fellow Irish pilgrims that, shortly before their arrival, a tradition of evening processions had been introduced to Lourdes. The processions – lit by thousands of torches and accompanied by the singing of hymns – became one of the great hallmarks of Lourdes.

In 1872, the first torchlight procession was held at Lourdes. Since then, thousands of pilgrims have assembled each evening near the grotto, where they light candles and form a parade of light. The effect is spellbinding. The long line of pilgrims becomes a river of flame, glowing, shimmering, as it eases along in the fading evening light. Prayers are said, hymns sung, intentions invoked, as this solemn, moving ribbon of light brings the day's events at Lourdes to a close.

In 1887, an English Jesuit with Irish connections witnessed one of the processions and recorded his impressions in a book. The man was Fr. Richard F. Clarke, a former Anglican clergyman who had converted to Catholicism and become Fellow and Tutor at St. John's College, Oxford. Four years earlier, he had spent time in Ireland investigating the distress and destitution of its famine-stricken population. His sympathetic report was followed by his account of Lourdes, notably his description of "the crowning ceremony of the day" – the evening procession of light.

The torchlight procession – *la procession aux flambeaux* – has always begun from near the grotto, where the pilgrims assemble for the much-anticipated event. As Fr. Clarke describes it, each of them holds a torch – a white candle, with blue rings, enclosed in a paper shield to shelter it from the wind. They have bought them from candle-sellers, who all afternoon have been plying their wares from the roadsides of the town. At the time of his visit, 7,000 pilgrims stood in the dim twilight awaiting the order to set the candles alight.

Suddenly, a single candle is lit, followed by some more, then thousands more, until with the fading light as a backdrop it seems as if the whole sky becomes a garden full of dancing golden flowers. "The crowd becomes simply a sea of light, or rather a sea of stars," notes Fr. Clarke. "It looks as if all the stars had come down from heaven and gathered there to honour the Queen of Heaven."

At 7.30 pm, the signal is given for the procession to begin. The vast sea of stars takes on a new form, slowly working its way into a thin band of light as the parade takes shape. The basilica's lamps come on. They twinkle in the evening sky, outlining the contours of the church in a soft golden glow. "This band gradually spreads up the zigzag path leading up to the basilica, until there is a zigzag stream of moving stars marching in curious zigzag pattern up the side of the hill," Fr. Clarke observes.

Like a luminous river, the procession threads its way to the basilica. It is no longer a line of silent people; instead, the pilgrims have begun to sing. At first, they intone in a low murmuring hum, but gradually the volume increases. "Ave, Ave, Ave Maria," they chant, "Ave, Ave, Ave Maria," the sound increasing in volume as they march along. The melody is haunting, the repetition enthralling, and the image memorable for the rest of the pilgrims' lives.

"Altogether there are nigh seven thousand persons taking part in it, all singing lustily," Fr. Clarke recalls. "In the midst is a brass band, which varies the harmony, but is sometimes a trifle too noisy, and drowns the voices in its vicinity. The effect of the body of sound rising simultaneously from all points of the procession is most curious and most effective."

Like a stream of molten lead slowly oozing from a red-hot furnace, the procession winds its way down the other side of the basilica and assembles by the Rosary Church. It takes some time for those who are at the rear to arrive. As the pilgrims gather together, the orderly line dissolves and once again the procession moulds into a mass of flickering lights.

"After a time, there is a new sea of light, into which the stragglers hurry up at double-quick time, until all are there," according to Fr. Clarke. "Then there is a short pause, and on that still autumn evening there rise through the air the vigorous tones of a bishop belonging to one of the pilgrimages. It is so quiet that I can catch most of what he says, though he must be a quarter of a mile away. The topic is ever the same, Our dear Lady, Our Lady of Lourdes."

Finally, the *Credo* is sung and the candles are extinguished. The bishops who are present bestow their joint blessing. There is a discernible hush. The hush persists, as Lourdes begins its night of sleep and silence. "By this time it is past ten," Fr. Clarke notes, "and the assembly breaks up to refresh their weary limbs with sweet repose. Such is a pilgrim's day at Lourdes."

Another early Irish traveller to Lourdes was the author Hugh Caraher. He visited the shrine in 1877, less than two decades after the apparitions.

At 5 o'clock, on the morning of 31 July 1877, Hugh Caraher arose from his bed at Lourdes. There was glorious sunshine outside his window. Crowds were already milling on the street, most of them either walking to or returning from the famous shrine. The Irish author was rested, having reached his hotel the evening before. It had been a long journey, but he was wide awake, dressed and ready to go.

It had taken Caraher five days to travel from Liverpool to Lourdes. He had chosen to travel by the Pacific Company's mail steamship *Sorato*, which was bound for the west coast of America, via Bordeaux. "With a fine evening and a noble ship, all was joyousness on board," the author said of the boat's first hours at sea. Unfortunately, conditions deteriorated and, as he put it, "the *mal de mer* had paid a visit to the pillows of many." Very few passengers were to be seen on deck the next day, he noted.

Although most of his fellow travellers had been bound for Spain or the Americas, not a few were on their way to Lourdes. Among the latter were two devout Catholics – the grandson of the Liberator, Daniel O'Connell, who, as we saw earlier in this chapter, had been in Lourdes the year before; the other was the grandson of Charles Bianconi, the entrepreneur who, in the days before railways and motor cars, had transformed transport in Ireland with his network of horse-drawn carriage services.

While pleased to meet his fellow countrymen on board ship, Caraher was even more delighted by the number of Irish people he encountered on arrival at Lourdes. On his second day, he bumped into two of them. The first was a Dublin-born Jesuit, Fr. Christopher Carton, who was working as a confessor at the shrine. In his mid-40s, he belonged to one of Dublin's most respected families and, as one acquaintance remarked, was "universally esteemed." How this man, who has largely been forgotten by history, ended up in Lourdes is completely unknown today; how much he knew about Bernadette and the shrine is also long forgotten.

On the day Caraher met him, Fr. Carton was sorting out the problems of another Irishman, who had got himself into a bit of a mess. His name was James Talbot, from Clonmel, County Tipperary. Having lost the full use of his right side, he had come to Lourdes in search of a cure. His trip had been partly paid for by friends. A bit of a bewildered, lost soul, his adventure had turned into something of a nightmare.

Talbot had taken a wrong turn *en route* to Lourdes, ending up in Toulouse, where he thought the shrine was located. Having only one word of French – "Irlandais" – he was eventually put on a train and arrived at the correct destination. The man was now not only totally confused but penniless. That's when Fr. Carton stepped in, paid for his accommodation, and bought him a ticket back to Clonmel. "All who know Father Carton will say, 'It's just like him,'" Caraher remarked of this kindly priest.

Even at the time of Caraher's visit – less than two decades after the apparitions – Lourdes was a fast-changing place. Business was booming and the streets were full of stalls. "The nuisance created by the noise of the vendors is very distracting," the author remarked. Yet, the town still had its appeal. Caraher lyrically observed "the leafy bowers surrounding the church and grotto" which, he said, "shone out in all their various tints of shade."

He also noticed the beauty of the women who, because of the town's close proximity to Spain, had "a tinge of Spanish features."

It would be impossible to visit Lourdes without encountering cures. Caraher's visit was no exception. In a four-week period overlapping with the time he was there, no less than 35 miracles were reported, he later pointed out in his book *A Month at Lourdes and its Neighbourhood*. One of them involved an obstinate Irishman, who was determined not to leave the shrine until he was well.

The man had travelled to Lourdes to seek relief from what Caraher described as "a long-endured infirmity." During his time at the shrine, he was fortunate to achieve his goal. He began his return to Ireland a happy man, travelling by rail to Bordeaux, where he boarded the steamship for home. As the steamer sailed down the Garonne, his former illness returned. Thirty miles later, the ship stopped at Pauillac. The man decided to forfeit his fare, leave the vessel and return to Lourdes.

Asked why he was leaving, he said: "I came from Ireland to the shrine of Our Lady at Lourdes, to be cured, and I will go back to that blessed spot and make the Blessed Virgin cure me!" That's exactly what he did. Back to Lourdes he went, he prayed and prayed, and eventually his infirmity disappeared. Caraher reported that, at the time of writing, the man's malady had not returned.

As the title of Hugh Caraher's book implies – *A Month at Lourdes and its Neighbourhood* – his time at the shrine was limited and he would soon have to return home. During his visit, he had traversed some of the most beautiful parts of France. He had witnessed fierce thunderstorms and basked in glorious sunshine. He had seen the mountains, valleys and woods of the

River Gave. But, most of all, he had been to the place of his dreams – that charming place, he concluded, where "I had spent the happiest weeks of my life."

During his visit to Lourdes, Hugh Caraher also was struck by a newly-composed hymn sung by pilgrims. Composed in 1873 by a French priest, Abbé Jean Gaignet, it was known as the Lourdes hymn or, more commonly, as the *Ave Maria*.

Although Hugh Caraher might not have appreciated it at the time, the simple, compelling melody commonly known as the *Ave Maria*, with its repetitive, hypnotic refrain – "Ave, Ave, Ave Maria" – would become the undisputed anthem of Lourdes during the next century and a half. He initially heard it at the torchlight procession. Conducted in the evening darkness, and set in a blazing sea of light, the highlight of the event was the new hymn.

As it was being sung, the basilica was encircled with robes of light. Thousands of candles burned before the shrine of Our Lady. Six thousand people held lighted torches in their hands. But the brightest light was "the melody of the thousand voices of priests and people" singing the *Ave Maria*. It was a scene, Caraher remarked, "which anyone who had the privilege of witnessing can never forget."

The *Ave Maria* hymn was written by the priest and seminary director, Abbé Jean Gaignet, from the town of Luçon, in western France. He was a devout cleric and scholar, tall and strong, and described as austere yet open-minded. He suffered tragedy in his early 30s, when his two brothers were killed in the Franco-German War of 1870. To recover, he travelled to the south of

France – to the Pyrenees – and was captivated by the hymns and melodies of the area.

It was a fortuitous visit, as Luçon – the ancient seaport he came from, which was set in the Vendée region of France – was providing many early pilgrims to Lourdes. Wishing to furnish them with a hymn of their own, he recalled a traditional Pyrenean melody and superimposed on it a series of eight verses. The resulting hymn, the *Ave Maria*, immediately became popular with pilgrimages to Lourdes.

There was good reason for its immediate success. It had a beautiful melody and it was easy to sing. Everyone could remember, and deliver, the chorus. No matter how many people were singing it, the verses all seemed to roll together in one wonderful patchwork of song. Soon, Abbé Gaignet was being asked to extend the number of verses, to accommodate the ever-lengthening evening processions. He did so, writing 120 in all. Although not everyone could remember them, no one would forget the chorus, "Ave, Ave, Ave Maria."

Within a few decades, the *Ave Maria* was copper-fastened as the symbolic hymn of Lourdes. All nationalities sang it – at the evening procession, in churches, on the trains and boats that brought them to the sacred shrine, occasionally on the streets or in hotels where they would spontaneously burst into delivering its captivating refrain. Irish pilgrims sang it as they departed by boat from Dublin, or on their later return. It was eventually sung by pilgrims on planes and in high-speed TGVs as they hurtled southwards through France.

Irish newspapers first remarked on its popularity in 1875. *The Freeman's Journal* commented on the chanting of the hymn and how "four lines of a popular hymn to the Blessed Virgin were sung in unison" at Lourdes. A later newspaper report described how pilgrims intoned the hymn as they arrived at the shrine: "We crowded to the carriage windows and sang again the Lourdes hymn, 'Ave, Ave, Ave Maria,' while tears came to many eyes and the train entered the station."

In 1928, John Gibbons, an English author who travelled in and wrote extensively about Ireland, also wrote about Lourdes and the *Ave Maria*. "The thing is all over Lourdes," he observed. "They sing it on the trains as they leave Victoria Station in London, they sing it on the boat, they sing it down the twenty-two-hour rail journey through France, and they are singing it harder than ever as the train gets into Lourdes.

"They sell the score of it at the one little official shop, and at a hundred shops in the town they sell images which when you wind a screw in the base turn into musical-boxes and play always the same tune. The hymn is the key-note of all Lourdes. Somewhere in the distance down the line is a band playing the thing. It is a good half-bar in front, but with all the priests' frantic efforts as, walking backwards, they beat time frenziedly at their flocks with their hands, it is impossible to keep a score of nationalities all correct to the very note."

Almost 150 years after it was composed, there is hardly a country in the world that hasn't translated the Lourdes hymn – the *Ave Maria* – into its respective language, although the refrain of "Ave, Ave, Ave Maria" is always kept the same. Indeed, the hymn has spread so widely that a relative of its composer – Abbé Olivier Gaignet – encountered it in Africa, in 1977. On arrival in Mali, he was received by the Archbishop of Bamako. "During our conversation, the chime of his clock played the *Ave Maria* of Lourdes," he recalled.

The hymn's composer, Abbé Jean Gaignet, died in 1914, aged 75, leaving behind one of the most memorable hymns in

Church history. Although regarded today as a universal symbol of Marian devotion, it is in Lourdes that it retains its ultimate potency and power. The diocesan bulletin of Luçon put it well in 1925: "The *Ave Maria* would not exist without Lourdes. But it can be said that the pilgrims of the world cannot imagine Lourdes without the *Ave Maria*." The link is as strong as that.

Another feature of Lourdes – the baths – was becoming world-famous by the 1890s. It was there that many cures were taking place.

Louise David was 16 years of age when she was immersed in the baths at Lourdes. For two and a half years, she had suffered from a lesion of the spinal column. Confined to bed during the 30 months, she had developed internal sores, one of which had formed at the root of her spinal nerves. As a consequence, her left leg had been turned inward and could only be straightened with great effort. Moreover, her side had become so sensitive that the slightest touch caused intense pain.

In August 1895, Louise was brought to Lourdes, where she was twice immersed in the baths. So painful was the shock caused by the cold water that the women attending her cried out of compassion. Immediately after emerging, Louise was brought to the procession of the Blessed Sacrament. Lifted in her father's arms, she kissed the monstrance three times. Suddenly, she exclaimed to her father, "Let me down. I am going to walk!" And she did. "She had been cured in an instant," a subsequent report explained.

By the mid-1890s, extraordinary cures following immersion in the water of Lourdes were being reported on a regular basis. The first description dated back to the time of Bernadette's apparitions; since then, numerous accounts had been recorded. It seemed as if every believer who was sick sought to follow Our Lady's words to Bernadette: "Go and drink at the spring and wash yourself there." In time, the one distinctive feature that marked out Lourdes compared to other religious sites was arguably the presence of its miraculous water.

The authorities at Lourdes were excited by the first reported miracles associated with their newfound spring. The mayor, spotting a commercial advantage and hoping that the town might rival other spa resorts in the region, commissioned an analysis of the water's properties. The first authoritative report was clear in its conclusions – "This water contains no active substance capable of endowing it with marked medicinal properties." In other words, it was just ordinary water. It followed that wherever the cures came from they didn't come from the water – instead, people said, they must have derived from God.

Lourdes water started out as a tiny trickle discovered by Bernadette on 25 February 1858. A basin – or pool – was soon hollowed out by quarry workers. That pool, in which Justin Bouhort was cured, became the first nominal baths. A few years later, it was replaced by a wooden shed constructed near the grotto. Each of its two compartments contained a bowl into which water was pumped by hand. Further refinements followed until, in the early 1890s, a structure containing nine baths was put in place. The demolition of that structure, in 1955, broke many hearts due to the cures reported within its walls.

In the 1890s, the scene at the baths was colourful, if intense. Outside could be seen a long row of carriages, stretchers, chairs and portable beds carrying the sick. Inside, in the plain stone baths, were the ill and infirm seeking cures. The dense mass of people outside, their arms outstretched, prayed for those inside. "All day long these unceasing prayers go up to heaven," one Irish pilgrim commented at the time.

If a cure was declared, the place erupted with joy. Hymns were chanted, faces suddenly lit up. "The strange surroundings – the living faith you see – the hope on the faces of the sick; the subdued joy on the face of the cured; the chant gaining fresh strength in open air as it spreads from group to group all along the baths by the grotto; all this forms an experience for you, which you can and must feel, but which you can badly describe," the Irish pilgrim said.

Pilgrims also either drank the water or filled their bottles to bring copious amounts back home. The water – initially made available in a number of crude receptacles – was eventually provided in a marble container known as "the fountain". The fountain is "just to the left of the grotto," another Irish pilgrim observed in the 1890s. "Some drink from pretty shells that are sold as souvenirs of the place, and some from the metal cup chained to the marble which now encloses and preserves the fountain." In time, the fountain was replaced by taps.

"Nearly every pilgrim had brought home a large tin or bottle of Lourdes water," a journalist noted as he watched passengers from Lourdes disembark from their boat at Dublin's North Wall. The containers were decorated in blue and white. "People were there begging of the pilgrims a little of the water, and though loath to part with it, some in their generosity could not refuse." Other people had water delivered to their homes, either by hand or by post. Through this method, Joseph Dalton – a Waterford man living in Australia – had his sight miraculously restored. "I was thunderstruck," he said of his cure.

Towards the end of the nineteenth century, it was with the legendary baths that the cures and revivals were mostly related. Although freezing cold, those immersed in the water never died of shock. Neither had anyone caught a chill or cold from their immersion. Nor had they fallen sick from any diseases, even though the water was not changed during a bathing session. The water was "much polluted with all types of germs," the Irish prelate, Msgr. Joseph Deery, wrote in his book, *Our Lady of Lourdes*, "yet no disease has ever been contracted from it."

Why the water was so powerful, so miraculous in its impact, yet so benign after being frequented by people with diseases and illnesses, was an easily-resolved conundrum, said Msgr. Deery. No one refuted that it was just ordinary drinking water, he pointed out. Therefore, he said, there is only one conclusion: "The physical cures obtained through its use must be attributed solely to a supernatural power given to it by God: and taking all the circumstances into account, this divine intervention must be ascribed to the intercession of Our Lady of Lourdes."

The spring water of Lourdes was the main reason why two young ladies from Boyle, County Roscommon, undertook one of the strangest, and most circuitous, visits to Lourdes in 1893.

It's a long way from Boyle, County Roscommon, to Lourdes – more than 2,000 km by road. The trip felt even longer back in the 1890s, when travel was more arduous than today. The journey was even more painful if you travelled in the wrong direction, had to rectify your mistake, and ended up zigzagging your way to south-west France!

That's exactly what happened to two girls from Boyle, County Roscommon, in 1893. Their names were Mary Anne and Bridget who, by all accounts, were responsible, well brought up, and boasted a not-inconsiderable supply of poise and sophistication. Unfortunately, when it came to foreign travel, all these qualities seemed to desert them.

Having journeyed through Ireland, Wales and England, they became a trifle confused when they reached France. Instead of heading south from Paris, they took a train in the opposite direction, to Brussels. From there, they headed to Bordeaux, pointed themselves in the general direction of the Pyrenees, and eventually, with much good fortune, arrived at Lourdes.

"How these selected pilgrims from Boyle ever did reach Lourdes still remains a mystery to me," wrote Stephen Bonsal, a 28-year-old American writer who was visiting the pilgrimage site to compile a feature report. Although the girls couldn't have guessed it at the time, Bonsal was already on his way to becoming a highly-regarded war correspondent, author, diplomat and translator, and would eventually go on to win a Pulitzer Prize. Throughout his career, he reported from war-torn Cuba, China, Japan, Macedonia and Russia. In time, he visited every country in Europe, most of Asia, and travelled through South America.

At Lourdes, Bonsal spent "many hours" listening attentively to the girls' adventures – a most agreeable task, he said. Their story began on a "proud day" on the village green, at Boyle, when a Fr. O'Brien selected them from a class of 38 to travel to Lourdes on an errand. Their job was to bring back jugs of holy water, along with "great bundles of rosaries, chaplets, and beads that had been blessed by the priest of the grotto, and rendered sacred by being rubbed up and down against the walls of the cave." They had been chosen, Bonsal said, because of "the superior excellence of their maidenly deportment."

Although Bonsal restrained himself from going into detail, he explained that the girls experienced some misadventures in Paris, where they "nearly cried their eyes out." Their worst misfortune was when they took the express train from Paris to Brussels instead of the "rapide" for Bordeaux. Things weren't helped, they said, by the "astonishing ignorance of English which the French invariably displayed." Having finally reached Bordeaux, they drifted into the valley of the Pyrenees and arrived at Lourdes with a "crowd of pilgrims."

"Early in the morning and late in the evening I saw them drawing water from the miracle spring and carrying it up the hillside and into the city in earthenware jars," Bonsal later wrote. "In their lodgings they had placed a score or more of mammoth milk cans in which they intended to transport the waters back to Boyle. It was weary, slow work."

One afternoon, Bonsal stumbled across information which stopped the girls in their tracks. He had spotted some important Irish news in *La Croix*, "the church organ which was our only channel of communication with the outside world," as the journalist explained. The news was dramatic, to say the least – Gladstone's second Home Rule Bill had passed the House of Commons.

"We made merry as best we might in the shadow of the holy places," Bonsal recollected. "But on the part of the colleens the gaiety was forced and far from real. Tears came into their eyes as they thought of what they were missing, in being absent from Ireland on such a memorable day. 'There will be many a bonfire around Boyle tonight,' said Bridget, regretfully. 'And maybe there will be a little fighting down in the market place,' added Mary Anne, right ruefully."

For the record, that House of Commons vote was passed on 1 September 1893 by a majority of 301 to 267 votes. Six months later, at the beginning of March 1894, Stephen Bonsal's article was published in the highly-influential, upmarket periodical, *The Century Magazine*. Although the girls featured prominently, he never disclosed what happened to them following that fateful day when it looked as if Ireland might achieve Home Rule.

In the following years, Stephen Bonsal went on to enormous success, serving as a journalist and foreign correspondent for *The New York Herald* and *The New York Times*, becoming a Lieutenant Colonel with the American Expeditionary Forces during World War I, and acting as President Woodrow Wilson's translator at the Paris Peace Conference in 1919. His book, *Unfinished Business*, which was published in 1944, won him a Pulitzer Prize for History.

As for the girls, they disappeared from view. We can only speculate that they returned to Boyle, County Roscommon, with their rosaries, chaplets and beads, not to mention their milk cans containing Lourdes holy water. Hopefully, these "two green-eyed Irish girls," as Bonsal called them, had an easier, smoother, more direct journey home, via Paris and not via Brussels or some other city east of the Volga!

A book published in 1894, which was written by the French novelist Émile Zola, questioned how miracles at Lourdes came about. A bitter debate pitting science against faith ensued.

The 1890s was a great decade for writers. Tolstoy, Ibsen and Twain were still at work in their respective home countries. Conan Doyle, Kipling and Wilde were on the go, too. In France, Émile Zola was the man everyone talked about. Not only was he acclaimed, but he was controversial. Indeed, Zola was so controversial that when Catholics heard he was interested in tackling the issue of Lourdes, they erupted in an uncontrolled rage.

"The news that M. Zola intends laying his polluted hands on the sacred shrine and associations of Lourdes will be received by Catholics with feelings of indignation" was how one Irish newspaper, *The Freeman's Journal*, put it. Harsh though that remark might seem, there was worse to come. Another Irish newspaper, *The Drogheda Independent*, dismissed Zola as an author "who has carried his diagnosis of human degradation to the most revolting point of cynical brutality." The message was clear – the French author wasn't welcome poking his nose into Lourdes.

The truth was that Zola didn't put much store in religious belief or faith. Instead, he took a scientific view of matters, arguing that all things could be explained rationally. Spectacular cures might happen, but the explanation was to be found in science and not in God. Be realistic, he declared, how could anyone in an era of steam engines and the telegraph believe that the Virgin Mary had appeared in the little French town of Lourdes? How could anyone believe that miracles had ensued, as a result? The truth, he said, lay elsewhere.

To find out the "truth," Zola travelled to Lourdes to witness the religious phenomenon and conduct interviews. His most important visit was in 1892, when he accompanied a pilgrimage to the shrine. "I am like St. Thomas," he said. "I must touch and see for myself, put my hands into the wounds and feel for myself that they are really healed." Newspaper editors raised their eyes to heaven anticipating what was in store. "It is feared that Zola's presence in a pilgrimage will put a strain upon the forbearance of the devout," Dublin's *Evening Herald* acidly remarked.

Things didn't go exactly as planned for the writer. At one stage, while visiting the town's hospital, he had an experience which upset him greatly. Stopping by the bed of a young boy dying of TB, the little patient said: "Is it true you are going to write against Our Lady of Lourdes?" "No, my child," Zola responded, "who told you so?" "One of those gentlemen," the child said, pointing to the stretcher-bearers.

The boy then said something strange: "If I am not cured it is because I wish to remain ill." "Why?" Zola asked. "When they told me a great writer was here to write against the Blessed Virgin, I made the sacrifice of my life and asked that instead of being cured, Our Lady might convert him," the young lad said. Zola, who was deeply moved, presented his hand to the boy with emotion.

Zola also witnessed an extraordinary cure. He was with the recipient – an 18-year-old girl – when it happened. She suffered from advanced lupus, TB and enormous leg ulcers. Her face, he remarked, "was a frightful distorted mass of matter and oozing blood." After entering the baths, the girl was completely cured. Zola wasn't impressed. If he was to believe, he said, he would have "to see a cut finger dipped in water and come out healed." He then walked away.

Zola's book – which was simply called *Lourdes* and published in 1894 – was true to form. Although written as a novel, it was based on the real-life events he had witnessed at the shrine. The results weren't to Catholic tastes. Cures happened, he argued, but they had scientific roots such as hypnotic suggestion or faith healing. They did not originate from supernatural sources. "Were I to see all the sick at Lourdes cured, I would not believe in a miracle," he declared.

The reaction of Catholics was scathing. Not only was Zola's work "ponderous fiction," but his interpretation of the history of the famous shrine was "almost beneath contempt," according to *The Freeman's Journal. The Cork Examiner* said it was a "scoffing novel." To make matters worse, Zola was sued for libel over remarks related to Lourdes which he made in the Parisian literary periodical, *Gil Blas.* The book was placed on the Vatican's index of banned books.

Pope Leo XIII became involved in the controversy, accusing Zola of causing "great pain to all Catholic hearts" and of having contemptuously trodden truth underfoot. The French author counterattacked, arguing that the Pontiff was merely defending pilgrims because of the financial contributions they made to Rome. Come to think of it, Zola said, Rome wouldn't be a bad subject for his next book. "To write it I shall make a rather prolonged stay in the Eternal City," he dryly remarked. He would also seek an audience with the Pope. Although it seemed only like a threat at the time, for his next book Zola actually did focus on Rome, even though he never got that audience with the Pope!

The controversy over Zola raged for decades. That it did so was not surprising, as the issues were fundamental to society's views about the nature of faith. At stake was the battle between science and religion, the veracity of miracles, and the truth or otherwise regarding the existence of God. That conflict, which was also about the validity of Lourdes, has not gone away even today, and it was all started by a man who once declared that while many people might believe in Bernadette's visions, "I do not, and that is all about it."

Émile Zola inspired a generation of writers, including Dubliner James Joyce. Although Joyce eventually became hostile to Catholicism, in his youth, in the 1880s and '90s, he was a devotee of Our Lady and was strongly influenced by events at Lourdes.

You would be hard-pressed to believe that James Joyce was ever a devout Catholic. In his writings and conversations as an adult, he presented a virulent disdain and hostility towards the faith of his youth. He railed against the Church's "Roman tyranny" and declared "I make open war upon it by what I write and say and do." His erstwhile educators, the Jesuits, shunned him. University College Dublin, where he had studied, turned their back on him. Rightly so, they believed, as Joyce was not pious enough to be remembered as one of their own.

It wasn't always so. As a boy, Joyce was not only religious – he served as an altar boy – but was a great devotee of Our Lady. When he was aged 13, in 1895, he was elected to the Sodality of Our Lady at his school, the Jesuit-run Belvedere College, Dublin. Membership of the sodality, which was founded by the Jesuits in the sixteenth century, was a mark of honour. Members prayed, said novenas and dedicated themselves to the Blessed Virgin, whose popularity had grown exponentially since the Lourdes apparitions. Many sodality members went on to join the priesthood.

Joyce also grew up in a Dublin where Lourdes dominated conversations in tea rooms, gentlemen's clubs, smart suburban parlours, and in the city's slums. There were reports of cures including numerous cancerous tumours vanishing, deformities disappearing, rheumatics no longer feeling pain, blind people having their sight restored, and the lame casting off their crutches and walking. The news was dramatic, to say the least. Allied to Lourdes pilgrimages, lectures, sermons and novenas, together they formed part of an atmosphere that profoundly influenced the young James Joyce.

Years before he became famous – when he was still in his 20s – Joyce set about earning money by opening Ireland's first dedicated cinema, the Cinematograph Volta, at 45 Mary Street, Dublin. He was careful to include Lourdes among films he presented during his short time in charge. *Sister Angelica, a Legend of Lourdes* – a tragic love story – was featured during his tenure. Even though his experiment at providing cinematic "exhibitions" was deemed by critics to be successful, he retired from the project after seven months and directed his talents elsewhere.

After exiling himself to the continent, Joyce returned to Dublin for visits, although these ceased for good after 1912. He lived in Trieste, Paris and Zurich, and published his great literary masterpieces, *Dubliners* (1914), *A Portrait of the Artist as a Young Man* (1916), *Ulysses* (1922) and *Finnegans Wake* (1939). Even when writing abroad, his works were firmly rooted in his native Dublin. "I always write about Dublin," he once said, "because if I can get to the heart of Dublin I can get to the heart of all the cities of the world." Of course, the Dublin he knew was a Dublin obsessed with Lourdes.

Many references to Lourdes appear in his writings, most amusingly in a scene in *Ulysses*, where two pious, elderly ladies – Anne Kearns and Florence MacCabe – climb Dublin's Nelson's

Pillar. They waddle slowly to the top, out of breath, "praising God and the Blessed Virgin" as they painfully thread their way up the steps. Anne, we are told, has "the lumbago for which she rubs on Lourdes water, given her by a lady who got a bottleful from a passionist father." Seemingly, the Lourdes water works, as the pair reach the pinnacle where, tired and fearful of the height, they proceed to eat a bag of plums!

Leopold Bloom, the hero of *Ulysses*, additionally mentions Lourdes when referring to the Catholic Mass. He compares it to the "Lourdes cure" and the "waters of oblivion." It reminds him of the Knock apparition, statues bleeding, an old fellow asleep near the confession box – "hence those snores." Stephen Dedalus, again in *Ulysses*, describes a midwife he sees on the beach as swinging her bag "lourdily."

Once more, in *Ulysses*, we read of Bloom who, when working as a bill collector, failed to collect a debt from a convent. The nun who refused him payment was young, attractive and aroused his desires. She was also unavailable and uninterested, and described in the book, in Joyce's inimitable style, as: "Tranquilla convent. Sister Agatha. Mount Carmel, the apparitions of Knock and Lourdes. No more desire.....Only the ethereal." Even in *Finnegans Wake*, the cry "My Lourde! My Lourde!" is used instead of "My Lord! My Lord!"

As far as Joyce was concerned, referencing religion was one thing; practising it was another. In spite of the all-pervasive presence of Catholic symbolism and practices in his works – including a large number of priests featured in *Dubliners* – he turned away from the religion of his youth as he progressed through life. For the remainder of his days, he fought a private war against Church dogmas, refused to be married in a church, didn't have his children baptised, and didn't receive the last rites or a Catholic funeral.

Following his death, on 13 January 1941, Joyce was buried in Zurich. The ceremony was "simple, with no clergyman, no scripture reading, and no prayer," the *Irish Independent* noted. No Irish state representative attended, and later requests by his wife to have his body repatriated to Ireland were turned down. We don't know if anyone prayed for Joyce's soul at Lourdes. But we do know that his sister – Sr. Mary Gertrude, a Mercy Order nun in New Zealand – remembered him at her convent, where she had prayed for him daily, and whose prized possession was the surplice he wore as an altar boy when he was young!

By the end of the nineteenth century, Lourdes had developed into a thriving urban centre and pilgrimage site, according to newspaper reports from the time.

In 1895, the prestigious American newspaper *The Boston Pilot* – edited by Laois man, James Jeffrey Roche – provided a fascinating description of the progression of Lourdes from a modest country market town into a flourishing urban centre. Since the apparitions in 1858, Lourdes had become "a splendidly laid out city, with fine streets, spacious gardens, magnificent houses and hotels, the whole lighted by electricity," the newspaper remarked. Its growth, it continued, was "as great a wonder as the miracles that occur here."

The commentary – published less than four decades after the apparitions – highlighted how popular Lourdes had become. The basilica was filled with offerings of gratitude for favours received, left there by pilgrims. There were officers' epaulettes, swords, military decorations, Crosses of the Legion of Honour, and other civil decorations. Most moving of all were "thick coils of hair, woven into a sort of rope," which were the offerings of five Hungarian women who had nothing of greater value to give. The hair, the newspaper remarked, was "the richest treasure they possessed."

By the close of the century, pilgrims were coming in huge numbers. Formal pilgrimages during the high season amounted to around 150, embracing in the region of 125,000 people. The annual number of pilgrims who travelled on their own or in small groups amounted to probably as many again. One pilgrimage, consisting of men from the different provinces of France, was 40,000 strong. Around 400,000 communions were distributed each year to the pilgrims, and more than 25,000 Masses were celebrated at the shrine.

During the French national pilgrimage, close to 1,000 sick people were attended to in the hospital. In one year alone, a staggering number of sick women, amounting to around 50,000, had immersed themselves in the baths, together with upwards of 20,000 men. More than 3,000,000 petitions to the Blessed Virgin were received from all parts of the world, including almost 50,000 thanksgivings for favours received.

Staggering though those numbers were, they were matched by the lavish gifts donated to the shrine. The offerings included a magnificent monstrance, hundreds of jewels, together with the ornate insignia and military medals mentioned earlier. The Catholics of Brittany had erected a monument in marble representing the crucifixion. New marble altars had been added to several of the chapels, and the Church of the Rosary had been adorned with mosaics.

News of further miracles and cures was also emerging as the century came to a close. One woman, aged 25, with an unknown disease, arrived at the shrine pallid, speechless, skeletal, looking like a corpse. She weighed only 40 lbs, around the weight of a child of six. She was unable to eat or leave her bed. On her departure for Lourdes, her doctor had given her 15 days to live. As the Blessed Sacrament was brought past her at the grotto, she rose from her stretcher and exclaimed, "I am cured!" A few months later, she weighed 110 lbs and had gained three inches in height.

A young boy, whose arm was paralysed, withered and dead, was also cured. The skin on his arm had become discoloured and was falling away in scales. He had been treated at a hospital, but without any satisfactory result. Once again, as the Blessed Sacrament passed him, he instantly felt a violent shock in the withered arm; motion, heat and life returned to it, he took off his splints, and he was cured.

A 12-year-old boy, lying nearby, had suffered from TB of the hip joint since infancy. The hip was oozing pus. Again, as the Blessed Sacrament was brought past him, he caught on to the vestment of the priest and would not let go. "I will not let go unless I get up cured," he shouted. A moment later, he rose to his feet healed.

So great was the number of cures that a returning pilgrim highlighted them, in September 1899, in *The Cork Examiner*. Not only did he describe how one young girl had discarded her crutches following immersion in the icy pool, but he went on to outline how the general area was littered with mementoes of miraculous revivals. "The crutches, testamentary evidence of many cures, make a heap that fills the whole side of the grotto, and outside are crutches, iron frames, litters, and other appliances of the sick, piled as high as a house," he said.

Perhaps the most telling insight to the progression of Lourdes was provided by the marble tablets lining the walls of the basilica, which recorded the visits of private pilgrims and public pilgrimages. They told of individual cures and expressed the gratitude of people who received miracles, *The Boston Pilot* informed its readers.

Those tablets, the newspaper said, were the outpouring in enduring marble of the gratitude of those who came to Lourdes in search of a cure through "Our Lady's powerful intercession, and who have gone away healed." As the century drew to a close, the author of the article was able to conclude: "If the unbeliever desires proof of belief, here it is."

SEARCHING FOR CURES

Irish miracles at Lourdes regularly appeared in the national press during the opening decades of the twentieth century. Recoveries from paralysis, TB, deafness, nerve pain, spinal disorders and many other illnesses and diseases were featured. So widespread were the reported miracles that, in 1913, a *Daily Mail* correspondent wrote that Lourdes was "ringing with the news" of Irish cures.

Drawn by the extraordinary attractions of the shrine, Irish pilgrims set off on long, tiring journeys to south-west France. It took two and a half days to reach there and the same to return. They came from all four corners of Ireland – from Wexford to Donegal, from Kerry to Antrim, and from all the counties in between.

Many participated in the unforgettable 1913 Irish National Pilgrimage, which was the first organised pilgrimage to leave for the shrine from Irish shores. Representing every diocese in the country, it was said that "there had been nothing like it in the whole history of Lourdes."

The first Irish National Pilgrimage to Lourdes, which departed in 1913, marked the most profound public display of devotion seen in Ireland up to that time.

More than 3,000 Irish men, women and children of all ages converged on the country's main ports in September 1913. There were people on stretchers and in wheelchairs, nuns, priests, doctors, nurses and ambulance men, not to mention ordinary Catholics who were just plain curious or devout. Most had left their tiny parishes and villages for the very first time. Some had never been on a train or a boat, or seen the streets of a town or city. All were heading on the adventure of a lifetime to a faraway place called Lourdes.

The atmosphere during their departure was electric. Pilgrims crowded the decks of their ships from bow to stern, waving to those onshore. Their friends and relatives waved back. As the steamers weighed anchor, the crowds on the quaysides sang the *Ave Maria*, *Hail Glorious St. Patrick* and *Star of the Sea*. The hymns were taken up by those on board. A mighty explosion of song rang out, echoing over the sea as the ships withdrew farther and farther from the shore.

This mass accumulation of people – many of them severely incapacitated – eventually made its way to England and onward to Paris, Bordeaux and Lourdes. "It was only when we arrived and saw the passengers disembarked that we realised the number of helpless invalids that had come that long journey from different parts of Ireland," Rose Lynch, the Cork author, who was on the pilgrimage, later wrote.

"No one looking at that moving hospital could help marvelling at the courage and faith that had carried them so bravely, so patiently, through the fatigue and sufferings of that long trying journey. No wonder a great love and pride welled up in my heart for my own dear Irish people when a French abbé, glancing around at the large number of invalids, turned to me, and, raising his hands and eyes to heaven, said: 'All these have crossed two seas? Impossible, Mademoiselle, impossible!'"

The mass movement of people from all corners of Ireland was a triumph for the pilgrimage's Irish organisers. The logistics involved in conveying so many invalids across three different countries, onto and off trains, into boats and to their rooms in hotels – all done without ramps, elevators or other aids that are now available – is hard to imagine today. That it was achieved with the 1913 "lockout" as a backdrop – with its strikes, travel disruption and general upheaval, never mind the hunger and deprivation it caused – was a miracle in itself.

What made the trip an ultimate success was the camaraderie and selflessness of those who participated. "A sight met my gaze that I shall never forget as long as life lasts," Rose Lynch recalled. "Out in the courtyard of the hospital, partly sheltered by trees from the fierce sun, were a crowd of invalids, some on stretchers, others in bath-chairs – in a word, all those who were too ill to be moved into the refectory for dinner. Ladies were passing to and fro among them, helping them."

Close to Rose was "a beautiful young girl, dressed in white, with roses in her belt. She was seeing after a woman far gone in consumption. Presently she slipped her arm underneath the tired head, and, raising her up, fed her spoonful by spoonful, just as if her patient was a little child. I saw the wealth of pity and tenderness in the young girl's eyes, and God's love seemed very near."

There were numerous memorable highlights from that 1913 pilgrimage. The pilgrims marched in procession to the grotto – each contingent arranged behind its diocesan banner – attended an open-air Pontifical High Mass, performed the Stations of the Cross, and were received by the Bishop of Tarbes, before whom they sang *God Save Ireland*. They also presented a large Celtic cross, made of limestone, to the shrine. But the highlight, as ever, was the torchlight procession, with all who took part carrying lighted candles and singing the *Ave Maria*.

"The exteriors of the three churches were brilliantly illuminated," Rose Lynch recalled of the night the procession took place. "It was a beautiful sight to see that long line extending on and on until it looked like a running stream of light flowing through the wide avenues of trees, and then the singing grew louder and louder while the procession wound back and drew up opposite the three churches, which were ablaze with light. Then the majestic strains of the *Credo* arose on the still air from the lips of the assembled multitude. It was a wonderful profession of faith, a wonderful example of the Church, Catholic and universal."

The Irish National Pilgrimage eventually returned to Ireland, with each pilgrim proudly wearing a green poplin badge to which was attached a silver medal of Our Lady of Lourdes. It was not just a simple memento of a wonderful trip but a badge of honour, a symbol of a long and rewarding journey to a mystical, magical destination far away. Many people who had received cures were aboard, as we shall presently see. Also standing on deck was Rose Lynch, who was on her way back to her native Cork.

"What stands out on my mind most is the wonderful happiness and peace that pervades Lourdes, and that everyone feels there," Rose wrote in her book *The Story of Lourdes*, which was published in 1921. "I never met a man, woman, or child who did not love Lourdes, who did not want to prolong his or her visit there."

"Why should that be so?" she wondered. Partly, she said, it was because the Queen of Heaven chose Lourdes to visit, not once but 18 different times. Just as important, she said, was that Our Lady of Lourdes had brought to all who came to visit the happiness and peace that "passeth all understanding." It proved to be the ultimate achievement of the 1913 pilgrimage.

Twenty-one-year-old Grace Moloney, who had a chronically disabled right knee, was stretchered to Lourdes as part of the 1913 Irish National Pilgrimage. She returned home cured.

Among the pilgrims standing on the deck of the *Cambria* as it berthed at Dublin's North Wall, in September 1913, was a young woman, Grace Moloney, from County Clare. Small in stature, dressed in a plain blue serge skirt and wearing strong leather boots, she had rough hands, a comely face, and eyes described as not quite blue but yet not grey. That she was smiling brightly was no surprise because, as one newspaper put it, her "marvellous recovery from paralysis of the knee" had been the outstanding feature of the pilgrimage.

Grace was bashful and reserved. "When several newspaper photographers sought to take a photograph of her and asked that she would come to the front, she modestly retreated into the background," noted a reporter for *The Freeman's Journal*, who witnessed the ship's arrival. "Her friends induced her to come forward and the pictures were obtained. A cinematograph operator, with an eye to dramatic effect, asked her to wave a handkerchief, but she shyly shook her head. She walked along the deck and down the gangway with as much freedom as the healthiest person on board."

That she could walk with ease was remarkable; some would say even miraculous. For 11 years, she had been crippled as a result of a tubercular swelling of the right knee joint. Although treated for disease of the bone, including undergoing a number of operations, her knee remained swollen and painful. When walking, she had a noticeable limp. Her condition had been declared incurable.

Grace had always maintained that if she could only reach Lourdes, Our Lady would intercede for her and she would be cured. Her chance came in 1913, when she joined the Irish National Pilgrimage. Aged 21, she departed Dublin without the use of her right leg. Observers noted that, following years of pain and suffering, her features were drawn and she was haggard beyond her age. "She was carried on a stretcher bed the whole way from Killaloe to Lourdes, and so painful was her knee that she could not even allow it to be touched," one newspaper reported.

We do not know precisely what produced Grace Moloney's sudden recovery at Lourdes. She certainly entered the baths; we do know that. We also know that, a short time afterwards, at Mass, something strange happened. "I felt a sudden pain climbing up my leg," Grace later explained. "When the pain reached the knee the stiffness suddenly passed off. I straightened my leg for the first time for many years and walked without limping."

A priest, Fr. Lynch, added: "I was beside her myself at the time. She took an awful pain in the knee and two ladies were supporting her. They were afraid she would not be able to proceed further. Suddenly she walked up to the altar rails. The people cried out that there was a miracle, and the crowd pressed around her so much that two priests took her across the altar to the vestry. I have seen her frequently since, and she hasn't had the slightest return of the stiffness or paralysis in the knee. She can walk as well as anybody."

The accuracy of Fr. Lynch's eyewitness account was verified by a special correspondent writing for the *Sunday Independent*. "I am enabled to quote the Very Rev. Canon Fagan, Father Lockhart, Father Myles Ronan, C.C., Pro-Cathedral, Dublin; the girl's aunt (Mrs. Maurice Cosgrave), and Dr. Fitzgerald," the correspondent wrote, supporting Fr. Lynch's description of events. The writer went on to conclude that the case was a wonderful manifestation of the "power and influence of the Blessed Virgin Mother."

On Grace Moloney's return to Ireland, among those who commented on her case was the noted physician Sir Alexander Dempsey. A founder member and later president of the North of Ireland branch of the British Medical Association, he had been knighted in 1911. As a Catholic, he took a keen interest in the pilgrimage and accompanied it to Lourdes. On its arrival home, he was asked for his medical opinion of Moloney's revival.

"There has been a good deal of discussion about the remarkable case of Grace Moloney," he observed in an interview with the *Daily Sketch*. "She had been operated upon by Dr. Blayney, of Dublin, for tubercular disease of the femur. She had a contraction of the knee joint as a result of the disease, probably due to the tightening of the tendons. For years, she has only been able to walk on the tips of her toes. She suddenly got well, and now walks as well as you or I.

"I examined her knee, which is now as supple as my own. There is no ankylosis – adhesion which prevents movement," he said. "There is no medical explanation for this sudden cure. Anybody can question it as much as they like, but it is there."

An article published in *The Southern Star* also addressed the issue of Moloney's recovery. The author said he was "dazzled, dazed, bewildered" by what he had witnessed – "a little country girl hobble painfully assisted by her friends to the waters of the sacred grotto. We have seen her walk away from the grotto with firm tread and unaided." He added that, whatever doubters might say or sceptics believe regarding her cure being a miracle, all you had to do was look at the once-damaged Grace Moloney who could now "run around, and looks a bright, healthy girl of 16." That, he concluded, was proof enough.

Patrick Casey, a blacksmith from County Longford, likewise received an exceptional cure having travelled to Lourdes with the Irish National Pilgrimage of 1913.

Patrick Casey, from Gortgallon, Lanesboro, County Longford, was a long-time sufferer from a crippling, painful disorder known as acromegaly. The disorder caused shocking swelling of his joints and paralysis of his limbs from the hips down. Doctors gave him little or no hope. The best he was offered by a Dublin specialist was an operation to take out his thigh joints and pare their ends to make them small enough to fit into their sockets. To put it mildly, Patrick Casey was in a bad way.

"I sat here for hours at a time it was such a labour to rise from my seat," Casey said regarding his condition. "For two and a half years I was forced to use two sticks. I could not manage without them, and badly I could manage with them; to attempt to lift my foot off the ground without the aid of my two sticks meant that I would fall helpless."

Casey was so unwell that, on the day of his departure to Lourdes, he had to be helped into the train at Longford station. John Leavy, a popular and prosperous trader in Lanesboro, was one of those who assisted him: "He was unable to help himself into the train that day, being as bad as I have seen him for the past two years. With the aid of another man I succeeded in getting him into the carriage by lifting him into it bodily and placing him in a seat.....in short, he had all the appearance of a hopeless cripple."

The morning after Casey's arrival at Lourdes – Friday, 12 September – he was wheeled to the grotto, bathed in the holy waters, and received communion. This pattern was repeated throughout his four-day stay. Each time, he had to be helped from his invalid chair and helped back in again. Things changed, however, on the final day, when a remarkable event occurred.

"I approached the rails of the grotto with the aid of my sticks and the attendant," Casey recalled. "Standing at the rails I fervently implored Our Blessed Lady of Lourdes to accept my two sticks and to give me the use of my two limbs to work and walk, and then hung them on the rail of the holy shrine. A thrill passed through my whole frame at that moment and suddenly I found myself able to stand up straight without any aid, and I turned and walked back to my chair that I had left a few minutes before an invalid, now a cured man."

On the advice of the attendants, Casey allowed himself to be wheeled back to his hotel as if nothing had happened. He entered the hotel dining hall, where breakfast was being served. "I got out of the chair without assistance and walked up through this long hall," Casey remembered. "The majority of people who did not know me passed no remark, but as I proceeded through the long rows of tables I heard several calling out, 'Where are your sticks?' I said, 'I left them at the holy grotto.'"

By the time he arrived at Lourdes railway station, the news had spread. "A great crowd surged around the station," Casey recalled. "There was wonderful commotion about the platform. Everyone wanted to shake hands with Casey the cured man, those who saw me less than half an hour before with my sticks being the more impressed with the great change that had come over me.....I soon became husky in the voice from answering questions."

On his homecoming to Ireland, Casey was greeted by scenes of great joy. At Longford station, he was met by a large crowd who were accompanied by the Irish National Foresters Band. There was a torchlight procession. Numerous bonfires blazed throughout the countryside. Lanesboro chapel, where he had stopped off to pray, was illuminated.

"Having spent a reasonable time in prayer," he said, "we again mounted the motor car and, followed by a torchlight procession of huge dimensions, which was accompanied by the Clontuskert Band with its fine rousing music, we proceeded through Lanesboro, which was all illuminated.....Everyone was bidding a hearty welcome home to Casey, and expressing their thanksgiving for the great blessing bestowed on him."

Nothing could match the excitement of Casey's arrival at his thatched home in Gortgallon, where he was met by his wife and four children. It was "a touching scene," he recalled. Although his family had heard the happy news beforehand, they feared they might be disappointed. "When they saw the complete change in my condition their joy was even greater than mine," Casey said. "It knew no bounds."

In the following days, Casey's revival was commented upon by doctors who had known and cared for him. One doctor – Dr. McDonnell, from Dublin – said: "Casey's is a very remarkable case. He is a man of unusually clear intelligence and I never knew a man of stronger faith in the goodness and charity of Our Lady of Lourdes. He told me he has been eleven years an invalid, but always asserted that he would leave his crutches at Lourdes and walk home. It is extraordinary."

Another doctor – Dr. J. A. O'Halloran, the Lanesboro doctor who had treated him for three years – wrote: "I did everything that it was humanly possible to do for him. I literally regarded his case as absolutely hopeless. If it is proved that Mr. Patrick Casey is now able to walk after his visit to Lourdes, the proof will carry the further proof that the said Patrick Casey has been cured by miraculous means, for he could not possibly be cured by human means."

As for the proof that Casey could walk again, the evidence was plentiful. A journalist from *The Longford Leader*, who interviewed him at his home, was crystal clear: "After my first visit to Mr. Casey yesterday at his humble home at Gortgallon, I was fully convinced, and I am proud to be in a position to state, that his is a positive cure." The final words, however, should be left to John Leavy, the Lanesboro shopkeeper who helped Casey board the train on the day of his departure. Asked if Casey's condition was much improved since he came back from Lourdes, he replied: "Much improved? Why, it is nothing short of miraculous."

The demand for brancardiers, or stretcher-bearers, increased rapidly with the growing number of pilgrimages arriving at Lourdes. One of the earliest Irish brancardiers was an eminent politician who had taken part in the War of Independence and Civil War. His name was P. J. Little.

We can imagine the shock on the faces of Irish pilgrims when spotting one of the country's best-known politicians caring for the sick and disabled at Lourdes. Year after year, from his first-reported visit in the late 1920s to his last in the late 1950s, this well-regarded national figure travelled to the grotto. There, he rose before dawn, helped carry stretchers to wherever they needed to go and provided general support for the infirm. One would be hard-pressed to identify any present-day politician who could match what P. J. Little, through his activities at Lourdes, contributed to those less fortunate than himself.

Little's role as a brancardier – a French word for "stretcher-bearer" – was an arduous one. The job was thus described in the 1940s: "There is little or no rest for a 'brancardier' and the heat of a Lourdes summer can be almost overpowering, which doesn't improve things for him. He, like Caesar's wife, is expected to be 'all things to all men.' He is at the beck and call of everyone. He rises at an unearthly hour, frequently has to go without meals, and is the last to retire at night." Not surprisingly, many brancardiers come home "considerably lighter in weight," the commentator pointed out.

There was no better man than P. J. Little to undertake these selfless, onerous tasks. A veteran of the War of Independence and Civil War, and a founder member of Fianna Fáil, he was known for being resolute and tireless. The son of a former Premier of Newfoundland, P. J. studied at University College

Dublin and eventually became a lawyer, journalist, diplomat, politician and government minister. Although from Dundrum, County Dublin, he served as TD for Waterford, and was best-known for his role as Minister for Posts and Telegraphs from 1939 – 1948, a record-breaking period for the office that survives to this day.

"Paddy" Little, as he was sometimes referred to, had an extraordinary life. Éamon de Valera, who was both a friend and admirer, chose him for delicate overseas diplomatic missions in the troubled era of the first Dáil. He was sent to South Africa in 1921, where he tramped through the country wearing an Irish tweed suit while promoting Irish industry. In America, he was followed by British agents – and almost caught – before absconding for Argentina on a Japanese ship. There, he was welcomed by Argentine families of Irish descent.

Those who knew him remarked how P. J. always undertook these responsibilities with a smile on his face. He "kept the faith and kept his good humour also. Nobody can remember Paddy Little in bad humour," a journalist acquaintance recollected. Beneath the good humour, however, was a man of steel. During his visit to South Africa, the *Cape Argus* newspaper noted his "self-restraint" and "resoluteness of purpose." Rounding off the picture, Éamon de Valera described how he was "gentle and noble" and "occupied himself chiefly with the things of the soul – religion, philosophy and the arts."

It was this diverse combination of personal traits – a bright disposition combined with a single-minded determination and a sensitive nature – that turned the mind of P. J. Little to Lourdes. He genuinely cared for the sick and unwell. "One of the most quiet and modest people in the Dáil," as *The Irish Times* called him, he felt obliged to help those less fortunate than himself. With the exception of World War II and occasional ministerial duties, nothing could stop him from undertaking his annual visits to the shrine, where he dedicated himself to his worthwhile endeavours.

Even compared to the exhausting graft of politics and high office, his daily routine at Lourdes was tiring. He not only looked after the transporting and general care of the sick but performed a multitude of additional services, as well. He served meals, shaved male invalids who could not shave themselves, washed dishes and filled Lourdes water containers. He posted letters, having sometimes written them on behalf of the disabled. He searched for missing children, purchased items for the bed-ridden and accompanied people who were partially mobile on visits to the shops. "There is nothing they are not prepared to do," it was once remarked of brancardiers.

His work continued a tradition set in place in 1884, when a French nobleman went to the assistance of a feeble old woman pilgrim who he noticed at the railway station. He helped her towards the grotto, enlisting the aid of two young men along the way. The three talked it over and decided to establish the function of brancardier, known for their "bretelles" or shoulder straps of canvas and leather. One of the first to join was a 27-year-old member of the local landed gentry, Count Étienne de Beauchamp, who served as a brancardier for 72 years. P. J. Little didn't quite achieve such longevity, but his tenure was remarkable all the same.

Not only did P. J. know Count de Beauchamp, but in 1935 he was decorated by the count in his capacity as President of the Hospitalité Notre-Dame de Lourdes. The decoration he received was the silver medal of the Hospitalité, the highest gift to be awarded by the organisation. It was just one of numerous awards and accolades that he would receive throughout his life in recognition of his work at the shrine.

Back home, after retiring from politics in 1954, P. J. dedicated himself to the arts. He had already become the first Director of the Arts Council, having been appointed to that role in 1951. Along with his love of all things connected to Lourdes, he also enjoyed his new work with the council. Indeed, it was said that had Ireland been free and at peace during his peak years, he would have eschewed politics and devoted his talents to bringing the finer arts to increasing numbers of people.

P. J. Little passed away at his County Dublin home in 1963, aged 79. President Éamon de Valera and Taoiseach Seán Lemass attended his removal, as did many other notables from Fianna Fáil. Not many connections from his Lourdes days were present, but that doesn't mean that his association with the shrine was forgotten. It was always said that Irish invalids felt happier when cared for at Lourdes by any brancardier from home, but at the time of his death many said P. J. Little had been the best of them all.

One of the most impressive cures to occur at Lourdes took place in 1923. The beneficiary, John Traynor, from Liverpool, was born to an Irish mother and an English father.

Forty-year-old John Traynor was in very rough shape when he arrived at Lourdes in 1923. His right arm was paralysed and shrivelled, both his legs were partly paralysed, and he was experiencing up to three epileptic fits a day. He had a gaping hole in his skull, into which a silver shield had to be inserted so that his pulsating brain could not be seen. He had to be lifted into a wheelchair from his bed each morning, with the reverse procedure being executed at nightfall. Not surprisingly, his doctors declared him to be "completely and incurably incapacitated."

Traynor's infirmities dated back to World War I, throughout which he had fought gallantly with a number of military units including the 1st Battalion Royal Dublin Fusiliers. Eventually, at the notoriously vicious Battle of Gallipoli, in 1915, he almost lost his life. During a bayonet charge, he was hit in the head and chest by sustained machinegun fire. One bullet tore through the inner part of his upper right arm, causing paralysis. Attacks of epilepsy soon followed, as did five major operations. By the time he had arrived home to Liverpool, he was described as "a human wreck."

There was little for him to fall back upon, apart from his disability pension and his faith. The latter he had inherited from his Irish mother, who had died when he was young. A devout Catholic, she had instilled in him a belief in the importance of Mass and Holy Communion. She had also inspired in him a devotion to Our Lady. It was that belief that prompted him to consider going to Lourdes, although he had neither the health nor sufficient money to do so.

In July 1923, a neighbour called to the Traynor home and mentioned that a Liverpool diocesan pilgrimage to Lourdes was being organised, at a cost of £13 per head. A down-payment of £1 would secure a place. John called his wife in from the yard and told her about it. He asked her to go upstairs, where they kept a sovereign coin given to John by his brother. It was on standby for emergencies. With the coin, along with money raised through the sale of household belongings, including jewellery pawned by his wife, he secured his ticket.

The pilgrimage reached Lourdes on 22 July, where Traynor was taken to the Asile hospital. "I was in a terrible condition," he eventually remarked, "as my wounds and sores had not been freshly bandaged since I left Liverpool." He was desperately ill, had several haemorrhages, along with a number of epileptic fits. A strange thing did happen, though – on the second day, after entering the baths, his fits stopped. Then, on the fourth day – once again in the baths – his paralysed leg became violently agitated. On that same day, his right arm moved, and for the first time in years he blessed himself.

That evening, Traynor was sedated, to keep him calm and to force him to sleep. The next morning was the most dramatic of all. At the last stroke of the basilica's chimes, which played the *Ave Maria*, he opened his eyes and jumped from his bed. "First, I knelt on the floor to finish the rosary I had been saying, then I dashed for the door, pushed aside the two brancardiers and ran out into the passage and the open air." How John did so was remarkable as he hadn't walked in eight years and his weight was down to eight stone.

He continued: "I ran the whole way to the grotto without getting the least mark or cut on my bare feet. The brancardiers were running after me but they could not catch up with me. When they reached the grotto, there I was on my knees, still in my nightclothes, praying to Our Lady and thanking her. All I knew was that I should thank her and the grotto was the place to do it. The brancardiers stood back, afraid to touch me."

Word spreads rapidly, especially when it comes to miracles. There was mayhem in Liverpool, as a massive crowd awaited

Traynor's arrival home by train. People waiting at the railway station knew what had happened from reading the evening papers. "It seemed as if all Liverpool had gathered there," he recalled. Even his wife was there, not sure of what to expect. Extra police had been called in, and railway officials had to stop people from rushing the train.

"When I did appear on the platform, there was a stampede," he remembered. "The police had to draw their batons to force a passage for my wife and myself to a taxi. My brother got a blow on the side of the head before he could fight his way into the taxi with me. We drove home, and I cannot describe the joy of my wife and children."

John Traynor eventually entered the coal and general haulage business, building up a fleet of four trucks and employing a staff of 12. "I lift sacks of coal weighing around 200 pounds with the best of them and I can do any other work that an able-bodied man can do," he said at the time. "I am now comfortably situated, and my children are all well provided for. Three of them have been born since my cure, one a girl whom I have named Bernadette."

He died in 1943, aged 60, from an illness unconnected to his previous afflictions. In the meantime, he had been assessed many times by the medical experts at Lourdes. They found no trace of epilepsy or paralysis, his right arm worked freely, he could use his right hand, and his shoulder and chest muscles were fully restored. The only trace left of the hole in his skull was a slight depression that could be felt in the bone.

The biggest surprise was the right arm, where the nerves had been severed for eight years. Four operations had failed to reunite them. But, then again, as the official Lourdes Medical Bureau report on Traynor's case declared, on 2 October 1926: "This extraordinary cure is absolutely beyond and above the powers of nature."

Five hundred invalids were ferried by transatlantic liner from Dublin to Lourdes, via Bordeaux, in 1924. It turned out to be a memorable trip.

The brightly-lit *Chicago* departed Dublin port soon after 11 pm, on 29 September 1924, and headed out to sea. The conditions were grim, the winds strong, reaching gale force at times, and the Irish Sea ahead was rough. Most of the pilgrims were below deck, huddled in their bunks. Others stood and watched as the ship began to leave.

There wasn't much to see through the misty, inky darkness – only vague black shadows on the shore. Suddenly, through the mist, came the sound of voices. Ears picked up below deck; eyes up on deck tried to focus. People smiled, some cried, when they heard the strains of women and girls, back on land, singing the *Ave Maria*. Soon, men and boys joined in. Then they heard the sound of bands. Their able-bodied friends and families on shore were bidding them *adieu* – God speed, safe voyage, good health, we will be thinking of you far away from home.

That night, the *Chicago* ploughed, dived and rolled its way into the breaking seas. On its starboard side, all along the coast, people bade farewell. Bonfires blazed, rockets flared, a line of fire traced the ship's course as it headed past Dun Laoghaire and the coastline of County Wicklow. The invalids who were not visually impaired witnessed the spectacle through their portholes. Those who could hear noted the singing. It must have been a moving departure for those who were on board.

The passenger list was mixed and varied. One little girl had been maimed in an ambush during the recent troubles; she had lost her eyes. A man had been shot in the neck. Another man – a member of the old constabulary – had an eye blown out. A further passenger – a little boy – travelled alone. He had a tag in his buttonhole, with his name. He troubled nobody, smiled a lot, and was always cheerful – a human cork on a vast ocean, like a piece of luggage labelled and lost.

Yet another passenger – a disabled little boy – attracted the attention of a brawny French sailor, fuzzy-haired and bearded, who worked on board. He loved taking the boy in his arms and feeding him, as a mother would her child. A further sailor, from Brest, tended to a disabled little girl, whose big eyes looked haunted and holy but whose disposition was always joyful. "Ah, my little child," the sailor would say, in French, as he made her comfortable and tucked her in.

Two days later, on Wednesday, the weather improved and Mass was celebrated on deck. Almost all the pilgrims grouped themselves around the altar. "Here was a spectacle that has rarely been witnessed in the history of the Catholic Church," a correspondent wrote for the *Irish Independent*. "If the spirits of those who go down to the sea in ships haunt the waters of the Western Atlantic and Bay of Biscay, what did they hear that morning? The choral glories of holy Mass."

Witnessing the coast of France brought forth strong feelings. The invalids were assembled on deck. Many had never seen the sea or observed the vastness of an ocean. Others had never sat in the sun. The choir on board began to sing. Some of the invalids began to cry, overwhelmed by their emotions. They badgered each other, embarrassed, for being "so foolish." All enjoyed the rest, the air, the light, the calm serenity which, in many cases, had never been experienced before.

On they travelled to Bordeaux. An abbé and a curé awaited them at the pier. They waved in welcome. The choir on board assembled on deck and responded in song. They sang *Regina Coeli, Hail Glorious St. Patrick* and the *Ave Maria*. The abbé waved his appreciation. Later, he returned and asked for more. The choir reassembled, the pilgrims crowded around, and the abbé was happy – tears rushed from his eyes and coursed down his cheeks. He then gave the pilgrims his blessing.

From there, it was on to Lourdes. The journey was long and tiring, departing at 9.15 am and arriving at 7 pm. Soon, the waters of the Gave were in sight. The rosary was said all along the train. Then, suddenly, into sight came the grotto, and what did they do but sing. And, of course, they sang the *Ave Maria*. Tonight they would sleep in the home of Mary; tomorrow they would experience Lourdes.

They did everything at Lourdes but, most memorably, they participated in the torchlight procession. The torches flared, the basilica glowed with a brilliant flame of red and green. Lights appeared from everywhere – from the churches, convents and monasteries. A cross stood on its rocky peak, burnished gold against the blackness of the mountain behind it. Once again, they sang the *Ave Maria*, the refrain, at one stage, ricocheting off the Rosary Church and reaching bystanders in layers and billows of thunderous noise.

They arrived home on Friday, 10 October. Many miracles were claimed. One man, whose hand was once pronounced incurable, had reclaimed its use. Another man, who earlier could barely walk, now walked with ease. Yet another recovery was claimed by a woman who was previously without hearing and speech. At the suggestion of a friend, she delivered a song at the quayside – and what else was the melody she chose but the *Ave Maria*!

John Gibbons, an English writer with Irish connections, discovered in 1928 that Lourdes wasn't all about physical cures.

On his 1928 visit to Lourdes, the author John Gibbons met a likeable young couple. The man – who the author guessed was a poorly-paid clerk – told him bits of his story. The couple were madly in love, engaged to be married, and were saving up to buy the hire-purchase furniture. All of a sudden, tragedy struck when the young man's intended bride – who Gibbons believed might have been a typist – became seriously ill.

They went from one doctor to another, but with no success. The first doctor, from the suburbs, passed them on to a specialist, and they both said the young woman's prospects were hopeless. The consultant recommended some manner of very expensive treatment which "might possibly" save her. They took their furniture money, tried the treatment, but it didn't work. By this time, the woman had left her job and was forced back home to live with her parents. Things were tight, and the future looked bleak.

"Then it occurred to the man that they both were Catholics, and what about Lourdes?" Gibbons later remarked in a book about his visit. The fare cost £10, which included boat, train and hotel. They had to borrow to help pay for it. Gibbons noted that they had no extra money to buy new clothes for the journey. After all, he said, a woman was likely to wear her best dress, but what she wore was far from the best. "I think they had about come to the end," he concluded.

Gibbons spotted the couple again on the return trip out of Lourdes. He noted the young woman's difficulty in boarding the train. She couldn't manage the step from the platform to the carriage. Clearly, there had been no miracle. "One would have thought that Our Lady might have spared ever such a little one for them," the author said to himself. "How long did she have left?" he wondered. He then remembered the man had said about two years. "She would have to die now," Gibbons noted sadly.

On board the train, the author dropped by to the couple's carriage to say hello. What he encountered shocked him. "They both were absolutely radiating happiness," he remarked in his book, *Tramping to Lourdes*, which was soon followed by a companion book, *Tramping through Ireland*. "I do not think I ever saw two people quite so happy. Not happy in the religious sort of way at all, with tranquil faces and an air of resignation, but secularly happy.

"I mean – with the entirely human sort of happiness that goes to the pictures on Saturday night and holds hands all the time in the dark. For he was looking at her and holding her shabby little glove – I could not help noticing it, though I am sorry – and she was looking at him and simply beaming all over. And yet she was going to die. There had been no miracle cure. All their poor little pinchings and savings had been wasted."

Gibbons noted that it was the same with almost all the other pilgrims on the trip. Sure, there had been some minor "cures". One man was wandering through the train telling everybody about something to do with his ear, and his middle-aged wife was making sure he didn't go near a window in case he would get caught in a draught. There was another minor cure, too, it seems.

From the outsider's point of view, these recoveries were not startling, Gibbons said, "for with all the money that had been spent on fares, all the tiredness of the two journeys, the night in the train and all that, all the thousands of prayers that had gone so hopefully up, the truth was that we were going back with only two cures."

In contrast to those who received cures, the rest of the train was filled with people who had received no good news at all. At the end of the train, there were two long carriages full of stretcher-cases who had travelled out physically unwell and were travelling back in the same distressed state. There were people with lesser complaints, involving deafness and bad eyes, and most were returning empty-handed. The truth regarding miracles, he said, was that "half the people who had gone to Lourdes had wanted one, either for themselves or for somebody else. It was no use saying that they had not. And they had not got one."

Yet there was something about all of them – including the young couple he had befriended – that was hard to define, something that wouldn't quite come to mind. Suddenly, the elusive feature they shared in common struck him – he had never seen such a happy group of people. Everyone on the train was happy. "Here were the people who had saved up and spent their money and then had not their cure, and they were as happy as possible about it," he remarked. One person might shrug their shoulders and say, "It was not Our Lady's wish this time." Another would shrug their shoulders and say they had been coming year after year but would only get a cure when "Our Lady wished it." And that person was happy, too.

"But why were they all so happy?" he asked. He found the answer in the young couple he had met earlier on the train, who seemed radiant and untroubled even though they were travelling home clearly bearing nothing but bad news. "Understanding came like a thunderclap," Gibbons said. "What had happened was this: they had had a glimpse through that hole in the clouds that we call Lourdes, and through it had seen into Eternity. There they would be for all the time that there ever was going to be, together with one another and with God and the Mother of God."

What did it matter to them, he wondered, about a few poor miserable years in wherever they lived? "They had their miracle after all," he wrote. "Their money had not been wasted. Only it had not been a miracle to the body." Instead, it was a miracle of another kind. It explained things, he felt, "and it explained things all down that long train." It explained things on the boat, too. It was all about absolute belief in a happier place. That, he concluded, was why an "uncanny happiness lasted every mile of the way."

A novel Irish Schoolboys' Pilgrimage departed for Lourdes in April 1928. They had a whale of a time, by all accounts.

No one knows how the Cobh schoolboy nicknamed "Buttons" acquired his masterly skill on the slot machines. He possibly developed his uncanny talent in his native County Cork. More importantly, we were told, his family had recently moved to County Dublin – to Dun Laoghaire – and it was there, perhaps, that he had acquired his golden touch. Either way, there he was, on the Irish Schoolboys' Pilgrimage of 1928: the boy with silken skills, whose flair and versatility on the slot machines had never before been witnessed in Lourdes.

So impressive was his dexterity that his hotel at Lourdes had to prohibit him from playing their machine. "His success in extracting francs through a system of his own invention" was so impressive and "so great the probability that he would break the bank" that the alarmed management at his hotel took the only course of action they could think of – they shut the machine down.

Given that those quotes were written by the Rev. Canon Breen, from Killarney, who was one of the supervisors on the tour, signifies the gravity of the situation. The fact that the boy in question was hardly four feet tall and only five stone in weight was irrelevant. The reality was that he was a genius on the gaming machines!

It was inevitable that when 500 Irish schoolboys assembled for their journey to Lourdes in 1928, some colourful, exciting moments were all but guaranteed. The boys had gathered at the port of Rosslare, County Wexford, on Holy Thursday, 5 April. Accompanied by two doctors and six nurses, together with priests, brothers and lay teachers from their respective schools, they set off for Fishguard, London, Newhaven and Dieppe, before heading all the way to Lourdes. Boys being boys, they wiped out supplies of confectionary and fruit at a Lyons' Corner House in London, which they discovered along the way.

At Lourdes, the Irish contingent met up with 5,000 French schoolboys, 300 more from Belgium, and a further 300 from Spain, who had arrived for this special event. The convergence of so many boys was a bit like a "perfect storm", where warm air from a low-pressure system meets cold air linked to a high-pressure front, causing chaos and havoc.

To begin with, the Irish boys detested the strong local coffee, preferring instead to drink tea. They searched out the two best places in Lourdes providing tea – the Café de la Terrasse and the Patisserie Labourdette. They favoured the former for the crowds and the view, the latter for its sweet confectionary obtainable for one shilling a go.

They also developed an exotic sartorial style based on the beret, the ordinary headgear of Lourdes, which was worn by all of the French schoolboys. The fashion craze began on the second day, when some of the Irish boys discarded their college caps and replaced them with the distinctive French headgear. They were not finished yet. They next purchased long streaming ribbons in green, white and gold, which they attached to the middle of the berets.

The fashion took off. Soon, 500 Irish boys were ransacking shops in search of similar attire, and they wiped out all the stock. From then on, shopkeepers shrugged their shoulders and remarked that they had no more supplies, while humorously suggesting that the boys might prefer English colours instead. "Such a riot of colour one rarely sees as when, thereafter, the Irish boys marched in a body, two deep, to and from the bishop's palace, church or grotto," Canon Breen remarked concerning the new fashion trend.

The boys – like the Irish girls who had travelled a year earlier – visited all the major sites at Lourdes. They went to the grotto and all the various churches, did the Stations of the Cross, participated in the torchlight procession – where the gusting winds made it difficult to keep the torches alight – and attended Mass. The Tuesday benediction was particularly memorable. "What touched the chords of the heart was not so much the thunderous volume of the hymns from the throats of 500 boys as the simple solo '*Ave*', sung by Willie Dunn, of Belvedere College. It stirred all present to the depths of their hearts," Kevin Kenny remarked in a special message sent to the *Irish Independent*.

The unique pilgrimage departed Lourdes on the Friday and worked its way home. The boys' last act was to sing the *Ave Maria* on the train as the town vanished from sight. Apart from bad weather and rough seas on the crossing from Dieppe to Newhaven, the trip back was largely uneventful. Soon, the boys were arriving at their home railway stations, to tumultuous welcomes. A packed Glanmire station, in Cork, exemplified the excitement. "As the train emerged from the tunnel loud cheers were raised by those waiting, and as the boys got on to the platform there were many happy reunions," *The Cork Examiner* reported.

The pilgrimage certainly left its mark on all those who had participated, both students and supervisors alike. Canon Breen, who had carefully watched over the boys, noted how they were "splendid young fellows" and he wondered if there could be "anywhere the world over, such boys as these?" For six days, in the interludes between their religious exercises, they had delighted the people of Lourdes and the town's visitors by their "innocent, boyish pranks, in hotel and in street, in shop and in café," he reflected.

He had also noted their sense of wonder at the sanctity of Lourdes – how, singly, "they stole away from their companions' play, overcome by the lure of the grotto, and for long spells at a time stood gazing wistfully into the sightless eyes of the venerated, miraculous image of their Immaculate Mother, praying earnestly that those dear hands might fashion their life's future and pour out in a rich torrent the spiritual favours and the temporal blessings which they and their loved ones at home so badly needed for life's journey."

On a much lighter note, he also referred to the accomplished "Buttons" from Dun Laoghaire, who was originally from Cobh. No doubt this "trim, dapper figure in long pants," who was so proficient on the slot machines, was also warmly welcomed home. Although he had honed his skills at Lourdes, he had failed to profit from them. Instead, he had acted honourably by handing over his substantial winnings for the repair of the Lourdes basilica. Whether he did this voluntarily or not, we don't know, but what we can surmise is that he returned home broke!

Unlike the highly-accomplished "Buttons", many Irish pilgrims who travelled to Lourdes in the 1920s experienced culture shock on their journeys. For the vast majority, it was their first time outside Ireland and an eye-opening introduction to the wonders of cities like Paris.

More than 2,000 Irish pilgrims descended on Paris in October 1928, where they spent the best part of two days on their journeys to and from Lourdes. Coming from all four corners of Ireland – including small towns, villages and remote parishes – they were astonished by this city of fashions and fads. Paris, at the time, was enjoying its so-called "crazy years" as a hub of literature, art, music and cinema. James Joyce was living there; so were George Orwell and Pablo Picasso. George Gershwin was there, too, composing *An American in Paris*. The place was buzzing, the bars and bistros were full, and the visitors were shocked by the spectacle.

After travelling for 16 hours by sea and rail, it was a relief to be able to explore the Parisian boulevards by night. "The chief attraction was the movements of motor cars, motor buses and trams," one Irish pilgrim recalled in a news report written anonymously for the Irish press. "With an apparent recklessness that the dizziest of cinema productions cannot excel, they plunged across streets and boulevards at all angles, each driver animated, as it were, with a homicidal passion and actuated with no desire but to puncture the vehicle nearest him, and yet when we were on the point of being horrified at a terrible scene of blood and wreckage, he pulled up within a fraction of an inch and everything went smoothly."

There was no traffic problem in France, the writer argued; instead, there was "a traffic mystery." Even the policeman who directed the traffic had no effect; instead, the traffic directed itself. Cars went "scorching by," one after the other, and "in the midst of this sea of mechanism the crippled and the aged stroll carelessly from one side of the street to the other, confident that their lives are quite safe." It certainly was enough to "excite curiosity and wonderment," the author remarked.

Parisian fashion was notable, too, and a far cry from the clothing back in Ireland. There were high fashions in the shop windows – "whole streets of them," the correspondent noted, "ready for export" – although he felt the standard of dress on the city's footpaths was less than impressive. No doubt he was referring to the "liberated" look of the era – straight waists, short hemlines, cloche hats and short hair. Either way, he was unenthused: "There is more 'style' to be seen in a small street of a small town in Ireland than, in proportion to its size, is to be met with in the whole vast stretch of Paris."

The food also was a novelty. As the pilgrimage – which was run by the Catholic Truth Society of Ireland – made its way by train to Lourdes, it stopped for refreshments. The stopping-off point was Mont-de-Marsan, about 140 km from the shrine. Breakfast – "pardon the word," the author exclaimed – was awaiting the visiting party on improvised tables placed on the station platform. Passengers weren't familiar with French fare, as the breakfast consisted of "vile" coffee "in small bowls, and long bread rolls slit down the centre, with a piece of butter shoved in between the two halves, which were not parted." The concept of coffee and baguettes would take many more years before entering the Irish gastronomic consciousness!

Lourdes, when the pilgrims reached there, produced other surprises, most notably its weather. Although it had been sunny for days, things changed in an instant, as might be expected so close to the Pyrenees. "Suddenly the sirocco gale swept across the vale, hurtling traders' outdoor furniture in all directions," he wrote. "The sky darkened, lightning flashed and thunder rolled, and torrential rain and hail and pieces of ice descended on what was a smiling landscape a few minutes earlier. For two hours the downpour lasted.

"It was amply proved to us that every country has its dis-advantages as well as advantages of climate and that the rain we often complain about in Ireland is one of our greatest blessings, giving us abundance of vegetation that is not known to the dried lands of France, and making the Emerald Isle of history one of the richest of the earth's agricultural countries."

There was another comparison he noted, but this one was less favourable. It concerned the Irishman's lack of fluency in his native language. When prayers were recited in English or French, the noise was "thunderous," he remarked, but when uttered in Irish things went mute. "Many of us, of course, were able to render a fair account of ourselves, but, as a body, ignorance of our own language in the presence of foreigners was humiliating." It was a matter "greatly to be deplored," he concluded.

After five hectic days in Lourdes, the Catholic Truth Society pilgrimage wound its way back through Paris and London, and arrived home to Ireland. It had been a colossal undertaking, involving an enormous number of people, but it was an admirable success. The pilgrims arrived in Dun Laoghaire on "a grey, wet morning" – a jolting contrast to the scorching weather they had experienced in France.

"We steam into Dun Laoghaire singing *Sweet Star of the Sea*, and soon, as a priest humorously put it, we are on 'terra cotta.' Now the fields are no longer parched, the grass no longer brown, and, despite the rain, everything is fair and lovely. All were satisfied. We had endured much weariness, but we experienced great joys," the correspondent reflected. "All are glad to be home, our only regret being that we have left Lourdes behind."

As the 1920s came to a close, a young Dublin woman, Nancy Walsh, met the love of her life in Lourdes. The couple became a cornerstone of the local business community in the decades ahead.

The word in Paris was that there was only one proper cup of tea to be obtained in France – and that was at Walsh-Douly's in Lourdes. Many testified to the accuracy of the claim. Among them were visitors from home, who loved their cup of tea. The British did, too. So successful was the tea shop that, by late 1952, it had already served an estimated three million cups of golden brew to its Irish and British customers.

Run by Dublin woman Nancy Walsh and her French husband Felix Douly, the tea shop was an add-on to the couple's souvenir store, St. Laurence O'Toole's. Commonly known as "The Irish Shop", newspaper readers were encouraged to pay a visit to it in advertisements in the Irish national press. They were also advised to visit the couple's Hotel Gallia – "first class, with moderate terms, entirely renovated." No doubt about it, the Walsh-Douly partnership had a lot going for it in Lourdes.

Their story was a tale of enterprise and romance. In 1929, Nancy Walsh, from Dundrum, County Dublin – a charming young lady, by all accounts – travelled to Lourdes to help the sick. One of the first members of the Irish Hospitalité, Nancy visited Lourdes for a month each year as a volunteer. There, she met the jovial Felix Douly, who she married three years later. For the rest of their lives, the couple lived in Lourdes, ran their various enterprises, and raised their four children.

Their first souvenir shop – "The Cross of Jerusalem" – was a commercial success. Waves of Irish pilgrims visited it. To them, Nancy was a reassuring presence. Her accent was comforting, her knowledge priceless, her welcome a solace to those feeling lost in a foreign land. One Irish woman, who arrived in 1933, on a bleak, cold, leaf-strewn December day, with its "dull, forbidding sky," later expressed her relief at encountering a friendly face from home.

The woman said that from her taxi seat she spotted "scores and scores of shops" devoted to the sale of religious emblems and souvenirs. Out of the corner of her eye, a sign – "The Irish Shop" – caught her attention. "As best I could, I navigated the taxi-man back to where I remembered 'The Irish Shop' was. How delightful to hear again the Dublin accent after spending several weeks abroad; how welcome it was to hear English spoken with the *blas* that one comes to appreciate only when one is in exile."

Another pilgrim spotted the "Céad Míle Fáilte" scroll – in genuine Irish letters – above the premises. "I entered the shop," he said, "and was asked in Irish what I wished to buy. I stated what I wanted in Irish, and the negotiations for the purchase were conducted in that language. 'How is it that you can speak Irish?' I asked the girl, who was conversing with me. 'Oh,' said she, 'I am from Dublin.'"

The shop also caught the attention of two Irish journalists who visited in 1952. "The Irish pilgrim is well catered for in Lourdes," they wrote. Not only were they impressed by the cups of tea – agreeing they were the best in France – but they also liked the staff's grasp of the Irish language. "Connemara and other Gaeltacht area pilgrims" would have no problems in Lourdes, the reporters emphasised, as assistants at the tea shop "were there to welcome them with 'Dia is Muire dhuit.'"

Everyone was drawn to the premises and paid a visit, even Cardinal Joseph MacRory, Primate of All Ireland. In 1933, the *Irish Independent* stated how, one day, Mrs. Walsh-Douly was "deeply touched when his Eminence unexpectedly appeared amongst the Irish pilgrims who were making purchases in her shop. His charm of manner quickly put everybody at their ease, and after a brief stay he left as quietly and unobtrusively as he had arrived."

The couple knew everyone in Lourdes. They were especially close friends with François Soubirous, the grand-nephew of St. Bernadette. His father was the son of Jean-Marie, Bernadette's elder brother. He was close to Mrs. Walsh-Douly, who persuaded him to visit Ireland in September 1947, when he was aged 19.

"It is my first visit to Ireland," François Soubirous commented during his stay in the country. "I came because I had heard a lot about Ireland from the Dublin wife of M. Felix Douly, who owns St. Laurence O'Toole stall, known as 'The Irish Shop', in Lourdes.....I have been to Athlone, Westport, Galway, Ennis and Limerick, and I visited a number of colleges and convents." He was impressed by the colleges and said there was nothing to equal them in France. After a two-week stay, he returned to Lourdes.

Throughout her life, Nancy was also known for her visits to Ireland, which were frequently reported on in the press. She returned to Dublin almost every year, where she customarily stayed with her brother in Dundrum. It was in Dundrum, too – at the Holy Cross Church – that she was married in 1932. Her attendance at Dublin events was deemed worthy of favourable mentions in newspaper reports. In her later years, her daughters accompanied her on these visits.

The visits – and her life – came to an end in October 1964, with her untimely death at the age of 58. Obituaries in Irish newspapers emphasised her many achievements – her efforts on behalf of the Irish Hospitalité in Lourdes, her work retailing "religious books, emblems and souvenirs" but, most notably, stressing how she would be missed by Irish pilgrims. Following Solemn Requiem Mass, she was laid to rest at the Old Cemetery, Lourdes, where, seven years later, she was joined by her husband Felix, bringing to an end one of the most famous business partnerships in the history of the iconic shrine.

MASS APPEAL

That John F. Kennedy regarded Lourdes as a must-see during his 1937 visit to Europe tells us much about the growing popularity of the shrine. From 1930 – 1950, pilgrims poured in from all parts of the world. Many were Irish-Americans. One was a famous Irish-American Hollywood star who gave up the bright lights and set out to become a nun.

With the exception of the war-torn years from 1939 – 1945, the shrine became more accessible. Transport conditions improved. The expansion of air travel enhanced matters greatly. The first Aer Rianta charter flight from Dublin to Lourdes took place in September 1947. A further air pilgrimage departed from Belfast two years later.

Bernadette's canonisation, in 1933, raised the shrine's profile, as did the release of the blockbuster Hollywood film, *The Song of Bernadette*. Reports of cures continued to emerge – from heart trouble, strokes and kidney disease, among many other complaints. Some of them were Irish, as we are about to see.

James Francis O'Kane, from Derry, walked unaided for the first time in three years after visiting Lourdes in 1932.

The year 1932 was no time to be without a job in Northern Ireland. This was the pinnacle of the Great Depression, with record unemployment and widespread distress. Almost 80,000 workers were idle, with 20,000 of them denied poor relief.

There were no jobs available. The Belfast shipyards were at a standstill due to lack of orders for new shipping. Things were so depressed in Derry that an open-air meeting called for the use of physical force.

It was bad enough for the able-bodied, but it was even worse for the sick or infirm. Those who were ill or unwell, incapacitated or disabled had no chance of finding employment. Competition for the few available jobs was far too intense. They suffered exceptional hardship, with bare cupboards and not a penny of income. Forecasts were that as 1932 progressed their problems would intensify and their circumstances become even worse.

James Francis O'Kane, from Derry, wasn't the worst off – at least, by 1932, he ran his own shop after almost killing himself in a work accident three years earlier. In 1929, he had fallen 54 feet from the masthead of a ship in Belfast docks. He sustained multiple injuries, principally to the spine and hips. Despite six months' treatment in hospital, his mobility was restricted and he could barely walk.

At the beginning of 1932, doctors advised him that only by amputating his right leg could his life be spared. O'Kane wasn't impressed. "I would rather die with two legs than live with one," he said. He refused the operation, deciding to seek a cure elsewhere. As it happened, the Catholic Travel Association had organised a five-day Easter pilgrimage to Lourdes, via Paris and Bordeaux, second-class travel, departing London on 24 March. O'Kane made sure he was on board.

"I left Londonderry for Lourdes on March 24," O'Kane recalled later on. "At that time, I had no control whatever over my feet and was only able to slide along with the aid of a stick."

On the journey out, he walked painfully and, although he had to be helped by other members of the travelling party at railway stations and hotels, he had a great sense of hope: "I knew that if I reached Lourdes I would be made fit and well."

Things turned out exactly as expected. Immediately after his arrival, he noticed an improvement in his mobility. "I thought I felt slightly better," he said. The following day – a Sunday – he felt even stronger. "I walked from my bed to the dressing table on Sunday morning – the first time I had walked unaided from the date of the accident," he reflected.

On that day, he also walked to the grotto. He did so without using his stick. He brought it with him, however, but only to discard it. After adding his stick to the pile of crutches – and having offered thanks to Our Lady – he then walked away unaided. "The pilgrims who saw him on the outward journey are astonished at his present condition," a special correspondent for *The Universe* wrote in an article reprinted in *The Donegal Democrat*. "They have signed a statement setting out the facts. One of the signatories is a doctor."

O'Kane's wife was overjoyed to see her husband on his return. She had gone to the railway station to meet him. "I was looking into the carriage windows to see where he was and help him out and get his bags," Mrs. O'Kane remarked. "When he went away he was on sticks, and could only walk with difficulty. Imagine my feelings when I saw a smiling man walking fit and well towards me. I could hardly believe it was my husband. I could hardly keep from crying with joy."

O'Kane was overjoyed, too, and remained in perfect health. When visited by a reporter at his shop, he was described as not looking "in the least an invalid." His case also made him quite famous. "Derryman at Lourdes Recovers Full Use of his Limbs," declared one banner headline. "Cripple Walks Unaided after Lourdes Visit," stated another, using the language of the time. "Disabled Derryman: Condition Improved at Lourdes," a further headline proclaimed.

O'Kane seemed unmoved by the media commotion, pointing instead to what he believed was the cause of his cure. "I hope to visit Lourdes next Easter, in thanksgiving to Our Lady of Lourdes, and if possible each succeeding year," he said, not long after his return. Like so many others who were restored to good health, he was clear about where, and to whom, his gratitude was due – Lourdes and the intervention of Our Lady.

A young, terminally-ill Dublin woman left her baby daughter and husband behind and travelled to Lourdes knowing she had little chance of returning home alive. The year was 1933.

We will never be certain of what ultimately drove 30-year-old Celia MacMahon to set out for Lourdes in September 1933. Despite the parlous state of her health, maybe deep down she harboured a vague hope of obtaining a last-minute cure. More likely, she knew death was imminent and wanted to end her days in peace and calmness, in the embrace of Our Lady. Either way, in September 1933, she said goodbye to her husband and 18-month-old daughter, and headed for Lourdes.

Celia suffered from tubercular laryngitis – a by-product of that terrifying and potentially-fatal disease, TB, caused by the insidious bacterium *mycobacterium tuberculosis*. The disease, which had spread from her lungs to her larynx, was rampant in

Ireland in the 1930s and resulted in numerous painful and often premature deaths. Whatever chance Celia had of recovering from her primary symptoms, she had little hope of surviving its later spread. She and her doctors knew she was dying.

When Celia was lying in her bed at Our Lady of Lourdes Hospital, Dun Laoghaire – just down the road from her home in nearby Blackrock, County Dublin – she expressed the wish that, if she were to die, she wanted to do so at Lourdes, on the Feast of Our Lady's Nativity, and that she wanted to be buried close to the shrine. The timing was providential, as a national pilgrimage was scheduled to depart on Wednesday, 6 September, bringing 2,500 people from all parts of Ireland to Lourdes. Despite her failing health, Celia was determined to join it.

It must have been heart-wrenching for this young mother to say goodbye to her husband and daughter as she departed Dun Laoghaire on that autumn day in 1933. The trip was arduous. "The long journey by sea and rail racked her body with pain," one news report commented. Throughout the journey, she was looked after by the chief medical officer assigned to the pilgrimage and by a parish priest who stayed with her.

Shortly after her arrival in Lourdes, Celia was brought to the baths and from there to the hospital, where her health continued to deteriorate. Knowing that the end was near, she made her will. Her engagement and wedding rings she bequeathed to her husband. Her Lourdes badge, which she had proudly worn, she willed to her daughter. Finally, in deference to her love of the Blessed Virgin – and in recognition of where she lay dying – she asked that her daughter's name should be changed to Mary. Shortly afterwards, she succumbed to her illness and passed away.

The news came as a shock to the other pilgrims, who were notified about Celia's death by the leader of the pilgrimage, Cardinal Joseph MacRory, after a sermon he delivered the next morning. "She had expressed before leaving home a desire to die in Lourdes, and God has quickly given her her wish," he said. He then proceeded to ask for prayers from all present for the repose of her soul. The decision was taken to bury her, as she had wished, at Lourdes.

The funeral, which took place in beautiful sunshine, was uplifting. An estimated 1,000 Irish pilgrims marched for two miles to the graveyard, together with 40 men from the Army Medical Corps. Cardinal MacRory and a number of bishops, all dressed in their ceremonial robes, marched, too. They were joined by two senior government representatives – the Minister for Justice and Government Chief Whip – who were in Lourdes at the time.

Following French custom, the last prayers at the grave were chanted. When they were finished, Celia's local parish priest from Blackrock dropped a sod of clay on the coffin. Some 20 priests stood nearby. Observing the moving occasion, a reporter for the *Irish Independent* commented: "The funeral was one of the most impressive tributes to the dead that I have ever witnessed."

And so it was, on that bright Saturday in 1933, that Celia MacMahon, a young mother, aged 30, was buried far from her homeland, in the new cemetery at Lourdes. There, in the shadow of the Pyrenees, she lay peacefully having got her three wishes – she had died at Lourdes, was buried near the shrine and, just as she had asked, had passed away on 8 September 1933, on the Feast of Our Lady's Nativity.

The canonisation of Bernadette, which took place in Rome in December 1933, was a spectacular occasion. It was attended by many visitors from Ireland.

A glittering array of sartorial styles was to be witnessed in Rome during the canonisation of Bernadette on 8 December 1933. The colourful regalia of cardinals, archbishops, bishops, patriarchs and mitred abbots could be seen, not to mention the eye-catching ensemble of the Pope. Adding to the scene were the blue, red, orange and yellow dress uniforms of the Pontifical Swiss Guard, and the rich black velvet and jewels of the gentlemen-in-waiting.

On that occasion, however, it wasn't the usual suspects who caught the attention – instead, it was the women and girls from Lourdes. On another day, they, like all women, would have been expected to wear lace mantillas, which are the normal fashion accessory used in the presence of the Pope. Instead, they were given a special dispensation to wear black Pyrenean *capulets* – headdresses shaped a bit like a monk's hood – which were the customary, everyday head cover worn by Pyrenean peasant women, including Bernadette.

These Pyrenean *capulets* – made of cloth, worn diagonally on the head and hanging down at each side over the shoulders – were both striking and unique. "I have observed women walk with a smarter and more erect carriage when supporting this curious burden," an English woman travel writer observed in 1847. She added how impressive it was "to see old dames" rushing about a marketplace, with this article of dress "resting on their heads, immovable as if it were by nature a part of them." A Pyrenean female would no more go outside her door without wearing one than "a respectable woman in England would walk without a bonnet," she stiffly remarked.

How the Irish delegation reacted to this strange headdress has been lost to history. At least there were enough of them there – Dr. Mulhern, Bishop of Dromore, representing the Irish hierarchy, the Parliamentary Secretary to President de Valera, the Free State chargé d'affaires, and a host of other Irish priests and pilgrims. It was no surprise that in a private audience Pope Pius XI remarked to Dr. Mulhern: "I have always said that the Irish are like Divine Providence; they are everywhere."

The Irish, together with 50,000 other pilgrims, awoke to a dark, rain-swept morning on the day of the canonisation, with the steady downpour making the darkness even darker. There was no dampening of enthusiasm as many departed for their early-morning Masses. Others started queuing at St. Peter's, standing under umbrellas to protect them from the rain. "The Irish pilgrims didn't mind; they are used to nice soft weather," remarked a correspondent for *The Standard*, a weekly newspaper which served Irish Catholics from 1928 until it ceased publication in 1978.

The atmosphere inside St. Peter's, as the huge congregation awaited the Pope's arrival, must have been electrifying. Fifty thousand people were there, of whom 20,000 were French. Bernadette's sister-in-law was present, accompanied by three of Bernadette's nephews and other members of her extended family. The Superior General of the Sisters of Charity of Nevers had arrived, along with 160 of her nuns. Archbishop Lemaître, Primate of Africa – whose recovery from a decade-long illness had been attributed to Bernadette – was in attendance. His was one of the two certified cures that had underpinned the canonisation.

The famous silver trumpets announced the Pope's arrival, causing a tremor to run through the crowd. He was accompanied by a retinue of 20 cardinals and over 100 bishops, including Dr. Mulhern, Bishop of Dromore. Great cheering immediately rang out. "Evviva il Papa" ("Hurray the Pope") the congregation roared, as he was carried up the aisle in his gestatorial chair. "Like the waves of the sea, that cheering echoed through the vast building, and followed him like a rising tide in a storm until it reached the pitch of thunder as he was borne past the transepts where the greatest numbers were gathered," according to *The Standard*.

Following the many Church rites that precede canonisation, the great moment eventually arrived. All rose as the Pope stepped forward. There was a great silence. "We define and declare the Blessed Marie-Bernard Soubirous a saint," he announced, his voice cracking with emotion, "and we enrol her in the catalogue of saints, ordaining that her memory shall be piously celebrated in the Universal Church on April 16th of each year, the day of her birth in heaven."

The Pontiff intoned the first notes of the *Te Deum* – the beautiful early Christian hymn of praise – which was then sung by the choir together with the congregation. It was delivered with huge enthusiasm and a great sense of devotion. The great bells of St. Peter's rang out, and all the church bells of Rome rang out in reply. Then, a magnificent painting, representing Bernadette kneeling during one of the apparitions, was unveiled in a dazzling splendour of light. The French in attendance were overwhelmed by the moment. Many of them, particularly the nuns of Bernadette's old order, were in tears.

The memorable event – which had begun at 8 am – didn't conclude until after 1 pm. By then, the Pope had once again been carried down through St. Peter's in his famous chair. The noise was deafening – more and more ovations for the Pontiff, drowning out the fanfares of the silver trumpets. And then came the all-defining moment when the congregation spontaneously burst into song. And what did they sing? What else but the *Ave Maria*, appropriately concluding an event that had lifted so many hearts on a rain-sodden day in Rome.

The first official Irish cure at Lourdes took place in September 1936. It involved a Dubliner, Charles McDonald, who had been given up for dead having contracted TB.

Dull skies and showery weather cast a shadow over the pilgrimage departing Dun Laoghaire for Lourdes on 3 September 1936. Moderate south-west winds, with local fog, were encountered by the steamship as it made its way across the Irish Sea. The schedule for the 330 pilgrims was intense – first to Holyhead, onward to London, then to Paris via Folkestone, and finally to Lourdes.

It must have been an arduous journey for Dubliner Charles McDonald. Suffering from advanced TB, the disease was active in four locations in his body – lungs, shoulder, kidneys and spine. For five years, he had been an invalid and had spent 13 months on his back. Doctors could offer no hope. They recommended hospice care, but he opted to go home to die.

It was then that McDonald decided to travel to Lourdes. "I made application for a place on several pilgrimages, but each refused, as I was too far gone," the dying man, who weighed less than six stone, later recalled. Among those who rejected him was the St. Catherine's branch of the Catholic Young Men's Society, Thomas Street, Dublin. Their quota was full. By chance, one of their members took ill and died. "I took his place on the pilgrimage," McDonald recollected.

McDonald was transported to Lourdes on a stretcher, his intention being to remain inactive and say the rosary and pray throughout his stay. On the first morning, he was stretchered to Rosary Square for Mass and communion, and from there he was brought to the grotto. "When I got in front of the grotto I felt the presence of Our Blessed Lady there," he said. "I knew she was there at that moment, and anybody who has had the privilege of being there will realise that Our Lady's presence is really felt."

He was then taken to the baths. "My first immersion nearly killed me," he remembered. "It was icy cold. I was taken out trembling all over. It left such an impression on me that I was afraid of the following morning." The next day's immersion proved to be less painful: "I was pleasantly surprised to find the water not so bad as I anticipated.....It was after that bath that I felt so well."

McDonald found he could suddenly move his arm without pain: "I had been in pain for years, and at this moment the pain disappeared." He could also loosen his stretcher straps and raise his shoulders right off the pillows. "I felt I could have got off the stretcher and played a game of football.....I knew then Our Lady had answered my prayer," he later said.

The improvement continued the following day, the birthday of Our Lady: "I threw the bed clothes off me and sat up. They helped me to dress and put me in an invalid chair. I remained up for fourteen and a half hours, had three good meals, and had no sign of weakness or sickness." The next 24 hours brought even more good news: "I walked around Rosary Square, and on two occasions I walked through the grotto quite unaided. I came home as an ordinary passenger on trains and boats."

The excitement back in Ireland was palpable. Everyone was delighted with the news. They were particularly surprised to hear that, on arrival in Dublin, McDonald had travelled home by taxi and not in an ambulance. His doctor ordered X-rays, which showed that everything that was active before was negative. The sores from which he had been suffering as the pilgrimage commenced had healed.

The following year, McDonald returned to Lourdes, where he was examined by 32 doctors at the Lourdes Medical Bureau, which investigates apparent miraculous recoveries. "The result of their investigations showed that my condition was such that the cure could not have been brought about by medicine or science, but only by supernatural intervention," McDonald remarked. On a subsequent visit, in 1938, the cure was officially passed and registered by the bureau.

The revival made headline news in the Irish press. "Dublin Man Tells of Lourdes Miracle: Years of Suffering Ended," proclaimed one national newspaper. "Miracle at Lourdes Grotto: First Irish Cure to be Officially Passed," trumpeted another.

"The Only Irish Cure at Lourdes: Dublin Man's Wonderful Experience at World-Famous Shrine," yet another broadsheet declared.

Not surprisingly, McDonald became something of a national celebrity. He appeared on Radio Éireann, where he appealed on behalf of the Lourdes Invalid Fund. He lectured throughout the country, including in Tralee, County Kerry, where he "held the large attendance in thrall until the final sentence." There, he reminded the audience that it is not always the most worthy who are cured; why the unworthy are selected is just as big a mystery as the miracles themselves. Finally, he never forgot Lourdes, to which he returned as a stretcher-bearer in the years following his miraculous revival.

In November 1938, McDonald put in another appearance, this time at a meeting in Dublin's Gresham Hotel, where 600 people had gathered to celebrate a recent C.Y.M.S. pilgrimage to Lourdes. The entertainment was provided by none other than Mr. Charles McDonald who, according to a press report, "sang several songs in a robust baritone voice." His state of health, that night, was a far cry from the time he was carried to Lourdes on a stretcher as a dying man.

The following night, he turned up in the Parochial Hall, in Dublin's Glasnevin, where he gave a talk about his remarkable cure. He spoke so simply and charmingly – especially when he described himself as "an ordinary working fellow, and by no means pious" – that the crowd burst into enthusiastic applause.

Always a modest person, McDonald apologetically asked that he should not be applauded. "Instead," he said, "all praise and tribute should be given to the Mother of God." As a newspaperman who was present reported, Charles McDonald was, after all, "a glorious manifestation of the kindness and the triumphant power of Our Lady of Lourdes."

President John F. Kennedy visited Lourdes as a 20-year-old student during a European tour in 1937.

In July 1937, John F. Kennedy set out from the seaside town of Saint-Jean-de-Luz, in south-west France, and headed east for Lourdes, about a two-hour drive inland. On the journey, the 20-year-old future President of the United States and his friend Lem Billings no doubt discussed the film, starring Pat O'Brien, which they had seen the previous night. The Irish-American actor, whose grandfather came from County Cork, was famous for his Irish roles. In this dubbed film, however, they were "plenty amused" to hear O'Brien "spouting French."

On the day they drove to Lourdes – Tuesday, 27 July 1937 – the two young men were three weeks into a grand European tour. It was a wonderful adventure, spanning five countries – France, Italy, Germany, Holland and England – and including visits to Paris, Biarritz, the Riviera, Monte Carlo, Florence, Rome, Munich, Amsterdam, London and, of course, Lourdes. It had all begun on 7 July when the pair stepped ashore from the *S.S. Washington*, at Le Havre, having "stayed up to see Ireland," as Kennedy remarked.

We can only imagine the duo as they approached the grotto at Lourdes. The pair of former Choate schoolboys, who were both studying at prestigious universities back home, arrived in Kennedy's two-tone Ford convertible, which he had brought with him from New York. Kennedy had neatly packed into the car six tailor-made suits, 14 shirts and a supply of monogrammed silk pyjamas – hardly a case of roughing it on tour! Above all, though, he was pleased to be at the wheel of his prized, much-loved convertible. He had a lifelong love of open-topped cars that would prove fatal in Dallas, Texas, 26 years down the line.

Lourdes meant a lot to the Kennedys. Rose Kennedy, the matriarch of the family, had been enthralled by the story of Bernadette and the Marian apparitions. A devout Catholic, she had visited Lourdes, among other French Catholic shrines. Her daughter Kathleen – known as "Kick" – inherited the gene. She, too, was captivated by Lourdes – a place, she said, that was "really worth seeing." The fascination had also rubbed off on Jack, who had made it a must-see during his 1937 tour.

Arriving in Lourdes around the same time as a pilgrimage from Cork – involving 26 people and organised by Heffernan's Tourist Agency, based in the South Mall – Kennedy and Billings set about doing all the things visitors would normally do. Most importantly, they headed for the baths – which no doubt proved of interest to Kennedy, whose childhood illnesses had included whooping cough, measles, chicken pox and scarlet fever, and who in his prep-school and college years suffered from acute intestinal ailments, infections, and what doctors feared for a time to be leukaemia.

It was all "very interesting," Kennedy wrote in his 1937 European tour diary, a small, leather-bound journal, titled *My Trip Abroad*, which was donated to the John F. Kennedy Library by Jacqueline Onassis in 1975. Lourdes, he remarked, was "the scene of thousands of sick people seeking cures." Unfortunately, he explained, the idea of a cure being realised by either him or his friend seemed to "become reversed," as

Lem Billings "became quite ill after leaving." Lem ended up, he said, with a temperature of 103° Fahrenheit.

Perhaps providing some sort of measure of Jack's less-than-intense Catholicism, he was said to have laughed out loud at his friend's predicament; no doubt the irony of reaching Lourdes and becoming sick struck him as amusing. In many ways, it was similar to the manner in which he later practised his faith – attending Mass, receiving communion and going to confession combined with an exceptional facility for promiscuity and an ability to sin with gusto. It was a contradiction that would characterise him for the rest of his life.

The pair didn't remain long in Lourdes; instead, they left that evening for Toulouse, then on to Cannes and Monte Carlo, followed by Milan and Rome. The religious theme continued, with visits to churches and to cathedrals, although they also stopped at palaces, castles and museums along the way. They took time out for gambling and womanising on the Riviera and at Monte Carlo. They also had a private audience with Cardinal Pacelli at the Vatican. Less than two years later, Pacelli, who was a friend of Kennedy's father, became Pope Pius XII.

On 25 August, Kennedy and Billings left for England, where they met up with Kennedy's sister "Kick" and his brother Joe. Replicating Lem's sickness at Lourdes, Kennedy became ill in London. His face "puffed up and he got a rash" and "terrible asthma," Billings noted. In his diary, Kennedy, who was forced to see a doctor, complained of hives and a low blood count. It wasn't until 1947 – a decade after his return from the 1937 tour – that doctors in Boston identified the cause as Addison's disease.

Illness continued to dog Kennedy for the remainder of his life. Bobby, his brother, later recalled: "At least one-half of the days that he spent on this earth were days of intense physical pain." The Catholicism which had brought him to Lourdes in the first place also pursued him, particularly during the 1960 presidential election. Even his post-Lourdes rendezvous with Cardinal Pacelli became controversial. But all that lay ahead – more than two decades after he paid a short, but memorable, visit to the shrine at Lourdes, the details of which are poignantly recalled in his diary.

In the late 1930s, a recently-established American magazine, *The Catholic Digest,* **published the story of a young boy's cure at Lourdes. Although the boy's family came from England, they had Irish roots.**

One summer, an English doctor, of Irish heritage, named Dr. Ryan, took his wife and partially-paralysed son, John, on a motoring holiday through France. Their final destination was Biarritz, the fashionable seaside resort on the Atlantic coast, where they planned to spend about a week. The trip was going smoothly, the weather was good, and the car – a relatively new one – was performing well.

Suddenly, on the outskirts of Lourdes – about 160 km from Biarritz – the car broke down. On enquiry, they discovered it would take three days to repair. They had no choice but to get the job done, and meanwhile booked into a hotel. While there, the young John Ryan befriended a French boy by the name of Jean Patou, who was the son of the hotel's chef. John's parents were pleased, as the newly-discovered friend not only spoke

English but shared with their son an enthusiasm for stamp collecting.

On their first day together, Jean Patou noticed that his new friend's left leg and arm were paralysed. He told him about the Lourdes shrine and how people had been coming to it, unable to move properly, and had departed perfectly healed. John was amazed by the news, which raised his hopes. That night, he spoke to his father and asked if he would take him there. The father laughed, patted his son on his head, and spoke of many things, including "superstition." John didn't quite understand what he meant.

The following day, John mentioned to his friend about what his father had said the night before. The friend replied, "Well, then, I'll take you myself." John pointed out that he would find the journey difficult. Without his crutches, he couldn't walk; even with them, he struggled. The friend thought for a while and remembered that his father had a large wheelbarrow. "You can climb into that and I'll wheel you down," he said. He added that coming back would be easier because, by then, John would be able to walk.

The next morning, just before sunrise, the two boys set out on the short journey to the grotto. They cut a strange sight – the pale-faced young boy, John, sitting in the wheelbarrow, being pushed by his friend, Jean, who was sturdy but small. The pair arrived just in time for second Mass. Jean pushed the wheelbarrow into the back of the church and helped his friend onto a seat. Jean told him to watch the Mass and he would do the praying.

During the Mass, John was enthralled by what was going on, and at the elevation of the host and chalice he rose from his seat to see better what was happening. "It's all right," Jean whispered. "You must kneel now because Our Lord is present. You'll be able to walk afterwards." John obeyed him. A short time later, the Mass ended. At that very moment, something extraordinary took place. John whispered, "I can walk." "Of course, you can," his friend replied. And the two friends left the church together.

They walked back to the hotel, pushing the wheelbarrow before them. On the way, their conversation turned once again to stamps. John recalled that, back in London, he had four new stamps from Ceylon, and he promised to send Jean two of them. Jean, in turn, offered to send his English friend a stamp from China which had been given to his father by a priest. Caught up in the conversation, they failed to notice the two figures coming towards them. It was John's mother and father, hurrying down the street, alarmed and searching for their son. "Thank heaven, it's John," Dr. Ryan exclaimed loudly. "He's walking," the mother cried out, speaking louder still.

Jean, who had heard the mother's remark, replied: "Why, of course. You see, I took him to the grotto because I knew Our Lady would help him to get strong again. She's helped such a lot of people, you know." Dr. Ryan stared at the two boys, especially his son. The doctor was frightfully pale and without understanding. A short time elapsed. Mrs. Ryan was the first to break the silence and said to the boys: "I think breakfast is ready. You'll come and have some with us, won't you, Jean?" The French boy replied, "I'd like to. I'm very hungry."

"And there the story ends," *The Catholic Digest* remarked in conclusion. Whether you believe the account or not is up to you, the reader of this book. It is worth noting, however, that the publication is a reputable one, still in existence, and prides itself on being not only "America's most popular Catholic magazine" but that it always uses "stories of real people" to show that "a life guided by faith can be exciting, challenging, enlivening, and joyous."

As for the happening at Lourdes, the magazine remarked in conclusion: "Nothing is known at Lourdes about the miracle, except perhaps at the hotel. The faith of the children was so great that it did not occur to them to make a fuss about something they knew would happen, and the doctor and his wife, though deeply grateful and very mystified, were nevertheless not willing to attribute the perfect cure of their boy to Our Lady of Lourdes. That would, of course, be 'sheer superstition.'"

Lourdes suffered badly during World War II, which resulted in the cessation of international pilgrimages. One Irish group was lucky to escape before hostilities commenced in 1939.

An eight-month-old girl was among 66 Irish invalids, including seven stretcher cases, who made a hasty escape from Lourdes in late August 1939. The pilgrimage they were part of – organised by the St. Vincent de Paul Society – faced being pinned down in France as the country prepared for imminent war. With the army being mobilised, and trains about to be commandeered, it was feared that the 400-strong party might be trapped in the country. Advice was issued to get out of Lourdes – indeed, get out of the country – and do so fast.

It was obvious to the Irish pilgrims that the atmosphere around them was darkening, and darkening quickly. Private overseas telephone calls were immediately suspended, while strict rules were introduced requiring telegrams to be in plain language and not in code or cipher. The press was about to be censored. Exporting maps from the country was banned, especially those used by the army or identifying the position of factories, mines or train lines. France's first and second division soccer matches were cancelled for the weekend. Trouble was certainly afoot, and it was time to get out.

The pilgrims departed Lourdes on Sunday, 27 August, just as wartime contingency plans were being put in place. As they sped through the French countryside, the rail network and the borders around them were closing down. The Italians had just shut their frontier with France. Plans were put in place to seal off the French border with Germany. The pilgrims were like animals being caught in a net, their escape options gradually narrowing, and their hopes of making it home diminishing with the passage of each mile.

As their train hurried through the French landscape, the 400 Irish pilgrims were cared for by 22 priests, two doctors and a group of nurses. They sang the *Ave Maria* and *Salve Regina* as they scurried along. The priests held an hour of prayer in each train compartment, to compensate for the Holy Hour which the passengers were missing at the shrine. Back home, Radio Éireann broadcast an emergency announcement advising relatives to make their way to Dun Laoghaire, to meet the boat. Everything was heading towards a safe arrival, but there was still some distance to go.

The pilgrims reached Calais after a tense, 22-hour, non-stop train journey. There was mayhem at the port, with businessmen and holidaymakers rushing for home. Long queues had formed for the cross-channel steamers, with passengers waiting several hours before being permitted on board. Boats were densely packed, and a large number of travellers had to stand during the crossing. The *Golden Arrow* train service, via Calais, was crowded to capacity. Even air services were completely booked up, with wealthy travellers who asked for special planes being told that owing to the European situation no machines were available.

Having eventually crossed from Calais to Dover, the pilgrims were brought by special train to Holyhead, and then ferried home. When they arrived, they "looked well, if tired," one reporter noted. It was by the skin of their teeth that they had made their escape. Within 72 hours of their return, German aircraft bombarded Poland. Forty-eight hours later, Britain and France declared war on Germany. The next scheduled Irish pilgrimage – organised by the Catholic Young Men's Society – was cancelled, "owing to the present international situation," their executive committee explained.

For the next six years, Irish connections with Lourdes came to a standstill. Pilgrimages ceased completely. Communications were cut. News of events at the shrine dried up. Even in 1945, when the war finished, travel proved difficult. Train transport was poor and food was in short supply. Many visitors were forced to stay in hospitals, convents or wooden huts.

Despite these impediments, the first small group of Irish men and women left for the shrine in September 1946. Ten people departed in all. They included P. J. Little, Minister for Posts and Telegraphs, who we heard about earlier, a doctor, two priests, and two women from Dublin who had been there many times before. Also in the travel party were representatives of the St. Vincent de Paul Society and the Catholic Young Men's Society, checking on the viability of future pilgrimages to the shrine.

There was also a noble purpose to the visit – to assist at what turned out to be one of the most moving and edifying pilgrimages ever to reach Lourdes. That September, in 1946, some 90,000 ex-prisoners of war walked, cycled, drove or travelled by train from all parts of Europe to offer thanks to Our Lady. Some came from concentration camps run by the SS. Many were maimed or unwell. All had promised to travel to Lourdes if they survived the war. "It was a most inspiring example of devotion," said Mr. R. F. Murphy, who was a member of the Irish party.

Another member of the party, Mrs. Kathleen Lynch, met up with an old friend – businesswoman Nancy Walsh-Douly – who we were also acquainted with earlier. "She was delighted to meet friends from Ireland again," Mrs. Lynch said. She was even more pleased to discover that Irish pilgrimages would be beginning again the following year. Even if those who travelled would need to bring supplies of condensed milk for their cups of tea – "employ a tin opener while there, and use it as required" was the advice – the next year, 1947, would see the pilgrimage trail in action once more.

The good news was that the first Irish pilgrimage in 1947 was organised by the Catholic Young Men's Society – the very same group whose 1939 trip was cancelled at the last moment due to the outbreak of war. Because of travel complications, the tour was restricted to invalids only. A small group of 116 people travelled. It was a great success. In Lourdes, they joined 150,000 people from all parts of the world, and were the only country to display a national flag. Eight years after the beginning of World War II, Ireland's connection to Lourdes was back on track.

The celebrated movie, *The Song of Bernadette*, enthralled Irish cinemagoers following its release in Ireland in March 1944.

In October 1943, a senior executive from 20th Century Fox arrived in Dublin to announce the American studio's forthcoming blockbuster movie, *The Song of Bernadette*. The production, he said, had cost a staggering three million dollars, of which one-quarter of a million dollars was spent on music. Thousands of actors and extras had been employed, many of them French. He emphasised at a reception in Dublin's Gresham Hotel that the film's magnificent scale was "in keeping with the great religious theme which it sought to portray on the screen."

That the Hollywood executive happened to be Mr. Murray Silverstone, the Vice-President of 20th Century Fox, not only indicated the importance of the pending production, but also highlighted the significance of the Irish market. Although he referred to Dublin as the "greatest cinema city for its population in the world," he neglected to mention that the illustrious Hollywood studio expected huge financial rewards in Ireland because of the country's predominantly Catholic ethos.

How right he was! From the moment *The Song of Bernadette* opened at the Metropole Cinema, Dublin, it drew crowds in record numbers. The hype was enormous. The premiere was attended by members of the government, diplomatic corps, judges and politicians. Critics were there, too. "Screen triumph," one reviewer exclaimed, praising the production for its "calm dignity," "quiet restraint" and "exquisite simplicity." Another critic wisely noted that the film "should have a greater run in Dublin than any picture for many years."

With admission prices increased to 2/6, 3/9, 5/6 and 8/6, the studios, distributors and cinema owners pocketed handsome profits. The high prices, they pointed out, were due to the length of the film – more than two and a half hours – which restricted the number of showings. Others argued that cinemagoers were being exploited, with one newspaper columnist declaring that "the chappie who sits under the screen and sees the Lourdes grotto as in a glass, darkly, will pay a half-a-crown and no deduction for eye-strain."

The film opened in classic Hollywood style. The introductory title card read: "Twentieth Century Fox presents Franz Werfel's *The Song of Bernadette*." Audiences were then advised: "This is the story of Bernadette Soubirous who lived in Lourdes, a village in southern France close to the Spanish border. For those who believe in God, no explanation is necessary. For those who do not believe in God, no explanation is possible." Something mystical and profound was clearly in store.

What followed was the narration of Bernadette's life story "with delicacy and fidelity to truth," as an *Irish Independent* reviewer put it. "We see Bernadette first in her humble home," the critic wrote, "see her long struggle against the doubts of Church and State, the amazing response of the peasants, and her death in the convent. The photography is beautiful and acting of the many minor characters excellent, and in Jennifer Jones the producer found an actress who could reach the acme of simplicity the part required."

The film catapulted the unknown Jennifer Jones to instant worldwide stardom. As the *Irish Independent* film reviewer explained: "She had to convey to us something of the exalted divine love that had inspired Bernadette. Perhaps that was impossible, but at least I know no actress who would have come nearer success than Jennifer Jones did in *The Song of Bernadette*." For the Roman Catholic-raised Jones – who came from Oklahoma and whose real name was Phylis Lee Isley – her onscreen achievement was remarkable indeed. On her twenty-fifth birthday, she won the Academy Award for Best Actress for her interpretation of Bernadette Soubirous.

The film also enhanced the fame of the Cork-born priest, Monsignor John J. Devlin. A former seminarian at All Hallows College, Dublin, he had moved to America in the 1920s, where he founded the Los Angeles chapter of the Legion of Decency. In his role as director of the chapter, he rated Hollywood movies for their moral content and became a much-used script consultant. He soon became known as Hollywood's "Padre of the Films".

Devlin, whose brother was manager of the Savoy Cinema in Waterford, had acted as "technical advisor" during the film's production, vetting the Catholic content of the movie and ensuring that its message was in accordance with Church teaching. One negative word from Devlin and *The Song of Bernadette* would have been subjected to a mass boycott by American Catholics. Without his approval, the ambitious production would have flopped.

The movie also invigorated the career of Franz Werfel, the Prague-born author who had written the novel on which the movie was based. In June 1940, after the collapse of France, this Jewish author and his wife had sheltered in Lourdes as he attempted to escape from the Nazis. Having become acquainted with Bernadette and the wondrous healings of Lourdes, he vowed that one day, if he reached America, he would sing as best he could "the song of Bernadette." His subsequent novel, of the same name, was a runaway success, and continued to sell in vast quantities after the film's release.

The truth is that everyone, including 20th Century Fox and its Vice-President, Murray Silverstone, did well from the movie. It won four Academy Awards and it was nominated in eight further categories. It was also awarded a Golden Globe as the best picture of 1943. Most of all, it left its mark on millions of cinemagoers and, in later years, on viewers of the film on TV. And it did all this, as the *Irish Independent* reviewer put it in 1944, by telling "one of the most extraordinary stories in the history of mankind in the only way it could be told – with absolute simplicity."

What follows is the story of a Hollywood film star, June Haver, with Cork roots, who gave up her acting career after becoming a Catholic and visiting Lourdes. She shocked her fans by joining a convent and setting about becoming a nun.

She was beautiful, blue-eyed, small – just 5ft 2in – and blonde, and was hired by 20th Century Fox as rival and successor to Betty Grable. In the 1940s and early 1950s, she became a Hollywood screen idol, starring in a dozen major films and eventually earning $3,500 a week – a fortune for its time. It says something of her stature as a star that 20th Century Fox replaced her with Marilyn Monroe. Eventually, she gave it all up for something entirely different and, as a result, her amazing story deserves to be told.

June Haver was born in Rock Island, Illinois, in 1926, and had a grandmother who came from Cork. A child prodigy, she made her stage debut aged six and had her own radio show at the age of eleven. Signed by 20th Century Fox, she went on to feature in a succession of musical films which, though largely forgotten today, were enormously successful in their time. Among them were *Irish Eyes are Smiling* (1944), *I Wonder Who's Kissing Her Now* (1947), *Oh, You Beautiful Doll* (1949) and *The Daughter of Rosie O'Grady* (1950).

Although a worldwide star – and, according to her sister, "very self-assured" – Haver was regarded by all who met her as approachable, modest and unassuming. A reporter from *The Cork Examiner* described her, during a visit to Ireland in 1950, as not only fashionable – dressed in "a navy-blue fitted coat, and chic jersey stocking cap to match" – but having "a charming personality." A journalist with *The Kerryman*, who spoke to her during the same trip, later recalled her "quiet, unassuming manner" and how, in her short visit, she "cultivated a friendship with a great many."

Despite surviving at the highest level in Hollywood for more than a decade, she eventually tired of the film industry and all it entailed. Her private life was troubled. Marriage to a trumpet player proved short-lived – she called it "the biggest mistake of my life." A follow-up relationship with a dentist ended abruptly, after he died during routine surgery. She felt that she needed something new in her life, and she found it in Catholicism.

"It was Father James McGovern, an Irish priest, who was instrumental in bringing about my conversion to the Catholic faith," she later explained. She first met him after attending Sunday Mass at a church near her Hollywood home. She had gone there with friends. On learning of her interest in religion, he offered to give her instruction, which she duly accepted. She was eventually received into the Catholic Church.

In November 1950, Haver travelled to Lourdes, where Irish pilgrims were assembled to commemorate the Holy Year. On that trip to Europe, she also visited Assisi and Rome. At the Vatican, she had a semi-private audience with the Pope. Arriving in Ireland on the TWA Constellation *Star of Indiana*, on her way back to the USA, she spoke of her European tour and her Irish friends at home, including the Mayo-born "Rosary Priest" Fr. Peyton and the Dublin-born film star Maureen O'Hara. She gave no inkling, whatsoever, of what was about to happen next in her life.

In 1953, the 26-year-old Haver issued a statement through her Hollywood studio, which came as a shock to her fans. "I am going away to prepare myself, by several years of prayer and study, for something I have been contemplating for the past two years," the statement read. "I am determined to be a Sister of Charity, with the grace of God and the approval of his church, and to consecrate my life to the service of God. To do this will take more ability than I have. That is why I am going to prepare myself in a novitiate of work and prayer."

Haver became a novice in the order of the Sisters of Charity, in Kansas, where, despite being locked away from public view, the press pursued her. The news agency, Reuters, reported that she was "waiting at tables" in the convent "in return for room, board and schooling." They also spoke to one of the Sisters, who described Haver as the least sophisticated of her group, adding: "She is sweet, earnest and sincerely fits into her training here. Everybody loves her."

Despite finishing her probationary period and donning the habit of a Sister of Charity, Haver eventually succumbed to ill-health. After seven and a half months in the convent, she returned to her family home. "I have no regrets," she said. "It was a beautiful life – everything I had hoped it would be. But I didn't have the physical strength to withstand the strain of a religious life. Many people seek to do God's will as they understand it. That is all I did. I don't think I failed."

Almost immediately, speculation was rife that Haver would make a quick return to the silver screen, but it didn't turn out like that. Instead, at a birthday party for John Wayne, she was reacquainted with Fred MacMurray, an actor and singer she had worked with before and who had recently been widowed. The couple immediately fell in love and were married a month later, in California. They adopted two children and then lived happily ever after, remaining together for 37 years.

As for Haver, she never worked in films again, arguing that she had decided to retire from the business "while I was still under, rather than over the hill." Instead, she remained at home and looked after the couple's two girls. When MacMurray developed throat cancer, she helped look after their ranch and extensive property holdings. She also took care of him until his death in 1991. His last words, as he lay dying, were: "I love you, Junie." She had at last found the happiness that had eluded her throughout her extraordinary life.

The name Bernadette became hugely popular in Ireland in the 1940s and '50s. By then, the saint had become a cultural icon.

Civil rights activist and former politician, Bernadette Devlin, was born on 23 April 1947. At the time, her Christian name had become a much-favoured choice among Irish parents. The reason was the relatively recent release of the film *The Song of Bernadette* and the book by the same name which had been published a few years earlier. Both film and book would result in Bernadette becoming the fifteenth most popular name in Ireland – a ranking that seems inconceivable today. In 2014, for example, just four children were christened Bernadette.

Devlin came from a very religious family, with a mother who she described as "despairingly Christian." In her autobiography, *The Price of my Soul*, she explained: "You could have kicked her fifty times a day and she would still have turned the other cheek." Not surprisingly, the mother chose religious names for her children, including Mary, Marie and, of course, Bernadette. Her choices, no doubt, were helped by the fact that she herself was named Elizabeth Bernadette, harking back to an earlier era when the saint's name was first becoming popular.

Prior to 1900, Bernadette was a virtually non-existent name in Ireland, with only seven references to it turning up in a search of births at the time. There was good reason for that – it had no connection with the country. Instead, it was of Germanic origin, a feminine version of Bernard, meaning "brave as a bear." It had eventually worked its way into France, but even there its use was relatively rare. The French preferred names like Marie, Jeanne, Marguerite and Madeleine.

It remained that way up to the Lourdes apparitions, when the young Bernadette Soubirous entered the scene. She had been named Marie-Bernarde after her aunt and godmother, the relatively wealthy tavern owner Bernarde Castérot. She quickly became known as Bernadette, the pet form of the name. Following the apparitions, her name gradually became a popular choice among French parents. By 1914, at the start of World War I, it had risen to number 68 in the national charts. After that – mainly following her beatification (1925) and her canonisation (1933) – it took off.

The big boost came when the film *The Song of Bernadette* was released in 1944. Huge numbers of French parents chose to call their babies Bernadette, and the name entered the top 20. By 1960, however, things were changing. New entries, like Brigitte – related to the growing fame of Brigitte Bardot – became chart toppers. Bernadette's decline was spectacular after that – she did not even feature in the top 500 by 2014.

The popularity of Marie experienced similar fortunes. Back in 1900, it was the dominant French chart topper. It was the same in 1914, and again in 1939. Even by 1949, nothing had changed. Then, in the mid-1950s, Marie, too, began to decline, and by 2014 it was languishing at number 49. The three most popular girls' names in that same year, 2014, were Jade, Louise and Emma.

The situation was comparable in Ireland, with Bernadette first growing to prominence in the early twentieth century. Notable people born in that period include the Radio Éireann announcer Bernadette Plunkett. In 1938, when in her early 20s, she joined the national broadcaster and was known for her first news bulletin – a remarkable 40-minute broadcast concerning the infamous Munich Agreement which, according to British Prime Minister Neville Chamberlain, would guarantee "peace for our time." Plunkett went on to become one of the best-known Bernadettes of her era.

Another widely-known Bernadette – born slightly later, in 1924 – was the celebrated Irish actress Bernadette O'Farrell. From Birr, County Offaly, she became famous in Britain and America for her role as Maid Marian in the TV series *The Adventures of Robin Hood*. With O'Farrell playing alongside Richard Greene, who performed the lead role, the show had a weekly audience of more than 30 million viewers. She left after 78 episodes, fearing she was becoming typecast, although she received sacks of mail begging her to stay. The problem, she said, was that even her shopkeeper started addressing her as Maid Marian.

One of the better known of the final wave of Bernadettes was Bernadette "Bernie" Nolan, the former lead vocalist of the girl group, The Nolans. Born in Dublin, in October 1960, her parents moved to Blackpool, where the girls began performing as The Nolan Sisters and later as The Nolans. After seven Top 20 UK hit singles, including *I'm in the Mood for Dancing*, she became an actress, appearing on *Brookside* and in the stage musicals *Blood Brothers* and *Chicago*. She died from breast cancer in July 2013.

There are many reasons for the demise of Bernadette as a popular name. To begin with, fashions change. This was particularly true in the 1960s, when a new popular culture swept away old customary ways. People became less hidebound by tradition and gravitated towards distinctive, individualised names. The declining influence of the Church also had an effect, particularly in the move away from naming children after saints. Populations became more mobile and diverse, with notable foreign influences coming into play.

Those who already possessed the name became part of an ever-growing minority. They were often referred to by abbreviations or nicknames, including Bernie, Bern, Bennie or even Bunny. In Bernadette Devlin's case, she was not infrequently called "St. Bernadette" by her avid supporters, who idolised her. Not everyone felt the same way, though. As one newspaper letter writer declared in 1970, her time was past and she had persisted beyond her hour of need. Clearly, he was not enamoured. But, then again, as his home address made clear, he lived in a house called "St. Jude's"!

History was made in 1949 when the first pilgrimage by air departed Belfast for Lourdes.

A dense fog delayed for three hours the departure of the first-ever pilgrimage scheduled to leave Belfast for Lourdes by air. Visibility was so bad that the incoming chartered aircraft – a Sabena Skymaster, arriving from Brussels – had to circle Nutts Corner Airport for just under an hour before it could land. Forty-four pilgrims, including invalids and stretcher cases, waited patiently in the terminal building for the aircraft's arrival. Having looked forward to this moment for months, no amount of fog could dampen their optimism or high spirits.

On that bleak Thursday morning, in August 1949, the 44 pilgrims cheered as the Skymaster broke through the fog and landed in Belfast. One by one, the sick and unwell were helped onto the plane. It was no easy job. Some had not left their beds for years, much less their homes or towns. One girl, who was paralysed, had been forced to lie down face-forwards for two years. A 60-year-old woman had been bedridden for two decades. They were accompanied by a blind girl, along with sufferers from heart trouble and TB – all sharing in common the intense faith necessary to undertake this arduous journey.

Relatives and sightseers enthusiastically sang the *Ave Maria* as the pilgrims boarded the plane. The mood inside the aircraft was equally joyous, with one observer noting an atmosphere of "eagerness and buoyant cheerfulness." Then, just after noon, on that foggy day – some of the worst fog ever seen in Ireland, it was said – the 44 members of the Down and Connor diocesan pilgrimage were on their way. All going well, they would soon join the other 900 members of the pilgrimage – those less physically distressed – who had travelled ahead by land and sea.

The aircraft flew low, travelling unpressurised at just over 4,000 feet, in consideration of those aboard who had heart trouble or suffered from pulmonary TB. The plane, as a result, bore the brunt of any low-lying bad weather. The captain – a war veteran – did his best to avoid the worst of the unsettled conditions. Any drops or bumps only evoked smiles and jokes among the passengers. Matters were helped by the food – milk, cakes and fruit flown in that morning from Belgium – which was far better than anything available back home, where post-war rationing was still being enforced.

Activity on the plane was frantic. Four nurses – only one of whom had flown before – administered medicine, rearranged pillows, and took care of their patients. The steward took care of the food. "Serving invalids is obviously a new experience for him," D. J. Hayes later reported in *The Irish Press*, "but it is doubtful if his usual opulent passengers ever got more attention or courtesy. As he distributes second helpings he shakes his head and admits that the experience is not one he wants repeated: 'It makes me sad,' he admits, 'to see so many sick people travelling so far.'"

There's no doubt the pilgrims aboard were unwell, all in different ways. D. J. Hayes noticed "a blind girl whose face is serene as a child's asleep" and a disabled young girl "with flowing brown hair" whose friends had oversubscribed to send her to Lourdes. There were the cardiac patients, TB cases, the congenitally disabled, no two the same. Seven invalids were lying on their stretchers near the rear door. There was also, he humorously observed, "an old lady of nearly seventy from the Falls Road, whose only worry is that she disgraced herself by falling asleep while the priest was reciting the rosary a while ago."

Owing to the fog, the airplane was late arriving at Tarbes airport, although that did nothing to dampen the cheerfulness or high spirits. The pilgrims were pleased when Dr. Mageean, Bishop of Down and Connor, boarded the aircraft to greet them. With him was the Commander-in-Chief of the French Army, who had come to Tarbes to witness the event. Once loaded onto a bus, the pilgrims then proceeded to Lourdes.

There are no reports of any miracles associated with that 1949 pilgrimage, but the participants did see a person who had received one. They saw her only hours after their arrival. While travelling from the airport to Lourdes, their bus was halted by a commotion that had spilled onto the streets. At the centre of the disturbance was a seven-year-old girl, Jacqueline Gaudier, a Belgian, who had been paralysed since birth.

The girl could neither walk nor stand because of a paralysed left arm and leg. During High Mass, in the Lourdes basilica, she suddenly turned to her mother and said: "I feel I am going to walk." After leaving the basilica, she got out of her "pram" and, clutching its handle, walked 100 yards. Then, exhausted by her efforts, she returned to her pram, leaving her mother in tears. It was that same girl who had caused the stir around the Irish pilgrims' bus.

"I saw her face amid the crowd that surged around her and halted our bus," D. J. Hayes remarked. "I shall never forget the incandescent light of joy in her eyes as she laughed and gave thanks with the thousand friends she had at that moment." No doubt, all the other occupants on the Irish bus were equally overjoyed – perhaps hopeful, as well, of what lay ahead.

For six days, the Down and Connor pilgrimage remained in Lourdes, visiting the grotto, entering the baths, attending at Masses, participating in the many ceremonies including the torchlight procession, and praying to Our Lady. They were given the honour of leading the torchlight procession, walking or being carried ahead of the 90,000 pilgrims from European countries who took part. Then, on 1 September, they returned home.

Words failed D. J. Hayes in describing the venture. He tried "important" and "wonderful," but in the end he settled on something else. More pertinent, he said, was "the faith that moves sick people to make the long journey to Lourdes; it is the faith that transcends the physical risks that the journey entails, and even the knowledge that at its end there is no guarantee of cure." That, he said, was the mark of what the invalid air pilgrimage from Belfast, in 1949, was all about.

Dr. John Charles McQuaid, Archbishop of Dublin and Primate of Ireland, led his first diocesan pilgrimage to Lourdes in 1949. Up to the time of his death, in 1973, his name was inextricably linked with the shrine.

Archbishop Dr. John Charles McQuaid was one of the most controversial figures in twentieth-century Irish Catholicism. He was loved and admired by some; hated and reviled by others. His critics accused him of being conservative, authoritarian and strict; his proponents praised him for being gentle, kind and good to the sick. Whatever might be thought of him, McQuaid had one distinctive feature – he loved Lourdes and did more than any other Irishman to promote the shrine.

Those who knew McQuaid described a shy, retiring individual who was happiest by his own fireside, well away from the glare of publicity. On the other hand, he was forceful and manipulative, a thorough manager, always striving to be in control. Perhaps it was that combination of disparate traits – his reserve allied to his impressive organisational skills – that brought out the best in him when he departed Ireland on his annual pilgrimages to Lourdes.

Having led his first Dublin diocesan pilgrimage to the shrine in 1949, McQuaid became inextricably associated with the annual event. The pilgrimages were highly complicated, most of them involving 1,000 or so subscribers, their operation requiring high-level coordinating and management skills. Although the archbishop possessed all these abilities in spades, it was the emotional aspect of the visits that appealed to him most. Even after that first pilgrimage in 1949, his only thoughts were of the courage and the cheerfulness of the pilgrims towards each other, and especially towards the sick. "There is a grace of peace in Lourdes which cannot be defined," he remarked.

It was said that McQuaid's face lit up at the mention of Lourdes. He was no sooner home from one diocesan pilgrimage than he was planning another. They became his obsession. Stories are told of how he would whip out a map of Lourdes, spread it across the floor, kneel down in front of it, and point out the town's features and layout to anyone who would listen. Others described how, once he arrived at Lourdes, he became a different man. The place seemed to draw him out of himself, relieve him of his worries, and allow him to engage with his fellow pilgrims.

The Jesuit, Fr. Roland Burke Savage – editor of the influential journal *Studies* and who knew McQuaid – witnessed him at the shrine. "As I watched him, night by night, sit at the bedside of one invalid after another, perfectly at home with all types, cracking jokes, giving spiritual counsel, praying with the sick, helping and encouraging the band of schoolboys who, year after year, do such notable and yet so unobtrusive work with the sick on the Dublin pilgrimage, I saw the truly human touch of Dr. McQuaid, made all the more lovable because it was inspired by Christ-like charity."

We can speculate that at least some of McQuaid's sensitivity derived from the death, aged 22, of his mother, Jennie, a week after his birth in Cootehill, County Cavan. His father, Dr. Eugene McQuaid, married again, but it was not until his teenage years that John Charles discovered that his biological mother was dead. Whatever the root source of his subsequent reserve and shyness, it did little to impede his stellar rise through University College Dublin, where he received a first-class honours degree, and the Gregorian University in Rome, where he was awarded a doctorate in theology.

It was not until1940 – on his appointment as Archbishop of Dublin – that the authoritarian, manipulative and manoeuvring side of McQuaid's personality came to the fore. He scuppered Minister for Health, Dr. Noel Browne's Mother and Child Scheme, which would have provided free medical care to mothers and their children; enthusiastically implemented a ban on Catholics entering Trinity College; and forced the Football Association of Ireland to cancel a scheduled match against "communist" Yugoslavia. Even before becoming archbishop, he had played an active role in ensuring the presence of Catholic values in the drafting of the 1937 Constitution.

Lourdes provided the perfect antidote to McQuaid's backroom scheming. Everything about the place – the holiness, the camaraderie, the religious fervour, the tranquillity – appealed to him. "One can describe Lourdes," he said, "but one must live at least some days in Lourdes in order to understand the meaning of that shrine. I do not now refer to the undoubted cures. I refer rather to the vast number of confessions heard, to the vast number of communions distributed for hours on end each morning.

"In Lourdes, as always, Our Lady leads us sinners to the feet of her Divine Son. There is thus in Lourdes a serenity, which is the peculiar grace of that shrine, for there we feel that she

160

obtains for us from her Divine Son the grace to bear our daily cross with a new courage and a new love."

Up to 1971, Archbishop McQuaid continued to visit Lourdes, leading pilgrims from his diocese to the shrine of Our Lady. In his later years, his closing remarks to his fellow pilgrims seemed almost prophetic, hinting that his days on earth hadn't long to run. He once commented how he looked forward to meeting Our Lady, just as Bernadette did. "But we know that to see her, death must intervene," he said.

On Saturday, 7 April 1973, Archbishop McQuaid, aged 77, died after experiencing two heart attacks. His body was interred in the vaults of the Pro-Cathedral, Dublin, following Solemn Requiem Mass. During his last pilgrimage, in 1971, he said goodbye to "the company of the kindly pilgrims" who had each year travelled with him to the shrine. His final address was delivered with great sadness. The moment had come, he said, "to say farewell to Lourdes."

MODERN TIMES

Transport improvements made in the 1950s and 1960s transformed the shrine at Lourdes. Boat and train travel became faster. Upmarket liner passengers arrived via Bordeaux. Most important of all, travel by air grew rapidly. "Shining silver aeroplanes sweep across the sky; stately ships sail seas, stormy or serene, long diesel trains roar and rattle through the countryside at dead of night, or in full moonlight, all converging on Lourdes," one pilgrim wrote in the 1950s, capturing the mood.

Irish travel agencies vied with each other for the growing pilgrimage trade. Companies offering package deals included Joe Walsh Tours, Bon Voyage Travel and the Catholic Travel Service, all based in Dublin, along with Heffernan's in Cork and McGuills in Dundalk – the latter promoting a novel "pay later" plan for its customers. Lourdes welcomed millions of pilgrims. Popes and a future Pope paid visits. Even film stars and celebrities dropped by, some of them causing mayhem, as you will see in our first story.

Author Brendan Behan went on a pilgrimage to Lourdes in 1950. He linked up with the pilgrimage in Paris, where he was living at the time. As with most of Behan's adventures, it turned out to be a chaotic affair.

Brendan Behan enjoyed living in the Latin Quarter of Paris. Situated on the left bank of the Seine, it was home to artists, writers, students and numerous poseurs. The place suited his temperament and financial constraints, with its second-hand bookstores, bars, cafés and cheap accommodation. While there, he got to know Samuel Beckett and Albert Camus, and was entertained by Norman Mailer. He drank hard and worked hard, even making a first stab at what would be his eventual masterpiece, *Borstal Boy*.

From 1948 – 1950, Behan supported himself in Paris by working as a house painter and, as he claimed himself, a pimp. Along with an American friend, Ronny Thirst, he spent many hours scrounging food and drink when times were hard. The couple frequented popular bohemian establishments, hoping to encounter generous and gullible souls. Given Behan's fertile imagination, verbal dexterity and larger-than-life personality, free drinks and plates of food were all but guaranteed.

It was in one such establishment – a "bistro," Behan called it – that plans for an ill-advised visit to Lourdes were hatched. The year was 1950, which had been declared a Holy Year by Pope Pius XII. Irish pilgrims were making their way in droves to Rome, Assisi, Fátima, Lisieux and, of course, Lourdes, to commemorate the event. Most stopped off in Paris on their way, primarily to visit the city's holy sites but also, as Behan had hoped, to visit the bars and bistros where they might buy him a drink.

One night, Behan was treating one such establishment to a rendition of *The Holy City*, when he was approached by an Irish priest. His name was Fr. Flynn – "a gentle country priest," Behan later recalled. Obviously impressed by Brendan's voice, not to mention the old religious ballad he was singing, the cleric wondered if the two friends might be interested in joining his pilgrimage to Lourdes. "I'd like to, but we'd feel badly," Behan said sheepishly, testing the water. "Ronny and myself have no money at all. I wouldn't like to be living off you. Good God, on a sacred thing like this, you'd want to pull your own end of things."

No problem, the priest said, although he did have a favour to ask. He wondered if Behan, who was robust and strong, might carry a cross for the final journey into Lourdes. The plan was simple – the group would head south from Paris and then stop at a town 20 miles from their destination. From there, the following morning, they would march the remainder of the way to Lourdes. Behan would lead them while carrying the cross. "How big is this cross?" Behan wondered. "It's nothing. Just a couple of sticks tied together," he was assured. "I'll do it," the Dubliner responded, confident of free hospitality along the way.

The group left Paris and arrived at the little town. After a promising night of drinking – having "a few gargles" was how Behan described it – he arose the next morning to be confronted by a surprise. "What did I find?" he later asked. "Two monster railway ties, nailed together!"

Behan didn't really have much choice. He was in the middle of nowhere, with no money, and there was no turning back. Lifting the cross, he set off with the pilgrims on the final lap of their journey. Within an hour, he was no longer leading from the front but had fallen back about a mile behind the main body of pilgrims. Within another hour, he was about five miles behind. "The going was slow, real slow," Behan later reflected.

At around the third hour, they arrived at a bridge and sat down. Fortunately, Behan's companion had a bottle of whiskey, which provided some relief. The companion – Ronny Thirst – then looked Behan straight in the eyes and with deep reverence said: "Brendan, for the love of Jesus, throw that cross in the river!" Together, they heaved the cross into the water and it floated away. Brendan and Ronny then finished the bottle of whiskey.

The duo eventually arrived in Lourdes just as High Mass was about to begin. Groups of pilgrims from all over the world had already taken their places. The only group that hadn't were the Irish – they were waiting for Brendan at the edge of town. They demanded their cross. "I hate to tell you what went on," Brendan ruefully recollected. "There were bad words. Real bad words." Someone came up with a solution. "A cross was bought in a religious store – and I carried it the last stretch," Behan said.

Perhaps it was the holy atmosphere in Lourdes that did it; or maybe some sort of sense of forgiveness; or, dare we suggest, the influence of a few drinks, but by that night Brendan was pardoned by the pilgrims he had so badly let down. Brendan had his own take on what happened: "That night, I made up for the trouble by singing *The Holy City* – 135 times!" Either way, the drink flowed. That was one thing about the Irish pilgrims, he remarked, "they surely knew how to break out the gargles once all the religion was out of the way!"

The spontaneous disappearance of a cancerous tumour is rare, but that's exactly what happened in 1950 to a woman with strong Irish roots. Her miracle followed immersion in the baths at Lourdes.

Winifred Feely was a sickly child, born with a curvature of the spine requiring surgical intervention. "I'd been a semi-invalid," she later said. "I had three major operations, spent a year suffering from lung trouble. I was always ill." As if that wasn't sufficient, she later developed a cancerous growth in her chest, which doctors had told her was "inoperable and inaccessible." The prospects were catastrophic.

By that stage, Winifred was in her early 50s and married. "The growth in my chest had affected my throat. My voice had gone. I was beyond medical aid. There was no hope for me," she explained. "What troubled me most at the time was not the thought of death but the knowledge that I had done so little with my life."

Winifred had been born in China, where her parents lived, but she had Irish roots on her grandmother's side. Her husband was from County Tyrone. Although born a non-Catholic, she had converted to Catholicism while attending a convent school. As a result, she was well aware of Our Lady and was conscious of what was happening at Lourdes.

The unfortunate woman had no opportunity to go there at first, but in time the chance came. "When I came as an invalid I was a very sick woman," Winifred reflected. "My only request was for a happy death and for a short time of life to devote to others and show some gratitude to God for all that I have received from him."

While at the shrine, Winifred attended all of the important religious services and prayed intensely. Although she wasn't, as she said, praying for a cure but only for a happy death, things worked out very differently. The first time she was immersed in the baths, nothing happened. She hesitated about taking a second bath, as she found the cold water disagreeable. She changed her mind, however.

"I decided that there was little enough I could do and that I could offer up the second bath as a penance for others," she remarked. Once she had emerged, she realised that something dramatic had occurred and she had been cured of all her symptoms. "Soon after I came out of the baths I discovered I could walk and run freely. I had no more pain. There was no longer any difficulty in breathing. My voice came back. I felt suddenly completely strong, and at the same time utterly unworthy. I knew I was cured," she said.

Shortly after her miraculous revival, Winifred suffered a further misfortune – her husband died. "God's ways are strange and wonderful. I had no children, so when my husband died soon afterwards, I returned to Lourdes. I felt if I worked there I might have an opportunity of helping others. It was the only way I knew of saying thanks. This was how I began working at the Medical Bureau. Our Lady didn't give me this great grace just to sit around and do nothing," she explained.

In the following years, Winifred devoted her energies to the Lourdes Medical Bureau – the official organisation within the sanctuary which investigates apparent cures and claims of inexplicable healing. She was well-qualified to undertake the job as she had, by then, become a Doctor of Law. She was also fluent in a number of languages, so she spent part of her time on the international lecture circuit.

She also travelled to Ireland, most notably in 1961, when she delivered a lecture in aid of St. Joseph's School for Blind Boys, at Grace Park Road, Drumcondra, Dublin. On that occasion, she spoke on the theme of "Suffering and Lourdes." She lectured there again in 1972, when her appearance raised the princely sum of £100, which enabled the centre to send two extra blind boys to Lourdes, in addition to the four already scheduled to go.

During both visits, Winifred was free of cancer and looked well. A gossip columnist from *The Irish Press* who bumped into her at the Moira Hotel, in Dublin's Trinity Street, during one of those visits, wrote: "If you saw Mrs. Winifred Feely in the foyer of any hotel, or in the lounge of any airport, you'd admire her elegance, and probably type her as having something to do with fashion.

"Tall, silver-haired and distinctive, unless you knew she was a noted lecturer on Lourdes, unless you knew she was instantly cured there of a fatal cancerous growth in 1950, you might easily accuse her of never having been ill in her life, she looks so healthy."

During that brief encounter, Winifred Feely explained how fortunate she was to have received her miraculous cure. "Though I'm not young, and I'm always on the go, I've never been a day ill since I was instantly cured in 1950. Prior to that, I'd been a semi-invalid," she remarked.

More importantly, she explained how she was acutely aware of the bigger miracle that defines Lourdes. That miracle isn't just about rituals or cures, she said; it is about selflessness, the desire to give and to help others, the willingness to take care of people who are battling life's troubles.

"So many people see Lourdes in terms of torchlit processions, which admittedly are tremendously edifying," Winifred, who eventually died in her 96th year, reflected, "but to me one of its great marvels is the hundreds and hundreds of voluntary workers who pour in every year. To witness, as I so often have, the dedicated unselfishness of doctors, nurses and those who come to help, to see in turn the tremendous spiritual graces given to the sick, this is the miracle of Lourdes so many miss."

Two young Irish journalists, John Healy and Kevin O'Kelly, who would later develop notable careers, visited Lourdes in 1952. Their subsequent report was published in *The Irish Press.*

Arriving at Lourdes by night can be an awesome experience. It is particularly the case if your train happens to arrive during the torchlight procession. A long, meandering stream of light, created by thousands of shimmering candles, is the first image you see. As you emerge from the train, you hear thousands of voices – sometimes tens of thousands of voices – singing the *Ave Maria.* The volume becomes even louder as the procession comes to a close. Not many experiences can match the shock created by such a breathtaking sight.

This was the remarkable vista confronting Irish journalists John Healy and Kevin O'Kelly as their train entered Lourdes in 1952. They had gone there to compile a feature for their employers, the Irish News Agency. Healy would in time write the Backbencher column for *The Irish Times.* O'Kelly would become the Religious Affairs correspondent with Radio Telefís Éireann. In the meantime, their mission was to produce a colour piece for the government-subsidised agency which, in its day, operated as a state news propaganda machine. Their article was later published in *The Irish Press.*

"In a sense, the pilgrim does not come to Lourdes, Lourdes seems to rise up out of the dusk to meet him," observed John Healy of their late-evening arrival by express train from nearby Pau. Healy, who was doing the writing, while O'Kelly took the photos, then described, in vivid prose, the torchlight procession – "a long, winding river of flickering lights which ends in front

Marino Branch
Brainse Marino
Tel: 8336297

of Rosary Church, where 50,000 full-pitched voices thunder the *Credo*. It swells and swells, rising up to the purple night sky and the trembling stars, until it ends in a lingering *Amen*."

Minutes later, the sound was reduced to a buzz – the buzz of conversation rising up from Rosary Square. It was the sound of people in casual conversation, exchanging gossip, meeting friends, returning to their hotels, or heading off to the grotto to say late-night silent prayers. The following day, it was again ordinary people who caught the reporters' eyes – the milling crowds, the 50,000 pilgrims in prayer, the helpers and, above all, those who were sick and unable to care for themselves.

"They're the aristocracy of Lourdes," the article noted of the invalids, "for from early morning to late at night hundreds of pilgrims, doctors, nurses and nuns are constantly attending to them. Where others have to queue, the invalids are given free passage. At the grotto, the baths, and in Rosary Square. And many who come to Lourdes to gaze have stayed to pray after seeing the invalids pray: their tortured, pain-filled eyes turned hopefully towards the grotto statue of the Blessed Virgin. For nobody can see their twisted and broken bodies, their resignation and faith in God, and go unmoved."

The helpers, too, were everywhere. "Take Joe Dirrane, for instance," Healy remarked. "Joe was the only Aran Islander on this year's Galway pilgrimage and his French was limited to 'Merci.' But at the end of five days, the jovial-faced Joe was being hailed in the streets of Lourdes by pilgrims from Spain, France, Belgium, Italy, Corsica and Switzerland as 'Monsieur Irlande.'

"His friends were the pilgrims and invalids he had helped during his 16-hour-a-day stint at the hospital, the grotto and at the springs. After a day of reciting rosaries for the invalids, pilgrims were always sure of finding him at the holy springs, filling water bottles for pilgrims who said 'thanks' in half-a-dozen languages, or just smiled gratefully at him. And if Joe said 'Ná bac leis,' they always seemed to know just what he meant."

A highlight for both helpers and invalids was the Blessed Sacrament procession, held in Rosary Square. "The procession moves off at 4.30 no matter what the condition of the weather," the article observed. "It's headed by Children of Mary members from all over Europe with the different pilgrimages following, led by their flag-carrier. It takes an hour for the procession to wind from the grotto, around the Esplanade and into Rosary Square for the blessing of the sick.

"Here again the invalids have the spotlight as the bishop carrying the host blesses them under the chestnut trees lining the square while 50,000 people pray for them. Every day Lourdes comes to a standstill for this hour. The taxis stop their clamour of horn-blowing; the streets are empty, and above all is the 50,000-strong 'voice' of the pilgrims singing the *Lauda Sion*, their hosannas filling the warm air."

Their visit finished, the two journalists returned to Dublin, where their Irish News Agency report was published by *The Irish Press*. Both went on to develop noteworthy careers in journalism. Not only did John Healy win widespread praise for his Backbencher column in *The Irish Times*, but he also published a remarkable book, *The Death of an Irish Town*, chronicling the economic and social decline of his native Charlestown, County Mayo.

Kevin O'Kelly became a noted broadcaster with Radio Telefís Éireann where, in 1972, he hit the headlines when sentenced to jail for contempt of court for refusing to disclose information regarding an interview he had conducted with IRA Chief of Staff, Seán Mac Stiofáin. He later became RTÉ's Religious Affairs correspondent.

From the tenor of their report, both journalists had clearly been impressed by their visit to Lourdes. It left many memories. One stuck out – "out of all the splendour and spectacle that is Lourdes, the words 'Ave Maria' remain in the pilgrim's mind for after five days listening to it 16 hours a day from the sidewalk musical statues with their delicate, fragile-sounding notes; from the dining room clock at mealtimes; from the milling crowds winding to and from the grotto – it goes on to be repeated, unconsciously, a prayerful souvenir of Lourdes...Ave...Ave...Ave Maria."

A British Railways ferry, the *Princess Maud*, became famous in the mid-twentieth century for carrying tens of thousands of Lourdes pilgrims across the Irish Sea.

On Monday, 11 August 1952, excited families and well-wishers waited at Dun Laoghaire port for the arrival of the *Princess Maud*. They were there to welcome 1,000 members of the Derry diocesan pilgrimage, which had chartered the steamer for the Irish Sea portion of their visit to Lourdes. A tiny speck on the horizon soon became a full-sized ship. Gradually, almost imperceptibly, those with good hearing could discern the Lourdes hymn being sung by passengers lining its deck.

A few hours later, after the Derry contingent had disembarked, another 1,000 pilgrims boarded the ship. These were members of the Dublin diocesan pilgrimage, who in turn had chartered the steamer for the first leg of their trip to Lourdes. Some struggled with their luggage. Others – the stretcher-bearers – negotiated difficult gangways and narrow passageways as they carried invalids on board. Then, as the Lourdes hymn rang out again, the good old *Princess Maud* – "the pilgrim ship," as many called her – headed back out to sea.

It was once billed as a "magnificent steamer," but the truth is it was anything but. Without stabilisers, it was open to the vicious mercies of the sea. When tackling violent storms, and being buffeted by strong crosswinds, the decks would be awash the entire way across the Irish Sea. If it developed mechanical trouble, it had to turn back. On occasions, it ran aground. One passenger remembered travelling on it as "a journey from hell," with people getting sick all over the floor.

People experienced some genuinely horrific voyages. During a storm in January 1947, the ship was tossed around like a cork on the ocean. One deckhand said the *Princess Maud* rolled so heavily that on many occasions her masts touched the water, and he thought she was going to turn over. The crew said it was the worst crossing they had ever experienced.

On yet another occasion, in March 1950, having developed steering-gear trouble off Tuskar Rock, the boat had to travel backwards as it attempted to complete its journey. The captain turned the vessel around, put the engines to full speed astern, and in heavy seas and a south-westerly gale headed in reverse for the safety of Rosslare. "Foaming breakers buffeted the ship and frequently threw her off her course, but she kept on going," one of those onboard later recollected. Thanks to the captain's skill, the *Princess Maud* made it all the way into port.

It wasn't as if the *Princess Maud* was unused to adversity. In fact, it had served during World War II as a troop carrier. The ship famously took part in the evacuation of British and French soldiers from Dunkirk, in 1940, and was one of the last to leave during that history-making event. "Dunkirk was being shelled and bombed," 17-year-old crew member, Bill Birtles, later recalled. "How we got out, God only knows." It rescued over 2,000 troops from the advancing German army.

In June 1944, the ship was involved in the D-Day landings, ferrying an assault company to Omaha Beach. On board were several hundred American troops, most of them demolition men landing in advance of the main force with the aim of clearing obstacles from the beach. They made their final approach to the shore in mechanised landing craft. "With three foot waves and a heavy swell, it was a very tricky operation," an American soldier recollected.

After carrying almost 1.4 million troops during her war service, the *Princess Maud* was assigned in 1946 to the Larne – Stranraer route. She was then relocated to Dun Laoghaire – Holyhead where, in the following years, she ferried ordinary passengers and pilgrims. Unfortunately, on the Irish Sea, she developed a dreadful reputation.

Passengers were known to avoid travelling on her, waiting instead for the more comfortable *Hibernia* or *Cambria*, which also operated the route. One passenger later reflected how his "mother's heart always fell" when she arrived in Holyhead or Dun Laoghaire and spotted the *Princess Maud*. On a blustery winter's night, she knew she was in for "a rollercoaster of a ride." At least she boarded the ship, unlike other passengers who walked away and awaited the next sailing.

The ship's Lourdes pilgrimages also had harrowing crossings. They came from Dublin, Derry, Limerick, Armagh and Galway, and from numerous dioceses throughout the country. One of them, from Down and Connor, had it especially tough, with the *Irish Independent* reporting "a fairly rough crossing from Holyhead" and that "some of the pilgrims were ill and a number who lived in Dublin were conveyed to their homes by ambulance." An Armagh pilgrimage had a similar experience, having been buffeted by strong winds and with her decks awash all the way home.

The torture was terminated in the early to mid-1960s, when decisions were taken to phase out the *Princess Maud*. Not only was the steamer very expensive to maintain, but it had also become irretrievably unpopular with passengers. Eventually, it was sold, renamed *Venus*, and relocated to the Mediterranean. Her story came to an end in 1973, when she was shipped to Spain and scrapped. Some people remembered her fondly, recalling life-affirming pilgrimages to Lourdes. Others never forgot the sensations of terror and travel sickness they experienced while tightly gripping the handrails on deck!

The introduction by Aer Lingus, in 1954, of a scheduled new service to Lourdes changed the pattern of Irish travel to the shrine.

The sun shone from a crystal clear, cloudless blue sky on Tuesday, 14 September 1954. The Dublin streets were sparklingly clean, having been washed by the previous day's thunderous downpours

175

which had spilled from a dark, overcast sky. Today, there was a sense of freshness in the air. People were happy. The mood was bright. Even the white-gloved Garda on traffic duty had a smile on his face.

It was the perfect day for flying, thought Fr. Philip O'Boyle, the County Donegal parish priest who was making his way to Lourdes. His first job was to negotiate his little Austin through the early-morning traffic as he headed from Dublin city centre to Collinstown Airport. He motored past Nelson's Pillar, up Dorset Street and out the north road. Soon, the airport was in sight. On arrival, he encountered a courteous official who he had casually met many years before. The gentleman insisted on parking his car. It was that kind of airport in those days.

"All is activity at the airport," Fr. O'Boyle noted. Buses were arriving. People were sauntering about. Crowds occupied the airport balcony, where they watched the departure of planes containing their loved ones. The priest checked in. There was the short walk to the plane, the *St. Colmcille*, a DC-3 prop plane named after a saint with connections to the priest's home county of Donegal. The plane taxied, engines raced, and "before we realise it we are in the air," he remarked.

Fr. Philip O'Boyle was one of those Irish pilgrims who, back in 1954, were shunning travel by boat and train to Lourdes and opting instead for the more comfortable method of flying there by plane. So promising was the new fashion that, in 1954, Aer Lingus introduced the world's first scheduled air service to the shrine. Using propeller-driven DC-3 and Wayfarer planes, the fare cost £29 and eight shillings and the flight time, with stop-offs, was 11 hours. The price was competitive and the journey was a lot quicker than by boat and train.

The new schedule proved a rage with pilgrims. In June 1954, it was estimated that in the region of 1,250 passengers would use the Lourdes service up to October, when it would close for the winter months. Instead, more than 6,000 people flew the route. It was also believed that the number of flights would be 50, but the figure quickly grew to 240. At the beginning of October, instead of closing down, the schedule was extended into November.

Pilgrims, particularly those who were disabled or unwell, quickly recognised the comforts of travelling by airplane. "The introduction of air travel has made the journey vastly more comfortable for the sick, and many who will now make the pilgrimage by plane will draw comparisons with the days, not so many years ago, when not even dining cars were provided on the continental trains and there was no special accommodation for stretcher cases," wrote a journalist at the time.

Of course, demand was helped by the fact that 1954 had been declared a "Marian Year" by Pope Pius XII, the first in Church history. Marian "fever" was everywhere – at shrines, in churches, and at social gatherings and events. The Pope had encouraged visits to Lourdes where, he pointed out, "there is such ardent devotion to the Blessed Virgin Mary." This special year had encouraged Fr. O'Boyle to make his visit. But the boost to numbers visiting Lourdes was no mirage as far as Aer Lingus was concerned – after 1954, the number of travellers continued to spiral.

In time, the shaky, prop-driven DC-3s and Wayfarers were replaced by a new fleet of Vickers Viscounts, which proved to be noticeably more comfortable. Passenger numbers were boosted further. "Those who have flown in one of these aircraft can indeed say that it is not merely flying in comfort, it is flying in luxury," an Irish journalist wrote after experiencing the new technology. "Flying over the lovely east coast of Ireland one was immediately struck by the almost complete absence of vibration. Public Relations Officer David Hayes balanced a coin for this writer on its edge as the plane flew several miles up. This gives an indication of how smooth is the flying."

So novel was the Viscount that the people of Lourdes flocked to see it when Aer Lingus landed one there for the first time in May 1957. It had "the latest and most expensive fittings," "every possible accommodation" and its lavish catering was "excellent," as one passenger remarked. "We had a delicious lunch served during our journey," he added. The excitement was even more palpable in 1972, when Aer Lingus landed the first Jumbo jet to touch down at the airport. By then, the airline was the No. 1 customer at Lourdes, ferrying around 50,000 passengers there each year.

All that was well into the future as far as Fr. O'Boyle was concerned back in 1954. His visit over, he returned home by the same route as he had arrived. There were stops at Bordeaux and Rennes, and then the plane headed directly for Ireland. It flew low over the streets of Dublin, before landing at Collinstown Airport.

Once more, it was back into the little Austin followed by a non-stop journey to County Donegal. The roads were dry, the evening was lovely, and the priest's mind was a whirlwind of impressions and sensations. But one image predominated and he couldn't erase it from his mind – the grotto at Lourdes, which preoccupied him all the way home.

But for a visit to Lourdes by Prince Rainier of Monaco, his marriage to Irish-American actress Grace Kelly might never have happened. The visit took place in 1955.

Prince Rainier of Monaco was seen as "the catch of the century." Not only was he handsome and sophisticated, but he was also powerful and rich. As Prince of Monaco, he ruled over 22,000 subjects, owned a 200-room palace and 300-ton yacht, possessed a fleet of racing cars, and laid claim to a sizeable portion of the revenues from the principality's main attraction, the casino at Monte Carlo.

By the mid-1950s, aged 32, Rainier was in search of a wife. Numerous names were suggested, including Princess Margaret, the movie stars Natalie Wood, Deborah Kerr and Eva Marie Saint, and allegedly even Marilyn Monroe. Nobody quite fitted the picture, not even the French actress Giselle Pascal with whom he had a long relationship. In 1955, however, he was introduced to the Irish-American, Oscar-winning actress Grace Kelly, and suddenly things began to look up.

Kelly had all the right credentials. Just like Rainier, she was a Roman Catholic. Her Irish-American father, John Kelly – whose own father had emigrated from County Mayo – was a self-made millionaire and Olympic gold medallist for rowing. Grace was beautiful, famous and had a string of successful films, including *High Noon*, *Dial M for Murder*, *Rear Window* and *The Country Girl*, for which she won an Oscar.

Rainier was smitten, but he still wasn't sure. He spoke at length to his personal chaplain and advisor, Fr. Francis Tucker, a lively priest in his 60s who had been sent to Monaco by the Vatican. Tucker – known as "Fr. Tuck" – thought Kelly was a good idea. Yet the prince still hesitated. He organised a private viewing of the films *The Country Girl* and the recently-released *To Catch a Thief*, both starring Kelly, but even that didn't do it. There was only one course of action, he told Fr. Tuck – we're off to Lourdes and the Blessed Mother will guide me!

The two friends departed for Lourdes by car, a seven-hour journey across the south of France, past Marseille, Montpellier and Toulouse. They talked along the way about the qualities required for an ideal partner for Rainier. The standards were high – not only would she need to be a good wife and mother, but also a good princess and a representative of all that was beautiful about Monaco. We will find her with the help of the Blessed Mother, Fr. Tuck advised. Yes, the prince mused, "either prayer works, or it doesn't. And I believe it works."

The praying did work. On his return from Lourdes, not only did Prince Rainier propose to Grace Kelly but, after a year-long courtship, they got married in 1956. In the interim, Fr. Tuck spoke to Grace about the visit to the grotto and explained its role in Prince Rainier's decision to ask for her hand in marriage. She was amazed by what he told her. "Why, Father," she remarked, "you will never believe this, but my confirmation name is Bernadette!"

The marriage was known in the press as "The Wedding of the Century." Everybody who was anybody was invited, from Bing Crosby to the Aga Khan. There was dancing in the streets, parades, processions, a trapeze artist performing while hanging from a helicopter and much, much more. Six hundred to seven hundred invitees made their way to Monaco. Grace arrived in style. "From next Thursday – when bride-to-be Kelly and a party of between 60 and 70 friends and relatives arrive in Monaco on the liner *Constitution* – until the post-wedding champagne party, Monaco is going to be a very dressy place," one newspaper remarked.

On the big day, the route from the palace to the cathedral was lined by Monégasque schoolgirls attired in satin dresses of red and white – the national colours – a gift from Prince Rainier. The Pope sent an envoy. Prince Rainier was overjoyed. He thanked Fr. Tuck for all he had done, especially for helping him find Grace. "Oh, no," the priest replied. "Do you remember our pilgrimage to Lourdes? Well, this is the 'Grace' the Blessed Mother gave to you and to you alone."

In the following years, Prince Rainier never forgot the important role of religion in his life. He presented his new wife to Pope Pius XII. The couple made state visits to the Vatican for audiences with Pope Paul VI and Pope John Paul II. The Rainiers were also proactive in ensuring that Monaco remained one of the few sovereign states to retain Catholicism as its official religion.

The couple also never forgot the shrine. In 1958, Rainier contributed a handsome sum to help pay for construction work at the basilica of Lourdes. Three years later, when they visited Ireland, one of their most treasured engagements was a stop-off at Our Lady of Lourdes Hospital, Drogheda, where they were given a tremendous welcome by one of the biggest crowds ever gathered in the town. Rainier presented a cheque to the hospital before leaving.

In July of that year, 1961, Grace made a pilgrimage to Lourdes, and she did so again in 1979. She also paid a private visit to Ireland in 1979, during which she and her husband dropped by to her ancestral home in County Mayo. Unfortunately, she didn't live long after that visit – just three years – and she died in a car accident in 1982.

Her funeral, in Monaco, was attended by numerous well-known names, including Cary Grant, Princess Diana and Nancy Reagan. But it was another one of her friends, the actor James Stewart, who provided the most poignant words at a memorial service in Beverly Hills. "You know," he said, "I just love Grace Kelly. Not because she was a princess, not because she was an actress, not because she was my friend, but because she was just about the nicest lady I ever met.....No question, I'll miss her, we'll all miss her. God bless you, Princess Grace."

You could meet anyone in Lourdes, as a lucky Irish journalist discovered in 1958 when he bumped into a future Pope.

There was much anxiety in France – especially in Lourdes – at the beginning of the centenary year of the apparitions. The principal concern was whether the reigning Pope – Pope Pius XII – would be paying a visit. To put it mildly, he was unpopular in France because of his stance during World War II. What had he done to condemn Nazism? Why did he maintain silence in the face of genocide? Why had he been impartial throughout the war, yet was fervently anti-communist now that the war was over?

That the French didn't warm to Pope Pius XII was obvious, but now that the anniversary of the apparitions was about to take place, it seemed unavoidable that he would have to pay a visit. Even Air France had made contingency plans, assigning a Caravelle jet airliner to ferry him from Rome to Lourdes. At the last minute, wisdom prevailed and the Vatican designated an altogether different representative. His name was Cardinal Angelo Giuseppe Roncalli, the one-time Apostolic Nuncio to France. Within seven months of his visit to Lourdes, he would become Pope John XXIII.

Cardinal Roncalli was affable, cheerful, and well able to engage with the ordinary man. He had spoken humorously about his humble beginnings in a tiny village near Bergamo, northern Italy. "In Italy, there are three ways of losing one's money: women, gambling and farming. My father chose the most boring of the three. He became a farmer," he once said. Later, when he became Pope, one of his first actions in the Vatican was to increase the salaries of its officials, especially the carriers of the sedes gestatoria, or portable Papal throne. Referring to his rotund shape, he explained: "Gentlemen, the weight has been increased, so I had better increase your wages."

The French loved Cardinal Roncalli. Despite the last-minute announcement of his arrival, thousands of people congregated at the airport to welcome him. They cheered as his Caravelle jet airliner – the same model as assigned to the Pope – swept down from the clear-blue sky. They cheered even louder as the unmistakably rotund cardinal emerged from the airliner and walked briskly across the tarmac. One man must have cheered louder still, at least inwardly – *The Irish Press* reporter, Michael O'Halloran, who had a special invitation to attend the reception arranged for the visiting dignitary in the sealed-off airport lounge.

"It was an informal reception and the air was full of Gallic excitement," O'Halloran later wrote in a retrospective article for *The Kerryman*. "Suddenly, beside me in the crowded lounge of Lourdes Airport was the guest of honour, Cardinal Roncalli, the Papal Legate. With an all-embracing smile he greeted everybody near him individually and from that moment the occasion was serenely happier. The smile was reflected back from every face within range.

"Here he was now, the man who had won the love and respect of all sections of the French nation. Smiling and jovial, he moved among the guests and immediately it was no longer a semi-formal reception, but rather a happy family reunion, such as you would find in a Kerry home at Christmas.

"I moved back to make way for others who pressed forward to be near him and drank the glass of champagne that was thrust into my hand as I watched an extraordinary scene. As he moved around the crowded lounge, talking easily in French, there was a glow of happiness in the faces of the people immediately around him. It was as if a broad-beamed spotlight followed wherever he moved."

It was no surprise to O'Halloran that Cardinal Roncalli was accompanied to the shrine – and to the reception – by Msgr. Donal Herlihy, Rector of the Irish College in Rome. In truth, Roncalli loved everything Irish. For a time, during World War II, the Tipperary-born Msgr. Thomas Ryan was his private secretary and constant companion. Their friendship continued after he became Pope, with Msgr. Ryan acting as his English teacher and his interpreter. During Roncalli's time in Paris, he never missed a St. Patrick's Day reception at the Irish embassy. In his first St. Patrick's Day address after he became Pope, he prefaced his remarks with "Dia is Muire dhíbh."

In Lourdes, in 1958, things were altogether more French. People shouted "Vive le cardinal" from the moment Cardinal Roncalli emerged from the plane to the time of his departure. Hundreds of thousands turned out just to wave to him as he travelled the seven-mile stretch from the airport into town. Almost a million people crowded into Lourdes that day – one of the largest influxes of pilgrims in the history of the shrine.

The cardinal's primary formal function was to perform the consecration ceremony of the new basilica, the second-largest church in the world. To do this, the French had provided him with an open-topped, gleaming-red sports car. He willingly travelled in the automobile, standing upright in the back, as he traversed the vast outside circuit of the structure, wielding a sprig of hyssop. The same red sports car carried him as he blessed the walls of the inside of the basilica, on both occasions travelling at speeds of more than 15 miles an hour.

At the central altar, he then presided at the Mass of consecration. Celebrated 100 years after the "beautiful lady" had informed Bernadette that she was the Immaculate Conception, it was a remarkable and historic occasion. Twenty thousand people received communion, all of them in the presence of Roncalli. "It was a memorable sight and he was a memorable man," Michael O'Halloran recollected: "Short months later France and all the countries and all the people who had ever contact with him rejoiced when he was made Pope. But soon afterwards the whole world knew him and loved him as their own."

Cardinal Roncalli never forgot Lourdes. Later on, after he became Pope, he delivered a radio message marking the close of the centenary year. He referred to a place where "the sick received, if not always a cure, at least resignation and serenity in offering their sufferings, whilst the dying learned there to make peacefully the sacrifice of their lives." He asked: "How many unsteady wills have received the strength to persevere?" as a result of visiting Lourdes. He wondered, in conclusion: "How many in darkness received light at Lourdes?"

It was strange to think that, back in March, Cardinal Roncalli was visiting Lourdes as a relatively unknown churchman; but now, here he was, at year's end, as Pope John XXIII, expressing his admiration and love of the shrine. From then until his death in 1963 this "memorable man" with the "all-embracing smile," as the journalist Michael O'Halloran put it, always retained a love for Lourdes.

A poignant song, *The Village of St. Bernadette*, sung by Anne Shelton, became a huge chart hit from late 1959 to early 1960. The English performer, whose grandfather was Irish, toured Ireland on the back of the song's success.

The cold spell that brought freezing weather to County Mayo had mellowed by Thursday, 21 January 1960. The treacherous ice on the roads was thawing, and the snow on the hills was melting, as revellers made their way to the dance hall at Tooreen village. They were heading to an event that had been billed for weeks as "the talk of the province" – an appearance by the "world-famous screen, radio and TV star," Anne Shelton.

Tooreen was very lucky to get Shelton, as the English singer, whose grandfather came from Limerick, had recently been receiving massive publicity for her single *The Village of St.*

Bernadette. The record was riding high in the charts, vying for top spot with *Travellin' Light* by Cliff Richard, *Little White Bull* by Tommy Steele, and *Mack the Knife* by Bobby Darin. It was no surprise that, wherever she went, including Tooreen, huge crowds greeted her non-stop 45-minute show with ecstatic applause.

In retrospect, it seems appropriate that the main highlight of Shelton's show in Tooreen was a song about St. Bernadette and Lourdes. After all, the building of the village hall had been organised by the curate Fr. James Horan who, just months before her arrival, had been transferred from Tooreen to Cloonfad, County Roscommon. Not only was he a devotee of Our Lady, but he later became famous for his role in developing Knock shrine – "The Lourdes of Ireland" – and was the inspiration behind Knock airport. He died while on a pilgrimage to Lourdes in 1986.

No doubt, Fr. Horan was as enthralled as the rest of the Irish population by Shelton's song concerning Bernadette. It had a beautiful, melodic air and wistful lyrics proclaiming a person's love for the little town they would never forget – Lourdes, the village of St. Bernadette. The longer version of the song spoke of weary pilgrims, rich and poor, healthy and lame, arriving to praise Our Lady's name. Both the longer and shorter versions described the grotto at night as being aglow in the light. Both versions included the well-known refrain, "Ave, Ave, Ave Maria," taken from the Lourdes hymn.

Not only did the song become a No. 2 hit in the UK for Anne Shelton, but another version, sung by Andy Williams, became a No. 7 chart success in the USA. It won an Ivor Novello Award

– the prestigious British award for songwriters and composers – for being "the outstanding song of the year" in 1959. Just as important, from the Lourdes point of view, it kept the shrine in the public eye at the cusp of a decade – the 1960s – that would bring many changes in people's lifestyles, including those pertaining to their religious practices and beliefs.

At least on this side of the Atlantic, Anne Shelton was already famous when her song burst into the charts. She was the first female British star to headline at the London Palladium; had appeared in the Royal Command Show at Buckingham Palace; had toured Australia and New Zealand; and had appeared in India, Singapore and Germany. Her show on Radio Luxembourg – *Anne Shelton's Song Parade* – was attracting a listenership of 19 million; and, just to crown things off, she had already sold eight million records and was a chart topper.

A vital personality, Shelton "gives her songs that individual treatment that has won her much popularity," one Dublin critic wrote. Another person, who met her – J. J. Walsh, the proprietor-editor of *The Munster Express* – said that she was "even more charming" than she had seemed to be in a weekly half-hour programme she presented on BBC TV. Yet another commentator praised her for devoting "much of her time and talent to works of charity." The truth of this latter observation was borne out by her willingness to forego payment for appearing at Clery's Ballroom, Dublin, on behalf of the Polio Fellowship, during one of her Irish tours.

The composer of the song, Eula Parker, had a more chequered career. An Australian, she had entered the music business in the 1930s with her sisters Pat and Marie. Together, they performed as the Parker Sisters, until Eula's sisters decided to marry. Eula then departed for the UK, where she joined a vocal group called The Stargazers. Although they became well-known, especially on BBC radio, it was only when Eula composed *The Village of St. Bernadette* that she achieved international fame.

While it must have been thrilling for Eula to see her song vying at the top of the charts, she must have been equally delighted to hear of the enthusiastic response it was receiving in Irish dance halls. Everywhere that Anne Shelton went, her audiences loved it. On that January night in 1960, it was wildly applauded in Tooreen. It was also acclaimed in Carlow, Navan, Listowel, Millstreet, Strabane and Dublin, among other places she appeared in during that early 1960 tour.

So positive was the reaction that Anne was back again in September and October of that year, this time appearing in Cork, Galway, Dublin, Drogheda and Castleblayney, among other locations. Notably, she was also back at Tooreen. Her visit there, just eight months earlier, had been such a success that they wanted her to perform there again. What they wanted most of all, however, was to hear her singing about that little town that nobody could ever forget – Lourdes, the village of St. Bernadette.

A Donegal woman living in England had a miraculous cure from cancer in 1962. The recovery happened during a visit to Lourdes.

The family of Sally McCloy, in County Donegal, woke to grim weather at the start of the August Bank Holiday back in 1962. A north-westerly airstream was passing over the country, bringing heavy showers, fresh winds, with gale gusts in northern areas. Where Sally lived – in Coventry – conditions weren't much better. The Bank Holiday was a bit of a washout there, too.

The bad weather didn't matter to Sally as she was far away, having just arrived in Lourdes. There was no sense of her visit being any sort of a holiday; things were a lot more serious than that. She was suffering from cancer, weighed five-and-a-half stone, and had been carried by boat and ambulance train all the way from Coventry to the shrine. She was desperately seeking a cure.

On leaving Coventry, Sally was in severe pain. It had "wracked" her body for many months, she explained. "I had a feeling like being squashed all the time," she said. Her health was so bad that she feared she could not endure the long journey through England and France. "I knew that I was not expected to live," she remarked. "The children expected me to come back cured, though no one else thought I would survive."

Sally's visit to Lourdes had been arranged by her parochial church, Christ the King, in Coventry. From its official opening in 1933, the church – and the parish it was based in – was Irish to its core. Its first parish priest was named Fr. Rooney, who had been "sent to Coventry" by his Vicar General, Msgr. Cronin. The first curate was named Fr. Bernard McKenna. It was that sort of church, in that sort of parish, containing hard-working, honest people who looked after and cared for each other.

Sally, who came from Letterkenny, County Donegal, where her family still lived, was married and had four children. Her husband, Dan, worked as an aero inspector at the Alvis Car and Engineering Company in Coventry. Although she was dying from cancer, it was her husband and children, and not herself, she was worried about. She "accepted" her illness and "never moaned about it," she said. "My prayers were always for my husband Dan and the children."

Lourdes was a busy town when Sally arrived back in 1962. On the Friday of her arrival, a 350-strong Irish pilgrimage, organised by the Oblate Fathers, was beginning its five-day visit to the shrine. Forty Dublin boy scouts, along with their relatives and friends, were about to join them. They planned to see the usual places – the grotto, the baths and the basilica, among other destinations.

It was during the procession of the Blessed Sacrament that something extraordinary happened to Sally. "There was like a sudden burst of light," she recalled. She instantly felt free. It was as if a weight had been lifted from her body. The pain that had afflicted her for months was gone. "I knew I was healed," she said. Feeling good and being free of pain was one thing; being cured from cancer was another. She feared, on her return to Coventry, what her medical specialist might say.

Her appointment with the consultant was terrifying. Sally told him she had been to Lourdes and felt well. "He examined me and for a minute didn't say anything," she recalled. She was certain the news was bad: "I had a terrible feeling that although I felt well and the pain was gone, that he hadn't found any change." But he had. What he said next came as a shock: "This isn't imagination; it's absolutely wonderful." The cancer was in remission. It would soon be gone.

It wasn't long before Sally was back to full health. She was restored to her normal weight of 8st 3lbs. She put her miraculous recovery down to faith. Maybe her own prayers had helped, she reflected, because they had been directed to her family and not herself. Her family's prayers had possibly helped, too, as had those of people at home in Letterkenny. But there was no doubt the visit to Lourdes was central to her cure – that's where the miracle had happened.

Over the following three years, Sally was investigated by the Lourdes Medical Bureau, which took an interest in her case. A panel of doctors, mostly non-Catholics, from all over the world, questioned her and examined her medical records. Her visits to the bureau took place on an annual basis. The bureau finally verified her cure, pronouncing her completely free of cancer.

There was another happy ending for Sally, which occurred in 1969. In June of that year, seven years after her cure, she attended the wedding of her daughter, Olive. The marriage ceremony was held at the church of Christ the King in Coventry. Newspaper reports remarked on how Olive and her husband Anthony were not only prominent in the Coventry Samaritans, but for several years had been helping to look after Birmingham area pilgrims to Lourdes.

The reports also mentioned that Olive's mother, Sally, had a history at the shrine, that she once had cancer and had received a miraculous cure. What they didn't need to mention – as it was clear from the photograph of the ceremony – was just how well she looked. They also didn't need to tell us how good the weather was – again, that was obvious from the photo. As a check of weather reports revealed, Coventry was basking in a heatwave, with dry, sunny days and clear blue skies. It was nothing like the weather when Sally had left for Lourdes in 1962. There must have been some significance to that!

Eddie Cleary left for Lourdes in a wheelchair but returned a cured man. The year was 1977.

"I still don't know what happened but I just felt the urge to get up and walk." So said former Carlow butcher Eddie Cleary, who was speaking on his return from Lourdes in 1977. Having left Ireland in a wheelchair, he had arrived home unaided. His remarkable recovery not only made headline news but became one of the standout Irish recoveries at the shrine in the second half of the twentieth century.

Some three years before his departure for Lourdes, Eddie's legs had been shattered in a traffic accident. He suffered several compound fractures, leaving him in severe pain and with an inability to move about unaided. He could not bend his damaged legs. "I was able to hop around but not very far. The pain was pretty hard," he remarked in a press interview following his return home. For those three years, he was either confined to a wheelchair or forced to use crutches or a walking stick.

Despite spending weeks in hospital in Dublin and Kilkenny, and undergoing several operations, this former physically-fit Wexford footballer, who was 6ft 4in, was forced to quit his job as a butcher and was effectively confined to his home. There, he was cared for by his wife, Susan, who worked as a nurse. "He was in very bad pain and could do very little. He could only hobble around on a stick, and it took everything that was in him to stand at the sink and peel a few potatoes. He could never move properly," she said.

Encouraged by some close friends, Eddie agreed to join a pilgrimage from Carlow to the shrine in July 1977. His wife remained in Carlow, to mind the couple's three children. Led by local curate, Fr. John Fingleton, the group departed from Dublin Airport, where Eddie was helped onto the plane. On arrival, he was helped off the plane again, and was cared for by the friends who had inspired him to travel.

At Lourdes, he visited the grotto at least twice a day, being wheeled there from his hotel by his friends. Nothing of note happened until the last night of the pilgrimage. Throughout that day, he had participated in the usual events held at the grotto, including a recital of the rosary and the torchlight procession. After returning to his hotel, he joined in a singsong, but then decided – as it was his last night – to revisit the grotto and light some candles.

"I was in the wheelchair in front of the grotto," Eddie later recalled. "I took a crutch and walked round the grotto and I sat back in the chair again. After a while, I said I would like to walk again. I felt the urge to do it. I got up and walked without using the crutch. I suddenly found I could walk very comfortably without any pain. I felt relaxed and full of confidence."

Newspaper reports later said that Eddie pushed one of his friends back to the hotel in the wheelchair. That was not true, he later remarked. Instead, he walked about halfway to the hotel, but then took his friends' advice and travelled the rest of the way in the wheelchair. The pain had disappeared from his legs, and he could walk again unaided. "I didn't really know what had happened," he said, and as a result "got a bit frightened." But he was delighted with what had occurred.

The following day, the Carlow pilgrim returned home to a fanfare of newspaper publicity. "Agony Turns to Joy as Wheelchair Man Walks at Lourdes," one headline proclaimed. "Lourdes

Cure Man is Talk of Town," another one declared. "Accident Victim Describes 'Urge to Walk,'" a further one revealed. The reaction was enormous, but it was nothing compared to the impact the cure had on Eddie's life.

Although he never returned to his job as a butcher, from then on Eddie lived a normal, active life. He took care of the home, while his wife continued to work as a nurse. He looked after the three children, did the housework, went shopping, drove the children to school and dropped his wife off to work. He went for walks again, without ever needing the wheelchair or a walking stick or crutches.

"Even if I hadn't been cured, I'm really happy I went," he reflected shortly after his return. "Lourdes is a wonderful place and since my visit I have terrific peace of mind. I went hoping to get peace of mind and I am a changed man now. Since then, the pain has not come back and I can walk with great comfort."

Twenty years after returning from Lourdes, when in his mid-60s, Eddie Cleary suffered from complications with his spine, which may or may not have been connected with his earlier traffic accident. Throughout the two decades up to his new illness, while perfectly well, he had great devotion to Our Lady and was a regular attendee at Mass. His devotion continued after the new ailments surfaced, and he lived a fruitful life up to 2016, when he died, aged 82.

His case remains one of the most notable recoveries of the 1970s and beyond. Quite simply, he was transformed from a man who had once struggled to stand, never mind walk, into a man who, on his last morning in Lourdes, walked confidently into the hotel dining room, where he was greeted by jubilant applause. "Faith in God," he said, was what brought about his recovery.

Poet Seamus Heaney, who won the Nobel Prize for Literature in 1995, often recalled a visit he made to Lourdes as a teenager. It was one of the fondest and most influential memories of his life.

In 1958, Seamus Heaney joined 1,000 fellow pilgrims on a famous Derry diocesan pilgrimage to Lourdes. Not only was the pilgrimage the largest-ever from Derry, but it was memorable as it commemorated the centenary year of the apparitions. The visit wasn't Heaney's idea; instead, it came from his Aunt Jane, who paid the fare. No doubt, the prospect of such a special adventure – his first abroad – must have thrilled the recent school-leaver who had just begun studying at Queen's University Belfast.

Like most Irish people at the time, Heaney was well aware of the country's fascination with Lourdes and St. Bernadette. Pictures of the saint on bended knee before the grotto, beads in hand, her eyes fixed upwards to Mary, who was dressed in blue and white, were everywhere to be seen. Framed images of the apparition scene hung in countless family homes. People spoke of miracles and cures. None of these images had escaped the notice of Heaney as a boy.

Nor, in later life, had the excitement of preparing for the pilgrimage left his mind. He once recalled a conversation with Benedict Kiely, the County Tyrone-born author, journalist and critic, about his need to secure a passport for the trip. For sheer convenience, living in County Derry and studying in Belfast, he opted for a British one. Ever the cynic and always capable of a sardonic remark, Kiely responded that had Heaney lived in the Republic no passport would have been required as Lourdes lay within its jurisdiction!

On Tuesday, 5 August 1958, the main body of Derry pilgrims – including Heaney and his cousin, Michael Joyce – wound their way by steam trains from Derry to Dun Laoghaire, and from there to Holyhead, Dover, Calais, Paris, and onward to Lourdes. The trains leaving Derry were symbolically decorated in blue and white, the colours of Our Lady of Lourdes. Papal bunting adorned the route. Invalids were spared the overland journey and transported instead by planes from Ballykelly military airport. The Lourdes hymn was sung, and ovations rang out, as the entourage departed.

Heaney worked as a brancardier, wearing the trademark coloured bandolier, on that famous 1958 Derry visit. He bore the sick on their stretchers to the grotto and to the baths. The word "cure" was everywhere in the air. Later, he recalled images of rosaries and mantillas, prayers recited out loud or in hushed tones, members of sodalities wearing their sashes, banners and pennants and, most of all, the enduring image of Lourdes – discarded crutches, hanging near the grotto, having been left there by those who found they could miraculously walk.

The weather was sizzling, the hottest of the year. On the day of the eucharistic procession, the sun burned down. At one stage, Heaney almost fainted from the heat and fumes. For the Stations of the Cross, the weather was cooler, which helped as they had to climb up the hill. Seamus was in his element, ferrying the infirm on stretchers, pushing wheelchairs, serving as an altar boy and carrying the thurible with its incense during the various ceremonies. The images were powerful and potent, momentous and memorable, and imprinted themselves on his mind for the rest of his life.

There were three Masses at the grotto, two High Masses in the Rosary Church, and a Mass in the new basilica. Most of all, there were crowds – "crowds like a human tide that flows from every direction in the morning to the grotto area, back again into the streets at noon, returning again to the grotto in the afternoon for the procession of the Blessed Sacrament, and again at night for the torchlight procession. Such a crowd as this can, I imagine, be seen nowhere else in the world," a Derry pilgrim later remarked.

Nationalities from all corners of the globe mingled together. They came from the Orient, dressed in their brilliantly-coloured silken robes, from the Tropics wearing sandals, from Europe wearing heavy shoes and sombre costumes. Their numbers were of a magnitude never seen before, crammed into the precincts of the grotto, on the streets, everywhere. Even the 1,000-strong Derry contingent seemed lost in the area of the basilica so great was the attendance at Mass.

After four days at the shrine, Seamus Heaney and the Derry diocesan pilgrimage wound their way back to Ireland. They met English Channel gales and Irish Sea fog on their return, but nothing could dampen their spirits. Heaney arrived bearing a container of Lourdes water, a brancardier shoulder strap to show to his priest, a globe with snowflakes for somebody's mantelpiece, and a certificate testifying to his stretcher-bearing work. But he came home with a lot more than that.

In time, Lourdes would appear in Heaney's poetry, notably in *Brancardier*, with its images of carrying the sick to the bleak concrete where they awaited their baths; of Belgian miners in their blue dungarees, marching in procession, with their brass lamps; of the distinctive Catholic acoustic in the basilica; and, most of all, of the powerful impact Lourdes has on those who pay it a visit. The images remained with the poet up to the time of his death, more than half a century later, in August 2013.

In 2004, an ailing Pope John Paul II visited Lourdes. It turned out to be one of the most moving pilgrimages in the history of the shrine.

With his speech slurred, hands trembling and rigid posture, the 84-year-old Pope John Paul II had to be brought by wheelchair to the Lourdes grotto in 2004. Tired and frail, he cut a sad figure. Aides assisted him from his chair onto a kneeler before the shrine. Within a minute, he slipped. Aides rushed forward to steady him and to support him back into his chair. He was obviously unwell.

On that wonderfully sunny day at the shrine, the Pope was clearly overcome with emotion. He prayed to Our Lady, just as Bernadette had done almost a century and a half before. At one stage, he sipped water from the spring. "Kneeling here, before the grotto of Massabielle, I feel deeply that I have reached the goal of my pilgrimage," he remarked. "Good Mother, have mercy on me; I give myself entirely to you."

The Pontiff had arrived earlier that day on a two-day visit to Lourdes. Three hundred thousand people had come to join him. Loud cheers broke out everywhere he went. Church bells pealed. Yellow-and-white flags hung throughout the town. The crowds seemed to love him more than ever, perhaps because of his long battle with Parkinson's disease. "Dear brothers and sisters who are sick," he said, "how I would like to embrace each and every one of you with affection, to tell you how close I am to you and how much I support you."

The Pontiff's visit had a purpose and meaning much deeper than his state of health. It marked the culmination of a life dedicated to the Blessed Virgin. Following his mother's death, when he was aged eight, he had turned to Our Lady for solace. He would frequently be seen praying at one of her statues in his parish church. In later life, he remarked: "This woman of faith, Mary of Nazareth, has been given to us as a model in our pilgrimage of faith. From Mary, we learn to trust even when all hope seems gone."

He also credited his survival from an assassination attempt in 1981 to Our Lady of Fátima. The event took place on her feast day, 13 May. It happened when he was greeting a crowd in St. Peter's Square. Not only was he shot twice in the abdomen, but a bullet had missed his heart and aorta by inches. "It was a mother's hand that guided the bullet's path," he later said. In gratitude, he placed one of the bullets in the crown of the statue of Our Lady of Fátima in Portugal.

An estimated 1,000 Irish pilgrims, and two Irish bishops, joined the Pope for his open-air Mass at Lourdes. The Irish were dwarfed in the 300,000 crowd, many of whom were ill or disabled. John Paul struggled once more with the occasion, which took place over three hours in the blinding midday heat. "Help me," he whispered despairingly, at one point, while delivering the homily. The crowd repeatedly burst into applause, trying to encourage him. Many pilgrims were moved to tears by the effort he was making.

He also attended a torchlight procession. It was a spectacular and moving occasion. Standing at the head of the procession, he held a flaming torch in his hand. He then delivered a prayer while tens of thousands of worshippers held up torches in his direction. "Holding in our hands the lighted torch, we recall and profess our faith in the risen Christ," he said. "From him the whole of our life receives light and hope."

Pope John Paul II's pilgrimage "was one of the most moving celebrations ever," a Belgian cardinal stated. Back in Ireland, where the Lourdes visit had been broadcast live on TV, hopes were high that an equivalent event might be arranged to commemorate the Irish visit he had made 25 years earlier. Unfortunately, it wasn't to be. The Pope's health was slipping and his pilgrimage to Our Lady's shrine was to become "his goodbye to Lourdes and maybe also to his life," as the Belgian cardinal put it.

As predicted, Pope John Paul II's health further deteriorated following his return to the Vatican from Lourdes. In time, he developed breathing problems, necessitating the insertion of a breathing tube, and found it difficult to swallow – both problems being caused by his Parkinson's disease. He was weak and not eating. Although he was suffering, he was doing so with dignity, a close friend said.

By the beginning of April 2005, not much more than seven months after his Lourdes visit, it was clear the end was near. Outside his apartment window, St. Peter's Square was packed with pilgrims. Some sang hymns, more prayed, others stayed silent respecting his final moments. He was conscious of their presence, at one stage reaching out with his arm as if to touch them.

Inside the apartment, his friends and aides were by his side. He was heard saying, in a weak voice, "Let me go to the house of the Father." Following Polish tradition, a solitary candle illuminated the twilight of his room. It seemed to those outside that the room was in darkness. Then, shortly after 9.37 pm, on 2 April 2005, the lights in the apartment came on.

Everyone in St. Peter's Square understood the significance of what had just taken place. There was silence. Then, something unexpected happened. The whole square burst into sustained spontaneous applause. There was to be no miracle, as many had hoped. But, as one pilgrim said, there should be no sadness, either. Pope John Paul II, the pilgrim pointed out, was already "hearing the angels" and had joined his beloved Blessed Virgin in heaven.

ACKNOWLEDGEMENTS

We are fortunate that two eminent French authors met Bernadette and wrote about events at Lourdes. One of them, Henri Lasserre, was a lawyer and an author of national significance. He had good reason to believe in the power of the shrine, having recovered the use of his failing eyesight after paying it a visit. His book, *Notre-Dame de Lourdes*, became a massive French bestseller on its publication in 1869. It later became an international success when published in English.

Louis Veuillot was an equally formidable figure in French publishing circles. He was widely known for his work with the popular Catholic newspaper, *L'Univers*. He, too, visited Lourdes where, having met Bernadette, he became convinced of her story. His articles and other publications had a major impact in France. Both Veuillot and Lasserre were instrumental in bringing the shrine to worldwide attention. Their works were vital in the writing of this book.

Few people knew Bernadette better than Jean Baptiste Estrade. He befriended her and witnessed many of her ecstasies. Although neither a writer nor journalist, we are lucky that he documented his memories in *Les Apparitions de Lourdes: Souvenirs Intimes d'un Témoin*. Those recollections were particularly important when we dealt with the seventh apparition. While Estrade was still living, another French author, the controversial Émile Zola, spent some time at the shrine, resulting in his fact-based novel, *Lourdes*.

There are lots of general books about Bernadette Soubirous, but not all are worth reading. Among the best is *St. Bernadette: The Child and the Nun* by the authoritative 1903-born author Margaret Trouncer, whose maiden name was Lahey. Another fine research source is *Saint Bernadette Soubirous: 1844 – 1879* by Abbé François Trochu, the eminent historian who produced masterly biographies of religious figures. An additional excellent work is *Bernadette of Lourdes* by René Laurentin, the French theologian who wrote more than 150 books.

There are also numerous general works about the events at Lourdes. The French academic, Prof. Georges Bertrin, published *Lourdes: A History of its Apparitions and Cures* in 1908. The Danish writer, Johannes Jörgensen, who was nominated five times for the Nobel Prize, wrote an influential book simply titled *Lourdes*. Fr. Richard F. Clarke authored *Lourdes: Its Inhabitants, its Pilgrims, and its Miracles*; while Dublin's own Msgr. Joseph Deery also produced an excellent work called *Our Lady of Lourdes*.

There are two further interesting publications of note from an Irish perspective. Each was helpful in its own way. The first was written by Kerry landowner Denis Shine Lawlor, who travelled to the grotto in 1868. His *Pilgrimages in the Pyrenees and Landes* is comprehensive and passionate but its style is overblown. The second, *A Month at Lourdes and its Neighbourhood*, was written by Hugh Caraher and published in 1878. His book is a work of great importance.

The wonderful Cork woman, Rose Lynch, wrote two titles on the shrine – one a guidebook, published in 1924; the other

The Story of Lourdes, published in 1921. In the latter, she recalled the 1913 Irish National Pilgrimage. Some of Rose's reflections featured in an earlier chapter. Not only did she travel to Lourdes on numerous occasions, but she lived there for six months. She died in Cork in 1940.

Regarding Fr. Philip O'Boyle's trip by air in 1954, we are fortunate that he committed his story to paper. His booklet, *My Marian Year Pilgrimage to Lourdes*, is essentially a short pamphlet, running to no more than 20 pages. It was printed and published by The County Donegal Printing Co., Ltd. and sold for a mere sixpence. Unfortunately, the booklet has all but disappeared, although we were lucky to source a copy at the National Library of Ireland in Dublin.

As we mentioned earlier in this book, John F. Kennedy's tiny diary, which briefly chronicles his 1937 visit to Lourdes, was donated by Jacqueline Onassis to the JFK Library in Boston. Without it, the details of his visit might have been lost to time. We used many other sources for this story – to mention just a few, *John F. Kennedy: A Biography* by Michael Meagher and Larry D. Gragg; *The Kennedys at War: 1937 – 1945* by Edward J. Renehan Jr.; *Rose Kennedy: The Life and Times of a Political Matriarch* by Barbara A. Perry; and *Kick: The True Story of JFK's Sister and the Heir to Chatsworth* by Paula Byrne.

Other famous people appeared in earlier chapters and credit needs to be given. The book *Stepping Stones: Interviews with Seamus Heaney*, by Dennis O'Driscoll, and Heaney's poem *Brancardier*, helped steer our section on the eminent poet. Bernadette Devlin's *The Price of My Soul*, Maurice Gorham's *Forty Years of Irish Broadcasting*, along with numerous other sources including Irish Central Statistics Office and French data, were helpful in ascertaining the popularity of the name Bernadette.

Few people were more famous than Grace Kelly, and her story was a pleasure to research. Two works stand out as being helpful – J. Randy Taraborrelli's *Once Upon a Time* and *Grace: A Biography* by Thilo Wydra. Regarding actress June Haver, *Hollywood Songsters* by James Robert Parish and Michael R. Pitts was an important resource. Irish author John D. Sheridan wrote about Lourdes for the *Irish Independent*; while Malcolm Muggeridge was interviewed in *Cara* magazine.

Further specific sources that proved invaluable include *The Catholic Digest* for its narrative about John Ryan's cure in the late 1930s; *Tramping to Lourdes*, by John Gibbons, for his remarkable visit in 1928; the gossip columnist from *The Irish Press* who bumped into Winifred Feely in 1961, prompting our interest in her cure; and the article by D. J. Hayes in *The Irish Press* regarding the first air pilgrimage from Belfast in 1949.

Our gratitude also to Rory Childers, Professor of Medicine at the University of Chicago, whose discussion with Brendan Behan provided the basis for the story regarding the author's chaotic pilgrimage in 1950. His outline of that discussion was first published in *Chicago Today* in 1966. It was later reprinted in 1982 in *Brendan Behan: Interviews and Recollections* by E. H. Mikhail. Another useful text for that story was *Brendan Behan's France: Encounters in Saint-Germain-des-Prés*, by Jean-Philippe Hentz, Université Strasbourg II.

Regarding the celebrated miracle of John Traynor in 1923, thanks are due to Fr. Patrick O'Connor who interviewed him in 1937 and whose subsequent chronicle of their conversation was, with Traynor's cooperation, released to public view. Traynor also delivered a very interesting lecture in the Savoy Cinema, Waterford, in March 1939. By all accounts, his talk that night was good value for the 1/6 (balcony) or 1/- (stalls) entrance fee.

Details regarding Msgr. Capel's visits to Bernadette were in danger of being lost to time and took a lot of work to unearth. We sourced material from numerous editions of old newspapers and from census documents. We are also thankful to Arthur Warren's *London Days*, the *Oxford Dictionary of National Biography* and the *Dictionary of National Biography*, 1912 supplement.

Information on the *Ave Maria*, and its composer Abbé Jean Gaignet, was equally sparse and has mostly been lost to the dark recesses of history. However, we are eternally grateful to the newspaper *Ouest-France*, which contained a fascinating article in French and which we translated for the purpose of this book. We are also grateful to the diocesan bulletin of Luçon for the year 1925.

The connection between two other Irishmen and Lourdes required considerable research but produced interesting results. Numerous sources were used in the case of James Joyce, but in the end the most important insights came from a scrutiny of *Ulysses* and *Finnegans Wake*, while other material was drawn from *Dubliners*. *James Joyce's Ulysses: Critical Essays*, edited by Clive Hart and David Hayman, was among other texts that proved useful.

Regarding Archbishop John Charles McQuaid, three main sources were of value – the first being Roland Burke Savage's article The Church in Dublin: 1940 – 1965 in *Studies: An Irish Quarterly Review*, Vol. 54, No. 216 (Winter, 1965); John Cooney's *John Charles McQuaid: Ruler of Catholic Ireland*;

and Francis Xavier Carty's *Hold Firm: John Charles McQuaid and The Second Vatican Council.*

Many Irish daily newspapers were of immense help to our research. *The Freeman's Journal,* which folded back in 1924, took an enthusiastic interest in the shrine, as did *The Irish Press, Irish Independent, Sunday Independent, Evening Herald, The Dublin Evening Post, The Dublin Evening Mail, The Evening Packet, Belfast Telegraph, Belfast News Letter, The Belfast Daily Mercury, The Irish Times, The Cork Examiner* and its later manifestation the *Irish Examiner.* The weekly newspaper, *The Nation,* was also useful.

Of all the main news outlets, a few need to be singled out for particular mention. Michael O'Halloran provided priceless eyewitness reports for *The Irish Press* of Cardinal Roncalli's arrival at Lourdes in 1958; incidentally, he also compiled a retrospective for *The Kerryman* at the time of Roncalli's death in 1963. The Irish News Agency must be credited for the superb story on Lourdes, in 1952, by John Healy and Kevin O'Kelly. Regarding the account we wrote about these two talented journalists, John Horgan's paper Government, Propaganda and the Irish News Agency, published in the *Irish Communication Review,* Vol. 3, 1993, was most useful.

The British newspaper industry also took a keen interest in Lourdes, most notably in Ireland's fascination with it. The old London evening newspaper, *The Globe,* was a valuable resource, as were *The Daily Telegraph, The Independent, Daily Sketch, The Guardian,* Scotland's *Daily Record, The Scotsman, The People* and *The Daily Mirror.*

Both *The Coventry Evening Telegraph* and *The Birmingham Daily Post* were especially valuable regarding the Sally McCloy miracle in 1962. Our gratitude also to the *Gloucester Citizen*, *Lincolnshire Free Press*, *Bristol Evening Post*, *Hull Daily Mail*, *Derbyshire Courier*, *Thanet Advertiser*, *Hampshire Telegraph* and *York Herald*.

Many American news outlets were additionally crucial to our work – among them *The New York Times*, *The New York Herald*, *The Boston Pilot*, *Life* magazine, *Rome News-Tribune*, *The Century Magazine* and NBC News. Other international sources included the *Cape Argus* from South Africa. Our thanks also to many religious publications including *Lourdes* magazine, *The Catholic Digest*, *Catholic Standard*, *Catholic Advocate* and the Catholic News Agency.

From the beginning, local Irish newspapers were enthralled by the activities at Lourdes – including *The Cork Constitution*, whose staff set up the rugby club of the same name. Other invaluable local publications were the *Dundalk Democrat*, *Strabane Chronicle*, *Limerick Leader*, *Drogheda Independent*, *Connaught Telegraph*, *Connacht Tribune*, *Tuam Herald*, *Mayo News*, *Fermanagh Herald*, *Westmeath Independent*, *Waterford News and Star*, *Derry Journal*, *Donegal News*, *Nationalist and Leinster Times*, *Sligo Champion* and *Munster Express*.

As with all matters religious, County Kerry had an insatiable appetite for information about the shrine. Stories turned up with regularity in publications such as the *Kerry Evening Post*, *Kerry Sentinel*, *Kerry Star*, *Kerry Weekly Reporter*, *Kerry News*, *The Kerryman* and *Liberator* (Tralee). Other publications around the country were helpful, too, including the *Leitrim Observer*, *Donegal Democrat*, *Mayo Examiner*, *Ballinrobe Chronicle*, *Western People*, *Ulster Herald*, *Londonderry Sentinel*, *Meath*

Chronicle, Nenagh Guardian, Anglo-Celt, Leinster Express, Longford Leader and *Southern Star.*

Before ending, it is worth noting some good books that are available in bookshops or on the internet. We would recommend Thérèse Taylor's scholarly biography *Bernadette of Lourdes: Her Life, Death and Visions*; Prof. Patricia McEachern's *A Holy Life: The Writings of Saint Bernadette of Lourdes*; and Jean-Pierre Harris's *Sainte Bernadette: L'âme Soeur*, if your French is up to it. It goes without saying that the film and book of *The Song of Bernadette* are also worth considering, as they have stood the test of time.

Our friendship with the legendary Kerry broadcaster and footballer, Weeshie Fogarty, likewise stood the test of time, until his death in November 2018. Weeshie was a gentleman, kind, wise, with a heart of gold, and is a great loss. We extend our gratitude also to Professor Con Timon for his continued support. Further thanks to Linda Monahan and Barbara Ryan, of Typeform, for their first-rate work in the design and layout of this book.

Two other good friends – Dorothea and Jeremy – did some exceptional work in unearthing what, to our knowledge, is Ireland's first cure associated with Lourdes. They also led us to a fascinating book, *Mother Mary Arsenius of Foxford*, by Rev. Denis Gildea B.D., which was published in 1936. Their research provided the missing link in our understanding of the early Irish connection with the shrine. We are indebted to them for their exertions on our behalf.

In conclusion, we would like to acknowledge a story we encountered in the course of our research. It is the story of a young disabled man who went to Lourdes, full of hope, in search of a cure. He didn't get what he sought, but he did find something else. "Before going to Lourdes, I often kicked against my fate," he said. "I often grumbled and bemoaned my lot. I was often jealous of those who had greater physical strength and powers than I had."

A five-day visit to Lourdes changed everything. The young man found peace and contentment. "I never wanted to leave it," he said. "I never experienced the same peace anywhere else in the world, and the same feeling returned each time I went to Lourdes. It was always the same. Peace, complete peace of mind and soul." Echoing the views of so many who have visited, he concluded: "Those five days were the five happiest days of my life."

THE LITTLE FLOWER ST. THÉRÈSE OF LISIEUX

THE IRISH CONNECTION

Colm Keane & Una O'Hagan

St. Thérèse's suffering as a nun, the bullying she experienced at school, her intense holiness and details of her tragic death, aged 24, are revealed in this groundbreaking book.

You will read about her miracles, including cures from cancer, arthritis, meningitis, infertility and septicaemia. Devotion to this modern-day saint who became a nun aged 15 is described.

The Little Flower's blueprint for a good and fulfilling life – her "little way" – is explained. Everybody is important, she said. Every little deed matters. All things are part of a greater scheme.

This powerful and inspiring book gives you an intimate insight to one of Ireland's favourite saints whose relics created a national sensation during their visit in 2001.

Reviews of *The Little Flower: St. Thérèse of Lisieux*

'Great book' *RTÉ Radio 1*

'Compelling read' *The Connaught Telegraph*

'Excellent' *Tipp FM*

PADRE PIO
IRISH ENCOUNTERS
WITH THE SAINT

Colm Keane

Padre Pio, the man, his miracles, priestly life, loves and hates, are described in this book. What he was like, his moods and personality, his holiness and sense of humour are featured.

You will read about his stigmata, powers of bilocation, ability to read minds, his Masses and confessions. The saint's views of women, new fashions and even his interest in football are outlined.

The man who bore the five wounds of Christ is described by those who knew, met or witnessed him.

Padre Pio: Irish Encounters with the Saint brings you up-close to an extraordinary mystic and wonderworker in a way you have never experienced before.

Reviews of *Padre Pio: Irish Encounters with the Saint*

'Fascinating book' *Belfast Telegraph*

'Couldn't put it down' *Radio Kerry*

'Reads like a thriller' *WLR Radio*

GOING HOME

IRISH STORIES FROM THE EDGE OF DEATH

Colm Keane

Going Home contains the most comprehensive insights ever provided by Irish people into what happens when we die.

Many of those interviewed have clinically died – some after heart attacks, others after long illnesses or accidents. They have returned to claim – 'There is life after death!'

Most have travelled through dark tunnels and entered intensely bright lights. Some have been greeted by dead relatives and met a superior being. All have floated outside their bodies and watched themselves down below.

Those left behind describe visions of relatives who passed away. The book also acquaints us with the latest scientific research.

Award-winning journalist Colm Keane has spoken to people from all corners of Ireland and recounts their stories.

Based on years of research, Going Home provides us with the most riveting insight we may ever get into where we go after death.

Reviews of *Going Home*

'Fascinating' *Irish Daily Mail*
'Intriguing' *Sunday World*
'A beautiful, satisfying, comforting book' *Radio Kerry*

THE DISTANT SHORE

MORE IRISH STORIES FROM THE EDGE OF DEATH

Colm Keane

The Distant Shore is packed with a wealth of new Irish stories about life after death.

Extraordinary accounts of what takes place when we die are featured throughout. Reunions with deceased relatives and friends, and encounters with a 'superior being', are included.

Visions of dead family members are vividly described. The book also examines astonishing premonitions of future events.

This compilation was inspired by the huge response to Colm Keane's number one bestseller Going Home – a groundbreaking book that remained a top seller for six months.

Containing new material and insights, The Distant Shore is indispensable reading for those who want to know what happens when we pass away.

Reviews of *The Distant Shore*

'Amazing new stories' *Irish Independent*

'Terrific, wonderful read' *Cork 103 FM*

'A source of genuine comfort to anyone who has suffered a bereavement' *Western People*

FOREWARNED

EXTRAORDINARY IRISH STORIES OF PREMONITIONS AND DREAMS

Colm Keane

Did you ever have a feeling that something bad was going to happen? Perhaps you dreamt of a future event? Maybe you had a 'gut feeling' that an illness, death, car crash or some other incident was about to occur?

Most Irish people, at various stages of their lives, have experienced a forewarning of the future. It may reveal itself as a sense of unease. Alternatively, it may be more intense and involve a terrifying foreboding. Perhaps it brings good news.

Forewarned is the first Irish enquiry into this intriguing phenomenon. Crammed with fascinating stories, the book also presents the latest scientific evidence proving that the future is closer to our minds than we think.

Reviews of Forewarned

'Amazing stories' Belfast Telegraph

'Authenticity of experience is written all over these reports' The Irish Catholic

'A fascinating read' Soul & Spirit

WE'LL MEET AGAIN

IRISH DEATHBED VISIONS
WHO YOU MEET WHEN YOU DIE

Colm Keane

We do not die alone. That's the remarkable conclusion of this extraordinary book examining deathbed visions.

Parents, children, brothers, sisters and close friends who have already died are among those who return to us as we pass away. Religious figures appear to others, while more see visions of beautiful landscapes.

Riveting case histories are featured, along with numerous stories from those left behind who describe after-death visitations and many other strange occurrences. The latest scientific evidence is discussed.

We'll Meet Again, written by award-winning journalist Colm Keane, is one of the most challenging books ever compiled on this intriguing theme.

Reviews of *We'll Meet Again*

'A total page-turner' *Cork 103 FM*
'Packed with riveting case histories' *LMFM Radio*
'A fascinating book' *Limerick's Live 95FM*

HEADING FOR THE LIGHT

THE 10 THINGS THAT HAPPEN WHEN YOU DIE

Colm Keane

This explosive book reveals the truth about what happens when we die.

The ten stages we go through when we die are outlined for the very first time. They establish conclusively that death is a warm, happy experience and is nothing to fear.

Based on five years of research, the author has drawn from the real-life stories of people who have temporarily died and returned to life.

This definitive book provides you with all you need to know about the stages of death as we head for the light.

Reviews of *Heading for the Light*

'Absolutely fascinating' *RTÉ One*
'Provides much pause for thought' *Sunday Independent*
'The mysteries of dying and death from those who know'
The Irish Catholic

Capel Island Press
Baile na nGall, Ring, Dungarvan,
County Waterford, Ireland
Email: capelislandpress@hotmail.com

HARP & MAIDEN

Ladder of Charms

HARP MAIDEN

Ladder of Charms

JACKIE BURKE

LINDON BOOKS

First published by Lindon Books in 2022
9 Raheen Park, Bray, Co. Wicklow
Web: www.grindlewood.com
Email: jackieburke@grindlewood.com

Paperback	ISBN: 978 1 78846 264 8
eBook – ePub format	ISBN: 978 1 78846 265 5
Amazon paperback edition	ISBN: 978 1 78846 266 2

Produced by Kazoo Independent Publishing Services
222 Beech Park, Lucan, Co. Dublin
www.kazoopublishing.com

Kazoo Independent Publishing Services is not the publisher of this work. All rights and responsibilities pertaining to this work remain with Lindon Books.

Kazoo offers independent authors a full range of publishing services.
For further details visit www.kazoopublishing.com

Cover artwork © Rachel Corcoran, 2022
Printed in the EU

BOOKS BY JACKIE BURKE

HARP MAIDEN SERIES
Harp Maiden
Harp Maiden: Web of Secrets
Harp Maiden: Ladder of Charms

and

GRINDLEWOOD SERIES
The Secrets of Grindlewood
The Secret Scroll
The Queen's Quest
Zora's Revenge
Othelia's Orb

ABOUT THE AUTHOR

Jackie grew up with her sister and three brothers in Dublin. An avid reader and writer since her early school days, she only recently began writing children's stories, having dreamed of doing so for quite some time. *Harp Maiden: Ladder of Charms* is the third book in Jackie's second series for children, following the hugely popular *Secrets of Grindlewood* series.

The magical, mystery tale of the *Harp Maiden* was inspired by Jackie's other great love, music. She is also greatly inspired by her love of nature, gardens, forests, wildlife and of course magic! Reading, hill walking, music and baking are just a few of her other many interests and hobbies. Jackie divides her time between writing and giving creative writing workshops to children in schools and libraries around the country. She lives with her husband in Bray, County Wicklow. They share their home with a big fluffy cat called Millie.

CHAPTER ONE

Evie couldn't sleep with the oppressive heat. Even at two o'clock in the morning it was incredibly warm. She got out of bed, dressed quickly, and crept downstairs. She took the harp from the parlour and went outside.

Outdoors, there was no relief from the heat either, not even a gentle breeze. Evie walked the short distance to the park, deciding to try to find a new spot for the rituals. Better to do it at this unusual hour rather than wait until the morning when the park was crammed with people, she told herself. Deep down she knew she was being silly, reckless even, but a stubborn mood had overtaken her and she disregarded all sensible thoughts of returning home immediately.

For weeks now, the weather had been unusually hot and there had been no rain since the end of May. Everyone in the town was worrying about a drought and crops failing. The looming crisis was on the front page of every newspaper for the last few weeks. Water was going to be rationed soon and food shortages could be expected in the autumn and winter.

But Evie could fix that problem at the next full moon, or rather the magic in her harp could. She had already gathered everything she needed and packed her satchel ahead of time too. The sheet of parchment, the neatly tied bundle of dry twigs for the fire, the matches, and a new thick felt cover she had made for the harp – all were ready. She had written the next wish on the parchment: for enough rain to fall to fill the rivers, wells and reservoirs and save the farmers' crops. It was a good wish that would help so many people. The rain might arrive the next day, if not within hours of her making the wish.

Tonight, however, Evie was irritated from lack of sleep and frustrated at the thought of all she had to do. She hoped that playing the harp, even briefly, in the park – should she find a suitable spot – would help her to relax. For some time now, Evie had been building the little fire she needed at the full moon in the same spot, and she knew that it was time to move to a new location. The earth was scorched and dry from the repeated fires, and she feared that the next one she lit might spread. It was a miracle no one had spotted and reported the ash and burned grass. 'Tonight is as good a time as any to find a new space,' she said out loud, still trying to convince herself that she was doing the right thing.

But Evie didn't find the tranquillity she craved or the new location she needed. Whenever she stopped to try out a new spot and strum the harp, she thought she heard a rustle, a tiny twig crack, or a leaf flutter. Something always seemed to be moving nearby, as if following her, from the cover of bushes. She dismissed the idea at first, but by the fourth time she couldn't. What would be out in isolated areas of the park at this time of night? Was it a mouse, a rabbit, a fox? Somehow Evie didn't think so.

Evie stiffened. There it was again, a noise and a definite

movement this time, and it was coming from the thicket beside her. For a horrible moment Evie thought it might be Volok, the demon lord who she knew would sooner or later seek her out. Suddenly Evie wished she had never left the safety and comfort of her bedroom. How foolish of her! As she held her breath she could feel beads of perspiration pricking at her temples and one drop was annoyingly trickling slowly down the back of her neck. Oh, how she desperately wanted to reach the safety of her home, run inside, shut the door, bolt it tight and ensure the harp and everyone was safe!

But no, Volok wouldn't skulk around, she thought, trying to calm herself. He would pounce and roar, grab her and the harp and run back to his cave, or wherever he was hiding now. Olga, the demon-ogress and Volok's servant, was dead, so it couldn't be her either. So who was watching her? Her thoughts raced through several possibilities, including that it was just some vagrant. She should have considered that before and must include some means of defending herself in future, bring a weapon of some sort to fend off unwanted company.

Whoever it was, it was a pointed reminder of how much danger she and her family and all those close to her would soon be in. A confrontation with Volok was edging ever closer, and soon his search would lead him to Evie.

After a seemingly long and agonising wait for someone or something to emerge from cover, Evie stood, grabbed the harp and broke into a run. But she didn't run straight home. If someone is following me, she thought, I'm not leading them straight to those I love most in the world.

Evie hurried as best she could, but it was difficult. The

harp, though unusually small, was surprisingly heavy and awkward. At the same time, she was trying to lift the hem of her skirt to allow her to run at all. She soon grew tired and very hot, her blouse sticking to her back as she hurried through the park, down several narrow laneways, then circled around and eventually arrived at the rear of her house. She stumbled through the back gate, not bothering to stop to close it properly, and finally arrived out of breath at the back door.

Evie's hand was trembling as she lifted the key to the lock. In her haste, she dropped the key. Letting out a groan of frustration at her carelessness, she bent down to pick it up and bumped the harp against the door with a whump, bumping her head at the same time.

Cross now, and fumbling with the key, Evie heard a tiny squeak. Was that the gate? She didn't look behind to find out, but tried the key again. Successful this time, she almost fell through the door once it opened. She whirled around the door and into the boot room behind the kitchen, almost forgetting to shut the door *quietly*, pausing just in time to prevent a loud bang that might wake half the household. Evie leaned against the door with relief but was startled by another sound. Footsteps. *Is he really coming all the way up to the house?* she asked herself in disbelief.

Tightly clutching the harp, Evie backed away from the door. Frantic thoughts raced through her head, wondering what she should do, yet not wanting to call out for help and put her family in danger.

But Evie couldn't just run and hide, and her curiosity was burning. She stopped retreating and began to walk slowly towards the back door again. By the glow of the moonlight outside, Evie could make out a shape behind the frosted pane of glass on the upper half of the back door. A dark shape, not overly large – another reason it was unlikely to be Volok. She watched as a lighter patch moved closer to the glass – a face. First the nose pressed tight to the glass, then the mouth and stubbled chin. *He's trying to see inside*, Evie thought. *He wants to get in, come after me and the harp, perhaps my entire family. Maybe even murder us all!*

Evie gritted her teeth, then placed the harp carefully on the floor. Clenching her fists, Evie was just two steps away from her pursuer behind the door, when she stopped abruptly. He was pressing the whole of his face hard against the window now and Evie could see his eyes. No! Not his *eyes*, just *one* eye, wild and staring.

Evie knew exactly who it was.

CHAPTER TWO

Still unsettled by the mysterious spy, Evie was unable to sleep long after he had left and she had retired to her bedroom. She got out of bed again, lit a candle and opened the bottom drawer of her dressing table. She reached into the special drawer where she kept private things under lock and key, and took out a small bundle of letters. Matthew had written every week since he left after the Easter break. Evie always wrote back straight away and was looking forward to his return in just over two weeks' time, at the end of July. She reread his letters. They were mostly about boarding school, his upcoming exams and graduation, and his exciting plan to open a music academy with his father.

How Evie wished she could tell Matthew about the harp and its magic, that she was the Harp Maiden with enormous responsibility and a long list of problems that she didn't really know how to solve. Yet there was still that niggling doubt about Matthew's father and his former friendship with Lionel Thorn, who had been her tutor and was a secret demon. Matthew's father, Mr Reid, was now Evie's new music tutor. He had once known the real maestro, under normal circumstances. But their old acquaintance was still a connection to Dower Hall and to all the horrors connected with that place, a fact that unsettled Evie. Still, it wasn't Matthew's fault.

Evie returned the letters to the drawer and pulled out her personal diary. Looking over the recent entries, she reminded herself of both the good and the not so good that had happened since she became the Harp Maiden over six months before. There was still no sight nor sound of Volok, which was both a relief and a concern. The man who followed her tonight could only be his spy, just as he had once worked for the ogress Olga. 'It must be him, the sneaky, one-eyed man I saw before,' she whispered to herself. 'He's probably working with Volok now that Olga's gone.' Evie shuddered, remembering her involvement with Olga's awful death – how, on the sorceress Nala's instructions, Evie had used the Black Ruby to fire a lightning bolt of black magic at the evil ogress, destroying her and saving Evie's life. Evie hadn't known what magic the Black Ruby could perform, but it repulsed her to think that she had committed such an act, though it had been necessary to escape alive.

She felt a twinge of sadness as she read her notes about Charlie McGinn's family, from the full moon in May. 'At least I could use the harp's magic to help his sons, do something in return for the help he gave Lucia all those years ago,' she whispered, thoughtful. 'And for helping me too.' Without Charlie, Evie might never have known Nala's notebook even existed, and therefore never would have known about the Ladder of Charms, the path to earning powerful magic that could destroy demons and the Black Ruby.

Evie's thoughts returned to more immediate concerns when she heard the night nurse leave her father's bedroom.

It was very late; her father must have needed something to help him sleep. The professor's speech had improved quickly after his stroke, but he tired easily, and walking was risky, even with assistance. He would probably always need to use a walking stick now. Evie hated the sight of it, knowing how her father detested it too. It was a constant reminder of the upheaval in his life, in all their lives. Evie preferred to remember him as the big, strong, able man, always busy, absorbed in his historical work, excited by his research and his journeys to far-flung places.

Evie felt sadder still to think of her mother. Since the professor's sudden illness, Mrs Wells had fallen into another deep melancholy. She was prone to worrying more than ever about absolutely everything, frequently retiring to her bedroom, tearful. She fussed over Evie's father, plagued the nurses with too many questions and often annoyed Dr Elliott, who was only doing his best. No one was able to cheer Clara Wells. Evie was upset that these were matters she couldn't fix with her harp magic, as she had already wished for both her parents and could not do so again.

Evie turned the pages and reread her account of the full moon in June. How she had longed to wish for her friend Grace that night, but it had been cloudy and windless all day and heading out into the night, Evie wasn't optimistic that the moon would appear at all. After sitting for hours waiting and hoping, Evie had to admit defeat and returned home bitterly disappointed. No visible full moon meant no magic.

Evie had hardly seen her friend of late. After returning from her aunt's funeral at the end of May, Grace had several appointments with an eye specialist. Her eyesight had always been poor, but it had deteriorated in recent months. An operation was now critical to saving her sight. But Grace's father wanted a second opinion, and then a third. After that, Evie heard nothing, wondering if Grace had gone ahead with the operation or whether she and her father were still considering what to do.

Evie desperately needed to talk to her. It was well past the time to tell her best friend her secret, and she was worried that Grace was becoming increasingly suspicious and hurt at being left out of something clearly occupying so much of Evie's time and attention. Grace might be so upset as to not want to be friends any more, a thought that filled Evie with even more dread.

CHAPTER THREE

Evie had been forced to avoid Dower Hall for weeks as there were too many people working there, removing the rubble and levelling the site, perhaps to prepare for a new manor house to be built, though no one was sure. Anything of interest that had been salvaged from the manor before the demolition began, was now sitting in a sealed crate in Evie's father's study waiting to be sent to the museum.

At last, she received some news she had been waiting for. Grace's father and local magistrate, Mr Finch, informed Evie's father during one of his visits that the workmen had left Dower Hall, their job complete. Next, ownership of the estate had to be established, and so far, it was proving exceedingly difficult to trace any relatives of the late owner. But now that the workmen had left the site, Evie could finally take another look around and then carry on to the caves. Having already found the Black Ruby, she wanted to find Volok's talismans, treasures he had collected over his lifetime. They would play a part in resurrecting his wife, Madruga, from the dead. The two caves that the demons had used as hideouts were obvious places to search. She assumed Volok must still be in one of them, giving his spy instructions, preparing the way for the return of his queen, but above all, searching for the Black

Ruby: the ruby Evie had hidden in an enchanted casket in her house.

Evie had enjoyed taking horse-riding lessons with Freddie, and it provided a welcome distraction from all the serious and dangerous aspects of her role as the Harp Maiden. They were both progressing quickly and competitively too. It annoyed Evie that she had to ride side-saddle – more silly rules for girls, she thought. Her newly ordered jodhpurs could not arrive too soon from the family's tailor.

During the summer there was the usual break from school lessons for six weeks, and with both her parents indisposed, Evie's governess Julia was effectively running the household. Relations between Evie and Julia had been prickly for a while as they didn't always agree on aspects of Evie's new role. So, to avoid any further rows with her governess over how dangerous a journey to Dower Hall might be, Evie decided to say nothing and to ride alone at dawn.

It was a glorious summer morning, the sky still a soft mauve with wispy clouds tinged with pink slinking slowly across it. Evie felt free from all her cares as she galloped down country lanes and across fields to Dower Hall, her first horse ride unaccompanied. Her horse, Chestnut, wasn't bothered by the terrain and responded well to Evie after all the lessons, feeling as confident with her as she was with him.

Evie pulled up just short of where the manor house had once stood. The workmen had done a thorough job. There was barely a trace of debris, just a few patches of scorched earth where the fire had been particularly intense. Evie dismounted and led the horse over to the same little copse of trees where she had left a carriage on previous visits. She tied

Chestnut securely but loosely enough so he could munch on some grass while he waited for her. With a gentle pat on his nose, Evie left him.

Winding her way through the trees, Evie felt strange returning to the scene of so many awful events. She was glad to exit the darkness of the forest, its peculiar trees still a mystery to her. After walking through the open fields beyond them, she pressed on towards the caves. As she neared the first one, Evie slowed, watchful in case she suddenly needed to take cover. She stopped about a hundred feet away and looked around. Straining to hear every sound, she looked full circle then waited. Nothing at all but the gentlest breeze whispered through the long grass.

Evie was strangely unnerved by the quietness of the place. It was as if Volok had vanished and the silence was peculiar, puzzling. 'Where are you?' she murmured, gazing around again. 'What are you up to?' A raven cawed noisily above. Evie watched it circle then fly away. She cautiously approached the cave.

It was exactly as she remembered: the big yawning entrance, the boulders, many of them smashed and scorched after Volok's furious attack on Olga, and later, Evie's magical lightning strike. Stepping in and around the pieces of debris, Evie saw a scattering of bones that Volok must have tossed away after finishing some prey. A sudden shiver ran the length of her spine, and she felt goosebumps rise on her arms as the temperature dropped in the gloomy cave. Despite feeling a little uneasy, Evie ventured further in.

Though Evie didn't know exactly what they were, the five primary talismans were important to demons, and very important to Volok. He had to have hidden them somewhere safe. She knew he had them because she had heard him boast about it. Perhaps he had hidden them in this cave or the other one further down the gorge. 'Well, I'm here now,' Evie whispered to her surroundings, 'so I'm going to take a good look.'

She searched every nook and cranny, behind and beside every lump of rock, stumbling around and climbing over boulders to check every possible hiding place – even around the spot where Olga had died. To Evie's great relief there were no remains to be seen, just dark stains of dried black demon blood.

After the partial collapse, the roof of the cave seemed to have settled, albeit at a strange angle. It was lower now, making the cave darker and cooler than before. There was evidence of bats roosting, their droppings making the ground sticky and squelchy. Some of Olga's torn clothes lay tossed in a dirty heap, and more bones were piled up at the back of the cave. To one side, Evie saw what must have been the ogress's bed: branches roughly torn from trees dumped together, covered with a layer of bracken and ferns. The cave stank, and Evie often had to hold her nose. The further in she went, the worse it became, with fresh air unable to penetrate its farthest reaches. Just when Evie thought it was getting too dark to see, she slipped and fell hard.

Her cry of pain turned to a yell of disgust, as she pressed her hands on the ground to push herself up. Great dollops of bat poo lay all about, and the smelly muck was now on her hands, the cuffs of her clean blouse, her skirt and all over her laced-up boots.

'Ugh! Aaaaghhh!' she cried crossly.

She tried to get up, but the bat droppings were so skiddy Evie couldn't get a grip with her hands or her shoes. Finally, she rolled over onto her knees, ruining her skirt completely, awkwardly grasping the nearest rock to support herself. But she lost her balance again, her feet kicking out one at a time as she rocked and wobbled. She slid, snatching desperately at anything to steady herself. Her arms waved about to correct her balance without success, then she shot forward and tumbled over a long, low boulder, landing beside Olga's old bedding.

Grimacing at yet another awful smell, Evie was about to let out a groan when she held her breath and froze. A distant voice. Mutterings. Someone was coming. Partially hidden by the boulder she had fallen over, Evie crouched as low as she could and looked frantically around for the best place to hide. She looked towards the huge rocks that crashed down in the collapse. Maybe over there, behind them, she thought. Maybe not. There? No. She glanced at the entrance; the voice was getting louder. A man was entering the cave.

The bedding was thick and dry, and feeling the brushwood and heathers, Evie thought it might work. With no more time to decide, Evie burrowed into Olga's old bedding, covering herself with the largest of the ferns, hoping that would be enough to hide her. She lay still, though the smell was even worse underneath, and the bracken and ferns were probably brimming with insects. She quickly ignored her discomfort, her curiosity bursting. And there was just enough of a gap in the bedding for her to peep . . .

The voice grew louder still, the footsteps too. The man

was alone and vaguely familiar. Him again! The skinny, one-eyed man she had seen with Olga, the same man who had followed her home, the man who had been spying on her was here in the cave. Evie could see his face now, his expression suggesting he was in another world, his own crazy mixed-up world. His face was animated, something excited him. Even though he was close now, his words were hard to make out. He was rambling, not making any sense. But what he carried in his arms was of much greater interest to Evie than any of his silly mutterings.

Chapter Four

The one-eyed man set down the wooden crate he was carrying and began to empty it. He was so close Evie was terrified to move a single muscle or even blink through the foliage covering her. When the man spoke next, he began to make more sense.

'Hmph, wooden ornaments – boring,' he muttered.

Taking them out of the crate one by one, he dropped them casually on the ground beside him.

'What's this?' He turned a white object around in his hands. 'A horn?' He wrinkled his nose. 'I suppose someone might pay good money for it, if it's ivory. I could always say it was ivory.' He chuckled, placing it more carefully on the ground. 'Ah, this is more like it! And real gold too.' His smile showed bad teeth as he stuffed a gold locket into his pocket. He delved back into the crate, more encouraged. 'Pearls. Hmm, not bad, not bad at all!' He held them up then stuffed the triple string of pearls into his other pocket. 'Silver cutlery,' he said, pulling out a bunch of knives and forks. 'Always popular. They should fetch a good price.' He placed them beside the horn.

Evie felt disappointed. These things were too ordinary, definitely not what she was looking for. The five primary talismans would be at least unusual, at best spectacular. She grew impatient, wishing the one-eyed man would hurry up and find something interesting.

Then she almost jumped out of her hiding place.

'Aaghh!' the man screamed, quickly sucking one of his fingers. As he peered into the crate, Evie watched his expression change from irritation to pure delight.

'Aha! Gotcha!' he cried, pulling out a dagger. Holding up the weapon to admire it, the man then tried to polish the blade on his sleeve. The steel shone brightly. 'I know just the buyer for this,' he said, smiling broadly at the thought of a windfall. Evie's interest was also hooked. The dagger looked like a real artefact. It could even be a talisman, a *magical* artefact. She wondered if the one-eyed man was aware of this too.

Evie wondered why Volok had trusted this strange man with something potentially so important. Then it struck her: maybe Volok didn't know about these items. Maybe it was Olga who had given them to the one-eyed man in payment for his earlier assistance. Or perhaps, once he heard that Olga was dead, he simply stole them. If so, there could be more, and if not here, then perhaps in the other cave on the far side of the gorge – the green cave, as Evie called it – the one where Madruga's heart was still beating in a murky, green pool.

The one-eyed man stood up, stretched his arms, flexed his fingers and cracked his knuckles. He put everything except the locket and the pearls back inside the crate, taking greater care with the more valuable items, then closed the lid with a bang and carried it into the darkest part of the cave. Evie waited for him to leave, then got up and brushed herself down. She tried to make the bedding look untouched, though

Volok would probably pick up her scent, given his keen sense of smell. There was nothing she could do about that. Cross with herself for not bringing a candle or even a single match, she now had to grope her way around in the darkness to find the crate.

Slowly feeling her way around the back of the cave, Evie eventually located it, wedged tightly in between two great boulders. With barely any light at all, she heaved the crate out and lifted the lid. Trying to avoid being cut by the dagger, the horn or the cutlery, she felt around carefully. Frustrated, she realised that the dagger must have slid right down to the bottom.

'Ouch!' she cried, annoyed at herself for being impatient.

She glanced towards the entrance, worried the one-eyed man could still be within earshot or that the cave might echo. But it did not, and there was no sign of anyone. She took out the offending object, the horn. The sharp tip had pricked her finger. Evie could feel a sticky trickle of blood. Quickly, she wrapped her handkerchief around her finger, then reached into the crate again. Finding each object with her right hand, she passed it to her left hand to put to one side, as she continued to stare into the crate, willing her eyes to adjust to the gloom. Finally, she felt the bejewelled handle of the dagger, then she recognised the cool, smooth steel. She removed it, closed the lid and, pressing her shoulder to the crate, she pushed it back into the tight space with a few hefty shoves. Rubbing her shoulder, she let out a sigh of relief. One talisman. One. Hopefully it was one of the five primary talismans. She would have to do some research to be sure, but it was a start.

After checking the coast was clear, Evie left the cave and hurried back across the field and through the forest. But she got a shock when she spotted deep cart tracks and hoof prints. Lifting her skirt a few inches, she ran faster, fearing for her horse until she heard his familiar whicker. The animal turned to greet her, completely undisturbed. Evie rode home feeling excited, the dagger secured safely in the pouch at the back of her saddle. She looked down at her ruined clothes. 'Oh my goodness, what will Mrs Hudson say?' She decided to let the mud and muck dry then try to brush it off in the garden when no one was looking. She would have to really hurry to her room to change before anyone saw her in such a state!

The morning sun was higher now and it was already warm. Her tummy rumbled loudly for breakfast while her head buzzed with even more questions and plans.

Despite the beautiful day, Evie couldn't spend much more time outdoors. She had promised to spend the later part of the morning helping her father with his speech exercises. He had not been able to leave his bedroom yet as he was too unsteady on his feet. Despite everyone trying to please him, the professor was proving to be a difficult patient, easily bored and frequently frustrated.

Evie needed to spend time with her mother too, though Mrs Wells didn't feel like doing anything much, even talking. The doctor said it would take time and the family must be patient. Julia had organised activities to keep Freddie busy now that formal lessons were over for the summer, but it was the stable boy, Jimmy, who occupied more and more of his time, teaching Freddie all about the horses and their care.

Evie hoped that by evening time she would have time to practise more harp music for the charms. In between all of that, she wanted to consult her father's books about the dagger she had found, and perhaps pay a visit to the local library to find out more. Evie knew her father's collection of books well now, having read quite a few over the last couple of months. Ancient daggers had been mentioned in three different books, but without any drawings she couldn't be sure that the one she took from the cave was one of the five primary talismans she needed. Looking at the carriage clock on the mantelpiece in the study, there was just enough time to run down to the library and see if there was anything there that might help confirm the dagger's importance.

Being a very punctual and strict librarian, Miss Grimes was already starting to tidy up when Evie whirled through the door five minutes before closing time. There were no other patrons, so Evie ignored the sign that said, 'No talking, only whisper if you really must!'

'Good afternoon, Miss Grimes,' Evie said. 'I'm so sorry to bother you this late.'

'Good evening, Miss Wells,' the librarian said tersely. 'I was just about to lock up.'

'Would you have any books on ancient weapons, um, decorated daggers, ornate objects, that sort of thing?' Evie asked.

'The professor is studying a lot during his recovery,' Miss Grimes said. 'I hope he's not overdoing it.'

'Oh, not at all,' Evie said, smiling sweetly. 'I'm just trying to keep him occupied, otherwise he is finding it rather difficult being cooped up.'

'I can imagine,' Miss Grimes muttered. 'I'll check what I have on the shelves.' She turned neatly on her heels and headed down one of the many aisles brimming with books.

Evie waited impatiently, drumming her fingers on the desk, wondering what the librarian would say to her father when he eventually asked to be taken to the library. But she could worry about that later, along with several other things.

Miss Grimes appeared beside her quicker than expected, frowning at Evie's tapping fingers.

'At present, I have only one book on that subject that might interest the professor,' she said, peering at Evie over her small, round spectacles.

'Only one?' Evie said, a little disappointed.

'Yes,' Miss Grimes said, as she heaved the great book onto the desk. It landed with a whump. 'Most of the books the professor inquires after are immense.'

It was difficult for Evie to hide her excitement once she saw the title: *The Almanac of Talismans*. *Perfect!* she thought, and there was even a colour picture of a dagger on the cover – *her* dagger.

'Not all talismans are daggers, of course,' Miss Grimes said pointedly. Evie realised she had been staring rather obviously at the deadly weapon. 'Such things were popular in ancient times. Barbaric people used them for all sorts of dreadful reasons, including the dark arts, the occult, various rituals and the most horrible murders.'

'They might have been put to good use too,' Evie said.

'I doubt it,' Miss Grimes said, as she recorded the book as 'borrowed'.

'Thank you so much, Miss Grimes,' Evie said. 'I won't

keep you any longer.' Evie lifted the book off the desk, almost staggering under its weight.

'Be careful with that,' Miss Grimes said. 'I expect all my books to be returned in perfect condition.'

'Of course.'

Evie headed home, grunting occasionally under the weight of the precious book. She was dying to examine it. With a picture like that on the cover, surely she would find what she was looking for. Perhaps she would also learn what the other four talismans were. She hoped they wouldn't be difficult to find. There always seemed to be something to search for, which led to something else, then to something else. When would it all end? When would life return to normal? Probably never. She staggered on, trying to convince herself that all her efforts would be worth it in the end. Hopefully, what she was about to read in the great book would propel her farther along in her quest, and quickly.

CHAPTER FIVE

After dinner, Evie returned to the study where she had left *The Almanac of Talismans*. She sat down at her father's desk and opened it. With the turn of every page, it smelled old and musty, yet also strangely sweet and perfumed. It was a very beautiful book, full of detailed descriptions and colour pictures of every talisman it listed.

'Artefacts,' Evie muttered to herself. 'Old and rare, often of great value. What I'm looking for are talismans, magical artefacts with real magic, whether the historians believed in magic or not. Hmm, I wonder if any of them did believe in magic.' Further on she was pleased to read that the authors of *The Almanac of Talismans* had indeed included objects considered to be magical too. Evie was soon engrossed in the book and didn't notice the hours ticking by.

The birds were beginning to sing in the trees outside in the early summer dawn when Evie finally closed the book. She rubbed her tired eyes and yawned. Feeling satisfied with her night's work, she crept up to her bedroom to catch a couple of hours' sleep.

Later that morning, Evie left Freddie and Julia to finish watering their newly planted herb garden. She practised the flute and the harp, then returned to her bedroom. After taking out her notebooks and diary, she spread them across her bed. She wanted to compare the notes she had made to those Lucia had written all those years ago. There were similar highs and lows, despite being from a different time and in different circumstances. Evie read them again in the hope that she had missed something. In particular, she wondered how high up the Ladder of Charms Lucia had reached. Her predecessor had never mentioned the charms and Evie was disappointed that there were no references to them in her diary. The charms were especially secret, but perhaps Lucia hadn't come across Nala's notebook until quite late and was then forced to entrust it to Charlie for safe keeping while she was being pursued. Or perhaps Lucia chose *not* to attempt the Ladder of Charms. Maybe she had tried and failed. There was so much Evie would never know, and it irked her.

She picked up Nala's notebook and reread the secret revealed after Evie had completed step three. It was a bold command.

> *Find the five primary talismans so cherished by the demon lord and destroy them. To do so, you must list them on parchment, wrap them in ferns and burn all five together under a full moon – after you make the full-moon wish. Collecting the correct talismans will be a challenge and may take some time, but you must persevere.*

It had taken three very testing pieces of music to complete step three and reveal that single troubling instruction back in June. 'Why on earth does it not say where they are?' Evie asked herself wearily. 'I suppose they could be moved, over time,' Evie muttered, cross at her silly outburst. At least she had one of them, and she knew what the other four were now. *The Almanac* had specifically named them, which was a great relief after all her researching and wondering.

The Dagger of Dower. 'Dower,' Evie whispered, wondering if there was a connection to Dower Hall. The others were Galen's Goblet, Portia's Plate, Xavier's Stone and Marielle's Mirror. Evie had the dagger, there was no doubt. *The Almanac* provided proof with a detailed description and more pictures inside as well as on the cover. But where were the others? *Volok must be keeping them close*, Evie thought. *I must go to the green cave as soon as possible*. The five primary talismans might be an additional aid to smooth Madruga's return to the land of the living, or to present to her as a gift on her return, or for some other reason. Evie didn't know for sure, but none was as important as the Black Ruby, the only talisman that could bring the demon queen back to life. Without it, Volok's whole plan was doomed. He would undoubtedly come after her once his search for the ruby led to nothing.

Evie felt excited by her task, even though she knew it would be dangerous, probably difficult, and definitely urgent. The pressure was mounting to complete the Ladder of Charms so she could destroy the ruby. Then, there would be just the two of them: Evie and Volok. She shuddered, wondering exactly how that terrifying encounter would unfold.

CHAPTER SIX

Ever since her last visit to the cave, Freddie had been hounding Evie with questions, wanting to know exactly what she was up to. Julia was inquiring too.

'I have many duties as a Harp Maiden,' Evie said evasively. 'There are some things I must do on my own.'

'Dangerous things, no doubt,' Julia said.

'Sometimes,' Evie admitted. 'And some things can only be done by me. Nala made that quite clear.'

'But I could help you,' Freddie said earnestly.

'No!' Julia said. 'You cannot both go riding off into danger. It's bad enough that Evie won't listen to sense!'

Freddie looked surprised by Julia's outburst, and turned to Evie, pleading, 'Let me go with you the next time,' he said. 'Please.'

'I'm sorry, Freddie,' Evie said. 'I'm not sure that's such a good idea. Let me think about it.'

Evie rode off alone at dawn the next day. She felt cross. Although not wanting to put Freddie in danger, she could also have done with his help. She felt confused about whether he should come with her or not, and there hadn't been enough time to think about it properly. Julia's attitude was annoying her too. Didn't her governess realise she had a lot to think about and a lot to do? And her riding jodhpurs still weren't ready! A skirt was such a ridiculous thing to wear riding a horse! The tailor was working terribly slowly, even if these were the first jodhpurs he was making for a young lady, as he had informed Evie and Julia on his visit. He had nonetheless promised to have them ready by today, but he was never going to have them delivered early enough! Riding side-saddle in a long skirt was so awkward and even looked stupid. Evie scowled and galloped faster.

She left Chestnut in the same spot and headed off along the top of the gorge, then followed the winding rocky path that led to the cave with the green pool, Volok's lair. As she neared, Evie was intrigued to hear more than one voice.

'What else did the ogress give you, Simeon?' Volok asked.

'Junk, mostly,' Simeon said. 'I doubt if any of it will make me much money.'

'Money, bah!' Volok said. 'You people always want money.'

'What else would anyone want?' Simeon said. 'Except maybe a second eye.'

Volok snorted. 'Bring me everything Olga gave you. Everything. There may be something I want back.'

'Want back?' Simeon cried. 'But we had a deal!'

'Maybe with that disloyal wench, but not with me!' Volok roared.

From her crouching position just outside the entrance Evie watched Simeon raise a protective arm and lean back, withering at the demon lord's bellow.

'Bring me the crate, the *full* crate, then I will decide what you may keep and what you may not.'

'It's in the other cave,' Simeon said. 'And it's heavy.'

'Go!' Volok bellowed. 'Get it now!'

Simeon scurried out of the cave, a look of confusion and fear etched on his weaselly face. He stumbled very close to where Evie was hiding, but he was so eager to get away he didn't notice anything.

Returning her focus to the cave, Evie heard a rustle in the grass behind her. And again. She didn't move a muscle. She waited, silently, patiently, wondering whether Simeon had in fact spotted her. After a few more seconds, she couldn't bear it, she had to know. Slowly, Evie turned her head but there was no one. Or was there something? Was that a wisp of blond hair? Then two wide blue eyes peered guiltily through blades of long grass.

'Freddie!' Evie whispered, accusingly. 'What are you doing here?'

'I told you, I want to help,' he whispered, crawling towards her.

'Stay down and stay quiet,' Evie whispered, aware that she must be glaring furiously, though she couldn't really be angry with him. She knew he meant well, and his curiosity was as keen as her own.

'I remember that man with the eye patch,' Freddie said. 'But I can't think from where.'

'Volok called him Simeon,' Evie said. 'I think he was in the Crompton Arms the day we met Charlie. He was working for Olga before, and now it seems for Volok.'

Evie and Freddie both ducked when they heard a loud crash, then several more. They looked at each other. Freddie made a questioning face.

'He must be smashing boulders again,' Evie whispered, perplexed.

'Why?' Freddie mouthed.

'Something must have angered him,' Evie whispered.

'Let's look,' Freddie whispered, moving forward.

Evie tried to grab his jacket to haul him back, but Freddie was too quick. He scurried past her and she followed as quickly as she could, frustrated again by her clothing. They huddled together at the entrance and risked a peek.

After smashing another boulder Volok stretched to his full height. Evie glanced at Freddie, wondering how he would react. Freddie's eyes were wide with interest, but his expression was otherwise calm and focused. This was so new for Freddie, and Evie marvelled at his bravery.

Then to their great surprise, Volok suddenly jumped down on all fours and began to dig into the ground like an animal, his nails lengthening to ferocious claws, long and hooked. His huge arm muscles rippled as he carved into the earth.

Freddie looked at Evie. 'What's he doing now?' he mouthed to her.

Evie shrugged, and they continued to watch. It didn't take long for a huge mound of earth to pile up behind the demon as he dug a great hole. When he was finished, Volok stood up and admired his work. It worried Evie that he looked so pleased. She glanced again at Freddie.

'I have a bad feeling about this,' she whispered.

'Me too,' Freddie replied.

Volok stretched his arms wide and began a peculiar incantation. It was the first time Evie had heard the demon conjure a spell. She felt her heart quicken, knowing that it couldn't be a good sign. Together Evie and Freddie watched and waited. Nothing was happening, yet Volok looked extremely satisfied. He walked over to a large boulder and heaved it off another hole, one he must have dug some time ago, Evie thought. Volok picked something out of the hole, and then Evie realised she had been right all along. Volok had the talismans. He kept them hidden in a pit under a huge boulder in the cave, right beside Madruga's heart.

Volok picked up one item after another, admiring it or frowning at it. He appeared to be selecting just a few. Then he roared angrily; something was wrong. Evie felt a tingle of dread surge through her body.

Frowning fiercely, Volok picked up four items and brought them to the newly dug hole. He dropped them inside. There was a burst of hissing, which then faded to silence. Volok rolled the boulder back over the remainder of his collection, then returned to the new hole. But he was still angry. He stared into the pit and punched his fists on the ground, snorting loudly. After roughly covering the new hole with some of the soil he had dug up, he stormed out of the cave.

Evie and Freddie ducked instinctively, though they were not directly in the demon's path. He thundered out, disappearing around the boulders outside. After a moment, Evie and Freddie stood up, turning to watch Volok clamber along the edge of the gorge, up to the higher ground and off towards the field, and presumably through the forest.

'Wow!' Freddie said. 'That was weird.'

'Now you understand why I wanted to come alone,' Evie said.

'No way!' Freddie said. 'I should have been with you all the time.'

Evie smiled. 'Maybe you're right.'

'Let's look in that pit he dug,' Freddie said. 'Quick, before he gets back.'

They ran inside, skidding to a halt. A blast of fierce hissing erupted immediately they entered, echoing all around the cave.

'Snakes!' Freddie cried. 'Hundreds of them!'

'Run!' Evie said.

Black asps poured through the loosened soil and over the top of the pit. Evie and Freddie bolted out of the cave and ran as fast as they could as far as they could. After a few minutes, they stopped to catch their breath and risked a look behind. They saw a wall of snakes poised aggressively at the entrance to the cave, on guard.

'We should hurry,' Evie said. 'We can't be sure some of them aren't still slithering after us. They've been enchanted and might never stop chasing us. Come on! Let's go!'

They arrived breathless and shaken to find both horses safe. It was a relief to mount and turn them towards home. Evie saw her hands were shaking as she took the reins, and Freddie had needed three attempts to get into his saddle. They rode home at a fast gallop without saying another word.

CHAPTER SEVEN

E vie barely noticed Julia standing watching them, while she and Freddie dismounted in the stable yard. 'Are you all right, Freddie?' Evie asked, turning to him.

'I'm fine,' Freddie said. 'I'm supposed to meet Jimmy soon. He's going to teach me all about horseshoes today.'

'We'll talk later, then,' Evie said. 'All of what happened is—'

'I know,' Freddie said. 'Another big secret.'

He ran off to get the horses some water and feed before his lesson, and Evie walked over to the boot room.

'Your father was asking for you,' Julia said, stepping out of the doorway. 'I told him you went out for an early ride. It seems I was right.'

'Yes, it was lovely being out so early,' Evie said.

'And yet you look flustered,' Julia said. 'Did something happen? Was there trouble?'

Jimmy, the stable boy, passed by as they paused at the back door.

'You're back then,' he said cheerfully.

'Freddie's waiting for you in the stable,' Evie said. 'He'll be glad to see you. He's looking forward to his lesson.'

'And I'm very glad to see you,' Julia said quietly.

'Is Father all right?' Evie asked, trying to avoid further questions.

'A little cranky, but otherwise well,' Julia said. 'He has a lot of correspondence from the museum, but his hands become stiff after writing just a few sentences. I offered to write the letters for him, but his pride won't let him accept much help.'

'I offered too and got the same response,' Evie said. 'I'll go and see him now.'

'Meet me in the parlour afterwards,' Julia said. 'I'd like to hear what's going on, Evie. We don't seem to talk as much as we used to.'

Evie nodded, and they went inside.

Julia hadn't been her usual self for the last couple of weeks. Her cough came and went, a little worse each time it returned, and her complexion was dreadfully pale. Her overall form was somewhat 'off' at best. Evie knew that crankiness was a sign that Julia wasn't feeling well, and it had been difficult to persuade her to see a doctor. She would try to raise the subject again.

Evie changed her clothes and went to sit with her father for a while. She managed to ease his irritation by distracting him with a game of chess. Afterwards, she brought him up some more books from the study and left him to read and doze.

Julia was sitting in the parlour, deep in thought, when Evie entered.

'Before you say anything,' Julia said, coming out of her reverie, 'I saw the doctor early this morning. As you know, I thought it ridiculous to visit a doctor for a cough in the summertime, but I finally went, and he wants to conduct some tests. He thinks I may be a little rundown. Nothing to worry about.'

'Finally! I am glad,' Evie said. 'I didn't want to bother you with my concerns while you were clearly feeling unwell.'

'And when we weren't exactly seeing eye to eye,' Julia added. She gave Evie a wry smile.

Then Freddie burst in. 'Have you told Miss Julia what happened?'

'Freddie! Shh!' Evie said. 'I'm about to.'

'Oops, sorry.'

'Haven't you got a lesson with Jimmy?' Evie asked.

'Mr Hudson asked him to fix a wheel on the carriage first,' Freddie said.

'So, you went on a mission,' Julia said. 'And you went together, ignoring my advice.'

'No, I went alone, but Freddie followed me,' Evie said, then she brought Julia up to date.

'Oh, my word!' Julia said. 'Even worse than I imagined!'

'Nobody died today,' Freddie said pragmatically.

'Well, thank goodness for that!' Julia said.

Freddie shifted uncomfortably on the settle.

'And hopefully no one else will,' Evie said gently. 'But I must go back for the talismans, Julia. I only have the dagger and I must have all of them.'

'The mirror could be big,' Freddie said. 'We might even need a cart to carry it.'

'You're right, it might,' Evie said. 'The picture in *The Almanac of Talismans* didn't mention its proportions.'

'Just a moment,' Julia said. '*We?*'

'Freddie was very brave, Julia,' Evie said.

'We all know that Freddie is a very brave boy,' Julia said. 'But really, I must insist—'

Julia suddenly succumbed to a coughing fit, and Evie went to the sideboard to pour a glass of water for her.

'When are you having these tests?' Evie asked.

'Next week, in the hospital,' Julia said.

'The hospital?'

'Yes,' Julia said. 'Dr Elliott said it would be easier to do them there rather than in his rooms.'

'I see,' Evie said. 'Perhaps you should lie down for a while. I need to practise for the fourth step of the charms. I'd like to pass the test on the first attempt.'

'And what will you be doing, Freddie?' Julia asked.

'Jimmy is going to show me how to reshoe a horse today. I think I should go and see if he's ready now.'

The room felt unusually quiet after Freddie ran outside.

'You know I wish I could be of more help,' Julia said after a moment. 'I'm so tired all the time, and this annoying cough is wearing me out.'

'Then let the Hudsons look after the house,' Evie said. 'You really don't need to.'

'I promised your mother,' Julia said.

'She would understand,' Evie said. 'The Hudsons know they must defer to you on any important decisions while Mother is indisposed. Anyway, Freddie and I are fine, even if we are, um, busy.'

To Evie's surprise Julia nodded without further protest, which worried Evie even more.

*

Evie received another letter from Matthew, confirming when he would be home, saying he was relieved his final exams were over and reminding her how excited he was about the academy. His father would be overseeing his music diploma studies from September, which was both a blessing and a curse, he joked. Evie was looking forward to seeing him and felt a distinct lift in her mood as the days ticked by to his return.

Freddie had begged to accompany Evie at the next full moon on 16 July, and she had agreed, suspecting that he might follow her anyway. He was very excited, and Evie repeatedly stressed the importance of being quiet and careful at all times.

'It would be very difficult to explain what we are doing,' Evie said.

'I'd think of something,' Freddie said. 'I always do.'

Evie had to stifle a laugh, knowing that was true. They walked quickly to her usual spot in the park.

'I need to find a new location soon,' Evie said. 'Someone is bound to notice all these ashes and the scorched grass.'

'Someone else, as well as the one-eyed man?' Freddie asked.

'Yes, I could get into trouble, and awkward questions would be asked,' Evie said.

'There should be lots of hiding places in this park,' Freddie said. 'We should probably look in the daytime, go for a walk and look around. Julia might be able to come too.'

'Good idea,' Evie said, setting out her things.

'Hopefully she'll feel up to it,' Freddie said.

'I hope so,' Evie muttered. 'Now, the moon has to be fully

bright before I play, but the sky is completely clear tonight so we shouldn't have long to wait.'

'It gets bright so early in the summer,' Freddie said.

'Another reason not to delay, if at all possible,' Evie said. 'We might be seen if someone is out very early.'

Freddie was remarkably patient throughout the ritual. Evie could see he was enjoying the music as she wished for the rain to fill all the rivers and wells, save all the crops and the farms. She felt pleased that so many people would be helped by her wish. Then Evie remembered her last visit to the park, and she told Freddie how she thought that someone had been watching her.

'It was probably Simeon,' Freddie said. 'I haven't seen or heard anyone tonight, though.'

'Neither have I,' Evie said, 'but if you do, don't speak. Raise a hand and point.'

They began the walk home through the park, keeping close to the trees to provide cover if someone happened to be out for a very late or very early stroll.

Crack!

Then a voice said, 'Drat!'

Without a second's hesitation, Evie and Freddie ducked into a thicket to hide. Evie held the harp close. To her surprise she saw Freddie was trying to protect it too, clasping it tightly. Then, there were more noises, rustling. Someone or something was moving through the cover of foliage.

Suddenly, Freddie let go of the harp, burst out of the thicket, broke a branch off the nearest bush and charged in the direction of the noise, arm and weapon raised. Evie could only gasp and stare before running after him. She stopped suddenly when Freddie stopped to listen, looking around at no one, nothing.

'He's gone,' Freddie said.

'Good. Home. Now,' Evie said. 'As fast as we can.'

'That man must be very interested in the harp,' Freddie said. 'Or very interested in you, or both. What a creep!'

So true, Evie thought. A sneaky, greedy creep, who would report their every move back to Volok. Simeon didn't seem that bright, but he would do anything for money. He had practically admitted that in the cave. Evie was glad she hadn't come out alone this time.

CHAPTER EIGHT

The rain finally came. It poured for a full week, followed by sunshine and thundery showers for another week. Throughout the town and county everyone was relieved that the drought had finally ended. Evie couldn't help feeling chuffed and her spirits were high. But there was another reason for that. Matthew was due back that evening, and in his final letter he asked if he could call to see Evie the next morning.

Matthew arrived punctually at eleven o'clock. Evie had asked Mrs Hudson to bake a lemon cake, Matthew's favourite. Mr Hudson opened the door with his usual formality. Evie stood in the hall feeling a bit silly, knowing she was beaming from ear to ear and unable to hide her delight. Freddie was hopping beside her, excited to see Matthew too. Despite the age difference, they got on very well. Matthew didn't mind Freddie's antics, and Freddie loved the interest Matthew took in him, asking him questions and making suggestions about all the things he should think about doing, including some mischievous pranks.

Julia joined them in the parlour, but she didn't talk much while the other three chatted merrily for an hour or so.

'I wanted to see you as soon as I returned,' Matthew said.

'I'm going to be very busy setting up the academy and I was hoping to get your advice on a few things.'

'Oh? And what might that be?' Evie asked.

'Well, um, the choice of music for different students, beginners, intermediate and advanced, for example. And, um, the pacing of learning, you know how every student is different, and we must try to understand their learning requirements. Then there's the layout of the music rooms, and um, so on.'

'Won't you be learning all that in your diploma?' Evie asked, suspecting that Matthew was just finding excuses to involve her, though she was rather pleased.

'I should think so,' Matthew said. 'But it's good to talk these things over with a fellow musician. And a young person too. So many music tutors are old and boring, and lessons can sometimes be old-fashioned and boring too. My father is extremely knowledgeable, but I'd like to introduce some new ideas, keep the academy modern and fresh.'

'Don't let your father hear that!' Evie said, laughing. 'But of course, I'd be happy to advise on anything you think I can help with.'

'Excellent. Thank you,' Matthew said. 'My father is becoming very stressed about the whole project, you know. He's quite overwhelmed by it all and has a long list of things for me to do.'

'Then you're back just in time,' Evie said. 'Is it shaping up as you hoped?'

'From what he told me last night, yes, I think so,' Matthew said. 'But I hope he'll listen to my suggestions. It will help if I say you have ideas too, and perhaps Miss Pippen might like to contribute?'

'I'd be delighted to help in any way I can,' Julia said, though her enthusiasm sounded a little watery.

Freddie changed the subject. He had been dying to tell Matthew all about the horse riding lessons.

'That's marvellous,' Matthew said. 'We should go for a ride together someday. Perhaps I could teach you how to jump over hedges.'

'We're not quite at the jumping stage,' Evie said.

'Yes, I am!' Freddie said.

'Oh?' Evie said.

'Jimmy taught me last week,' Freddie said. 'I did my first jump, though it wasn't very high.'

'Well! I didn't know I had so much catching up to do,' Evie said.

'It seems we both do,' Matthew said. He smiled. 'Perhaps I could call again, and we could play a duet, piano and flute. You're welcome to call to my house, but it's rather upside down at the moment, papers and plans everywhere!'

'Of course we could practise here,' Evie said. 'Both my parents are quite confined at the moment, as I explained, but they love the sound of music in the house. We won't be disturbing anyone.'

'Would that be all right with you, Miss Pippen?' Matthew asked politely.

'Oh, yes, of course,' Julia said, distracted. 'It was very nice to see you again, Matthew. Would you excuse me, please?'

Matthew stood up as Julia left the room. Evie explained that her governess hadn't been feeling well and that she wasn't being rude.

'No need to explain,' Matthew said. 'I hope she'll feel

better soon as there is no one better at calming my father. Now I must be going too. I'll try to arrange some time off, then I'll send you a note about that practice, Evie. We should have afternoon tea again with Grace too. How is she?'

'She's been out of touch for a while,' Evie said. 'When she returned from her aunt's funeral, she wrote to me saying her eyes were giving her trouble. Her father took her to see a new specialist and he was considering an operation. I really should call to see her, but I didn't like to disturb her. It must be weighing on her mind a lot.'

'That's awful. I hope she'll recover in time to play at the academy's grand opening,' Matthew said. 'My father wants the Hartville Ensemble to give a concert to mark it "open for lessons". We're hoping for autumn, but a lot depends on the refurbishment. Oh! I really must hurry. We're meeting the builders for an inspection. It was great to see you Evie, and you too, Freddie.'

They said their goodbyes and repeated their tentative plans to meet.

'Matthew really likes you,' Freddie said.

'He likes you too,' Evie said, blushing.

'We should go riding with Matthew,' Freddie said. 'It would be fun.'

'Yes, it would,' Evie said. 'But I have other things to do too, like returning to the cave.'

'What about all those snakes?' Freddie asked.

'I'll think of something,' Evie said. 'Now, I must write to Grace and post it immediately. I really shouldn't have waited this long.'

*

Grace replied quickly to Evie's letter, apologising for her silence too. She had some news, but it could wait until they met.

A week later, Evie, Grace and Matthew met for afternoon tea in Hartville. It was one of those mixed-weather days. The sun was shining warmly as it normally would at the end of July, but there were frequent showers too, keeping the water levels where they should be, just as Evie had wished.

As they arrived at the tea rooms, Charlie McGinn's two sons walked by. They nodded, then stopped to talk.

'Hello,' Evie said, a little unsure. 'We were very sorry to hear about your father.'

'Very sorry,' Grace said.

'It was a terrible shock,' one of the brothers said. 'But he wanted to do what was right, despite any risk to himself.'

'He was a very brave man,' Evie said.

There was an awkward pause. The McGinn brothers were blocking the door to the tea rooms without realising it.

'He would have been so thankful for this rain,' the other brother said. 'Our crops would have been ruined without it.'

'Aye, it arrived just in the nick o' time,' the first one said, nodding meaningfully to Evie.

Evie looked from one to the other. *Charlie must have told his sons a lot*, she thought. *They may even know I'm the Harp Maiden. I hope they won't blurt it out, not now, not ever.*

'Um, yes,' she mumbled. 'The rain saved everyone a lot of hardship.'

'Aye, thank you again, and good day, Miss.' The brothers tipped their caps like their father used to, then continued on their way.

'Mr McGinn, he was the man who was murdered, wasn't he?' Matthew said.

'Yes, they're his two sons,' Evie said.

'They were with him in the inn when we met,' Grace said. 'Though we didn't speak with them then.'

'They recognised you quickly,' Matthew said. 'In fact, it sounded like they were thanking you for the rain, Evie. What a strange pair.'

'Me? The rain? Oh, why not?' Evie said. But her joke sounded odd, and Evie could feel her friends' confusion. 'Em, shall we go in?'

Over tea, Grace explained why she had been out of touch.

'I must apologise,' she said. 'I had so many medical appointments and I was very anxious about all of them. Actually, I was terrified. My eyes are much worse than I've been letting on, worse than the doctors told me at first. Anyway, we've decided that I will have the operation, but there's no guarantee that it will be successful. In fact, I may lose my sight for good.'

'Oh, Grace, how awful!' Evie said, taking her friend's hand. 'Are the doctors sure? I mean, won't the operation fix the problem?'

'They're not certain, so they told me to be prepared,' Grace said. 'But it's the only chance to save my sight, or some of it. I'm absolutely dreading it.'

'I'm so sorry to hear that,' Matthew said. 'If you'd rather not talk about it, we'll understand.'

'Of course,' Evie said. 'We don't want to spoil your afternoon, but, Grace, is the operation soon?'

'Next week,' Grace said. 'And you're right, I do need

some distraction. I've been worrying and fretting so much. Let's talk about everything else, starting with the academy. Matthew, tell us your latest news.'

Matthew filled Grace in on what he had already told Evie, but he had some other news as well. His father had been approached by a local earl, Lord Moffat. A generous supporter of Mr Reid's new academy, the earl had requested a favour in return: a private recital for his wife's birthday party in August.

'My father wants me to play piano,' Matthew said. 'And he would like you, Evie, to play the flute, if you'll agree.'

'I'd be delighted,' Evie said. She glanced at Grace, who looked very tense.

'I'm sorry, Grace, I hope you don't mind,' Matthew said.

'Not at all,' Grace said. 'How could your father not ask you to play piano? Anyway, I couldn't play so soon after my operation. You will make a lovely duet.'

Evie felt herself blushing again, as Matthew continued the story.

'I think you may have met the earl's son and daughter before,' Matthew said. 'Cedric and Cecilia Moffat.'

'Oh!' Evie and Grace said together, and they couldn't help but laugh.

'Lord Moffat mentioned the auditions last September, but not your names,' Matthew said. 'I put two and two together based on what you and my father had told me. I see that you do remember them.'

'We met only very briefly,' Evie said.

'They didn't talk much to anyone at the auditions,' Grace said.

'No, they just complained rather loudly about everything!' Evie said.

'Oh,' Matthew said. 'Well, they are a very influential family. Lord Moffat is supporting the academy financially, and he is also interested in my father's scholarship idea. We felt obliged to agree to this request.'

'I expect it will be quite formal,' Grace said. 'You must wear something really special, Evie.'

'A good excuse for something new,' Evie said.

'Actually, Grace is right,' Matthew said. 'It is an evening event, so it will be formal, but we should have all the details soon. I'll let you know.'

The tea ended with a promise from Grace to write if she could, or at least send word as to how her operation went, and for Evie to tell her all about the recital.

'We'll need to rehearse a few pieces,' Matthew said. 'Would a couple of evenings suit you, Evie? It'll be difficult for me to get away during the day, I'm afraid.'

They arranged some practice times and parted with warm smiles. Evie stood watching Grace as her family carriage drove her away. She was dreadfully worried for her friend. If Grace lost her sight, her life would be changed forever. Evie must make that wish for Grace at the next full moon, 13 August. It was the same night as Lady Moffat's birthday. What a busy evening that promised to be.

CHAPTER NINE

Cedric and Cecilia didn't recognise Evie from the previous September, but Evie didn't mind. The siblings were so busy readying themselves and fussing about, they hardly noticed 'the hired musicians' for their mother's birthday party. There were about forty close friends and family attending, most around the same age as Lord and Lady Moffat – middle-aged or older – and all of them oozing wealth and power as displayed by their clothes, jewellery, poise and demeanour. It was quite the occasion and all in a sumptuous setting.

Evie was delighted with her new turquoise silk evening dress which beautifully complimented her rich auburn hair. It was her first formal evening gown, and she couldn't help but notice the admiring look on Matthew's face when he and his father collected her. Evie's mother had barely registered her request for a new gown. She was sleeping a lot, drowsy from new medications Dr Elliott had prescribed. Evie's father, on the other hand, was so delighted she had been invited to play at a private recital, Evie thought he would have agreed to buy her absolutely anything. The dressmaker was summoned to the house and the new gown was made.

The carriage ride to the Moffats' grand estate took about

half an hour. When they arrived at the imposing castle, Evie, Matthew and Mr Reid were ushered into the library where the recital would be taking place.

It was a magnificent room. A huge fire was lit despite it being August, blazing brightly and giving a merry welcome. Ornate candelabras were lit on every occasional table in addition to an enormous amount of electric lighting from sparkling crystal chandeliers. Elegant, cushioned chairs were set out in rows for the select audience. But Evie marvelled most of all at the towering bookcases lining every available wall space, right up to the richly decorated, corniced ceiling. She wondered for a moment what Lord Moffat might like to read and how she would love to browse through his collection of books.

Evie stood by the grand piano and Matthew sorted their music sheets. They warmed up their fingers with a few scales, while Mr Reid chatted nervously with Lord Moffat. As soon as the guests began to arrive, the lord excused himself and went to greet them with his wife and two children. Cecilia smiled sweetly, flinging her ringlets about her shoulders at every opportunity. Cedric set out to impress in his own way, trying to converse like a learned young man, a lord in waiting.

Waiters shimmied around the room in their pristine livery, quietly and efficiently ensuring every guest was being looked after. Lord and Lady Moffat chatted and smiled as guests congratulated her ladyship on her birthday, as birthday gifts were discreetly whisked away from any prying eyes by the attending fleet of servants.

Evie, Matthew and Mr Reid stood quietly together, feeling a little nervous as they waited to perform. Mr Reid was in a dither and kept repeating how important it was that the evening should be a success, how they must make a good impression, and how he was sure they would. He remained distracted, however, terrified of missing a signal from Lord Moffat that it was time to begin. Evie and Matthew were amused by the snatches of conversation they overheard as the guests circulated around the room.

'What a novel idea to invest in a music academy!' one heavily bejewelled lady announced.

'Ah, Lord Worthington, how are you? I missed you at the cricket club!'

'Did you read about those snakes in the newspapers? How perfectly horrible!' a duchess shrieked. 'Snakes, I tell you! Who would have thought? I won't be stepping outside of my carriage in the countryside for a while, and I'm glad we live on the other side of . . .'

Evie's ears pricked up at the mention of snakes, wondering if they were the same asps she had seen in the cave. Were they leaving the cave now, or had Volok created another swarm somewhere else? This was not good news.

After a few more exclamations, Evie drowned out the mutterings of the guests by playing some practice trills on her flute. Matthew did likewise with a few chords on the piano. He smiled warmly at Evie, then resumed a look of complete composure when his father approached with Lord and Lady Moffat. He stood to be introduced.

'Welcome,' Lord Moffat said. Lady Moffat smiled delicately. 'We are looking forward to hearing you perform. My wife adores the flute – which is why you are here.' He glanced at Evie, then turned back to Matthew. 'We have been

– 55 –

looking forward to hearing you play, and I hope tonight's concert will help you to attract some students to the new academy. If you impress their parents, of course. Ha ha, ha ha!'

'Thank you, your lordship. We will do our very best,' Matthew said. 'It is an honour to play for you on such a special occasion.'

'Are we ready to begin, your lordship?' Mr Reid asked.

'I think so,' Lord Moffat said. He turned to wave the butler over.

'Shall I ask the guests to take their seats, your lordship?' the butler asked.

'Do that, Reeves,' Lord Moffat said. 'Mr Reid will introduce the duet.'

Without even glancing back at Evie and Matthew, Lord Moffat promptly led his wife to the front seats, leaving Mr Reid looking a little lost for words. Clearly, he had hoped that Lord Moffat might make an introduction. Evie cast a nervous look at Matthew, who leaned towards his father, pressing his hand reassuringly on his shoulder. Mr Reid cleared his throat and clasped his hands together for courage.

'My lords, ladies and gentlemen,' he began. 'We are delighted to have been invited by Lord Moffat to bring beautiful music into this magnificent house tonight, to honour Lady Moffat on her birthday.'

Polite applause.

'I am deeply grateful for his lordship's generous support of my – of our new endeavour, The Reid Academy of Music.'

Polite applause.

'We might have to reconsider the name, but carry on, Reid,' Lord Moffat joked.

Tittering laughter.

'I now give you two members of the Hartville Ensemble, my son, Matthew, on piano, and Miss Evelyn Wells on flute.' He bowed to the guests and moved into the shadows. Matthew began with the piano introduction, then Evie joined in.

After the performance, the butler informed Evie and Matthew that they were required by his lordship to circulate at the fringes of the party to answer any questions the guests might have about their performance and the academy. Surprised, Evie and Matthew obliged, but most of the time they were left alone, receiving the occasional nod or smile from the guests and catching more snippets of gossip from some of the more vocal ones. It was then that Evie overheard something that would throw her head into another spin.

The gowns and jewellery on display around the room were simply dazzling. Evie was admiring the ladies' finery when Matthew nudged her gently.

'Here comes his lordship,' Matthew said. 'Oh, relief! He's been distracted by that pompous Lord What's-His-Name with the enormous moustache!'

'Matthew!' Evie whispered, as the two of them tried not to laugh.

Lord Moffat began chatting to another lord close to where Evie and Matthew were standing. The lords were sipping wine from magnificent crystal glasses. As they spoke in loud projecting voices, it was impossible not to hear their conversation.

'Although the rain has come and solved the problem of drought, we've had more drama on the estate today,' Lord Moffat said, irritably.

'How so, Atticus?'

'One of my tenants' children was involved in an accident on one of the holdings.'

'How careless!'

'Yes, the labourers are most distracted, yet again.'

'Any excuse to avoid honest, hard work.'

'They say the child is in a coma and may die,' Lord Moffat said. 'That will mean more delays for a funeral and what not.'

'These labourers are a troublesome lot, but it's all part of being lord of such a vast estate.'

'Quite so.'

Evie was disgusted by what she heard. Glancing at Matthew, she saw he was fuming. He turned his back on the gathering and looked at Evie.

'How dare they speak about their tenants like that!' he whispered through gritted teeth. Evie had never seen him angry before, his brows knotted and his face taut. 'That poor, unfortunate family,' he continued. 'Their child may die and it's *inconvenient* for these blundering . . . Pardon me, Evie, but it's disgraceful to speak of people like, like they're cattle instead of human beings!'

'I totally agree,' Evie said, 'but we can't make a scene. Your father would faint or have a heart attack. Perhaps we should play some more music, something soothing?'

'Good idea,' Matthew said. 'Even if they don't expect it.'

Evie needed something to soothe her feelings too. Her thoughts were whirring, knowing she could save the child with a wish, but that would mean putting off Grace for a third time. But the child's need was greater and more immediate, it was literally life or death. She hoped that waiting another few hours to make the wish later that night wouldn't mean it was too late.

Matthew sat at the grand piano and shuffled through his music sheets, finally selecting something soft and light.

'Mendelsohn,' Evie said, looking over his shoulder. 'Perfect.'

The guests seemed a little surprised when the music started up again, pausing only briefly in their conversations, before resuming them. The gentle, flowing piece was the perfect choice, and simply beautiful. Evie was at her artistic best, while Matthew played minimally to allow her to show off her talent. When they finished, there was an awkward moment of silence, then someone generously cried, 'Bravo!' It was followed by a smattering of clapping mixed with the clinking of glasses. But that word still made Evie flinch, the same word that Thorn used to say to her on that fateful scholarship almost a year ago.

Lord Moffat, however, didn't look altogether pleased at the unexpected change to the programme. Stony-faced, he approached the piano to speak to a trembling Mr Reid.

'I thought you had finished earlier,' Lord Moffat said, in clipped tones. 'But that was – quite nice.'

'Papa, why don't I play a duet with Matthew?' Cecilia said, flouncing over and plonking herself down beside Matthew on the piano stool, causing him to stand up with a start.

'There's plenty of room on this stool for two,' Cecilia said, beaming at him. 'Do sit down, Matthew. Papa and Mama like duets. Cedric and I play together sometimes, so we have always had a double-width piano stool.'

'Perhaps Master Cedric would like to accompany you now?' Matthew said.

'Actually, I would like to play solo,' Cedric said, shouldering his way around Matthew.

'You can play later, Cedric,' Cecilia said sharply. 'I'd like to play something with Matthew first. Can't I, Papa? For Mama's birthday?'

'If you're going to play with – Matthew, is it? – then I shall play *solo* afterwards,' Cedric said. 'I'll play something powerful, Beethoven perhaps, it's my *forte*. You two can play something light and frivolous if you wish.'

'Very well, children,' Lord Moffat said. 'For your Mama.'

Evie noticed Mr Reid giving Matthew a pleading look.

'Whatever Lady Moffat would wish on her birthday,' Matthew said, placatingly.

Everyone turned to the lady of the house as she joined her husband.

'I'd like to hear Cecilia and Matthew play,' Lady Moffat said, beaming at her daughter.

Cedric sighed loudly. 'Very well. I once wished to be a concert pianist, you know, though I never, ever considered being a mere *accompanist*. I'm so glad I didn't take the scholarship with that what's-his-name nobody, Thorn. It would have been such a waste of my time and my talent. Señor Perez, however, my new tutor from Seville –'

'Shall we begin?' Cecilia asked, interrupting her brother. She sat closer to Matthew, too close, as soon as he reluctantly sat down at the piano again.

Matthew played like he didn't want to be there, but somehow, he got through it. He forced a watery smile at the end, stood up quickly, made a short polite bow, then stepped away from the piano to allow Cecilia all the attention she craved. There was rapturous applause for Cecilia, who enjoyed several bows and smiles, which she followed up with a ridiculous twirl and a final deep bow to all the guests.

Cecilia was enjoying so many compliments that she completely forgot about Matthew, and after playing a short sonata on her own, she moved flirtatiously around the room among the guests. Cedric, meanwhile, glowered as he thumped his way through a heavy piece by Beethoven.

'Father,' Matthew whispered. 'Why are we really here? Cedric and Cecilia could have played for the entire evening. They really didn't need us at all.'

Evie had been wondering the same thing.

'Because his lordship requested it, Matthew, and we need his financial support to get the academy up and running,' Mr Reid whispered in reply. 'Lord Moffat is a huge supporter of the arts. It is a great honour that he decided to support us. He could have chosen any number of other projects.'

'I hope he won't interfere in the running of things,' Matthew said. 'Cedric and Cecilia are able to wrap him around their little fingers, Cecilia especially. Heaven knows what ridiculous plans she might have for our academy.'

'They are a precocious pair, I agree – vain, rude and lacking in any real talent,' Mr Reid whispered. 'But we will remain polite and patient as always, and get through the evening, having made a very good impression on everyone. With a bit of luck, his lordship will leave us alone to do our work, at least most of the time.'

The evening passed without further incident, and it was late when they finally left. Playing music was always a pleasure for Evie, and for Matthew too, she was sure. But on the way home, she could see that Matthew was tiring of his father's justifications as to why they should be tolerant of the Moffats – all of them, and anyone like them.

'Some of our future students will be demanding too, you know,' Mr Reid said. 'We must learn to be forever tolerant and patient, and to treat everyone with respect. Give each student the attention they need to become the best musician they can be. They must enjoy coming to their lessons or they won't come at all!'

'I understand all that and I agree,' Matthew said. 'Thankfully, I don't expect the Moffats to be wanting any lessons. I just think their behaviour is abominable and I'd rather be as far away from them as possible.'

'Yes, well, leave them to me,' Mr Reid said. 'Thank goodness the evening went well and seemed to be enjoyed by everyone.'

'Of course, and if it helps the academy then I'm glad we were asked,' Matthew said, calming down. 'In fact, I think we play very well together, Evie.'

Evie blushed. 'I enjoyed it too, very much, and um, and playing with you.'

'You both played beautifully,' Mr Reid said.

'Did Lord and Lady Moffat actually *say* they were pleased?' Matthew asked.

'Oh eh, yes, I think they were delighted,' Mr Reid said. 'But you know the gentry, they ration their compliments and their appreciation.'

'That's absolutely fine,' Matthew said. 'We don't want them asking us every year, do we?'

Evie couldn't hold back a giggle, then Matthew and his father joined in.

'Goodness me, they are quite a family!' Mr Reid said. 'Thank you both for putting up with their nonsense. I promise, you can leave all the bowing and scraping to me.'

'Oh, we will!' Matthew said, winking at Evie.

As Mr Reid chatted with Matthew about the academy and their plans, Evie's thoughts turned to her next task: to make a wish under the full moon to heal the injured child. There was no doubt that this was a dire need and she dearly hoped she wasn't too late to save the child. Afterwards she would play the four pieces of music for step four on the Ladder of Charms. It had taken an enormous amount of practice, but she had finally learned each piece by heart. Already, she could feel her excitement building, eager to know what secret or instruction would be revealed this time. It was going to be a very long night and a lot was at stake.

Chapter Ten

Matthew walked Evie to her hall door and said goodnight. Hudson let her in; everyone else had gone to bed. Evie wanted to head back out and make the wish immediately, but first she went to check on Julia.

As expected, her governess was still awake. Julia always tried to stay awake the night of a full moon until Evie returned home after the ritual. Evie told her quickly about the Moffats' party, then helped herself to more parchment from Julia's writing desk. Evie paused before she wrote the new wish, disappointed once again that she had to postpone helping her friend. In front of Julia, Evie wrote down her wish for the injured child she had heard about at the party.

'I know it's disappointing,' Julia said, 'but you are doing the right thing.'

'At least Grace doesn't know I could have helped her tonight, and then didn't,' Evie said.

'You will next month,' Julia said. 'And it won't be too late for Grace.'

Evie nodded meekly and said goodnight. As she passed Freddie's room, she thought she saw light seeping out from under the door. She stopped and peeped in. He was sitting on his bed reading by candlelight.

'Can't you sleep?' Evie whispered.

'No, I'm coming with you,' Freddie said. 'You need a lookout.'

Yes, I probably do, Evie thought. 'It will take a bit longer tonight,' she said. 'Are you sure you want to come?'

'Very sure,' Freddie said. 'What's different about tonight?'

'I have to play four charm pieces to complete step four,' Evie said. 'They're quite tricky and I mustn't make a mistake.'

'What will happen after you play them?' Freddie asked.

'I only know that the charm will be revealed when I'm finished,' Evie said. 'It could be a secret, some information or another instruction to do something. I never know for sure in advance.'

'And the wish?' Freddie asked.

Evie briefly mentioned what had happened at the party then held out the piece of parchment. Freddie took it and read it.

'Wow! It was lucky you heard about this accident at all!' he said.

'Very lucky,' Evie said. 'I'd like to go right away.'

'I'm ready,' Freddie said, putting his book away.

'I'll go and change,' Evie said. 'Once we're sure Hudson has gone to bed, we'll head out.'

The practice took a while. Evie had a few problems with part of the second piece and wanted to make sure she had it right before starting the ritual. Then they had to wait for the moon to be clear of all traces of cloud. It took well over an hour and a half before she could make the wish for the injured child, and then follow it with the four pieces of music for the fourth charm. But Evie was glad of Freddie's company, and he stayed alert for any unwelcome sounds or sightings the whole time. She began to wonder if perhaps Freddie should always accompany her, make it a permanent arrangement.

With great relief, Evie accomplished her task. Now it was time to burn the parchment to seal the fourth charm. She had written the first line of music from each piece she had to play on a second page of parchment, as instructed in Nala's notebook. Placing the parchment on the reducing flames, she felt excited and a little nervous.

'You'll find out the next secret now,' Freddie said, sounding very excited too.

'I hope I like it,' Evie said.

They watched the parchment shrink into its final curls, blacken and burn to ash, then disappear into the embers. The fire went instantly out, leaving only a tiny wisp of white smoke rising straight as a needle into the night sky before disappearing.

'Is that it?' Freddie whispered.

'That's it,' Evie said. Then, 'Oh! Oh!' She felt a little sting in her fingertips, then more stings, lots more, like a million tiny bees were jabbing her. Lifting her hands, she turned them over and back to look. She stared at her fingertips, curious, baffled, feeling like she wanted to run away from this invisible, stinging swarm of miniature bees, but there wasn't any swarm. There were no bees. There was nothing to see at all.

'What is it?' Freddie asked.

'My fingers feel so strange,' Evie said. 'They were stinging, all of them, now they're throbbing, and they feel really hot.'

'Maybe that's a good thing,' Freddie said.

'Really?' Evie said.

'Oh, wow!' Freddie cried.

'What – is – this?' Evie gasped. 'What's happening?'

As well as the throbbing and the heat, a glow began to radiate from each of Evie's fingertips.

'Oh no,' Evie said. 'The stinging is back, but it's different. It's, it's spreading up my arms, everywhere. Something must be inside me. What is it?'

The look of puzzlement on Freddie's face didn't help Evie to feel any less concerned. Then suddenly Evie stiffened from head to toe and keeled over onto the grass as the tingling sensation surged through her entire body.

She lay there dazed and confused, Freddie's voice suddenly sounding remote.

'Evie, Evie, wake up!' he cried.

Evie turned her head slowly to look at him, feeling very disorientated.

'Evie!'

She looked down at her left arm. Yes, it was moving, but she wasn't moving it. She blinked a few times, trying to focus. Her arm. Yes, she felt something. Oh! It was Freddie. Freddie was shaking her arm. *He's here, he's beside me. He's not far away at all.*

'Oh!' she cried, sitting up with a start.

'Evie, what happened?' Freddie asked.

'It's all right. I'm back, I think,' Evie said. 'That was so strange.'

'What was? What do you mean, "back"?' Freddie asked.

'I'm not sure,' Evie said. She reached for the notebook and

turned the pages to see the next revelation. 'There's nothing here, nothing at all.'

'But your fingers were glowing,' Freddie said. 'And stinging. And you fell over, stiff as a pole!'

'So very strange,' Evie mumbled.

'Maybe that's the message,' Freddie said.

'What possible message could this be?' Evie asked, holding her hands up.

'I don't know, but I'm sure you'll find out soon,' Freddie said.

Evie didn't like to say because she wasn't sure. Then she felt she knew. She had magic inside her now. Perhaps it was only a little. Perhaps the magic would come to her gradually, a little bit with each step from now on. But something about her was different, she could feel it, and though she couldn't quite understand it yet, she thought she liked it.

CHAPTER ELEVEN

Evie's mother was very down. She would sit in the parlour listening to Evie play her favourite pieces, then retire quietly to her bedroom looking sad and tired. Evie was at a loss as to what to do. In contrast, she saw improvement in her father's condition, though Professor Wells was now worrying about Mrs Wells and thinking less about his own difficulties. His walking was still stiff but more stable. His hands and fingers ached but weren't too bad, and his speech was back to normal. Aches and pains were a problem, but only because he was trying so hard to be well.

Freddie joined Evie in her father's bedroom where they had been playing chess.

'We're having a family meeting in the parlour before lunch today,' Evie's father said.

Evie was surprised. 'Is anything wrong?' she asked.

'Is it good news?' Freddie asked.

'You'll hear all about it at the meeting,' Evie's father said.

'Are you able to come down the stairs?' Evie asked.

'Oh, yes! I've been practising with Hudson,' her father said. 'I want to dress fully today after my exercises. I've had enough of all this lounging around in bed.'

Evie and Freddie left the room, passing Hudson and the

day nurse on the way in, punctual as ever for the professor's mid-morning exercises. Julia joined the family in the parlour for the meeting, and the news was indeed a surprise.

'Mrs Wells and I have decided to enrol Freddie at an excellent boarding school,' Evie's father said. 'In fact, it is the same one Matthew Reid attended.'

Evie was shocked. Freddie looked bewildered and Julia disappointed.

'But why?' Evie blurted out. 'He's doing perfectly well here with Julia.'

'Very well indeed,' Evie's father said. 'But it's better for boys to attend school with other boys as they grow up rather than being stuck in the house all the time. I think you'll enjoy it, Freddie. It's a very good school. You'll make a lot of new friends. What do you say?'

'I don't know, Uncle Henry,' Freddie said. 'I've never been away to school before. What's it like?'

'Wonderful fun,' Evie's father said. 'It was for me, and you can ask Matthew about it too. He seems to have enjoyed it very much.'

'When will he start?' Evie asked.

'We haven't decided yet,' Evie's mother said. Everyone looked at her, surprised she had spoken at all. 'Your father and I haven't agreed if it will be this coming September or when Freddie turns thirteen, when he would begin secondary school.'

'Not this September, please, it's too soon,' Evie cried. 'Surely when he is thirteen would be soon enough.'

'Evie, it's your parents' decision, not yours,' Julia said quietly, but firmly.

'We haven't made a final decision,' Evie's father said, 'but it's good to have his name on the list. We will talk about it with Freddie, of course, and with you all. I was hoping to visit the school with Freddie over the summer, but we'll have to see if I'm up to it. The headmaster said he won't mind if Freddie joins a little later in September, if necessary.'

'It would be better if he started with all the other boys,' Julia said. 'From an educational point of view, that is.'

'Yes,' Evie said. 'And I need him here, um, we all do at the moment.'

Evie squirmed under her father's enquiring look. 'We have to accept our new circumstances, Evie,' he said. 'Your mother is feeling rather delicate, and I have my own challenges to overcome. We must ensure that Freddie has the best education possible so he will grow into a fine young man. Julia is looking after you very well, but Freddie must have his chance too.'

'I understand,' Evie said impatiently, 'but –'

'Your mother and I will discuss it, then we will have another family talk,' Evie's father said, casting Mrs Wells a doubtful glance. 'Nothing is definite yet. We just wanted you to know what we were thinking.'

Evie's mother went straight back to her bedroom. Evie thought of following her to talk her round, but Julia motioned her not to. Deep down, Evie knew her governess was right. Mrs Wells wasn't well enough for any arguing and Evie was clearly rattled by the news. She would have to pick the right moment to talk to her father about it, let alone upset her mother. She retreated to the garden to stroll and think. Just when she thought Freddie could be more involved, he was about to be sent away. It was a great opportunity for him, of course it was, but she had never seen this coming.

Both Evie's parents had lunch in their bedrooms. Lunch in the dining room for everyone else was unusually quiet until Freddie burst out with a pile of questions.

'What's boarding school like? How many boys will be there? Will I do sport as well as studies? Can I go riding? What else happens at boarding school? How often can I come home?'

Julia answered his questions as best she could, but Freddie always had more. Evie didn't speak for a long time.

'Uncle Henry will have all the details for you soon,' Julia said. 'You can ask Matthew about it too. He's just finished six years there.'

Freddie turned to Evie. 'I'd prefer to stay here and help you, until, you know, the mission is over. Then I could go. But we can't explain that to Uncle Henry, can we?'

Mr Hudson entered the room.

'Miss Evie, your father wishes to speak with you upstairs after luncheon,' he said.

'Thank you, Hudson,' Evie said.

'And he asked that you bring the notebook.'

Evie stared at the butler as he turned and left the room. Nala's notebook. She had hoped her father might have forgotten about it. No chance.

'Evie. Evie!'

'Sorry, Julia, I was just thinking,' Evie said.

'Listen to what your father has to say about the school before bamboozling him,' Julia said. 'He wants to do his best for Freddie, though I believe I can manage his tutoring perfectly well until he is thirteen, and I shall tell him so when I get the right opportunity.'

'I know you can,' Evie said, distractedly, suspecting that wasn't the only thing her father wanted to talk about.

Evie knocked on her father's bedroom door and entered, relieved to see him smile at her. She sat on a chair beside the bed.

'I'm sorry that announcement took everyone by surprise,' Evie's father said. 'I really didn't think it would. Although I am improving, thank goodness, I want to ensure Freddie has a good education and plenty of activities to make up for all that he has lost. With my new restrictions, I cannot be as actively involved with Freddie's development as I would like.'

'I understand,' Evie said. 'But you are making progress. It won't be long now before you're back to your old self. It's just, well, this September is so soon. Can't he wait until he's thirteen, when he would be starting secondary school anyway? It's only just over a year and a half away.'

Her father thought a moment.

'Perhaps you're right,' he said. 'I suppose I didn't think of what his absence might mean to you quite as much as I should have. I'll write to the headmaster again this afternoon and ask his opinion. Did you bring the notebook?'

Evie handed it to him.

Her father took it and opened it again. He looked up, surprised.

'There are notes and music in it,' he said, perplexed. 'I thought it was empty before. Did you write this?'

'Um, sort of, um, yes,' Evie mumbled, swallowing uncomfortably.

'You realise this is an ancient artefact, and yet you wrote in it?' her father said.

'I, um, it didn't do any damage – did it?' Evie mumbled again.

Her father stared at her. 'I thought you would know better, Evie. You have to handle ancient things so carefully. Writing on them is really out of the question!'

'Sorry, I should have thought . . .' Evie said, unable to explain to her father how the diary wrote itself. 'I love that diary. I wanted to make it my own. Lucia said it belonged with the harp, and that music is for the harp, and, and –'

'It's very artistic, very decorative writing and music,' her father said. 'Perhaps you are an artist as well as a musician.'

'Hmm, maybe,' Evie said, trying to only half-lie rather than tell a complete untruth.

'Well, there's no point in sending it to the museum now,' her father said. 'They would be horrified. But it belongs with the harp, you say. Why, that makes it nearly four hundred years old! And you're right, it doesn't look damaged by the new ink. Is that really new ink? It looks rather like an ancient mix.' He peered closer at the musical notes and staves, Evie hoping fervently that he wouldn't turn any more pages or ask her to fetch his magnifying glass.

'It's my, um, calligraphy quill and ink,' Evie said. 'I thought it looked nice on the old parchment.'

'My dear, you really should have checked with me first,' her father said. 'Never mind, there doesn't appear to be any damage. Very lucky. Pure magic, I'd say!'

Evie gulped.

'Are you all right, dear?' Evie's father asked. 'I didn't

mean to shout at you, but this is a delicate thing, or rather, it should be. It really is remarkably robust.' He frowned at the notebook.

'Who was it that told you I had the notebook?' Evie asked.

'Ah, yes. That surprised you, didn't it? It was Jimmy,' her father said, still frowning at the cover.

'Jimmy, our stable boy?' Evie said, surprised.

'Yes. No, I mean his cousin,' her father said. 'He's a stable boy in Crompton. A cheeky fellow if I remember rightly. He saw Mr McGinn give it to you, told Jimmy, who told Hudson, who told me.'

'Oh, I see,' Evie said. She needed to change the subject quickly. 'Um, Father, do you remember you were going to tell me a story, something you came across a few weeks ago? You said I would enjoy it, like the old stories you used to tell me when I was little.'

'Yes, I do remember,' her father said. 'Pass me that book from the dresser, dear. It's all about talismans, which are in fact artefacts – that is, important ancient objects. However, talismans are *magical* artefacts, and that difference is important.'

'I know, I mean, I remember you telling me before,' Evie said.

'Did I? Oh! Good,' her father said. 'Well now, you are going to love this!'

CHAPTER TWELVE

Evie's father had asked Hudson to bring more books up to his bedroom from the study. Evie took one of those books from the top of a pile in the corner of the room and handed it to her father.

'Thank you, dear. I suspect you have looked at the great *Almanac* already,' he said.

'I couldn't resist,' Evie said. 'The drawings are beautiful and there are excellent descriptions too.'

'Indeed,' her father said. 'It's an enormous weight so we'll look at it properly in the study. This little book here has intrigued me for years.'

'It has no cover,' Evie said.

'It's such a shame but that's how I found it,' her father said. He turned the pages of the book in his hands. 'I came across this particular story on a number of occasions. It kept popping up, but the first time was on one of my early trips to Mesopotamia with the museum. Unfortunately, I couldn't give it the time it deserved, as I was involved in other research.'

Evie nodded, remembering his stories from the ancient territory with the strange-sounding name.

'There were a number of junior scholars on that trip,' her

father continued. 'Each of them keen as mustard, competitive too, vying with each other to make a notable discovery. All of them were carrying far too many books in the oppressive heat.'

Evie was all ears.

'We were examining the trail of a particular demon lord from ancient times – Vodor, I think. No. Volok. Yes, that was it. His name sounds almost as scary as the stories told about him. Ha!'

Evie nearly choked on her own breath.

'Are you all right, my dear?'

'Just a tickle in my throat, it's nothing,' Evie said.

'Apparently he was a terrifying demon, on this earth to wreak havoc and build an empire, or so the story goes. I suspected that at least part of the story was based on some violent brute who was terrorising the area, but everyone else dismissed it as nonsense. I was hooked, however, and determined to follow it up as soon as I got the chance.'

Evie managed to stifle a groan.

'Apparently this Volok was obsessed with collecting the five primary talismans. These objects were revered throughout history, Evie, believed by some to be powerful *magical* artefacts, and by others as important examples of ancient art and craftsmanship. Volok collected such items, and he wanted these particular talismans desperately, no doubt to help him do his dreadful deeds. But the important thing is that these five primary talismans were found, lost, found, and lost again. A few historians like myself have been convinced that if they are found again, they should be put safely where they belong – in a museum. For some, it has been an obsession, a lifetime's work to find them. Each of the five is considered priceless, a tremendous find for any historian or archaeologist – if only they could be found.'

Evie almost melted.

'I thought you would be more excited, dear,' her father said.

'Oh, I am!' Evie said. 'I'm dying to hear more.'

'Good. Well, as we know, people with all sorts of intentions chase after such objects, but only one of the five primary talismans has been found in modern times, and only very recently.'

'Oh? Which one?' Evie asked.

'The goblet, Galen's Goblet to use its proper name,' her father said. 'According to legend, several copies of the goblet were made to fool thieves, but only the real one has a small opal studded into the base of the cup.'

Evie hadn't noticed an opal on the goblet Simeon had taken out of the crate, but it had been hard to see in the dim light of the cave.

'Where is the goblet now?' Evie said.

'In our museum,' her father said, beaming with pride. 'My friend Howard Carter unearthed it a couple of years ago. It took a long time to persuade the Egyptians to allow it out of the country, and only with a promise to return it at some point. I still haven't seen it. It arrived just when I fell ill, and I was so looking forward to examining it. Hopefully soon, though, when I'm a little more mobile.'

Evie's mind was spinning. She would have to go to the cave as soon as possible to see if Volok had the real one, or if the real one was in the museum like her father said. And if the real one was in the museum, how on earth would she take it out? This time it really would be stealing. Evie shivered. She would actually have to commit a serious crime in order to retrieve it. But it couldn't be helped. She had to destroy the *real* talismans, not fakes. Suddenly, she felt like laughing. How shocked would her father be if he knew her plans? And where oh where were the remaining three talismans?

'Evie, dear, are you sure you're feeling well?' her father asked. 'You seem very out of sorts today.'

'Sorry, no. I'm fine. I was just thinking about what you said,' Evie said.

'Yes?'

'Would it be possible for me to see Galen's Goblet?' Evie asked. 'It would be so exciting to see such an important find. Freddie would love it too. He hasn't been to the museum yet, and I haven't been there for ages.'

'I was hoping to bring you both over the summer,' her father said. 'But then my health suffered and now I have all this resting to do.' He shook his head in despair. 'And all this catching up on my work to do too.'

'The more you rest, the quicker you will recover,' Evie said.

'As I am repeatedly reminded,' her father said. 'It's really not the same trying to work from this bed.'

'Julia and I could take Freddie the first time,' Evie said, hoping her father wouldn't want them to wait until he could go. 'It would be a nice day out. I would ask Grace to come too, but she's having an eye operation and will be confined to her home for a few weeks afterwards. You could take us again when she's well enough to come and introduce Freddie to some of those eccentric friends of yours. He'd be thrilled.'

'Not a bad idea,' her father said. 'Yes, Mr Finch told me about Grace's operation, most unfortunate.'

'Then it's settled,' Evie said. 'Julia and I will take Freddie to the museum soon, and you can come with us as soon as you feel able. And Grace too.'

Evie smiled uncomfortably as her father eyed her a little suspiciously. *He really is so clever*, she thought, and changed the subject.

'What about the rest of that story?'

'Where was I?' her father said. 'Ah yes, I wrote a lot of notes on that trip to Mesopotamia and on every trip since, come to think of it.' He reached for another small, well-worn book on the bed quilt. 'Ancient history is full of tales of magic, prophecies and superstitions. Whether you believe them or not is up to you. As an historian I must weed out the fact from the fiction, so I like to check out everything *very* carefully – unlike some people. I have always believed that those primary talismans were tied to some particular purpose, a ritual, probably something nasty, but very important to ancient people, nonetheless. So far, I have not been able to discover what that might be. And out of that, my dear, came the myth about the dreadful demon, Volok.'

Evie felt jittery, somewhere in between excited and very nervous.

'Goodness! Was it really that long ago?' her father muttered, as he read over some of his old notes. He read some more, frowning as he went. He stopped, snapping the book closed, and picked up Nala's notebook. He flicked through the early pages. 'Of course! That's it!'

'What is?' Evie asked, a little worried.

He turned to her, excitement in his eyes.

'One of the students at the museum asked me about it a few months ago,' her father said. 'You remember Edward Hill, don't you? I've mentioned him before. He's an enthusiastic student and a good researcher, happy to put in extra hours.'

'Extra hours for what?' Evie asked.

'Doing research, my dear,' her father said. 'Research on the story of the Harp Maiden.'

Evie nearly fainted. 'The wha-aa-at?'

'The same words are written in the opening pages of your notebook,' her father said. He pointed. 'Look! No wonder it belongs with the harp, when it says "Harp Maiden" on the very first page!'

Evie sat staring at her father, unable to speak. Luckily, he put down Nala's notebook and began flicking through his own notes again.

'Edward was fascinated by that story and spent a lot of personal time delving into it,' her father continued. 'He was going to tell me what he had found when I had this silly stroke. I knew it rang a bell when I saw your notebook the first time. I must ask him more about it. You'd like to know about it too, wouldn't you, dear? It might tell you more about your notebook and your harp.'

This was way too close for comfort for Evie. She needed an escape. 'Yes, um, that would be lovely, but you must be tired now, Father. I'll leave you to rest a while. I have some music practice to do.'

'Oh, already?' he said.

'Yes, you need to rest,' Evie said, 'and I must arrange that visit to the museum too.'

'Very well,' her father said. 'I'll write to Edward and tell him to expect you soon. Let me know what day suits after you check with Julia. I hope she'll be well enough to accompany you. Edward will show you around and tell you all about the museum's latest findings and displays. You can ask him about the Harp Maiden story too. He'll be delighted!'

Evie left the room startled, but with another plan beginning to hatch in her brain.

CHAPTER THIRTEEN

Very early the next day, Evie left the house quietly and unnoticed. She had already told Julia her plan the night before, which no doubt condemned her governess to a sleepless night, but it couldn't be helped.

Freddie was already waiting for her in the stable, the horses ready. He stuffed a piece of cold toast into his mouth.

'Was Miss Julia cross?' he mumbled, munching.

'More worried than cross,' Evie said. 'Have you got something to carry the talismans if we find them?'

Freddie pointed to a sack on the ground. 'I'll stuff it inside my jacket.'

'Make sure it doesn't fall out,' Evie said.

'Don't worry, I will,' Freddie said. 'Do you think we'll find them all?'

'I really hope so,' Evie said. 'Are we all set?'

Freddie nodded, they mounted the horses – Evie wearing her new jodhpurs at last – and they headed off to the green cave.

Evie decided they would leave the horses in a different spot, well out of sight, then continue on foot along the top of the gorge before climbing down to the stony pathway that led to the green cave. For a change, she was hoping Volok would be there. He was, but he seemed preoccupied.

'What do we do now?' Freddie whispered, as they crouched outside.

'We watch for a little while,' Evie said. 'If we're lucky, we'll spot the goblet and be able to make out if it's the real one or not.'

'That could take ages,' Freddie said. 'What about the snakes?'

'There's no reason for them to strike while Volok is in there and we're out here.'

Freddie looked at her doubtfully.

'I know,' Evie said. 'It's always like this: keep your fingers crossed and hope, and then hope some more.'

'Then maybe that's enough,' Freddie said, shrugging his shoulders.

Simeon was in the cave too, sitting quietly on a boulder to one side. Volok stood over the pit of snakes. He stared down with eyes that glowed bright yellow, their glow bathing the pit in two beams of yellow light. He waved a huge hand in wide sweeping gestures, mumbling all the while. Another spell, Evie thought, wondering how many he could do and what this one was about. There was a tremendous hiss and the asps appeared, hundreds of them standing up in a ring around the edge of the pit like a black curtain. They parted to allow Volok retrieve what he wanted.

'Soon you will know just how powerful I am,' Volok said, glancing at Simeon. 'Especially when you see me bring my queen back from the dead.' He dumped a selection of items beside where he stood and began to rummage through them.

Simeon whimpered something inaudible. Freddie pointed.

Evie followed his direction with her eyes and saw that Simeon's knees were bobbing up and down and his feet were tapping the ground.

'He's terrified,' Freddie mouthed.

Evie nodded. *And well he might be*, she thought. *Volok won't tolerate him for long.*

'What's that awful smell?' Freddie mouthed, wrinkling his nose.

Evie sniffed, leaning forward to catch the odour, then she nearly sneezed, quickly clasping her hand over her mouth and nose to stifle it. Luckily the snakes were hissing loudly as they retreated down the pit, their noise disguising any snorting sounds Evie made as she tried to calm her nose.

'It's coming from Simeon,' Evie whispered in Freddie's ear. 'It's disgusting.' She continued pinching her nose, afraid of a loud sneeze.

Then Simeon spoke. 'I always knew magic was real,' he said meekly. 'And why have any kind of magic but the darkest type? Heh heh! Bringing people back from the dead – heh, how clever!' He laughed a silly, squeaky laugh.

'Not *people*,' Volok said, 'a pure, black-blooded demon, my wife and queen. Do not speak of her again. Watch, listen, and above all, remember.'

Simeon gulped and nodded vigorously.

Volok lifted each primary talisman high, naming and explaining each one.

'This is Galen's Goblet, for my beloved to drink from the spring of life,' he announced with unusual formality.

Evie cringed at the thought that the gloopy, green pool could really be a 'spring of life'. Drinking from that stinking goo would be utterly revolting.

'Portia's Plate,' Volok said, holding it up, 'for when she will take her first meal. Marielle's Mirror, so she may see proof that she is whole again, to watch as her beauty returns, and most importantly, to see visions of her future. And Xavier's Stone, the most ancient talisman I own. It will store my queen's magic until she is strong enough to wield each of her powers again.'

Evie stared at the goblet. Was it the real one? Did Volok even know there were fakes? She couldn't see any opal, not at that angle and distance. She would have to get closer or hope that Volok would turn it over so she could see for sure. Either option would mean going into the cave. And a mirror to see the future! If only she could use it now.

'And finally,' Volok continued, as he rummaged in the pile at his feet, firing unwanted objects behind him as he searched. 'The dagger. Where is it? WHERE IS IT?'

He turned around and glared at Simeon, who gulped again.

'I, I don't have it, my lord,' he squeaked. 'I haven't seen any of those items before.'

Volok's nostrils flared, and his eyes turned momentarily bright orange.

'I need that knife to draw blood,' he said.

Simeon began to shake uncontrollably.

'She must drink a potion made from my blood once she returns,' Volok continued. 'It is an important part of the ritual.' He approached his trembling servant.

'I need that KNIFE!' he roared into Simeon's face, and was about to wallop him with his fist, but he paused, sweating, causing another bad smell to waft through the cave and drift out onto the breeze. He lowered his arm. 'There can be no more delays,' Volok said quietly but fiercely. 'I have worked long and hard for this. I want to give my wife a taste of what is to come. Her form will only be ghostlike at first, but so much better than just a beating heart in a green pool.' He stared at the pool for a moment, then returned his gaze to Simeon. 'You,' – he pointed a huge, long-nailed finger at Simeon – 'you will find the Dagger of Dower and the Black Ruby and bring them to me. I must attend to the preparations for her return without further interruption. Go! Now! Olga said she had the dagger, so it must be here or in the other cave. Search until you find it. She had the ruby too, but she lost that as well! Bah! Aaaagghhhhh! Be quick, Simeon, or I will not be pleased.'

'Yes, my lord.'

Simeon scurried out of the cave, passing perilously close to the pit. A few snakes rose up and hissed at him but recoiled quickly. He squealed like a pig and Volok laughed.

'I told you,' he roared after him. 'That herbal paste I gave you will keep the snakes at bay. They don't like your new stink!'

Evie and Freddie ducked as Simeon hurried by, almost tripping over them as he dared to look behind, unsure whether Volok was joking about the snakes or not.

Evie looked at Freddie. They both knew they had to get closer. Freddie nodded and Evie led the way, crawling slowly, steadily around the mouth of the cave. She remembered where the best hiding places were and headed for the last big boulder sitting just outside the entrance. Freddie tucked in beside her.

Volok had moved over to the green pool. It was surrounded by mounds of pungent herbs and a collection of flora and fauna that Evie couldn't quite make out. Peeping around the boulders, Evie and Freddie could also see a row of small, glass bottles, full of either a black or a green liquid. Beside the bottles lay another array of talismans, some of which she had seen in her father's library book, as well as four of the five primaries – though Evie still couldn't be sure if the goblet was the real one.

Volok sat beside the pool and closed his eyes. He folded his hands and sat there humming for a full ten minutes. Evie and Freddie were getting anxious and uncomfortable by the time Volok finally moved. He took a deep breath through his nose, stretching his nostrils wide, then he let out a long groaning sigh. Kneeling over the green pool he began a strange incantation, his muscular arms held high.

Bubbles appeared in the thick green water, small and few at first. Then Volok started adding the ingredients from all around him: the herbs, the flora and fauna, as well as the strange liquids from the bottles, one after the other. The bubbling increased steadily until the water was almost spilling over. It looked thicker, sticky and slimy. Volok reached for the smaller talismans. Evie couldn't make them out in his huge hands – some appeared to be made of wood, others of pottery or glass.

Volok chanted briefly over each one, invoking whatever power or benefit it had, before tossing it into the green pool. Within seconds, the smaller talismans were spurted up on a jet of green water before being sucked back down and swallowed by the pool. The primary talismans, however, were ejected out of the green water, each one landing safely nearby. They would be needed again as Volok had said once Madruga returned.

Evie tried to remember where each one had fallen, not wanting to waste time if she got the chance to snatch them.

'The first stage has begun, my love,' Volok said into the pool. 'You have accepted my gifts and you have seen four of the five primaries. The fifth will be here soon, as will the Black Ruby. Be patient, my love. Your heart will soon be joined to the rest of your body, and we will reign together again, forever invincible.'

Volok stood up without taking his eyes off the steaming green bubbles as they slowly subsided, then the pool was still. He stomped out of the cave, his broad face thoughtful. Once outside, he broke into a run.

Evie couldn't believe their luck.

'Quick!' she said to Freddie. 'Grab the plate and the mirror, and I'll get the stone and check the goblet.'

'I'm glad that mirror is small,' Freddie said. 'It even has a handle!'

'Yes, thank goodness,' Evie said. 'Quickly, now.'

They ran inside. Freddie gathered the plate and the mirror which had both landed a little further inside the cave. The smooth stone had rolled around, stopping at the edge of the green pool. The goblet had bounced and rolled slightly further to the side. Evie reached down for the stone and grabbed it, then she froze. Something was rising out of the murky green pool.

CHAPTER FOURTEEN

Madruga's shadowy form was secured by a twisting string of green slime anchored to the depths of the green pool somehow, making it impossible for her to escape, for the moment. In a flash, Evie remembered only too clearly when Volok had been attached to the harp in a similar way. The demon queen shuddered and swayed then collapsed back into the pool, her gurgling cries disappearing into the pool.

Recovering her composure, Evie spotted the goblet and ran over to pick it up. She turned it upside down but there was no opal set into the base, not even a dent where it might have been.

'It's the wrong goblet,' Evie said. 'Volok mustn't know there are fakes, or he would never have risked throwing the wrong one into the pool. But Madruga might have sensed it, and she will tell him as soon as she comes out of the pool again.'

'If she can talk,' Freddie said. 'But we should take it anyway, even if it's the wrong goblet.'

'You're right,' Evie said. 'All these things belong in a museum, not with demons.'

'We can give them to Uncle Henry,' Freddie said. 'Tell

him we found them, because we did.'

'Maybe we could do it anonymously, just leave them outside the house,' Evie said.

Freddie looked doubtful.

'If we hand them over, he'll ask us where we found them,' Evie said.

'And then he'll send a team of excavators to look for more,' Freddie said.

'Exactly,' Evie said.

'I guess it's another secret, then,' Freddie said.

'Come on,' Evie said. 'We should go.'

They took the four talismans and shoved them into the sack Freddie had brought. But as they turned to leave, their way out of the cave was barred. Hundreds of asps had silently left the pit. In all the excitement about the talismans, Evie and Freddie had forgotten about them. Quite ridiculously, Evie wondered why they hadn't come out of the pit sooner. Perhaps they were trying to trap them inside the cave.

Neither Evie nor Freddie moved an inch. One asp slithered closer, hissing, baring its fangs. Another followed, then another. The leaders were larger than the rest, with long, curved yellow fangs, the same yellow as Volok's eyes. More heads popped up from the pit. Suddenly there was another swarm gathering behind the first swarm, then a third line rose up, all jostling for position, pushing each other forward, their hissing loud and menacing.

'F-Freddie,' Evie said. 'They're getting ready to attack.'

'Mm-mm,' Freddie muttered. 'I kno-o-ow.'

'Walk very slowly towards me and around me,' Evie said, 'and leave.'

'I'm not leaving you with them!' Freddie said.

'Go. Now!' Evie said with a strange calmness she didn't understand, given the circumstances.

'No way!' Freddie cried. 'We should turn and run. Like this!'

Freddie snatched Evie's arm, pulling her right along the wall of the cave, scraping both their hands and elbows. They scrambled up and over boulders, heading towards the way out. But Evie shook herself free of his grip and stopped. She turned back, focusing on the huge swarm slithering towards her, dozens of asps rising aggressively, others keeping low, but together they moved like a shiny black tidal wave preparing to strike.

Behind her Freddie screamed. 'Evie! No! We have to run!'

Evie closed her eyes, suddenly feeling incredibly composed. She began to hum a little tune she didn't know she knew. Far away in the back of her mind she wondered why she was doing that as there were hundreds of deadly snakes about to attack. The snakes surrounded her, touching her clothes, slithering over her shoulders and around her neck. Soon, she was completely hidden from Freddie's view.

Opening her eyes suddenly, Evie flung her hands into the air, knocking several snakes off with the movement. She began to move her fingers in the air and they began to glow. She held her position for another moment, still humming, her eyes half open, half closed, and slowly the asps retreated into the pit.

There was a moment of silence, until Freddie broke it.

'Wow!' he gasped. 'You did it! I mean, you did something!'

He ran to her, grabbing her arm again as she slumped to the ground.

'What just happened?' Evie asked.

'You used magic! You saved us!' Freddie said, excited. He leaned over her, then glanced back at the pit to make sure.

'What? That's impossible,' Evie muttered. 'I can't do magic, can I?'

'You have to get up,' Freddie said, pulling her arm. 'We have to go before Volok comes back or the snakes change their minds, or both.'

'Magic,' Evie mumbled. 'Nala was weak after using magic.' She looked vacantly at Freddie. Something in her head was telling her to get up and get moving, but she felt so tired.

'That was when she was in the casket,' Freddie said, as he helped her to stand up. Evie did her best, but their progress was worryingly slow.

'Please, try harder,' Freddie said. 'You can rest when we reach the horses.'

'I'll be fine,' Evie said, as she stumbled along.

Somehow, Freddie managed to hold on to the four talismans in the sack – three plus the fake goblet – as well as Evie, and eventually they reached the copse where the horses were waiting.

Evie slumped to the ground, breathless. 'I'm not sure I can move another inch,' she gasped.

'You're not used to using magic, that's all,' Freddie said.

'I think I might be too weak to ride,' Evie said. 'I hope it doesn't always feel like this. Oh dear! Oh no!' She swooned.

'It was that last charm,' Freddie said. 'The night of the full moon. It must have given you magic after you finished step four. Remember, when your fingers glowed the first time?'

'Maybe. I don't know,' Evie said, trying to sit up. 'Something has made me feel really awful.' She slumped back onto the bracken again. 'I hope this wooziness will pass quickly.'

'It must be magic, your fingers are glowing again,' Freddie said.

'Really? Oh! Don't worry,' Evie muttered. 'I'm sure it will pass in a moment, I'll be fine. Really. I just need to rest for a few minutes, just a few minsss . . .'

Then Evie lost consciousness.

Chapter Fifteen

Someone was shaking her arm. Opening her eyes, Evie saw two blurry faces.

'Oh! What? Who are you?' she cried.

'It's all right, Evie,' Freddie said, coming into focus. 'I've got Danny with me. Danny McGinn. You remember, Charlie's son. He's going to help us.'

'I . . . oh!' Evie tried to sit up, but her hands landed on the talismans in the sack beside her, then her head spun, and she fell back again.

'Stay still,' Freddie said.

'How long have I been like this?' Evie asked, placing one hand on her brow. Her head was pounding.

'About half an hour,' Freddie said.

'Are you all right, Miss?' Danny asked.

'I suppose I must have fainted,' Evie said. 'I have *never* fainted before.'

'You did,' Freddie said. 'Then I had to leave you to get help. But I wasn't away for long. Luckily, Danny was coming down the road in his cart.'

'Here, take a drink,' Danny said, handing Evie a small flask of water.

Evie took a few sips. The cool water felt good, reviving.

'I told Danny about the snakes,' Freddie said. 'And how those artefacts were stolen from the museum.' He held Evie's gaze.

'The rumours about the snakes were true then,' Danny said. 'I'll make sure the whole town knows. Someone will be arrested for putting them there, and for the thieving too!'

'The snakes scared us a lot, especially Evie,' Freddie said.

Evie shot him an indignant glance, then realised he was just trying to cover up what they were really doing.

'Um, yes, I remember now,' she said. 'Yes, I was very scared. Um, my father will be pleased we found those, um, those things. He's a professor of history.'

'Very good, Miss,' Danny said. 'Now, I'll tie your horses to the rear of the cart. They'll trot along fine.'

'Thank you, Danny,' Evie said. 'I don't think it would be safe for me to ride just yet.'

'Not likely, Miss,' Danny said. 'You'd risk a bad fall. Young Freddie is a good rider, though. Handled his horse very well.'

'Yes, um, he is,' Evie said, sounding woozy again.

'He galloped along the Crompton Road at quite a speed,' Danny said, helping Evie to her feet.

'Well done, Freddie,' Evie said, as her legs buckled.

'Woops!' Danny said. 'We'll get you home quick as can be.'

Evie had to swallow her pride and let both Freddie and Danny help her into the cart where she lay down on a dirty rug, still feeling annoyingly weak. When her head settled a bit, she saw that Freddie was staring at her, a mighty frown on his small face.

'I'll be fine,' Evie whispered. 'We know what this is. It can't last forever.'

'There's no chance you got bitten, is there?' Danny asked as he tied Evie's and Freddie's horses to the back of the cart.

'None at all,' Evie said.

'We ran away as soon as we saw them,' Freddie said.

'Just a bad fright then,' Danny said. 'Nothing good food and sweet tea won't fix. Hold on now, it might get a bit bumpy.'

Danny got into the driver's seat, turned the cart around and headed back to the road.

Evie was glad her parents were both resting when she and Freddie arrived home. It was bad enough to see the horror on Julia's face. As usual, the governess had been imagining all sorts of terrible things and had assumed something dreadful had happened.

'I'm fine,' Evie said. 'We both are. I just felt a little faint, that's all.'

'You? Faint?' Julia said.

'We were riding very fast,' Freddie said. 'It was great, but it was really hot, and we forgot to bring water. We stayed out too long. Evie got dehydrated, then Danny helped us.'

As usual Freddie rushed out with all the details – which Evie had prepared with him. She didn't want to talk about being able to do magic with Julia until she was sure. After all, she hadn't finished the Ladder of Charms yet. Evie suddenly felt an urgent desire to look at Nala's diary. First though, she really needed to eat and get some proper rest. Then she would try to figure out exactly what was happening to her.

Freddie kept the chatter going during a late breakfast, in between gobbling his food down in no time at all. Evie was very hungry too and felt the better of a good meal. Julia eyed them both with growing concern.

'You should take it easy and make sure you go to bed early tonight,' she said. 'Both of you. You should lie down for a while once you finish breakfast, Evie. I'm sure you'll feel better after some rest.'

'I feel fine now that I've eaten,' Freddie said.

'I feel a lot better too,' Evie said. 'Please don't worry, Julia. It was just too much sun and an empty stomach. I should have worn a wide hat for shade.'

'We'll bring water and biscuits next time,' Freddie said.

Evie retired to her bedroom for a while, glad that her parents were both occupied, her mother not wanting conversation and her father writing a whole pile of letters. Hopefully Julia would keep her promise not to tell them anything about her 'fainting spell'. How she hated covering things up, but that was how it had to be. She groaned and plonked onto her bed, though not at all in the mood for a nap. A few minutes later, Freddie knocked gently on her door. Evie opened it to see him standing there, three talismans and the goblet in his arms.

'I didn't want to leave them in the stables because Jimmy might find them, and I had to return the sack,' Freddie said, pushing past her. 'Where shall we put them now?'

'I thought perhaps your toy box would be best,' Evie said.

'It's full,' Freddie said. 'What about a drawer? One that Tilly doesn't tidy.'

Evie went to her secret drawer where she kept her diaries

locked away. She took the key from the chain around her neck and opened it.

'The mirror, the stone and the plate will fit if I take out a couple of things,' she said, removing some older journals and framed photographs. She placed the talismans inside. 'That'll do,' she said. 'Now, the fake goblet. Hmm, it's a more awkward shape.'

They both looked around the room. Then Freddie picked it up and placed it on Evie's dressing table.

'How about here?' he said. 'Could you put something in it?'

'Why, yes!' Evie said, immediately placing her hair pins, clasps, two brooches and a few ribbons inside. 'There, that looks almost normal.'

'Where will you say you got it?' Freddie asked.

'I'll say we found it when we were out riding,' Evie said.

'Just checking,' Freddie said, grinning.

'By the way, I told Father you'd like to go to the museum with me,' Evie said. 'You would, wouldn't you?'

'Oh, yes!' Freddie said. 'Uncle Henry said he wanted to take me there, but I thought it wouldn't happen now.'

'Well, we are going, and Julia too, as soon as possible,' Evie said.

'Why the hurry, though I don't mind?' Freddie asked.

'Because I have to get the real goblet,' Evie said.

'You mean, it's in the museum!' Freddie squealed.

'Shh, yes,' Evie said. 'And once I have it, I have to burn all five talismans together.'

'Burn them? Really?' Freddie said. 'So, you're going to swap the fake for the real one? That's, isn't that –'

'A crime? Yes. Though I hadn't thought of *swapping* one for the other,' Evie said. 'I was just going to steal the real one. But that's a very good idea, Freddie!'

'It'll be tricky,' Freddie said.

'And it's definitely a crime,' Evie said.

'Is it really a crime if you're stealing it to finish the Ladder of Charms so you can destroy the demons who will otherwise destroy the whole world?' Freddie asked.

'I'm afraid so,' Evie said. 'Unfortunately, not everyone will see it the way we do. I need a good plan, a very clever and cunning plan to pull this off.'

'Then I'll start thinking too,' Freddie said.

'Think hard and let me know what you come up with,' Evie said. 'I'll talk to Julia tomorrow and we'll arrange the visit to the museum. Father said he would write to someone called Edward who could show us around. Though with a guide it will be more difficult to swap the fake goblet for the real one. Oh well, I'll just have to figure it out.'

Later that night, Evie took out the talismans for another look. Xavier's Stone was rather plain and round, smaller than the palm of Evie's hand, cream in colour with a few speckles on its surface. It was exceptionally smooth, and shaped a bit like a scone, Evie thought. Portia's Plate was round, about the size of a side plate. It wouldn't hold much food for a demon, Evie thought with a shiver. It was solid silver and needed a good polish. The decoration around the edge was very unusual, more like an ancient language. Evie thought her father would probably recognise it. Marielle's Mirror was more intriguing, and Evie wondered if it really could tell the future. She picked it up. A hand mirror, the handle and back were also decorated silver, very ornate. The looking glass itself was somewhat tarnished but Evie could make out her image well enough. She wondered what she had to do to see a vision of the future. Did she have to ask it out loud? Did she merely gaze into it?

Evie decided to try both, but neither worked. She turned it over in her hands. The ornate handle had different carving on it and was rather grubby. Taking a handkerchief she rubbed the handle gently at first, then vigorously. It soon shone, revealing beautiful craftsmanship. Evie rubbed some more, front and back till it was gleaming. Then she saw it. The image in the mirror was changing from her reflection to something else, something blurry at first, then it formed a new image, which in turn became a moving picture.

CHAPTER SIXTEEN

I n Marielle's Mirror Evie found proof of her magic. She saw herself stopping the snakes, yet it felt strange to watch how she controlled them. But this was the past. What about the future? Clearly there would be another visit to the cave, she thought, and soon enough, her confrontation with Volok . . . She longed to know how that would turn out.

The next image was very different. Madruga rose out of the green pool, looking triumphant. She was powerfully built, muscles bulging on her arms and shoulders, even her neck. Her head was hideous, its shape and expression like a gargoyle. Her wiry hair stood out from her head like a bunch of twisted sticks. Evie immediately thought of Medusa, the demon with snake hair whose gaze turned her victims to stone.

Then in quick succession, Evie saw the devastation the demon queen would wreak on the world. Strangely, Volok was often positioned behind her as she led an army of demons into battle. So, Madruga was the true leader of the demons after all, the fiercer of the two, the one to truly 'beware', as the message on the piece of silk Evie had found had forewarned. The scenes of slaughter and violence were shocking as Evie watched the horrors unfold. The importance of stopping Volok from bringing Madruga back to life could not be clearer. Then he too would have to be stopped. Killed. Would that make Evie a murderer as well as a thief? She thought of Olga – was Evie already a murderer? Suddenly, stealing a goblet didn't seem so bad. She gulped loudly, as if trying to swallow all these horrible thoughts.

Evie lowered the mirror and the images disappeared. She returned it to her private drawer with the other items, covering them up with folded handkerchiefs and silk scarves. She opened Nala's notebook. Somehow, she sensed there would be a new message, and her suspicion was correct. She read it eagerly.

> *By now you will have witnessed and felt the first drops of magic you have been given. The magic will strengthen as you complete the Ladder of Charms. Tread carefully, respect this new gift, and use it well. Moon magic will come if you really need it. If you try to abuse it, it will desert you.*

There was no doubt at all. Evie had magic and there was more to come. She was full of questions, but there was no one to explain any of it now. She only had these occasional messages and the knowledge that she must finish the Ladder of Charms. She wondered if the magic would desert her after her tasks were complete, or would it remain, slowly turning her into a sorceress like Nala. She turned the page to find the instructions for step five.

> *Between the Harvest full moons of August and September you must play the harp without error,*

stoppage or sustenance all night from dusk till dawn. You may choose the music yourself but choose wisely: every piece must be of the same standard as anything you have played for the fourth charm and should be of a suitable length to keep you playing all night long without pause. The harp will release more magic to you once you have completed step five. It will be stronger magic. Be aware of the changes within you and use it cautiously until you master it.

'Changes?' Evie whispered. 'What does that mean?' It struck Evie that she didn't want a life like Nala's, nor Lucia's for that matter. They were both so alone, living in strange places, always on the move having to leave everyone they loved behind, and always in danger. But wasn't that one of the vows Evie had made? Perhaps she secretly hoped to change that pattern somehow and live out her role in her own way. But would that be possible?

Evie felt flustered. A tiny thought crept into her head that she had brushed aside before. Doubt. Should she really have started down this path? But of course she should. No one else but the Harp Maiden could play the harp to complete the charms and use the magic to stop the demons. Cross with herself, she closed the notebook and secured the buckles. It was time to banish all niggling doubts. Every single one. But like most things, it would be easier said than done.

It took two nerve-wracking attempts to play the chosen pieces from dusk until dawn without error, food, water or a break of any kind – not to mention falling asleep. The first time, Freddie accompanied Evie to their new location in the most isolated area of the local park. Luckily it had been a showery day, keeping most people indoors as dusk approached.

Julia had prepared several excuses should Evie's parents inquire after them during the evening. After the first few hours Evie was doing well, but then the wind picked up and the showers returned, making it most unpleasant. Freddie huddled into his light summer coat and cap but began to shiver as the wind blew surprisingly sharp and cool for late summer. Evie struggled on with the five pieces of music she had chosen, eventually succumbing to the inclement weather and overwhelmed by irritation and tiredness. Once she made an error, that was it. She had to admit defeat.

'How stupid of me, and so close to the finish!' she cried. 'All those hours for nothing.'

'At least you know what it'll be like now,' Freddie said. 'You couldn't practise for that long at home without being asked a lot of questions.'

'I suppose so,' Evie said, grumpily. 'But I have to get it right the next time. I feel like I'm running out of time.'

'Maybe we should pick a night with better weather,' Freddie said. 'Even if you have to wait a couple of extra days. It could make all the difference.'

'You speak a lot of sense, Master Freddie,' Evie said, more cheerfully. There was little point in allowing her disappointment to annoy her for long. 'Come on, let's go home and get warm and dry. Really, such weather!'

At the second attempt, Evie was more prepared and more

resolute. She had tried to persuade Freddie *not* to come, but once again he had spoken sense.

'You need me to keep a lookout,' he said. 'You can't move or stop playing for anything, so you need me with you.'

And so, they went out together again, Evie determined that she would accomplish her task and Freddie upbeat as usual, certain that Evie would succeed. The evening was calm and mild, with no threat of rain this time. Evie hoped the pleasant conditions would last until dawn.

Evie was concentrating very hard, and barely noticed when Freddie got up twice to peer through the bushes or look behind a tree, checking some noise or other. Despite her determination, at the back of her mind was the same concern Freddie had, that someone might spy on them. She hadn't seen Simeon for a while now, but she would have to let Freddie deal with that problem if it arose.

Thankfully, Evie was successful, finishing all five pieces she had chosen to play, repeating each one three times to fill the hours, and without error.

'Whew!' she said, hugging the harp with relief after plucking the last note.

'Well done!' Freddie said, delighted.

She looked at him, bleary eyed from lack of sleep.

'Oh! That was weird,' she said, staring at Freddie and he stared back.

'What is it this time?' he asked.

There it was again, the same tingling sensation she had experienced after finishing step four, only this time it was stronger, deeper, and frightening.

'What's the matter, Evie?' Freddie pressed.

'I feel strange, really peculiar,' Evie whispered. 'Something is happening to me.'

'What? Tell me,' Freddie said.

'I don't know,' Evie said, a tremor in her voice. 'I'm tingling again, all over this time. It's like something is surging through my veins. It's scary, it feels like my blood is boiling, or like poison is shooting up and down my arms, my legs, everywhere, like I might explode!'

'No way, it can't be anything that bad,' Freddie said. 'It's magic, that's all!'

Evie knew he must be right, but she felt so peculiar she didn't know what to do. She looked at her hands – they were glowing bizarrely, pulsing like lighthouse beacons.

'Look,' she said, holding them up for Freddie to see.

'Oh wow!' Freddie whispered, then his expression changed.

'What is it? What do you see?' Evie asked.

'You're, um, I think you might be glowing all over,' Freddie whispered, his eyes almost popping out of his head.

Evie pulled up her sleeves and looked at her arms. She removed her shoes to look at her feet. They were glowing too. She looked at Freddie who was nodding at her. 'Yep,' he said. 'Your face and neck are glowing, and I'll bet the rest of you is too!' He tried to stifle a giggle.

'Freddie!' Evie said. "This had better stop. I can't go around glowing forever!'

'Of course it will stop,' Freddie said.

Evie looked at him, unsure.

'It did before,' Freddie said.

'Yes. Yes, it did,' Evie said, trying to calm herself. 'Let's just sit here for a few minutes and wait for it to pass.'

They sat quietly, listening to the early-morning birdsong. After about twenty minutes, Evie's hands were almost back to normal.

'How is my face?' Evie asked.

'Perfect,' Freddie said. 'It seems to start and end with your hands.'

'No glowing of any kind on my face or neck?' Evie asked, turning her head from side to side. She reached down to check her feet again, then her arms.

'No, all perfect,' Freddie said.

'That's a relief,' Evie said.

'How do you feel inside?' Freddie asked.

Evie thought for a moment. 'Stronger,' she said. 'Yes, I feel stronger, more certain, and . . .'

'And?'

'Something else,' Evie said. 'I don't know. Braver?'

'That's good,' Freddie said.

'But I'm not sure, it's hard to explain,' Evie said.

'Not to worry,' Freddie said. 'You'll know soon.'

Evie picked up the harp, Freddie carried her satchel and they headed for home. They hurried along as it would be bright soon, and a few people were already entering the park for an early walk. Evie suddenly grabbed Freddie's arm, stopped walking and stared, or rather glared.

'What is it now?' Freddie asked.

'We're being followed,' Evie said.

'I didn't hear anyone,' Freddie said.

'Nor did I,' Evie said. 'I felt it. Someone is near us who shouldn't be.'

'Who?' Freddie asked.

'It's – it's – it's Simeon,' Evie said as she turned around. 'There he is!' she cried, and started to march towards him, her face taut with anger. 'What are you doing? Why are you following us? Go away! Leave us alone!'

Simeon peeped out from behind a tree a few yards away, his mouth hanging open in surprise.

Evie strode towards him, Freddie almost jogging to keep up. Two gentlemen out for a walk stopped to stare, as Evie shouted at Simeon again.

'Leave us alone!' she cried. 'Go on, go away. Don't you dare follow us again!'

As the two gentlemen approached to see what was going on, Simeon turned on his heels and ran. Evie stopped walking and stood frowning after him.

'I'm impressed!' Freddie said.

'So am I,' a familiar voice said.

Evie whirled around. 'Matthew! Oh, um, good morning!'

'Are you both all right?' Matthew asked. 'It's early for you two to be out – and with your harp too.'

'Evie likes to play when the birds start singing,' Freddie said.

'What a lovely idea,' Matthew said. 'Don't the birds sing in your garden?'

'Yes, of course,' Evie said, a little flustered. 'But I –'

'There are lots more out here,' Freddie said. 'And it's lovely being up early in the summer. We like to go horse riding early too. You should come with us some time.'

'I'd love to,' Matthew said, raising his eyebrows at Evie.

'We were just heading home,' Evie said. 'I thought that

awful man was following us. I just reacted without thinking. I shouted at him, hoping he would go away. And, well, luckily he did.'

'You were lucky,' Matthew said. 'And brave. You never fail to surprise me, Evie. You too, Freddie. I'm glad you were with Miss Evie to protect her.'

'Thank you, Master Matthew,' Freddie said.

'May I introduce Mr Humphrey,' Matthew said. 'He's in charge of the refurbishment of the academy.' They exchanged polite greetings. 'We decided to get some fresh air before we begin a long day inside our very dusty building.'

'But we are making good progress,' Mr Humphrey said pointedly.

'We are indeed,' Matthew said. 'Perhaps I should escort you two home in case that rascal is still lurking about.'

'Shall I see you at the academy in say, half an hour?' Mr Humphrey asked.

'Perfect,' Matthew said, as Mr Humphrey tipped his hat and walked on.

'Evie, who was that scruffy, skinny man with the eye patch?' Matthew asked. 'And what's all this about playing the harp in the park at dawn? Seriously?'

'It's a long story, Matthew,' Evie said. 'Could we talk about it another time? We're both very tired, and I'm sure Freddie is hungry. We were out all – um, very early.'

'I'm absolutely starving!' Freddie said.

Matthew laughed. 'Very well. Perhaps I could call on you some afternoon this week. I'll try to escape my father and Mr Humphrey for an hour.'

'That would be nice,' Evie said, stifling a yawn.

'You really do have some unusual secrets, Evie,' Matthew said quietly. 'I am intrigued.'

Evie smiled and blushed as Matthew left her and Freddie at their front gate. He waved goodbye, and as she watched him walk away, Evie wondered when she might be able to tell him all her secrets, or even some of them. But then, should she tell him anything at all? Ever?

CHAPTER SEVENTEEN

Evie was annoyed that Simeon had been once again so close to her home, and it worried her that he could have been spying for some time now and might know all about her family. Still, she had enjoyed shouting at him and scaring him off. She felt proud of her show of courage, even though it was probably the sight of Matthew and Mr Humphrey that finally sent Simeon running.

Freddie went straight into the dining room. Evie put the harp away, then walked straight into Tilly, the maid, who was about to take an early breakfast up to Evie's father.

'Good morning, Tilly,' Evie said. 'I was out for an early walk this morning. I'll take breakfast in the dining room with Freddie and Julia as usual, then I'll be studying in my bedroom for a while. No need to come and tidy today, thank you.'

Evie hoped Tilly would take the hint that she didn't want to be disturbed – while she caught a few hours' sleep.

'Of course, Miss Evie,' Tilly said. 'Everything is ready in the dining room, as the professor wanted an early start today as well. He says he will be coming down for breakfast soon. It's wonderful to see him getting back to his old self.'

Evie was of course delighted to see her father improving

daily now, but it meant it would be more difficult for her to go about her business without being noticed, suspected of something or questioned directly about what she was up to. But enough worrying, she thought. There were things to do and things to organise: the trip to the museum to find the goblet, going back to the green cave, and writing another letter to Grace – or perhaps she should visit. She hadn't seen her friend for weeks now.

Mr Hudson interrupted her thoughts.

'Your father was asking for you, Miss Evie,' he said. 'He didn't see you yesterday, apparently.'

'I'll go up shortly,' Evie said, noting his disapproving tone.

'And the doctor is visiting Mrs Wells at eleven o'clock,' Hudson said.

'I see,' Evie said. 'Thank you, Hudson.'

After breakfast, Evie went upstairs to see her father. She knocked gently on the door and entered.

'Evie, my dear, come and sit,' her father said.

'I see you have a lot of letters,' Evie said, noticing the pile sitting on her father's bedside table.

'Some are from well-wishers, others are from the museum, but this one will interest you,' her father said, picking one up. 'It's a reply from Edward. He says he will be delighted to show you and Freddie around the museum when you visit. I asked him if he could bring me the goblet, here, to this house, so I can examine it without delay and in private.'

'Really? Here?' Evie was taken aback.

'Cheeky of me, I know,' her father said with a glint in his eyes, 'and Edward will have to ask special permission, so I have to fill out this silly form. I'm doing that now. Wouldn't it be marvellous if the request were approved? It would be such a privilege. Yes indeed!'

'Yes, indeed,' Evie muttered, amazed at her father's bold request but excited by it too. This could give her a second chance to snatch the goblet, or perhaps a better first chance. Maybe she shouldn't try to take it from the museum at all. Her thoughts were in a whirl.

'I hope it won't take too long to catalogue,' her father continued. 'That must be done first, as it is part of a very important consignment that arrived from Egypt. These things can take ages.'

'Oh, perhaps a few weeks then,' Evie said.

'You sound almost as disappointed as I am,' her father said. 'Well, I'm going to give you another letter asking him to make it a *priority*. I know that should be obvious, but it's better to state it in writing for the curator. He must sanction it, you see. Making it more official should mean it will arrive sooner. If the curator agrees. Yes. If. Oh, well, it's all I can do.'

'How much sooner?' Evie asked.

'Who knows?' her father said, spreading his hands. 'You can ask Edward if he has heard anything when you see him on Friday. I'll be dying to know.'

'This Friday?' Evie asked.

'Yes, he just confirmed it,' her father said. 'I take it that will suit all of you?'

'Oh, yes, of course,' Evie said, hoping it would suit Julia, though she couldn't see why not once she was feeling well enough.

'Good.'

They chatted for a while, but Evie was distracted, thinking about the real goblet that she needed to steal from the museum, from this Edward fellow, or perhaps later from her father. She didn't like either option, but she also didn't want to wait days or weeks to get it, and Friday was tempting. As her father wittered on in his excitement at examining the goblet in his own home, Evie made a mental note to check on the ruby later, just to see it and make sure it was safe, undisturbed in Freddie's toy chest.

Mr Hudson knocked on the door and entered.

'Excuse me, Professor, but there is a young man at the door asking for Miss Evie,' he said.

'Really? Who?' Evie's father asked.

'A Daniel McGinn,' Hudson said. 'He wishes to speak with her urgently.'

'Who is this fellow, Evie?' her father asked. 'Do you know him?'

'It must be Charlie McGinn's son,' Evie said. 'You remember, Charlie McGinn from Crompton.'

'The man who was murdered?' her father asked. 'What does his son want with you?'

'I have no idea,' Evie said. 'I'll go down and see.'

Evie hurried out of the room, leaving her father and Hudson bewildered.

Danny was standing awkwardly in the hall, twisting his cap nervously in his hands, just like his father, Charlie, used to. He looked hugely relieved to see Evie.

'Danny, what is it?' Evie asked quietly.

'I need your help,' Danny said. 'Me, my brother Martin

and a few friends went hunting those snakes.'

'Oh dear,' Evie muttered. 'What happened?'

'We found them, hundreds of them, thousands maybe,' Danny said, his mouth twisting in disgust. 'They had huge fangs! And there was this man, a huge, strong, terrifying lump of a man. While we were trying to dodge the snakes, my friend Bart got too close to the big man and was slashed across the chest. The doctor stitched him up, but the wound looks terrible, it must have been a poisoned blade. I'm afraid Bart will die. Can you help my friend, Miss Evie? Please. My father said you can do special things. Is it true? Can you? Can you save him?'

Evie led Danny outside onto the porch.

'Yes, Danny, I can do certain things,' Evie said, 'but usually only when there is a full moon.'

Danny stared at her. 'But Bart mightn't last till then. Can't you do something for him now?'

'No. I mean, I don't know,' Evie said. Her mind was telling her no but her heart was saying yes. She felt confused. Then she remembered one of the pieces of advice from step one on the Ladder of Charms: 'Be true to your heart.'

'Well, perhaps, yes,' Evie said. 'I'll try, Danny, but I can't promise anything.'

'But you *will* try?' Danny said.

Evie glanced back into the hall. Hudson had come downstairs and was fussing about, probably trying to overhear their conversation. Evie made up her mind.

'Where is your friend now?' she asked quietly.

'He's at our place, in Crompton,' Danny said.

'I see,' Evie said, thinking.

'I'm coming too,' Freddie said, joining Evie and Danny.

'It's agreed, then?' Danny said, looking hopefully at Evie for confirmation. 'My horse is outside. We three can ride together.'

'Yes, let's do that,' Evie said. 'Give us a moment to change, Danny, and I'll have to make some excuse. Wait for us over in the stables.'

Danny nodded and hurried down the driveway and around to the back of the house.

CHAPTER EIGHTEEN

They rode fast to Crompton, Danny leading the way. The horses were steaming when they left them in the McGinns' stable. Freddie stayed behind to give them some water while Evie rushed into the farmhouse behind Danny. A fair-haired young man was lying on a mattress in a downstairs room. He was sweating and delirious. Danny's brother, Martin, was attending him. The local doctor was standing at the end of the bed looking grim.

'I'm sorry, there is nothing more I can do,' the doctor said quietly. 'The infection in the wound is spreading fast. Try to keep him cool and make him drink some water. I'll check back on him in a couple of hours.'

The doctor left and Evie approached the bed.

'His fever is very high,' she said, feeling Bart's forehead with the back of her hand. She knew her previous wish to look after the McGinn family had probably kept the two McGinn brothers safe, but not their friend Bart. Evie had decided not to tell them about the wish. If they began to feel invincible because of it, they might end up taking unnecessary risks just like this.

Martin dabbed a damp cloth on his friend's face to try to soothe him. Then Bart began rambling about monsters and snakes.

'We can't let anyone hear what he's saying, no matter how silly it sounds,' Evie said.

'The other lad who helped carry him here heard some of his ravings already,' Danny said. 'But he won't think much of the mutterings of a wounded man.'

'Tell me how it happened,' Evie said, as Freddie joined them.

'There were six of us,' Danny said. 'We split into two groups of three. Bart was tracking just ahead of me and Martin when that big ugly man came out of nowhere, bellowing nonsense, then the snakes came out of the ground in a giant swarm. The big fella went completely wild. He charged at us, roaring and lashing out. Bart fell like a sack when he was hit, slashed right across the chest. It was sickening to see him bleeding so badly. Then some of the snakes broke from the swarm and headed towards me and Martin. I shot some of them and Martin clubbed a few. I don't know how we did it, but we managed to grab Bart under the armpits and drag him away. We were lucky that big, freaky fella didn't follow us. He just stood there laughing, then he whistled, and the snakes turned around and followed him, just like a dog would. It was so creepy. We called to the other lads to leave immediately, hauled Bart over his horse, tied him securely with some rope, mounted our own horses and rode away as fast as we could.'

'Wow!' Freddie said.

'You mustn't tell anyone else about this,' Evie said. 'It's really important.'

'Did you know that fella was there?' Danny asked.

'We only just found out,' Evie said, avoiding the question. 'This must be kept a secret or more people may die.'

'You mean, like our father did,' Danny said.

Evie nodded.

'He used to say there were strange things at work in the world, things best left alone,' Danny said. 'We'll put the word out to avoid the area, but something must be done to keep people safe.'

'Trust me,' Evie said. 'Something is being done, but I can't tell you what that is right now.'

'I see,' Danny said, though he sounded doubtful.

'You'll need to think of some explanation to keep your friends from going there again,' Evie said. 'They may be curious after what they saw.'

'They didn't see too much,' Danny said. 'Only me, Martin and Bart saw the man and the snakes. The other lads had gone in a different direction. Afterwards, I just told them someone jumped us and attacked Bart with a knife.'

'Good,' Evie said.

'If you need to,' Freddie said, 'you could say that Bart was bitten by one of the snakes, and the snake venom made him sick and caused temporary madness. That would explain anything strange he might say.'

'That's a very good idea,' Evie said, looking keenly at Danny. 'Freddie's excuse will stop awkward questions being asked and curious people ending up in the same situation, or worse. Better not to mention the, um, the big fellow at all.'

'I'll promise you anything if you can save my friend,' Danny said. 'Can you?'

'I don't know,' Evie whispered, wondering if her new magic could help. She desperately wanted it to work, but she wasn't quite sure what to do. She sat on the bed looking at Bart, thinking.

'Don't think,' Freddie whispered to her after a couple of minutes. 'Just believe it'll work, and it will.'

'Believe what?' Danny asked.

'In magic,' Freddie said.

Danny looked at Evie.

'It's true,' she said. 'Are you sure you want me to try, now that you know what's involved?'

Danny looked bewildered, almost scared. Then he nodded, and Evie turned back to Bart. She took his hands in hers, closed her eyes, and believed.

Evie woke on a chair in a corner of the room, a blanket over her legs and a cushion supporting her head.

'What happened?' she asked groggily.

'You were holding Bart's hands, then you started humming,' Freddie said. 'And glowing.'

'And then?' Evie asked.

'It went on like that for about five or six minutes,' Freddie said. 'Then you swooned.'

'Not again!' Evie said. 'How long ago?'

'About half an hour,' Freddie said.

Evie sat up straight, shook herself awake and looked around. Martin was washing Bart's face. He checked the wound dressing, then lifted him slightly as Danny held a cup of water to his lips. Danny turned to Evie, smiling.

'He's weak but awake, and I think he looks better,' he said. 'Whatever you did helped him.'

Bart gave Evie a weak smile.

Martin settled him back onto the pillow and tucked a blanket around him. Danny went over and crouched down beside Evie.

'You saved him, Miss Evie,' he said. 'I thank you from the bottom of my heart. We all do.'

'I'm so glad he's doing better, but it may take time for him to heal fully,' Evie said.

Freddie handed her a glass of water. 'Are *you* feeling better?'

'Just a little light-headed,' Evie said. 'Not as bad as last time.'

'You must be getting used to it,' Freddie said.

'Have something to eat before you go,' Danny said. 'You need to be feeling well to ride home.'

'Thank you,' Evie said. 'Anything at all would be nice.'

'I really believe Bart is on the mend,' Martin said from the bedside. 'His fever has broken, and you saw him drink. He wouldn't take any water before.'

'Aye,' Danny said. 'I think he's drifting off to sleep now.'

'His colour is better, less poisoned looking,' Martin said. 'It's a miracle.'

'No, it's magic,' Freddie said. 'And remember, you can't tell anyone.'

'Miracle, magic, they're the same thing to us,' Danny said, and Martin nodded. 'Don't worry, this family knows how to keep secrets.'

After some tea and thick slices of bread smothered with strawberry jam, Evie felt well enough to ride. But they didn't go straight home. So close to Wick's End – Witches' End – Evie felt revived enough and determined enough to risk another visit to the green cave and check on Volok's preparations for Madruga's return.

*

They left their horses in the usual spot and hurried on to the green cave. They hunkered down a short distance away, not wanting to disturb the snakes. Evie hoped they would see something that would tell them if Volok was making progress or not.

'Can he bring her back without the Black Ruby?' Freddie whispered.

'I don't think so,' Evie said. 'But he seems to want to prepare the way before he uses the ruby. Or maybe it's to give her hope, or just part of some ancient ritual. I'm not sure, but he will want the ruby soon. I wonder if he knows we have it, or if he's still spending hours every day searching.'

There was no sign of activity.

'Let's go in,' Evie said.

'What about the snakes?' Freddie asked.

Evie was surprised by her recklessness. 'Oh!' she said, ducking down into the long grass again. 'Sorry, I don't know what I was thinking.'

'Maybe you don't need to think,' Freddie said.

'What?'

'Maybe you just know what to do, like instinct, or believing,' Freddie said.

But Evie was hardly listening. Her eyes locked on the cave. She stood up and walked straight towards the entrance, ignoring any danger.

The snakes came in droves, hissing and lunging aggressively, their yellow fangs looking even longer and sharper than the last time. Evie stood her ground as they surrounded her again. Calmly, she raised her arms, stretched out her fingers and began to hum. Her humming grew as loud as the hissing, creating a peculiar din. Evie waved her arms slowly from side to side, her hands glowing. The snakes quietened, cowered, and withdrew to the pit. Silence.

'Brilliant!' Freddie exclaimed, running towards her.

Evie turned to him. 'I don't know what I just did or how I did it.'

'Who cares! It worked!' Freddie cried.

Evie looked at her hands. They were very hot, and she wasn't surprised to see that they were still glowing. She watched the bright glow fade then disappear. She liked how she felt this time, calm, powerful, in control, and there was no negative reaction, no weakness, even though she had used magic twice in the one day.

'Come on,' Freddie said, bringing her back into the moment.

They entered the cave and went straight to the green pool. The remains of more ingredients were floating on the gooey water, some of which had splashed over the edge and solidified like candlewax. Inside the pool the liquid bubbled gently, but the stink was far worse than before.

'Volok did something,' Evie said. 'He's taken the ritual another step closer to the end.'

Evie leaned over the pool and peered down, trying to see into the depths. Mere seconds passed before she could just make out the ghostlike image hovering beneath the surface, dark gaps for eyes staring up, perplexed.

'Look, Freddie,' she said. 'She looks stronger, less wobbly, at least when she's in the pool. How desperate Volok must be to get his hands on the ruby now.'

Freddie knelt beside Evie.

'That's bad, really bad,' he said. 'We really need to finish this.'

They both started at the voice that suddenly boomed around the cave.

'I knew you would come,' Volok said. He laughed evilly. 'You just can't resist. Your curiosity always leads you into trouble, Evelyn Wells.'

Evie spotted Simeon creeping around behind Volok, a sickly smile on his scrawny face.

'I was right, my lord, they had been here before,' Simeon said, gloating.

'I knew that long before you did,' Volok said. 'I could smell the scent they left behind. But I didn't care that you had trespassed on my dwelling, Evelyn. I wanted you to come, and now you are here. You see, I always get what I want.'

'You're running out of time, aren't you?' Evie said. 'You must be getting anxious now, worrying that your plans will be messed up again at the final moment.'

'Again? No, no,' Volok said. 'Soon, I will have everything I need to accomplish my goal.'

'I don't see how,' Evie said. 'You don't have the ruby and you can't complete the ritual without it, not properly.'

'How do you know I don't have it?' Volok asked. 'Ah, because *you* have it, don't you?'

'No, we don't!' Freddie cried. 'You'll just have to keep looking for it, if it takes you forever! But I doubt if Madruga has forever to wait!'

'Don't speak my wife's name, and don't lie to me!' Volok roared. 'Who else would have the ruby? Who else even knows about it?'

Evie wished her magic would do something now. She willed it, she believed it, but it didn't come. For some reason, she couldn't even hum properly when she tried.

'I will give you one last chance to bring me the ruby and the other talismans you stole from me,' Volok said. 'I know it was you who took them. No one else knew they were here, except Simeon. And your scent was all over this cave. Simeon has been following your movements and keeps me informed of everything you do and everyone you see.'

Simeon smiled sickly.

'Now,' Volok said, 'you will bring me everything I want – or else!'

'Or else what?' Freddie asked boldly.

'Or – you – will – die!' Volok roared. Reaching out with remarkable speed, he snatched Freddie, and held him in a tight grip.

'Let him go!' Evie cried. 'This is about me and your plans for resurrecting Madruga. It has nothing to do with him. He's just a boy!'

'It has a lot to do with him now,' Volok roared. 'Bring what belongs to me, or I will kill the boy. Simeon will accompany you. GO! NOW! BRING ME THAT RUBY!'

There was a sludgy, sucking noise as Madruga's ghostlike form rose out of the green pool. Volok was instantly distracted.

'My love, no! You must not emerge too often,' he said, in a surprisingly tender voice.

Freddie immediately saw his chance and wriggled out of Volok's grip. Evie grabbed him by the hand, and they charged straight at Simeon, knocking him out of the way. Exiting the green cave, Evie and Freddie ran for their lives.

CHAPTER NINETEEN

G lad to be home, Evie and Freddie left the horses with Jimmy and hurried inside. They had an excuse prepared for their delay, but it wasn't needed. The doctor had been to see both Evie's parents: Professor Wells had overdone his exercises which caused severe pain in his legs, and Evie's mother was feeling particularly down. The nurse was fussing, annoying the Hudsons with her demands. No one took any notice of Evie and Freddie, except for Julia.

'Something has happened,' she said. 'You both looked mightily relieved to be home.'

Evie was startled, but not so much by what Julia said. Her governess looked extremely pale and drawn.

'Are you all right, Julia?' Evie asked.

'Just a little tired,' Julia said. 'Let's go into the parlour and you can tell me about your latest adventure.'

The three of them sat down, and Evie related a shortened version of what had occurred.

'This saga only gets worse!' Julia said.

'We're nearly at the end,' Evie said, trying to sound reassuring. 'All the danger and the worry will soon be over.'

'Until the next demon attack!' Julia said.

Freddie was bursting to tell the best bit. He looked at Evie, and she nodded, knowing she might need Julia to cover for her if she had to use magic.

'Evie can do magic now,' Freddie whispered.

'What?' Julia said, her eyes wide with surprise.

'Nala made it part of the charms,' Evie said. 'After step four, I could do small things, sense things. And I feel stronger, braver. I think I have the ability to heal.'

'You were always brave, so being braver may not be a good thing,' Julia said. 'And are you sure that's what it is – healing?'

Evie hoped her governess wouldn't start arguing again.

'What will happen once you finish all the charms?' Julia asked after a moment's silence.

'I'll be able to use magic to destroy the Black Ruby, which means Volok can never bring his wife back from the dead,' Evie said.

'How will you do that?' Julia asked. 'And what about those five talismans you mentioned?'

'I don't know how I'll do it, at least not yet,' Evie said. 'Perhaps something will appear in the notebook to guide me. As for the talismans, they must be destroyed so Volok can never use them for his evil deeds. Every single one of them must burn in the fire at the next full moon.'

'If they are so important, will fire be enough to destroy them?' Julia asked sarcastically. 'I mean, will they simply *melt*?'

Evie tried her best to ignore her governess's bad mood.

'It's magic, it'll work,' Freddie said. 'They'll be destroyed forever, and Evie will be a hero.'

'The female word is heroine,' Julia said.

They turned as Hudson, looking equally hassled, entered the room.

'Master Matthew Reid is here,' he said. 'He asks if he may come in.'

'Of course,' Evie said. To her annoyance, Hudson looked to Julia for confirmation. Julia nodded and Evie went quickly out to the hall.

'Hello, Matthew,' Evie said. 'Please, come into the parlour. Mr Hudson, would you ask Mrs Hudson to bring us some tea please?'

'Of course,' Hudson said.

Matthew followed Evie inside.

'I hope I'm not interrupting,' he said. 'I was on my way back to the academy after an appointment, and I thought I'd see if you were in.'

'I'm glad you did,' Evie said.

'Hello, Matthew,' Julia said. 'Do sit down.'

'Hello, Miss Pippen. Hello, Freddie. Doing any exploring lately?'

'Oh yes,' Freddie said. 'Lots!'

'Excellent!' Matthew said.

When Mrs Hudson arrived with the tea, Julia excused herself, saying she had a headache and needed to lie down. After chatting for a while, Evie and Matthew played a duet in the drawing room – Evie on the flute, Matthew on the upright piano. It was relaxing, especially for Evie after quite a disturbing morning.

Freddie returned to the parlour and became absorbed in one of his books while Evie and Matthew walked around the garden for a while. Evie told him about the upcoming visit to the museum.

'Would you mind if I came too?' Matthew asked. 'I've been promised an afternoon off as I've been working most weekends. We could have tea in town afterwards if you like.'

'That would be lovely,' Evie said. 'I would ask Grace too but she's not going out just yet. She wrote to me, saying her eye is very sore after the operation, and some medication she must take is making her feel ill. She's very anxious about her follow-up appointment with the specialist too.'

'It must be so hard waiting to know the outcome,' Matthew said.

'Absolutely awful,' Evie said. 'She sounded very worried. I'd really like to visit her soon.'

'Hopefully the operation will have been a success,' Matthew said. 'It can take some time for eyes to heal, but please let me know if you hear anything.'

'I will.'

They arrived at the museum on Friday at two o'clock sharp – Evie, Freddie, Julia and Matthew. Julia walked up to the porter, still looking pale and drawn despite putting some extra rouge on her cheeks.

'We have an appointment with Mr Edward Hill,' she said.

The porter checked the book. 'The Wells family?'

'That is correct,' Julia said.

'Wait here a moment, please.'

Edward arrived quickly. He was a dark-haired, wiry young man, about twenty-two, with lots of energy about him.

'Good afternoon, and welcome to our wonderful museum! I am a great admirer of Professor Wells,' he said. 'What a wonderful mind, so much knowledge packed into such a small space!' He tittered. 'Such a colourful career in exploring too. His stories and adventures are legendary around here. I do so want to follow in his footsteps!'

'He asked me to give you this letter,' Evie said, handing it to him.

'Another letter? He is keeping busy! Thank you, Miss Wells,' Edward said, taking the letter and putting it in his pocket. 'May I call you Evie?'

'Of course,' Evie said.

'I am Miss Pippen, Evie's governess,' Julia said firmly. 'This is Master Freddie, and this is Master Matthew Reid.'

'Please forgive my manners!' Edward said, giving them each a short, sharp bow and shaking their hands one after the other.

Matthew raised his eyebrows, making Freddie giggle uncontrollably. Evie stifled her own giggles with a polite cough. She could see that Julia had taken an immediate dislike to Edward. Her governess always hated precociousness and Edward came across as very pushy, and he had certainly taken an immediate shine to Evie, that was obvious. He could hardly take his eyes off her, and every time he spoke, he directed his comments to her alone. Evie noticed that Matthew had spotted this behaviour too.

'Let us begin our tour,' Edward said, turning smartly and leading the group briskly up a wide polished staircase to the first-floor exhibits.

After wandering around listening to Edward for nearly an hour, Evie decided she had to do something or they might have to leave before she even saw the goblet, let alone managed to steal it.

'Tell me, Edward,' she began.

'Yes, Evie?' Edward said, coming to her side.

'Where is Galen's Goblet that my father told me so much about?' Evie asked. 'I believe it was being catalogued and that you were organising for it to be sent to him for a full examination. Could we perhaps see it now?'

'Your wish is my command,' Edward said. 'This way.'

At last, Evie thought.

'I'll wait for you in the hallway,' Julia said. 'I need to sit down for a few minutes.'

'Oh, very well, Miss Pippen,' Edward said. 'This way, everyone.' Edward took the rest of the party down a long stuffy corridor and around a corner. 'The goblet is in here.' They stopped outside a big wooden door with an enormous lock. Edward took a bunch of keys from his jacket pocket and opened the door. He led the party into a long, narrow room, and threw a switch on the wall before closing the door.

'The electricity is deliberately at a low voltage in here so as not to damage the artefacts with too much bright light,' Edward said. 'It can affect the colours and materials very badly, and would be a sacking offence should it happen.' He made a mock serious face.

'I'm sure you are always extremely careful,' Matthew said.

'Absolutely,' Edward said proudly. 'I take the utmost care in my work.'

He went over to a packed table and picked up a lidless wooden crate, strands of straw poking out of it here and there. He carried it over to the only empty table in the room and placed it down carefully.

'Here it is,' he said. 'Galen's Goblet, the real one.' He lifted the goblet out of the crate and placed it gently on the table. It was tall for a goblet, almost double the size of a normal drinking goblet, as Edward explained. Evie walked around the table to look at every inch of the famous talisman.

'What is it, Evie?' Matthew asked.

'Miss Evie is looking for proof,' Edward said smugly. 'And here it is.'

Edward picked up the goblet and turned it over. The opal was shaped like a teardrop, milky white, set cleverly into the centre of the base so as not to disturb the balance of the goblet.

'I think Miss Evie already knows,' Edward said, 'but the rest of you might like to learn that the real Galen's Goblet has this opal set here.' He pointed. 'Professor Wells discovered this important fact. Several fakes have been made, mostly to thwart thieves. Some were very good, except for the lack of an opal set into the base, of course. Their owners still like to believe they have the real one, when all they have is a piece of junk.' He laughed his silly laugh again, wrinkling his nose in disgust at such appalling ignorance.

'Very interesting,' Matthew said. 'Does your father have a special interest in this goblet, Evie?'

'Professor Wells is an expert,' Edward said, before Evie could answer. 'He is interested in everything to do with ancient history. It is his specialty.'

'Yes, he cannot wait to see it,' Evie said. 'Though I think the fakes are maybe a tiny bit shorter in height.'

'Indeed!' Edward exclaimed. 'How clever of you! How did you know, Evie?'

'Oh, I saw a picture in one of Father's books,' Evie said,

annoyed at her little slip. ' And I think Father might have mentioned it.'

'He is the expert!' Edward said. 'It's such a pity he is indisposed at the moment. His work is invaluable to the museum.'

'As you know, Edward,' Evie began, 'my father has requested that the goblet be sent to our home so he can begin his examination without delay. However, that could take a long time to arrange. Is there any way you could speed things up? He is very impatient, and I know he would appreciate it enormously. He is always saying what a wonderful researcher you are. Why, he would expect no less of you, I'm sure!'

Matthew turned an astonished gaze on Evie, which she acknowledged with a discreet raising of her eyebrows.

'Well, I – um, that's very kind of the professor,' Edward muttered, though clearly flattered. 'I would have to see, eh, eh, fill in forms, yes, more forms, and get permission from my superiors.'

'I thought my father had already filled in the necessary form,' Evie said. 'And he is also one of your superiors, isn't he? I think he made this new request very clear in the letter I gave you, the one you haven't opened yet.'

'Ah, yes, I see. I would, um, have to speak with, um, my, um, superiors, again, the ones here in the museum, you understand,' Edward continued bumbling, stalling while he thought of what he would do. Clearly, he didn't want to let the professor down, nor Evie. Everyone was looking at him, waiting for a decision.

'It would be wonderful if you could ask someone now,' Evie said, 'anyone who might look on the request favourably.'

'Yes, quite,' Edward muttered.

'We don't mind waiting in here,' Evie said.

There was an awkward silence.

'I, um, well, I . . .' Edward was in a quandary.

'It's a good idea,' Freddie said. 'You should ask right away, then we can tell Uncle Henry the good news when we get home.'

Edward looked down at Freddie's eager expression, as he continued to struggle to find a sensible reply.

'I agree,' Matthew said. 'Off you go, Edward. No time like the present. We'll wait here and admire the goblet while you get permission.'

Matthew ushered Edward to the door before he could convincingly protest and closed it quickly after him. He grinned at Evie.

'That was fun!' he said. 'Well done both of you!'

'I know it sounded awful, but my father really wants to see it,' Evie said. 'Though I think it unlikely Edward will get permission straight away. Artefacts rarely leave the museum except on an official tour, sometimes even under armed guard.'

'I think Edward is keen to impress you,' Matthew said. 'He'll do his best.'

Freddie nudged Evie and pulled her aside.

'Use magic,' he whispered. 'We really need that goblet now.'

Evie pretended to be looking at a few other items displayed on tables and stacked on shelves, tagged with names, dates and places of origin. Concentrating on what was needed – permission to take the goblet out of the museum – Evie tried to keep her humming low, while Freddie babbled on to Matthew about horse riding.

After about fifteen minutes, Edward whirled back into the room.

'Good news and bad,' he said.

'I hope you're not going to disappoint Professor Wells,' Matthew said pointedly.

'Of course not,' Edward said, sidestepping him to face Evie. 'I couldn't find my superior. Apparently, he has left for the afternoon. However, I have taken it upon myself to sign out the goblet for three days to allow Professor Wells to undertake the important examination of such a prestigious artefact.'

'Three days?' Evie said, sounding as disappointed as possible. 'He will need at least three weeks. Can't you amend the dates, Edward?'

'Well, I suppose I –'

'Marvellous,' Matthew said. 'Well, aren't you going to parcel it up?'

'Absolutely not,' Edward said. 'It must be done properly, paperwork, tagging, wrapping and packaging, that sort of thing. I shall deliver it myself to the Wellses' house this evening.'

'How kind of you,' Matthew said.

'Thank you, Edward,' Evie said. 'What time shall we expect you?'

'About eight I should think,' Edward said.

'And don't forget – three weeks not three days,' Matthew said.

'My father will be so grateful,' Evie said, followed by a winning smile.

They each thanked Edward for showing them around, and then headed back to Hartville with Julia, where there was just enough time to visit the tea rooms before Matthew would have to dash off.

'Edward was so keen to impress you, Evie, he was even prepared to break the rules,' Matthew said. 'I never doubted once you asked, he would simply have to give in.'

'Keen to impress my father, you mean,' Evie said, with a blush and a smile.

'He is certainly a very exuberant young man,' Julia said.

'I hope he won't be late tonight,' Freddie said. 'I'd like to see Uncle Henry's face when he receives the goblet.'

As will I, Evie thought, *but then I have to steal it.*

CHAPTER TWENTY

E dward kept his word and arrived at the Wellses' house at the appointed time. Evie's father insisted on dressing and coming downstairs to meet with him in the parlour. After a brief conversation, Edward left looking rather uncomfortable. Evie, however, was as delighted as her father.

'How exciting!' she said.

'Indeed,' her father said. 'Would you carry it to the study, dear? I want to begin my examination right away.'

'You're going to start now?' Evie said.

'Absolutely! I've waited too long for this and I've been too long in bed too,' her father said, struggling to get out of the armchair. Evie assisted him, calling for Hudson to take her father's arm, while she carried the goblet in its crate to the study.

It was another two hours before Evie and Mr Hudson could persuade the professor to return to bed.

'You'll be fresher in the morning, sir, after a good night's sleep,' Hudson said.

'All right, stop fussing,' Evie's father said, placing the goblet back in the crate, and into a cabinet, which he then locked. 'I'm surprised young Edward let me have it, despite my pleading letters. I count myself very lucky.'

'He appreciates your expertise, sir,' Hudson said.

'I think it far more likely that Evie persuaded him,' Evie's father said, winking at her.

'Well, I agree with Hudson,' Evie said. 'Now, Hudson will help you upstairs and I'll tell the nurse you're on your way up to bed.'

Evie went to bed herself soon after, wondering when and how she would steal the goblet and burn it with the other four talismans at the next full moon – 10 September, just over a week away. She would wish for Bart to be restored to full health if he wasn't completely well by then, and if he were fully recovered, she would make the wish for Grace.

Evie wanted to talk to her father again about Freddie's schooling. A thought had occurred to her: why couldn't Freddie attend the local school here in Hartville? He could always go to boarding school after that, and Julia would still be tutoring Evie for another year anyway. Then, out of the blue, she suddenly doubted that somehow. It was a thought and a feeling that disturbed her.

Evie groaned, realising she might have to use magic to persuade her parents about Freddie. She didn't want to manipulate people, especially not her family. As time went on and her magic increased, she wondered if she would be able to call on the magic at any time, or only when it was important. Something from Nala's notebook rang a bell in her head, and she remembered that that might not always be the case. 'The magic will decide,' it had written. Strange. She went immediately to her private drawer and took out the notebook.

Fewer pages were blank now that Evie was progressing through the charms. Although the secrets disappeared after she read them, they reappeared again once she completed the next step on the Ladder. Maybe the notebook would wipe itself clean again once it was passed to the next Harp Maiden, who would have to work through the charms from scratch. Evie wondered how and if she would meet her successor someday and if she would recognise her somehow.

Despite feeling this new magic within her, Evie remembered the warning she had read, not to abuse the magic or she would find herself corrupted. Evie didn't like that word, 'corrupted'. It sounded like she might succumb to some dreadful temptation, using the magic for herself instead of others, something she had already vowed not to do. But making a vow didn't mean it would be easy to keep. Perhaps she would have new doubts or make mistakes. She couldn't allow the magic to change her. But Nala had told her she would be 'a changed person if she succeeded'. So how exactly was that going to work?

Evie turned the page to read the sixth charm again. To reach the highest step on the Ladder, she had to play the harp 'alone in the wilderness for a full day and a night'. She would have only one chance to get it right this time, no second attempt, and she must remain without food, water or shelter for the duration. To accept the final challenge, Evie must recite a vow at the next full moon. After that, there was no backing out, but she could undertake the challenge whenever she felt ready, within three months.

'Ready?' she exclaimed. 'How do I know when I'm ready? All this time, I've just been stumbling along!'

Evie felt cross with herself for her outburst, hoping no one had heard it. She turned the page to look at the music she would have to play.

'Oh dear!' Evie whispered, watching the next few pages fill with the most intricate lines of music. 'I'm not sure I'm a good enough musician to play that, and it will be very, very long.' She checked all the way to the end of the notebook, but many pages were blank. 'But that's not long enough to play for twenty-four hours! Oh, I see, I'm only allowed to see a sample,' she said, thinking aloud. 'Then I can only rehearse such a small amount! The music might only appear as I play it, one page at a time. What a nightmare this will be!'

Evie wondered where this 'wilderness' was. Did she have to choose the location or would it be revealed? No food, water or shelter for a full twenty-four hours, and in the autumn too. She tried to think she was lucky as the winter would be worse. She took a sharp breath as Nala's handwriting began to fill a blank page with yet more instructions.

> *To succeed at step six, the final step on your journey, you must truly believe in the harp's magic with all your heart. Once you pass the full-day challenge you will be endowed with magic that can destroy the Black Ruby and the demon lord. But receiving this special gift comes at a cost, especially if you must use it to take a life – any life – so prepare yourself well.*
>
> *Good luck, Harp Maiden.*
>
> *Always believe.*

Evie closed the notebook and sat at her dressing table, staring into the mirror. A year ago, she hadn't even gone to the auditions in Dower Hall. She hadn't even heard of the place nor the maestro. Now, she wondered if she was turning into a sorceress. *Why me, why really?* she wondered. 'I am not Nala,' she whispered to her reflection in the mirror. 'I am Evelyn Wells, a girl who loves music. I am also the Harp Maiden, but I am not a sorceress. I will keep my promise to play the harp under the full moons to make wishes to help people. I will finish this quest. But after that, I don't know. Murder is still murder, even if the victim is a demon and the reason for such an abominable act is to protect everyone – isn't it? I'm not sure how much magic I want in my life, outside of my duty as the Harp Maiden. I will have to think about it again after step six. Then I will make a final decision.'

CHAPTER TWENTY-ONE

The news from Grace was not good. After visiting her specialist doctor again, the eye operation was deemed a failure. There was nothing they could do; Grace was going to lose her sight. Evie could tell from her friend's letter that Grace was terribly upset, and disappointed also to read that Grace didn't want any visitors. Evie was unsure what to do. Although she desperately wanted to make a wish for Grace, she was going to have to postpone it *again* until the October moon, as Evie had also received a note from Danny McGinn.

Danny wrote to thank Evie for her recent healing, saying Bart was still improving but was by no means fully well. He begged Evie to heal his friend at the full moon as she had said she could. He hinted that she owed the McGinns a favour after all the years they had helped Lucia, and for coming to Evie's aid recently. Despite the rather pointed request, it was a thoughtful letter, understanding how it was a lot to ask but pleading Bart's case, nonetheless. Evie felt she could hardly refuse, but she was heartbroken for Grace and decided that she couldn't stay away while her friend was in turmoil. She sent the stable boy Jimmy with a note to the Finches' house, saying she would call on Grace that afternoon regardless of her request for solitude.

Grace's father was out, and their butler showed Evie into

the parlour. Grace was sitting at the piano. She had been crying. After some more tears and hugs, Grace told Evie the full story of her time with doctors, her stay in hospital, and how annoying it was to wear a thick bandage over one eye, while her other eye was constantly watering.

On her way over, Evie had made up her mind to tell Grace her secret – not all of it and not in too much detail – but enough to reassure Grace that Evie could save her eyesight, and so her friend needn't fret over it any more.

But Grace's response was a complete shock. She wasn't delighted as Evie had expected, she was horrified, frightened and more than a little doubtful.

'You can't be serious, Evie!' she cried. 'Magic? That's spooky and weird, and, and I don't believe it! How could you say such a thing? Did you think a joke like that would cheer me up?'

For a moment, Evie didn't know what to say.

'I'm telling the truth, Grace,' she said, after a strained silence. 'This magic is real. I can repair your sight completely.'

'Then you should have *asked* me, Evie, not told me!' Grace said, completely flustered, almost hysterical. 'Anyway, I don't believe you! I can't believe you!'

Evie barely recognised her friend, but she held her nerve. 'Then I'm *asking* you, Grace,' she said gently. 'Will you let me help you?'

'I don't know, I can't think,' Grace shrieked. 'I'm so afraid, Evie, so desperately afraid.' Grace was trembling, wringing her handkerchief in her hands.

Evie took Grace's hands in her own to steady them. 'You

have a little time to think about it,' she said. 'It wouldn't be for over a month yet.'

'You mean October?' she said wearily.

'Yes, at the full moon on 8 October,' Evie said.

'Do you know how crazy that sounds?' Grace asked. 'That you can actually perform magic under a full moon?'

'I know,' Evie said. 'I've had a lot of secrets to keep since I was kidnapped, and this is only one of them.'

'Oh, I see,' Grace said. 'Even *this* has something to do with Dower Hall!'

'That is where it all started,' Evie said. 'At first, I thought the idea of having magic was crazy too, even impossible. Then it intrigued me though it scared me. Now I'm getting used to it, though there is still so much to learn.'

'But it sounds so strange, so dark,' Grace said. 'I was always afraid of stories about witchcraft.'

'The harp's magic does only good,' Evie said, 'and if the doctors can't help you, then why not let me try? Please say you will. All I have to do is play the harp under the full moon and wish for your eyesight to be restored. You don't even have to be there.'

Grace looked at Evie directly for the first time since she had entered the room, one watery eye appearing huge behind her glasses, the other covered with a thick padded bandage.

'At least tell me you'll think about it,' Evie continued. 'But let me know, soon. And Grace, please understand that this is an enormous secret. You must never tell anyone any part of it, even if you don't want me to help you. Will you promise me?'

Grace nodded. 'I am so sorry,' she whispered. 'It must

have been so hard for you all these months, and I must seem so ungrateful now. Of course, I promise to keep it secret, but I will need to think about it.'

Mr Finch arrived home and entered the room.

'Hello, Evie, I'm glad you came to visit,' he said cheerfully. 'Grace has been hiding away for too long. What is it you must think about, my dear?'

Grace blew her nose while Evie thought of an answer.

'I was inviting Grace to come to tea, and I thought we should invite Matthew and Samuel as well,' she said. 'They would love to see you, Grace. They ask about you all the time, Julia and Freddie too.'

Mr Finch nodded his approval. 'An excellent idea!' he said. 'You must go, Grace. It will do you the world of good. Poor Samuel must be pining for you, judging by the pile of letters he has been sending.'

Evie followed Mr Finch's gaze to the sideboard where several letters lay neatly tied together with ribbon.

Grace tried a little smile. 'I would like that, Evie,' she said. 'Very much. I'd love to hear everyone's news. It seems like ages since we've been together.'

Evie was relieved to see her friend react more normally. She leaned over and gave her a hug. 'We will meet soon,' Evie said. 'I'll send you a note.'

Mr Finch led Evie out to the hall.

'She's fretting dreadfully,' he whispered. 'She avoids seeing people because they remind her of all she will miss when her eyesight fails. Some of the pain medications the doctors gave her make her feel quite low, not herself. She can be tearful, fearful, even tetchy – it's difficult, you understand.'

'It's awful for her,' Evie whispered. 'Perhaps something will turn up that will help, luck, a miracle, anything.'

'I hope so,' Mr Finch said. 'You are very kind, Evie, and such a good friend to Grace. Please arrange that get-together, won't you? I worry about my darling daughter.'

'I will, I promise,' Evie said, and they said their goodbyes.

On her way home in the Finches' carriage, driven by their butler at Mr Finch's insistence, Evie felt unsettled. She could understand Grace's nervousness about magic but this was a wonderful gift and the harp's magic could cure her. Surely that was different from spooky and weird? Suddenly, after Grace's unusual response, Evie was worried about telling anyone else in the future. She had hoped to confide in Matthew someday, but what if he reacted like Grace? Or reacted even worse? Telling Samuel was out of the question. He would think it his duty to scour the countryside looking for Volok and hundreds of people would end up dead. That is, if he even believed her. Evie hoped that in all her distress Grace wouldn't let such a big secret slip.

With everything in her life so precariously balanced, and with still so many problems to overcome, Evie was beginning to feel like the whole world was falling in on top of her. But things were about to get even worse.

CHAPTER TWENTY-TWO

Much to Evie's disappointment, the get-together was delayed. Samuel was busy organising search parties for 'strange sightings' in Wick's End, including hunting 'vicious reptiles' after a confirmed sighting by a local man from Crompton. His friend had apparently been bitten by an extraordinarily large, yellow-fanged snake, whose venom had poisoned his brain, causing him to rant and rave, according to the local doctor.

Pictures on the front of the local newspapers showed Samuel shaking the doctor's hand, thanking him for his assistance. 'Residents need not be alarmed,' it quoted the constable as saying. 'Everything is under control.'

Grace had already told Evie that Samuel hadn't had a day off in weeks and was unlikely to be free to meet them. Clearly, the authorities were busy trying to hide the fact that there was an ongoing search for a dangerous killer, as well as for snakes. Evie had listened politely, thinking of Volok, his raging temper and volatile nature. Her quest was becoming more urgent by the hour. She didn't blame the McGinns. It was very likely they couldn't keep all their friends quiet. It might even have been someone else who leaked the story to the newspapers.

Matthew and his father were putting the final touches to the academy but there had been one or two last-minute hitches. Despite the delays, Matthew had promised Evie and Grace a special preview and Evie was looking forward to it, hoping she would be able to find the time. Rehearsals would be starting soon for the concert the Hartville Ensemble would be giving at the grand opening. A date was still not set but was likely to be in November. Matthew sent a note to say he hoped to have more definite news soon.

Evie visited Grace again and was relieved to find her friend in improving spirits. The visit was brief, however, as Evie was now in training. The sample music for the sixth charm had alarmed her, and she decided to challenge herself with difficult pieces of music to sharpen her skills, and that meant many extra hours of practice. Evie also had her regular duties of care for both her parents, and she still hadn't figured out how she was going to manage to 'head off into the wilderness'. Where exactly was that going to be? And what reason could she give for disappearing for a whole day with so much going on at home? So far, she had dismissed all her ideas for excuses as either useless or ridiculous.

With Julia keeping more and more to herself, Freddie was Evie's main source of encouragement and sense, and she was glad to include him more and more in her secret activities. This meant additional cover-up stories were needed – for both of them, not just for Evie – and sometimes there were some narrow escapes within the household. With the Black Ruby hidden in his toy box, he had become rather possessive of his bedroom, as Tilly had noticed.

'Master Freddie is growing up fast,' she said to Evie one

day. 'He doesn't like me tidying his things any more, or even going near his room. I haven't pressed him to let me in, but I do hope he's not hiding a dreadful mess!'

'He's just being a boy,' Evie said, smiling uncomfortably. 'I'll keep an eye on him, and his room.'

Evie's mother was at last feeling a little better and began to spend more time up and about, sitting in the parlour listening to Evie practise the flute and the harp, even walking around the garden on her better days. It made the house appear almost normal again, and it made Evie's father more determined to get back to his routine too. He was desperate to return to work full-time and insisted on examining the goblet for hours every day in his study, including doing a mountain of research.

'Enough of this bedroom!' he had announced. 'Time to push myself harder and get back to work! Yes, work. It never did anyone any harm!'

Every day, Evie helped him get organised in the study once his exercises were over. She was still trying to decide how she would remove the goblet from right under his nose, as well as under lock and key. Edward had said he would collect it in two weeks, not three, unless the professor was finished with it sooner. Hardly likely, Evie thought. Her father would want to keep it as long as possible. But it gave Evie a little time, and perhaps her father would discover something important about it. Her only hope would be to sneak it away at night, unobserved. But then her father instructed Hudson to always check that he had remembered to lock it away in his safe, rather than his cabinet each evening, and Evie knew it would be impossible to crack that open.

Julia had been spending her time quietly, reading and taking short walks in the garden, still looking pale and off form. Then, she fell ill. With the first change in the weather, the governess developed a chest infection and was confined to bed. After a week she hadn't improved and her cough had worsened, so Dr Elliott was called to see her. He instructed Julia to remain in bed, ensure she got plenty of rest, hot drinks and good food, and not to consider doing anything until he pronounced her well enough. Tuition for Evie and Freddie would not be resuming yet even though it was a week into September.

Evie needed to discuss a few matters with her father. *I must handle this carefully*, she thought, hoping that her magic would help her. As she knocked on the door of his study, she was already feeling guilty. Trust the magic, Nala had said. But perhaps the magic would decide who Evie could persuade, and if it wasn't meant to be then Evie would have to accept it. She rolled her eyes in frustration, crossed her fingers, and entered.

The professor was taking his regular afternoon tea and biscuits at his desk.

'Come in, dear,' he said. 'You caught me at a good moment. This goblet is fascinating. As soon as I'm finished, I will explain everything. I think you'll be enthralled.'

'I can't wait,' Evie said. 'You're not working too hard, are you?'

'Not at all,' her father said. 'I love my work. I'm convinced it keeps me alive! And this goblet is so special. I am really enjoying it.'

'Well, try not to overdo it,' Evie said. 'Dr Elliott must

think our home is more like a hospital at the moment, he has so many patients here.'

'Don't count me as one, not any more,' her father said. 'I'm a bit wobbly on the legs, but otherwise I'm fine.'

'Do you really mean that?' Evie asked.

'I'm a little tired sometimes, but yes, I'm fine,' her father said. 'Just fine.'

'Good, I'm glad,' Evie said.

'Well, what is it?' her father asked. 'I can tell you want to ask me something.'

'Yes. Yes, I do,' Evie said. She decided not to beat around the bush and got straight to the point. 'I know you said you hadn't decided anything yet, but I'd really prefer if you didn't send Freddie to boarding school. Please, not yet.'

Her father paused before biting into his biscuit. 'I see. Why is that exactly?'

'Not till he's older,' Evie said. 'Freddie hasn't lived with us that long, so it wouldn't be fair to send him away so soon. And I like having him around, we all do. It would be so lonely here without him.'

'Rest easy, my dear,' her father said, raising a hand. 'I have come to the same conclusion.'

'You have?' Evie said, and her whole body relaxed with relief. 'But I thought you had more or less made up your mind to send him away.'

'Dear me! Your mother and I aren't monsters, you know! We were simply worried that with both of us under the weather, too much would be on Julia's shoulders, and yours too. It wouldn't be fair on the Hudsons to fill in, and Freddie has a lot of energy as you well know. I'm much better now and your mother is doing better too, thank goodness. But you're right, Freddie needs stability in his home life. When he's thirteen, he will cope better with boarding school.'

'I am relieved,' Evie said.

'Good. Now, what else did you want to ask me?' her father said.

Evie knew the surprise must have shown on her face.

'I always know when you have something on your mind,' her father said. 'The look is still there in your eyes.'

'Do you? Is it?' Evie asked nervously.

'Always,' her father said. 'Out with it! Come on!' He smiled encouragingly.

'Well,' Evie began slowly, 'even though Julia won't be back on her feet for a few weeks, I was hoping you wouldn't hire another governess.'

'And why is that?' her father asked.

'I know you must have thought of getting a substitute,' Evie said. She was worried about a replacement arriving, another person to keep away from her secrets.

'Your mother and I have already spoken about it,' her father said. 'We would never ask Julia to leave while she is unwell, but your education is important. Go on, explain your thoughts.'

'I believe I can manage my studies myself and I can help Freddie with his too,' Evie said. 'It probably won't be too long before Julia returns to her duties, anyway, hopefully. But also, I've decided that I want to have a career in music. I have some ideas about that, but, well Matthew has asked me to consider being a tutor at the academy. Not yet of course. I'd have to do some training, but I'd like that very much. So, the rest of my studies won't be so important, especially as I only have a year of tutoring left and I'm not terribly keen on going to finishing school. Mother can teach me all that I need to know.'

Evie paused as her father nodded, considering her words.

'There's a music teaching diploma starting in the new year,' Evie continued. 'In the academy. With Mr Reid. Matthew has already completed the first year of it while he was at boarding school. He studied for it at night. He'll be a little over a year ahead of me, but that means he can help me with it, if I need help.'

Evie looked at her father, hoping he wouldn't shoot down the idea along with her rambling explanation.

'You are very young to be making such a big decision, Evie,' her father said, after a pause. 'Are you really sure? Matthew is three years older than you and has finished all his schooling.'

'I'm very sure,' Evie said. 'I've given it a lot of thought, really I have. I want to be a music teacher. My studies will take about two years, maybe three, but I can assist part-time after I complete the first year. Perhaps, like Matthew, I could study at night, until I finish regular studies next July. Mr Reid wants to arrange more concerts, and I can help him with that too. It will be a wonderful career doing what I love.'

'I can't say I'm totally surprised, you have a great musical talent,' her father said. 'But you're only fifteen. Aren't you taking this leap just a little too soon?'

'Nearly sixteen,' Evie said, indignantly. 'And no! Why should my age matter where music is concerned?'

'With your exceptional talent, you make a good point,' her father said.

'I will concentrate on the flute first, but I'd like to play the harp more too,' Evie said. 'Maybe take some formal lessons. I'm really self-taught, after all.'

'You are a remarkable young woman, Evie,' her father said. 'Your mother and I have always wanted you to follow your heart's desire, and we would like Freddie to do so too. You have just confirmed to me that music is at the centre of all you wish for.'

'It is,' Evie said. *It has to be*, she thought, but didn't say.

'You already know how I feel about women following their own path in life,' her father said. 'If this is what you want, then so be it. But you are young, and I don't want you to regret it. Think on it some more, and by all means send in the application to Mr Reid. I will sign it, but that will give you time to make a final decision by the end of the year.'

'All right,' Evie said. 'But I already know what my decision will be.'

Her father smiled. 'Does that mean your interest in my work is over?' he asked.

'Oh no!' Evie said. 'I love it. The discoveries, the mysteries, the history, all of it. I'd like to learn more, though as a hobby rather than a career.'

'I see you have thought about this too,' her father said.

'I have,' Evie said. 'Things have changed a lot over the last year.'

Her father nodded wisely.

'I'm glad you understand,' Evie said. 'I was worried you might not.'

'Really? Never!' her father said. He smiled. 'But we will talk about it again just as soon as I finish my report on this goblet. Come, take a look at it with me.'

Evie left her father engrossed in his work an hour later, satisfied that she had achieved at least some agreement regarding Freddie's schooling and little or no argument about her own plans, just a sensible caution. Now, she needed to come up with a plan to steal the goblet from her father and destroy it. She hoped its disappearance wouldn't break her father's heart.

CHAPTER TWENTY-THREE

Neither Evie nor Freddie gave much thought to the studies they were missing while Julia was ill. Both of them loved to learn and always enjoyed reading, but there were more pressing issues to take care of. After over a week of demanding harp practice, Evie felt she had really improved and was ready for any challenge the final charm could throw at her.

Matthew, Grace and Samuel were due to arrive for supper. The idea of meeting for tea in the morning or afternoon had been too difficult to organise for everyone, and an early evening arrangement was the next best option. (Samuel was surprised and delighted to be given special permission by Mr Finch to have the evening off!) Julia was still in bed, but Evie's father didn't insist on a chaperon. Evie knew he would pop in to say hello at least once, and Hudson would no doubt hover nearby. It would be Grace's first time out of her house for ages, and Evie wanted to make it especially nice.

After supper, the friends relaxed in the parlour, and Evie related some of her recent conversations with her father.

'Good for you!' Matthew said. 'Standing up for what you believe!'

'I'm glad too,' Freddie said. 'I'd prefer to wait until

secondary school before boarding. My best friend, Philip, told me he'll be going then too.'

'That's great,' Matthew said. 'The two of you will start together. You'll be friends for life.'

'What about now, while Miss Pippen is unable to teach?' Samuel asked. 'Will a new governess be appointed?'

'No. We'll continue with our studies as best we can,' Evie said. 'Hopefully, it won't be for too long.'

'And you're sure you want to be both a musician and a tutor?' Samuel asked.

'Very sure,' Evie said. 'It's what I've always wanted.'

'We will be lucky to have you at the academy, Evie,' Matthew said. 'Lucky to keep you too. You might decide to spread your wings after a few years, perhaps travel, perform solo.'

'I really haven't thought that far ahead,' Evie said.

'My father will be delighted with your decision,' Matthew said. 'At the moment, all he can think about is getting ready for the opening. He is fussing unbearably.'

'Have you a date yet?' Grace asked.

'Still looking like late November,' Matthew said. 'We might promote it as an early Christmas concert. It would add a nice atmosphere.'

'Everyone in the town will come,' Evie said. 'I'm sure it will be a great success, and a wonderful way to promote the academy.'

'You should put posters up all around the town and other towns too,' Samuel said. 'I could help with that.'

'Excellent! Thank you,' Matthew said. 'I've already warned several of my friends that I will be counting on their support.'

Grace had fallen quiet, and everyone knew why. With her

eyesight failing, she probably wouldn't be able to take part.

Matthew bravely broke the silence. 'There would be a place for you in the academy too, Grace, when you feel ready and if you wish it. Your marvellous memory means you can play everything. You mustn't give up the piano.'

'I won't give up,' Grace said, glancing at Evie. 'I'll just have to get used to it, I suppose.'

'You've been very busy lately, Samuel,' Matthew said, changing the subject. Grace was looking so forlorn.

'Yes, sightings of snakes, vandalism, a madman on the loose and a murder still unsolved,' Samuel said. 'A policeman's work is never done.'

'Are you still hoping to become a detective?' Evie asked.

'That is my ambition,' Samuel said. 'I think it would be a more rewarding career in the long run.'

He was about to launch into the merits of detection when Hudson knocked on the door and entered quickly.

'Excuse me, Miss Evie, but I've had to send for the doctor,' he said. 'Tilly was just with Miss Pippen, and it appears she has taken a turn for the worse. Your parents are upstairs talking with the nurse.'

The gathering broke up immediately, and everyone said hurried goodbyes.

'Write to me, Evie, or send the stable boy with a message if it's really urgent,' Matthew said at the hall door. 'Let me know how Miss Pippen is and whether you need any help, or some company.'

'Thank you, Matthew,' Evie said. 'Thank you all for coming. I really enjoyed the evening and I'm so sorry to send you away with more bad news.'

'It was lovely, Evie,' Grace said. 'It meant a lot. I'll write soon, and you must call on me again when you can.'

'I will,' Evie said.

The doctor arrived soon after Evie's friends left. The news was worrying – Julia's infection had turned to pneumonia.

'Nurse Stanley will keep an eye on Miss Pippen tonight,' the doctor told Evie and her parents, the nurse looking stern, standing beside him. 'I'll check on her again tomorrow.'

Julia's temperature was high, and in her delirium she began to mutter about full moons, magic and demons, snakes and even resurrection. Evie was sitting with her father in his study, and nearly choked on her biscuit when the nurse came in to report on Julia's condition and her latest ravings.

'You mustn't let it bother you, Miss Evie, nor you, Professor,' Nurse Stanley said confidently. 'I've heard things like this before. It comes from all the reading and learning a governess does. All those books have given her a vivid imagination!'

But a few minutes later, Tilly mentioned it too.

'I don't like what Miss Pippen has been saying, sir,' Tilly said.

'Oh? And what was that, Tilly?' Evie's father asked.

'Something about witchcraft, sir,' Tilly said. 'I'd rather not say, exactly. Excuse me, sir, but I'd prefer if only the nurse went into Miss Pippen's room for the next while.'

The professor was taken aback but he agreed. On her way to bed, Evie decided to find out what had frightened their maid so much.

CHAPTER TWENTY-FOUR

Evie stood outside Julia's bedroom and put her ear to the door. Inside Julia was mumbling but it was hard to make out any words. Evie knew she could enter safely without risk of infection, because a Harp Maiden will only die of old age not of illness. But she didn't want to be spotted entering and then have to make up more excuses.

Evie opened the door a couple of inches. The nurse was mopping Julia's brow, trying to cool her fever. She came quickly to the door.

'You shouldn't come in, Miss Evie,' the nurse said. 'The professor said there were to be no visitors. Miss Pippen is very ill. I think it likely she will go to the hospital tomorrow for some new treatment the doctor mentioned, and to keep everyone in this household safe.'

'How awful,' Evie said. 'The fever is making her rave, isn't it? What is she saying?'

'Oh, the stuff of fairy tales, mostly,' the nurse said. 'I don't pay any attention to ravings like that.'

'All right, then. Thank you, Nurse,' Evie said. 'Please let us know if there is any change.'

'Of course,' the nurse said. 'I'm updating Professor Wells regularly.'

Evie turned to go.

'Oh, Miss Evie, I need to go into town to collect more of the sedatives the doctor prescribed from the apothecary,' the nurse said. 'I won't be long. I don't trust the servants to do that sort of thing. You understand.'

'Um, oh, all right, thank you, Nurse,' Evie said.

Evie returned once the coast was clear and this time she went into the room. Approaching Julia's bed, she was alarmed to see how frail her governess had become. She was tossing and turning, muttering all the things that should be kept secret. There was only one way to soothe her. Evie sat down on the edge of the bed and placed a hand on Julia's forehead. Closing her eyes, she thought only of how desperately she wanted to soothe her governess, her friend, who had suffered so much this last year, and who, despite all her concerns, had remained steadfast and loyal if a bit cantankerous at times.

When Evie opened her eyes, Julia was in a deep sleep, though her forehead was still burning. She thought of the Ladder of Charms and felt guilty that she hadn't finished it yet. Perhaps then she would have enough magic to heal Julia, though she wasn't entirely sure if that would be the case. Her thoughts switched to the ruby and her guilt turned rapidly to anger. Was Julia's illness part of the ruby's ancient curse?

Evie left Julia and went straight to Freddie's bedroom. She opened his toy chest and took out the casket. Peeping around the door, she checked to see that the way was clear, and returned to her own bedroom. Placing the casket on the floor, Evie opened it. She removed the package, opened out the shawl and took out the Black Ruby of Yodor.

'How dare you!' she whispered to it. 'How dare you

curse innocent, good, kind people!' And then in an angry, bitter voice, 'I will destroy you forever. Soon, very soon, I promise. You will never hurt anyone again. Your curse will be destroyed with you, and you will never bring demons back to life to wreak havoc in this world, not now, not ever!'

Furious, Evie was about to throw the ruby at the wall when there was a knock on her bedroom door.

'Evie?' her father said. 'May I come in?'

The professor entered before Evie could answer.

'I thought I heard you in some distress,' her father said. 'Oh my! What is that?'

'Um, nothing,' Evie said, stuffing the ruby under the shawl. 'I was just going through some old things, muttering to myself.'

'Aha! Tilly was right,' her father said, his gaze moving from the shawl to Evie's dressing table and the fake goblet.

'About what?' Evie asked.

'She said you have a goblet just like the one I have been examining,' her father said. 'An exact replica, she said. Might I take a look?'

'Of course,' Evie said, and went over to the dresser. She took her pins, brooches and ribbons out of the goblet and handed it to her father. 'Freddie and I found it when we were out riding.'

'Why didn't you tell me?' her father asked as he studied it.

Evie didn't reply.

'Where exactly?' her father asked.

'Near Dower Hall, well, not far from it,' Evie said.

Evie watched, irritated, as her father turned the goblet over in his hands. Then he put it gently back on the dressing table. Evie's anxiety soared as she waited for what could only be a difficult question – or several.

'Tell me, Evie, why are you really so interested in Galen's Goblet, the real one, or this fake one, for that matter?' her father asked. 'The truth, please, Evie. And where did you get that?'

Aided by his stick, he walked stiffly over to her bed and lifted the shawl. He turned his head and looked directly at her. For the next few seconds, Evie felt like she was suspended in time – time she needed to think what to do and what to say. Could she really lie her way out of this? Surely her father was too clever to fall for any excuse she could think of. If she could even think of one.

Her face must have said it all, and she slumped onto the bed. She was so cross with herself and so desperately disappointed to have let her guard down. There was no going back now.

'Oh, my darling girl,' her father whispered. 'What a burden you have had. I knew there was something strange going on ever since those awful events last year. I know about the legend, Evie. I'm an historian, for goodness' sake! That story I didn't finish – well, you know it all, don't you, because it's true and it's happening right here and now, isn't it?'

The professor sat down on the bed beside her.

'What do you mean, which story?' Evie asked, clutching at the last straw, hoping her father had jumped to some other conclusion.

'The story of the harp and the Harp Maiden,' he said gently. 'But more importantly, that *you* are the Harp Maiden.'

Evie gasped as she looked up and stared into her father's

face. She had never expected him to say that, and certainly not right now. Looking into his eyes, she tried desperately to read what was there. Was it anger? Fear? Dread? No, it was pride, mixed with a deep concern.

'I, I, um . . .' Evie really didn't know where to begin.

'I was going to tell you the rest of the story of the Harp Maiden, the legend, I mean,' her father said. 'But you knew it already, better than anyone. How did I not see what was right in front of me for so long?'

'But how did you know?' Evie asked, perplexed.

'Certain details I found in my research, your recent interests and behaviour, and even the words you spoke just now,' her father said. 'I asked Edward to bring the research notes he had collected on the Harp Maiden story, they filled in a few gaps for me.'

Evie stared at her father.

'So, you don't deny it, then?' he asked her.

Evie shook her head slowly, without saying a word.

Her father took one of her hands in his. 'The harp legend was always assumed to be connected to the demon legend, though a lot of details became entangled over the centuries,' he said. 'If I'm not mistaken, that is the Black Ruby of Yodor.'

Evie thought she would collapse. She still couldn't speak, and luckily her father didn't seem to expect her to.

'I heard a little of the story many years ago, when I was researching something entirely different, as I told you,' her father continued. 'Bit by bit, I gathered a lot of information, but I never got the chance to put it together properly. It always seemed to me to be like a tricky jigsaw puzzle, and there were so many gaps. Then Edward brought his notes with him the other night, and in those notes I found a lot of the answers I had been looking for. There was the harp, of course, the ancient notebook you are so protective of, the primary talismans, including that goblet, and the infamous Black Ruby. My oh my! Is that a Mesopotamian casket?'

'A what?' Evie asked.

'It is,' her father said, running his fingers along the carved wood. 'You kept the ruby in there?'

'You were really able to figure it all out?' Evie asked, barely hearing his question.

'That's my job, dear, my life's work,' her father said. 'The truth is always there if you are patient and know where to look and probe. Putting all the bits and pieces together when the facts are so scattered puts many people off. The facts in this puzzle were in quite a jumble, which is why no one ever fully pieced the story together. They *chose* not to believe what might be hidden amongst all those strange clues because it was easier, and then they just let it go. But eventually I cracked it, though not the biggest revelation of all – you, Evie.'

'What do you know about the Harp Maiden?' Evie asked.

'Are you finally admitting it?' her father said, eyeing her inquiringly but gently.

'If you know the whole story as I do,' Evie said, 'then you know that the Harp Maiden is duty bound to follow her path, use the harp's magic wisely, protect the harp at any cost and do whatever it takes to rid the world of evil.'

The professor's eyes nearly popped out of his head, and his spectacles slid down his nose and fell into his lap. Evie swallowed hard. Had she spoken too soon? Perhaps her father didn't know as much as he thought, as much as *she* thought.

How could she have been so reckless again?

'Evie, I know enough about magic to understand that it doesn't just come with privilege but with obligations too – and usually a lot of danger,' her father said, putting his spectacles back on.

'I have so much to tell you,' Evie said, almost ready to burst.

'Hudson wants to talk to me about something,' Evie's father said. 'Let's talk when I'm finished with him. Does Freddie know about this?'

'Yes, all of it, so does Julia,' Evie said.

'Well, I'm glad you had some confidantes,' her father said. 'Otherwise, it would have been a heavy and lonely burden.'

'It was,' Evie said without thinking. 'I mean, it can be sometimes.'

'Join me in the study in half an hour,' her father said gently. 'Then you can tell me everything. We'll share all our secrets then.'

Evie looked at him, wide-eyed.

'Oh, yes! I have a few too, but don't tell your mother!' her father joked. 'And bring that fake goblet down, will you? I want to look at it with my magnifying glass.'

The professor went to meet Hudson, leaving Evie with plenty to think about for the next thirty minutes.

CHAPTER TWENTY-FIVE

U nable to think straight, Evie spent the time brushing her hair and tidying away her ribbons and brooches. Then she took out Nala's notebook and sat down on her bed again. She opened it, sensing that there might be another message for her – she was getting good at that. A few more pages had been rescripted, confirming her progress up the Ladder of Charms. Skimming through the now familiar pages, she found the new message.

> *The magic within you may come when you call it, or it may not. Learn to accept the choices the magic makes, for it will not always give you the answers you seek. If it is time for someone to pass on to the next life, then so it shall be. The magic will know best because it knows the future. It knows all – your destiny, and everyone else's.*

Evie gasped. It was as if the diary knew what was happening in her life right at that moment. Could it really be time for Julia to pass on? Who else could it be referring to? Her governess had looked dreadfully ill even after Evie had soothed her with what little magic she had. Perhaps the magic had chosen not to heal Julia because it wasn't her destiny, or perhaps it was the ruby's curse. Evie couldn't know for certain. Her bottom lip began to tremble as she fought back tears at the thought, the most awful thought . . .

Evie stood up abruptly, slapping the notebook onto the bed. Why couldn't *she* decide? Whoever heard of magic deciding anything? Suddenly feeling both angry and defiant, Evie refused to wallow in sad thoughts. She smoothed her skirt, tidied her hair, picked up the goblet and the notebook and marched downstairs to her father's study. She took a few calming breaths before entering to compose herself.

'Good, you brought them,' her father said, entering the room a few minutes after Evie. 'We can talk about them in a moment. Let's sit on the sofa and I shall listen to *your* story. Please, my dear, tell me every little detail. Don't leave anything out.'

To her surprise, Evie's father listened patiently and calmly from start to finish, only wincing occasionally when she told him of the more dangerous events, even though she chose her words carefully.

'If I didn't understand this stuff so well, I'd be an absolute wreck after hearing all that,' her father finally said. 'Or I wouldn't believe a word of it!'

'But you do believe me, don't you?' Evie said, suddenly worried.

'Absolutely, my dear,' her father said. 'I have all the proof I need in my books, and from all my years of learning. I have believed in magic in all its forms since attending university when I began to delve into all these myths and legends. I wanted to know the truth then and I still do. Unfortunately, it is a truth many people want to avoid. Some of the stories were only hearsay, of course, exaggerations to impress, or simply wild imagination, but others, well,' – he shook his head – 'I just knew they had to be true or partly true. I always wondered if I would encounter magic one day and here it is.'

'Why didn't you tell me this before?' Evie asked.

'I didn't discuss it with anyone except one or two colleagues, and that was a long time ago,' her father said. 'Magic is too difficult for most people to understand, and too frightening for others, even for some of my most learned friends in the museum.'

'There's more,' Evie said, squirming. 'And you're not going to like it.'

'Let me be the judge of that,' her father said, putting down his teacup.

Evie finally got to the part about Nala and the casket, and her instructions to finish the Ladder of Charms, so she could destroy the Black Ruby and Volok.

'Volok really was a *demon*?' her father asked incredulously.

'He *is*,' Evie said. 'And he is determined to resurrect his wife.'

'A *real* one, I mean, two demons? Here?' her father asked, his eyes almost popping out with surprise. 'And a head in a casket? Good grief!'

'I'm afraid so,' Evie said.

She explained some more.

'Oh no, not the talismans!' her father said. 'Do they really have to be destroyed?'

'Yes, all five of them together and soon,' Evie said. 'On the night of the full moon. I must do it or Volok will come after them and use them. He's also desperate to get his hands on the Black Ruby and use it to resurrect his queen. If he succeeds, together they will–'

Her father raised a hand. 'I understand,' he said. 'But goodness me! How I underestimated my own daughter, my lovely Evie.' He cupped her cheek gently in his hand. 'When I put enough of the clues together, I didn't want to believe you could be the Harp Maiden, caught up in so much danger. But it all fits, every little piece, right down to your birthday, your talent, your endless curiosity and bravery.'

Evie smiled gently at him, hoping this startling revelation wouldn't undo her father's recovery. 'You mustn't worry about me,' she said. 'If this is meant to be then I am able to do it. I know what I must do, and I am close to the end now.'

They were both silent for a long moment. Evie hoped her father wouldn't raise some major objection to her continuing the quest. If he did, she would have to ignore him and press on regardless.

'I think I understand it all now,' her father said. 'Normal policing won't stop this creature. Our brave constabulary is no match for dark magic. But to know that it must be *you* that stops him, *you*, Evie. Is there no other way?'

'No, no one else,' Evie said. 'It's my duty, part of being the Harp Maiden. I must see this through.'

Silence.

Evie's father stood and walked slowly with the help of his stick back to his desk. He slumped awkwardly into his great chair, dropping his stick on the floor. 'Bring that other goblet over here, would you, dear?' he asked.

Evie brought the fake to him. Standing beside the real one, it looked identical except for the opal set into the base of the real one, and they were slightly different in height. Evie walked around the desk and opened her notebook.

'Look at this,' she said. 'You saw some of these notes before but look how many there are now. Each step on the Ladder of Charms reveals a secret, information or instructions from Nala, the sorceress who made the harp. I cannot turn my back on all this. This is real.' Evie paused but couldn't wait for her father to comment. 'Even if I wanted to, I couldn't. And you can't order me to, and I can't obey you even if you do order me. Really, I can't. I won't!'

The professor turned in his chair and took Evie's hands in his.

'My dear, I understand,' he said gently. 'You are incredibly precious to me, and now I see that you are incredibly important to the whole world too. I admit this will be extremely difficult for me to accept, but now–'

'Now what?' Evie interrupted.

'Now,' her father repeated, then paused. 'Now, you must let me help you with your destiny.'

Evie lunged forward and hugged her father tightly.

'Thank you, thank you!' she said, bursting with relief.

'My goodness!' her father said. 'I can hardly believe I am agreeing to all this. Nor can I believe what I am about to do.'

'What are you about to do?' Evie asked.

'My dear,' her father said. 'I have just thought of a very naughty plan that concerns these two goblets. Something I never in my life thought I would ever do.'

CHAPTER TWENTY-SIX

The professor explained his idea to exchange the real goblet for the fake one – *after* inserting an opal belonging to Evie's mother into the base of the real one.

'That way I can claim it was the best fake yet, and do so somewhat honestly,' Evie's father said. 'What do you think?'

'I think it's a great plan,' Evie said. 'In fact, Freddie had a similar idea.'

'Did he indeed?' her father said, sounding rather pleased. 'He's going to be a fine young man one day!'

Evie couldn't help smiling. She was glad that her father had also come up with the idea to swap the goblets. Adding her mother's opal was even better. It made what they were about to do seem less like a crime and made her feel a little less guilty too.

'This opal belonged to your grandmama,' her father continued. 'Your mother won't notice it's missing as she hasn't worn this brooch in years. This will be another secret, Evie, at least until I can think of a good excuse for its disappearance.'

Professor Wells was quite the craftsman. He delicately removed the opal from the brooch and set it into the base of the fake goblet, where he had hollowed out a little indent for the stone with one of his excavation tools. It was a perfect fit. Using a very stinky glue, he lightly touched the back of the opal and pressed it firmly into the prepared space, then held it steady for a couple of minutes. Taking his hand away carefully, he watched to see if it was secure.

'You did it!' Evie said.

The professor leaned back and admired his work.

'We should let it sit undisturbed for a few hours,' he said. He handed the real goblet to Evie. 'Do what you must, my dear, though it pains me to say so.'

'Thank you,' Evie said. 'I hated the thought of stealing it from you, but I would have done it.'

'I know,' her father said. 'Wrong as that might seem to some, what you are about to do is more important than having that goblet sit in a museum for all eternity. Take it, fulfil your destiny and your promise to the sorceress.'

He kissed Evie on the forehead.

Evie took Galen's Goblet and turned to leave the study, when she stopped.

'Would you like to see the other talismans?' she asked. 'Before I—'

'I would adore to, my dear, but I must say no,' her father said. 'One day, in my discussions with my colleagues, I might let it slip and then where would we be? In big trouble, to put it mildly.' He leaned back in his chair. 'Go, do what you must to save the world, my darling.'

'What will you tell Edward, and the museum?' Evie asked.

'I'll tell them the truth – that they have a fake!' her father said.

Evie couldn't stifle a giggle, and her father smiled back, shaking his head. She left the study and returned to her bedroom with the final primary talisman safe in her arms.

Freddie was delighted when Evie asked him to help her on the night of the full moon. Instead of going to the park, however, she decided they would ride out of town as she would need a bigger fire to burn the talismans once the wish was made. As soon as Jimmy had finished his chores and left for the day, they went to the stables to prepare.

'I kept another one of these sacks for the talismans,' Freddie said, lifting up a slightly grubby canvas bag.

'Good thinking,' Evie said. 'What was in them, horse feed?'

'Yes, they're all a bit smelly but very sturdy,' Freddie said.

'Perfect. We can pack everything now and head off once the moon is up,' Evie said. 'It should light our way easily as the sky should stay clear tonight.'

'Volok will be so furious when he realises what's happened,' Freddie said.

'I know,' Evie said. 'It will be much more dangerous from now on.'

'Did Uncle Henry want to see the other talismans?' Freddie asked.

'No,' Evie said. 'He said he wants to make sure he never lets it slip that he ever saw them at all, and in his house too!'

'But he must have been dying to see them,' Freddie said. 'How could he resist?'

'I know,' Evie said. 'It was very generous of him, a big sacrifice. I didn't tell him you were coming, by the way, just that you were helping me to get ready.'

'I'd better make sure he sees me going to bed, then,' Freddie said. 'Before I get up again and leave with you!'

'We won't go too far,' Evie said. 'Just to the edge of the forest out on the road to Crompton. We shouldn't be seen or heard out there.'

'Are you going to wish for Danny and Martin's friend?' Freddie asked.

'Yes, I promised I would,' Evie said. 'It's only fair as he's still not back to full health.'

'I think the McGinn brothers will help us again if we need them,' Freddie said. 'Maybe Bart will too.'

'Let's hope so,' Evie said. 'Though I don't want too many people knowing what I'm doing, what we're doing.'

Freddie grinned at her, looking chuffed.

Evie secured the satchel behind her saddle and the sack carrying the talismans on the back of Freddie's saddle. Next, Freddie helped Evie to strap the harp to her back with long lengths of rope, his lessons in tying rope knots coming in very handy. It was a little after three in the morning, a late moon rise, when they were finally ready to go.

They rode slowly at first to keep the noise of the horses' hooves to a minimum, and for Evie to become accustomed to the extra weight she was carrying on her back. Once out of town, they galloped for about ten minutes, their route through the countryside illuminated by a rising full moon.

Evie led the way into a copse she remembered, having travelled that road many times now. It was thick with ferns too, another reason why she chose it. The ferns would be needed to wrap the talismans before they were burned.

Freddie tied the horses to a low, sturdy branch and removed the satchel and the sack and placed them on the ground. Evie untied the knot of rope at her waist, allowing the harp to slowly slide down her back and onto the grass. Freddie then gathered ferns as well as extra twigs for the fire as it would need to burn hotter and for longer than normal.

'I'm glad to take the harp off my back,' Evie said, stretching her arms and rubbing her neck.

'Was it very heavy?' Freddie asked.

'Not at first,' Evie said. 'It felt heavier as we rode, bumping into my back and neck all the time. I was nervous the rope might come undone, and it would fall off.'

'No way,' Freddie said. 'Jimmy showed me how to tie knots really well.'

'Good for Jimmy,' Evie said. 'Good for you!'

'The moon looks extra brilliant tonight,' Freddie said. 'Maybe it knows what you're about to do.'

'I wonder,' Evie murmured, gazing up. The stars were twinkling like diamonds making the sky look especially magical.

They sat down and Evie lit the fire. She placed the wish for Bart on the flames and played some lovely melodies on the harp. When she stopped, neither Evie nor Freddie could hide their excitement.

'The talismans,' Freddie said. 'I can't wait to see this.'

'This is a really big step,' Evie said. 'We were so lucky to find them all.'

'What will happen when you burn them?' Freddie asked.

'I don't know,' Evie said. 'But we should be ready for anything.'

Freddie added more wood to the fire to boost the flames and placed more stones around it to keep it controlled. It burned merrily, its crackling and the occasional hoot of an owl the only sounds in the remote surroundings.

Evie wrapped each talisman in ferns, covering them completely. Then she placed the second piece of parchment on the flames, listing the names of each of the five. She picked up the dagger and dropped it into the now roaring blaze. The fire hissed and grew smoky. Sparks flew off in several directions, then the flames erupted into a tall column of fire before retreating back to normal. The same reaction occurred with the stone and the plate. But Evie hesitated when it came to burning the mirror. For a second she thought it might be useful to see the future again. How a magical object could tempt you, she thought, looking at her own reflection. The image in the mirror began to blur, then change. She was curious to know what it might show her this time.

'Evie, finish it,' Freddie said.

Resisting the allure of the magic, Evie tossed Marielle's Mirror into the flames. When the column of fire reduced once more, she picked up the goblet. Her father's heart must be breaking no matter what he had said. He would have received much praise for his research work, more recognition too, maybe even a medal. But like the other talismans, the goblet had to burn.

Evie dropped the goblet into the fire. This time it exploded into multiple forks of red flames, hissing and spitting as all five primary talismans melted down, even the stone disintegrated, crackling and smoking as they were each consumed by the flames. Then the fire suddenly went out, leaving only pillars of black smoke drifting towards the moonlit sky. It was over.

'It was sparkier and smokier than I expected,' Freddie said. 'I hope nobody noticed.'

'They'll only find the ashes if they come looking,' Evie said, 'and we'll be long gone.' She peered into the dying embers one last time. There was no trace of what had been burned.

'All the powerful magic is on our side now, isn't it?' Freddie said.

'Let's hope so,' Evie whispered. She stood up and gathered her things. 'Right then, help me strap the harp onto my back and we can go home.'

They eased up the pace as they approached the town, keeping the horses as quiet as possible. The moon was lower now though still bright, and dawn wasn't far off. Some early birds had already begun their song. But there was commotion at their house. They trotted unseen around the back of the house and into the stables. Their household was abuzz; someone was being taken away in a hospital wagon. Evie's heart began to pound faster and faster.

'What's going on?' Freddie asked.

'I don't know but it doesn't look good,' Evie said. 'Let's hope no one notices us in all the fuss.'

'We can leave everything in the boot room,' Freddie said. 'There's loads of stuff left there all the time.'

'Good idea,' Evie said. 'I even polish the harp in there sometimes to avoid making a mess. And, um, try to look like you're just out of bed. You know, sleepy, dressed in a hurry, and yawn a few times.'

'I will,' Freddie said, and followed Evie inside.

They joined the rest of the household in the hall. Evie looked first for her father. He was as glad to see her as she was to see him, standing up looking strong and alert, though frowning. He stared when he saw Freddie clearly faking a few yawns, then he looked to Evie hoping for some indication of what had happened. Evie nodded slowly to reassure him her task was done and was glad to see her father look relieved for a moment. Evie and Freddie made their way over to where the professor was standing. Everyone was looking towards the hall door and beyond, all of them having dressed in a hurry to be ready to help.

'What happened?' Evie asked quietly.

'Julia is gravely ill,' her father said. 'Tilly woke on hearing a noise, and found Julia at the bottom of the stairs, delirious. She woke the Hudsons, who woke me, and I sent Hudson for Dr Elliott. He insisted that Julia be taken to the hospital immediately.'

'Oh no!' Evie said. 'Will she be all right?'

'The doctor was quite concerned yesterday afternoon,' Evie's mother said. 'He was thinking of admitting her to hospital today, but she clearly worsened overnight. Julia needs more care than Nurse Stanley can give her here.'

Evie looked around at the anxious faces as the hospital wagon drove off with Julia inside, Dr Elliott following in his own carriage. Evie's magic hadn't put her governess on the road to recovery at all. She remembered with horror the recent message in Nala's notebook: '*If it is time for someone to pass on to the next life, then so it shall be.*'

Evie sat down heavily on the bottom step of the stairs. Freddie snuggled in beside her. Everyone was quiet, worried, returning to their rooms only slowly. Despite the harp's magical wishes, and now with her own developing magical powers, Evie found it difficult to accept there was nothing she could do for Julia at all, except hope.

CHAPTER TWENTY-SEVEN

No one was allowed to visit Julia in the hospital due to the infectious nature of her pneumonia and the seriousness of her condition. The doctor called to the house a few times to update the family, but it always sounded either vague or grave. Evie was desperately worried, but also about her mother. After making some recovery, Mrs Wells plunged yet again into more sadness, keeping mostly to her room, worn out by stress headaches.

One evening, the professor spoke to Evie in his study.

'This is a terrible business,' her father said quietly. 'Is there anything you can do, my dear? Anything at all?'

'No,' Evie said, sadly. 'My first wish was for Julia and Freddie back in January, and only one wish is allowed in each person's lifetime.'

Evie hadn't told her father about the magic within her. It was the only thing she had withheld from him, and she didn't mention it now either.

'So, there are rules,' her father said. 'I suppose I shouldn't be surprised.'

'Quite a few, unfortunately,' Evie said.

Silence.

'I wished for your arthritis to heal,' Evie said after a

moment. 'Last February, and for Mother in March. Which is why I can't wish for either of you again. I am sorry.'

'You cannot blame yourself,' her father said. 'You didn't choose the rules of this magic. I'm sure they were set a long time ago.'

Another silence.

'Will Julia live?' Evie asked, her voice trembling. 'The doctor doesn't say much. I wonder if he even knows. Did he tell you anything?'

'He said her lungs are weak, that they always have been,' her father said. 'We must prepare for the worst and hope for the best, as always.'

Evie poured some tea but neither of them felt like drinking it.

'You managed to destroy them, then,' her father said after another minute. 'All five talismans are gone?'

Evie nodded. 'Yes, but I didn't enjoy it as much as I thought I would.'

'It disappoints me to lose such important artefacts,' her father said. 'But if it is for the greater good then we can't complain.'

'Have you told Edward yet?' Evie asked.

'No, I've been trying to craft an appropriate letter,' her father said. 'I'll keep it brief and stick with the "it's a fake" story. It's true after all.'

'The whole museum will learn of it,' Evie said. 'Edward might have to report it to the police as well as the curator. I hope he won't get into trouble.'

'Don't worry,' her father said. 'I'll say it's the best fake I've ever seen.'

'Will any of this be awkward for you?' Evie asked.

'I don't see why,' her father said. 'They should be glad I discovered the fraud before it went on display!'

'I suppose,' Evie muttered.

'What is it, Evie?' her father asked.

'There is something else, but I don't want you to worry about it,' Evie said in a rush. 'It's something I have to do, and you are already working too hard, doing far too much. You know you have to pace yourself or you'll have a relapse.'

'Now you sound like Dr Elliott,' her father said. 'Enough about me. Tell me about this other thing.'

'Mother needs us too, she's terribly down,' Evie said, preparing herself by wittering on. 'I think she's retreating into herself again. I hope we're keeping the nurse on. We could do with the extra help, and I'll be—'

'We are keeping the nurse,' her father said. 'That is one argument with your mother I already lost, but I conceded so long as she concentrates on looking after Clara instead of me. What is it, Evie? What's this thing you must you do?'

Evie took a deep breath and launched into a fuller explanation of the Ladder of Charms, and in particular, step six.

'It's the final and most difficult step,' she said. 'I have to play music for a full day and night – very difficult music which I can't even practise properly! And I must play without stopping, eating, resting, and – and I have to do it outdoors.'

'That sounds horrendous!' her father said. 'What about your safety? And the weather?'

'I can choose the day, so I'll wait for a fair-weather day

– and night,' Evie said. 'But I can't wait too long, a day or two, maybe.'

'Well, you can't do it alone,' her father said.

Evie looked her father squarely in the face.

'You're not going alone!' her father said, looking horrified.

'I'm afraid I must.'

Evie spent hours trying to decide where she would take the final step on the Ladder of Charms. It had to be away from any interruption, and somewhere Volok wouldn't find her. Finally, she consulted a map of the area, then made her decision: she would spend a day and a night on Little Island, in the middle of Ladies' Lake. She had only been there once before when she and her brother, Ben, were very young. It wasn't easy to reach so it should be deserted. It was her best bet and she set her heart on it.

It was a beautiful autumn day, the best she could have hoped for, and Evie was optimistic that the weather would hold long enough for her to complete her task. Only Freddie and her father knew what she was doing and where she was going. Her mother would be told that Evie was spending a day and night with Grace, the servants likewise.

'Good luck, my darling,' her father said, the night before. 'I won't get up when you leave in the morning. I would only disturb the whole house and there would be awkward questions.'

'I understand,' Evie said.

'Is everything ready?' her father asked.

'All done,' Evie said. 'Freddie helped me. Thank you for asking Mrs Hudson to prepare that sumptuous dinner last night. I don't think I've ever eaten so much.'

'It'll be a while before you eat again,' her father said.

'You can have triple breakfast when you come home tomorrow,' Freddie said. 'I will too!'

Evie smiled. 'We'll see who can eat the most, won't we?' she said.

'We'll be waiting for you,' her father said, and he gave her a long hug.

Evie went to bed early, intending to rise in the dark and be on her way to her destination an hour before dawn. Freddie rose early to help Evie strap the harp on her back and attach a larger satchel to the saddle. Inside was her notebook, a rug and a flask of water. It was all she was allowed, according to the short message that appeared in Nala's notebook the day before. Again, it felt a little creepy how the message always appeared just in time.

'Good luck, Evie,' Freddie said. 'You'll do it. I know you will.'

'Thank you, Freddie, you've been such a big help,' Evie said, and gave him a tight hug. 'I'll see you tomorrow morning for that big breakfast.'

It wasn't a long ride and Evie knew the way well after checking it carefully beforehand. It was a clear night, and though still dark when she arrived, the waning moon was still shining and dawn wasn't far off. She tied her horse securely but loose enough to allow him to move around while she was occupied. The grass was still lush close to the lake, so he wouldn't go hungry. After untying the satchel from the saddle, Evie carried it in her arms and headed down to the water's edge. There were two small rowing boats waiting there for anyone who needed to cross to the tiny island. Evie chose the sturdier of the two, climbed in – glad she was wearing her jodhpurs and riding boots – and settled herself. She untied the boat, took up the oars and pushed off.

Due to her lack of rowing practice, Evie took it slowly. Fortunately, the water was very still, and the journey across only took about ten minutes. She secured the boat, gathered up her things, stepped up to the landing deck and walked inland. Evie had been there before as a six-year-old, when her brother Ben was only three. For that reason, it held a special place in her heart, a place filled with happy but sensitive memories. She was pleased with her choice of location, and relieved to see the island remained wild and natural, largely undisturbed.

She kept walking until she found a clearing close to a huge bank of rhododendrons that would provide some shelter should the wind pick up. Evie spread the rug on the grass, then untied the harp from her back and let it slide down onto the rug. She sat down and looked up. The sunrise was just beginning, the first cracks breaking low in the sky. It was glorious, a perfect setting for playing beautiful music. She guessed it was around 6.30 a.m. She took a long drink of water and settled into a comfortable position. After a few calming breaths to still her whirring thoughts and fluttering heart, Evie warmed her fingers with some practice scales and trills, then began.

By midday, Evie was already finding it hard. Her back and shoulders were getting stiff, and despite her big dinner the night before she was feeling the first pangs of hunger. She was thirsty too but wouldn't be able to drink another drop until she finished – in about eighteen hours. She tried not to think about it.

Nala's notebook lay on the rug before her, the pages turning automatically as she progressed through the challenging music. For an instant she wondered if the notebook would contain enough pages for all the music she would have to play, but of course it would, it was magical.

There were a few nervous moments during the afternoon when Evie nearly lost concentration. Luckily, she perked up in the nick of time, but it made her fearful that the remaining hours would be unbearably difficult.

To her surprise, that was not entirely the case. There were even moments that were quite blissful. As with the sunrise, the sunset threw cheerful splashes of gold, pink and lilac across the sky, and the birds twittered merrily in the trees before settling for the night. Though the day was drawing to a close, Evie didn't feel cold yet. Her surroundings were so beautiful and tranquil that she drew strength and comfort from them. As she plucked the strings of the harp, Evie felt cocooned in a world of her own, in a special place, a privileged one. She was enjoying it in an odd sort of way.

It was autumn, however, and despite the lovely day, once darkness fell it grew cold. Evie's fingers pained due to the length of time she had been playing the harp and the rapid fall in temperature. She shivered a few times and almost plucked the wrong string. Guessing it was only ten or eleven o'clock, there were many more hours ahead and she worried that she might fail at the last moment. Her tummy was roaring with hunger now, and her mouth was bone dry. She could feel her eyelids getting heavy. Occasionally she moved her head an inch or two in one direction, then the other, to try to ease the increasing aches around her neck and shoulders, while not losing her place in the music. Sometimes the notes seemed to blur in front of her eyes, but she held her nerve, willing her concentration to return and remain strong.

Despite the aches, the hunger and the cold, Evie's eyes were causing her the biggest problem. The moon was past its highest point, but it was still bright enough to enable her to see the music. It was an increasing strain, however, and she felt her eyes squinting, then half closing, and she began to drift, then almost sink into sleep. It took barely a second, but it startled her greatly.

'Awake! I must stay awake!'

Evie's mouth and throat were so dry her words came out as a croak, then she coughed, and nearly lost her balance, using her foot to stabilise the harp as it tilted briefly. She steadied it, somehow continuing to play as her heart thumped wildly in her chest.

The birds were quiet now and there was no sound at all except Evie's harp playing. She wished she could play something more vigorous, something to make her think of parties, celebrations, anything to keep her alert long enough to finish. No matter what trick Evie tried, in the final stretch every minute felt like an hour.

'When will the dawn ever come?' she croaked, her bleary eyes glancing up briefly for the first hint of sunrise.

In the final hour, Evie was wracked with pain, including a piercing headache. Her stomach was not only desperate for food, but nauseous now too. Her eyes ached from extreme fatigue, but worse than that, tears were threatening to fall.

Finally, one came, then a second and a third, warm drops rolling slowly down her cold cheeks.

'No! No! I must not weep!' Evie told herself inside her head. A flood of tears would make it impossible to see the music. She shook her head briefly, sniffed loudly and encouraged herself through gritted teeth. 'Come on, Evie, nearly there!'

Her feet and legs were numb and had been for an hour at least. Her fingers were so cold they were stiffening, and she wondered how long she would be able to continue plucking the strings without a mistake.

Evie let out a squeaky cry of relief as the new dawn broke, but she had to keep playing until no more music appeared on the notebook. It must be a full twenty-four hours. Finally, she saw that only one and a half pages remained. She watched her fingers strum the last few notes while the mellow warmth of the breaking sunrise bathed her in soft light. Finally, she stopped, and clutching the strings tightly, she watched a magnificent sunrise explode across the icy-blue sky. Beside her, from the top of the giant rhododendron, a blackbird sang lustily, heralding the new day. Evie slumped over the harp and wept tears of joy and relief, as the final piece of music written in Nala's notebook disappeared.

Chapter Twenty-eight

The first bright shafts of sunlight stung Evie's weary eyes. *What sort of fantastic sunrise is this?* she wondered, squinting at the sky, raising her arm to use her hand as a shade. The sun was above the horizon and shining brightly, but it wasn't the sun that was so dazzling. It was Evie herself, and all around her. She was ablaze with a tremendous white light. She felt wave after wave of energy surge through her, and for a moment her entire body was illuminated. Was she imagining it or was she floating off the ground? No, it was real. The harp had slipped from her arms and Evie was suspended in the air, the white light enveloping her like a radiant cloud. A new and exciting energy pulsed strongly through her body. There was nothing she could do but surrender to it.

It was warmer when Evie woke feeling refreshed, calm and unhurt, lying on the rug on the grass, the harp and her satchel beside her. The sun was a little higher. It must be almost half past eight, she thought. She had slept for an hour and a half. Examining herself, she looked normal and she felt well. Somewhere in her tummy she knew she was hungry, but it didn't bother her. She reached for the bottle of water in her satchel and took a long drink, thinking she should, but her thirst didn't seem so urgent any more either. Despite playing the harp for a full twenty-four hours, she wasn't tired. 'It's the magic,' she whispered. She knew it, she felt it. But she couldn't stay there and marvel at what had just happened. It was time to go home, reassure her father and Freddie, and then plan for what she had to do next.

Freddie ran out to greet Evie when she rode into the stables. Jimmy looked up from his work, surprised to see her. Her father was standing at the back door, fully dressed.

'Thank heaven!' he cried.

'Evie, you did it! I knew you would!' Freddie cried and ran over to hug her.

'Are you all right, my darling?' her father whispered with some urgency as Evie came to the back door.

'I'm fine, everything's fine,' Evie said. She could feel an enormous grin on her face and didn't try to hide it.

'Hurray! It's finished!' Freddie cried. 'Let's have some breakfast!'

'You mean you actually waited for me?' Evie said.

'I was so dreadfully worried,' her father said, frowning then breaking into a broad smile. 'Um, yes, can you believe it? Freddie couldn't eat a thing this morning. First time ever, I'd say! Never fear, I think he'll make up for it now, and so shall I! No, all three of us! I told Mrs Hudson to prepare extra helpings this morning. She thinks we've gone food-crazy!'

Evie gave Freddie and her father brief details about her time on the island, careful not to let anyone overhear them. Then everyone had to go back to their normal routine as if nothing unusual had occurred. Freddie spent the afternoon with Jimmy, changing his first horseshoe under supervision, and learning how to fix a harness. Evie's father completed his exercises with Hudson as usual, and Evie joined him in the study after sitting with her mother for a while. It was a lovely autumn afternoon, so before dinner she put on her coat and took a book out to the garden to read. She felt the need to reflect on her achievement, relax a little, then set her mind on the task ahead.

Evie slept deeply that night and woke with a start.

'Oh! What?' she cried. Her pulse was racing; it must have been a nightmare. But it wasn't that: something felt off. The sun was high, she had slept late. Why had no one woken her? Evie got up, dressed hurriedly, and went downstairs.

'Hudson, where is everyone?' she asked the butler as she entered the dining room. He was beginning to clear things away.

'The professor and Mrs Wells both had breakfast in bed,' Hudson said.

'Father too?' Evie asked, concerned.

'Professor Wells overdid his exercises again and is feeling a little sore,' Hudson said. 'I don't think he's been sleeping very well these last few nights. He says he will be up in an hour, but I think he needs to rest.'

'I see,' Evie said. 'And Mother?'

'Mrs Wells was very distressed on waking,' Hudson said. 'The nurse gave her a tonic to calm her. She took a light breakfast and is sleeping now.'

'I'll go and check on them both after I have some breakfast,' Evie said. 'Oh, and Master Freddie?'

'I haven't seen him, Miss Evie,' Hudson said. 'Not since

he ran out to the stables very early. He said something about one of the horses making a racket and went to check on the animal.'

'Thank you, Hudson,' Evie said.

It felt strange to be sitting in the dining room alone. Evie found she couldn't eat much. Something was bothering her, something felt wrong. She abandoned her breakfast and went out to the stables.

To her horror, she found Jimmy on the ground, groaning. There was blood on the side of his head where he had a nasty wound.

'Jimmy!' Evie cried, running to him. She looked quickly around wondering where Freddie was. 'What happened? Where's Freddie? Freddie, where are you?'

Realising Jimmy was injured but alive and coming round, Evie left him sitting up against a bale of straw and ran into the stables, then all around the stables, but there was no sign of Freddie. She went back to Jimmy, who was wincing and holding his head.

'Tell me what happened,' Evie said, dabbing her handkerchief on the wound. 'Did one of the horses kick you?'

'No, Miss,' Jimmy groaned. 'There was this skinny man with an eye patch. He came into the stable while I was checking on the horses.'

Evie took a sharp breath and stared at the stable boy.

'He started talking to me first, all friendly, but there was something odd about him. When Freddie came out of the stable, the skinny man shouted, "There you are!" Then he punched me in the stomach and ran at Freddie.'

'What? No!' Evie shrieked.

'I'm sorry, Miss,' Jimmy whined. 'He was skinny like I said, but he was strong. I got up, grabbed him and hit him a few times and he hit me back, only harder. Freddie tried to fight him off too, but then the skinny man grabbed one of those logs and clubbed me on the head.' Jimmy pointed to where there was a pile of chopped logs.

'Sit still,' Evie said, dabbing at the wound again. She then closed her eyes and concentrated on healing him.

'Your hands are all tingly, Miss,' Jimmy mumbled. 'And warm. Whatever you're doing, it's easing the pain. I had a massive headache just now.'

'Jimmy, listen to me very carefully,' Evie said, removing her hands and looking straight at him. 'I have to find Freddie, but you must rest or you'll make yourself ill. Did the skinny man say anything else, anything at all?'

'I don't think so, I don't remember,' Jimmy said. 'I'm sorry, Miss. We should tell the police.'

'No, I'll do that later,' Evie said.

'Shouldn't we tell them right away?' Jimmy said. 'Hudson—'

'I'll deal with this, Jimmy,' Evie said. 'I think I know where that man might have taken Freddie.'

'You do? Where?' Jimmy asked. 'Do you know him?'

'Not exactly, but it sounds just like the man who was following us in the park recently,' Evie said. 'You stay here and keep watch in case Freddie comes back.'

'Comes back? But, Miss Evie, that man—'

'I'm sorry, Jimmy, I have to go,' Evie said. 'Do you feel able to help me with the saddle?'

Jimmy stood up gingerly and helped her to saddle her horse, then Evie mounted and rode off at a gallop.

CHAPTER TWENTY-NINE

Evie left her horse, Chestnut, in the usual spot and hurried on to the green cave. This time, instead of lurking behind rocks and boulders, Evie stood boldly outside. As expected, Volok and Simeon were there. Evie scanned the cave until she saw Freddie sitting quietly on the ground, over to one side.

Volok sniffed the air, stood up and made his way to the entrance. Evie didn't move, didn't flinch. She would not hide today.

The snakes rose from the pit, hissing loudly as they slithered to Volok's side. Several of them looked bigger, but Evie raised a hand and her magic halted them with one gesture.

'I knew you would come quickly, again,' Volok said. 'I let you enter the cave the last time you were here. The snakes would not have killed you – not yet.'

'I don't care,' Evie said. 'I only came for Freddie.'

'You can have the boy in exchange for the ruby and my five primary talismans,' Volok said.

'Those things don't belong to you,' Evie said. 'Now let Freddie go.'

'You are not in a position to bargain,' Volok said.

'Bargain?' Evie said. 'I thought you would already know!'

'Know what?' Volok said crossly.

'That the talismans are gone, destroyed,' Evie said.

'You're lying!' Volok roared.

'I saw them burn,' Evie said. 'No one can have them now, not you, not Madruga, no one.'

Volok looked ready to explode. His nostrils heaved, his eyes blazed, and his skin was turning purple. He clenched his huge fists.

'WHAT?' he roared. 'Those talismans are mine, I collected them for my wife! *My* talismans! MINE!'

'They were never yours,' Evie said. 'They belonged to an ancient people from an ancient time. They belong in a museum, only it's too late for that now because they are gone forever.'

'How do you know this?' Volok asked.

'Because I destroyed them,' Evie said.

'You! YOU!' Volok roared. 'How could you destroy something as magical as a talisman? You cannot–' He stopped abruptly, thinking. 'So, you have dark magic now.'

Evie didn't reply.

'Nala did this,' Volok said. 'This was her plan all along: to pass her magic to a Harp Maiden. Clever. Difficult. I underestimated that annoying little sorceress.'

'You underestimate me,' Evie said.

'I take it she is gone, then,' Volok said. 'No longer in the casket. Aha! The casket, of course!' He smiled savagely. 'That's where you kept the Black Ruby when Nala finally decided to depart this world. Who put it in the casket, Harp Maiden? Was it you?'

Oh no, Evie thought, *he's figured it out.*

'It was Charlie,' Freddie said. 'Charlie found the ruby in the rubble, and he stole the casket from the other cave. He took out Nala's head when she told him to, then he put the ruby inside the casket. He told us everything before Olga killed him. Didn't Olga tell *you*?'

Volok glowered at Freddie.

'Charlie's dead now,' Evie said, 'so no one can remove the ruby from the casket. It's stuck there.'

'Not even you, Volok!' Freddie cried.

'Maybe I believe you and maybe I don't,' Volok said. 'But we can test the truth of what you say.'

'No!' Evie cried, as Volok grabbed Freddie by the arm and threw him at the snakes. The asps wove around him at lightning speed, binding him tightly from his shoulders right down to his feet.

'Bring me the casket with the ruby inside and we shall see who really put it in there,' Volok said. 'If you refuse or try to trick me, the boy will die.'

'Don't do it, Evie. You mustn't,' Freddie cried.

At a wave of Volok's huge hand the snakes coiled higher, up to and around Freddie's neck. He coughed and spluttered as one covered his mouth.

Evie raised both her hands and tried to counter Volok's spell.

'You can't overpower me, not when you don't know how to use magic properly,' Volok said, sneering at Evie. 'It will take years of practice and learning and you're only a beginner.'

Volok twisted his outstretched fingers, and Freddie

wheezed, struggling to catch a breath.

'Stop!' Evie cried. 'I'll do it. I'll bring the casket.'

Another wave of Volok's hand and the asps retreated from Freddie's neck and face, but not from the rest of his body.

'Get it now,' Volok said. 'Simeon will go with you.'

Evie glared at the one-eyed man, as he emerged from the shadows, looking annoyingly smug.

'Bring me the ruby and the casket or I will go to your house and kill everyone there, *after* my snakes finish the boy,' Volok said. 'GO!'

Evie took one more glance at Freddie and left the green cave. All the way home, Simeon was in hot pursuit on Freddie's horse, which annoyed Evie greatly. What was she going to do? How was she going to get out of this dilemma? She couldn't give Volok the casket, but she couldn't let Freddie die either. It was such a horrible, horrible choice and yet, there could only be one outcome.

Evie returned with the casket. Simeon had loitered outside her back gate while she went inside to get it. Luckily, she didn't bump into anyone and did not have to explain herself. But when they returned to the cave, Volok was preoccupied, distracted by the wailing, writhing, green, ghostlike image of his wife, Madruga.

'Uh oh, oooh,' Simeon stuttered nervously, taking a few steps back. 'You called it out again, then.'

Volok turned and glared.

'Quiet!' he bellowed. 'My wife is a superior being – a queen, you fool! Do not refer to her as "it".'

Despite his confident roars, Volok looked worried. Evie

had never seen him like that before. But his demeanour quickly changed when he saw what she was carrying.

'Bring the casket over here,' he said.

Evie was about to move when the ghostly form wailed piteously again.

'What is it, my love?' Volok said, turning swiftly to his wife. 'Why do you wail and cry? The preparation is done. The talismans would have been my special gift to you, but all we really need now is the ruby and you will be whole again, in time. See, it is here.' He turned and pointed to the casket in Evie's arms.

Evie guessed the reason for Madruga's cries: Volok had made a grave error. The goblet he had dipped into the green pool with the other primary talismans was the wrong one – one of the fakes created to fool thieves and perhaps demons too. Madruga seemed to know it was wrong. Perhaps it had more importance than Volok realised.

It was risky, reckless, downright dangerous, but Evie couldn't resist.

'She is wailing because you threw the wrong goblet into the pool,' she said. 'Your wife recognised it for what it was – a fake. Strange that you didn't spot it. Are you sure the others weren't fakes too? This ruby, for example?'

'Aaaggghhh!' Volok roared, turning around to face Evie. 'You lie! The goblet was real. They were all real, and that ruby had better be real. I warned you, don't try to trick me.'

'I'm not lying,' Evie said, cool as ice. She took a few steps forward. 'The real goblet has an opal set into the base of the cup. Do you remember seeing an opal?'

A look of horror crossed Volok's face. Evie could almost

hear him screaming inside his head, thinking, calculating. Madruga's ghost-form let out such a piercing wail, another deep crack appeared in the ceiling of the cave.

'Yeeesssh, the gob-bl-let wasshh a faaaaake!' she screeched.

For a second, Evie thought Volok would collapse. He swayed on his feet, stunned by this revelation, and his face darkened like thunderclouds. He hunched his shoulders, clenched his fists and let out a terrible roar. His eyes bulged and turned bright orange as he stared at Evie. She recognised at once that he was trying to hold her in a trance. But it didn't work any more, her magic enabled her to resist it.

'Bah!' Volok cried, giving up. 'Give me that ruby!'

'We told you, we can't,' Evie said. 'Charlie put it there so only he can remove it from the casket, and Olga killed him, remember?'

In a sudden leap, Volok ripped the casket from Evie's hands, set it down and opened the doors. He was about to reach inside but stopped. He looked over at his wife. She was barely hovering over the putrid green pool, only managing to wave as if on a breeze, her form becoming frailer, her cries fainter.

Then, to Evie's horror, Volok roared in Freddie's direction. The snakes slithered quickly away and Volok pulled Freddie towards him. As he held Freddie in a tight grasp with one arm, Volok used his other hand to force one of Freddie's arms to straighten out, and he stuck it into the casket.

'Close your fist, Freddie, close it tight,' Evie screamed. 'Don't touch the ruby. Don't touch it!'

'I won't take it out, I won't,' Freddie cried. 'I'll never do it. Never!'

'Yes, you will,' Volok roared.

'He can't, you fool!' Evie cried. 'He didn't put it in there!'

'I don't care!' Volok roared. 'Take it out! Now! Take it!'

Madruga was sinking lower and lower into the green water, wailing mournfully. It seemed to urge Volok on, in a sort of panic.

Evie rushed forward, yelling. 'Freddie can't take the ruby out of the casket because he didn't put it in. Let him go! Let him go!'

'He *can* take it out,' Volok said, 'but it will kill him. Ha! You didn't know that, did you?'

'Stop! No!' Evie tugged at Volok's muscular arm, hopelessly trying to free Freddie from his powerful grip. She closed her eyes and tried magic, but before she could even concentrate, Volok switched position, and holding Freddie down with his knee instead, he freed one arm and punched Evie away.

Freddie continued to resist bravely, but then Volok tricked him.

'Your precious Evie can't help you,' he said. 'Look over there, she's dead.'

'No! No!' Freddie cried, unable to see exactly where Evie was.

The shock was enough to make him release his fist, allowing Volok to plant Freddie's hand over the ruby and pull it out of the casket. Volok promptly ripped it out of Freddie's hand, and Freddie collapsed in a heap.

CHAPTER THIRTY

Volok's eyes gleamed with delight as he held up the Black Ruby triumphantly.

'Madruga! My love! I have it, just like I promised,' he said. He stomped over to the green pool where Madruga's withering form was no longer upright but floating on the water. She was silent. He bent down, whispering tenderly to her.

After landing heavily from Volok's wallop, Evie was dazed. As her head began to clear, she saw Freddie lying unmoving a few feet away. Volok was leaning over the green pool, completely distracted, but Evie knew she had to act quickly. She put her hand to her head to heal herself, then rushed over to Freddie. He looked frightful and she feared the worst. She placed her hands gently on his head, then his chest to reach his heart.

'Freddie, wake up!' Evie whispered. 'Open your eyes. Please, Freddie, please.'

Evie choked back a few tears, then held her breath to listen. What was that sound, that whisper? She looked around thinking someone else must be there. Volok's full attention was on Madruga, Simeon was nowhere to be seen. Evie stood, searching with both eyes and ears trying to find the source of that eerie sound. Freddie lay quietly, his eyelids flickering. Volok began tossing herbs into the green pool with one hand, still holding the ruby in his other outstretched hand. Evie heard him tell Madruga to sink back into the pool and rest, that he would drop the ruby in once the bubbles had settled.

Then, that sound, that whisper.

'There is no more time,' it said. 'Do it, Evie, hurry!'

Evie looked from Freddie to Volok, back and forth.

'Leave the boy!' it said.

Then she knew. It could only be Nala.

'Destroy the ruby,' she said. 'Destroy it now, or nothing else will matter.'

Suddenly, somehow, Evie knew exactly what to do. She stood up straight, clasped her hands together, interlocking her fingers tightly. The tingling returned, then the glow, but it was so much more than a glow this time. Her hands became as bright as the brightest moon could ever be, and a ball of brilliant light surrounded her fists. Without further thought, Evie flung out her hands, discharging the magic directly at the Black Ruby, still sitting in Volok's hand as he cooed to his wilting wife.

It was a perfect shot.

Time slowed to a crawl as Evie saw the moment unfold. The streak of light stretched out like a giant arrow. It hit the ruby with a tremendous blast. An explosion of light, bangs and cracks followed, then a gurgling scream from Madruga. Volok roared as the hand that had held the ruby was burned off in a great flash. The Black Ruby had been obliterated.

Evie ignored Volok's roaring and returned her attention to Freddie, patting him on his face to try to wake him. He came round slowly but was very groggy. She dragged him out of harm's way, as Volok roared and stumbled about, clutching at his wrist that had no hand any more, trying to stem the black blood gushing from the open wound.

Madruga had landed awkwardly after the explosion caused a splash in the green pool, and was now stuck half-in, half-out of the water. She gurgled something indiscernible as she reached out with a few trailing green strings for help. Volok staggered over to her and pushed her back under the water. But as he did so, Evie could see that Madruga's peculiar form was rapidly coming apart. The demon queen would never be whole again, now that the ancient gemstone was gone, blasted to smithereens for all eternity, and having taken Volok's hand with it. That left only the demon lord to deal with. But first, Evie had to get Freddie to safety.

While Volok was distracted by his injury and distraught at his wife's disintegrating form, Evie whooshed Freddie off the ground and they staggered towards the exit. But Freddie was too weak to walk, making their progress awkward and slow.

Volok yelled to Simeon, who peeped from behind boulders where he had been hiding throughout the unfolding drama.

'After them, you fool!'

Simeon looked from Volok to Evie and back, unsure who was going to emerge the winner of this contest. Trembling and whimpering, his wits seemingly gone, he decided to make a run for it. With another roar from Volok, the snakes rose out of the pit and blocked Simeon's way.

'That protective balm I gave you doesn't last forever,' Volok roared.

Evie grimaced in disgust as the snakes swarmed around Simeon, wrapping tightly around his body. They carried him, slithering together like a shiny black sheet, down into the dark pit. Simeon's screams were loud and hysterical at first, then they faded to just a couple of garbled whimpers. Then nothing.

Madruga managed a last gurgle on the surface of the pool, demanding Volok's attention again. He bent down to tend to her, and Evie saw her chance.

After setting Freddie down gently behind a boulder, Evie stepped aside, clasping her fingers together until another ball of magic swirled around her hands. Opening them up, she flung it at Volok and Madruga, hoping to hit both of them at the same time. Volok bellowed and Madruga screamed as the light hit their faces. Madruga's peculiar green visage melted instantly like liquid wax, amid screeches and screams that nearly burst Evie's eardrums. The demon queen fell apart, her ghost-form body splattered all over the pool, on the ground around it and on the wall behind. A layer of lumpy green goo remained floating on the top of the pool, then slowly sank to the bottom.

Volok turned slowly to look at Evie, then staggered backwards till he fell against the splattered wall. Half of his face had burned away, leaving the remainder in a revolting mess of black blood, burns and bubbling flesh. He was beside himself with anger, pain and grief. He howled from his gaping, collapsing mouth, then grappled for rocks with his one whole hand and hurled them in anger. But in his weakened and agitated state, his aim was way off. Evie stood watching the demon's furious yet pathetic display, easily sidestepping any rocks that came close.

Worryingly, however, Evie began to feel a bit weak. She had used a lot of magic to destroy the ruby, and then used a second ball of magic to try to finish off both demons together. That action now seemed rather reckless. Her body hadn't fully adjusted to using magic yet; even Volok had known that. Perhaps it was too soon to risk trying to kill Volok now, because if she failed – and it wouldn't be an easy task, no matter how injured he was – it would leave Freddie and her family and friends entirely at his mercy. Evie felt frustrated, but she would have to be patient and pick her moment.

'Your heart, my love, I'll find it. I'll find it! We will try again, I promise!' Volok cried, as he staggered back to the green pool, and plunged his one good hand into the green goo.

Meanwhile, Freddie was more alert but still dazed. Evie hoisted him up and they hurried as fast as they could towards the exit.

The snakes rose in a hissing wall to stop them, but Evie batted them away with more waves of magic from her free hand. She felt the wobbles return but kept stumbling along until they made it out. She would deal with Volok later; she had to get Freddie to his horse, and away to safety.

Freddie suddenly moaned and sank to the ground. She placed her hands on the side of his head and kissed his forehead gently. A few tears rolled down her cheeks, landing on his ashen face. She wondered how much more magic she could use to help him.

'There is still so much I don't know, Freddie, but please, please be well,' she said. 'I love you and I need you. Please Nala, if you can hear me, heal him. I beg you, make him well or make me strong enough to do it.' Evie choked back the sobs that threatened to overwhelm her, and fought hard to banish the awful thought that another of the Black Ruby's curses was preventing her from healing Freddie's injuries.

Then she heard the whispers again.

'Believe, Evie. Remember, you must *believe*.'

She closed her eyes, breathed deeply and steadily, concentrating on healing, on believing she could heal and on her love for her adopted brother, Freddie.

After a moment, Evie opened her eyes with a start. There was noise. Loud noise, lots of noise, voices, horses and wagons! She stood up and looked across the fields to see at least a hundred men approaching on foot, and dozens more on horseback.

'Jimmy must have raised the alarm,' Evie muttered. She looked down at Freddie. He couldn't remain in the middle of what would become a war zone.

'Freddie! Freddie, wake up,' she said, shaking him.

'Ha! They are no match for me!' Volok roared, as he staggered out of the green cave. He boldly turned to face the approaching army. Alone but standing proud, he looked even more terrifying with his injuries.

At last, Freddie opened his eyes wide, and they were the brightest blue that Evie had ever seen.

'Oh, thank goodness!' she said. 'Freddie, look! The police will take care of you now. I must deal with Volok.'

'You can't, it's too soon,' Freddie croaked. 'You've used too much magic.'

'I'll be all right,' Evie said. 'Nala told me once I destroyed the Black Ruby, I would have enough magic to destroy Volok.'

'The ruby is really gone, for good?' Freddie said.

'Yes, completely destroyed, and so is Madruga,' Evie said.

'Are you sure you can kill Volok now, so soon after all that?' Freddie asked.

'I wanted to do it immediately, but I felt a little off and only wounded him,' Evie said. 'I'll be strong again in a few minutes. It'll be all right. I can do this.'

'But you don't know what it'll do to you, what it might cost you,' Freddie pleaded. 'Please wait till you're stronger, I don't want you to die.'

Tears fell down Freddie's cheeks, and in that moment, Evie realised she had never seen him cry before.

'Can't you destroy him another time?' Freddie pleaded.

'No, Freddie, I see now that it must be today, otherwise he will kill all these brave people coming to help us,' Evie said. 'I'll be fine. You'll see. This is what I am meant to do.' She looked at Volok, then at the approaching makeshift army. 'I'll try to draw Volok away, try to keep as much distance between him and all those constables. I have to go now. You stay here and wait for help.'

'Where are you going?' Freddie asked.

'To the forest,' Evie said. Somehow, she knew that was where this conflict had to end. She gave Freddie a quick hug and ran.

Chapter Thirty-one

Volok did not take the bait. He ignored Evie and waited for the small human army. The stump at the end of his left arm was now wrapped in a dirty rag, reducing the bleeding to just a drip. His one remaining eye blazed yellow, flickering orange now and again. His other eye was a melted mess. He flexed his huge arm muscles and roared like a lion.

'Come on, weaklings! I'm ready to fight!'

'Volok!' Evie screamed from behind the cover of a nearby tree, hoping the constables wouldn't see or hear her. 'Volok! Over here!'

But he continued to ignore her. He waved his good arm in a wide circle and then the hissing erupted like never before. The snakes burst out of the pit, out of the cave and slithered with surprising speed towards the oncoming constables. They were as big as vipers and cobras now, their fangs long, curved and shiny yellow. *He's used another spell*, Evie thought. *Maybe he'll let them do the fighting for him and he will follow me.*

'Volok!' she cried again, but still he did not respond.

The snakes headed straight for the advancing army. Evie watched wave after wave of slithering reptiles attack in packs, and it was then that Evie saw them: Matthew, Samuel and Mr Finch. She tried to halt the snakes with waves of magic of her own, but she couldn't let anyone see her do it, especially people she knew, nor could she let herself get too weak. Suddenly, her plan to complete her mission was a mess.

'No, no, no! This cannot be happening!' Evie cried, knowing it would be impossible to protect them all. While she dithered about what to do first – help the army or go after Volok – the battle began.

The snakes broke off into several swarms and attacked at different points. Evie stood her ground as one swarm reached her. It was so large, she had to create two smaller magic balls. She fired both at the asps, killing many of them instantly and sending the rest scurrying away mortally wounded. She staggered backwards before righting herself. Suddenly, she was very afraid that Freddie had been right after all: she might not have enough magic to deal with Volok if she kept using it to fight the snakes.

Evie stood for a moment wondering what to do: Volok to her right, the approaching police and her friends on her left. Some of the snake swarms had separated again and veered off in several directions. The army was in disarray trying to deal with them. Then Evie heard gunshots. The police had come armed; that was good, though she doubted the bullets would be enough.

Evie saw that two policemen had spotted Freddie and stopped to assist him. In that instant, she decided to stick with her original plan. She had to get closer to Volok and there could be no witnesses to what she must do. Skirting around trees and bushes, Evie moved to where Volok could not avoid her, his demon hearing still sharp.

'Volok! We must end this now!' she cried. 'You and me, no one else.'

'I want you to see this first!' he roared. 'Their deaths will be your fault. All you had to do was give me the ruby and mind your own business.'

Volok shot fireballs from his good hand, and men and horses fell everywhere. The snakes kept attacking. Screams and screeches filled the air, along with horses neighing and bucking, guns firing, magic blasting, trees and bushes bursting into flames. It was mayhem. Yet, Volok stood admiring the death and destruction he caused. Bullets were having no effect on him. All the damage was happening to the brave young men. When Evie looked back from behind the trees to survey the scene, she was horrified. Then, to make matters worse, she heard Mr Finch yelling orders to the constables to press forward.

'Keep advancing, men!' he cried. 'Kill those wretched snakes, apprehend that villain and round up any accomplices!'

'No! No! No!' Evie cried, her hands covering her face as Volok fired more magic fireballs, spears and lassos, laughing all the while.

'Evie! What on earth is going on?' Matthew shouted, running up behind her.

'Matthew! You mustn't be here. It isn't safe,' Evie said.

'Then what are *you* doing here?' Matthew asked, incredulously. 'Please, Evie, I must take you to safety, you and Freddie both. I found him lying half senseless and left him with two constables so I could come and find you.'

'He's all right now, just a bit dazed,' Evie said. She looked over to where Freddie was sitting up rubbing his eyes and face. One constable was bending down to check on him, the other was standing on guard, his pistol raised.

'Come with me,' Matthew said, taking Evie's hand. 'We'll get Freddie out of here together.'

Evie found herself momentarily unable to disagree. They ran back to Freddie, while all around them the constables were shouting, charging, and firing bullets at the enemy. Volok was waving his good hand, sending bolts of exploding magic towards the oncoming army who were completely unaware of who he was and what he could do. Some were speared with rods of magic, others were burned to a cinder by fire bolts. Many had fallen badly injured, and the death toll was rising rapidly.

'Freddie, you look a little better,' Evie said, kneeling beside him. 'Matthew is going to take you to safety.'

'I am,' Matthew said, 'and you're coming too.'

'I can't, I have responsibilities here,' Evie said. 'You must leave right away with Freddie. No arguments please, Matthew. I'll explain later.'

'Evie, look around us,' Matthew said, perplexed. 'This is unbelievably dangerous!'

'How did you know where to find us?' Evie asked, ignoring his protest.

'I knew there was something wrong when I saw that one-eyed fellow galloping after you through the town. I remembered him from the park, the day you shouted at him to leave you alone. I was worried and called into the police station. I suspected you might be out this way. It always seems to draw you back somehow.'

Evie stared at him, wondering if she should tell him something now, enough to make him believe her, take Freddie away and leave her to finish it. But she didn't.

'So many men are injured and dead already,' she said instead. 'It will only get worse, and I am the only one who can put a stop to this.'

'You can't possibly!' Matthew cried. 'I mean, how do you know this villain anyway? He's an abominable creature!'

'You mean monster,' Evie said, turning to watch as Volok roared and cast another fireball which blew a huge crater in the ground and sent dozens of men flying through the air.

'A monster, absolutely,' Matthew said, staring at Volok. 'He's using explosives!'

'No, really, I mean it, Matthew,' Evie said. 'Look at him. He is enormous and powerful. He's not human, Matthew. He really is a monster, a demon.'

Matthew stared at her, his look so intense, so full of horror.

'Right, we're leaving. All three of us,' he said firmly. 'The police can deal with this man-monster-demon, whatever he is. I'm taking you both to safety. Right now.'

'Evie can't leave,' Freddie said. 'Not yet.'

'What? You too?' Matthew cried.

'I can't help you this time, Evie,' Freddie said, turning to her. 'I'm feeling a lot better, but my head is still spinning.'

'I know, but you're going to be fine,' Evie said. 'I'm sure of it. You just need to rest, and as soon as you can, you should eat a lot!'

'Yes, I'll bet you're starving after all this excitement,' Matthew said. He looked at Evie, and she could see so many questions in his searching gaze.

More cries and screams disturbed their private moment. The three of them turned to see Volok lashing out wildly. He was roaring in a crazy, delighted way.

He's actually enjoying this, Evie thought.

'I can't let this go on any longer,' she said. 'I'm going to lure him to the forest. This must end today.'

'Evie! No!' Matthew cried.

Evie raised a hand. 'No. Don't tell me what to do, Matthew, and don't ask me any more questions. Please, just take Freddie to safety.'

Matthew's loss for words told Evie that he finally realised he would not be able to persuade her to change her mind.

Then Evie got an awful shock.

'Oh no! Mr Finch,' she cried, grabbing Matthew's arm. 'Matthew, look, he's being carried to one of the police wagons. Quick! Go with them. Take Freddie and Mr Finch and go to the hospital. Please.'

Evie was so insistent that it was Matthew who didn't argue this time.

'What are you going to do, Evie?' he asked gently.

Evie paused, then said, 'That demon is my secret, Matthew, or rather he has been a big part of it. I have to deal with him once and for all.'

Matthew stared, completely speechless.

'It's true, Matthew,' Freddie said. 'This is Evie's secret, but only part of it like she said. It would take all day to tell you everything. And you can never tell anyone about it. When you know the rest, you'll understand why.'

'He's right, Matthew,' Evie said. 'Not a word to anyone.'

'As you wish,' Matthew said, bewildered. 'I really hope you will explain it to me soon. And – please take care, Evie. I couldn't bear it, if–'

'She will,' Freddie said.

Evie looked at Freddie in surprise, then at Matthew, who was still staring at her.

'Is this really happening?' Matthew whispered.

'It really is,' Evie said, squeezing Matthew's hand. 'And I must go, now.'

Volok was firing fireballs at the remaining constables who had lost all coordination and were running helter-skelter and diving for cover even when they weren't being fired at. Now and then, there was a shriek or a yell, as a snake found another target. Evie cleared more of them away with waves of her own magic as she ran from Matthew and Freddie, directly into Volok's line of sight, making sure he saw her and not caring who else did.

'Aren't you bored with this yet?' Evie cried. 'Don't you want to know which of us will win, the demon or the weak, human girl?'

'I already know who the winner will be,' Volok roared confidently. 'I always win!' Despite his boast, this time he took the bait and ran after her.

CHAPTER THIRTY-TWO

As she raced through the forest Evie tried to come up with a plan for when they would face each other. Something was willing her to lead Volok into the forest though she wasn't entirely sure why. Her thoughts beyond simply being there were blurry at best. She wondered about the trees and whether they were still enchanted. If they were, did Volok control them, or were they still under Olga's old spell? If either were true, would they attack her again? If so, what on earth was she doing in there? If she had to use magic to protect herself from the trees, that would be costly too.

Ignoring the cuts and scratches on her hands and arms and the rips to her clothing as she pelted through the trees, Evie could hear Volok hot on her trail, bashing and thrashing his way behind her. Despite his blood loss, he seemed to be still extraordinarily strong. Panic started to churn in the pit of her stomach as she thought all might yet be lost. The tension grew and grew till it suddenly leaped up to her throat, and Evie thought she would gag.

'No! Go away, stupid thoughts!' Evie said aloud. 'I will not listen to you!'

Then she heard it again, the faraway voice, whispering.

'Hold on, it will soon be over.'

What will? Evie thought. *Am I about to die?*

Suddenly, she veered left. It seemed the correct thing to do. She ran on, then swung right. There was that voice again, guiding her; she could hear it whispering directions that she automatically followed, sometimes anticipated. It could only be Nala who was leading Evie somewhere, couldn't it? Not some awful trick of the mind, old witches' magic or one of Volok's spells?

Behind her, Volok was laughing as he neared, goading Evie, threatening her. It was time for Evie to make a stand.

She stopped abruptly at the edge of a circle of ancient oak trees, each one enormously tall, wide and deeply gnarled. She knew at once where she was. This was the place where Volok had been imprisoned for centuries. Evie entered the magical circle. Looking up and around, she saw the branches on the trees were still, there was not a single rustle. She turned to face her enemy.

Volok thundered to a stop at the edge of the circle of ancient oaks. Evie thought he looked wary; perhaps the memory of being imprisoned there still haunted him. She saw where a couple of trees had been felled. One of those must have been Volok's prison, the tree trunk that was later fashioned into the magical harp. Evie knew instinctively that she had to entice him closer. He had to be in the centre of the magical circle with her.

'You failed,' Evie began. 'You broke your promise to Madruga that you would bring her back. Now she is gone forever.'

'No. NO!' Volok snarled. 'There is still a chance. I can still bring her back.'

'What chance? How?' Evie asked.

'Her heart may still be beating at the bottom of the pool, and while it beats there is hope.'

'Hope? Is that all you've got now?' Evie cried.

'Other magic could do it,' Volok said, but he didn't sound so sure. 'The harp's magic mixed with my own, perhaps. I will find some other way. Nala's gift to you will come at a price, or didn't she tell you?' He sneered, looking even more revolting. The smell oozing from his burned and still-melting face made Evie wince. She clenched her teeth and swallowed hard.

'She told me,' Evie said. 'We both know that only the Black Ruby can resurrect a black-blooded demon. You can stop pretending. You're alone and a failure. You are injured, your most important talismans are gone, and the harp will never be yours to command. You should have stayed in your own world, because here you lost everything.'

Volok clenched his fists and glowered at Evie, but his one good eye wasn't able to flash any more. It bulged as if about to pop, as he stomped slowly, and it seemed reluctantly, towards her. The voice in Evie's head told her not to back away just yet. She had to time her next move perfectly.

'I never understood why we bothered with this pathetic planet,' Volok said. 'A simple crack in the universe allowed the first demons to reach earth, a weak planet with weak people. It should have been easy to crush, but we were distracted by those witches and the new magic we found. In the end, earth witches were no match for our might. We defeated them and forced their magic out of them. I should have left here as soon as I collected enough magic and talismans, including my ruby.' He moved slowly, snorting spurts of black blood from his missing nose.

'All this misery was just a waste of time then, was it?' Evie said, backing very slowly into the centre of the circle. 'Where might you have been more successful? Mars? Jupiter?' She laughed to annoy him.

Volok didn't answer, but his breathing grew louder.

'You wouldn't have been strong enough or clever enough to invade a real planet, is that it?' Evie asked cheekily, inching sideways and backwards, hoping he wouldn't notice. 'Or maybe you just weren't brave enough to go anywhere else. Because how could a demon lord fail so badly on such a pathetic planet full of weaklings?'

A blast of bloodied steam shot from Volok's nostrils, and his eye flickered a peculiar shade of orange. He was about to strike.

Evie stopped moving. Trying to remain calm, she mumbled, 'Nala, this is it, I am in the centre of the circle. Please, don't desert me. This – is – the –moment.'

'Not quite,' the voice said.

Evie felt a surge of anxiety.

'You think your friend Nala can help you now?' Volok asked, his hearing still sharp in one ear. 'She used you to get her revenge, you foolish girl. You took her side so easily. Did you not realise you were her pawn? Did you never stop to think it through?'

'I have thought and seen enough,' Evie said. 'How could I possibly be on *your* side? How could anyone? Even loyal Olga deceived you in the end. You and your beloved wife have been slaughtering innocent people for centuries!'

'And what was Nala? Kind, gentle, truthful? I don't think so,' Volok said. 'Demons existed long before any sorceress. The Black Ruby belonged to *my* people. Nala stole it from us, from me!'

'It was found in the desert,' Evie cried, doubts stabbing at her brain. 'It belonged to an ancient human tribe, long gone.'

'Ha! Is that what she told you?' Volok said, inching closer. 'Think about it, you weak, foolish girl – Black Ruby, black magic and black-blooded demons. It makes sense, doesn't it? Ah, yes, now you see the connection.'

For a split second, Evie had a terrifying thought that he could be right, or even partly so.

Suddenly, Volok reached out with one long, muscled arm and grabbed Evie, lifting her off the ground. As he slowly choked her, she had to think fast before she passed out, before she was strangled to death. His shovel-sized hand was immensely strong, and Evie could feel herself fading, unable to speak, and barely able to breathe. She could hear the trees though, their familiar swishing had begun. It sounded soft and gentle, almost lulling her to sleep. And the bark, she had seen it in her dreams, hadn't she? It was the same bark with those strangely twisted faces hidden among the craggy gnarls on the tree trunks. Those faces were looking at her now, their mouths were moving, speaking. What were they saying? Was any of this real?

But there was another voice that she could hear, mixed in among the swishing of the swaying branches. The movements in the trees grew stronger, the faraway voice clearer despite Evie's failing concentration.

'The trees are your friends, Evie, magical friends,' the

voice whispered. 'They are yours to command, as they once were mine. Olga enchanted them too, but her enchantment ended with her. They can obey you now, Evie, if you ask them. Your magic is strong enough and of the right kind.'

'Na-chla! Chlel-lp m-me.'

'What did you say, Harp Maiden? You want Nala's help? Bah! The sorceress can't help you now.'

'Use them, Evie, command the trees,' the voice whispered. 'Call to them from your heart. Call to them, Evie, Evieeee . . .'

Evie's arms lay limply by her side. Her vision blurred and her breathing stopped momentarily as she hung in the air in Volok's tight grip.

'Hold your breath, Evie,' the voice said. 'You can do this . . .'

With a tremendous effort Evie interlocked her fingers, squeezed them tightly and closed her eyes. Volok didn't notice, as he was too busy gloating, staring into Evie's face, smiling, waiting for her to die.

Evie heard the trees whisper her name, and that voice calling to her again. She remembered Nala's beautiful face, her soft dark eyes and smooth dark skin. Then she heard one last word: 'Believe.'

Volok slowly tightened his grip on her throat. Breathing was impossible now, and Evie had to act immediately. As her eyelids fluttered as if they might close for the last time, she raised her locked and glowing hands, then opened them slowly to release another ball of magic. She thrust it into Volok's chest, knocking him forcefully backwards. He slammed into one of the oak trees, stunned.

Evie dropped to the ground and staggered backwards. She

bent over and gulped in some air, then stretched her arms wide. The magic was in her, guiding her as she spun around and around inside the magical tree circle. Gradually standing up, she lifted her outstretched arms higher and higher as she twirled, calling on the magic of the ancient forest.

The great oaks responded immediately, swishing then thrashing from side to side but never touching Evie. The one nearest to Volok lowered its branches, reached out and wrapped the demon lord into a fierce clench. He roared at being captured and struggled to free himself, no doubt reminded again of his time imprisoned in one of those trees, trapped by magic passed down from ancient witches, and now under Evie's command.

Evie stood triumphant and quiet, then walked over to her prisoner. She was aware of the effort the magic had cost her, but her pride wouldn't let it show. At the same time, she felt a power she had never known before. In her mind she felt fearless, and in that moment, completely merciless. She understood the dangerous allure of magic and how easily anyone could be tempted by its power, how easily someone could be utterly changed by it. But there was no other choice, she had to finish it.

Standing before Volok, still held tightly in the grip of the tree, Evie interlocked her fingers and made a final magic ball. This time she blew it gently from her hands straight at Volok's face. It hovered for a couple of seconds before erupting with incredible force. In those long seconds, Evie stared calmly at her enemy through the light radiating out from the ball. Volok stared back in horror, fully aware of his fate.

The ball exploded. Volok was blasted into the tree that

held him, sucked inside through the splitting, breaking bark, shredded by the wood as he was swallowed. The trunk closed around his remains, crushing him and burying him forever. The last demon was gone. It was over and Evie was victorious.

Finally, Evie could give in to her overwhelming feelings of relief, horror and fatigue. She felt her knees buckle as she slowly lowered herself to the ground. Looking up at the tree again, she was horrified to spot two people running in the distance, coming towards her. Then she saw two faces that were so very dear to her. She began to tremble, hoping they hadn't seen too much, not more than she would have wished. Overwhelmed with emotion and the effort of using so much magic, Evie swooned.

CHAPTER THIRTY-THREE

When Evie woke, it took her a few seconds to realise that she was resting in someone's arms.

'Oh! Who, um?' she mumbled.

'Good, you're awake,' Matthew said. 'How are you feeling? We hoped it was only a fainting spell, not some awful head injury. We didn't like to move you too quickly, just in case.'

'Fainting sp-spell!' Evie spluttered.

'Don't worry,' Matthew said. 'We're here now, with some constables. Freddie has gone to find you some water.'

'Freddie!' Evie shrieked. 'Is he all right?'

'He's fine,' Matthew said. 'Someone gave him a bar of chocolate and he recovered almost instantly!'

Evie shook her head. 'Good. No! That's impossible!'

'Honestly, he's fine,' Matthew said.

'No, I mean, I've never fai– oh!' Evie suddenly remembered another little 'faint' not so long ago. She looked over at the huge oak tree, but it was gone.

'What happened over there?' Evie asked, pointing.

'There seems to have been a fire,' Matthew said. 'We pulled you out of the way before you caught fire too. You didn't light it, did you?'

Evie stared first at Matthew, then at where the tree had been, then back at Matthew again.

'Yes, right there,' Matthew said. 'The ash is still smoking.'

'Ash? Oh, yes, I can see it,' Evie said. 'You mean, the whole tree burned down?'

'Yes, it's amazing the fire didn't spread,' Matthew said. 'Are you sure you're all right, Evie? We were very worried about you. And where did the huge monster-man go? The constables haven't found him yet.'

Evie managed to sit up. 'He's gone,' she said.

'Gone where?' Matthew asked.

'You didn't happen to see him on your way here, did you?' Evie asked, wondering how much Matthew might have seen.

'No, we must have just missed him,' Matthew said. 'Freddie spotted a bright light through the trees and said it must be you. We arrived just in time to see the fire dying down and you flopping to the ground.'

Freddie appeared out of the trees with a flask of water.

'Ah, well done,' Matthew said, taking the bottle and helping Evie to drink.

'Wait a minute – what *are* you doing here?' Evie asked, spluttering. 'You said you would take Freddie home.' She looked accusingly at Matthew.

'I told you, he's perfectly recovered,' Matthew said. 'And like I said, we were both very concerned about you.'

'I'm fine, really,' Freddie said. 'I had some chocolate. It really helped, so I ran after you.'

'Then I ran after Freddie,' Matthew said, looking a little embarrassed.

'A few policemen ran after both of us,' Freddie said. 'They had that flask of water. They're just behind those trees, over there. They're still searching for V – for him.'

'The monster-man,' Matthew said.

Evie could hear more voices now. The police would be combing the area for some time helping the injured and trying to find Volok.

'We couldn't just abandon you while you were, well, while you were monster-hunting,' Matthew said.

'It's all over now,' Evie said.

'Thank goodness for that. I'm just glad you're safe,' Matthew said. 'You were right about Mr Finch, he was badly hurt. We saw him taken away in a police wagon.'

'Grace will be so upset,' Evie said.

'His injuries looked very bad, I'm afraid,' Matthew said.

'Poor Mr Finch, poor Grace,' Evie said. 'Thank you, Matthew. Thank you both for coming after me even though you really shouldn't have.'

'You know we had to,' Freddie said.

'Absolutely,' Matthew said.

'I'm so sorry all these people have been hurt,' Evie said. 'How many died?'

'Dozens, I should think,' Matthew said. 'More, if all the snakes hadn't collapsed and died suddenly.'

'Really?'

'It was so peculiar,' Matthew said. 'They killed and injured so many people but then just after Freddie spotted the fire through the trees, they all collapsed, dead.'

When Volok was destroyed, the snakes were destroyed too, Evie thought, but didn't say. She lowered her head to hide a few tears. She couldn't help but feel responsible for all the deaths and terrible injuries.

'You'll feel better after a rest and some food,' Matthew said gently. 'I'll bet Freddie is starving even after the chocolate!'

'Yes, I really am!' Freddie said. 'We should probably go now. You don't want to have to talk to all those constables, Evie. That could delay us for ages.'

'I certainly don't,' Evie said, rousing herself. She would think of some explanation for why she was there if she needed to. 'I think I'm all right now. I should be able to ride.'

'I'm not so sure,' Matthew said, frowning at her again.

'I am *very* sure,' Evie said. 'I must go and see Grace and tell her about her father.'

'Samuel will get word to Grace,' Matthew said.

'Oh, yes, of course. Good,' Evie said. 'But I must go and see her, at least try to comfort her. She might like to stay with me while her father is in hospital.'

'That's an excellent idea, but first I really must insist that I escort you both home,' Matthew said, helping Evie up. 'Your hands, Evie! Were you burned by that fire?'

Evie looked down. Her hands were still slightly aglow after using so much magic.

'No, they feel fine,' she said. 'Really. Um, we should leave.'

The constables finished checking the area and found nothing suspicious except for the pile of ash. Evie found her strength returning as they headed out of the forest, accompanied by a few policemen.

The three of them stopped for a moment before leaving the scene, to look back towards the green cave and its surroundings. Evie was shocked by what she saw. The whole area looked like a battle zone with so many badly injured, their cries and moans still loud and pitiful. At least forty men were dead, their bodies lined up waiting to be taken away. The landscape was completely scorched, a number of trees were still burning, and the cave had collapsed, the entrance completely blocked by fallen rock and other debris. *Some of Volok's fireballs must have misfired*, Evie thought. There was no way the green pool could still be intact, nor anything, or any part of anyone inside it.

'So, he's finally dead,' Freddie whispered.

'Dead and gone forever,' Evie said. She looked at Matthew standing beside them.

'Dead?' Matthew said. 'The monster-man is dead? How, Evie? You couldn't have, I mean, where's the body? The police will want to recover it as proof.'

'Trust me, he's definitely dead,' Evie said. 'Please, Matthew, I can't explain now. We'll talk in private another time.'

'Yes, yes, all right,' Matthew said, sounding a bit frustrated. 'But we really must talk, all three of us, right, Freddie?' He ruffled Freddie's dusty, tousled hair.

'Right, Matthew,' Freddie said. 'Gosh, I'm really starving!'

'I'll bring you home in our carriage,' Matthew said. 'You've had enough drama for one day, and you wouldn't want to risk falling off a horse as well!'

'Matthew, please don't fuss,' Evie said. 'There is one more thing I should do before we leave.'

'Now? What on earth could that be?' Matthew asked.

'I'd just like to see the wounded,' Evie said. 'I promise, I won't be long.'

'Well then, we're coming with you,' Matthew said.

Evie began wandering among the injured constables, quickly followed by her companions. Matthew was a bit bewildered, but Freddie realised what she wanted to do. Under the guise of saying a few comforting words, Evie took each man's hand in hers, closed her eyes and sent waves of healing magic to ease their pain, and hopefully, to heal their wounds. The constables who had been bitten by snakes were the easiest to help, though sadly, a few had already died of poisoning before Evie could reach them. Mr Finch had already been taken away to hospital, so she would try to see him later. He had been speared by one of Volok's fire bolts, according to one constable. Evie tried to convince herself he would be all right. Being such an important man, Mr Finch would be given the best of medical care without delay. There was nothing more she could do for him for the moment.

Twenty minutes later, Matthew escorted Evie and Freddie over to his carriage. He helped them in, covered them up with a couple of warm rugs, then tied their horses to the rear. As they drove away, there was another cave-in crashing loudly behind them, sending clouds of dust into the already dusty and smoky atmosphere, burying any remains or any evidence of Madruga even deeper. The Black Ruby was destroyed, and now so was Volok. It was over, yet Evie didn't feel nearly as jubilant as she thought she would. She put her arm around Freddie and he soon drifted off to sleep.

Soon, tiredness overcame Evie as well. She tucked the rug tightly around the two of them and tried to get comfortable. All she really needed to think about now was the harp, its magic, and her own personal magic. There were no more battles to fight, no more quests to complete. And yet, as Evie drifted off to sleep, she wondered how long it would be before she heard Nala's whispers again, and what the sorceress might say to her.

CHAPTER THIRTY-FOUR

By the time they reached Hartville, both Evie and Freddie were awake again.

'Uh oh!' Freddie said, looking out the window.

'What is it?' Evie asked.

'At our house, look,' Freddie said.

Professor Wells and Hudson were standing at the front door. Hudson was stony faced, but Evie's father looked bereft.

'Thank heavens!' he cried.

Matthew jumped down quickly from the driver's seat to help the others.

'I must apologise, Evie,' Matthew said quietly. 'I called to your house earlier to see if anyone knew where you were. I am so sorry. I don't know what I was thinking, worrying your family like that. But I was so worried about you.'

'It's all right,' Evie said. 'I'll explain, and we are all safe now.'

Evie's father hurried down the front pathway as fast as his stiff legs would allow, aided by his walking stick and a frowning Hudson shuffling along beside him, holding the professor's arm like his life depended on it.

'Matthew! You found them, and you brought them home!'

Evie's father cried. 'I am deeply grateful. Evie, Freddie, come here to me!'

The professor hugged them tightly, then shook Matthew's hand firmly.

'Come inside, you too, Matthew,' Evie's father said. 'I want to hear everything.'

Matthew hesitated, but Evie nodded to him encouragingly.

'Eh, thank you, Professor,' Matthew said, and followed the family into the house.

'Some tea please, quick as you can, Mrs Hudson. Thank you!' Evie's father said to the housekeeper as she rushed to the hall door. 'And rustle up something hot and filling for everyone please, poor Freddie must be starving!'

'I certainly am!' Freddie said, and everyone chuckled.

They chatted together in the parlour, and then enjoyed a hearty meal in the dining room.

'I was beside myself with worry,' Evie's father said. 'Luckily your mother spent the day in bed. I didn't dare explain that you were missing, and I don't think we should tell her anything now either.'

'She'll know something is up,' Freddie said. 'Aunt Clara is very clever.'

'How right you are, Master Freddie,' Evie's father said, smiling broadly. 'But your aunt has been over-anxious lately, and I don't want her to have any more upsets, if at all possible.'

Freddie nodded but Evie felt uncomfortable at that remark. What was it that was bothering her? What else could possibly go wrong?

'I had best be off and let you get some rest,' Matthew said.

'Thank you for that lovely meal, Professor Wells. I'll pop by tomorrow, Evie, to see how you both are, if that's all right.'

'I'd like that, Matthew,' Evie said. 'But are you sure you can? You were a long time away from your work today.'

'I'll squeeze an hour in somewhere!' Matthew said. 'I'll check in with Samuel too. He'll have heard how the injured constables are doing, and Mr Finch of course.'

'Dear me,' Evie's father said. 'Was he shot?'

'No, sir, he was stabbed,' Matthew said.

'Stabbed?'

'A spear wound, apparently,' Matthew said. 'Thrown by the criminal mons— madman.'

Matthew glanced furtively at Evie.

'How dreadful,' Evie's father said.

'I hope he'll be all right,' Evie said. 'Poor Grace.'

'Samuel said he would go to see her as soon as he returns from the scene, then he'll have to return to the police station to file his report,' Matthew said. 'I'll talk to him tomorrow and try to find out more.'

Evie's father thanked Matthew profusely again before he left, and everyone went to their rooms to rest.

'We'll talk when you're ready, Evie,' her father said outside her bedroom door. 'I know there must be more to this story, but right now all I care about is that you and Freddie are safe. You *are* safe now, aren't you? All is well?'

'Yes,' Evie said. 'We are safe, and it is over.'

Evie knew it would be a miracle if Grace's father could cling to life until the night of the next full moon. The hospital was doing all they could. As reported in all the newspapers, the local magistrate and leader of the local Hartville community had been 'speared by a strange weapon in battle, while attempting to capture the violent maniac terrorising the locality'. Unfortunately, they had mentioned Mr Finch's injuries too. They were described as horrific, and the doctors were not hopeful. Evie had visited Grace several times to try to comfort her but was unable to persuade her friend to stay in the Wellses' house. Finally, she explained what she could do for Mr Finch on 8 October, if Grace was agreeable.

'Even if you can help him,' Grace said, 'he may not last until then.'

'May I visit him?' Evie asked.

Grace looked surprised. 'I'm not sure,' she said. 'They barely allow me to go in, and not for long. I feel so helpless, seeing him so badly hurt and in so much pain. I'd prefer if he were at home, but the doctors said that he could need further operations at a moment's notice. At least he is in a room away from other patients. The doctors were worried he might pick up some infection.'

Evie took her hand. 'I might be able to ease some of that pain, Grace,' she said. 'If I could just see him. It might help him hold on until the full moon.'

'Could you really? But how?' Grace asked.

'I have healing power in my hands,' Evie said. 'I was able to help Danny's friend, Bart, making him more comfortable until I could wish for him at the last full moon. And I was able to help Freddie recover after he was hurt during that battle. I can't promise it will work, but it's worth a try. Isn't it?'

Grace stared at her, still fearful, so unsure. 'You actually have magic in your hands as well as in the harp?' she whispered.

'Yes, it's not the same, though,' Evie said. 'I don't really control the harp, I just play it and the harp's magic makes the wish come true. With my hands – well, when I touch people, they heal to varying degrees. I can't be completely sure how well it will work, so I would prefer to make a wish for your eyes at the full moon. But would you let me try to comfort your father? If only to ease some of his pain?'

'What would we tell the doctors?' Grace asked.

'Nothing at all,' Evie said. 'I would accompany you on a visit to your father to give you support. Here, let me show you what I would do. Give me your hand.'

Grace held out one of her hands. Evie held it gently and closed her eyes. Thinking of healing her friend's deep distress and mistrust, Evie's hands became warmer and warmer and then they glowed. Grace let out a little cry of surprise but did not pull her hand away. The warmth, the magic began to soothe her.

'I see what you mean,' Grace said. 'At least, I think I do.'
'Well, then?'

Grace hesitated, then replied. 'Yes! Yes, let's do it! Let's visit my father together,' she said. 'Any comfort you can give him would be such a relief.'

They paid a visit to the hospital the following afternoon. Evie was shocked to see Mr Finch bandaged up, tubes attached, an oxygen tank beside the bed, and several nurses fussing about. He was still unconscious, and his normally flushed cheeks were pale save for some awful bruises. Once the nurses left the room, Evie sat beside Mr Finch and held one of his hands, while Grace looked on. Concentrating hard, Evie's hands glowed brightly, and the warmth of healing seeped into his injured body. Evie stayed in that position for about half an hour, and only stopped when a nurse entered.

'What happens now?' Grace asked, once the nurse left the room.

'We wait and see,' Evie said. 'Try not to worry. It isn't too long until the full moon when I can wish that he will be fully well again.'

'If he can just hold on until then,' Grace said.

They left the hospital in hopeful mood.

Evie received a note from Grace two days later, saying the doctor thought her father was stable, and his wound was looking better. Evie was delighted by the news, but the October full moon still couldn't come quickly enough.

The next few days crawled. Finally, the night of the full moon arrived. The weather was dismal, cool and windy. It was more like winter than autumn, and earlier in the day, Evie had been fretting that the moon might not be visible. Fortunately, the wind picked up enough to fix that problem, blowing the clouds out of sight. Freddie was back to his normal lively self, and he accompanied Evie. The moon was shining brightly in the early hours and Evie didn't waste a moment. She made the wish 'to bring Grace and her father to full health in every way', wording the wish carefully to include Grace's eyesight as well as Mr Finch's life-threatening injuries.

'At last!' she said to Freddie when it was done. 'I cannot wait to hear the good news from Grace!'

CHAPTER THIRTY-FIVE

Once Mr Finch was out of danger and her eyesight was restored, Grace's reaction to Evie's secret completely changed. In fact, she was like a new person. She called to Evie's house, running straight past Hudson standing officiously as ever just inside the hall door, and gave Evie a huge hug.

'Grace! You must have good news,' Evie said, smiling. 'Come inside and tell me everything.'

Evie bundled her friend out of earshot, quickly closing the parlour door.

'Father is out of danger,' Grace said. 'They say he should make a full recovery.'

'That's wonderful!' Evie said.

'And look at me!' Grace squealed with delight. 'I don't need my glasses any more and no bandage either. Everything is so clear, so colourful and bright. The doctors can't understand it, and I don't care that they can't!' Grace gazed around the room, smiling the biggest smile Evie had ever seen on her friend's face. 'Oh, Evie, I don't know how to thank you.' She gave Evie a kiss on both cheeks and another big hug. When Grace finally released her, Evie could see that Grace was feeling very emotional. Tears were in the corners of her eyes, on the verge of overflowing as Grace reached into her pocket for her handkerchief.

'Forgive me,' she said, dabbing at her eyes. 'I don't know why I'm tearful. This is such a happy day.'

'I'm so pleased for you, and for your father,' Evie said softly. 'The harp's magic always works at the full moon, but this is really special.'

'I'm so very grateful,' Grace said. She paused, looking embarrassed. 'I'm sorry for reacting so strangely – no, rudely – before. I was frightened, Evie. Your story sounded spooky to me. I felt that I didn't know who you are. I almost wanted to run away from you.'

'I think I understand,' Evie said. 'Sometimes I'm not sure that I am the same me, even though I know I am.'

'I realise now how much good you can do,' Grace said. 'You have a wonderful gift, even if it isn't exactly normal.'

'No, it's not normal,' Evie said. 'It's a privilege but it can also be a burden. Keeping it a secret has been very hard, and you can never tell your father the part I played in his recovery.'

Grace nodded. 'I know.'

'My father knows about my secret, but only very recently,' Evie said. 'He figured some of it out through his work, and then I sort of let it slip.'

'Goodness, Evie! What did he say?' Grace asked.

'He took it rather well, but I know he's worried about what it will mean for me,' Evie said.

'He's bound to be concerned,' Grace said. '*I'm* concerned. Can you tell me a little more?'

'Well, I have a duty to perform at every full moon, as I

explained before,' Evie said. 'I have healing magic in my hands which I'm still figuring out. I don't know what I've become, Grace, but I believe I am still the same person deep down, even with this strange new path I must follow. Some of my life should remain normal enough, well, mostly normal – hopefully.' Evie paused, wondering if that were true. 'Say you'll always be my friend, no matter what happens. I am the Harp Maiden, but I'm also Evie, your friend, a girl who loves music.'

'We will be friends forever,' Grace said. 'Look at the gift you have given me and my father. I celebrate the day we met, Evie, how we became friends, all the help and kindness you have shown me, your encouragement and thoughtfulness. You are the best friend I could ever have. The doctors doubted they could save my father, and they failed to save my eyesight. It was you who changed everything for the better.'

Evie heard the tremor of emotion in Grace's voice. Tears were threatening to spill again, one or two escaping. Evie had to wipe some away too. Then they both giggled.

'How silly of me,' Grace said.

'And me!' Evie said. 'So much has happened since we met at the auditions last year. Well, we survived all of that, so surely we are due plenty of fun now.'

'Most definitely!' Grace said. 'Oh, I should have asked after Julia as soon as I came in. How is she?'

'She's still very ill,' Evie said, quietening down.

'Can you do anything to help her, you know, like you did for my father?' Grace asked.

'I tried, but I didn't have much impact,' Evie said. 'And I can't make a moon wish for Julia because I did before. Only one is allowed.'

'Oh, I see,' Grace whispered. 'How unfortunate.'

'We can only hope that the doctors can save her now,' Evie said.

The two girls were silent with their thoughts for a moment.

'Let's not talk of anything sad,' Evie said. 'Today, we should celebrate your good news.'

After some tea and fruit cake, and lots of talk about music, Evie saw Grace to the door.

'The new schedule for rehearsals will be sent to everyone soon, and then we'll have the grand opening of the Reid Academy of Music to look forward to,' Evie said.

'Let's hope Julia will have recovered by then, and can join in all the excitement,' Grace said.

'She would love it, and Mr Reid would love to have her help organising everything,' Evie said, then something niggled at her again.

'What is it, Evie?' Grace asked. 'Your brow is wrinkling. Try not to worry about Julia, hard as I know that is.'

'It's nothing,' Evie said, brushing it off. 'You must start practising on the piano right away! You have a lot of catching up to do.'

'I started this morning!' Grace said. 'We should practise together, and with Matthew too, if I'm not in the way.'

'You are definitely not in the way,' Evie said, feeling herself blush.

Evie smiled as she waved her friend off, and was about to close the door, when she paused and waited. Dr Elliott was hurrying up the driveway looking very grave.

Much to Evie's dismay, the doctor insisted on speaking with

her parents before breaking the news. She showed him into the parlour and went to find her father, after sending Tilly upstairs to see if her mother would be able to join them.

Evie's father was in the study, delving into the history of Evie's harp.

'Come in, my dear,' her father said. 'I found more references to those nasty characters you met recently while looking into the history of your harp. It took a while to untangle all the nonsense, but – oh, dear, what is it?'

'Father,' Evie said.

'More trouble?' her father asked, removing his spectacles. 'I can always tell.'

'Dr Elliott is here,' Evie said. 'He asked to speak with you and Mother right away.'

'Oh dear,' her father said. 'Is it Mr Finch? Julia? Someone else?'

'He wouldn't say,' Evie said. 'Oh, I should have told you immediately.'

'Told me what?' her father asked.

'Grace was just here,' Evie said. 'Mr Finch is out of danger and is expected to make a full recovery.'

'That is excellent news,' her father said. 'It must be Julia, so.'

'I hope not, he looks very serious,' Evie said.

'Help me up, dear,' her father said. 'I've been sitting here too long and I'm stiff. We mustn't keep the good doctor waiting.'

Evie's mother was entering the parlour, assisted by Tilly, followed by Freddie just ahead of Evie and her father. The doctor was standing at the window, looking out at the front garden. He turned abruptly when everyone came in. Evie found herself staring at his anxious face, his weak attempt at any kind of greeting making her feel even more anxious.

'I think everyone should sit down,' he said.

Evie remained standing.

'What is it, Dr Elliott?' Evie's mother asked.

'I'm terribly sorry to have to inform you,' the doctor said, 'that Miss Pippen passed away early this morning. There was nothing more we could do. Her illness progressed to the point where we could not save her.'

'No! Julia, no!' Evie cried, and this time the tears poured down her cheeks. Freddie ran to her side, also weeping.

'How absolutely dreadful,' Evie's father said.

'Dear Julia, so terribly sad,' Evie's mother said. She clasped her hands tightly, struggling to hold back tears. Evie watched through bleary eyes as her father tried to comfort her mother. It was as if she were watching some awful scene play out. Surely, this couldn't be happening to her family. It must be some horrid nightmare.

Evie heard a muttering about tea, something else about Freddie, then her father's voice, distant at first, then clear.

'Evie dear, I am so very sorry,' he said. 'This is a dreadful blow for all of us but especially for you and Freddie.'

As though in a daze, Evie watched Mrs Hudson and the nurse help her mother from the room. The doctor followed them upstairs to give Mrs Wells a sedative.

'You two, come sit by me,' Evie's father said.

Evie and Freddie moved to the settle and sat either side of the professor. He put a big comforting arm around them both. It was so terribly painful to hear Julia was gone, Evie's beloved governess, her trusted friend and confidante. And they hadn't even been allowed to visit her. When had Evie last spoken to her? When had she last seen Julia smile, heard her laugh? Asked her for advice, then ignored it?

Evie felt her whole body slump, then she cried bitter tears that stung her eyes and drenched her face. Her life had utterly changed again, and it cut her deeply. She had saved Mr Finch and restored Grace's eyesight, but despite the harp's magic and Evie's new healing powers, there was nothing more she could have done to save her beloved Julia.

CHAPTER THIRTY-SIX

The funeral was a very sad occasion. Grace and Matthew did their best to comfort Evie. Samuel would have come too, Grace told her, but he was on duty. All the members of the Hartville Ensemble were there, and Mr Reid was particularly upset.

'I was so very fond of her,' he said. 'Such a talented pianist and teacher, and such organisational skills! What will we do without her?'

Evie's parents led the mourners as Julia had no other relatives. She had made her life in Hartville with the Wells family over the last three years, and Evie hoped they had made her feel happy and welcome. Professor Wells stayed close by his wife, who was doing her best but was clearly slipping into another bout of melancholy. Freddie stayed beside Evie, holding her hand for comfort. The servants were all in attendance, every one of them shocked by Julia's passing. Once again, the whole household had been turned upside down by this latest tragedy.

It was a long and difficult day. Evie was grateful to all her friends for their comfort and support, though she felt her heart would burst with the pain. Later that evening, she sat on her bed with Freddie looking through books, talking sometimes, trying to distract each other from the sadness of the occasion. Freddie wanted to look at Lucia's diary again, so Evie opened her own diary and she set to writing. She didn't notice the time passing until she heard Freddie yawn loudly.

'It's very late,' Evie said. 'You should go to bed. I think everyone must be asleep by now. Go on, I'll pop in and say goodnight in a minute.'

When Evie peeped around Freddie's door a few minutes later, he was already fast asleep. She whispered goodnight and returned to her room. Though she was tired too, her thoughts wouldn't rest. She took out Nala's notebook. Evie didn't know what she was looking for, perhaps some comfort, but there were two new messages.

> *Personal magic comes at a price. Not the magic of the harp — I have protected that by tying it to the moon. But the healing magic I have passed to you is ancient magic, and sometimes it will demand that a price be paid. You will not know in advance what will be paid, nor by whom. Despite all the good that magic can do, we each have our destiny, and we cannot change it nor anyone else's. No matter what, our future lies in the stars and the moon.*
>
> *Using healing magic to destroy a life, however evil, will always come at great cost. This you must accept, even if you have righted a terrible wrong, even if you destroyed a demon who deserved his fate. Such is the way of powerful, ancient magic.*

'So, Julia's life was the price to be paid!' Evie whispered, astounded. 'If anyone should pay it should be me, not Julia.'

Then she wondered again if Julia's death might have been the last curse of the Black Ruby and not the price of using magic. If so, that would mean there was still a price to pay for destroying Volok. Evie might never know which theory was correct until the next tragedy.

The more she thought about it, the more shocked Evie felt. She really wasn't in control. Somewhere out there in the universe, the magic was in control, the magic decided everything.

After pacing her room for a few minutes, trying to find an explanation she preferred, Evie slumped down in the chair by her dressing table. She went over it again: First, Evie hadn't used the *harp's* magic to kill Volok, she had used *personal* magic and so, there was a price to be paid. That was clear. It was through the Ladder of Charms that Nala had bestowed this personal, ancient magic to Evie, *not* the harp. The harp was merely the means to climb the Ladder. Second, the balls of magic she used to destroy Volok and the Black Ruby had nothing to do with the harp; that was personal magic too. So, what further connection, if any, was there between the harp and the Ladder? 'Only Nala,' she whispered. She gazed into her mirror. Were Volok's taunts correct? Had Nala tricked her after all?

Perhaps there was some magical link between the two that Evie didn't understand, or that she hadn't discovered yet. She hadn't needed the harp when she called the trees to her aid. 'That was dark magic too, dark and personal,' she muttered. 'Nala whispered that I now had "the right sort of magic" to command the trees. Olga had used dark magic to enchant the trees, so I must have used dark magic too.'

Evie felt something between horror and anger. Doubt flooded her mind, doubt over whether she should ever use magic again. She felt so disturbed she forgot to read the second message. Instead, she went to her bedroom window and flung it open. Taking in gulps of cool, fresh air, she willed herself to calm down and think clearly.

After a few minutes, she closed the window and sat down. She wrote in her personal diary:

> *I am the Harp Maiden, and I vowed to use the harp's magic for good for the rest of my life. But gambling with dark magic and paying some unknown price is unacceptable. I will ever do that again. Perhaps that's why Lucia never completed the Ladder of Charms, she did not want that responsibility, that extra burden. Nala told me that no one had finished it, perhaps now I know why. Maybe Volok was right when he said that I had been foolish and naive.*

'But why would Nala trick me?' Evie whined to her mirror. But she already knew the answer. Evie was new to magic and therefore easy to manipulate. Nala didn't care what the price for killing Volok would be. She only wanted to defeat him, to win. 'You must finish this quest for me, Evie,' Nala had told her. Evie couldn't deny it: she had been used.

Evie couldn't stop another wave of tears, tears of sadness and grief, mixed with frustration at having been outwitted. She sobbed until exhaustion overtook her, and then crawled into bed. She fell asleep almost immediately, still in her funeral clothes.

*

A letter arrived for Evie the next morning. It was waiting beside her place at the breakfast table. She was startled when she saw the handwriting, and tore it open as Freddie leaned over her shoulder.

'Who is that from?' he asked. 'Wow! Is that—?'

'It's from Julia,' Evie whispered. The letter was dated four days earlier.

Dearest Evie,

I know I don't have long, and I understand that you cannot visit me. As we may not have the chance to meet again, I hope this letter may speak for me.

It has been the privilege of my life to be your governess. You have been the most excellent of students, talented, dedicated and with the passion and belief that you can always do better — the perfect recipe for success. Don't be sad for me. My time with your family has been my happiest by far. I have felt welcome, useful, cared-for and loved, and enjoyed every single moment.

Despite any recent differences we may have had, we both know that our hearts were in the right place and everything we did and said was always for the right reasons. I apologise for my more cantankerous behaviour! You were right, I was not well. I have been ill for a long time, and I knew there was nothing more the doctors could do for me. Not even magic can save me now.

Please tell Freddie to continue being the bravest

boy that ever lived, and to you both I send all my love forevermore.

Goodbye and good luck, my darlings,

Julia

Evie handed the letter to Freddie and ran out of the room.

CHAPTER THIRTY-SEVEN

The household was very subdued for the next few days, with everyone still recovering from the shock of Julia's passing. Evie didn't do very much, spending a lot of time in her room alone. Even Freddie was content to play by himself in his bedroom, or else join Evie for some quiet time reading or listening to Evie play the flute.

Evie's father called her to his study once he had pieced together more of the historical facts. For obvious reasons, he had been particularly intrigued by the references he found to a sorceress called Nala.

'Tell me about this Nala of Yodor,' her father had said, when Evie joined him for his mid-morning cup of tea in the study.

Evie told him all she knew, including Volok's final comments, suggesting that Nala had tricked Evie into helping her take revenge.

'It's possible,' her father said.

'Don't say that!' Evie cried. 'The idea disgusts me! Volok was a brutal, murdering demon, and Nala was a clever sorceress who imprisoned him.'

'Clever, yes, but perhaps not always an honourable sorceress,' her father said.

'Oh no. What did you find?' Evie asked nervously.

'Apparently, Nala had quite a reputation for sorcery, and not always the good and gentle kind,' her father said. Evie listened anxiously. 'She was powerful and skilful, but also ambitious. She convinced the King of Yodor to give her a special position, one of considerable influence in his court. The decision upset many of his courtiers and closest advisors. Nala ended up with more power than anyone except the king himself, some thought even more power because her influence swayed many of his decisions.'

'Go on,' Evie said, still nervous but also intrigued.

'Some of those decisions were about amassing power, building an empire, extending his territory – not unusual in those days, or in any century for that matter.'

'Exactly what the demons were doing,' Evie said.

'Indeed,' her father said. 'So, it's difficult to know whether her intentions were always honourable, but perhaps. She may have stopped the king doing terrible things, for all we know. You can read some of the examples yourself in these two books here.' Though he patted the covers gently, small puffs of dust spurted out from between the yellowed pages. 'It seems Nala had a change of heart when she discovered the Black Ruby. At first, she wanted it for herself, but when she realised what it could do and who would be after it, she wanted no one to have it. Owning a talisman that could bring demons back from the dead would only bring a lifetime of trouble. But for once, Nala could not convince the king of its danger.'

'That's more or less what she told me,' Evie said, slightly relieved.

'Whether the king banished her or she left of her own accord is not clear,' her father continued. 'Either way, she departed the Kingdom of Yodor leaving the king to deal with the destruction that would follow in the Black Ruby's wake.'

'You mean, Nala ran away?' Evie said. 'She abandoned her people to their fate?'

'It would appear so,' her father said, peering gingerly over his spectacles. 'But who are we to say what else she could have done? The king wouldn't listen to her any more, and the courtiers were probably glad to see her go, but it was her own fault that the king became obsessed with the Black Ruby in the first place.'

'How do you mean?' Evie asked.

'According to these accounts, she spent years convincing him of the importance of talismans,' her father said. 'She believed they could use talismans and her magic to make King Udil the most powerful of all kings.'

'Nala told me she made the harp *after* she left Yodor,' Evie said. 'Do you think that was to make amends?'

'It's possible,' her father said. 'She may have realised the error of her ways, but we may never know. There are more opinions in this book here.' Evie's father reached for a bland-looking book, very old, with equally yellowed pages, some ragged and torn, others loose. He placed it in front of her. 'Bear in mind that some of the historians who wrote these accounts have interpreted the facts from their own point of view. By a strange twist of fate, we have a better idea of what went on, even if we don't know everything.'

'They wouldn't have just made some of it up, would they?' Evie said, aghast.

'Let's call it jumping to a conclusion to finish the story and move on to the next project,' her father said. 'What is clear is that Nala trusted and believed in you.'

'She didn't have much choice,' Evie said crossly. 'I am the Harp Maiden. Who else could have helped her?'

'Your predecessor perhaps?' her father asked.

'I don't think Lucia even knew about the Ladder of Charms,' Evie said. 'All I do know is that she didn't complete it.'

Silence.

'Nala also left you her notebook,' her father said. 'That was a vote of trust, surely?'

'Lucia had it too,' Evie said. 'As did every other Harp Maiden before her.'

'But she believed you would reach the top of the Ladder of Charms,' her father said. 'Something you said no one else achieved. I think Nala meant it when she said you were particularly special.'

'You're biased,' Evie said, unable to hide a little smile.

'Naturally, but where history is concerned, I always deal with the facts,' her father said. 'Nala's story is part of history too, though not a part that everyone needs to know. We will keep it to ourselves as we don't want the trail leading back to you. None of my students showed any interest in this story except Edward, and after that fake goblet business, he will avoid me for a long time!'

'I thought Nala would only tell me the truth,' Evie said. 'I never stopped to question her motives, nor what she was asking me to do. It all seemed so obvious: the demons had to be stopped.'

'There is no doubt about that,' her father said. 'Nala may not have been entirely truthful with you, but we should not condemn her too quickly. I think you should give her the benefit of the doubt, if only to avoid torturing yourself about what you should or shouldn't have known or done. Look at what your last wish did for Mr Finch and Grace.'

'That was the harp's magic,' Evie said. 'The Ladder of Charms gave me other magic, ancient, personal magic. I didn't realise until today just how different they are.'

'So, there are two types of magic,' her father said. Evie nodded. 'Well then, let us hope you never have a reason to use magic for such awful reasons again.'

'I've made up my mind,' Evie said. 'There can *never* be another reason to use dark magic like that. Anyway, there are no more demons, so that's final. The harp is another matter. With the wishes at the full moon, I can do good things, help people. But I don't want anything to do with dark magic ever again.'

Her father smiled. 'Now, that is a real heroine talking,' he said. 'Choosing right from wrong, learning from mistakes, putting the greater good ahead of personal gain. Well done, my darling. Now, try to put that horrible episode behind you.'

He raised his eyebrows and gazed at Evie over his dangling spectacles. 'All of those horrible episodes.'

'I will,' Evie said.

Before Evie went to bed that night, she made another decision: she would heal all members of her household with her hands, using the personal magic one last time. They were all suffering Julia's loss and needed comfort. But that would be the last time she would call on her personal magic unless something truly awful occurred and she could help. But she would never use magic in any violent way again. She didn't want it to change her, and she certainly couldn't let anyone else pay the price for what she might do. Keeping her vow as the Harp Maiden was different, and she was only too happy to grant a wish at every full moon.

Feeling a little more relaxed, Evie drifted off into a deep and restful sleep that night. In the morning, she healed herself with her own hands, hoping to find peace and the ability to cope with the dreadful loss of her friend and governess. She used it on her father when she was sitting beside him in the study looking at more books. Taking his hands in hers she let the healing magic flow from her to him. Later that evening, when Evie's mother was asleep, she healed her too, sitting quietly by her bedside, holding her hand.

Freddie knew about Evie's healing hands and was happy to snuggle up beside her on his bed. They read together, Freddie holding the book, Evie reading, her hands covering his, allowing the magic to flow into him and soothe him. It was more difficult to hold hands with the servants, but as soon as she could, Evie found clever ways to make contact without making it appear strange. Soon, everyone was coping better, though Julia would always be greatly missed and impossible to replace.

After another conversation with her parents and Freddie, it was decided that Freddie would go to the local school until he was thirteen. Freddie was delighted to be staying in Hartville. Several of his neighbourhood friends were going to the local school already, so he would not find the transition too difficult. The plan for boarding school was still an option to be explored for the future.

Evie's parents also decided that there would be no more governesses in their home. Evie enrolled on the tutors' course at the Reid Academy, which would begin in January, and she would join the academy as a music teacher as soon as she qualified. She would be a part-time assistant to begin, as she would only be sixteen, and learn the business of running an academy. She would graduate to full-time tutor as soon as she turned eighteen and attained her qualification.

Matthew brought Evie to the academy for a preview after all the work was done. She was very impressed.

'It's fantastic!' Evie cried, looking around at everything. 'Even better than I expected! The music rooms are so spacious.'

'The acoustics are perfect,' Matthew said. 'But we must test them again together, Evie, before the formal rehearsals.'

'I'd love to,' Evie said. 'You should be very proud of all this.'

'We are,' Matthew said, beaming from ear to ear. 'All we need now is a huge turnout for the concert and lots of people enrolling for lessons.'

'We will, and you will, most definitely,' Evie said, making a mental note for the next full moon.

After one rehearsal, Evie and Matthew went for a walk in the park. It was a lovely late autumn day, the trees still a riot of colour. A carpet of fallen leaves in various shades of russet and gold lay on the ground, crunching under foot as they strolled. It was there that Evie told Matthew all her secrets. She waited nervously for his reaction, afraid even to look at him. They stopped walking and Matthew turned to her. Evie waited patiently for him to say something, fearing he might react as Grace had. He looked troubled, but before he spoke, Matthew suddenly gave her a hug.

'Forgive me, Evie, but how lonely you must have felt,' he said. 'Lonely and frightened, and with so many personal tragedies happening at the same time too. How on earth did you cope with it all?'

Evie felt suddenly tearful. As she struggled to compose herself, Matthew guided her to a park bench.

'Honestly, Matthew, I don't know,' Evie said. 'I suppose I just had to. After Dower Hall, I only slowly realised what playing that harp would mean for me. Once I started on this road, I couldn't go back.'

'It's extraordinary!' Matthew said. 'You should write a book about it, except that it must be kept secret.'

Matthew groaned, and Evie looked at him, surprised.

'I am so sorry, Evie,' Matthew said.

'For what?'

'The way I teased you about having secrets,' Matthew said. 'I meant it as fun, but I had no idea you were under such pressure. It must have made you feel so much worse.'

'Don't be silly, you couldn't have known,' Evie said. 'It was always going to be difficult for me not to tell anyone. I was just glad to have Julia and Freddie in on my secret right from the start.'

'No one else?' Matthew asked.

'Not until a few weeks ago,' Evie said. 'My father knows everything now. He was beginning to piece it together, then he caught me off guard and I had to tell him.'

'Of course, the brilliant historian,' Matthew said. 'How did he react?'

'Rather well,' Evie said. 'He even helped me fill in a few gaps.'

'Wow!' Matthew said. 'That is very understanding of him.'

'That's just it,' Evie said. 'He really does understand, perhaps more than I did at first.'

'And your mother?' Matthew asked.

'She doesn't know,' Evie said. 'Although she is feeling a lot better, and really looking forward to the concert, by the way, my father thinks we should wait a while before telling her my story, and I agree.'

When they arrived home, Evie's parents were sitting together in the parlour. From the hall, Evie and Matthew overheard some of their conversation, which was quite amusing.

'A telephone would be so convenient, Clara,' Evie's father said. 'It will mean less travelling to and from meetings, which is really important for me with these stiff old legs. I'll get so much more work done from the convenience of my study.'

'I don't want you working too hard, Henry,' Evie's mother said. 'If we have a telephone installed, people will be calling you night and day. Shouldn't we get the electricity extended to the upstairs of the house first? It would be so convenient for *everyone*.'

'We should do both,' Evie's father said. 'But the telephone first. Then we'll sort out the rest of the electricity. I'll look into both matters immediately.'

'Perhaps we could do something about the plumbing too,'

Evie's mother said. 'I believe there are marvellous bathroom suites available now.'

'Suites, Clara?'

'That's what they're calling them, Henry.'

'What a silly word for a bathroom!'

Evie and Matthew struggled to stifle their laughter. Composing herself, Evie coughed politely then knocked on the half-open door. They entered.

'Ah, Evie, Matthew, come in,' Evie's father said.

After chatting for a while, Evie's mother asked Evie and Matthew to play a duet and they moved to the drawing room. It was a beautiful piece by Chopin. Evie's parents smiled and clapped.

'Thank you, that's our favourite piece,' Matthew said. 'We're going to play it on the opening night. I hope you're both coming?'

'We wouldn't miss it for the world,' Evie's father said.

'I can't wait,' Evie's mother said.

'Excellent!' Matthew said. 'Well, I should be going. My father will have a list of final checks for me to do. We want to make sure everything is just right.'

Evie hadn't felt this good in quite a while. Her parents were happier, still dealing with Julia's loss, but coping so much better. Freddie had his sad moments too, but he was doing so well and enjoying his new school. With the opening of the academy and the concert coming up, Evie had a lot to keep her busy. The concert was just three weeks away, and there would be a lovely festive feel to it, kicking off the Christmas season, if a little bit early. Evie was looking to the future, and it was beginning to look a whole lot brighter.

Chapter Thirty-eight

Word spread fast. The academy received lots of enquiries from enthusiastic parents and hopeful students. Mr Reid asked Evie if she could start immediately, albeit part-time, understanding that she had a lot of responsibilities at home, and hadn't started her diploma yet. But such was the demand he needed her urgently and felt confident that she could introduce young students to the flute with ease.

Mr Reid was also keen to arrange more concerts to help raise awareness for the academy further afield, and he had more ideas about the scholarship too. Lord Moffat was keen to put his name to something lasting, but Mr Reid did not want the lord's influence to become too overbearing. Taking his son's advice, he resolved to tread carefully.

The academy would officially open for lessons in the new year, with enrolments taken from the start of December. The concert would be held in the academy's new concert theatre on 26 November. Everyone was very excited. Grace designed a lovely poster which was put up in every shop throughout the town, a larger one in the town hall and a smaller version popped into as many letter boxes as possible, thanks mostly to Freddie and all his friends. Evie even managed to persuade the mayor to put up the town's Christmas decorations one week early to add to the atmosphere around the town before the grand opening.

'Well done, Evie!' Mr Reid said. 'You have learned Miss Pippen's organisational skills.'

'I heard the mayor is a fussy fellow who doesn't like change,' Matthew said. 'How on earth did you manage it?'

'Actually, it was Grace's idea to ask,' Evie said. 'The conversation started out a little awkwardly, but I managed to convince him by letting him think we would put up our own decorations if he didn't agree. There was no way he would have wanted that!'

'Daring, but clever,' Matthew said. 'I like it!'

'That part was my idea,' Freddie said.

'Yes, it was,' Evie said. 'In fact, I think Freddie's ideas are always better than mine, just as Grace's creativity is superior.'

'Then well done Freddie and Grace too!' Matthew said. 'We'll have to find the right instrument for you to play soon, Freddie. How about the drums? Or the trumpet?'

'Oh no!' Evie cried. 'How about the violin, or the oboe?'

'I think I prefer horses,' Freddie said. 'But I like listening to all of you play.'

'Then that will do nicely,' Matthew said.

'For now,' Evie added, with a mischievous smile.

The Reid Academy's first concert opened to a full house, everyone dressed in their Christmas best. The town was glittering with lights and decorations thanks to the mayor, and the new concert theatre wowed the audience. Electric lights complemented with candelabras, sweetly scented Christmas wreaths and a huge, decorated Christmas tree welcomed the excited audience.

Everyone played beautifully, the grand finale being Matthew and Evie's piano–flute duet. They received a standing ovation. All the musicians joined them on stage for the encore and received another standing ovation. It could not have been better.

Refreshments with a Christmas theme were served afterwards: a variety of savouries, together with mince pies, Christmas fruit cake, Yule log, mulled wine, tea and juices. The curtains were drawn back from the windows, showing everyone that it had begun to snow, adding another special touch to a successful evening.

Evie and her friends mixed with the audience, glad to relax and chat with friends. Samuel was smiling and chatting animatedly with Mr Finch, who had made 'a remarkable recovery', thanks to his 'robust constitution'! Evie noticed how happy Grace was, delighted to be relieved of her heavy glasses and clearly very pleased that Samuel had the night off. Lord and Lady Moffat were in attendance too, together with their children, Cecilia and Cedric. Evie was glad to see that Cecilia wasn't interested in talking to Matthew any more, turning her attentions instead to none other than Edward Hill, from the museum. The siblings were soon bored, however, and persuaded their parents to leave at the first opportunity.

During the evening, Evie gave Edward a polite nod from a distance, but decided not to engage him in conversation which might turn to the unfortunate discovery of the fake goblet. Then Evie spotted the McGinn brothers moving through the crowd towards her. Their friend Bart was with them.

'It's good to see you again,' Evie said.

'Pleasure to see you too, Miss Evie,' Martin said.

'That was a lovely concert,' Danny said. 'You play the flute beautifully.'

'Thank you,' Evie said.

'I owe *you* a big thank you,' Bart said quietly. 'The boys told me that my recovery is all down to you.'

'You're very welcome,' Evie said softly. 'You were all very brave to hunt down those snakes, but I think we've seen the last of them now.'

'Well, thank you again, Miss Evie,' Danny said. 'Good luck with the new academy. If ever you need us, you know where we are.'

Over the coming months, Evie and Matthew's friendship deepened and an unspoken understanding was evident to anyone who saw them together. Grace and Samuel's friendship was developing too, though more slowly, as Grace was quietly building her new-found confidence. She wasn't ready to consider following Evie to train as a tutor, but Evie was delighted when Grace said she might be interested in some secretarial work at the academy instead. Naturally, she would be happy to take part in all the concerts too.

Evie had agreed with Matthew and his father that she would teach the flute to the younger students at the academy – but not the harp, though perhaps in time. She would only play the harp at home for the moment, and to fulfil her obligations at the full moons. Knowing that her closest friends finally knew her secret was a huge relief to Evie. They each accepted that it was a lifetime promise to keep it a secret.

Freddie was delighted to be appointed as Evie's official Harp Keeper. It was obvious that this was his role, just as Lucia's grandmother had once been, and Nala had confirmed it when Evie finally read the second message.

As well as Freddie's appointment as Harp Keeper, Evie officially made Grace and Matthew her trusted Harp Guardians and invited them to the ritual on the night of the full moon in late December. They each vowed to forever protect Evie's secret and help her in her duties as Harp Maiden. They wrote it down on parchment and watched the paper burn until the fire went out. It was two days before Evie's sixteenth birthday.

The harp sat in its usual place, on the table in the bay window of the Wellses' parlour. It waited for each full moon, when the most important Harp Maiden of all time would play it, bringing its magic to those in greatest need for as long as Evelyn Wells could stroke its magical strings.

There was only one more message from Nala, and it appeared in February:

> *Yes, Harp Maiden, I have made terrible mistakes. Some people use magic for good, others for evil. I have done both. I tried to make amends by stealing the Black Ruby from Volok, imprisoning him with the tree curse, and creating the magical harp. Perhaps it was not enough, but I tried to put things right, if a little too late. I hope you can forgive me for what the magic has cost you, and that you will use your gifts more wisely than I did. The choices*

are all yours now, there will be no more demands from me. Good luck, Harp Maiden, you deserve this gift. Always use it as you see fit.

Your friend forever in magic,

Nala of Yodor

Evie closed the notebook, secured the leather straps and locked it away in her private drawer. She went downstairs to where the others were waiting. It was Sunday evening, time for Evie to entertain the family by playing the flute and the harp. Despite all the tragedies of the previous year, Evie felt she was on the brink of a new and exciting chapter in her life. She stroked the strings, filling her home with exquisite music that night, and for many days and nights to come. Fulfilling her destiny as the Harp Maiden, she would do wonderful things in the world and make people happy, all the while safe in the knowledge that she would never have to do it all alone.

THE END

Acknowledgements

Once again, my heartfelt thanks to the wonderful production team: Rachel Corcoran (illustrator), Robert Doran (editor) and Chenile Keogh (Kazoo production). I want to thank the bookstores, schools and libraries that continue to support my work, and all the enthusiastic young readers who enjoy my stories. A special mention also for my friend who accidentally inspired me to think of the idea for *Harp Maiden* when she told me she was taking up harp lessons again! Finally, warmest thanks to my husband, Angelo, my biggest supporter, wisest advisor and best friend.

SLOW TRAVEL

Norfolk

al, characterful guides to Britain's special places

Laurence Mitchell

EDITION 2

Bradt Travel Guides Ltd, UK
The Globe Pequot Press Inc, USA

Bradt

Norfolk

Norfolk's landscapes are far more varied than many imagine. As well as the reed beds and waterways of the Broads, and the straight-as-a-die channels of the Fen region, the county also has the wet grazing meadows of the Waveney Valley and the forests and sandy heaths of the Brecks. Best of all, perhaps, is the glorious north Norfolk coast with its salt marshes, shingle banks, tidal creeks and vast sandy beaches.

1 Boats in the tidal creek at Burnham Overy Staithe. 2 Steam heritage railway between Sheringham and Holt. 3 The Cley Marshes are superb for birdwatching. 4 The Norfolk Broads offer plenty of scope for off-road cycling. 5 Boat trip at BeWILDerwood adventure park near Hoveton.

TOWNS & VILLAGES

Many of Norfolk's towns and villages are charmingly old-fashioned. Building styles vary from pebble-built on the north coast to flint, brick and half-timbered elsewhere. Most towns have a weekly market day, which is invariably the best time to visit.

1 The small town of Loddon lies next to the River Chet, a tributary of the River Yare.
2 The Waveney Valley town of Diss has an unspoiled historic centre and a lively Friday market.
3 Picture-perfect Blakeney, a former fishing village, is quintessentially north Norfolk.
4 Southwest of Norwich, Wymondham has a fascinating history, as illustrated by its village sign. 5 In the far west of the county, Downham Market is well known for its iconic clock tower.
6 The coastal village of Cley-next-the-Sea not only has birds galore, it has exquisite food, too.

NORFOLK COAST

With splendid beaches, salt marshes and cliffs, the Norfolk coast is one of the glories of the county. As well as having a unique landscape and rare and distinctive wildlife, there is plenty that characterises the coast in human terms too, with fine resorts, fishing villages and time-honoured maritime traditions.

1 Brancaster was once the location of the Roman Saxon Shore fort of Branodunum. **2** Cromer is famous for the deliciously sweet crabs that are caught offshore. **3** The North Norfolk Coast Path runs all the way from Holme-next-the-Sea to Cromer. **4** Common seals at Blakeney Point. **5** Mundesley beach with its colourful parade of beach huts. **6** Oystercatcher, a typical bird of the coast. **7** Tall ships at the Great Yarmouth Maritime Festival. **8** Fishermen collecting mussels at The Wash. **9** Happisburgh's distinctive red-and-white banded lighthouse on the northeast Norfolk coast.

10 Caister-on-Sea, near Great Yarmouth, has an excellent sandy beach. 11 Fishing boats are launched from the beach at Cromer.

AUTHOR

Laurence Mitchell has at various times worked as an English teacher in Sudan, surveyed farm buildings in Norfolk, pushed a pen in a local government office and taught geography in a rural secondary school. Having finally settled for the uncertain life of a freelance travel writer and photographer, he specialises in places firmly off the beaten track like the Balkans, Central Asia and the Middle East when not wandering around his home patch of East Anglia. As well writing several guides for Bradt, his work has appeared in publications like *Geographical*, *Walk*, *Discover Britain*, *Wild Travel* and *hidden europe*. Laurence is a member of the British Guild of Travel Writers and the Outdoor Writers and Photographers Guild. His website is ⌖ laurencemitchell.com and his blog is ⌖ eastofelveden.wordpress.com.

AUTHOR'S STORY

I am not a native of East Anglia but, in my defence, I have lived here a long time – since the 1970s in fact. I stayed on in Norwich after graduation from the University of East Anglia, like many other 'UEA refugees', unable – or perhaps unwilling – to go anywhere else. Months led to years, years led to decades and eventually I just merged into the scenery. I have also travelled widely in the interim period but Norwich has become the place to which I return.

I was delighted to be given the opportunity to write this guide. As someone who has written about some pretty odd, far-flung places, it seemed strange at first to be focussing so close to home. But this just made me take a closer look at my own back yard and helped restore an appreciation that I may have been starting to take for granted.

Researching this book's predecessor, I revisited old stomping grounds and also discovered places that I did not know existed. I had forgotten just how attractive the old part of King's Lynn is and how vividly maritime history permeates the very bricks of Great Yarmouth's rows. Since then I have taken every opportunity to find out more about my own patch; to visit villages that hitherto had merely been ink on a map, and reacquaint myself with places that had become just a vague recollection. It has been the small things, the things that you could not plan for, that have really brought home to me why I live in this eastern curve of the country: fresh details that reveal themselves on oft-trodden walks, serendipitous sightings of wildlife and magnificent fleeting skyscapes. In a way it feels like a homecoming.

Second edition published February 2018
First published March 2014

Bradt Travel Guides Ltd
IDC House, The Vale, Chalfont St Peter, Bucks SL9 9RZ, England
www.bradtguides.com
Print edition published in the USA by The Globe Pequot Press Inc,
PO Box 480, Guilford, Connecticut 06437-0480

Text copyright © 2018 Laurence Mitchell
Maps copyright © 2018 Bradt Travel Guides Ltd
Photographs copyright © 2018 Individual photographers (see below)

Project Manager: Maisie Fitzpatrick
Series Design: Pepi Bluck, Perfect Picture
Cover: Pepi Bluck, Perfect Picture

ISBN: 978 1 78477 073 0 (print)
e-ISBN: 978 1 78477 534 6 (e-pub)
e-ISBN: 978 1 78477 435 6 (mobi)

British Library Cataloguing in Publication Data
A catalogue record for this book is available from the British Library

Photographs
Photos © individual photographers and organisations credited beside images & also from
picture libraries credited as follows: Alamy.com (A), Awl-images.com (AWL),
Dreamstime.com (D), Shutterstock.com (S), Superstock.com (SS)
Front cover Cley Windmill, Cley-next-the-Sea (Alan Copson/AWL)
Back cover Hunstanton Cliffs (BBA Photography/S)
Title page Cromer pier (Gordon Bell/S)

Maps David McCutcheon FBCart.S

Typeset by Pepi Bluck, Perfect Picture
Production managed by Jellyfish Print Solutions; printed in India
Digital conversion by www.dataworks.co.in

ACKNOWLEDGEMENTS

My sincere thanks go to all the team at Bradt, in particular Adrian Phillips, Rachel Fielding, Anna Moores, Maisie Fitzpatrick, Carys Homer, Holly Parsons and Deborah Gerrard. Thanks are due to those who contributed boxes – Penny Edwards, Donald Greig, Poppy Mathews and Andrew Paxton. My gratitude also goes to those individuals who made suggestions, provided food for thought or were good enough to answer my questions – Annie Bird, Jason Borthwick, John Hiskett, Danielle Howard, Sheila Rattray, Caroline Davison and David Vince. Thanks go too to Wendy Ellis of Boydell & Brewer for permission to quote from John Seymour's *Companion Guide to East Anglia*, and to Henry Head at Norfolk Lavender. For this second edition I would also like to thank Emma Halford, Helen Paine, Vanessa Scott, Ben Jackson and James Knight for further feedback and suggestions. As always, I also owe gratitude to my wife Jackie for her unstinting support throughout.

FEEDBACK REQUEST & UPDATES WEBSITE

There are only so many special places and aspects of Norfolk life that you can focus on when limited by word counts and book length. Much as we'd like to include them all, it simply isn't possible. We've done our best to include a good mix and to check facts but there are bound to be errors (phone numbers and websites change with alarming frequency) as well as inevitable omissions of really special places. You can post your comments and recommendations, and read the latest feedback from other readers online at ⊘ bradtupdates.com/norfolk. Alternatively, email us at ✉ info@bradtguides.com.

SUGGESTED PLACES TO BASE YOURSELF

These bases make ideal starting points for exploring localities the Slow way.

NORTH SEA

WELLS-NEXT-THE-SEA pages 45–8
The perfect compromise for staying on the coast – a small resort and former fishing port with excellent walking close to hand and easy road access east and west to other parts of the coast.

CHAPTER 1
page 16

The Wash

Brancaster Staithe

A149

Wells-next-the-Sea

Cley-the

BRANCASTER STAITHE pages 56–7
One of several attractive villages on this lovely stretch of the Norfolk coast, it makes an ideal centre for walking sections of the Norfolk Coast Path. There are good bus connections along the coast in both directions.

HUNSTANTON

Snettisham

FAKENHAM

A149

A148

A1065

KING'S LYNN

A17

Norfolk

A1065

CHAPTER 3
page 104

A47

EAST DEREHA

CHAPTER 4
page 134

A47

A47

Great Ouse

A10

WISBECH

A47

A1122

SWAFFHAM

DOWNHAM MARKET

A1075

A1122

Watton

A134

A1065

A10

CHAPTER 7
page 228

SNETTISHAM pages 143–4
Nicely situated between King's Lynn and Hunstanton in northwest Norfolk, this characterful carrstone village is just a mile or two from the shore of the Wash and a stone's throw from the Peddars Way.

Little Ouse

A134

Brandon

THETFORD

Suffolk

A11

SWAFFHAM pages 233–6
This attractive market town between East Dereham and King's Lynn is well situated for exploring the Brecks as well as the coast and hinterland of northwest Norfolk.

EAST DEREHAM pages 129–30
About as central as it gets in the county, Dereham provides easy access to the whole of Norfolk and the town has plenty of historical interest in its own right.

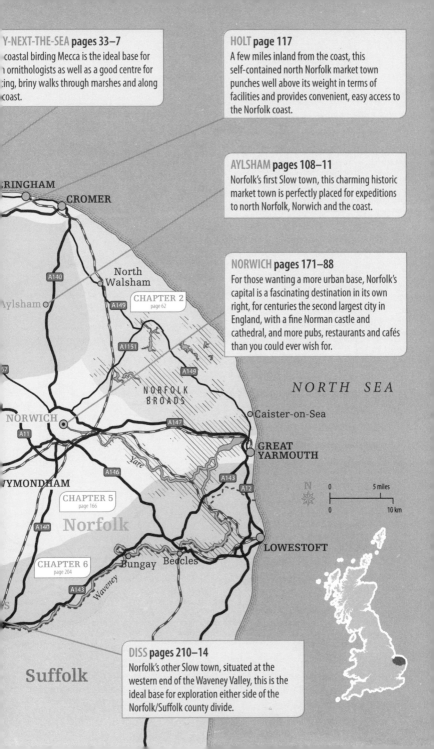

Y-NEXT-THE-SEA pages 33–7

coastal birding Mecca is the ideal base for
 ornithologists as well as a good centre for
 ng, briny walks through marshes and along
 coast.

HOLT page 117

A few miles inland from the coast, this
self-contained north Norfolk market town
punches well above its weight in terms of
facilities and provides convenient, easy access to
the Norfolk coast.

AYLSHAM pages 108–11

Norfolk's first Slow town, this charming historic
market town is perfectly placed for expeditions
to north Norfolk, Norwich and the coast.

NORWICH pages 171–88

For those wanting a more urban base, Norfolk's
capital is a fascinating destination in its own
right, for centuries the second largest city in
England, with a fine Norman castle and
cathedral, and more pubs, restaurants and cafés
than you could ever wish for.

RINGHAM

CROMER

A140

North
Walsham

Aylsham

A149

CHAPTER 2
page 62

A1151

A149

NORTH SEA

NORFOLK
BROADS

A147

Caister-on-Sea

NORWICH

A11

GREAT
YARMOUTH

YMONDHAM

A146

Yare

A143

A12

CHAPTER 5
page 166

N

0   5 miles

A140

Norfolk

0   10 km

CHAPTER 6
page 204

LOWESTOFT

Bungay   Beccles

A143   Waveney

DISS pages 210–14

Norfolk's other Slow town, situated at the
western end of the Waveney Valley, this is the
ideal base for exploration either side of the
Norfolk/Suffolk county divide.

Suffolk

CONTENTS

NORFOLK ONLINE

For additional online content, articles, photos and more on Norfolk, why not visit ⊘ bradtguides.com/norfolk.

GOING SLOW IN
NORFOLK

It is a piece of weakness and folly merely to value things because of
their distances from the places where we call home.

Martin Martin 1697

Why Slow Norfolk? Surely the county is 'slow' enough already? What is
so special about this part of eastern England? Well, for a start, the county
was largely bypassed by the Industrial Revolution. This is not to say it
had no part to play in shaping England's history – far from it – it is just
that Norfolk tended to have more political and economic clout back in
medieval times than it has over the last few hundred years. It may be hard
to believe but back in the 16th century Norfolk was the most densely
populated county in all Britain; nowadays, the county has the tenth lowest
population density in the country. Norwich, Norfolk's capital, was once
the second largest city in England; now it ranks as 26th. Clearly, much has
changed since medieval times but Norfolk's history has quite a tale to tell.

Norfolk is highly distinguished in terms of geography, too, and more
varied than most first-time visitors imagine it to be. In fact, there is
much to contradict the perceived wisdom that the entire county is as
flat as the proverbial pancake. As well as the lustrous lakes, reed beds
and waterways of the Broads, and the straight-as-a-die channels of the
Fen region, Norfolk also has the forests and dry, sandy expanses of the
Brecks and, perhaps best of all, the wonderful north Norfolk coast with
its shingle banks, salt marshes, tidal creeks and vast sandy beaches.

Connecting these disparate landscapes is a countryside filled with
rolling farmland, tracts of ancient woodland, meandering rivers and
hundreds of villages, each with its church. It may be a wealth of villages
that make the county what it is, each a self-contained microcosm of
rural life. As Reginald Pound, the author of *Scott of the Antarctic*, wrote,
'(Norfolk) is littered with villages but uncluttered by towns'. But there
are towns too, and by and large they are also handsome and distinctive.

As a rule, the built landscape reflects that which is found immediately beneath the surface: in the east of the county, thatch roofs and flint walls prevail; in the west, carrstone and chalk. Similarly, land use also depends on the soil and drainage of the area: the fertile black soil in the Fens of the west, the arable crops that thrive on the light land of north Norfolk, the sheep and cattle that predominate on the heavy clays of the south, and swathes of conifer forestry in the Brecks where sheep ranges and rabbit warrens once used to abound.

There is a common contention that Norfolk is forever a step behind the rest of the country; that it lies out on a limb at the end of a road to nowhere. And there is still sometimes a slightly sneering metropolitan view that the county is nice enough to visit but 'you wouldn't want to live there.' As for the people who do live here, 'Normal for Norfolk' remains a common jibe. It's good to see this expression being deconstructed and adopted in a non-pejorative sense as a slogan by World Class Norfolk, an enterprise that promotes business investment in the county. Of course, the fact that Norfolk remains one of just a few English counties without a motorway leading to it may be seen as an obstacle to progress by some. Others, though, see this as a virtue. Motorways and 'Slow' are not generally ideal partners.

I first came to Norfolk four decades ago to attend university. I went away for a year or two but I have pretty well based myself here since then, mostly in Norwich but also for a few years in south Norfolk. It has been a slow burn of appreciation. To be honest, it took a while for the subtle charms of the region to grow on me. Birdwatching on the north Norfolk coast and in the Broads got me out and about in the region, as did a bit of cycling around my own patch in Norwich and south Norfolk. Then, in the mid 1980s, I got a job as team leader on a project that was carrying out an extensive survey of farm buildings and agricultural practices in Norfolk. This got me interested in vernacular architecture and the way that the rural landscape had been shaped by farming and feudalism. I interviewed many north Norfolk farmers as part of this work and some of these were just old enough to remember working with horses.

Even just 30 years ago, things were different. Large-scale agribusiness had not taken such a firm hold and the majority of the farms were family-run, 200-acre affairs that, besides mechanisation, were not managed all that differently from the way they had been in the inter-war period. Memories of many of the farms I visited have blurred with the passing of time but I vividly recall one small and rather old-fashioned place near North Walsham, more of a large smallholding than anything else, which was lovingly farmed by a wonderful old couple. After I had looked around, the farmer gave me a mug of tea and took me to one side, 'Some people might cart right across the world looking for beautiful scenery but we are blessed, we've got it right here.' He gazed across a dung-covered farmyard alive with feeding swallows, past a rickety old barn to the fields beyond. 'Have a look at that view, will you? Have you ever seen anything better than that? Me and the missus never go on holiday and we've never been abroad either. What's the point

THE SLOW MINDSET

Hilary Bradt, Founder, Bradt Travel Guides

> We shall not cease from exploration
> And the end of all our exploring
> Will be to arrive where we started
> And know the place for the first time.

T S Eliot, 'Little Gidding', *Four Quartets*

This series evolved, slowly, from a Bradt editorial meeting when we started to explore ideas for guides to our favourite country – Great Britain. We wanted to get away from the usual 'top sights' formula and encourage our authors to bring out the nuances and local differences that make up a sense of place – such things as food, building styles, nature, geology, or local people and what makes them tick. Our aim was to create a series that celebrates the present, focusing on sustainable tourism, rather than taking a nostalgic wallow in the past.

So without our realising it at the time, we had defined 'Slow Travel', or at least our concept of it. For the beauty of the Slow movement is that there is no fixed definition; we adapt the philosophy to fit our individual needs and aspirations. Thus Carl Honoré, author of *In Praise of Slow*, writes: 'The Slow Movement is a cultural revolution against the notion that faster is always better. It's not about doing everything at a snail's pace, it's about seeking to do everything at the right speed. Savouring the hours and minutes rather than just counting them. Doing everything as well as possible, instead of as fast as possible. It's about quality over quantity in everything from work to food to parenting.' And travel.

So take time to explore. Don't rush it, get to know an area – and the people who live there – and you'll be as delighted as the authors by what you find.

when you've got all this on your doorstep?' I didn't have the slightest doubt about his sincerity – and he was absolutely right, it was a lovely view in a bucolic, John Constable sort of way. He was a wise and happy man, this old farmer; perhaps the perfect ambassador of what the Slow outlook is all about.

Hamish Fulton, whose art results from the experience of walking, once staged an exhibition entitled *An Object Cannot Compete with an Experience*. It's a mantra that stands me in good stead. The Slow movement is all about savouring the moment. A good meal taken slowly is an experience, so is a long walk with never-to-be forgotten views. So is a conversation that gives you an insight into someone else's life and celebrates a shared humanity. It's about a sense of being where you are, what makes it special, what makes it unique.

While I was researching the first edition of this book, I was fortunate to attend a talk by the writer Richard Mabey who was discussing the paintings of Mary Newcomb, a recently deceased local artist whose works were on display in a special exhibition at Norwich Castle Museum. Mary Newcomb's gloriously naive, almost Zen-like, paintings, along with Richard Mabey's insightful appraisal, helped me realise that an appreciation of the subtle beauty of rural East Anglia depends on having an eye for detail and a fondness for the drama of small events.

Perhaps that is what the essence of Slow is: finding the extraordinary in the commonplace – that which makes a place distinctive, the unique patina of time and custom that makes somewhere special. Everywhere has these qualities to some extent; it is just that, in terms of distinctiveness, Norfolk probably has more than its fair share. Let's not get carried away, there are places here as humdrum as anywhere else but the thing to do is to scrape away the veneer a little and see what is beneath.

People who have close contact with the land generally know this. The Northamptonshire shepherd poet John Clare, who modestly and perhaps disingenuously claimed, 'I found the poems in the fields, and only wrote them down', extolled the spirit of Slow when he wrote:

O who can pass such lovely spots
Without a wish to stray
And leave life's cares a while forgot
To muse an hour away?

I hope this book will help to inspire some happy musing.

A TASTE OF NORFOLK

With something like 90 miles of North Sea coastline it is hardly surprising that Norfolk has a wealth of seafood to savour. Probably the most highly regarded are the Cromer crabs (pages 22–3) that are caught just off the north Norfolk coast. There are plenty of lobsters and shellfish too, the most famous being 'Stewkey Blues' (page 44) – a type of cockle – and tasty fresh mussels from Brancaster. The wet fish options are also excellent; cod and haddock especially, and herring too, a nutritious and plentiful fish for which the port of Great Yarmouth was once world-famous (page 197). Several smokehouses around the coast, like the one at Cley-next-the-Sea (page 37), make good use of such provenance and produce all manner of delicious goods like kippers and smoked mackerel.

To complement your seafood you may wish to try a seasonal favourite, marsh samphire (page 43), a salty delicacy that grows in abundance in the saltmarshes of north Norfolk in the summer months.

For committed carnivores Norfolk meat is a treat too, especially that which comes from some of the county's rare breed varieties, like beef from Red Poll cattle. Many Norfolk restaurants make use of locally reared meat on their menus, but the county also has a large number of farm shops and farmers' markets where such products can be purchased for home consumption.

With a relatively dry climate and a tendency towards arable, Norfolk is not really much of a place for dairy farming, but the county does produce a number of cheeses with a distinctive local flavour. Probably the best known are those made by Mrs Temple's Cheeses at Wighton in north Norfolk, especially Binham Blue, which is made with vegetarian rennet and milk from British Holstein cows.

Vegetarians are well provided for as a rule: the county has a wealth of fresh vegetables and there are a number of organic providers, too. A decent number of restaurants also specialise in, or serve only, vegetarian food. This is particularly true of Norwich, the county capital. Asparagus is one of the county's specialities, abundant in early summer, especially in those areas that have light, sandy soil.

NORFOLK TIPPLES

Contrary to expectation, Norfolk actually has a few vineyards – some of the most northerly in the country – one of which has produced prize-winning wines (**page** 189). Overall, however, it is probably fair to say that the county is better celebrated for its beer. Norfolk has a plethora of small-scale real ale breweries scattered around the county – Woodforde's (**page** 97) from Woodbastwick, Wolf from Norwich, Yetman's from Holt and Humpty Dumpty from Reedham, to name just a few. If these are not enough to quench your thirst then there are always Adnam's or St Peter's Brewery ales from over the Suffolk border.

Surprisingly, perhaps, the county is also a whisky producer, with the English Whisky Company (**page** 243) distilling a range of hand-crafted whiskies conjured from Norfolk barley and deep aquifer water at its base in Roudham in the Brecks.

HOW THIS BOOK IS ARRANGED

This book divides Norfolk into seven fairly distinct geographical areas starting with the north Norfolk coast and ending with the Brecks in the southwest of the county. *Chapter 1* covers the north Norfolk coast and its immediate hinterland between Cromer in the east and Holme-next-the-Sea in the west. This coincides to a large extent with the boundary of the Norfolk Coast Area of Outstanding Natural Beauty. *Chapter 2* deals with the northeast coast between Overstrand and Caister-on-Sea as well as the Norfolk Broads that lies inland. *Chapter 3* (North Central Norfolk) covers the area south of the north Norfolk coast and west of the Broads as far as the Fakenham area to the west and East Dereham to the south. *Chapter 4* includes the rest of the Norfolk coast that faces west across the Wash as well as the borderland Fen region, while *Chapter 5* covers the River Yare valley from west of Norwich to the coast and includes both the county capital and Norfolk's second largest settlement, Great Yarmouth. *Chapter 6* covers that part of south Norfolk that lies close to the border with Suffolk along the course of the River Waveney, while *Chapter 7* includes Thetford and the area west and north of it as far as Swaffham. Both of the last two chapters make occasional short forays across the border into Suffolk.

MAPS

Each chapter begins with a map with **numbered stopping points** that correspond to numbered headings in the text. The featured walks have maps accompanying them.

Norfolk is a large county and requires a total of seven 1:50,000, Landranger OS maps to cover it fully. One very useful map to have is the double-sided 1:25,000, scale OS Explorer OL40 The Broads map, which shows much interesting detail and has plenty of walker- and cyclist-friendly information. Similarly, the three 1:25,000 OS Explorer maps of the Norfolk coast (West 250, Central 251 and East 252) are a boon to walkers or anyone with an interest in exploring the geographical and historical features of the area.

FOOD & DRINK

I've listed some of my favourite pubs, cafés, tea rooms and places to eat, favouring those places that serve local produce or are worth a visit for some other reason, such as appealing quirkiness or distinctive character.

ACCOMMODATION

Accommodation has been recommended on the basis of location and because it embraces a Slow approach either in its 'green' ethos or its overall feel. Hotels, B&Bs and self-catering options are indicated by the symbol ⍭ after town and village headings, and campsites by ⍍, with a cross-reference to the full listing under *Accommodation*, pages 256–8. For full descriptions of these listings, visit ⊘ bradtguides.com/norfolksleeps.

GETTING AROUND

Cycling and walking are the ideal methods of Slow travel. I'd like to encourage people to **visit without a car** but I appreciate that this can be difficult in some parts of Norfolk, particularly in those areas of the county that lie well away from the primary routes. Details of how best to get around are given in each chapter. Below is a brief overview and suggestions of how to reach Norfolk from other parts of the country.

A useful website for **planning journeys by bus or train**, or a combination of the two, is ⊘ travelineeastanglia.co.uk.

TRAINS

There are regular rail services between Norwich and Great Yarmouth, Norwich and Cromer and Norwich and Thetford. Norwich is connected to London by direct trains from Liverpool Street station and to the Midlands and North by means of a change at Peterborough or Ely.

Direct trains that stop at Manchester, Sheffield, Derby and Nottingham also run between Norwich and Liverpool. King's Lynn can be reached by direct trains from London via Cambridge and Ely. Within Norfolk, there are also short preserved **heritage railways** like the Mid-Norfolk Railway between Wymondham and East Dereham, and the North Norfolk Railway between Sheringham and Holt, as well as narrow gauge lines that connect Wells with Walsingham and Wroxham with Aylsham.

BUS & COACH

Norwich has regular long-distance coach services with National Express that connect the city with London, the major airports and other cities around the country. Several bus companies provide routes within the county, most notably First in Norfolk & Suffolk, Konectbus, Stagecoach, Anglian Bus and Sanders Coaches. Bus travel details for a locality are given at the beginning of each chapter.

WALKING

Norfolk abounds with walking potential, from linear coastal strolls to circular walks through forest and open farmland. As well as walking suggestions made at the beginning of each chapter a number of personal favourites are offered throughout the book together with a sketch map and directions for the walk. Walking in Norfolk is rarely very demanding thanks to the reasonably flat topography. The going is mostly easy and so walkers just need to decide how far they are prepared to walk if attempting a route. Any obstacles, such as they are, are limited to nuisances like overgrown nettles, hungry mosquitoes, obstructing herds of cows or the occasional recalcitrant bull. Otherwise, it's ideal, especially when a walk takes in a country pub and/or an interesting village church to explore *en route*.

Several notable **long-distance paths** run through the county. The best known of these is the **Peddars Way** between Knettishall Heath near Thetford and Holme-next-the-Sea close to Hunstanton. This route connects with the **Norfolk Coast Path** to continue to Cromer and beyond. Cromer is also the start of the **Weavers' Way**, which meanders through the Broads to finish at Great Yarmouth, where another route, the **Angles Way**, leads back to Thetford using paths on both sides of the River Waveney and the Norfolk–Suffolk border. As well as these routes that combine together to effectively circumambulate the county there is another succession of routes – **Wherryman's Way, Marriott's Way, Wensum Way** and **Nar Valley Way** – that connect together to pass through the middle of Norfolk linking Great Yarmouth with King's Lynn. Lesser routes in the county include the **Tas Valley Way, Boudicca Way** and **Kett's Country,** all in south Norfolk, and the **Paston Way** in the Broads. For a useful overview of the various walking options in Norfolk on offer, consult the Norfolk Trails website at ♂ www.norfolk. gov.uk/out-and-about-in-norfolk/norfolk-trails.

CYCLING

Norfolk has plenty to offer cyclists, from quiet country lanes and disused railway lines to off-road routes that follow bridleways and forest tracks. Details of suggested routes and areas with good potential for cycling are outlined at the start of each chapter, as are local outlets for cycle hire. The website ♂ cycle-route.com has many good suggestions for routes in the county. For off-road cycling probably the best part of the county to head for is the Brecks, where a large number of routes criss-cross Thetford Forest.

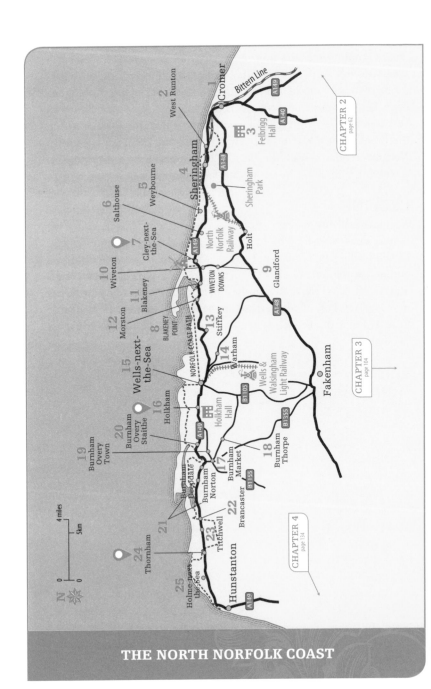

THE NORTH NORFOLK COAST

1
THE NORTH
NORFOLK COAST

From the slightly faded Victorian resort of **Cromer** to the village of **Holme-next-the-Sea**, the north Norfolk coast stretches resplendently east to west (which is how this chapter is ordered): a classic landscape of wide beaches, salt marshes, offshore sandbanks, muddy tidal inlets and all-too-rare harbours. This is the Norfolk that most city-dwellers hanker after: big skies, golden beaches and neat pebble-built cottages; mewing gulls and fishing boats beached in the mud. This stretch of coastline is quite unlike any other place in the British Isles, and has been designated an AONB (Area of Outstanding Natural Beauty). The icing on the cake is that there are even some modest hills here, with **Beacon Hill** near Cromer – 345 feet high – marking the highest point of the ridge where the southbound glaciations of the last ice age finally gave up the ghost as they deposited chunks of Scandinavia and North Sea seabed on Norfolk soil.

In spring, the road verges are emerald green with alexanders, a plant related to celery (of which it tastes strongly) that is particularly abundant at the coast and was recently considered for selection as the county flower of Norfolk. Predictably, the powers that be chose the poppy instead – a safe, if less representative, choice. In summer, the saltings glow purple with large swathes of sea lavender, and, with bright blue skies, the coastal marshes become an Impressionist painting of sea, sand and sky. Autumn brings waves of migrating birds, and the bushes twitch with freshly landed migrants at this time of year, as do the salt marshes where exotic waders feed cheek by jowl much to the delight of birdwatchers. In winter, the sky is often alive with noisy flocks of geese in their thousands. In fact, if you can put up with onshore wind that seems to hail directly from the Arctic, a bright, crisp winter's day is hard to beat for a bracing walk along the seashore followed by lunch in a cosy pub.

With a range of distinct habitats for wildlife that include salt marshes, sand dunes, pebble banks, reed beds and woodland, it is hardly surprising that birds – even some rarities – are found everywhere, and that conservation bodies like the RSPB and NWT (Norfolk Wildlife Trust) have several reserves along this coast, as does the National Trust. In fact, **Cley-next-the-Sea**, a village with the vast **NWT Cley Marshes Nature Reserve** of salt marshes and reed beds, has long been considered one of the best sites for birding in the entire British Isles. Seals are easy to see too, and a boat trip out among them is invariably a hit with visitors of all ages.

This coast is largely a place of small fishing villages that have turned, in part at least, to tourism. Flint and pebble rules supreme, with whole villages – houses, pubs, churches, even bus shelters – constructed out of these plentiful beach materials. It's almost a surprise that public phone boxes aren't made out of them – since public conveniences generally are.

GETTING AROUND

PUBLIC TRANSPORT

This is surprisingly good – far better than the dire situation a few decades ago when travelling along the coast required either a car or a willingness to hitchhike. Thankfully, the excellent and convenient **Bittern Line** (⌒ bitternline.com) links Norwich with Cromer and Sheringham on the coast. A **Bittern Line Ranger ticket** entitles unlimited travel at weekends and any time after 08.20 Mondays to Fridays, as well as free travel on the Coasthopper bus service – a veritable bargain. Trains run more or less hourly during the daytime and evenings Monday to Saturday, with a slightly reduced service on Sundays.

The Bittern Line connects with the superbly useful **Coasthopper** bus service that runs regularly – every half hour or so in summer – between Sheringham and Hunstanton. It calls at each village along the way as well as stopping on request – very useful indeed for walks along the coast. Easy connections can be made from Hunstanton down to King's Lynn, which is connected to Cambridge (but not Norwich) by rail. Coasthopper drivers are generally excellent ambassadors for the north Norfolk coast and are courteous and helpful in the extreme, so if you are unsure as to where to get off, just ask.

As well as the Bittern Line, there are a couple of short-distance, privately owned heritage railway lines that, while tourist-oriented, can sometimes come in useful for getting about. The **North Norfolk Railway** (✆ 01263 820800 ✎ nnrailway.co.uk), also known as the **'Poppy Line'**, runs between Sheringham and Holt (see Sheringham) and the **Wells and Walsingham Light Railway** (✆ 01328 711630 ✎ wellswalsinghamrailway.co.uk) plies the eight miles between Wells-next-the Sea and Little Walsingham.

WALKING

Exploring on foot can be sublime along this stretch of coast. It's flat certainly, but here you'll find some of the best marsh and coast walking anywhere in the country. And away from the coast, three magnificent estates have free year-round access for walkers, with lots to look at: **Felbrigg**, **Holkham** and **Sheringham Park**.

The **Norfolk Coast Path**, which links to the **Peddars Way** at Holme-next-the-Sea before meandering 44 miles eastwards to Cromer, takes in nearly all of the best bits: the whole thing, known rather clumsily as the Peddars Way & Norfolk Coast Path, is a National Trail, with the route shown with acorn markers. Since 2016 the coast path has been extended to follow the northeast Norfolk coast as far as Hopton-on-Sea

NORTH NORFOLK COAST WALKING HIGHLIGHTS

- **Cromer to Sheringham**, following the Norfolk Coast Path, which ventures inland to take in some modest hills and Norfolk's highest point. Returning from Sheringham, you can either take the train back or walk along the beach beneath the cliff.
- **Blakeney to Cley-next-the-Sea**, following the North Coast Path, taking the dyke out through the marshes to Cley Channel before heading inland towards Cley village along the bank of the River Glaven.
- **Cley-next-the-Sea to Salthouse**, alternating between the beach and sea wall.
- **Burnham Overy Staithe to Holkham Gap**, walking along the dyke and beach, then returning by bus. You can extend the walk through the Holkham Estate, across fields to Burnham Overy Town, and back.
- **Burnham Deepdale to Burnham Overy Staithe**, along the dyke, returning by bus.
- **Holme-next-the-Sea to Thornham**, following the North Coast Path along the beach and dykes, perhaps having a drink at the Lifeboat on the way back.

at the Suffolk border south of Great Yarmouth. Quite a lot of the coastal portion leads along grassy sea walls that zigzag between drained grazing land (much of it drained by Coke of Holkham, the agricultural pioneer) and vast expanses of seemingly impenetrable salt marsh cut by countless creeks and gulleys. Sections of the Peddars Way and Norfolk Coast Path make for excellent day walks, although circular walks will sometimes entail a stretch along the busy A149 coast road, which is tolerable but not really that much fun. With the exception of the paths through the Holkham Estate and the sandy heaths behind Cromer and Sheringham, the walking is not nearly so good away from the coast anyway, even if you do manage to avoid the awful coast road. This is where the Coasthopper bus service really comes into its own: walk in one direction along a stretch of coast and take the bus back – the ideal solution. Those expecting stereotypical Norfolk flatness may be surprised when they venture a little way inland from the coast, but ropes and climbing gear are not required.

CYCLING

Along the coast itself the prospects are not as good for two wheels as they are for two legs. The Norfolk Coast Path is a footpath, not a bridleway, and so it's out of bounds to cyclists (and horses). In summer, the A149 has far too much motor traffic along it to be enjoyable for most cyclists, and inattentive holiday drivers rubber-necking the scenery are an additional hazard.

A better bet is to make use of the **Norfolk Coast Cycleway**, a 59-mile route just inland from the coast that links King's Lynn with Cromer (and Great Yarmouth), using National Cycle Network Route 1 between King's Lynn and Wighton (southeast of Wells-next-the-Sea) and Regional Route 30 on to Cromer and Great Yarmouth. Felbrigg and Sheringham Park estates also have some very family-friendly traffic-free cycle routes.

The **Norfolk Coast Partnership** (✆ 01263 513811) publishes a map of the entire Norfolk Coast Cycleway (£2.50 from tourist information centres or direct by post from them; postage is extra). Ten Explorer tours of between six and 40 miles are also offered as circular day routes.

CYCLE HIRE

Deepdale Cycle Hire Deepdale Backpackers, Burnham Deepdale ✆ 01485 210614 🖱 deepdalebackpackers.co.uk/bike-hire. Provides bikes for hire complete with lock, pump, repair kit and helmet. They can also offer cyclists free route planning and advice.

Holkham Cycle Hire Holkham Hall, Wells-next-the-Sea ✆ 01328 713071 🖱 holkham. co.uk. Adjacent to the car park in Holkham Park, they have cycles for hire between April and October and can suggest routes around the estate.

Holt Overland Cycles 34 Norwich Rd, Holt ✆ 01263 713293 or 07733 445511. This cycle shop has a variety of bikes – mountain bikes, tandems, etc – for hire. Helmets and panniers provided free.

On Yer Bike Cycle Hire Nutwood Farm, Wighton ✆ 01328 820719 or 07584 308120 🖱 norfolkcyclehire.co.uk. Situated on Norfolk Coast Cycleway Route 30, they have bikes for hire that may also be collected from, or delivered to, tourism businesses along the coast.

THE END OF THE LINE: CROMER & SHERINGHAM

Cromer and Sheringham, the last places on the Bittern Line, are a long way from any notion of wild, remote Norfolk. With origins as modest fishing ports they were both developed as resorts during the late Victorian period. They were fashionable once but nowadays are often dismissed as old-fashioned or faded. I still have a soft spot for them both, though – especially Cromer, and especially out of season when winter wind whips up the sea and rattles the pier.

1 CROMER

🏠 **Gunton Arms** Thorpe Market, near Cromer (page 256)

'I am not enjoying myself very much,' a young, homesick Winston Churchill once wrote home to his mother regarding his stay in Cromer. For some reason – hurt pride, perhaps – Cromer's town council have seen fit to commit this to posterity and Churchill's youthful words are now engraved in the town's seafront promenade just in front of the pier entrance. As they say, there is no such thing as bad publicity.

Cromer became popular as a family resort in the late 19th century when the **railway** link to Norwich and London was established and those who could afford it would escape the capital's infernal smog and come here to grab a healthy lungful of north Norfolk air. Cromer's first railway station came into service in 1877, somewhat inconveniently located at the town's outskirts, but ten years later 'Cromer Beach' station was opened right in the centre of town.

Even before the steam age, city dwellers had come to Cromer to breathe its bracing salt air. Daniel Defoe came here in the 1720s and Jane Austen visited in the early 19th century and later wrote of it in *Emma*: 'Perry was a week at Cromer once, and he holds it to be the best of all the sea-bathing places.' Although popular in the Victorian period with the families of Norfolk's banking aristocracy like the Gurneys, it took a prince – and a railway – to really put it on the map. The future King Edward VII did just that when he started coming here to play golf at the end of the 19th century (probably one of the more innocent activities that the prince got up to whilst gallivanting in Norfolk away from the watchful gaze of his mother and wife).

CROMER CRABS

Cromer crabs may be a little on the small side but they are universally loved for their plump, sweet meat. The best come from the waters just offshore from Cromer and Sheringham. The crabs are *Cancer pagaraus*, exactly the same species as other British edible crabs, so it is hard to tell what it is that makes them so special and distinctive in taste. It may be that they are especially slow growing and so fill their shells with meat more plentifully, or that they contain sweeter white meat than their counterparts do. Alternatively, it may be that the seabed here has less mud than other parts of coastal UK and this influences the flavour. Whatever it is, their reputation has ensured a decent living for Cromer and Sheringham's small crabbing community over the years. Not that long ago, around 50 crab boats used regularly to put out to sea from Cromer's beach, but these days just a handful remain.

Crabbing technique involves the setting of long lines of baited pots called 'shanks' in the rocky offshore waters. These are marked with buoys and left overnight, to be hauled in again the next day and re-baited with white fish once the catch has been removed. Men work in pairs to haul in the lines, remove the crabs and re-bait the pots. Sorting takes place at sea and a good four-fifths are returned to the water simply because they are too small.

The crabbing season usually begins in March when crabs can be found relatively

Around the same time, the journalist, Clement Scott, started to write about the resort in the London papers and inevitably, with its easy access by train, and prior royal approval, it soon became a popular holiday resort with the late-Victorian chattering classes. The German Kaiser, Oscar Wilde and the aforementioned Winston Churchill all subsequently came to see for themselves.

These days, Cromer is probably best known for two things: crabs and its pier. **Crabs** are still caught here and are as sweet and delicious as ever. The **pier**, however, has had a rather troubled life over the past half-century or so. It was badly damaged by storms in 1953 and 1989, and in 1993 suffered the ignominy of being sliced in half by a storm-tossed drilling rig that had broken adrift. Currently it is in rude health and one of the few places in the country where you can still take in a genuine end-of-the-pier show of the likes of the Grumbleweeds or a Patsy Cline tribute show, or the annual **Folk on the Pier** weekend held in May (⌂ folkonthepier.co.uk); these take place at the **Pavilion Theatre** (✆ 01263 512495 ⌂ cromerpier.co.uk). Otherwise just do what everybody else does and take a stroll along it. Looking back towards land from its

close to shore – they tend to retreat further out to sea to deeper waters during the colder months.

The season lasts until the autumn, although there is a lull in high summer when the crabs breed and grow new shells and sensibly tuck themselves away from the reach of preying lobsters.

Because it is on a relatively small scale, crabbing is also reassuringly sustainable, but in recent years, there has been concern about dwindling stocks, probably the consequence of offshore dredging and rising seawater temperatures caused by global warming disrupting breeding patterns. There may also be competition for food and habitat from velvet crabs, which are usually found in the southwest but have been moving north thanks to warmer sea temperatures.

The crabber's secret, of course, is to know exactly where to lay his pots, and when to check them: the sort of thing that can only be learned by hard experience. Some Cromer crab dynasties like the Davies family have been catching and selling crabs – and manning the lifeboat – for generations. Cromer has a number of marvellous fish shops and the same families that catch the crabs often run these – Bob Davies' excellent fish shop is a case in point. Whether boiled or dressed, the important thing is freshness, so buying and eating one here is about as close as it gets to crustacean perfection.

end you can admire Cromer's grand neo-Gothic hotels along the clifftop beach road with their towers, turrets and elegant picture windows. Sadly, with British seaside holidays spiralling out of favour over recent decades, many of Cromer's hotels have gone the way of those in other resorts and struggle for business. Directly facing the pier, the **Hotel de Paris** manages to maintain an air of slightly faded elegance. Very much a Cromer institution, this may not be the most up-to-date of hotels but it is hard to imagine a better view of the pier and North Sea than that provided by one of its upper sea-view rooms. TV polymath Stephen Fry claims to have worked here as a waiter in his youth.

The true heart of Cromer is not in the narrow streets of the railway-age resort that stretch behind the main promenade, pleasant though they are, but in the far older **fishing community** that lies immediately east of the pier. This is Cromer's 'crab central', where small, clinker-built boats are launched from the beach, and where Cromer's inshore lifeboat, *George & Muriel*, dedicated in June 2011, is housed (the offshore lifeboat station is, of course, at the end of the pier). The indisputable hero of the Cromer Lifeboat tradition is Henry Blogg (1876–1954), who remains the most decorated of any lifeboatman in the United Kingdom. Cromer's central **church of St Peter & St Paul** has a stained-glass window commemorating the man (and another lovely window by Burne-Jones) as well as the tallest church tower in the county. The Burne-Jones window was damaged in a 1942 air raid but has since been fully restored. The **RNLI Henry Blogg Lifeboat Museum** (✆ 01263 511294 ⌔ rnli.org/henryblogg) is dedicated to the history of the Cromer Lifeboat and, naturally enough, Henry Blogg also figures prominently. There is a life-size figure of the former coxwain with his dog here, as well as the *H F Bailey*, a rescue vessel that came into service in 1935 and saved over 500 lives during its tenure as the town's lifeboat. The **Cromer Museum** (✆ 01263 513543 ⌔ museums.norfolk.gov.uk) also has some absorbing exhibits, mostly concerned with the Victorian 'bygone days'. These include old photos of Cromer folk of yore, including a fisherman with the unfortunate sobriquet of 'Belcher'. Its geology gallery features a few bones from the famous West Runton Elephant, whose skeleton was found propping up the cliffs just west of here (page 26). The museum also has a permanent display that features the work of Olive Edis, a pioneering local woman who photographed the full spectrum of British society at the beginning of the 20th century, from royalty to fishermen.

If you are in Cromer on New Year's Day, you can witness one of the best firework displays you are ever likely to see. The pyrotechnics, which take place over the North Sea from the end of the pier and usually coincide with a town fun run, are impressive enough to temporarily scatter the local gull population and probably send Cromer's offshore crab population scurrying to safety along the sea bed towards Dogger Bank. Be sure to come early for a good viewing position on the promenade.

⊺¶ FOOD & DRINK

Cromer is not a place for fancy dining, rather it's somewhere for fish and chips on the promenade or afternoon scones in a tea shop. Of the fish and chip shops, **Mary Janes Fish Bar & Restaurant** (27–29 Garden St ☎ 01263 511208) is considered by many to be the best. Not surprisingly, the town is also a good place to buy wet fish and especially crabs. **Davies' Fish Shop** (7 Garden St ☎ 01263 512727) is claimed by many to be the best place to buy freshly boiled or dressed crabs. The Davies family have been catching and cooking them for generations. Lobsters and wet fish are also available. For a meal or snack with a sea view, the **Rocket Café** at The Gangway (☎ 01263 519126 ⊘ rockethousecafe.co.uk) is a bright, modern café and restaurant conveniently situated directly above the Lifeboat Museum. Here you can have your coffee outside on the balcony and watch the crab boats go about their business.

Crabs are central to the Cromer psyche. In late May, Cromer is gastronomically linked to its fishy neighbour Sheringham by the annual **Crab & Lobster Festival** (⊘ crabandlobsterfestival.co.uk), which since its launch in 2009 has celebrated the fine crustacean produce of these two resorts. It's all great fun – there's a restaurant trail, cookery destinations, taster sessions, street theatre and lots of free events to raise money for charity.

2 WEST RUNTON

The A149 coast road runs west through East Runton and West Runton to Sheringham, along manicured green cliff tops that are home to regimented caravan sites and golf courses. Arriving by train on the Bittern Line gives a slightly different perspective, and you may notice that West Runton station with its pretty garden has won several awards for 'Best Unstaffed Station of the Year' and 'Best Small Station'. There is even a small 'wildlife area' to attract butterflies and the like. The West Runton station adopters, who are responsible for the floral flamboyance on display, are so enthusiastic about their station that they hold an annual tea party on August Bank Holiday weekend – all proceeds to the upkeep of the station garden of course.

A choicer but slower route to Sheringham is – tide permitting – on foot along the **beach**. Here you'll find chalky rock pools and soft crumbling cliffs that are home to fulmars and the odd fossilised mammoth. The so-called **West Runton Elephant** was discovered in the cliffs here by two locals back in 1990. The 'elephant' was, in fact, a steppe mammoth and turned out to be the largest, near-complete *Mammuthus trogotheni* skeleton ever found. The 600,000-year-old beast, which would have stood 13 feet tall and weighed around ten tons, twice the weight of an African elephant, was not fully excavated until 1995. Because of its weight and size, it is not possible to see the animal in its full, reconstructed glory but a few selected bones may be viewed in the Cromer and Norwich Castle museums.

"Here you'll find chalky rock pools and soft crumbling cliffs that are home to fulmars and the odd fossilised mammoth."

Elephants aside, West Runton's other taste of fame comes from once being home to the **West Runton Pavilion**, a venue that was used back in the 1970s and early 1980s by big-name rock bands wishing to begin national tours in a no-pressure, rural location. The Clash, Joy Division, Slade and, most famously, the Sex Pistols all played here in their heyday – not bad for a village of 1,600 with a rather elderly demographic. The venue was demolished in 1986 but is commemorated by a blue plaque on the wall of the Village Inn today.

West Runton is also the base of the **Norfolk Shire Horse Centre** (✆ 01603 736200 ⬧ hillside.org.uk ⊙ Apr–Oct), which operates under the auspices of the Hillside Animal Sanctuary at Frettenham near Norwich. The centre, close to the railway station, has five breeds of heavy horse – Shire, Punch, Clydesdale, Percheron and Ardenne – as well as a collection of old farming machinery. Ploughing demonstrations are held each day and special blacksmith days and sheepdog events are organised from time to time. Shire horses are magnificent creatures and farmers used to form strong bonds with their beasts of burden. Horse ploughing was a common practice right up until the 1950s in some parts of Norfolk. I can remember talking to some older farmers back in the 1980s who spoke fondly of their working horses: the unquestioning companionship that these gentle giants offered ('gentle giant' may well be a dreadful cliché but here it is wholly appropriate), and the magic of the farmyard at dusk when the horses settled down for the night, snorting with satisfaction at the prospect of fresh hay and a warm stable.

West Runton parish is home to Norfolk's highest point – **Beacon Hill** – which rises behind the southern reaches of West Runton as part of Cromer Ridge. The views from here, as you might expect, are good, as 345 feet of elevation counts for quite a lot in vertically challenged East Anglia. **Roman Camp**, just to the west, belongs to the National Trust and, despite the name, is not Roman at all but a set of Saxon and medieval iron workings. The Norfolk Coastal Path doesn't follow the coast hereabouts but instead passes just south of the camp *en route* to Cromer.

3 FELBRIGG HALL

Felbrigg NR11 8PR ✆ 01263 837444 ⊙ early Mar–end Oct, parts of house closed Thu & Fri; National Trust

This 17th-century Jacobean country house is a magnificent National Trust property, just south of the A149 coast road and the rolling, rather un-Norfolk-like slopes of the hall's 380-acre Great Wood. Felbrigg's construction straddled the period of the English Civil War and the house's elegant Stuart architecture is beautifully complemented by its sumptuous Georgian interior and Gothic-style library. Outside are a nicely restored, and still productive, walled garden and a splendid 18th-century dovecote that stands centrepiece to a kitchen garden with potagers. Extensive orchards are filled with traditional 19th-century fruit varieties, a fine collection of camellias, an 18th-century orangery and a Victorian pleasure garden. The 5,200 acres of parkland, lakes and mature woodland have a number of waymarked trails allowing free access for walking and cycling in daylight hours and, with reasonably priced parking at the hall, make a worthwhile destination in their own right.

4 SHERINGHAM

🏠 **Pirate House** (page 256)

As with Cromer, Sheringham is a crab- and lobster-fishing centre that became a resort with the arrival of the railway. Like supporters of rival teams at a local football derby, the Cromer and Sheringham crabbing communities were historically antagonistic towards each other until the realities of modern life required them to co-operate.

Although Sheringham has its neon-bright amusement arcades and might seem a bit tacky and 1960s in feel it is a nice enough place for gentle pursuits like walks on the beach and afternoon tea, and does have tangible civic pride. 'Twixt sea and pine' was the slogan chosen for

EINSTEIN ON THE HEATH

A couple of miles southeast of Felbrigg Hall is the village of Roughton on the Norwich to Cromer road. Although the village is unremarkable, Roughton Heath just to the north was the unlikely residence of Albert Einstein for a few weeks in 1933.

The celebrated German physicist was brought here under tight security to live in a small hut on the heath after fleeing Nazi Germany. While living in his modest hut, Einstein continued with important work that would later be put to use developing the world's first atomic bomb. The scientist also found time to pose for a sculpture by Jacob Epstein. It was this brief episode by the Norfolk coast that provided inspiration for Philip Glass's opera *Einstein on the Beach*.

A blue plaque commemorating Einstein's short-lived residence on the heath adorns the wall of the New Inn in Roughton village, although the whereabouts of the hut itself is not known.

the post-war British Railways travel poster and in fairness Sheringham today does not look so very different from the scene on the poster during its 1950s heyday – just fewer fishing boats on the beach and more flesh showing on the holiday makers. The same evocative slogan now adorns the sea wall along with murals detailing the town's fishing history. In many ways the town is like a smaller version of Cromer, but without the pier and the large seafront hotels. Plaques outside the Poppy Line station boast that Sheringham has won numerous Anglia in Bloom awards and, in season, the town has more bedding plants than you can shake a trowel at. For entertainment beyond pubs and strolls, the **Sheringham Little Theatre** (✆ 01263 822347 ⌨ sheringhamlittletheatre.com) in Station Road is just that: a 170-seat regional theatre that manages to survive by putting on a mixture of repertory plays, blockbuster Hollywood films and live screenings. Sheringham's museum (⌨ sheringhammuseum.co.uk), known as '**The Mo**', has interesting displays on the town's fishing and lifeboat history. There are good views to be had too, of the North Sea and the town's narrow streets, from The Mo's viewing tower.

August sees the **Sheringham Carnival**, and July the **Lobster Potty Festival** with enthusiastic Morris dancing in the traditional Norfolk style. Late May has the **Crab and Lobster Festival**, which the town shares with Cromer (see Cromer). The town also boasts its very own sea shanty choir, the **Sheringham Shantymen**, who perform frequently in the north Norfolk area as well as further afield. The choir does plenty of fundraising work for the RNLI; a proud claim is that they are the only organisation, other than RNLI branches, that is allowed to wear the RNLI badge on their uniform – there's even a lifeboat named *The Sheringham Shantymen* in their honour in Wicklow, Ireland. Mick Holford, their treasurer, told me that they also had close connections with Fisherman's Friends, the well-known shanty choir from Port Isaac, Cornwall, who are probably about as famous as it gets in the contemporary sea shanty world. 'We got invited to a sea shanty festival in Cornwall once that was co-sponsored by a brewery and a Cornish pasty company. Imagine, free beer and pies for three days – just perfect.'

Sheringham Park

Sheringham Park, Upper Sheringham NR26 8TL ✆ 01263 820550 ⊙ year-round dawn–dusk, visitor centre open daily mid Mar– end Sep, plus weekends in winter; free access; National Trust

West of Sheringham, south of the coast road, lies Sheringham Park, landscaped by Humphry Repton in 1812 and with a dazzling purple display of rhododendrons in early summer. It is often considered to be Repton's finest work – he described it himself as his 'favourite and darling child in Norfolk'. There's an exhibition of the landscape architect's life and work at the Wood Farm Barn visitor centre at the southern edge of the park. The park surrounds Sheringham Hall,

MYSTERIOUS SOUNDS AT KELLING HEATH

Andrew Paxton

We were camping at Kelling Heath at the beginning of July and had been having a bit of a snooze before popping down to the pub. It was just turning dusk when I became aware of a sort of raspy, mechanical noise that rose and fell, and then stopped for a few minutes before starting again. Initially I thought that it was some kind of pump in one of the nearby campervans and was becoming mildly irritated at this intrusion on an otherwise peaceful evening. Then I realised that the noise was coming from several directions at once, so unless it was pumps communicating with each other, it must be something else.

On the way to the pub we could hear the same mysterious noise all about us as we walked through the heath although we couldn't spot anything.

Later, I read that the area was noted for nightjars and so when I got home, I checked out the song on the RSPB website. Yes, definitely nightjars – unmistakable, unforgettable, and no longer irritating!

which is privately owned and not open to the public, but high above the hall there's a hilltop gazebo worth the climb for its views along the coast and the wooded country behind it. As well as numerous waymarked walks through the extensive woodland at the south of the park, there's a Tree Trail taking you past some rare and unusual trees.

North Norfolk Railway

✆ 01263 820800 ⌁ nnrailway.co.uk
⛺ **Kelling Heath Holiday Park** (page 257)

Right next to Sheringham's main railway station, the terminus of the Bittern Line from Norwich, is the privately run Poppy Line station of the North Norfolk Railway that runs between Sheringham and Holt, with an intermediate station at Weybourne and a request stop at Kelling Heath. Both diesel and steam trains ply this route regularly in summer and there are special events like steam galas and family days held throughout the year. Weybourne station is convenient for Sheringham Park (a 1-mile walk to the entrance), while the request stop at Kelling allows for strolls among the heather and gorse bushes of Kelling Heath, which has a nature trail and offers a reasonable chance of witnessing nightjars whirring around at dusk in high summer, an extraordinary noise (see box, page 29). Other specialist heathland birds like stonechat, woodlark and Dartford warbler can sometimes be seen here too.

🍴 FOOD & DRINK

Station Road has a selection of cafés, fish and chip shops and pubs scattered along its route down to the sea.

The Lobster 13 High St ✆ 01263 822716 ⌁ thelobsterinn.co.uk. This family pub just off the seafront has decent pub grub, a good range of beers and sometimes live music in its courtyard in summer.
Whelk Coppers Tea Rooms 25 The Driftway ✆ 01263 825771. In an interesting pebble-built building (actually three former fishermen's cottages built in 1630, restored 1934) overlooking the beach, this is the place for tea and cakes with a great sea view from the outside terrace. Inside, there's an open fire in a wood-panelled room during winter.

5 WEYBOURNE

Weybourne is a pretty, leafy village with a windmill on the twisting coast road just west of Sheringham. Weybourne's North Norfolk Railway station lies a mile or so from the village. The station's greatest claim to fame is its use as a location for an episode of *Dad's Army* ('The Royal Train'). Norfolk featured quite prominently as a backdrop for this classic TV series – more on this elsewhere (page 248).

The shingle beach at **Weybourne Hope** lies just north of the village past the ruins of an Augustinian priory founded in 1200. The beach is sloped steeply here, with relatively deep water offshore, enough to allow invading Danes to bring their boats right up to the shoreline in the 9th and 10th centuries. Such vulnerability was well-noted and, in keeping with an old saying that claims, 'He who would all England win, should at Weybourne Hope begin', defences were built in the 16th century to prevent possible attack by the Spanish Armada. The Spaniards never came but smugglers did, bringing 'tax-free' gin and tobacco to shore here, taking advantage of the ideal natural facilities of the beach and, indeed, all the coast between Sheringham and Weybourne. This strategic nervousness continued into the 20th century, when World War II anti-invasion measures included pillboxes, barbed wire and landmines. The garrison here, Weybourne Camp, became a top-secret military site during World War II and a training ground for anti-aircraft gunners. The camp continued with fresh intakes of national servicemen until it closed in 1959, a year before conscription was abolished.

> *"The Spaniards never came but smugglers did, bringing 'tax-free' gin and tobacco to shore here."*

SALT MARSHES & SAMPHIRE: FROM SALTHOUSE TO STIFFKEY

West of Kelling, the north Norfolk coast starts to take on the character that brings delight to so many: glistening silver channels snaking through salt marshes, marram-tufted sand dunes and shingle banks. And, then there are the birds, of course – mewing, piping, quacking and warbling – everywhere, birds.

6 SALTHOUSE

Salthouse is a typical north Norfolk coastal flint village with an impressive church for such a small place. Its name actually does derive from 'salt' as salt-panning was a viable industry in medieval times all along England's

A BEGINNER'S GUIDE TO NORFOLK BIRDERS

So what differentiates a birder from a twitcher? If you are visiting Cley for the first time then it is better that you know. Simply put, a common or garden **birder** is someone who is knowledgeable about birds, likes them, wants to protect them and goes out of his (and increasingly *her*) way to seek them out in their natural habitat. A **twitcher** is all of the above, but with the extra dimension of being preoccupied with listing new and rare species. Of course, the really rare species are in anything but their natural habitat – they are supposed to be in a North American forest or the Siberian taiga rather than stranded in a lonely north Norfolk marsh with no ticket home. The defining characteristic of a twitcher is his (and rarely *her*) 'list', or rather,

lists: UK list, Norfolk list, year list, life list, etc. Some twitchers will also extend their lists to other life forms such as butterflies or dragonflies (or more personally, to girlfriends or real ales sampled). It is a man thing: try not to judge them too harshly. Occasionally, the live theatre of a 'twitch' can be seen being played out at Cley or its environs. It is an easy phenomenon to identify: a murmuring green-camouflage army, brandishing telescopes like bazookas, will remain motionless and silent for some considerable time before a sudden flurry of activity occurs and there is a mass movement to a fresh viewpoint. The simple explanation: the elusive and rare bird that had fled from view some time ago has just been 'relocated'.

east coast. Being this close to Cley-next-the-Sea, this is superb birding territory and the Norfolk Wildlife Trust owns the salt marshes behind the shingle bank. In winter, large flocks of Brent geese cloud the sky here, and a variety of slender waders probe the marshes for food. Even more exotic, Arctic species like snow buntings and shore larks can be found on the beach at this time of year. Other migrants often turn up in the marshes and dunes on passage. As with all of this coastline, the quietest time of year in avian terms just happens to coincide with that which is busiest for human activity – August.

¶¶ FOOD & DRINK

Cookie's Crab Shop The Green ☏ 01263 740352 ⌖ salthouse.org.uk. Cookie's is well known locally as a place to buy shellfish and order seafood platters, sandwiches and salads. Many people travel some distance to sample the good-value seafood here, so it can be hard to find a table at weekends (a lot of customers simply take their platters out on the green and sit on the grass outside). Cookie's is nothing fancy but it does offer very good value and wholesome locally sourced food. Although the premises are not licensed, customers are welcome to bring their own drinks.

7 CLEY-NEXT-THE-SEA

Cley Windmill, **Little Orchard** & **Rhu Sila** (all page 256)

As anyone with even a passing interest in birds will tell you, Cley is the birding Mecca. All of the north Norfolk coast is good, of course, but Cley-next-the-Sea has that bit extra, those few essential ingredients: a wide range of natural habitats for breeding and feeding, a prime position on bird migration routes, sensible and long-established farming practices and, above all, plenty of goodwill towards feathered creatures. At peak times of spring and autumn migration, Cley can get very busy, with cars nose-to-tail on the A149 and the NWT car park filled to bursting. Usually, it is perfectly manageable though; the reserve is a big place and, with wonderful walks across the marshes and along the pebble bank and out to Blakeney Point, there is something for everyone here, even those who don't quite know their dunnocks from their dunlins.

The state-of-the-art, eco-friendly **NWT visitor centre** and car park are on the A149 just east of the village, with the entrance to the reserve and access to some of the hides just across the road. You'll find a very decent range of bird books and birding paraphernalia at the visitor centre, while the café has a choice view over the reserve's marshes. You can peruse the bird log at reception.

With birders in abundance, most of the colour on show in the Cley area is green – ex-military camouflage clothing, green binoculars (preferably Zeiss) and probably a 'scope and tripod. It must be said that the total value of the 'optics' (for that is what birders call their 'bins' and telescopes) on display here at any given time probably exceeds the GNP of a small African country.

This is birding nirvana. There cannot be many places where you can savour a Danish pastry and cappuccino while enjoying the spectacle of dense flocks of Brent geese rising above the marshes, avocets tirelessly scything the mud or even the rare public appearance of a bittern. If this is not enough you can always peruse the bookshelves and fantasise about the exotic birdlife of southeast Asia, where kingfisher species run to dozens.

Cley-next-the-Sea has far more than just birds, of course. It is a charming flint and pebble village with wonderful walking potential right at its doorstep. You could easily enjoy a stay here without having the remotest interest in birdlife.

Cley Mill, the windmill here, is a north Norfolk landmark, featuring in innumerable guidebooks and articles about the county. It is, indeed,

A walk to the sea & back from Cley

✳ OS Explorer 24 or Landranger 133; start: NWT visitor centre car park, ♀ TG054440; 3.5 miles; easy

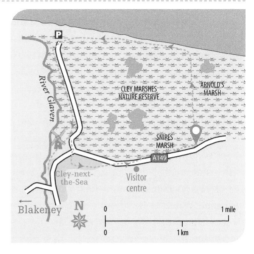

A recommended walk from Cley is to follow the footpath across the nature reserve from the pond (Snipes Marsh) on the main road, about half a mile east of the NWT visitor centre. To reach Snipes Marsh, cross the road and turn right from the visitor centre and follow the footpath that runs parallel to the coast road east. Just before the shingle bank is a large shallow pond called Arnold's Marsh, which is often full of wading birds. Climb up the shingle bank and admire the view back over the marshes to the low hills behind the village then follow the bank west to the beach car park.

The nature reserve is spread out beneath you as you walk, scrunching gravel to the low background roar of the seas. In summer, there will be yellow horned poppies emerging improbably out of the shingle, seemingly existing on nothing other than stones and salt; in winter, you are likely to see small flocks of snow buntings flittering about like sparrows dipped in icing sugar. The onshore wind can be pretty keen in winter, vicious even, but it is my favourite time to be here when the elements seem to be at their most primordial. Even then, it is never completely deserted – this is Cley and birders are a tough breed.

At the beach car park, a road follows the course of a dyke back into Cley, where, just before the village, a footpath (part of the Norfolk Coast Path) veers off to the right to skirt the windmill before returning to the High Street. You'll then need to follow the coast road east back to the Visitor Centre. You might well prefer to avoid the A149 as much as possible – it is, after all, rather a busy road. One alternative might be to skip the little detour to the windmill and instead return directly to the A149 by way of the beach car park road, cross over the coast road and take the little road left that runs parallel to it. This will bring you back to the A149 just before the Visitor Centre at the junction with the curiously named Old Woman's Lane.

rather beautiful, and, serving as a B&B, a wonderful place to stay (page 256). Otherwise, just stand back, admire, and take your own souvenir photograph. The mill dates from the 18th century and first went up for sale in 1819. It changed hands frequently over the next hundred years, eventually falling into disrepair after World War I. In 1921, the mill was converted into a holiday home by Sarah Maria Wilson, who later passed it on to her grandson Hubert Blount in 1934. Although the 1953 floods damaged the building, it managed to survive and, in 1979, Charles and Jane Blount, parents of the army officer turned singer-songwriter James Blunt, took over the running of the place. It passed into its present ownership in 2005.

Cley's High Street has some lovely buildings and a handful of quaint shops that include an excellent **smokehouse** and **delicatessen** (page 37). There is quite a diversity of building styles: a mixture of flint and brick, with some pebble-dash and the odd Dutch gable. The terrace next to the George pub even has an interesting art deco front to the street. The so-called **Whalebone House** on the High Street, which used to be the post office and later a tea room and restaurant, really does have bones set among its elegantly knapped flints – in the cornice and in a pattern around the windows. These are not, in fact, whale bones at all but the vertebrae of sheep and horses, a reminder of the bonemeal fertiliser industry that once thrived in these parts.

It is Cley's unsung nooks and crannies that make it such a pleasure to wander around. There is a heavily weathered stone arch on the High Street – the entrance to two cottages – that has a framed poem on the wall inside: *The Hardest Heart* by Anne Clark. Elsewhere, charming little alleyways lead down to the mill and marshes from the High Street. If you head down the one that lies opposite Crabpot Books, turn around after passing under the archway to see the panel of St George and the Dragon set in the wall above.

Strictly speaking, Cley (pronounced 'Cly' by the way, not 'Clay') is no longer 'next-the-Sea', but it once stood at the mouth of the River Glaven. Although it is hard to believe looking at it today, in the Middle Ages the river was navigable for even quite large boats as far as Glandford. Cley subsequently became a prosperous port exporting wool, grain and fish to the Low Countries until it began to silt up in the 17th century, mainly the result of unsuccessful land reclamation work carried out by Sir Henry Calthorpe.

St Margaret's Church

A little way along the Holt road stands St Margaret's Church, the largest in the Glaven Valley, overlooking the village green with the Three Swallows pub (✆ 01263 740526) – the perfect name for bird-mad Cley. Appropriate too, as swallows – usually far in excess of three – tend to gather on the telegraph wires above the green, taking turns to swoop down for flies.

Back in the days when Cley served as a port the church would have looked straight down on the harbour. Silting up has left this magnificent building high and dry, and it is sobering to think that it would have been even larger and more impressive had work not ceased when the Black Death devastated the village in 1349. The church has a bright, unusually cheerful interior, with graves among the flagstones and secondhand paperbacks for sale. In July both this and the churchyard are used as an exhibition space for contemporary artists. Its porch, stained glass and carved bench ends are all of interest but some might find themselves more drawn to the display that documents the arrival of an American white-crowned sparrow to the nearby garden of retired vicar, the Reverend Richard Bending, in January 2008. Naturally, the arrival of this extremely rare bird, which looks rather like an ordinary sparrow wearing a cycle helmet, heralded a vast influx of birders eager to tick it off their lists. The sparrow was amenable enough to hang around until March of that year, although there was much nervousness as to whether a local cat, 'Hooligan', might end up making a meal of it. The rare visitor is now immortalised in a stained-glass pane of the church's west window – a token of gratitude for the £6,400 the bird inadvertently brought to the church coffers in donations from twitchers.

I came across a local man in the church who had taken on the responsibility of managing the church's resident **bat population**. 'The bats are a real nuisance', he told me. 'There are two sorts – one that flies straight out after waking up, and another that needs to have a good old fly around before it leaves the church. We've got both sorts here and it's my job to clear up their mess.' The guano-removal man was eager to show me around, pointing out a wooden boss in the porch that depicts a country woman seeing off a fox attacking her goose – a charming vignette of no religious significance whatsoever. He took me back inside to show me the roof. 'It looks as if the walls are twisting outwards doesn't it? They're not of course – it's just an optical illusion. When they rebuilt the roof, some of the resin soaked into the masonry so they skimmed it and that created the effect of the walls falling outwards.' He went on to demonstrate the church's remarkable acoustics, which had not been lost on me anyway, as an acoustic guitarist had been using the church as a practice space since I had first arrived. As I made my move to leave, the bat-man chimed, 'It's a wonderful church, don't you think? So full of light.' He was quite right: the high clerestory windows seem to gather light of such quality that you can sense you are close to the coast without even stepping outside. Besides, a church that has resident bats and acoustic guitarists can do no wrong in my book.

FOOD & DRINK

Artemis Coffee Shop New Rd ℰ 01263 741674 ⬦ artemiscoffeeshop.co.uk. With undoubtedly the best view of all the Cley cafés – a terrace overlooking the marshes – Artemis serves locally roasted coffee, scones and cakes, as well as breakfasts and light lunches. There's even a bird sightings book for recording what you have seen. Situated behind the café is their own homeware and antiques shop.

Cley Smokehouse High St ℰ 01263 740282 ⬦ cleysmokehouse.com. This excellent Cley institution has a wide range of quality smoked goods, all hand crafted on the premises.

Picnic Fayre The Old Forge ℰ 01263 740587 ⬦ picnic-fayre.co.uk. This delicatessen, established in 1984, is the place where north Norfolk's foodies come for their cheese, wine and speciality breads. It also has a good selection of organic vegetables and sumptuous take-away pastries.

The Three Swallows Newgate Green ℰ 01263 740526 ⬦ thethreeswallows.co.uk. Facing the green by the church, this is an unexpectedly no-frills sort of place to find in a place like Cley. Serving unfussy pub grub and real ales, the ornate wooden bar here comes from a recycled ship's cabin.

8 BLAKENEY POINT

Blakeney Point is one of several spits along this coastline, the result of drifting sand and pebbles being deposited by offshore currents. The 'point' is a curious place that starts out as a narrow strip close to Cley beach car park before widening out to where marram-grass-covered dunes rise on its landward side opposite Blakeney harbour.

As Norfolk's most northerly point (admittedly, inaccessible Scolt Head Island does just have the edge, but we're talking yards here) this is the Ultima Thule of East Anglia – a genuinely wild place, with nothing but open sea between here and the Arctic.

DOGGERLAND

Although now an archipelago of islands, most of Britain was connected to mainland Europe not so very long ago. From the last ice age until about 8,000 years ago, a large land mass stood where the southern North Sea now lies. Slowly it became flooded by rising sea levels until Britain (that is England, Wales and mainland Scotland) became an island separate from the rest of Europe.

In recent years an increasing amount of evidence has shown that this former land mass, coined 'Doggerland' by archaeologists, was occupied by humans during the Mesolithic period that immediately followed the last withdrawal of the ice sheet. Fishing vessels working the North Sea have dragged up tools like barbed antler points and knapped flints as well as bones from animals like mammoth and lion.

The evidence suggests that Doggerland would have been a lush, food-rich environment for the hunters who lived there, with plentiful deer, aurochs and wild boar, not to mention an abundance of fish and birds to eat.

Dogger Bank, which usually gets a mention in the Met Office's Shipping Forecast, lies immediately north of the north Norfolk coast. These days it is a large submerged sandbank but once it would have been an upland area of Doggerland that remained an island for some time even after Britain had separated from Europe. Seven thousand years or so ago it would have been possible to walk all the way to Dogger Bank from Cromer; a millennium or two earlier, it would have been possible to walk to mainland Europe – a point worth remembering for those a little over-obsessed with our 'Island Race' credentials.

The end of the Mesolithic period saw Doggerland and other lowland areas of the ancient world flooded, never to surface again. Perhaps it is the folk memory of this apocalypse that lies at the root of the many flood myths in cultures around the world? Perhaps Doggerland is the original Atlantis?

The point's western extremity is curved like a bird's claw – quite fitting really – and home to a visitor centre and colonies of nesting terns, also both common and grey seals. From Cley, it is a marvellous walk out to the end of the point: about four miles each way, but quite a tough four miles, as for most of the way it is a matter of trudging along pebbles – noisy work and tiring for the feet.

Halfway along the spit is a hut called, rather unimaginatively, 'Halfway House'. Many years ago, I camped near here for a night (which I am not recommending, by the way: this is a nature reserve and, quite rightly, it is not now allowed). What struck me most was the eerie sensation of hearing the sea slap against the pebbles on both sides of me, inducing an odd sense of claustrophobia.

9 GLANDFORD

Cley lies at the mouth of the **Glaven River** and the village of Glandford immediately to the south stands on the same river. There is a ford here by the watermill, too deep and tricky for most cars, and a footbridge. It's a charming spot full of birdsong and buzzing bees and the perfect objective for a gentle circular walk that might also take in Wiveton village and Wiveton Downs.

It may be just a tiny estate village, with Dutch-gabled cottages dating from the early 20th century, but Glandford does have its very own **Shell Museum** (✆ 01263 740081 ⏏ shellmuseum.org.uk ⊙ closed in winter) next to the church – an eccentric place that has thousands of seashells in addition to quite a collection of fossils, birds' eggs and oddities such as a sugar bowl used by Queen Elizabeth I and a dried puffer fish. The museum also has a tapestry and painting by the much-lauded Norfolk fisherman turned artist John Craske. The **Natural Surroundings Wildlife Gardening & Wildflower Discovery Centre** (✆ 01263 711091 ⏏ naturalsurroundings.info ⊙ Tue–Sun, every day May to September) is located nearby, just south along the road to Letheringsett, within the walled confines of the Bayfield Estate, which also has a café. Follow the signs for 'Wildflower Centre' to find it.

FOOD & DRINK

Art Café Manor Farm, Glandford ✆ 01263 741711 ⏏ art-cafe.org. Located in converted farm buildings alongside other businesses like Cley Spy (⏏ cleyspy.co.uk), a specialist optics shop for birders, this is North Norfolk's only vegetarian restaurant. As its name suggests, this also doubles as an art gallery. Most food and drink supplies are Norfolk-sourced, with local cheeses, cakes from Fakenham and bread from Heydon. Vegetables come from a farm near Blakeney just two miles away.

10 WIVETON

A little inland from the coast on the Blakeney to Letheringsett road is the small village of Wiveton, with a church, an excellent pub and a neat row of cottages overlooking a village green – a sleepy place in the best sense of the word. You may notice a road sign here that says 'Slow You Down', which is Norfolk-speak for 'Slow'. Depending on your outlook, you might find this witty, slightly annoying or downright patronising. I tend to opt for both of the first two, while my wife, a Norfolk native, favours the third.

Wiveton Downs

Southwest of Wiveton stands the gorse-covered viewpoint of Wiveton Downs where there is an **esker**. An 'esker', as the information board will tell you, marks the past course of an underground river beneath a glacier. Some geologists scoff at this idea, however, arguing that if this were a true esker then it would be at right angles to the coast not parallel to it. Whatever, most locals come to walk their dogs rather than ponder Quaternary geomorphology. The gorse is particularly impressive here in spring, with a custard-almond pungency that almost knocks you off your feet. Come on a bright winter's day and you may well see a ghostly barn owl quartering the gorse looking for prey. The views are lovely too: Cley Mill and Blakeney's St Nicholas's Church are clearly visible, as is Blakeney's Old Rectory snuggled away in the lee of the hill behind the church. Looking inland, you should see a well-appointed metropolis of pigs just to the south; that is, unless the bottom has dropped out of the bacon market by the time that you read this.

11 BLAKENEY

The village of Blakeney slopes down narrow streets towards the harbour from the coast road where its magnificent 13th-century church of St Nicholas is located. This is quintessential north Norfolk, with all the classic coastal village ingredients: a tiny harbour, flint-pebble cottages, fishing boats and quaint little shops.

This was an active port far more recently than Cley, functioning as such until the early 1900s. Blakeney's eventual fate would be the same, however: the silting up of its estuary. It is this silting that characterises the coastal landscape here, with twisting muddy channels and creeks meandering out across the tidal flats of Blakeney Channel.

"This is quintessential north Norfolk: a tiny harbour, flint-pebble cottages, fishing boats and quaint little shops."

Thankfully, the channels out to the sea are still navigable for smaller private craft at high tide and this is where Blakeney really comes into its own, as the village has become a favourite of north Norfolk's yachting set both for its moorings and for the unspoiled feel of the village itself. It is undoubtedly lovely but just a little unreal: a well-behaved ghost of the thriving port that it used to be. Even John Seymour writing about Blakeney back in the late 1960s in his *Companion Guide to East Anglia* reflected that: 'Certainly no fisherman could afford to buy a

KAYAKING FROM BLAKENEY TO CLEY

Penny Edwards

I recently joined some friends on a Sunday morning in July when the tide was unusually high. We unchained the kayaks from the grassy area next to Blakeney Harbour and set off about 90 minutes before high tide, at about 09.00.

I had cycled out to Blakeney from Norwich and it felt good to be continuing to power myself, yet in a different medium. We made our way slowly past sailing boats and into New Cut – a channel joining Blakeney to Cley, created about three years ago to prevent flooding by the River Glaven.

It took us less than an hour to reach Cley windmill. We didn't disembark because we were aware that the tide would not remain high for long. On our return journey we stopped in New Cut to have a quick swim. We did this when the tide was near enough at its highest, and consequently the water was flowing so fast away from Blakeney that we found ourselves swimming on the spot making no forward progress whatsoever. After breakfast, I set off back to Norwich feeling as revived as if I had been away on a week's holiday instead of just out for the day.

"fisherman's cottage" today,' adding, 'Blakeney is now what is called "select",' meaning that many of its inhabitants have a lot of money. There is no "pin-table and Bingo culture" there'. Well, it is undoubtedly still select, and there is still no 'pin-table and Bingo culture' or 21st-century equivalent.

St Nicholas's Church, on the hill above the village, is well worth a look. You may notice something distinctly odd about this 13th-century church, sometimes referred to as 'the cathedral of the coast', when you first glimpse it. Above the chancel is a second tower that is much smaller than the main one to the west. This smaller tower was a 15th-century addition but its function is still a matter of debate. It used to burn a light as a beacon for Blakeney boats, but there is no reason why a second tower needed to be constructed especially for this purpose. Some think this incongruous addition may have been intended as a bell tower but, again, this makes little sense when the older, larger tower is far more suitable. The current church committee does not seem to have a firm opinion on this matter and invites visitors to write down their own suggestions on the pieces of paper provided. Wearing his church architecture expert hat, Simon Jenkins offers the thought that it may have been a private venture by a local patron wishing to rival the sponsor of the main tower. Undoubtedly, it does have something of the sense of a proud, if misguided, folly about it. Whatever the answer to this mystery, it is worth having a scout round and helping yourself to the generous free literature made available inside the church and, for a reminder of the long fishing tradition of this now somewhat sanitised village, take a look around the churchyard where you'll see plenty of fishermen's gravestones decorated with ropes and anchors.

12 MORSTON: A SEAL-SPOTTING BOAT TRIP

⋏ **Scaldbeck Cottage** near Morston (page 257)

Beans Boat Trips (✆ 01263 740505 or 740038 ⬧ beansboattrips.co.uk) run from Morston Quay, with one-hour trips to view the seals and longer ones that land on Blakeney Point and spend up to an hour there. Times are dependent on tides. **Temples Seal Trips** (The Street, NR25 7AA; ✆ 01263 740791 ⬧ sealtrips.co.uk) which has a ticket office in The Anchor pub, and **Bishop's Boats** (✆ 01263 740753 or 0800 0740753 ⬧ bishopsboats.com), operating from Blakeney Quay, both offer similar services.

There is not that much to Morston, another medieval port that has since silted up and now lies two miles from the open sea. Nevertheless, this is the place for boat trips out to Blakeney Point to see the seals.

Viewing these creatures is a slightly hit-and-miss business, despite their being 'guaranteed' by the boat companies. On an early May boat trip, Jason, one of the Beans Boats skippers, told me, 'We do get a few common seals but they come mostly later in the year. This time of year it's mostly grey seals – you can tell them from the common by their long, grey heads.' Out in Morston harbour, the seals were certainly a bit thin on the ground. 'You might want to call me a liar but, believe it or not, there are maybe around a thousand seals out around here altogether. They do well here – there's plenty of fish to eat and no predators for them.' Although the seals were not out in number, the birds certainly were. 'There's four sorts of tern out here. There's common tern, with their red beaks, and Arctic, who look pretty similar. Little terns are quite a bit smaller, of course, and then there's Sandwich terns, which are the biggest of all of them and have a sort of crest on their heads.' Terns were, indeed, everywhere, gracefully dive-bombing the water for sand eels, but I had also spotted some poetic skeins of sleek, dark geese flying about in the distance. 'They're Brent geese,' said Jason. 'They come all the way from Russia and they should have gone back home by now. I don't know what they are doing here this late. Maybe they know something we don't.'

Chugging back to Morston, past the bright blue warden's building on Blakeney Point, Jason tells me about Morston's maritime history.

MARSH SAMPHIRE

Half-way down,
Hangs one that gathers samphire; dreadful trade!
William Shakespeare, *King Lear*

The Shakespeare quotation above comes from a scene set near Dover and probably refers to the practice of gathering rock samphire, but it is marsh samphire (*Salicornia europaea*), sometimes known as glasswort or sea asparagus, that is the speciality of the Norfolk coast. The old name 'glasswort' comes from the medieval use of the plant's ashes to manufacture soap and glass.

Although it can be found at other locations around the British coastline, the finest samphire comes from the saltings of north Norfolk. Enjoyed as part of the local diet for centuries, samphire has started to appear on fancy upmarket menus in recent years, usually as an accompaniment to fish and seafood. It is harvested anytime between June and August before the plant flowers, but the sweetest is usually gathered early in the season. It is on sale at a limited number of outlets in north Norfolk in season but it is altogether more rewarding to forage for your own at low tide, providing you know what you are looking for and do not mind getting muddy.

Like most seasonal foods, samphire's short-lived availability is actually part of its appeal. It can be eaten raw in salads although the saltiness is quite pronounced; a light boiling or steaming helps to remove much of this. With its taste like asparagus dipped in seawater, eating samphire is a pleasure akin to stripping edible beads from a necklace with your teeth.

'That building was at the very end of Blakeney Point when it was first built but the spit has grown a lot longer over the last hundred years. Originally, it was a lifeboat station and the crew had to row 3½ miles out there from Morston just to reach it. They kept horses in stables out on the point and when the crew got there, they had to hitch the horses up to the lifeboat and drag it down to the shore. Then the crew had to row the lifeboat out to wherever the incident was. There was supposed to be a crew of 16 to man the boat but sometimes they had to make do with 12 or less. It took three or four hours just to get the lifeboat launched and when they had the job done they had to spend the same amount of time getting home again.' Clearly, the old days were not a time to be in any hurry to be saved. Still, the Morston lifeboat did manage to rescue over a hundred lives during its lifetime so it must have been doing something right. It finally went out of service in 1936 when Morston's rescue crew combined forces with the lifeboat at Wells.

13 STIFFKEY

Heading west from Morston towards Wells-next-the-Sea along a road bright green with shiny fresh Alexanders in spring, you'll pass through Stiffkey, a village with both an odd name and an eccentric reputation. It has earned local renown for being the home of 'Stewkey blues', blue cockles that are gathered on the salt marshes north of the village. It is said to be the mud that gives them their distinctive blue coloration.

The village is an attractive place of flint and pebble houses, and even the motor traffic on the busy A149 that passes right through can do little to assuage its obvious charm. The jury is still out on whether the village – and the river that passes through it – should be pronounced 'Stiff-key', as it is spelled, or 'Stew-key' in keeping with its famous shellfish. Opinions seem to differ, even between locals, so it's probably best to stick with the phonetic version lest you appear to be trying a bit too hard.

The east end of the village has the **church of St John the Baptist** alongside the ruins of an earlier church, St Mary's, in the same churchyard. South of this, **Stiffkey Old Hall**, the once spectacular property of the Bacon family, now lies in ruins and all that remains today is a gatehouse and part of one wing of the house. One of Stiffkey's former rectors, the **Reverend Harold Davidson**, who preached at the church and occupied the village's grand Georgian rectory during the interwar period, was a controversial figure who gained notoriety for attending the spiritual needs of fallen women from London. The Rector went on to become known as the 'Prostitutes' Padre' as a result – hardly the best moniker for a man of the cloth, especially in an isolated north Norfolk village. Such a crusade was an invitation to scandal whatever his true motives and, following accusations of licentious behaviour and falling out with the ecclesiastical powers that be, he was eventually defrocked at Norwich Cathedral and a more suitable replacement found. Bizarrely, Harold Davidson (no longer 'the Reverend' but still wearing full clerical regalia) met with a sticky end when he was mauled by a lion in a show at Skegness Amusement Park. His act had consisted of entering a lion's cage and talking about the injustices that had been meted out to him by the establishment. Unfortunately, one of the lions, Freddie, was unsympathetic to his plight and attacked him when he tripped over the tail of the other lion. These days, it is generally accepted that the charges against him were ill-founded and that he had inadvertently become one of the very first anti-celebrities created by the press.

Another controversial one-time resident of the village was Henry Williamson, the writer and naturalist alternately famous and notorious respectively for his admiration of both otters and Nazism. Williamson bought a farm in the village in 1936 and lived here during World War II before eventually moving to Devon.

14 WARHAM

Halfway between Stiffkey and Wells-next-the-Sea, and a little further inland, is the flint and cobble village of Warham, which has the site of an Iron Age settlement nearby. There were two parishes here before the reformation, hence the village's two churches. Half a mile or so south of the **church of All Saints**, along a quiet lane, lie the round grass-covered earthworks of the Iron Age camp. Covering three acres, this was built by the Iceni in the second century BC and is usually referred to as **Warham Fort**, although for many years it was known as 'Danish Camp' because it was thought to be the work of Viking invaders.

WELLS-NEXT-THE-SEA & HOLKHAM

15 WELLS-NEXT-THE-SEA

⌂ **The Merchant's House** (page 256) & **Albert's Cottage** (page 256)

> There are few places in England where you can get so much wildness and desolation of sea and sandhills, wood, green marsh and grey saltings as at Wells in Norfolk.
>
> W H Hudson, *Adventures Among Birds*

The largest settlement between Cromer and Hunstanton, Wells-next-the-Sea is also the only real working harbour along this stretch of coast, even though it stands well over a mile inland. Really the suffix 'next-the-Sea' might be better described as 'quite-near-the-Sea'. Wells has seen service as a port for at least seven centuries although, as with the rest of this coastline, silting-up has been a major problem over the years. Lord Leicester of nearby Holkham Hall constructed a high embankment ('The Bank') in 1859 to reclaim 1,970 acres of salt marsh and as an attempt to protect the harbour. Unfortunately, this proved ineffective against the floods that devastated the coast in 1953 and 1978. These days, **The Bank** is a favourite walk out to the beach, woods, and caravan and camping site that lie north of the town, and you can continue along the pine forest and on to the vast **beach** that extends past Holkham Gap. The Bank also marks the stretch of the Norfolk Coast Path that leads into Wells. A miniature railway runs alongside The Bank. This might be a little too quaint for some tastes, but don't let this put you off – Wells has plenty more to offer.

Considerably less precious than Blakeney, Wells is an appealing little town with narrow streets of flint houses and an atmospheric waterfront that still has vestiges of its former life as a busy port. Most prominent is the granary with its overhanging gantry, which has been converted into holiday flats. The granary building itself on Staithe Street, the town's main shopping street, now serves as a small theatre. This is the main venue for the annual **Poetry-next-the-Sea Festival**, featuring poets and writers from East Anglia and beyond.

You may observe that there are notably more bungalows here than in Blakeney, as well as a few amusement arcades and tacky gift shops along the harbour, but I think these humanise rather than devalue the place. One of the harbour fish and chip shops used to have a resident cormorant outside that would pester customers for a bit of cod as they sat on the quayside benches to eat. The bird has long gone but the chips remain as good as ever, as does the pleasure of tasting salt air along with your al fresco meal. In high summer there will inevitably be a queue snaking out of the fish and chip shops at the harbour, especially French's.

The harbour wall is also a great place for children who seem to love hoisting up small crabs on a line from the water below just as much as I did when I was a boy. On sunny days during the school holidays it can get so busy here that it is sometimes hard to find a space to dangle your line. These days, bacon seems to be the favoured bait.

Crabs and shellfish continue to be caught by local fishermen in Wells but **whelks** were the main industry here half a century ago when the port had its own fleet of special clinker-built boats. Once landed, the whelks were boiled in the town's boiling sheds close to the East Quay before being delivered around the country by train. Whelks are still brought in for processing today but the industry is a shadow of what it once was.

The strangely spelt *Albatros*, a 100-year-old Dutch clipper that resides in Wells harbour on a more or less permanent basis, has an interesting history. The boat may have been used to assist Jewish refuges escaping from Nazi Germany and to supply the Dutch resistance with weapons. It was used to ship soya beans from Belgium to Norfolk from 1990 to 1996 and since then she has seen use by Greenpeace as an environmental study centre for schoolchildren. The *Albatros* (⊘ albatroswells.co.uk) made her last commercial trip in 2008. These days she spends her days in Wells harbour moored at the quay near the fish and chip shops, selling beer and Dutch pancakes from its deck – something of a fall from grace for a sea-going vessel perhaps? At least the boat's bar has been consistently listed in the CAMRA *Good Beer Guide* for its range of local real ales since then, so it is not all bad news. Jazz, blues and folk musicians liven things up below deck on weekends. What I cannot understand is the choice of the boat's name. Have I, a confirmed landlubber, fallen into the trap of believing the old chestnut that the albatross is an unlucky bird for seafarers, or is it that Dutch sailors are exempt?

Apart from the quay itself much of the town's activity takes place along Staithe Street, which is lined with cafés, food shops, bookshops and gift shops. At the top, just beyond the Edinburgh pub, is a quiet Georgian square that has a leafy park at the centre of it – this is the Buttlands, where two of the town's best hotels and restaurants are located (see below). There is a stop for the Coasthopper bus service here, in addition to another down on the quay.

Wells & Walsingham Light Railway
⊘ 01328 711630 ⊘ wellswalsinghamrailway.co.uk

As well as the mile-long miniature railway that runs along The Bank, Wells is also the home station of the Wells & Walsingham Light Railway. This claims to be the longest 10¼-inch gauge steam railway in the world, running all the way to Walsingham, a scenic journey of some nine miles, along the track bed of the old Great Eastern Railway. The service operates between March and October and takes 45 minutes with halts made at Warham St Mary and Wighton *en route*. Christine's Buffet Bar next to the signal box at Wells is handy for a cake and a cuppa while you are waiting.

FOOD & DRINK

The Crown The Buttlands ⊘ 01328 710209 ⊘ crownhotelnorfolk.co.uk. Set in a 16th-century coaching inn overlooking the Buttlands, The Crown serves modern British cuisine and has a menu that includes a good selection of locally sourced fish and meat.
Globe Inn The Buttlands ⊘ 01328 710206 ⊘ theglobeatwells.co.uk. This 19th-century coaching inn, also on Buttlands Green and owned by the Coke family, has a restaurant that

serves excellent seasonal food, much of which originates from the Holkham Estate. There is a courtyard for sunny weather and Adnams and Woodforde's ales on draught.

Grey Seal Coffee 1 Quayside 🖉 01328 710051 🖉 greysealcoffee.co.uk. Grey Seal are award-winning coffee roasters based at nearby Glandford. This coffee shop, located beneath the overhanging gantry of the town's famous granary, is their main café outlet. As well as all manner of variations on the coffee theme there are also cakes and pastries, and a good choice of leaf teas too.

Mermaid's Purse 42 Staithe St 🖉 01328 711744 🖉 mermaidspurse.com. This coffee shop on the main street down to the quay doubles as a gift shop and and serves up a tasty selection of homemade cakes and scones for afternoon tea as well as delicious seafood platters in season.

16 HOLKHAM

The estate village of Holkham serves as a mere appendage to the extensive grounds of **Holkham Park** and **Holkham Hall**. It also allows access to the grandest of Norfolk's beaches. The hall and park have walled gardens, a lake and a deer park, garden centre, gift shop and café, in addition to a **Bygones Museum** filled with artefacts of every description. The hall's grounds are used to stage regular summer musical events that range from Jools Holland to José Carreras, while the marble hall is occasionally used for chamber music concerts.

COKE OF NORFOLK: THE GREAT AGRICULTURAL IMPROVER

With Holkham Hall finally built – it took 28 years in all – and the Coke family's vast art collection installed, later generations, most notably **Thomas William Coke** (1754–1842), Thomas Coke's nephew, concentrated on improving the estate itself.

Thomas was far more interested in earth than architecture and would subsequently become known as 'Coke of Norfolk'. He went on to become the standard-bearer for the Agricultural Revolution with his application of four-crop rotation, an innovation for which modern farmers and even humble allotmenteers owe a debt for today. Although often credited with inventing this practice, it was more likely that 'Turnip' Townshend of Rainham Hall was the actual innovator here.

To the north of the hall, a tall column with sheep and cows carved around its plinth serves as a fitting memorial for this agricultural aristocrat and, if stately homes do not float your boat, then you might enjoy this more. This being Norfolk, even aristocratic pronunciations are not all that they might appear to be: Coke should actually be pronounced *cook*.

Holkham Hall

NR23 1AB ✆ 01328 713111 ⬦ holkham.co.uk ⊘ end Mar–end Oct, Sun, Mon & Thu, noon–16.00, pedestrian access at all entrances 07.00–19.00, vehicular access at north gate only between 09.00 & 17.00

Holkham Hall, the property of the Coke family, is a Palladian mansion that dates from the mid 18th century, its construction inspired by the Italian travels of Thomas Coke, the 1st Earl of Leicester, whilst undertaking a grand tour. It is undoubtedly striking but perhaps not to everyone's taste: purists might consider an Italian-Renaissance-style house to be somewhat incongruous up here in north Norfolk.

Building began in 1734 under the guidance of Lord Burlington and the architect William Kent, who were both keen admirers of Andrea Palladio's Renaissance style. What is most impressive is that the hall remains completely unchanged from its original form. Its Grand Hall contains classical statuary and art, with paintings by Van Dyck and Rubens.

You can walk or cycle through the estate's extensive grounds (no charge) but since this is a working farm dogs have to be kept on a lead.

Holkham Beach

No question, Holkham Beach is one of the finest in all England: a wide swathe of glistening sand backed by dunes and a thick stand of Corsican pines; the sea, a softly lapping presence or a thin line on the horizon, depending on the tide. This is the very beach that Gwyneth Paltrow walked along in *Shakespeare in Love*.

"This is the very beach that Gwyneth Paltrow walked along in Shakespeare in Love."

Whatever the state of the tide, it's a wonderful beach for bathing and about as safe as it gets for children. Access is via Lady Ann's Drive opposite the Victoria Hotel and Holkham village. The provision for parking here is considerable but so are the crowds that come here on warm summer days. Once parked up, however, there is plenty of sand for everyone – the beach is a vast expanse that stretches as far west as the dunes at Gun Hill next to Burnham harbour creek, and east to The Run at Wells-next-the-Sea. Given the volume of traffic, arriving here on the Coasthopper bus makes an awful lot of sense, as long as you don't mind the half-mile walk along Lady Ann's Drive from the main road. You'll save paying quite a steep car park fee too.

¶¶ FOOD & DRINK

Victoria Park Rd ✆ 01328 711008 ⬧ holkham.co.uk/stay-eat/the-victoria-inn. This fully renovated and spruced-up brick and flint pub at the entrance to the Holkham Estate enjoys considerable repute as both a restaurant and a convivial place to stay. Fresh local produce features strongly – Cromer crabs, Brancaster mussels and beef, game and eel from the estate. There is also a simpler lunchtime bar menu.

A Holkham Beach walk

❈ OS Explorer 24 or Landranger 132; start: Holkham Gap car park, ♀ TF891450; 4 miles; easy

It can be breezy here – it usually is – and lazing on the beach may not be to everyone's taste. Birdwatchers should find plenty of interest in the pinewoods behind the beach – rarities have turned up here over the years – but otherwise the best thing to do after a swim or a picnic is to go for a stroll. An enjoyable four-mile walk that takes an unhurried couple of hours is to bear right at Holkham Gap and head along the beach as far as the lifeboat station by the embankment at Wells-next-the-Sea. Then, reversing direction, follow the way-marked Norfolk Coast Path back west, keeping the pine plantation to your right all the way to the car park at Lady Ann's Drive. A shorter alternative is to turn left at Holkham Gap and follow the track that leads along the southern flank of the pinewoods until you pass a large pond and reach a bird hide with access to the beach along a boardwalk. The path continues past the hide and Meals House until reaching a crossroads in the woods. Turning right here will bring you to the beach at Burrow Gap, from where you can turn right and walk back to Holkham Gap and Lady Ann's Drive. An even shorter option, about a mile, is to turn right at the boardwalk by the hide and return to the start point by walking through the woods or by turning right along the beach.

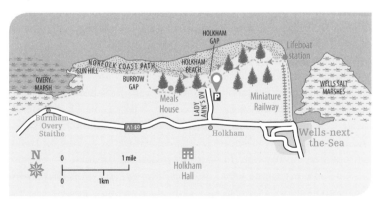

THE BURNHAMS

A whole family of Burnhams lie just west of Holkham in the valley of the unassuming River Burn: Burnham Overy Staithe and Burnham Norton on the coast road; Burnham Market, with its appendages of Burnham Westgate and Burnham Ulph, just to the south; and Burnham Overy Town and Nelson's birthplace, Burnham Thorpe, a little further inland. Burnham Deepdale lies a mile or two to the west of this group, and both Burnham Overy Staithe and Burnham Deepdale straddle the route of the Norfolk Coast Path. Such a tight cluster of villages means that six medieval churches lie within

"Such a tight cluster of villages means that six medieval churches lie within just three miles of each other."

just three miles of each other. Ironically, Burnham Overy Town is the smallest of the group, hardly a village, although it was once the port in the medieval period. Similarly, Burnham Norton also has little to it other than a round tower church with a restored rood screen (at the very edge of the parish, almost in Burnham Market). In contrast, Burnham Overy Staithe, with its delightful boat-strewn creek, is perhaps the very epicentre of northwest Norfolk's yachting set, although Brancaster Staithe, which adjoins Burnham Deepdale to the west, might also claim this prize.

It is the largest Burnham, Burnham Market, that seems to charm the most, judging by the traffic weaving through it and the impressive array of smart cars parked in its narrow streets on any given summer's day. It is here where people gravitate to 'escape London' and discuss skiing holidays in the village's posh eateries. You might even spot a famous face 'getting away from it all'.

7 BURNHAM MARKET

🏠 **Bagthorpe Treehouse** at Bagthorpe Hall (page 256)

A picture-perfect village of attractive Georgian houses surrounding a green – is it any wonder that Burnham Market is so popular? How many villages of this size have such a selection of galleries and boutiques and even a posh hat shop? How many have such potential for fine dining? And how many get labelled 'Little Chelsea' because of their unashamed metropolitan atmosphere (or 'Burnham Mark-up' because of its near-metropolitan prices, or even 'Islington-sur-Mer')? Burnham Market is so upmarket that you almost expect to bump into minor royals or

Hollywood A-listers whilst perusing the galleries here – in fact, there's a small chance that you might.

While it is certainly true that the village has attracted a disproportionate number of well-heeled second-home owners it is easy to see what all the fuss is about. If you are looking for a smart, yet unmodernised, rural idyll then look no further; if you seek the rural Norfolk of old then you might do better to try elsewhere. Either way, come and have a look around at least. The predominant dialect spoken around here may be that of South Kensington these days but that is not to say that genuine locals have disappeared from the scene altogether.

¶¶ FOOD & DRINK

Despite Burnham Market's haughty reputation you'll still find an excellent wet fish shop in the village, as well as an artisan bakery, a good bookshop – White House Books (✆ 01328 730270) – and even a couple of decent, unpretentious tea rooms. There is a **farmers' market** here on the first Saturday and third Friday of each month.

As well as the **The Hoste** (✆ 01328 738777 ⊘ thehoste.com), a long-standing favourite of the Sunday supplements at the heart of things in the village, Burnham Market has **The Burnhams Tea Room** (otherwise known as Lucy's Tea Shop) on the market place (✆ 01328 738908) for a light lunch or home-baked scones, **Gurney's Fish Shop** (✆ 01328 738967 ⊘ gurneysfishshop.co.uk) for locally caught wet fish, and **Groom's Bakery** (✆ 01328 736289) for cakes, pastries and 20 varieties of bread. **Humble Pie** (✆ 01328 738581) is a sumptuously stocked delicatessen and cook shop with lots of delicious Norfolk produce, a Mecca for foodies.

Located on the main road in the village of Stanhoe, 3 miles from Burnham Market, **The Duck Inn** (Burnham Rd, Stanhoe ✆ 01485 518330 ⊘ duckinn.co.uk) is an award-winning 'rustic-smart' gastro pub with creative and regularly changing lunch and dinner menus. The emphasis, along with inspired cooking, is on showcasing local produce like Norfolk crab and mussels and Holkham Estate beef. There's an extensive wine list and a choice of various East Anglian real ales.

18 BURNHAM THORPE

Horatio Nelson's birthplace no less and, although the original rectory in which he was born was torn down and replaced long ago, there is a plaque on the wall that commemorates the man whom many regard as one of the very greatest of Englishmen. The village pub, which unsurprisingly goes by the name of The Lord Nelson, does in fact date from Nelson's time and serves as something of a shrine to his memory with all manner of memorabilia and paintings of marine battle scenes on its walls. The **church** next to the Manor House has more: a crucifix and lectern fashioned from wood taken from *HMS Victory*.

FOOD & DRINK

Lord Nelson Walsingham Rd, Burnham Thorpe 🕿 01328 738241. This, the only pub in Burnham Thorpe, is both atmospheric and unspoiled, and despite its claims to be 'Nelson's local' remains remarkably unpretentious. The Lord Nelson serves pub grub with a Mediterranean flavour, and real ales from Woodeforde's and Heacham's Fox brewery. The pub's speciality is a herb and spice-infused brandy it calls Nelson's Blood – an allusion to the story of Nelson's body being preserved in a barrel of brandy whilst shipping home for a state funeral.

9 BURNHAM OVERY TOWN

In a car at least, by the time you have said the name you have driven through it. Burnham Overy Town does have the church of **St Clement's**, with its odd-looking squat central tower. Historically, this village on the River Burn served as the harbour but this function switched to Overy Staithe at the end of the medieval period. One of the small cottages at the road junction has some curious recycled classical statues flanking its front door and there are the remains of an ancient cross, now reduced to little more than a hitching post, in the middle of the junction's central reservation.

0 BURNHAM OVERY STAITHE

Along with Brancaster Staithe further west, this small coastal village is a favourite of the sailing set. The fact that it has a chandlery but no shop or café says it all. The creekside harbour may be modest in the extreme but the village's seafaring credentials are impressive: Nelson learned to row and sail on the creek here and Richard Woodget, captain of the *Cutty Sark*, retired here to farm. As elsewhere, the harbour has long since silted up and these days Burnham Overy Staithe sees a very different type of craft sailing up its creek.

A sea wall stroll to the beach

For a wonderful short walk out to the beach from Burnham Overy Staithe, take a stroll along the sea wall that starts at the end of the road by the little harbour and zigzags its way above the saltings to reach the dunes; to the left you can carry on round past a point known as Gun Hill. Over the water is Aster Marsh, the eastern end of **Scolt Head Island**, mauve with sea asters in late summer. Keep going past Gun Hill (or take a short cut through the dunes) and you're on the same beach that extends round to Holkham Gap (page 50). This walk is even better if you extend it and begin at Burnham Deepdale, following the Norfolk Coast Path at the church opposite Deepdale Camping. The handy Coasthopper bus service can be used to return along the coast road to the starting point.

¶¶ FOOD & DRINK

The Hero Wells Rd ✐ 01328 738334 ✐ theheroburnhamovery.co.uk. Burnham Overy Staithe's village pub is an unpretentious and cosy place for a drink or a tasty homemade meal after a walk.

CAMPING AT BURNHAM DEEPDALE

Donald (former Managing Director of Bradt Guides) and Darren (from the RSPB) spent a weekend polishing up their rusty camping skills in north Norfolk – and survived to tell the tale.

'Whether you're a seasoned camper or a first-timer just wanting to see what it's all about, the campsite (Deepdale Camping) at Burnham Deepdale is an ideal spot for a Slow experience. Days are filled with lots of low-impact outdoor activities, evenings are all about simple cooking on a stove or BBQ, or eating in one of the local pubs, and come bedtime you can retire weary but satisfied to the cosy interior of your canvas "bedroom".

We hadn't camped for more than 15 years when we visited for the bank holiday weekend at the end of May, but soon got into the swing of things. Over the three days we were there we walked, cycled, went birdwatching and took umpteen photographs of the timeless coastal and inland landscapes, with their ever-changing skies, historic flint-built houses and churches, and captivating light that has inspired generations of artists. One evening, we cooked easy but nutritious meals on our stove; another day we spent a wonderfully memorable evening in the conservatory restaurant of the local pub watching a brilliant sunset over the marshlands, and sat in the outdoors wrapped up in fleeces with a bottle of wine as dusk turned to night. By the time we left we felt as if we had had a complete escape filled with three days of really healthy living, and what's more, we didn't use the car once.'

Å See also listing on page 256.

21 BURNHAM NORTON & BURNHAM DEEPDALE

⅄ Deepdale Backpackers Hostel (page 256)

Coming from the bright, fashionable lights of Burnham Market, **Burnham Norton** has the roundtower church of St Margaret but no shop, café or pub. **Burnham Deepdale**, a little further on, has all of these facilities, along with the added appeal of easy walks out to the saltings and marshes. Other than that, the village centres on a strip of shops on the main road just before the eastern limits of Brancaster Staithe. Burnham Deepdale's **church of St Mary** is also well worth a look inside, having a Saxon round tower and a square Norman font that is carved to depict the Labours of the Months. Depending on the month when you visit, you can check what you ought to be doing in the agricultural calendar. In July, the 'labour' is mowing; in August, harvesting; winter is far more relaxed, with feasting in December and drinking in January.

Besides a handy garage and supermarket, there is a clothing store and a café here as well as the reception of the **Deepdale Backpackers Hostel** (page 256) and the excellent **Deepdale Camping** (see box, opposite) situated just behind it that offers the opportunity to stay in a heated tipi or Mongolian yurt. The reception doubles as the **Deepdale Information Centre** (✐ 01485 210256 ∅ deepdalebackpackers. co.uk), which has helpful suggestions for local walks and a good range of books and maps, including a stock of the wonderful hand-drawn Wilfrid George footpath maps. Deepdale Leisure Ltd, which runs all of these enterprises under the same green umbrella, promotes green tourism in the locality and organises a music festival in September and a Christmas market. Deepdale Hygge was inaugurated in March 2017, a weekend that pays tribute to the latest Danish craze and which is described as being all about connection to the environment and life's simple pleasures. Courses, guided walks and other activities are on offer throughout the year. Deepdale Camping was awarded the East of England Sustainable Tourism award in 2009 and the EDP Tourism in Norfolk Award in 2010.

⅋⅃ FOOD & DRINK

Deepdale Café Main Rd, Burnham Deepdale ✐ 01485 211 055 ∅ deepdale-cafe.co.uk. Serves everything from practical to posh, snack to slap-up. They usually open early (◔ 07.30) in good time to provide a full English breakfast for hungry cyclists and walkers.

BRANCASTER TO HUNSTANTON

22 BRANCASTER & BRANCASTER STAITHE

🏠 **The White Horse** & **The Maltings** in Brancaster Staithe (both page 256)

Further west along the A149 coast road, Burnham Deepdale morphs almost seamlessly into **Brancaster Staithe**, which in turn leads into **Brancaster** proper. These villages have developed more than most as smart holiday centres and have more than their fair share of holiday lets and weekend sailors. If you doubt this, try **The Jolly Sailors** for a drink or a meal on a Saturday night and see if you can detect many Norfolk accents. Despite this, Brancaster Staithe has not given itself over to leisure craft entirely and there is still a viable whelk and mussel industry here. Leisure craft and fishing boats have separate staithes linked by a path. To reach the fishermen's sheds walk down the lane opposite The Jolly Sailors pub. The neighbouring leisure-craft staithe has a highly attractive row of 17th-century cottages at its entrance; the National Trust owns the 'Dial House', the one with a sundial above its porch.

Brancaster Staithe Harbour is the place to come to catch a boat over to **Scolt Head Island**, formed as a spit but later isolated by the sea and made into an island. There are nesting colonies of Sandwich terns here in summer, the largest in the country. Branta Cruises (✆ 01485 211132 🔗 brantacruises.co.uk) operate a year-round (weather-dependent) guided boat service across to the island on the *Laura May*. Trips vary between 2 and 4 hours according to season and customers' interests. Sailings are according to the tide so it is necessary to phone and make arrangements in advance. There are also unscheduled ferries in summer to the eastern end of the island from Burnham Overy Staithe.

"Catch a boat over to Scolt Head Island, formed as a spit but later isolated by the sea and made into an island."

The Romans built a fortress, **Branodunum**, in what is now Brancaster and used it as part of its Saxon Shore fortification scheme to protect the Wash from invaders (another fort, Gariannonum, was built at Burgh Castle near Great Yarmouth). Apart from the outline of its ground layout, nothing remains to be seen today. Other than sailing, the biggest draw in Brancaster these days is the Royal West Norfolk Golf Club with a course that stretches with the sea on three sides nestled between the beach and the saltings, its clubhouse and car park by the dunes.

Up to Barrow Common

For a good overview of the coast at Brancaster, take a walk or cycle inland up Common Lane. In less than a mile, this narrow, Alexander-lined road leads gently uphill to **Barrow Common**, where there is parking, gorse bushes a-plenty and fantastic views over Brancaster harbour, Scolt Head, Brancaster golf course and even west across the Wash. On a clear day, you can easily see the wind turbines over on the Lincolnshire shore.

ACTIVITIES

Brancaster Millennium Activity Centre ✆ 01485 210719. Based in the 18th-century Dial House building at the entrance to the staithe, this centre organises a range of courses throughout the year that are mostly connected with art or wildlife. There are also activity days for children and family fun weeks that involve sailing, kayaking and mountain biking.

FOOD & DRINK

The Jolly Sailors Brancaster Staithe ✆ 01485 210314. This traditional 18th-century pub is known to everyone in these parts and has the advantage of a Coasthopper bus stop right outside its door. The pub has its own Brancaster Brewery ale and serves decent pub grub and pizzas.

The White Horse Brancaster Staithe ✆ 01485 210262 🖱 whitehorsebrancaster.co.uk. The interior is tastefully modern and the food good, featuring local seafood like oysters and mussels. The beers include Adnams, Woodforde's and Brancaster Brewery, and there is a lengthy list of wines from around the world. See also page 256 for accommodation.

3 TITCHWELL & 24 THORNHAM

🏠 **Titchwell Manor**, **Sea View** in Titchwell & **The Music Room** in Thornham (all page 256)

The coast road passes through **Titchwell** on its way here from Brancaster, a village with marshes that are home to a 420-acre **RSPB bird reserve**. The reserve has a swish modern visitor centre and offers a good chance of seeing bearded tits and bitterns among its many breeding species, and geese, plovers and harriers in winter. If you still have not seen an avocet, the graceful bird used for the RSPB logo, a sighting here is virtually guaranteed.

Thornham was once a busy port but trade peaked here back in the 17th century when the River Hun was diverted in order to drain the marshes. Predictably, silting, and the inevitable arrival of the railway, put an end to its harbour commerce. The massive floods of 1953, which washed away the railway line, sounded the final death knell.

A Thornham coastal walk

✵ OS Explorer 23 or Landranger 132; start: Orange Tree, Thornham ⚲ TF733433; 1.5 or 5 miles; easy – moderate

A pleasant, varied but easy, circular walk can be made starting at the Orange Tree at Thornham. The Coasthopper service has a bus shelter here. From the bus shelter by the Orange Tree pub, take Church Street north past the church, bearing immediately right at the junction to continue as far as the wood, bearing left at the edge of the wood along the signed footpath. The Norfolk Coast Path soon turns left over a stile. Follow this path alongside a vast reed bed where you may well see marsh harriers quartering for prey in summer – blissfully unaware that they are supposed to stay within sight of birders at the nearby RSPB Titchwell reserve. The path emerges close to the staithe, with its chalk-built coal barn, where you can have a look at the boats.

If you want to extend the walk, you can carry on westwards along the coast path from here, past Gore Point to Holme-next-the-Sea, and return the same way back to the staithe. Then from the staithe head along Staithe Lane, turn left along Ship Lane past the Lifeboat Inn and the wooded grounds of Thornham Manor before turning right at the end past the terrace of white cottages and back to the main road.

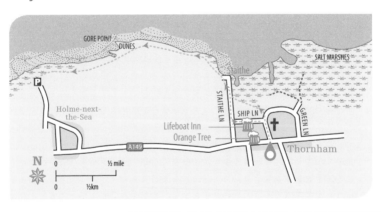

A spread out, quietly affluent place, the village marks the western end of the transition zone of north Norfolk's vernacular architecture. East of here, to well beyond Cromer, the building material of choice is mostly flint (although the transition starts somewhere around Brancaster); here at Thornham, chalk is the main material, a clue to the local geology.

FOOD & DRINK

Drove Orchards Thornham Rd ✆ 01485 525652 🖥 droveorchards.com. Drove Orchards cover 40 acres of orchard growing over 160 varieties of apple, of which 120 are East Anglian heritage varieties. There are also pears, plums, gages and soft fruit. You can pick your own fruit in season and the farm shop here stocks a wide variety of fresh produce along with local meats, cheese, breads and beers.

Lifeboat Inn Ship Lane ✆ 01485 512236 🖥 lifeboatinnthornham.com. This traditional 16th-century pub used to be the haunt of smugglers but these days it sees a more cosmopolitan clientele. The old bar has an open fire and gas lamps but there is also a new extension for swankier dining.

Shucks Drove Orchards, Thornham Rd ✆ 01485 525889 🖥 shucksattheyurt.co.uk. Located just off the A149 coast road between Thornham and Holme in, of all things, a large yurt, this cosy, quirky place serves 'honest rustic food' cooked by an award-winning chef who makes the most of local produce, especially vegetables from the Drove kitchen garden. Dogs and children welcome.

25 HOLME-NEXT-THE-SEA

Like Wells-next-the-Sea, Holme can hardly be described as 'next-the-sea'. The village is the point where the Norfolk coastline starts to twist south to face the Wash. It is also the 'elbow' of the combined Peddars Way & Norfolk Coast Path: the place where one ends and the other begins. It's a sudden change of coast and scenery, whichever direction you walk.

The village has a nice sandy **beach**, very popular on hot summer days, which can be reached by walking down Beach Road and turning right, or by turning just before the car park along a sandy path that leads through a NWT nature reserve. The boardwalk leads into a shady conifer plantation where the path continues to reach a sea defence bank near the tip of a pool called Broadwater. This path, the beginning of the Norfolk Coast Path, continues inland along sea defence walls to Thornham.

If you keep your eyes peeled on the beach, you may come across groups of what appear to be black peaty discs. These are the fossilised remains of a large, **prehistoric forest** that once extended across the North Sea. More of the same can be seen on the beach at Titchwell, just west of the sea wall and Brancaster golf clubhouse. The beach at Holme-next-the-Sea was put firmly on the map just over a decade ago with the discovery of a far more enigmatic arrangement of ancient wood, the so-called **'Seahenge'** (see box, page 60). A second timber circle has recently

THE SEAHENGE SAGA

Back in 1998, a particularly low tide at Holme beach revealed a circle of 55 oak timbers surrounding a massive upturned tree stump. The peat that had protected and hidden the circle for so long had been washed away by the tide and there were fears that further tides would sweep away the newly discovered site. As this was clearly some sort of ritualistic site, there was a strong argument for removing the timbers for preservation along with an equally vehement call to leave it well alone.

Debate raged as to what the original function was of what had become known as 'Seahenge' in the newspapers. Archaeologists suggested that the circle may have been a mortuary enclosure, while those of a less rigidly academic persuasion mooted more fanciful interpretations, such as a leyline centre. Spirits ran high and tempers frayed as those who would have the timbers removed clashed with those who wished to leave them be. Although this was mostly good-natured debate, the once-quiet beach at Holme became the setting for noisy argument between sensibly clothed archaeologists and dreadlocked, home-knitted jumper-wearing neo-druids, the latter performing improvised rituals accompanied by distinctly non-druidic instruments like didgeridoos and African drums.

The saga took an even more bizarre turn when, at a public meeting at the Le Strange Arms Hotel in Hunstanton, archaeologists, council officers and druids chanted together and used a 'talking stick' to symbolise the individual's right to speak uninterrupted. The meeting lasted five hours and reached some degree of accord but the circle's fate was already sealed.

The oak timbers were excavated and taken to Flag Fen near Peterborough. Analysis revealed that the circle was 4,500 years old and that the posts had not been positioned individually but placed in a circular trench. It was estimated that between 16 and 26 trees were used to build the monument, with at least 51 bronze axes employed, suggesting a community endeavour.

For many local objectors, the greatest fear was that the timbers might end up in the British Museum or somewhere similar, far away from Norfolk. These fears were unfounded, however: since 2008, the recreated Seahenge has taken pride of place in the Lynn Museum at King's Lynn (page 158).

been discovered nearby, this time dating back to 2400BC, which pre-dates Seahenge by several hundred years. Holme may well have several more like this buried away in its vicinity.

With a leisure beach and wildlife reserve located next door to one another, there has always been the potential for a conflict of interests at Holme. The discovery of Seahenge added further tensions to the people-versus-wildlife debate. The word on everyone's lips these days, though, is global warming and what can – or should – be done to protect coastal wildlife against the effects of **rising sea levels**. John Hiskett, Senior Conservation Officer at the Norfolk Wildlife Trust, gave me his view. 'As sea levels rise, higher tides will squeeze coastal habitats against the shoreline and this will mean fewer habitats for wildlife. The main losers will be those species that depend on these habitats and the bittern, for example, may be lost as a breeding species in north Norfolk if coastal reed beds disappear completely.'

So how can conservation bodies respond to this threat? 'We should help wildlife adapt to these changes by moving towards a more natural coastline.Freshwater habitats that are currently protected by sea walls will gradually be replaced by salt marsh – it is inevitable. At Holme, increased erosion means that we need to start considering some form of planned retreat now rather than live with the possibility of a catastrophic breach of the dunes sometime in the future.'

SEND US YOUR SNAPS!

We'd love to follow your adventures using our **Slow Travel Norfolk** guide – why not send us your photos and stories via Twitter (🐦 @BradtGuides) and Instagram (📷 @bradtguides) using the hashtag #Norfolk? Alternatively, you can upload photos directly to the gallery on the Norfolk destination page via our website (🖉 bradtguides.com/norfolk).

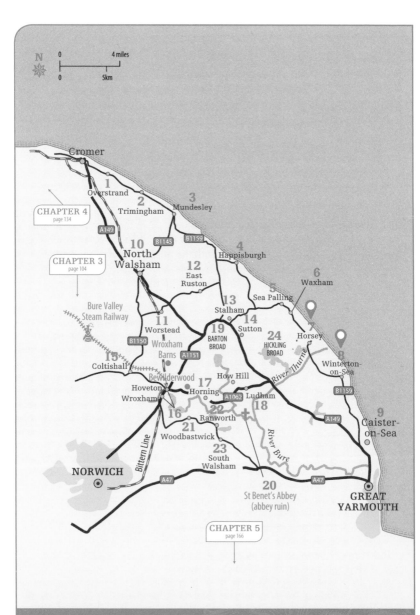

**THE NORTHEAST
NORFOLK COAST & THE BROADS**

2
THE NORTHEAST NORFOLK COAST & THE BROADS

East of Cromer, the north Norfolk coast curves gently southeast towards **Great Yarmouth** and the border with Suffolk. The coast here is less spectacular than that further west but provides locals with pleasant spots for dog walking and fishing, as well as sunbathing and swimming in the summer months when the wind drops. It is an uncomplicated, calming landscape of sand, slate-grey sea, pebble banks and dunes, set against a backdrop of fields of grazing cattle and great swathes of sugar beet and barley.

Thousands of hedgerows were enthusiastically grubbed out in this part of the county back in the 1960s but, that said, even some of the larger expanses of grain seen inland from the coast are a far cry in scale from the geometric prairies in the Fens further west.

With quiet, old-fashioned villages like Overstrand and Mundesley, along with the slightly more bucket-and-spade atmosphere of places like Sea Palling, Norfolk's northeast coast is likeable but it's hardly super-distinctive. Nevertheless, its safe sandy beaches and marram-grass-covered dunes make for great places for young families to potter about. The villages that punctuate this stretch of the coast have little of the cosmopolitan gloss of places like Blakeney or Burnham Market in northwest Norfolk, but there are enjoyable corners: this is workaday Norfolk, and there are far fewer incomers and second home owners than elsewhere in the county.

The timber groynes that push out to sea along the length of this shoreline – sometimes mysteriously erased from view by the frequent sea mists – give a clue to the nature of the coastline in these parts. West of Cromer, it is a landscape in the making, with transported sand creating spits and extensive offshore sands. Here, it is one of occasionally brutal erosion. Dotted sporadically along this stretch of coast are houses perched precariously on the edges of crumbling cliffs, with livelihoods hanging in the balance as the North Sea threatens to breach dunes and sea walls to flood valuable farmland. Measures to slow down the rate of coastal nibbling by the sea are hugely costly and ultimately don't often solve the problem. This can be hard to explain to those whose lives have always been based here.

Global warming is an altogether more sinister Sword of Damocles hanging over the region. With virtually all of northeast Norfolk sitting less than 20 feet above sea level, things do not bode well for the future. Worst-case scenarios suggest that much of this coastline may disappear underwater by the middle of the century: a radical redrafting of the map of lowland Britain. For many, it is more palatable to limit concern to receding cliffs and menacing high tides.

THE NORTHERN BROADS

Just inland from the coast is an area that really could not belong anywhere else in the country. **The Broads** dominate the landscape south of the small market town of Stalham: a sprawl of inland lakes linked by the River Bure and the shallow but navigable tributaries of the Thurne and Ant. Another collection of broads lies further south, east of Norwich along the River Yare, while a few more can be found across the border in Suffolk. They are all generally referred to as 'The Norfolk Broads'. For the purposes of this chapter, we will include just those northern broads clustered around the rivers Bure, Ant and Thurne – the very heart of Norfolk Broadland.

These sparkling bodies of water, previously assumed to be natural phenomena, were only proved to be manmade in the early 1960s, when research by Dr Joyce Lambert, a botanist, revealed that they had originally been medieval peat diggings that had become flooded over the centuries. With unique wildlife and landscape, and 28 Sites of Special Scientific Interest (SSSI) and nine National Nature Reserves within their boundary, the Broads have been awarded national park status, with the **Broads Authority** responsible for the area's management since its establishment in 1989.

The Broads are the one place that everyone associates with Norfolk (even though part of the area overlaps into Suffolk). Even David Bowie has made mention of them in one of his songs, although he was singing about 'Life on Mars' at the time. He also mentioned Ibiza in the same line, which hints at the frenzy that some parts of the Broads experience in high summer. At this time of year, the 'tourist honeypot' principle is amply demonstrated in the streets of Hoveton, where wannabe ship captains from the Midlands crowd the pavements, and Potter Heigham's medieval bridge has a lengthy tailback of floating gin palaces queuing to pass underneath. But this is just one face of the Broads; the other is a serene, watery wonderland of windmills, dykes and reed beds so rich with butterflies, dragonflies and exotic looking birds that it can feel almost tropical. It very much depends where you go … and when.

Not surprisingly, the busiest part of the Broads is around the boat hire centres – **Wroxham**, **Hoveton** and **Ranworth Broads**, and the River Thurne around **Potter Heigham**. Far quieter and more rewarding for landscape and wildlife are **Barton**, **Cockshoot** and **Hickling Broads**, the latter two having boarded walkways and water trails. **How Hill** near Ludham has special activities for children and a delightful walking trail through grazing marshes and woodland, and standing at a towering 40 feet above sea level, the highest point for miles, also offers one of the best panoramas in the area. It is also one of the most reliable places to see swallowtail butterflies around midsummer. Another excellent place for an overview of the Broads is the tower of **Ranworth Church**.

Few of the settlements in and around the Broads are particularly attractive. Red-brick rules supreme and bungalow estates are the norm – perhaps the reality of living at sea level inhibits the urge to build a second storey. **North Walsham**, just outside the Broads network, is an unremarkable but nice-enough market town, while **Stalham** is mostly bungalow-land centred upon a workaday High Street. **Wroxham/ Hoveton** is very much a holiday centre between Easter and September

A COUPLE OF NORFOLK TERMS

Carr

A carr refers to a boggy wooded area that represents an intermediate stage between a fen or bog and dry woodland. Carrs are typically characterised by alder, willow and sallow trees, which have high tolerance of waterlogged conditions.

Staithe

This term, used in east and northeast England, comes from an Old Norse word for harbour or landing place and refers to a narrow manmade channel where boats were landed and unloaded of goods. Norfolk staithes are often used as moorings today.

when the Broads cruiser hire trade is at its peak. Outside this season, it is pretty humdrum. What comes as a surprise is the lack of really good **pubs** in the region. The fringes of the Broads are more fruitful territory, and recommendable places for a drink can be found in Winterton, Horsey and Woodbastwick.

GETTING AROUND

Travelling around the Broads can be problematic, given so much water. It's far from ideal car-touring terrain as it is so divided by rivers and great expanses of wetland that long, circuitous detours are necessary to travel from A to B. More frustratingly, you see virtually nothing from a car, other than the number plate of the vehicle in front. This is low-lying terrain and it is rarely possible to get views over the reed beds to the water beyond even when a road does pass nearby. The good news is that you don't really need to travel the length of the Broads to get the idea: you can very much slow down and get the Broads flavour just by exploring a very small area in detail.

PUBLIC TRANSPORT

Luckily, a surprisingly decent **rail service** passes through the western part of the Broads, which, with a bit of ingenious bus timetabling and a willingness to walk, makes much of the region reasonably accessible. The more-or-less hourly **Bittern Line** train service (⊘ bitternline.com) links the Broads with both Norwich and Sheringham on the north coast. Salhouse station lies some distance away from the quiet broad of the same name, but Hoveton station, at least, is convenient for Wroxham Broad, the epicentre of boating activity in summer, and also handy for occasional bus links deeper into the Broads.

Particularly useful stations for starting **country walks** from include Worstead and Gunton. The steam-powered **Poppy Line** from Sheringham to Holt, and the **Bure Valley Steam Railway** (⊘ 01263 733858 ⊘ bvrw.co.uk) between Aylsham and Wroxham, also link with the Bittern Line.

Bus services are rather sketchy but the **First in Suffolk & Norfolk** 12 service runs from Norwich Castle Meadow, Monday to Saturday, to Wroxham, while **Sanders Coaches** 10 and X11 service runs between Wroxham and Stalham, Monday to Saturday. Sanders Coaches also run between Norwich, Wroxham, North Walsham, Mundesley and Cromer, while their 34 service running between Stalham and North Walsham along the coast calls at Sea Palling, Happisburgh, Mundesley and places in between. Please note that none of these operate on Sundays. However, **Konectbus** fills the gap here, with its 5B service between Norwich and Wroxham, which operates on Sundays and bank holidays.

RIVER CRAFT

Obviously, the very best way to see the Broads is on **water**. Self-drive **boat hire** options are numerous, and several companies like **Broad Tours** (✆ 01603 782207 ⊘ broads.co.uk) at Wroxham, **Richardson's** (✆ 01692 668981 ⊘ richardsonsboatingholidays.co.uk) at Stalham and **Ludham Bridge Boatyard** (✆ 01692 631011 ⊘ ludhambridge.co.uk) offer quieter and less polluting electric boats for hire. An even more eco-friendly boat excursion is to follow a wildlife water trail around How Hill National Nature Reserve near Ludham using the *Electric Eel* (booked from Toad Hole Cottage – page 91). There are also electric powered boat trips to be had at Hickling Broad organised by the **Norfolk Wildlife Trust** (✆ 01692 598276 ⊘ norfolkwildlifetrust.org.uk/hickling).

CANOEING

Paddling your way around by canoe is probably the ideal way to get the authentic Broads experience and is one of the best means of sneaking up on wildlife too. Canadian canoes are very stable and easy to paddle even for beginners. They can hold up to three people and can be great fun for children. Hire centres can advise on routes and suitability according to experience but, generally speaking, headwaters are the most rewarding for novices while lower reaches tend to require more experience – more strength too, given the need to cope with tidal waters.

Starting from hire centres, you might for instance try heading upstream along the River Bure from Wroxham Bridge past Belaugh towards Coltishall, or exploring the Dilham canal as far as the disused lock from Wayford Bridge, or south along the River Ant to reach Barton Broad. Staff at canoe hire centres are generally happy to advise on times and distances for planned itineraries. **Bank Boats & Canoe Hire** at Staithe Cottage, Wayford Bridge near Smallburgh (✆ 01692 582457 ⊘ bankboats.co.uk), **Barnes Brinkcraft** at Riverside Road, Wroxham (✆ 01603 782625 or 782333 ⊘ barnesbrinkcraft.co.uk), **Martham Boats** at Martham near Great Yarmouth ($\mathcal{O}$ 01493 740249 $\mathcal{O}$ marthamboats. com) and **Phoenix Fleet** ($\mathcal{O}$ 01692 670460 $\mathcal{O}$ phoenixfleet.com) at Potter Heigham all have canoes for hire, as does The Canoe Man at Wroxham (see below) and several other centres in the Broads.

PADDLE BOARDING

Stand up paddle boarding is starting to catch on as an alternative to canoeing and kayaking. **Martham Boats** ($\mathcal{O}$ 01493 740249 $\mathcal{O}$ marthamboats.com) offers two-hour beginners' sessions with qualified instructors while the **Norfolk Paddle Co** ($\mathcal{O}$ 07432 817495 $\mathcal{O}$ norfolkpaddleco.co.uk) sells and rents paddle boards and can provide tuition at a variety of locations in the Norfolk Broads. The Canoe Man at Wroxham (see below) also rents paddle board equipment and offers regular evening tuition sessions in summer.

CANOEING FOR NOVICES

For the uninitiated, canoeing is fairly intuitive really. I have a hopeless sense of balance but even I can manage it without too much trouble. The secret is to not stand up once you're in the canoe. It's best to make sure that anything that doesn't go well with water – cameras or electrical devices for example – is well-protected. In fact, it's easier just to leave these sorts of things behind.

Paddling is not especially hard work, although your shoulders and back may ache a bit if you are not used to it. Three hours is probably enough for novices – a six-hour canoeing session would leave most beginners pretty tired. Tidal currents should not present much of a problem unless you are a long way downstream but wind can slow you down and make it harder work just like on a bike.

As a humble canoeist, expect power boats to regard you in the same way that car drivers do cyclists – their attitude can range from courteous consideration to total and utter contempt. The further you can get away from them the better. Give anglers a wide berth, as canoes can scare away the fish.

The positives are considerable. You'll be getting good exercise and seeing river life close-up. You are likely to see plenty of kingfishers, herons and dragonflies and might even glimpse an otter.

One option is to take a **guided canoe trail** through the Broads, ideal for beginners. Mark Wilkinson, otherwise known as '**The Canoe Man**'

(✐ 0845 4969177 ☝ thecanoeman.com), offers a variety of guided canoe trails from spring to autumn between two and three hours' duration, more frequently during the school holidays. One- or two-night guided canoe and bushcraft trails take place about twice a month in the summer with camping or bivouacking on sites arranged with local farm owners ('wild camping' as such is not permitted in the Broads).

More comfortable are the canoe trails (from one to four nights) that make use of local B&Bs – these also offer an unguided option. Tipi camping trails that combine a Canadian canoe expedition with an overnight stay in a remote tipi lodge are another possibility.

WALKING

The **Weavers' Way** takes a meandering 58-mile route through the Broads from Great Yarmouth to Cromer following footpaths, bridleways, riverside tracks and the occasional minor road. The whole route takes at least three days, although sections of it are ideal for half-day or day excursions. A particularly enjoyable section is between Potter Heigham and Hickling Green, taking in a stretch of the River Thurne and snaking around the south side of Hickling Broad. The seven-mile section from Stalham and North Walsham is also appealing as it has decent bus links between the two.

Another walking route through the northern part of the region is the **Paston Way**, which meanders between North Walsham and Cromer, taking in 15 historic churches as it goes. The spidery, wandering route, waymarked in the North Walsham to Cromer direction, is anything but a straight line, but it does offer some rewarding walking and several intriguing detours.

The **Norfolk Coast Path** now extends all the way from Cromer to Hopton-on-Sea on the Norfolk-Suffolk border. The total distance from Cromer is 38 miles. In contrast to the rather linear walking available along Norfolk's northwest coast, the area has many other walking possibilities, and circular routes are easy to organise if you don't mind the odd short section of minor road. With few contours on the map, it goes without saying there are no uphill struggles. The downside of this is that, away from water, the terrain can sometimes be a bit dull, but alongside river or broad, it can be a delight. Several of the rivers have footpaths that follow them for miles but seeing the Broads themselves on foot is not so easy as most lack waterside paths.

i TOURIST INFORMATION

Broads website  www.broads-authority.gov.uk
Hoveton Station Rd ✆ 01603 782281
Ludham Toad Hole Cottage Museum, How Hill ✆ 01692 678763
Potter Heigham The Staithe, Bridge Rd ✆ 01692 756096
Ranworth The Staithe ✆ 01603 270453

CYCLING

Exploring the back lanes by bike is a delight, but not the busy main roads like the A149 and A1151. As the terrain is almost perfectly flat, you won't be needing those low gears. Using bridleways and minor roads, it is possible to travel around the region far more efficiently than in a car, avoiding long detours. There's still a lot of water to get round, though, and it takes very careful routing to avoid the main roads. Unfortunately, the former ferry across the River Bure from Woodbastwick Fen to Horning is no longer in service for cyclists or walkers.

For those without their own bikes, **cycle hire** is available at Clippesby Hall (✆ 01493 367800 ⚲ clippesbyhall.com), which incidentally has an excellent touring and camping park with pitches set out in natural woodland; Broadland Cycle Hire at BeWILDerwood near Hoveton (✆ 07887 480331 ⚲ norfolkbroadscycling.co.uk), who provide free cycling maps; Bike Riders in North Walsham (✆ 01692 406632); Ludham Bridge Stores (✆ 01692 631120); Sea Palling Cycle Hire (✆ 07747 483154 ⚲ norfolkbicyclehire.co.uk) at Waxham Barn, who offer a free delivery service within 6 miles of Waxham Barn for bookings of two days or more; and the tea rooms at Stokesby (✆ 01493 750470).

The **Bittern Line** is a highly convenient means of taking your own bike in or out of the area. Those turning up on the day can transport their bike on a first come, first served basis – each train is able to take up to four bikes. In summer it is probably best to book in advance (✆ 0845 600 7245).

The Broads Authority produce a useful **leaflet** called *The Broads by Bike* that can be picked up from any visitor centre or viewed online at ⚲ thebroadsbybike.org.uk. This shows an orbital cycling route around the Broads and suggests a variety of day and half-day itineraries. One really good ride of around 15 miles that takes in Potter Heigham,

How Hill and Ludham, begins and ends in Clippesby and gives a good overview of the region. A similar-length route starts at Hoveton's BeWILDerwood and follows quiet country lanes to Neatishead and Barton Turf where there is access to the boardwalk and viewing platform at Barton Broad. Another possibility is to follow the nine-mile Bure Valley Path that follows the Bure Valley Railway between Wroxham and Aylsham. Bicycles can also be carried on the Bure Valley Railway trains, space permitting, for £3.50.

THE COAST: OVERSTRAND TO CAISTER-ON-SEA

1 OVERSTRAND

🏠 The Green House (page 257)

Overstrand lies just two miles east of Cromer as the gull flies. Originally a place of crab fishing like its big-sister neighbour, it has slowly developed into a quiet resort with a safe, sandy beach. Much lauded in the writings of Clement 'Poppyland' Scott, the village was favoured by the Victorian upper classes and soon became known as 'the village of millionaires'. Some of its grandest buildings date from this period. Overstrand Hall was designed by a young Edward Lutyens for Lord Hillingdon, while Gertrude Jekyll is said to have been responsible for the gardens at The Pleasaunce. The rather grand Overstrand Hotel, built at the turn of the 20th century, became a very popular hangout for the aristocracy and upper classes, and one of the most prestigious hotels along the east coast. Unfortunately, the architects built it rather too close to the cliff edge and its foundations started to crumble within a matter of years. It finally collapsed in 1947, ironically as the result of a fire.

Erosion is a serious concern all along this coast. In the neighbouring village of Sidestrand, the village church was moved back, stone by stone, from the cliff edge in the 19th century, although the tower was left standing where it was. Overstrand's original church had been swallowed up by the sea centuries before, in the late 1300s. A new church, of the same name – St Martin's – was built in 1399 but this too fell into disrepair by the middle of the 18th century and was a ruin by the mid-1800s. A replacement church was built and consecrated in 1867 but this proved to be too small for local congregations and so in 1911 it was decided to restore and re-consecrate St Martin's.

A cliff walk to Cromer

A favourite outing from Overstrand is the walk along the cliffs to Cromer: a short, often windy, hike of just a couple of miles that offers a marvellous view over the resort and its pier as you approach from the east. This route, which also coincides with the last couple of miles of the Paston Way, is very popular all the year round. In autumn and winter, bushes that bear the brilliant orange berries of sea buckthorn

THE LEGEND OF BLACK SHUCK

And a dreadful thing from the cliff did spring, and its wild bark thrilled around, his eyes had the glow of the fires below, 'twas the form of the Spectre Hound.

Old Norfolk saying

Tales of Black Shuck, a dark ghostly hound with terrifying fiery eyes, are commonplace throughout East Anglia, especially along the coast. The legend may have arrived with Danish raiders, with 'Shukr' being the name of the faithful, yet ultimately abandoned, canine companion of the Norse god Thor. Alternative derivations may come from *scucca*, an Anglo-Saxon word that means demon, or even 'shucky', a local dialect word meaning 'hairy'.

One of Shuck's most notable appearances was at Blythburgh in Suffolk in 1577 when he appeared at the church and terrified the congregation, killing a man and boy, causing the tower to collapse and leaving scorch marks in his wake. Not content with this, Shuck was reported to appear at Bungay, also in Suffolk, the very same day and put on much the same sort of performance at the parish church.

The Overstrand version of the Shuck legend has it that two friends, a Dane and a Saxon, were drowned whilst out fishing

together with their dog. The Dane washed up at Beeston and the Saxon at Overstrand, while the dog's ghostly presence roamed the coast in search of both his masters. Anyone unfortunate enough to encounter Shuck on his nightly patrol would generally find himself dead within the year. Along with any number of supposed sightings elsewhere, Shuck was reported to have made his home in the ruins of Overstrand's St Martin's Church until the restoration work of 1911 drove him away. He is rumoured to haunt the coast road between Overstrand and Sheringham.

Legend or not, Shuck has been quite an influential figure in literature. Sir Arthur Conan Doyle probably heard of the legend whilst on a golfing visit to Cromer in 1901 and a terrifying spectral dog character subsequently appeared in his *Hound of the Baskervilles*, published the following year. The setting was transposed from north Norfolk to Dartmoor but the descriptions of fictitious home of the Baskerville family are strongly reminiscent of Cromer Hall.

flank the cliff top path. The berries look good enough to eat and they were, apparently, part of the diet of prehistoric man. Appearances can be deceiving though, as they taste unbelievably bitter – not the sort of things you'd want to put in a pie.

2 TRIMINGHAM

Further southeast along the coast road from Overstrand towards Mundesley, the village of Trimingham has the rather unusually named **St John the Baptist's Head**. The only other church in Britain with the same macabre dedication is in Kent. Needless to say, neither of these is the true repository of the apostle's cranium (which is supposedly at Amiens Cathedral in France): the name dates from a medieval scam in which hapless pilgrims were lured by the promise of holy relics. Certainly, as holy relics go, the head of St John would have been a very impressive attraction – if only it had been true. What would have once been on display here, and most probably destroyed during the Reformation, was a full-sized alabaster likeness – a superb 14th-century example, probably very similar to that on display at Trimingham, can be seen in London's Victoria and Albert Museum. The church itself is a little on the squat side but it makes up for this by standing, like Napoleon on a soap box, at one of the highest points along the northeast coast – around 200 feet above sea level.

"As holy relics go, the head of St John would have been a very impressive attraction – if only it had been true."

South of here, beyond tiny Gimingham, is **Trunch**, a place that sounds like a dull blow to the head but is, in fact, rather more pleasant. The gazebo-like, Gothic font canopy of Trunch's **St Botolph's Church**, carved with animals that include squirrels, monkeys, dogs and even a pig wearing a bishop's mitre, is by far the most striking feature of this 14th to 15th-century building, although its hammerbeam roof is quite splendid too. **Knapton**, the village immediately east of Trunch, also has the interesting **church of St Peter and St Paul**, with its early 16th-century hammerbeam roof timbers lavishly decorated with angels with outspread wings, 138 in total (according to architectural historian Nikolaus Pevsner), although the church itself claims 160 – or count them yourself and arrive at your own figure. The cockerel weathervane on the tower here is reportedly the design of the eminent Norwich School artist, J S Cotman, who gave drawing classes at nearby Knapton Hall.

3 MUNDESLEY & AROUND

Mundesley is more of a large village than a town. The railway station that brought the Victorian elite here in the 19th century has long since closed and the nearest station these days is the Bittern Line station in North Walsham. John Seymour describes Mundesley as 'a good solid respectable seaside town, and that is all there is to say about that.' He has a point, but it also has a fine Blue Flag beach for bracing walks and safe swimming – a great place for children to splash about. The very lovely beach, understandably very popular with local families on warm summer weekends, has a café and a shop selling the usual seaside requisites – flip-flops, beach balls and shrimp nets. On the concrete promenade next to the shop stands a neat terrace of brightly painted beach huts that add a splash of colour to an otherwise grey scene on an overcast winter's day. It may not quite have the grandeur of Cromer but at least it makes an effort. The tiny **Maritime Museum** (⟋ 01263 720879 ⌂ mundesleymaritimemuseum.co.uk ⊙ summer), on Beach Road and housed in an old coastguard lookout point, is worth 50p of anyone's money. Regrettably **Stow Mill**, a flour mill built in 1827 that lies just outside the village on the road south to Paston, can no longer be visited as it has, like so many historical agricultural buildings in these parts, been recently converted into a holiday let.

A little further along the B1159 coast road you reach the small village of **Paston**, where there is the magnificent flint and thatch **Paston Great Barn** built by Sir William Paston in 1581. At 160 feet long and 60 feet high this is one of Norfolk's largest barns. In recent years it has been fully restored by the North Norfolk Historic Buildings Trust. Paston Great Barn, now leased to Natural England, is also home to a maternal colony of very rare barbastelle bats and because of this the barn and outbuildings are closed to the public. Although the barn and courtyard cannot be visited, there is a small car park and interpretative panel on the eastern side of the barn and a footpath that takes you through the grounds to the south. The Paston family's dominant role in the village's history is brought to life through the legacy of the famous **Paston Letters**, a hugely historically important collection of 15th-century correspondence now kept in the British Museum and Oxford's Bodleian Library. The village's 14th-century St Margaret's Church has

"Paston Great Barn is home to a maternal colony of very rare barbastelle bats."

several memorials to the family; the most striking is that of Katherine Paston, sculpted in fine alabaster in 1628.

Bacton, a little further east still, is another small seaside centre but the name is more frequently associated with the enormous North Sea Gas Terminal that lies north of the village. The terminal is actually closer to Paston than Bacton. You can't miss it, as you drive right past on the coast road, although perhaps you might like to at least try to do so. Both Paston and Bacton are quite attractive villages in their own right, although it is hard to see the attraction of the caravan site that is right next to the gas terminal itself: it offers an industrial outlook that only those homesick for Teeside could love.

Just south of Bacton, the ruined **Bromholm Priory** was an outpost of the Cluniac priory at Castle Acre in the Middle Ages, and an important pilgrimage centre as it claimed to have a piece of the True Cross.

PIONEER MAN IN NORFOLK

In July 2010, the surprise discovery of more than 70 ancient flint tools on a Happisburgh beach pushed back the date of the first known occupation of Britain by up to a quarter of a million years. The stone tools discovered by British Museum archaeologists are thought to be between 840,000 and 950,000 years old, making them the oldest artefacts ever found in the country, indeed, in all of northwest Europe.

These were most probably the tools of *Homo antecessor*, a humanoid species that lived as hunter-gatherers in the flood plain of the ancient River Thames, which in those times flowed through the territory that is now Norfolk. *Homo antecessor* or 'Pioneer Man', whose remains have been found in Spain, is the only human species currently known to have existed in Europe around one million years ago. It must have been this same species that walked across the land bridge that connected Britain with mainland Europe at the time to become the first Norfolk settlers.

The Happisburgh discovery suggests that early humans must have been able to adapt to the cold as the winters here were cooler than they are now, although summers were much the same. These early settlers would also have had to share their terrain with mammoth, rhino, hyenas and sabre-toothed cats. Clearly, there was a plentiful supply of free-range meat available at the time, if precious little edible vegetation, but certain difficult questions remain: did the early Happisburgh settlers have shelter and clothes, could they control fire?

Before this find was made the earliest evidence of human activity in Britain – a mere 700,000 years ago – was from Pakefield in Suffolk. So, not for the first time, Norfolk has trumped its southern neighbour.

▌▌ FOOD & DRINK

Ship Inn Beach Rd, Mundesley ✆ 01263 722671 ⊘ mundesley-ship.co.uk. Above the beach, in an 18th-century flint and brick building, this friendly local pub serves Woodforde's Wherry, Green Jack, Winter's, Wolf and other locally brewed guest beers and ciders. The bar and restaurant menu offers well-priced food that uses seasonal, locally sourced ingredients; the Sunday roasts here are especially noteworthy. Both dog- and child-friendly, it has a cosy open-log fire in winter. The breezy beer garden with trestle tables overlooking the beach is home to a converted boat used for serving chargrilled burgers, kebabs and ice creams.

Corner House Café 2–4 Cromer Rd, Mundesley ✆ 01263 720509. This rustically furnished tea room near the seafront has good cakes, snacks and light meals as well as a wide selection of teas served from proper china teapots.

4 HAPPISBURGH

Continuing southeast along the coast past Walcott, which, frankly, is a bit of a grim low-rise sprawl next to a popular but bleak-looking beach, you arrive at Happisburgh, an instantly recognisable place thanks to its distinctive red and white banded lighthouse (painted in camouflage colours during World War II), the oldest working lighthouse in East Anglia. Happisburgh, pronounced 'Hazeboro', was put on the map back in 1990 when the repainting of the **lighthouse** became the object of a *Challenge Anneka* television programme, in which the presenter landed her helicopter and ran about badgering locals into revamping their village icon. The 'challenge' was to smarten up the dowdy-looking structure with a repaint in 48 hours. The task took almost two weeks apparently – although they didn't mention this in the television programme as this went rather against the spirit of things. They used the wrong type of paint too, which soon started to peel, so the lighthouse required an expensive repaint later on. They still talk about this event in the village – the next best thing to *Antiques Roadshow* coming to town. 'Put on the map' is perhaps an unfortunate choice of words as the twin threats of coastal erosion and rising sea levels currently threaten to erase parts of the village from the map altogether. Take a look at the cliffs from the end of Beach Road and you'll get the picture.

The lighthouse (⊘ happisburgh.org/lighthouse ⊙ summer Sun only), was built in 1791 following a severe winter storm off the northeast Norfolk coast in 1789 in which 70 ships were wrecked and 600 men lost. Before that, apart from distant light from Cromer and Winterton, the only navigation aid had been the tower of Happisburgh's **St Mary's Church**.

Happisburgh, perhaps more than anywhere else along this coastline, is where the effect of the raw power of the North Sea can best be seen, as every year, without fail, a little more land is chipped away by winter gales and high tides. The tenure of the caravan site next to the cliffs here looks increasingly precarious, and right next to this there is a tarmac road that, quite literally, ends at the cliff, crudely severed by gravity and deposited on the beach below. This is now a road going nowhere – concrete blocks have been put in place to block it just in case a mischievous sat nav encourages an innocent driver to follow it to the beach below. Coming here, you cannot but wonder how long the famous lighthouse will continue to stand. But the lighthouse, like the village church, stands on a low bluff a little way inland – both structures that will probably outlast the village itself. Having said all of this, the cliff top path at Happisburgh is an excellent place to walk on a crisp winter's day, when the sea is at its wildest and the brutal reality of coastal erosion is almost visceral. Hardy surfers in wet suits can sometimes be seen on such days – latter-day anti-Canutes who, rather than deny the incoming tide, embrace it.

5 SEA PALLING & 6 WAXHAM

Sea Palling, south of Happisburgh and four miles east of the market town of Stalham, is another fairly nondescript coastal village with a nice beach that has boasted a Blue Flag award for several years now. The drone of jet skiers speeding along the foreshore might help spoil your peace, however. Right next door is **Waxham**, a smaller village that has a partially derelict church (St John's) next to a 15th-century gatehouse that once belonged to Waxham Hall. Originally there were two villages, Waxham Magna and Waxham Parva, but the latter has gone the way of much of this coastline and been washed away to sea. Nevertheless, there's a nice small beach here.

Waxham Great Barn is one of the longest historic barns in the country. The building, which has featured in the BBC's *Restoration* series, was built in the early 1580s by the Woodhouses, a wealthy local family. Architectural salvage was common in those days if any material other than flint was to be used, and the barn's construction recycled parts of three monasteries closed by Henry VIII. The barn is actually a little larger than the slightly earlier one at nearby Paston and the roof may well have been built by the same carpenters.

Caroline Davison from Norfolk County Council's conservation department told me, 'The roof structure at Waxham barn is the same and was built only two or three years later. I like to think that the Woodhouses were making the point that they were the dominant family in the area, so they deliberately built their barn a bit bigger.' The Norfolk Historic Buildings Trust now manages the barn as a visitor centre on behalf of Norfolk County Council. It is open to the public in the summer months and on Sundays throughout the year and has a café adjacent to it.

🍴 FOOD & DRINK

Waxham Barn Café Coast Rd, Waxham NR12 0DY ✆ 01692 598824 ◷ early Apr–end Oct, closed Wed. Adjoining the enormous barn, this bright, family-run café uses locally sourced ingredients for its cakes, scones and lunches. From the café's courtyard tables you can enjoy the aerial spectacle of swallows and house martins swooping around the barn while you eat.

7 HORSEY

The coast road from Sea Palling turns inland slightly to pass through the village of Horsey, which has the best of both worlds in being close to the coast but also at the very edge of the Broads. Standing only a couple of feet or so above sea level, the village has always had a fractious relationship with the North Sea just over the dunes and was cut off completely for four months in 1938 when all of the villagers had to be evacuated. The village is tiny but manages to retain a pub, a nice old barn and thatched church, and easy access to a beach. Roman coins have been found in the area on several occasions and so despite its obvious vulnerability, Horsey has been settled for a very long time.

🍴 FOOD & DRINK

Nelson Head The Street ✆ 01493 393378 ◌ thenelsonhead.com. This country pub has a red telephone box immediately in front of the entrance, and a log fire and cheery, warm interior within. Outside is a huge beer garden. Fresh local food is served lunchtime and evening, all day in summer, and there's a selection of real ales including Woodforde's.

Poppylands Horsey Corner ✆ 01493 393393. Located on the coast road just before Horsey Gap, this popular tea shop serves coffee, cake, sandwiches and light meals. There's plenty of 1940s wartime memorabilia on display here, even down to the music played, because of the young owner's personal interest in the period. Thankfully, they draw the line at including wartime austerity dishes on the menu. Upstairs is a small gift shop.

A Horsey Mere circuit

❄ OS Explorer OL40 or Landranger 134; start: Horsey Mill car park, ♀ TG456223; 5 miles; moderate

One of my favourite walks in Broadland begins and ends at Horsey Mere, a broad just west of the village. The handy car park next to the staithe is alongside a four-storey windmill, restored by the National Trust. Horsey Mere, which also belongs to the National Trust, is a small, picture-perfect broad with thatched boathouses and sedge warblers calling from the reed beds. I have seen

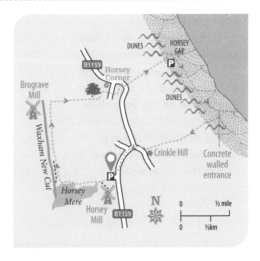

marsh harriers flying overhead here on several occasions – and, in the winter months you might spot hen harriers and day-flying barn owls. There is also a permanent colony of cranes in the fields around here, although they are not easy to see – I finally spotted two feeding in a field near the windmill on what must have been my tenth visit. The lovely thing about this walk, which is probably at its best on a clear, crisp winter's day, is that it gives you a taste of everything the area has to offer in the space of an easy five miles: reed beds, lake, river, farmland, marsh, beach, dunes and the North Sea itself.

A marked footpath leads through reed beds around the north side of the mere, along Waxham New Cut and over grazing marshes to a picturesque drainage pump before turning right to cross fields to the coast road. From here, a track leads over dunes at Horsey Gap to the beach, a favourite haunt of grey seals in winter. This is also highly popular with visitors in winter, especially during the week between Christmas and New Year. A mile or so southeast along the dunes, there's a muddy, pot-holed track that leads inland past an old World War II defensive pillbox to reach the road at Crinkle Hill. The 'hill' part of the name should be taken with a pinch of salt – round these parts 'hill' can mean almost anything above the horizontal; this one is about six feet above sea level, perhaps a little less. The road leads back to the village past the Nelson Head pub – a tempting stopping point before the short leg back to the car park.

8 WINTERTON-ON-SEA

Winterton's Holy Trinity and All Saints' Church is distinguished by its noticeably tall tower, the third highest in Norfolk, but steeples on steroids make good sense along this occasionally treacherous coastline: they stand out as beacons in this pancake-flat terrain. Local tradition sometimes claims that Winterton's church tower is 'a herring-and-a-half higher than Cromer'. Unfortunately, this is not true: it is, in fact, 35 feet shorter.

Daniel Defoe, who visited the village in 1722, remarked that all its houses seemed to be constructed out of the timbers of wrecked ships – a reflection on the hazardous nature of the coastline here. Most of the ones he commented on would have come from the fleet that was wrecked in the fatal storm of 1692. The danger of shipwreck can seem real enough if you come here on a winter's day when thick sea mist blankets the shoreline and stretches for a mile or so inland obscuring everything from view.

The **Winterton Dunes Nature Reserve**, north of the village, is a large hummocky stretch of sand dunes stabilised by marram grass that are

Winterton walk: dunes, fields & woodland

✳ OS Explorer OL40 or Landranger 134; start: Winterton beach car park, ♀ TG498197; 5 miles; easy–moderate

Starting and ending at Winterton, this rewarding circular walk takes in pretty well all that the area has to offer: sand dunes, wildlife, wind turbines and woodland. It is about five miles – two hours – in total, but easy going and varied. You might prefer to do the whole walk in the other direction if you want to keep the coastal stretch for the finale.

From the beach car park, head north towards Winterton Dunes Nature Reserve until you reach a marked footpath beyond the nature reserve sign. Continue along the sand dunes keeping the perimeter fence to your left. After a mile or so, the reserve ends at Winterton Ness; turn left here along the public footpath to Winterton Holmes. Turn left again towards the wind farm along a concrete farm road, which turns sharply right after another few hundred yards. When the track finally divides, turn left along the estate wall, heading towards the wind turbines alongside woods. At the end of a small plantation to your right, turn left and follow the path past the entrance and left towards Manor Farm. To the right, almost hidden, is the ruin of St Mary's Church. From Manor Farm, head east down Low Road past the duck pond to return to Winterton.

home to a large colony of rare natterjack toads. Plenty of birds nest here too – little terns, ringed plovers and stonechats – and dragonflies flit above the ponds. You can often see seals offshore here too: there is usually a colony of them on the beach to the north. In winter you might well see a flock of snow buntings on the beach. Other colonists found among the dunes to the north here are the odd naturist (and, perhaps, even odder naturalist) along with concrete pillboxes constructed during World War II as anti-invasion defences. In 2005, a landslide resulted in some of these toppling on to the beach near the car park.

> *"In winter you might well see a flock of snow buntings on the beach."*

Clearly visible from Winterton is the **Blood Hill wind farm** at nearby Somerton, one of the first erected in the UK, as well as the more extensive offshore wind farm at **Scroby Sands**, built in 2003 and 2004. Of course, wind farms are not popular with everyone, least of all those who fear living in their shadow. 'Nimby' might sound rather like a Danish place name but around here it means something completely different.

While Winterton retains the slightly isolated feel of the northeast coast, Hemsby, the neighbouring village, just a mile away, seems to belong firmly to Great Yarmouth's gravitational field. In Hemsby, you are starting to venture into a hinterland of caravan parks, amusement arcades and crazy golf that stretches all along the coast from here through Yarmouth and Lowestoft as far as Kessingland in Suffolk.

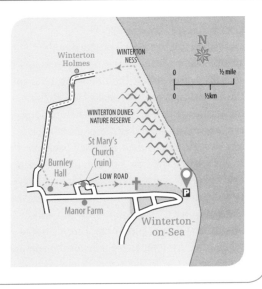

A CAISTER PHOENIX

As with all of the northeast Norfolk coast, erosion is a fact of life. The Manor House Hotel, a largish building that once stood proudly in the town, was finally abandoned to the elements during World War II after much of its shoreline had been destroyed by environmental erosion. The hotel is said to have completely disappeared from view by 1948, never to be seen again. But not quite: in March 2013, following a wild night of northeasterly gales, a large chunk of the hotel's brickwork dramatically re-emerged from the sands like a proverbial phoenix from the ashes. Elsewhere, at nearby Hemsby and Hopton, World War II concrete pillboxes were revealed for the first time in years. The huge amount of sand scoured from the beach to reveal these half-forgotten buildings is no doubt already halfway along the Norfolk coast, perhaps a future sand spit in the making.

¶¶ FOOD & DRINK

The Fisherman's Return The Lane NR29 4BN ✆ 01493 393305 ⏚ fishermansreturn.com. This 300-year-old traditional brick and flint pub has a good range of local ales, including Woodforde's and Blackfriars. 'Keeping it local' is the motto on the bar menu: fresh fish is delivered daily from Lowestoft while meat is sourced from local butchers.

Winterton Dunes Beach Café Beach Rd NR29 4AJ ✆ 01493 394931. This black-painted hut next to the dunes and beach car park does thriving business with local dog-walkers and summer beach visitors. No frills but freshly cooked food and good crab sandwiches.

9 CAISTER-ON-SEA

Virtually a suburb of Great Yarmouth, Caister offers much the same as Hemsby, except for the nearby remains of **Caister Castle**, a 15th-century moated castle built between 1432 and 1446 by Sir John Falstaff, the inspiration for the Shakespeare character. The Pastons inherited the castle from Sir John but before long the Duke of Norfolk, an enthusiastic and serial castle-grabber, took control of it having laid siege for a year. When he died, it passed back into Paston hands until the 17th century when the new London owner decided to tear most of it down. The castle (⏚ caistercastle.co.uk) now serves as home to the largest private collection of motor vehicles in Britain, and includes a minor star of *Chitty Chitty Bang Bang* and an 1893 Panhard et Lavassor, the world's first proper motor car. The 90-foot tower remains intact and can be climbed for a gull's eye view of the surrounding area. Caister is also well known for its lifeboat and never-say-die fishermen, whose slogan, 'Caister men never turn back', says it all.

The word Caister comes from *castrum*, the Latin for camp: hidden rather unglamorously behind back gardens of semis and bungalows are the labelled knee-height walls of the late Roman fort (free access), built as a defence against Saxon raiders around AD200 and in use until the end of the following century, that gives the village its name. This is not to be confused with another Roman 'Caister' in the county – Caister St Edmund (Venta Icenorum) close to Norwich, a Romano-British settlement which has altogether more impressive town walls.

INTO THE BROADS PROPER: NORTH WALSHAM TO THE RIVER BURE

0 NORTH WALSHAM

This market town, just beyond the Broads, is the most important urban centre in northeast Norfolk. Having said that, it is still pretty low-key. The Bittern Line between Norwich and Sheringham passes through the town, as does the Weavers' Way long-distance footpath. There is no river but the now-disused North Walsham and Dilham Canal, which connects with the River Ant and Broads system, skirts the town to the northeast.

"In keeping with Norfolk's radical tradition, the town became a focus for a rural uprising in support of Wat Tyler's Peasants' Revolt."

In keeping with Norfolk's radical tradition, the town became a focus for a rural uprising in support of Wat Tyler's Peasants' Revolt back in 1381, when a local dyer Geoffrey Litester headed a group of rebels calling for the abolition of serfdom. Workers' rights were not high on the agenda in the 14th century and, unsurprisingly, their pleas fell on deaf, and highly unsympathetic, ears. The rebels were attacked by none other than the Bishop of Norwich himself, Henry Despencer, who, if historic accounts are correct, rather enjoyed the bloodshed. The bishop, being a man of the cloth, was at least good enough to grant Litester absolution before having him drawn and quartered. Litester's quarters were subsequently dispatched to Norwich, King's Lynn, Great Yarmouth and his home village 'so that rebels, and those that rise above their place, may learn how they will end' – they did not do things by halves in those days. Bishop Henry erected three crosses to mark the crushing of the uprising, one of which can still be seen on the Norwich road just south of North Walsham.

THE NORTH WALSHAM & DILHAM CANAL

Few expect to find canals here in Norfolk, far away from England's industrial heartland, and this modest stretch in northeast Norfolk is the county's sole example. It was created by the canalisation of the upper reaches of the River Ant and the locks installed were made a little wider than average in order to accommodate Norfolk wherries. The canal is a little less than nine miles long and begins at Swafield Bridge, just north of North Walsham, ending where it reaches the River Ant at Smallburgh near Stalham. Opened in 1826, it was mainly used to transport animal bones and phosphates to the bone mills at Antingham, although grain, coal and building materials were also carried by the wherries. The canal was sold off in 1885, but the money from the sale – some £600 – mysteriously went missing in the care of the company solicitor. He was never seen again.

Today, very little of the original canal, last used for a cargo journey in 1934, is navigable – just a couple of miles at the Smallburgh end – although there are plans to restore some parts of it for pleasure craft. It is best explored by following footpaths along its banks south of the villages of East Ruston and Honing. A canoe is an even better option: hire one at Wayford Bridge and paddle along Tyler's Cut to reach the staithe at the Honing Road bridge at the end of the channel, from where you can easily walk into Dilham village with its Cross Keys pub.

Like Holt, most of Tudor North Walsham went up in flames, on this occasion in 1600, and most of the town's larger buildings date from the Georgian period. The town centre is a pleasant enough place to wander but the only real sights as such are the **Market Cross**, sometimes referred to locally as 'the gazebo', which has stood on the spot since 1550 but has been restored many times since, and **St Nicolas's Church** with its partially collapsed tower and rood screen covered in paintings depicting the apostles.

11 WORSTEAD

This solid, distinguished-looking village with its seemingly oversized church has a long historic association with the medieval Norfolk wool trade. The clue, of course, is in the name, as the village became well-known for producing a particular type of cloth. 'Walsham' cloth was light and for summer wear, while 'Worstead' was heavier. The first cloth description soon went out of common use, but the village still gives its name to worsted, even though it has not been produced in the village for centuries. Worsted cloth was introduced to East Anglia by Flemish immigrant weavers and the soft-textured but hardwearing material became highly sought-after from the 13th century onwards. Back in the medieval heyday of Norfolk's weaving industry, Worstead was a thriving place with two churches – more of a town than a village – but as the wool trade shifted to the mill towns of the north of England, its economy started to dwindle. There are still a few weavers' cottages there, characterised by their high ceilings, lofty enough to accommodate a loom. Perhaps more remarkable is that Worstead still has an active, if rather symbolic, Guild of Weavers who sometimes put on demonstrations of their ancient craft.

St Mary's Church, built with wool money in 1379, stands tall in the centre of the village and has a number of noteworthy features other than its sheer size: an impressive hammerbeam roof, box pews and a finely painted dado.

The **Worstead Festival** (worsteadfestival.org), the largest village festival in Norfolk, held each year on the last weekend in July, gives villagers the chance to show off a bit and makes for a fine day out. This is the perfect excuse for displaying rare breeds and prize farm animals and demonstrating country crafts from ploughing with heavy horses to sheep shearing, beekeeping and falconry. Classic farm vehicles and vintage cars are dusted off to take part in a parade and there is usually live music in the village square.

EAST RUSTON

Halfway between North Walsham and Stalham, close to the route of the Weavers' Way, this sprawling village is home to the **East Ruston Old Vicarage Garden** (01692 650432 e-ruston-oldvicaragegardens. co.uk), a rather special 32-acre garden open to the public from Wednesday to Sunday between April and October. It's less than two miles from the coast and vulnerable to onshore winds but the shelter of a belt of pines helps to maintain a relatively warm microclimate. Themed garden areas include the Californian Border and Desert Wash, a Tree Fern Garden, Sunken Garden and so on, as well as a wildlife flower meadow and cornfields sown with native species that have become rare in this age of herbicides. A pot of tea taken on the lawn here on a hot summer's afternoon with bees buzzing in the borders is an unbridled pleasure. The garden is not in the village itself but further east towards the coast along the Bacton Road, just beyond East Ruston church: there are guided tours on the second and fourth Tuesday of the month.

13 STALHAM & 14 SUTTON

These are two separate villages on the bend of the A149 at the northern limit of the Broads, both linked to the River Ant and Barton Broad by staithes. **Stalham High Street** is a hotchpotch of small shops and architectural styles but the town is probably best known locally for its supermarket that shall be nameless (but which rhymes with 'al fresco'), which, after years and years of planning permission being turned down, eventually took over the traditional saleground next to the bypass. It was inevitable, I suppose, that something as unfashionable as a weekly market and auction would finally give way to yet another 'out of town' shopping centre.

Stalham does, however, have an interesting **Museum of the Broads** (✆ 01692 581681 ⊘ museumofthebroads.org.uk ☉ Mar–Oct daily) down at the staithe, where you can see a mock-up of a wherry's cuddy (see box, pages 98–9) and plenty more relating to the working life of the Broads. The museum puts on occasional events in the summer and runs river trips on *Falcon*, a Victorian steam launch on some days. The tiny **Firehouse Museum** (✆ 01692 582781 ⊘ stalhamfirehousemuseum. co.uk ☉ Easter–end Sep) on the High Street is a fittingly eccentric place, the second-oldest fire station in the UK, built in 1833, with a 1902 fire engine and an array of fire-fighting paraphernalia on display.

Sutton has **Sutton Mill** just east of the village – at nine storeys high, the tallest remaining windmill in the UK (awaiting restoration and currently not open for visitors). The mill was built around 1789 on the site of a former tower mill.

15 COLTISHALL

🏠 **Norfolk Mead Hotel** (page 257)

Coltishall, better known as the site of an RAF base that existed to the north of here until recently, is actually quite a pretty village that sits in a bend of the River Bure. Formerly important for its malthouses and as a loading point for wherries travelling the Bure as far as Aylsham, the village's river trade fell into decline with the arrival of the railway line in 1879. Navigation beyond Coltishall became altogether impossible when the lock gates at Horstead were destroyed in a flood in 1912, and even today this remains the end of the line for boats venturing up from Wroxham.

Coming from Wroxham, the river bends sharply at **Belaugh** before it reaches Coltishall, and having passed the village meanders sluggishly

A riverside walk from Coltishall

✺ OS Explorer OL40 or Landranger 134; start: Coltishall bridge, ♀ TG267198; 4.5 miles; easy–moderate

An enjoyable **circular walk** from Coltishall is to follow the footpath along the north bank of the River Bure through woodland as far as Mayton Bridge at Little Hautbois, where you can cross the bridge to the south bank and cross fields via Hall Farm back to Horstead and Coltishall. I say 'enjoyable' but last time I walked it after a long period of rain the nettles along this path grew so tall that even my face got stung. Normally though, it is far more manageable and a lovely waterside excursion through dappled shade in the company of dragonflies. A lengthier alternative is to continue northwest from Little Hautbois towards Lamas and Buxton, then return along the river path on the south bank as far as Little Hautbois bridge before taking the route described above.

through lovely woodland west of **Great Hautbois** – superb, safe canoeing territory that is often frequented by school groups. Great Hautbois – pronounced 'Hobbis' – gets its odd name not from 'high woods' or oboes but from the Alto Bosco or Haut Bois family, who acquired land in the area just after the Norman conquest. The village of Great Hautbois was the head of navigation of the River Bure in medieval times. There's a Little Hautbois too, halfway to Buxton, a tiny place that consists of just eight houses, one of which used to be a pub. Formerly, it was important enough to warrant its own church. The church has all but disappeared today but traces of its foundations can apparently still be seen in the grounds of Little Hautbois Hall.

ⅱ FOOD & DRINK

A Piece of Cake The River Rooms, Church Close, Coltishall ✎ 01603 736090
🖉 coltishallcakes.co.uk. Established in 2010 by two local women, this traditional-style tea room on the High Street serves homemade cakes, light lunches and breakfasts. The tea room relocated in 2014 to new premises in what used to be the old Salvation Army hall. Depending on the weather, there are inside tables or an outside walled courtyard to choose from.
Recruiting Sergeant Norwich Rd, Horstead ✎ 01603 737077 🖉 recruitingsergeant.co.uk. In the village of Horstead, just south of the bridge that leads into Coltishall. The pub menu here makes use of Swannington Farm meat and local seasonal vegetables. Real ales include Adnams, Greene King and Woodforde's.

16 WROXHAM & HOVETON

These two villages are practically joined at the hip – or rather, at the bridge. Many people, especially visitors, tend to refer to the whole settlement as Wroxham, much to the annoyance of Hovetonites. Effectively, for those who come here to hire a boat, lick an ice cream or shop at Roys, the business end of the village is immediately north of Wroxham Bridge – in Hoveton.

Wroxham (I have lapsed already – it should actually be Hoveton) is famous for two things: as the epicentre of the **broads cruiser hire** trade and self-appointed 'Capital of The Broads', and for **Roys**, the 'world's biggest village store', a local enterprise that is ubiquitous hereabouts. Ask any local, 'Where's Roys?' and they will know what you mean, although they might be incredulous that you need to ask. They'll point you towards Roys supermarket, anyway.

Roys was founded back in 1899 by two brothers, Arnold and Alfred Roy, to meet the needs of holiday makers visiting the Norfolk Broads. Now it has branches throughout Norfolk and, to its credit, prides itself on selling locally sourced produce. Roys of Wroxham is well known throughout Norfolk but, technically, as all of the Roys commercial property lies north of the bridge, it really ought to be called 'Roys of Hoveton'.

Hoveton is anything but a typical sleepy Norfolk village. Once you cross the narrow bridge over the River Bure you'll find the place heaving with people in the summer. However, even if you do not wish to step out on to a motor cruiser here, it's still a good place to rent a canoe and paddle upstream. Canoeing downstream, alongside a flotilla of inexpertly, and sometimes erratically, piloted hire-boats on their way to Wroxham Broad is not everybody's idea of fun but to strike out north along the River Bure towards Belaugh and Coltishall is well worth doing. **Canadian canoes** can be hired from Barnes Brinkcraft at Riverside Road (✆ 01603 782625 or 782333 ◌ barnesbrinkcraft.co.uk) or The Canoe Man (✆ 0845 4969177 ◌ thecanoeman.com) at Norfolk Broads Tourism and Activity Centre right beside the road bridge.

Hoveton Hall Gardens

✆ 01603 784297 ◌ hovetonhallestate.co.uk

Popular for their azalea and rhododendron displays in late spring, these attractive and peaceful gardens are just north of the town. Various walks lead through woods and around a lake, and a walled garden has an ornamental wrought iron gate in the form of a spider. Tucked away in the woods is an 18th-century ice well, a brick-lined pit formerly used for storing ice for the house. The woodland has several adventure trails for children and there are suggestions as to what may be seen in terms of birds, butterflies and dragonflies along the way. Buzzards and hobbies are sometimes seen in summer, as are swallowtail butterflies occasionally.

BeWILDerwood

✆ 01692 633033 ⊘ bewilderwood.co.uk

A little way along the A1062 Horning Road, BeWILDerwood describes itself as a 'curious treehouse adventure park'. Certainly, it's designed to exercise and stimulate the mind as much as the body. It's a magical place for children – forest folk like Mildred, the vegetarian Crocklebog who lives in Scary Lake, and the Twiggles, litter-hating goblin-like figures, are BeWILDerwood residents, as is a giant spider called Thornyclod.

BeWILDerwood's environmental pedigree is certainly impressive too. The treehouses, ropewalks and boardwalks are all built from sustainable wood, while the 50 acres of marshland and woodland that make up the site are entirely pesticide-free, guaranteeing that no harmful chemicals leak into the broads. If that were not enough, some 14,000 broad-leaved trees have been planted since the park's creation and the food on site is mainly locally sourced and organic. BeWILDerwood won the British Guild of Travel Writers award for best new UK tourism project in 2008; as Jane Anderson, who nominated the park for the award, attests it 'harks back to a pre-PlayStation, pre-mobile, pre-iPod era' even if its creator Tom Blofield does admit to having been partly inspired by the 1990s computer game Myst. BeWILDerwood is open year-round and those under 92cm/3 feet tall go free. Bikes are available to rent at the **Norfolk Broads Cycling Centre** in the car park (*✆ 07887 480331 ⊘* norfolkbroadscycling.co.uk) which also provides useful free cycling maps.

Wroxham Barns

✆ 01603 783762 ⊘ wroxhambarns.co.uk

A couple of miles north of Hoveton along Tunstead Road, Wroxham Barns is a range of 18th-century barns and farm buildings that have been converted into craft workshops. Here, you'll find such things as woodturning, pottery and stained glass, all made on site with the finished goods being sold from the workshops. Several enterprises sell local produce, such as the **AppleShop** (✆ 01683 784876), which stocks both cider and apple juice produced by the Norfolk Cider Company and stages occasional demonstrations using antique apple pressing equipment. Animal-loving children are well catered for as well, with a **Junior Farm** that provides an opportunity for children to get up close to animals in a farmyard setting, offering activities like feeding rabbits and goats and grooming ponies.

BARTON BROAD, HICKLING BROAD & AROUND

17 HORNING

Heading east from Hoveton along the A1062 the first place that you come to is Horning, which, from a boating point of view, lies downstream along the River Bure beyond **Wroxham Broad**, **Hoveton Great Broad** and **Hoveton Little Broad**. Horning functions a little like a mini version of Wroxham. Firmly given over to the hire cruiser trade, it's all Edwardian thatch roofs and mock Tudor cottages but pleasant enough nevertheless. Sadly, the seasonal passenger ferry that used to cross the river here from the Horning Ferry pub to Woodbastwick no longer operates. From Horning, the River Bure meanders east through the Bure Marshes, with channels connecting it with Cockshoot Broad and Ranworth Broad, both ripe for exploration by curious boatmen.

18 LUDHAM, HOW HILL & AROUND

The next village reached by taking the road is **Ludham**, a pleasant, typical Broads village that does not sit on the river itself but just to the north of it. The village clusters around a crossroads with a pub and a church, and a road opposite the pub leads south past attractive houses with large gardens fronting on to **Womack Water**, a tributary of the River Thurne that serves as a staithe for boats. If you visit on Ludham Open Gardens Day, held every other year in June, you will get the chance to see some of these gardens. Horsefen Road, which leads south along the eastern bank of Womack Water, is similar, with some thatch-roofed barns, the parish staithe and a couple of boatyards. A staithe along here serves as headquarters for the **Norfolk Wherry Trust** (✆ wherryalbion. com) where the wherry *Albion* is moored when it is not out on charter.

Given so many water's-edge back gardens, it is perfectly possible for many Ludham residents to visit each other by boat, as I am sure some of them do.

The River Ant joins the Bure just south of Ludham and, a little way along this, How Hill rises above the river with its gardens, woodland and manicured lawns. Lest this sound too dramatic, I should add that How Hill, while undoubtedly the highest point for miles around, still only manages to reach about 40 feet above sea level. It is a hill, nevertheless – a welcome meniscus in this overwhelmingly two-dimensional landscape.

How Hill House is a residential Broads Study Centre that hosts courses and conferences and is not usually open to the public, although holiday courses and special events are organised by the **How Hill Trust** (✆ 01692 678555 ◌ howhilltrust.org.uk).

A narrow road with passing places leads up from a junction just before Ludham and there is a free car park on the left just before the main building. The large meadow here – Fisherman's Field – is a popular spot for locals to take picnics, play cricket and fly kites. A track leads across this down to **Toad Hole Cottage**, a small marshman's cottage containing a museum and information centre (✆ 01692 678763). A **wildlife walking trail** starts from here, but even better is the **water trail** that lasts for about an hour and makes use of the *Electric Eel* electric boat.

"It is perfectly possible for many Ludham residents to visit each other by boat, as I am sure some of them do."

A Broadland water trail on the *Electric Eel*

Maximum 6 passengers; book in advance at Toad Hole Cottage ◌ the *Electric Eel* leaves every hour on the hour 11.00–15.00 on weekends, bank holidays, Easter week & half terms in Apr, May & Oct, & Jun–Sep daily 10.00–16.00

Taking me out on the *Electric Eel* at How Hill in late May, Paul, the boatman, gave me the low-down on traditional Broadland ways and how, with encouragement from the Broads Authority, some aspects of the traditional economy are currently being revived. After gliding past a kingfisher's nest in the bank where, perfectly on cue, such a bird darted past us like a rocket-propelled jewel, Paul pointed out a couple of small windmills next to the water where the sails had been removed. 'Do you see what they've done there?' he asked, just a little exasperated. 'Would that be anything to do with Health and Safety?' I ventured.

'Yes, absolutely right. They said they were a hazard for walkers. Can you believe it? They're nine foot above the ground for heaven's sake.'

We soon turned off the River Ant down a narrow tributary to leave the diesel-engine throb of the motor boats far behind. This really was another world, a minimalist landscape of reed, water and a blue slice of sky. Reed has been harvested for centuries in the region for use as thatch but the industry went into decline back in the Victorian period when the railways made cheap pan-tiles and slate available to all. Nowadays, thatch is back in fashion, and there's considerable demand for reed harvested in the Norfolk Broads, as well as the sedge that is used to 'top' the thatch. Reed harvesting is clearly not an easy job. 'You need to be a special character to be a reed cutter,' said Paul. 'It's hard, laborious work and, in the winter when you have to do the cutting, it's freezing cold too. The sedge has to be cut in the summer months and that's just the opposite: there's mosquitoes to bother you and your hands get cut up from gathering the sedge.'

Although reed-cutting is clearly no career for lonely, work-shy rheumatics, there is enough demand for the Norfolk product that the Broads Authority have been training up the young and willing over the past few years and employment has been created for at least a dozen local cutters. There is no question about quality according to Paul. 'Polish reed is a bit cheaper but it doesn't last anywhere near as long. Most thatchers reckon that Norfolk reed lasts for anything between 80 and 100 years.'

After an hour of squeezing through narrow, reed-fringed channels, we head back to How Hill Staithe. On the way, we stop off at Reedham Broad, a recently reclaimed body of water that has resident bitterns and summer-breeding marsh harriers – a pair of which were quartering the reeds on the other side of the water, painstakingly searching for voles and mice. 'This was a reclaimed meadow with cows on it just 30 years ago but the Broads Authority have encouraged it to revert back to nature. It's manmade, I suppose, but then so are all the broads.'

¶¶ FOOD & DRINK

Alfresco Tea Room Norwich Rd, Ludham ✐ 01692 678384 ⊘ alfrescotearoom.co.uk. Opposite Ludham's St Catherine's Church, this is a fine place for afternoon tea and cakes. There's an indoor tea room and even a small, al fresco element – two tables outside in the back yard.

9 BARTON BROAD

The **River Ant** twists north past How Hill to open into Barton Broad, one of the finest and most unspoiled of all these bodies of water. Barton Broad is the second largest body of water in the broads system and is managed as a nature reserve by the Norfolk Wildlife Trust. Hemmed in by reed beds and swampy stands of alder, the broad is barely approachable by road and the only meaningful way to visit – other than walking along the short boardwalk – is by canoe or boat.

An excellent **boardwalk** starts from the car park near Gay's Staithe. To reach it, you first need to undertake a short half-mile walk along a footpath and lane to arrive at the start. The trail soon splits into two: one direction leads to a viewing point that looks over the southern edge of the broad, while the other takes a short circular course through the alder carr. It's very green and humid here, with warblers warbling in the trees, dragonflies hawking the moist air and yellow irises pushing up through the sedge. Watch out for mosquitoes though; they can sometimes be a nuisance on warm, still days.

"It's very green and humid here, with dragonflies hawking the moist air and yellow irises pushing up through the sedge."

A decade or so ago, Barton Broad was heavily polluted with nutrients from agricultural and sewage run-off but the multi-million-pound **Clear Water Project** has improved the water quality dramatically, even to the point of attracting otters back to the area. Back in the 1960s, the water here was a toxic chemical soup of phosphates (from sewage) and nitrates (from farms). Now, with investment from bodies such as the Millennium Fund and, fittingly, some detergent manufacturers, there has been a dramatic transformation. This is mainly thanks to painstaking suction dredging that has removed the nutrient-rich mud at the bottom of the broad and its channels. Although otters are present, you are far more likely to see herons, grebes, terns and a variety of ducks. Swallowtail butterflies are relatively common at the right time of year – between May and July – too. The waters of Barton Broad host an open regatta each August Bank Holiday organised by the Norfolk Punt Club, and the broad is also used by the Nancy Oldfield Trust to provide sailing and canoeing access for the disabled.

Barton Broad has three villages that just about touch it – **Irstead**, **Barton Turf** and **Neatishead** – none of which could be described as a metropolis, although Neatishead does have a pub and a shop.

Barton Turf has an interesting church with fine paintings on its rood screen but no other facilities whatsoever. Such a distinct lack of facilities may, in fact, represent a temptation for those in search of peace and quiet. A friend of mine who moved to Neatishead from London a dozen or so years ago told me: 'I've got used to living there; I've become a country boy now. Neatishead's got most things we need, like a pub and a restaurant. It's a lovely place to live. Every Saturday morning, we take the children for a walk along the boardwalk at Barton Broad and if we want a taste of big city lights then we just drive into Wroxham and go shopping at Roys. I hardly ever go into Norwich these days, let alone London.'

"The stretch of the bank between Barton Turf and Neatishead is known locally as 'Millionaires' Row'."

The stretch of the bank between Barton Turf and Neatishead is known locally as 'Millionaires' Row'. The posh, two-storey boathouses at the water's edge are just the icing on the cake, belonging as they do to large private houses in sumptuous surroundings set well back from the water. Barton Hall on the edge of Barton Turf village is where Lord Nelson's sister once lived and it is claimed that Nelson learned to sail on Barton Broad, presumably when he wasn't doing the same thing in Brancaster Staithe harbour.

Although it is hard to reach Barton Broad using public transport – Smallburgh or Stalham being about as close as you can get – the whole area west of Barton Broad makes for vintage cycling territory. With a bike, you might also wish to venture south of Neatishead to **Alderfen Broad**, another NWT reserve just outside **Irstead Street** – it's a decent circular walk too, starting in Neatishead. How Hill lies just across the marsh to the east but there is no direct way to reach it on either land or water.

Barton Broad by boat

I was lucky enough to tour Barton Broad by boat back in the days when the solar-powered *Ra* used to sail here (organised boat trips are sadly no longer available). As we progressed around the south end of the Broad, enjoying the sight of candy-striped grebe chicks riding on their parents' backs, Mike, the boat's skipper, pointed out a narrow channel leading off to the east. 'That's called Ice House Reach. There used to be an icehouse just down there. Ice was collected from the broad and stored there before it was transported all the way down to Yarmouth by wherry.'

Cruising up to the northern end of the Broads where the River Ant makes its entrance, we turned our attention to the water lilies dotting the water's surface. 'They're a really good sign of clean water', says Mike. Yellow water lily needs good water quality; white needs even better. What's remarkable is that they can lie dormant for years. Water lilies weren't here at all during the 1960s and 70s, when it was like a pea soup here. As soon as the water quality got better they started to appear again, growing from tubers that had lain dormant in the mud at the bottom for decades.'

The Broads, as everyone now knows, are a manmade environment, but it's easy to overlook the way that they have been altered to fit in with man's changing needs over the years. According to Mike, the River Ant did not originally pass through Barton Broad but passed just to the east of it. Irish workmen known as navigators were employed to cut a channel through to the broad so that wherries could be used to transport goods. 'Irish navvies did a lot of work in the Broads. They dug the channel here back in 1729 and there is even a Paddy's Lane in Barton Turf in memory of them.'

If you are up to it, an excellent way to explore the broad is to hire a **canoe** for the day from Wayford Bridge. To canoe south along the River Ant, cross Barton Broad, head up Lime Kiln Dyke to moor and visit Neatishead and perhaps have lunch before returning north, will probably take the best part of a day. It's a fairly energetic outing but, at the end of such a day, you will have better memories and a far more intimate impression of the Broads than will those who have chugged through them in a cruiser.

FOOD & DRINK

The White Horse Inn The Street, Neatishead NR12 8AD ✆ 01692 630828
⬠ thewhitehorseinnneatishead.com. This traditional inn tucked away in Neatishead village is probably the best bet for dining in the Barton Broad. It sources food from plenty of local suppliers, including Swannington Farm, Pye Bakery and Direct Seafoods, who provide many ingredients for its varied menu. The pub also has its own brewery producing a range of real ales. What's more, it makes its own 'Hopton Gin', which is infused with hops to create a unique flavour.

CANOE HIRE

Bank Dayboat & Canoe Hire Wayford Bridge ✆ 01692 582457 ⬠ bankboats.co.uk

20 ST BENET'S ABBEY

Guided tours led by volunteers available between May & end Sep, 14.00 Wed & 15.00 Sat & Sun; meet at the information board near the gatehouse

This atmospheric ruin was built on land granted by King Canute around 1020, probably on the site of a 9th-century pre-Viking hermitage. It's something of a rarity in having a pre-Norman origin and also for managing to survive the Dissolution. It did this by agreeing to a crafty swap of lands belonging to the Diocese of Norwich. The Bishop of Norwich continues to hold the role of abbot here and, once a year on the first Sunday in August, he arrives by wherry to preach an annual service at the site. The gatehouse contains a windmill, squeezed within its walls, that was put up by a local farmer at the turn of the 19th century. A more recent addition is the oak altar cross made from wood given by the Royal Sandringham estate. The Norwich School artist, John Sell Cotman, made a painting of the abbey in the middle of the 19th century, when it looked much as it does today, albeit with sails still present on the windmill. You can see this in Norwich Castle Museum in addition to another splendid painting of it by Henry Bright.

"St Benet's Abbey is at its best viewed from the banks of the river at dusk."

With a mysterious profile that combines these ecclesiastical and vernacular traditions, St Benet's Abbey is at its best viewed from the banks of the river at dusk, when long shadows help to enhance the numinous atmosphere.

For those lacking river transport, a visit to the site requires a detour south from the main road at Ludham – an easy cycle ride. The farm track that leads down to the abbey goes past a farmyard that has an enormous high midden of used car tyres of all shapes and sizes. So, if you were curious as to the fate of all the old tyres discarded in Norfolk, now you know.

In summer 2012, a two-year conservation project under the auspices of the **Norfolk Archaeological Trust** (norfarchtrust.org.uk/stbenets) began at St Benet's Abbey with the aim of not only conserving the remains of the abbey but also of providing more information on the site and improving access. A variety of special activities now frequently take place at the site – wildlife workshops, history days, wildlife surveys and storytelling.

HISTORY

Norfolk was first settled in prehistoric times. Both Romans and Normans left their mark on the county, with an extensive fortress at Burgh Castle (Gariannonum) and an impressive castle and cathedral in Norwich. A large number of medieval monasteries were established in Norfolk following the Norman invasion.

1 All that remains of the deserted medieval village of Godwick is a ruined church tower and field marks where the village streets once stood. 2 Burgh Castle near Great Yarmouth was built by the Romans to defend themselves against invaders. 3 Caister Castle was constructed by Sir John Falstaff in the mid 15th century. 4 Cart lodge built of local carrstone at Ringstead in northwest Norfolk.

EVENTS & COMMUNITY

Whatever the time of year, there is usually something going on somewhere in Norfolk. From weekly markets dating back to medieval times, to annual food and music festivals, as well as special arts and heritage events.

1 The Crab and Lobster Festival takes place each May in the streets of Sheringham. **2** The Norfolk & Norwich Festival held in Norwich each May features music, arts and plenty of street theatre events. **3** The Sheringham Shantymen bring songs of the sea to their home port. **4** Each September in Burston, participants march to commemorate the historic Burston School strike. **5** The Waveney Valley Sculpture Trail is an art and landscape event held in south Norfolk in late summer. **6** Courtyard Farm in northwest Norfolk is wildlife rich and welcoming to walkers.

HOUSES & GARDENS

A number of large estates with grand country houses and landscaped gardens were established in Norfolk from the 16th century onwards. The most famous are probably Sandringham House, a country retreat for the royal family since the mid 19th century, Holkham Hall, built for Thomas Coke, the first Earl of Leicester, in the early 18th century, and Blickling Hall built in Jacobean style in the early 1600s.

3

1 Sandringham House is set in 60 acres of landscaped gardens. **2** The Palladian mansion that is Holkham Hall has a library second to none. **3** The walled garden at Hoveton Hall in the Broads has splendid perennial borders. **4** Blickling Hall, near Aylsham, is a superb example of Jacobean architecture. **5** Felbrigg Hall, near Cromer, has walled gardens, orchards and 1,760 acres of parkland. **6** Oxburgh Hall, once home to the Bedingfield family, is everyone's idea of the classic stately home.

4

5

6

LANDSCAPES

The Norfolk landscape is far more varied than many outsiders imagine. Fairly low-lying but rolling in places, Norfolk is surrounded on three sides by sea and criss-crossed by slow-flowing rivers and shallow valleys. With its unique combination of inland waterways, marshes, reed beds, heaths and coastal salt marshes, Norfolk provides valuable habitat for some of Britain's rarest and most distinctive wildlife.

1 Flat-bottomed trading wherries were once a common sight on Norfolk's rivers and broads. **2** The winter rook roost at Buckenham Carrs in the Yare Valley is a timeless spectacular event. **3** Bearded tit is a rare reed bed species found in Norfolk. **4** Burgh Castle Reach near the confluence of the Yare and Waveney rivers. **5** Many windmills can be found in the Broads area, such as this one at Thurne. **6** The narrower waterways of the Norfolk Broads are ideal canoeing territory. **7** Humorous sign on a gate near Worstead, very Norfolk in tone. **8** Extensive salt marshes at Stiffkey on the north Norfolk coast.

Horse muck 40ₚ
Equine residue 50ₚ
Poo des chevaux €1·00

NORWICH

For centuries in the medieval period, Norwich was England's second-largest city. With a wealth of interesting architecture and more medieval churches than any other city in Europe, there is much to see of historical interest. The city has a modern face too, with a lively university and art school, and an exhaustive choice of pub, cafés and restaurants.

1 The clock tower of Norwich City Hall as seen from the River Wensum. **2** The charming Edwardian passageway of the Norwich Royal Arcade, supposedly home to a 'ghost shop'. **3** Norwich Castle, with its Norman keep, is now a museum. **4** Princes Street, close to Norwich Cathedral, is one of the city centre's many historic streets.

1 WOODBASTWICK

South of the River Bure, a minor road runs more or less parallel to the river and the A1062 beyond, connecting several villages on the southern fringe of the broads east of Wroxham. **Salhouse** village lies some distance from the broad of the same name – and its station lies even further away and is pretty useless for waterside exploration. **Woodbastwick**, the next village to the east, with a good pub and brewery, is an altogether better bet. Just east of the village, the road splits and a track leads down to the Bure where there is parking and a nature trail through the reed beds. **Woodforde's Brewery** (woodfordes.co.uk) next door to the Fur and Feather Inn runs occasional brewery tours that must be booked in advance (01603 720353). They have a shop and visitor centre too where, as well as bottles and beer-boxes, you can buy souvenirs that range from key rings to T-shirts.

FOOD & DRINK

Fur and Feather Inn Slad Lane NR13 6HQ 01603 720003 thefurandfeather.co.uk. A very popular thatched pub with a fireplace and newspapers but no pool table or juke box. The food is mostly hearty English – steak and kidney pudding, venison pie, fancy burgers and the like – while the beer is excellent, and so it should be with the Woodforde's brewery right next door.

2 RANWORTH

Ranworth is a charming, dinky little village right next to Malthouse Broad, little brother of neighbouring Ranworth Broad. Ranworth's **St Helen's Church** is well worth a visit, not simply because it has some of the best screen paintings in the county and a beautifully illuminated antiphoner (service book) on display, but because it has a feature that offers something that geology does not in this neck of the woods – elevation. A steep, tightly curving staircase leads up 89 steps to the roof of the church tower. It's very narrow so try to avoid two-way traffic if at all possible. The view is undoubtedly worth the climb: the broad and river are laid out in front of you and Broadland comes alive and suddenly means a lot more than just blue and green shading on a map. From here, as well as from Ranworth and Malthouse Broads immediately below, you can see the Bure and Ant rivers, How Hill, the wind turbines near Happisburgh and even the coast at Yarmouth. On a really clear day, Norwich Cathedral spire is said to be visible.

Ranworth Broad is a NWT reserve of some importance, with a visitor centre, boardwalk and child-friendly nature trail along with the usual range of Broadland wildlife: plentiful wildfowl in the winter months and dragonflies and swallowtails in summer. There's also an enormous roost of cormorants, one of the largest inland roosts in the country. During World War II, a number of wherries met their fate in the water here, by design rather than by accident, sunk to obstruct enemy hydroplanes attempting to land here. More wherries were sunk in the post-war years to prevent erosion of the broad's banks. Indeed, this is where the wherry *Maud*, now happily afloat again, was dredged up from in the early 1980s.

BLACK SAILS IN THE SUNSET – THE NORFOLK WHERRY

Undoubtedly the most iconic craft on the Broads system, the Norfolk Wherry evolved as a cargo boat based upon the design of the earlier Norfolk Keel, a square-rigged, clinker-built vessel. Norfolk Keels started to vanish from service around 1800 and were succeeded by wherries that could be sailed using a smaller crew. The typical wherry was a shallow-bottomed, double-ended, single-sail boat fitted with a gaff rig; its sail was black as a result of weatherproofing with tar and fish oil. The tall mast was fitted with a counterweight so that it could be lowered to pass under bridges. Most wherries were capable of transporting around 25 tons of goods, which they would carry from boats anchored off the coast at Great Yarmouth or Lowestoft upriver through the broads system. Although once a common sight, they were in steep decline by the 1940s as cargo was increasingly transported by road and rail.

Eight wherries survive in Norfolk today, one of which spent 40 years in Paris as a houseboat before its return to the Broads in 2005. A few have been lovingly restored in recent years. The 60-foot *Albion*, probably the best known, was originally used to haul coal between Bungay and Lowestoft. This vessel has had a colourful, if chequered, career: sinking near Great Yarmouth in 1929, to be raised three days later, and then losing her mast in 1931. Today, *Albion* is based at Womack Water near Ludham and has been maintained by the Norfolk Wherry Trust since 1949. The craft may be chartered with a skipper and mate for groups of up to 12 people, while members of the Trust have the opportunity to go on pleasure cruises several times a year at a reduced rate. In summer they hold open days when you can meet the crew and look around the boat for free.

As I was shown round the *Albion*, what impressed me most was learning that the 40-ton boat, and other wherries like it, were sailed using just a two-man crew. 'Man and boy, or man and wife, there was just two to

The **boardwalk** to the NWT visitor centre leads from the car park opposite The Maltsters pub, turning a corner past private moorings and continuing a little along the road before it leads into woodland. A magnificent, and very ancient, oak tree stands near the entrance of the boardwalk, which continues through alder carr (see page 65) until you reach the thatched visitor centre close to where Maltsters and Ranworth Broad meet. There's an observation point here and fantastic views over the broad and back to Ranworth church. A number of guided wildlife water trails run from the car park staithe (✆ 01603 270479), and there is a regular ferry service (10 mins) to the visitor centre as an alternative to following the boardwalk on foot.

sail it,' I was told. 'And if they didn't sail, they didn't get paid.' What goods did the wherry carry? 'It carried anything that needed to be carried – coal, bricks, flour, grain – and in the winter when there was ice on the broad it might carry ice down to Yarmouth too. This one worked mostly on the southern system – you know, on the Waveney – but it got about quite a bit.' Standing on the deck you can't help but be impressed by the enormous tree-trunk of a mast that stands proud on the deck. 'They lowered that while they were in motion as they approached the bridges. They were so good at doing it that they didn't even need to slow down.' Below decks, things are pretty cramped and you soon learn that the 'business end' of the boat – the storage area – is, in fact, most of the boat, and there is little space for frivolities like comfort. The sharp end has a tiny cabin called a 'cuddy' where there are two narrow bunks separated by a cast-iron stove – cramped but endearingly cosy.

Another wherry, the *Maud*, was moored in the next staithe, a slightly larger, 42-ton vessel. The skipper on board had sailed wherries in his youth, as had his father and grandfather before him. Massive rope-tying hands seemed to be part of the family inheritance. 'My dad used to carry a chain through the streets of Yarmouth on his way to the boat. He used to throw it in the water to slow it down.' The *Maud* worked right up until her demise in 1965 when she was sunk at Ranworth Broad as protection for the narrow spit of land separating it from Malthouse Broad. She was moved in 1976 to another part of the broad before being resunk. The boat was eventually rescued from the mud to be slowly and painstakingly restored by Vincent and Linda Pargeter between 1981 and 1999. Now she is back on the water once more – a floating museum piece with far more history in her timbers than the photographic display in the hold could possibly hope to relate.

23 SOUTH WALSHAM & SOUTH WALSHAM BROAD

⚐ **Clippesby Hall Touring & Camping Park** near Acle (page 257)

A mile or two south of Ranworth, **South Walsham** sits astride the old Norwich to Acle road. The village is a quiet, rural place, with a pub, a post office and some modern housing tucked away behind the old buildings.

The village is home to the lovely **Fairhaven Woodland and Water Garden** (✆ 01603 270449 ⌂ fairhavengarden.co.uk), which comprises over 130 acres of mature oak woodland (one tree is said to be 950 years old), and shady bluebell and candelabra primula-carpeted glades divided by waterways with footbridges stretching across them. I once inadvertently dropped a telephoto lens into the water whilst crossing a bridge here. I managed to retrieve it, but it was never the same again: every image I've taken since has a little speck of South Walsham silt floating in the frame. Moral: do not try to change lenses when crossing water.

The gardens lead down to privately owned South Walsham Broad from where, between April and October, it is possible to take a short boat trip out on to the broad, or a longer one across the broad and along Fleet Dike to get a view of St Benet's Abbey. The gardens are probably at their best in late spring when the naturalised candelabra primula and rhododendrons are at their prime, but every season has its charms, even winter. The Fairhaven Garden Trust has been run as a charity since 1975 and all gardening is done entirely organically using just leaf mould and compost as fertiliser. Both the trust office and the tea room are managed in a sustainable manner too.

Just north of the village, **South Walsham Broad** is linked to the River Bure by way of Fleet Dike. There's a footpath that leads past a boatyard all the way along the dike from a car park, and if you fancy making a **circular walk** from here it is quite a long six miles or so via the river and Upton Fen before you return to your starting point. There are no viable short cuts, but it is rewarding and varied.

From the car park, walk past the boatyard along Fleet Dike, where a number of hire boats are usually moored up. As you approach the confluence with the River Bure, you cannot help but see the unmistakable form of St Benet's Abbey ahead on the opposite bank; in fact, you will see it before you see the river itself. The path turns east and along the river, where there will be ditches full of reed and marshy grazing to your right and broads cruisers – and if you are lucky, possibly a wherry – plying the river to your left. Here and there, you'll pass clumps of gnarled old willows. In early summer, there'll be sedge warblers singing in the reeds, dragonflies darting through the air and tortoiseshell, and perhaps even swallowtail, butterflies flapping around.

As the river curves southeast past a drainage pump, continue until it curves the other way and you can see a concrete farm track striking off south across the marshes. Follow this for some way as it zigzags across the marshes away from the river and you will eventually emerge at the far eastern end of the boggy woodland that surrounds Upton Broad. Although the zigzags might persuade you that you are heading the wrong way, don't be tempted to deviate across the marshes until you reach this point: I tried to once and ended up walking through Norfolk's largest nettle colony … in shorts – not to be recommended! A footpath leads from the farm track through a corner of the Upton Fen woods before reaching a road. Walk west through Cargate Green and take another footpath on the southern flank of the woods until you pass a large modern farm, Holly Farm, which has is a fishing pond.

The entrance to Upton Broad and Marshes NWT reserve is just down from here along Low Road, an important wetland site with rare dragonflies and butterflies like swallowtail and white admiral as well as many scarce water plants. It's a good place to see water voles too, with a waymarked trail and boardwalk for visitors. Back on the road, head across the T-junction to Pilson Green then turn right along the edge of a field where the houses start. Turn right when you reach the road and continue north along it a little way before taking another footpath that leads west after Town House Farm. This will take you back to the South Walsham Broad car park.

24 HICKLING BROAD

A water trail takes visitors by electric boat across the broad to visit boat-only bird hides & the Tree Tower, a 60ft-high observation deck. Boat trips last 1 or 2 hours (✆ 01692 598276 ☉ Easter–Oct; booking is advisable during school holidays). You can also enjoy a combined water trail safari & supper on Tue & Thu evenings (Jun–Aug), 2-hour evening water trails (May–end Aug 18.00 Wed) & a dawn chorus water trail on selected dates in late Apr & May. Hickling Broad, the largest in all the system, is the classic Norfolk broad, with blue water, golden reed beds and white-sailed yachts bobbing on the water. It's off limits to power craft, and with a good footpath (the Weavers' Way) around its southern side, it is almost as enjoyable for walkers as it is for sailors.

The scope for **birdwatching** is excellent: you can often see marsh harriers hawking the reed beds here, and hear sedge, marsh and Cetti's warblers exploding with song within them. In summer, at certain times at least, swallowtail butterflies are just part of the scenery. Like Barton Broad, Hickling Broad is a nature reserve under the jurisdiction of the Norfolk Wildlife Trust, which has a visitor centre (☉ Apr–Sep) and bird observation hides here. A water trail takes visitors by boat across the broad to visit the Tree Tower, a raised observation deck only accessible by the water trail, from where you can get a magnificent view over the broad to the North Sea coast beyond.

"In summer swallowtail butterflies are just part of the scenery."

Early summer, when the swallowtails and dragonflies are out and about, is perhaps the perfect time to be here but even winter is good if you are wrapped up against the wind that blows straight from the North Sea (it is no coincidence that both sailors and wind-surfers favour this broad). In winter, there is a daily **raptor roost** at Stubb Mill in the middle of the marshes just north of the broad, where you can witness birds of prey flying in to roost at dusk. This can be spectacular at times, with combinations of marsh and hen harriers, merlins, cranes and pink-footed geese. To visit, it is necessary to park at the NWT car park and walk half a mile or so to the viewing area.

Hickling village, just to the north of the broad, is a pleasant enough place to stop for refreshment. The village is split neatly into two parts – **Hickling Heath** and **Hickling Green** – with the former being of most interest to sailors because it is closer to the staithe. The former pub here, the Pleasure Boat Inn, right by the staithe, used to serve the wherry trade. A young Prince Charles spent a night here back in 1961 when his shooting party could not make it back to base. Seemingly, he was told off by the landlady for making too much noise whilst having a pillow fight. Hickling Green is mainly residential but has its own local, the Greyhound Inn. St Mary's Church, which lies a little way north of Hickling Green, has the curiosity of a horse-drawn hearse inside. Visiting Hickling Broad without a car is a challenge but far from impossible. Hickling village has bus services from Great Yarmouth and North Walsham, from where it is easy to connect to Norwich and Cromer.

South of Hickling Broad, straddling the busy A149, is **Potter Heigham**, a village resolutely geared to the boat hire trade. The village is best known in these parts for two things: its medieval bridge, under which many an inexperienced skipper has come a cropper, and Lathams, a super-cheap discount store. Less well known is its lovely round-towered St Nicholas Church tucked away at the edge of the village overlooking fields. The bridge dates back to 1385 and has a very low arch that can cause headaches (quite literally) to novice sailors. Fortunately, there is a bridge pilot to help boats safely through. There are dozens of waterside bungalows along the River Thurne here; one of them, downstream from the bridge, known as the 'Dutch Tutch' or 'Helter-skelter House', is fabricated from the bottom half of a helter-skelter that used to grace the end of Britannia Pier at Great Yarmouth and was the first residential building on this stretch of the river.

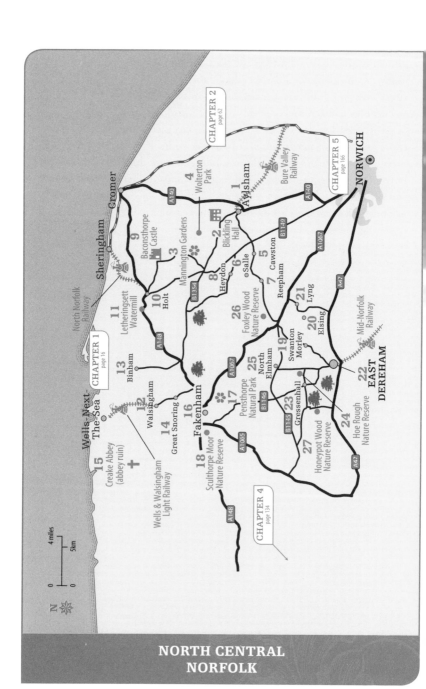

NORTH CENTRAL
NORFOLK

3
NORTH CENTRAL NORFOLK

Norfolk's wool country that once was – this chapter covers the north coast hinterland and the gently undulating landscape of what is sometimes cheekily referred to as 'upland Norfolk'. It's a region of small, solid Georgian towns and massive wool-trade churches, grand estates and country houses: an enclosed landscape with lighter soils and fewer hedgerows than further south. The area is bounded, more or less, by the market towns of Aylsham, Holt, Fakenham and East Dereham, although there will inevitably be the odd diversion. The main rivers here are the Wensum and Bure, which slowly converge as you head eastwards across the county, before coming together at Breydon Water outside Great Yarmouth.

Visitors tend to rush through this part of the county *en route* to the Norfolk coast, which is a pity because there's plenty of interest here. And it's true to say that you'll probably find more of the traditional spirit of north Norfolk away from the coast than at it. Holt is close enough to the fashionable north coast to have its own claim as an alternative base for visiting that region, a reality reflected in its range of smart shops and places to eat. Aylsham is more overlooked, despite the fact that the presence of Blickling Hall just down the road brings in quite a few visitors. This is a shame as, for my money, it's just as attractive as Holt. Fakenham and East Dereham are a little more humdrum, but both pleasant enough market towns with their own merits.

There are some highly appealing villages. Reepham and Cawston have imposing churches, while Salle is just an imposing church without a village. North Elmham has a Norman chapel and the site of East Anglia's former Saxon cathedral, while Little Walsingham, tucked away in lovely rolling countryside, has very much a living pilgrimage tradition. In between are sleepy villages like Heydon and even sleepier ones like, dare I say it, Great Snoring.

GETTING AROUND

This is straightforward enough: there are good roads to Aylsham and Fakenham from Norwich although it can take a long time to drive through the city's sprawling northern suburbs and satellite villages with their extensive new-builds. The main road to Holt branches off the Norwich to Cromer road at Norwich Airport and, once through a rather dreary commuter village, it's a nice drive through intermittent woodland and rolling farmland to reach the market town. East Dereham lies just off the A47 dual carriageway that links Norwich with King's Lynn. Away from these main roads, things are much, much quieter and you would get far more out of the experience by being on a bike.

PUBLIC TRANSPORT

The public transport network is reasonably good, with plenty of **buses** between Norwich and Aylsham, Fakenham and East Dereham, although Holt is better-connected with the coast than it is with the Norfolk capital. The fast, regular X1 service that links Great Yarmouth, Norwich, East Dereham and King's Lynn is ever-useful, as is the X29 that runs between Norwich and Fakenham. If you want to travel between towns within the area, like Aylsham and Holt for example, it's more problematic and will require a little more judicious juggling with connections; the website ⊘ travelineeastanglia.org.uk is useful. Two short **heritage railway** lines may also be of limited use: the Wells & Walsingham Light Railway (⊘ 01328 711630 ⊘ wellswalsinghamrailway.co.uk) between mid March and the end of October, and the Mid-Norfolk Railway (page 203), between East Dereham and Wymondham from late March to the end of October.

WALKING

This isn't vintage walking territory, but you can find plenty of pleasant enough options for casual wandering, with numerous circular walks possible around the small market towns. The 1:25,000 OS Explorer maps 238 and 251 pretty well cover it.

In 2013, a new walking route opened for business in this part of the county – the **Wensum Way** (pages 126–7). This 12-mile route, through fine central Norfolk countryside between Lenwade and Gressenhall, just north of East Dereham, is the final link in a cross-

TOURIST INFORMATION

Aylsham Bure Valley Railway Station, Norwich Rd ✆ 01263 733903
East Dereham Church House, Church St ✆ 01362 698992 🖥 dereham-tic.org.uk
Fakenham The Library, Oak St ✆ 07528 300103
Holt 3 Pound Lane, Market Pl ✆ 01263 713100
Walsingham Shire Hall Museum, 10 Common Pl ✆ 01328 820239

county route that combines with the existing Wherryman's Way, Marriott's Way and Nar Valley Way to provide a continuous footpath between Great Yarmouth and King's Lynn. Other than this, probably the most rewarding terrain lies in the area around Hockering and Foxley – both of which have gorgeous ancient tracts of woodland – or in open parkland of great **estates**, of which Blickling Park, Wolterton Park and Holt Country Park fit the bill nicely, with walks that take in lakes, pasture, woodland and sweeping views. You could also try sections of the Mariott's Way (see *Cycling*, below), or the Weavers' Way and Bure Valley Walk that both terminate in Aylsham, or the Nar Valley Way from Beetley, near Gressenhall, north of East Dereham, to Castle Acre and beyond.

CYCLING

Exploring by bike is idyllic along the back roads of north central Norfolk, and areas like the quiet lanes around Heydon, Reepham and Salle are perfect for casual exploration, with plenty of alluring churches to investigate, strategic well-placed pubs for refreshment and great views.

The **Marriott's Way** is an excellent off-road path on a disused railway track running between Norwich and Aylsham along a curving route that takes in Reepham and Cawston. The Way, one of the country's longest paths along a stretch of disused railway track, follows the River Wensum west out of Norwich before curving northwards at Lenwade. It's not exclusively meant for cyclists: it's used by all sorts – leisure cyclists, Norwich commuters, dog walkers and so on – and you really don't need a mountain bike as the surface is mostly pretty smooth, compacted sand or gravel, although it does get rougher after Whitwell. Indeed, the surface of this track was the subject of some controversy in its early days when its compacted sand was found to cause staining. One irate dog walker complained of her pooch turning irreversibly orange as a result, and for a while the route become known to Norfolk County Hall insiders as 'the Tango trail'. The Marriott's Way is improbably curved: the 180-degree Themelthorpe Curve that leads to Reepham was the sharpest bend in all of Britain's railway network. It was constructed in 1960 for moving freight, mainly concrete, from Lenwade but didn't stay in service for long as it was closed down in 1985.

AYLSHAM & NORTHWARDS

1 AYLSHAM

☗ The Gamekeeper's Hut Foulsham (page 257)

In many ways, Aylsham is the archetypal Norfolk market town. Sitting squarely between Norwich and the coast at Cromer, it is distant enough from both to have an independent life of its own and is far more than simply a dormitory town or coastal jumping-off point. The town's **market** originated in 1519 thanks to a charter from Henry VIII. The small market square remains the heart and soul of the town today and the oldest building around it is the Black Boys Inn that has stood on the same site since the mid 17th century. There used to be a Black Boys pub in Norwich's Pottergate too but this was renamed some years ago in a nod to political correctness (casual racism and pub signs are not

PROUD TO BE SLOW

Aylsham has admirable green credentials. It proudly became plastic-bag-free in 2008 and even the new Tesco supermarket, opened in July of that year, claims to be the 'world's greenest supermarket', constructed as it was from sustainable materials such as recyclable plastic. In recognition of Aylsham's enviable quality of life and very liveable nature, the town successfully became Norfolk's first **Cittaslow** (Slow Town) in 2004, the second town to do so in the country (Diss joined shortly after). Originating in Italy, the concept of a Cittaslow is that of a community that relishes good food, a relaxed living and

working environment, and a high quality of life above more mundane concerns like the availability of supermarkets and car parks. In Norfolk, both Diss and Aylsham have managed to fulfil these criteria with consummate ease, although both certainly have supermarkets and parking too. Aylsham had to change very little to become a fully-fledged member as it already quite effortlessly ticked all the right boxes. This is easy to believe: Aylsham has always been 'slow', although perhaps 'laid back' is a more fitting description for the town as it hurtles snail-like into the 21st century.

such strange bedfellows when you consider the number of Saracen's Heads and Turk's Heads found throughout the country that glorify the prejudices of the Crusades). The Black Boys would have always been the town's most prominent hostelry, serving as a coaching inn on the Cromer to Norwich run. Daniel Defoe is said to have stayed here – there again he did visit pretty well everywhere in the region.

There's a twice-weekly market in the square and a **farmers' market** on the morning of the first and third Saturday of the month. Equally well known, within the county at least, are the **Monday sales auctions**. Years ago, the Monday auctions used to bring all manner of old boys to town to buy and sell agricultural paraphernalia to each other. You could buy house-clearance rubbish for next to nothing. These days, it's quite a bit posher, with plenty of antique dealers perusing the items on offer. There's even a separate artworks sale that attracts national dealers.

Just north of the market square you'll find the **church of St Michael and All Angels**, where the landscape gardener Humphry Repton, who lived nearby at Sustead, lies buried in the graveyard. Repton's tomb has the following inscription, which celebrates the very essence of impermanence and the cycle of life, and perhaps anticipates the Slow way of thinking with its eco-centric, altruistic outlook:

Aylsham's Slow Town standing is closely linked to its Slow Food credentials. **Slow Food Aylsham** (⬡ slowfoodaylsham.org.uk) was formed in 2004 in anticipation of its coming Cittaslow status. Slow Food Aylsham actively supports local food producers and retailers and does its best to encourage people to shop locally. According to Slow Food 'convivium' leader Liz Jones, Aylsham sees itself as an 'unpretentious foodie town', and for a small town of just 6,000 to boast three butcher's shops, two greengrocers, two fishmongers, several cafés and a fortnightly farmers' market this seems a reasonable description. There's a food festival held in October that promotes local food businesses in addition to showcasing top local chefs in cooking demonstrations and highlighting the benefits of slow food to both the local environment and economy. The final event of the festival is The Big Slow Brunch held in the Town Hall on the Sunday morning.

Despite all these foodie wonders it is worth bearing in mind that Aylsham still follows the old ways, commercially speaking: Wednesday remains half-day closing day for most local businesses.

Not like Egyptian tyrants consecrate
Unmixed with others shall my dust remain
But mould'ring, blending, melting into earth
Mine shall give form and colour to the rose
And while its vivid blossoms cheer mankind
Its perfumed odours shall ascend to heaven.

The church itself is highly thought of too. Once, hovering at the church gate and dithering with a camera, I heard a voice in my ear exclaim: 'One of the best parish churches in Norfolk, that is. Well, according to Simon Knott anyway and he should know.' The voice came from a fellow visitor who, like me, was a devotee of Simon Knott's excellent Norfolk Churches website (norfolkchurches.co.uk), an online labour of love by a modern-day digital Betjeman who, while not shy of expressing an opinion, is wholly generous about the churches he describes, even the humblest. We chatted for a while about the great churches of central Norfolk – Salle, Cawston, Reepham – me nodding sagely for much of the time as I flounder under a friendly-fire barrage of architectural terminology. It was flattering to be identified as a fellow church fancier even if I cannot always tell my apse from my aumbry. But that's what you do in 'Slow' old-fashioned places like Aylsham: chat to strangers about the parish church and arcane local history, and if given the benefit of the doubt, hold your ground.

The town is small enough to walk around in half an hour or so and my recommendation, after the market square and church, is to wander down towards the watermill at **Burgh-next-Aylsham** a little further downstream along the River Bure. Surprisingly perhaps, the section of the Bure that runs through the town was not navigable until the 18th century and, even then, wherries from the coast would struggle to reach the staithe. You can reach Burgh-next-Aylsham by following the Bure Valley Walk from the Bure Valley Railway Station, where there's a tourist information centre. The railway is a good way to arrive from Wroxham and the Broads (pages 88–9). Heading southeast alongside the railway, turn left after about 1½ miles just before Brampton when you reach a small stream marked on maps as The Mermaid.

SHOPPING

At **Erpingham**, just north of Aylsham, **Alby Crafts & Gardens** (01263 768820
 albycrafts.co.uk) is a craft centre set in two courtyards of converted brick and flint

farm buildings. Here, there's a range of shops and galleries as well as working studios where woodturning, stained-glass making and sculpture take place, plus a tea room and gardens.

FOOD & DRINK

Biddy's Tea Room 16 Market Pl ✆ 01603 765766 ⌲ biddystearoom.com. Located almost adjacent to the church, this child- and dog-friendly tea room and bakery opened in 2014 following the success of their Norwich Lanes branch. This 'vintage inspired' tea room specialises in traditional afternoon teas served on tiered stands. Stocking 50 blends of loose tea (but only one type of coffee!), there are also breakfasts and light lunches to be had, as well as sandwiches and cream teas.

Black Boys Hotel Market Pl ✆ 01263 732122 ⌲ blackboyshotel.co.uk. Right in the centre of things, this long-standing hotel and restaurant serves a fairly traditional English menu that includes local produce such as aged English beef from Swannington Farm.

The Conservatory 3 Penfold St ✆ 01263 734433 ⌲ theconservatoryaylsham.co.uk. A bright café serving coffee and speciality teas, breakfasts, salads, jacket potatoes and afternoon teas, all using locally sourced ingredients wherever possible.

BLICKLING HALL

Blickling NR11 6NF ✆ 01263 738030 ⊙ Apr–Oct, closed Tue; weekends only in winter; National Trust

A couple of miles north of Aylsham, Blickling Hall has been in the care of the National Trust since 1940. Anne Boleyn may well have been born here, although there seems to be some uncertainty, but the building that you see standing today dates from after her time, the 1620s, and is a superb example of Jacobean architecture. The house attracts a large number of visitors, as do the formal gardens, but what cheapskates like myself often prefer is simply to walk (for free) the miles of footpaths that run through the estate. All manner of possible walks start either from near to the entrance or, further away, from the car park at Itteringham Common. Approaching the park from the Great Wood to the west allows for super views across oak-studded parkland to the lake and Blickling Hall beyond. You should also definitely check out **The Pyramid**, marked on most maps as a mausoleum. This is actually both of those things: a 45-foot high, pyramid-shaped mausoleum that holds the grave of John, the 2nd Earl of Buckinghamshire, who died in 1793. It's all rather esoteric and Egyptian in character, and quite a bizarre sight tucked away in this corridor of conifers and easily missed.

¶¶ FOOD & DRINK

The Bucks Arms Blickling ✆ 01263 732133 ⌗ bucksarms.co.uk. A 17th-century former
coaching inn close to the estate entrance that used to be known as the Buckinghamshire
Arms but which has since been rebranded simply 'The Bucks'. This has classic quality English
food and real ales represented by the usual suspects – Woodforde's, Adnams, etc.

3 MANNINGTON GARDENS &
4 WOLTERTON PARK

Contact details for both: ✆ 01263 584175 or 768444 ⌗ manningtongardens.co.uk

Not as well known as Blickling Hall but well worth a visit, nearby
Mannington Gardens and **Wolterton Park** both belong to the Walpole
family. Mannington Hall is not open to the public except by special
appointment but its gardens are open in summer and make for pleasant
walking. The Greedy Goose tea rooms located within the gardens are
open during garden visiting hours. If you just want to walk and not
visit the gardens there is a car park charge (free for garden visitors).
Wolterton Park, landscaped by Humphry Repton, is open year-round
and has walks of varying length along a good network of public rights
of way and permissive paths. There's the ruined tower of a church close
to the car park and the hall itself is also open for tours each Friday in
summer. **Barker Organics** (✆ 01263 768966) run the walled garden
belonging to the hall as an organic smallholding and have a few organic
open days each year.

Just south of Mannington Hall lies **Itteringham**, a charming small
village straddling the River Bure. The poet George Barker (1913–91),
much admired and financially supported by Graham Greene, lived here
for many years. His grave lies in the churchyard marked by a granite
book that bears the simple legend 'No Compromise'. George Barker's
daughter, the novelist Rafaella Barker, continues the family literary
tradition from her home in Cley-next-the-Sea.

¶¶ FOOD & DRINK

Itteringham Village Shop ✆ 01263 587325 ⌗ ourvillagestore.co.uk. A community
shop that also claims to have the smallest café in the county, this was threatened with closure
in 1994 after 350 years of business, but was bought out by the local community and has
been run by volunteers ever since. As well as delicious snacks and good coffee, the shop
defies its limited size by stocking an unreasonably wide range of greetings cards, art and
design books (including one on the history of the shop), gifts, vegetables, bakery goods,

bread, wine and beer, pretty well all of which is Norfolk produced. At the time of writing the shop's lease was about to end and its future was uncertain.

Saracen's Head Wolterton ✆ 01263 768909 ⌂ saracenshead-norfolk.co.uk. Tucked away on a quiet lane close to the Wolterton Estate, this isolated country inn serves up local produce like meat from Blickling and fish from the north Norfolk coast.

Walpole Arms The Common, Itteringham ✆ 01263 587258 ⌂ thewalpolearms.co.uk. The daily chalkboard here boasts an adventurous, seasonal menu that brims with local produce such as Cromer crab, Morston mussels and venison from the Gunton Estate. There's an impressive wine list, and Adnams and Woodforde's ales are on tap.

WEST OF AYLSHAM

West of Aylsham, the villages of **Reepham** and **Cawston** both have impressive, beautiful churches, while the massive wool church at **Salle** more or less stands on its own. **Heydon** is a handsome estate village. Reepham, Cawston and Salle all lie in close proximity to each other, which makes their oversized churches all the more remarkable.

CAWSTON

Cawston is a largish but compact village with a fascinating church. It lies in the heart of good cycling territory – the Marriott's Way goes right past the village and the local back roads are heaven-sent for those on two wheels.

The village's **St Agnes Church** is a marvel, certainly one of the most interesting in the county. Even before you enter, you encounter some fearful gargoyles on the parapets and a splendid Green Man and a dragon in the spandrels above the west door. Inside, there's a double hammerbeam roof strewn with huge angels, a rare 15th-century rood screen and wooden box pews. The local gentry had the comfy box pews while the hoi-polloi had to fend for themselves. The class system was as rife in church on Sundays as it was for the rest of the week outside. A friend from the village told me this that is where the expression 'go to the wall' comes from. 'If you didn't have a family pew in the church, you would have to "go to the wall". You'd have to stand up at the side for the service'. The stained glass is gorgeous but even better is the rood screen, created around 1460 and with about 20 paintings by Flemish artists – a series of saints, famous and less well known, including St John the Evangelist, St Jude and St Matthew (who wears glasses to read his book).

6 SALLE

There is not much to Salle village, a couple of miles west of Cawston, apart from a few cottages and a well-used cricket pitch. John Betjeman is reported to have said that, church-wise, you are either a Cawston or a Salle man. Really though, both have their charms and I would recommend visiting the two. On a bicycle, you could even make a three-cornered circuit through Reepham, Cawston and Heydon, taking in Salle along the way, using a combination of farm tracks, minor roads and a section of the Marriott's Way.

The spandrels above the door of **St Peter and St Paul's Church** here have no Green Man like at Cawston but, instead, a pair of scale-covered angels. Inside, there's a real sense of space, accentuated perhaps by the absence of stained glass in many of the windows. The church was in a terrible state at the end of the 19th century but restoration finally came with funds provided by Duleep Singh (the last Maharajah of Punjab) of the Elveden Estate in Suffolk. There is an enormously tall wooden font cover, supported by a sort of winch system, which dates from the 15th century, and distant angels and bosses high in the roof beams that retain some of their original medieval paint. If you want to see some bosses close up, go through the door at the northwest corner near the font where you'll find a narrow staircase leading up to a Lady Chapel, which has some wonderfully quirky bosses in the vaulted ceiling.

What I find most touching about the place are the carvings in the 15th-century misericord seats that have a variety of faces, some benevolent, some quite threatening. One looks like a tempestuous Greek god; another, a gentle monk, his head polished from hands gripping on to him over the centuries. The best are two facing corner stalls that depict two monks deep in conversation, their faces pure medieval but also there's something quite contemporary about them too.

7 REEPHAM

The largest of this trio, just south of Salle, Reepham is a small town with a fine marketplace that has the King's Arms, a 17th-century coaching inn, on one side, and what was once a brewery, the Old Brewery House Hotel, on the other. With a handful of old-fashioned shops meeting most of the needs of its residents, Reepham is a tidy, self-possessed sort of place – a bit like a smaller version of Aylsham just down the road. A market takes place here every Wednesday.

Reepham is rare in having three churches (one of which is ruined) side by side and sharing the same churchyard – reputedly one of only two places in Europe like this. St Mary's Church is joined to Whitwell St Michael by a vestry corridor, while the third church belonging to Hackford parish burned down in the 16th century to leave just a fragment of wall. This unusual state of affairs features on the town sign that also shows the three sisters who were supposedly responsible for building all three churches – complete nonsense of course as they were built over a much longer period. The three-in-one churchyard actually came about by all three churches being built on the intersecting point of the respective parish boundaries of Reepham, Hackford and Whitwell.

The town's successful **summer music festival** takes place in August; camping is available for the weekend at nearby Whitwell station.

3 HEYDON

North of Salle, Heydon Hall lies at the centre of a leafy estate of pasture and parkland. Over the years, the tiny estate village of Heydon, with its wide green and Earle Arms pub, has become well known, locally at least, as a popular focus for weekend outings. If anywhere in Norfolk deserves the accolade of 'hidden village', this does.

Heydon became Norfolk's first conservation area back in 1971 and has won a couple of Best Kept Village awards.

"In many ways, the whole village is something of a Victorian throwback."

Part of the explanation for the village's pristine status comes from the fact that there is no through road. You arrive at the village green by the pub, tea room and well and that's about as far as you can go on wheels. The estate's rented cottages that surround the green have attracted quite a bohemian community over the years and, in many ways, the whole village is something of a Victorian throwback. There's also a slightly feudal feel to the place, as everything in the village, including the pub, tea room, smithy and all the houses, is owned by the Bulwer Long family who have lived in the hall since 1640. This timeless quality has not gone completely unnoticed and Heydon's village green is beloved of movie location scouts – it has certainly featured in more than a film or two. If you remove the cars from the scene then nothing whatsoever gives the game away that Queen Victoria is no longer on the throne. The commemorative well in her name that dates from 1887 is, in fact, the village's most recent structure.

¶¶ FOOD & DRINK

Earle Arms The Street ✆ 01263 587376. With Adnams ales, a good selection of wines and decent pub grub mostly sourced from local ingredients, this pub on the green is very popular at weekend lunchtimes.

Village Tea Room The Street ✆ 01263 587211 ⌂ heydonvillageteashop.co.uk. Cosy tea room filled with china knick-knacks that serves light lunches, snacks and cream teas.

HOLT & AROUND

9 BACONSTHORPE CASTLE

The main reason for making a trip to the out-of-the-way village of Baconsthorpe is for a look at Baconsthorpe Castle, some way from the village along rutted farm tracks. The castle is more of a fortified manor than anything else. Henry Heydon started construction in 1486 and the Heydon family lived here for almost 200 years, expanding their property as their family wealth grew. It fell into ruin in the mid 17th century when the Heydon fortune went into decline and the family were obliged to take a sledge hammer to their property and sell it off for use as building materials.

The outer gatehouse, a later addition, has survived better than most, and this alone continued to be occupied until 1920 when one of its towers collapsed. It must have been an odd and slightly creepy place to live, so far from anywhere else other than the farm next door. With jackdaws noisily swirling around in the trees above the moat, it remains a lonely, atmospherically mysterious spot.

Half of the fun is getting here, along twisting country roads before striking out on farm tracks for the last mile or so. From the south you'll pass first through Plumstead, which just about typifies the rural landscape around these parts: a narrow sandy road and rolling fields; round bales of hay rising over a farmyard wall; an isolated phone box next to an overgrown churchyard; boxes of tomatoes and marrows for sale outside cottage doors. Cycle here and you will appreciate it even more, or you could drive here and then do a circular walk on arrival. There are even very occasional Sanders buses to the village from Holt, Cromer and Sheringham. The sign in the car park has some good walking suggestions including a circuit that takes in Hempstead and Baconsthorpe via Beckett's Farm and Ash Tree Farm. The nearest refreshment stops are Holt or Bodham.

HOLT

🏠 **Byfords Posh B&B** (page 257) & **White Horse Farm** (page 257)

More cosmopolitan than Aylsham, Holt stands *en route* to Norfolk's prestigious north coast, as an old market town that has found renewed life; there's a confidence and sassiness here too that comes from its proximity to places like Blakeney and Cley-next-the-Sea. Almost all its buildings were reduced to ash on 1 May 1708, when fire raged through the town. The subsequent rebuild has resulted in a handsome Georgian centre, although one survivor is Gresham's School, Norfolk's most prestigious public school dating from 1555, which brings a certain amount of gravitas to the community.

The town centre has elegant colour-washed frontages and a handful of narrow lanes running off the high street. Immediately apparent is the staggering number of **shops** and services for such a small place; not just along the main streets but also set back from the High Street in a procession of courtyards – Feather's Yard, Old Stable Yard and the largest, Apple Yard, which has the excellent **Holt Bookshop** (✐ 01263 715858 ✐ holtbookshop.co.uk). Two more lie just off Albert Street – Lees Yard and Chapel Yard. In addition to the newsagents, chip shops and greengrocers that you might expect in a small Norfolk town, there are also a surprising number of clothes shops, galleries, bakeries, kitchen shops and antiquarian bookshops. Nowhere of similar size in East Anglia seems to have quite such a concentration of cafés and tea rooms. In late July the **Holt Festival** (✐ holtfestival. org) brings together a wide range of musical, comedic and theatrical performances, along with literary events and lectures.

"Nowhere of similar size in East Anglia seems to have quite such a concentration of cafés and tea rooms."

FOOD & DRINK

Byfords 1–3 Shirehall Plain ✐ 01263 711400 ✐ byfords.org.uk. An all-day brasserie and deli that also functions as a 'posh B&B', Byfords is a Holt institution and serves up superb homemade food and snacks, and especially fine cakes and puddings. See also *Accommodation*, page 257.

Owl Tea Rooms White Lion St ✐ 01263 713232. On the corner of White Lion Street and Church Street, this busy place that has claims as Norfolk's oldest tea rooms – established 1929 – serves light lunches, snacks and afternoon tea in cosy rooms behind the bakery and also in the small courtyard garden.

11 LETHERINGSETT WATERMILL

Riverside Rd, Letheringsett NR25 7YD ✆ 01263 713153 ☉ 09.00–16.00 (15.00 in winter), closed Sun

Take the Fakenham road from Holt and you soon reach Letheringsett on the River Glaven, with a pub on the west side of the river and a watermill on the east. Letheringsett watermill sits behind a large millpond, a constant source of power for this, the only working watermill in the county. It's a solid, four-storey building with a shop on the ground floor that sells a variety of flours from the mill in addition to a range of whole foods. For a modest admission fee, you can visit the working parts of the mill, and there are occasional demonstrations of the milling process .

The present mill dates from 1802, although one stood on the same site at the time of the Domesday Book. The mill was converted to

NORFOLK'S DESERTED VILLAGES

Norfolk is estimated to have over 150 deserted villages within its borders – a figure that is greater than most other counties in England. This is commonly thought to be simply the result of the Black Death that ravaged the country in 1349 but often the reason for abandonment is more complex. Places that may have thrived in medieval times but which have long since been abandoned usually leave little evidence of their former existence other than crop marks in fields. Occasionally there is a ruin or two to mark the site. A good example can be found at Godwick close to the village of Tittleshall, a few miles south of Fakenham. **Godwick**, which was mentioned in the Domesday Book, existed as a village until the 17th century when it was abandoned after two centuries of gradual decline. Poor harvests and colder, wetter weather were probably the main reasons for the village's demise. Following its abandonment the land

belonging to the village was bought by the Coke family of the Holkham Estate, who in turn sold it in 1958 to pay for death duties. A solitary ruined church tower remains today surrounded by rough grazing land populated by indifferent sheep. Closer inspection of the site reveals earthworks that show where the houses, mill, village pond and street would once have stood.

Other villages in this part of north central Norfolk that were mentioned in the Domesday Book but deserted by the late medieval period include Little Bittering near Gressenhall and Pudding Norton close to Fakenham, where another ruined church tower stands near the roadside marking the site of the abandoned medieval village. Perhaps most evocative of all is **Egmere**, where the dramatic ruined tower of St Edmund's Church stands on a mound just south of the Little Walsingham to North/South Creake road.

diesel power in the 1940s but was reconverted to waterpower in 1984. Mike Thurwell, who started restoring it in 1987, had absolutely no experience of milling at all when he took the place on but today it's a highly successful enterprise. 'I can't keep up with demand,' he told me when I visited some years ago. 'We produce about 3½ tons a week at the moment but we could easily get rid of eight tons. We've just got two new millstones from Holland made from German quartz – they cost £3,500 each – but I don't know how good they are yet as I'm still running them in.' Running in new stones means that the flour produced needs to be sent off for inspection until it is declared fit for human consumption. 'The test flour can be used for pigs as they don't mind a bit of grit in their diet.'

Different millstones are used to produce different grades of flour. 'The French burr stones we use to make white flour, and we use the Derbyshire for wholemeal. With the new stones up and running we should be able to increase production up to about seven tons of flour a week.' Did the mill ever run dry? Was there ever a danger of power failure? 'You're joking,' says Mike dismissively. 'There's a million gallons of water out there in the millpond. Every bit of water in the river goes past this mill.' Mike passed away in July 2013 but his wife and daughter continue to run the business.

AROUND WALSINGHAM & FAKENHAM

2 WALSINGHAM

'England's Nazareth', it likes to call itself, although 'Norfolk's Lourdes' might be equally appropriate. Walsingham is actually two adjoining villages, Little Walsingham and Great Walsingham, and in true Norfolk topsy-turvy style, Little Walsingham is the larger of the pair.

The village has long been famous as one of Britain's foremost pilgrimage centres, a tradition that began just before the Norman Conquest in 1061 when a Saxon noblewoman had a vision of the Virgin Mary here. A wooden replica of the house of the Holy Family in Nazareth was constructed and an Augustinian priory founded in the 12th century to enclose the chapel. This set the ball rolling for what would become an important European pilgrimage tradition which continued until the time of Henry VIII when the shrine and priory were destroyed as part of the Dissolution, despite the fact that the monarch had made his way here from Cambridge in his youth. The pilgrimage was re-established at the end of the 19th century and has gone from strength to strength ever since.

Both Catholic and Anglican **pilgrimages** take place here. The largest annual event, the Anglican National Pilgrimage, takes place here each Whitsun, when there is usually a good deal of heckling from hard-line Protestant pickets who view the proceedings as shameless popery. Numerous other pilgrimages happen throughout the year and the quaint narrow streets of Little Walsingham are sporadically busy almost year-round. Summer attracts quite a number of non-pilgrim visitors too. Whatever your take on religion, Walsingham is certainly an attractive place that has not allowed itself to become too fazed by centuries of Marian mayhem. In fact, it is probably its very status as a pilgrimage centre that has, by and large, kept the village so untainted by modern development.

It's an interesting place to wander and reflect on what has or hasn't changed over the centuries. Today's pilgrims mostly come by coach or car and are generally better-scrubbed and less disease-laden than those who would have gravitated here in medieval times. No doubt the charlatans, quacks and dodgy corrupt monks who would have preyed on hapless pilgrims are thinner on the ground too. In terms of buildings, all that is left of the original Augustinian priory is a large arched window that stands in the abbey gardens,

"Walsingham has not allowed itself to become too fazed by centuries of Marian mayhem."

a Norman gateway and two wishing wells. You must pay to enter the abbey gardens and pass through the tourist office by the 'pump' to do so; it's sometimes mistaken for the Anglican shrine, which is in a modern building just down the road, while the Roman Catholic shrine is at the Slipper Chapel outside the village. The **pump**, in fact a 16th-century octagonal pump-house with an iron brazier on top, has pride of place in Common Place, the square that is Walsingham's heart, with the tourist office, Shirehall and Bull pub all surrounding it.

The **Shirehall Museum** served as a hostel in the 16th century but was converted into the Shirehall at the end of the 18th century. The courtroom is now part of the museum, which gives a good overview of the village's history as a pilgrimage site. The **High Street**, a very pretty street composed almost entirely of timbered houses, leads off Common Place. Along here, you'll find a few gift shops, the evocatively eroded Norman gate of the priory, a crocodile or two of pilgrims in peak season, and splendidly old-fashioned tea rooms like The Swallows and The Old Bakehouse. The gift shop on the corner has such a large choice of jam and candles that you could almost imagine this becoming a place of pilgrimage in its own right.

"There's such a choice of jam that you could almost imagine this becoming a place of pilgrimage in its own right."

A couple of miles south along a narrow road at **Houghton St Giles** you'll come to the **Slipper Chapel**, a restored 14th-century building that houses the contemporary Catholic shrine. This has long been considered the last staging point along the pilgrimage route to Walsingham and the done thing, for the pious at least, was to remove footwear here and continue the last stretch into Walsingham barefoot. Numerous kings have performed this act of piety in the past, even Henry VIII, although few do it today. While the hardcore devout may be thinner on the ground these days, they are certainly still out there. A few years ago, I remember seeing a man hauling an enormous cross along the hard shoulder of the Fakenham road just outside Norwich. Quite obviously, he was Walsingham-bound. The only concession that this modern pilgrim had made to ease his tough journey was to affix a little wheel to the bottom of his cross to make hauling slightly easier.

A pilgrimage footway still exists between Houghton St Giles and Little Walsingham but these days, rather than the road, the route follows the course of the former railway track that runs parallel. Following this firm-surfaced path brings you into Walsingham at the site of its former railway station, which now serves as a small **Orthodox chapel**, silver onion dome and all. I once met an Irish nun in an isolated Serbian monastery who, on hearing that I lived in Norfolk, asked me about Walsingham as she had lived here as a nun for several years. No doubt this would have been her former church. It's a small world sometimes.

FOOD & DRINK

Old Bakehouse 33 High St ✆ 01328 820454 ⌖ oldbakehouselittlewalsingham.co.uk. One of several old-fashioned tea rooms in Little Walsingham village. This one, which doubles as a B&B, has a cosy atmosphere with chairs around a fireplace – just the job in winter.

13 BINHAM

Guided tours of the church & monastery ☺ May–Sep 15.00 Sun & Tue

Turn right off the A148 just beyond Letheringsett and head due west and you pass through a landscape of big fields and small villages – Saxlingham, Field Dalling, Binham. It is well worth stopping at Binham to see the remains of **St Mary's Priory**, all the more remarkable because, although the rest of the priory lies in ruins, its church has been patched up and had its aisles removed to become the village parish church.

In a landscape of flint and brick, churches made of stone are rare, and this one is a monastic ghost that looks all the odder for the ornate windows of its façade being blocked up with workaday brick. An architectural historian might talk excitedly of the priory's west window being the earliest example of Decorated tracery in England but you do not really need to know this in order to appreciate just how atmospheric it all is.

Apart from the stone used for the church, the rest of Binham village is made almost entirely of flint – the extensive farm buildings, the cattle yard walls, the village cottages. You would be hard-pushed to find a flintier place, making the finely dressed imported stone of the priory church seem all the more precious as a result. With Blakeney port just down the road in one direction and the pilgrimage centre of Walsingham in the other, Binham with its priory must have been a bustling place back in the medieval period. Today, the village is the very antithesis of 'bustling'.

14 GREAT SNORING

Great Snoring isn't dull but it is certainly sleepy. It's actually quite a charming little village tucked into a fold of a gently sloping land. **Little Snoring**, close to the A148, is a little more wide-awake and, somewhat contrarily, quite a bit larger than its neighbour. Here, the rather unusual **church of St Andrew** is set slightly back from the village on a sloping site. The church has a round tower that has a windmill-like cap and what look to be dormer windows, but the really odd thing about the tower is that it is detached from the main body of the church, which is of a later build. The suggestion is that there may originally have been two Gothic churches side by side on this site although no-one seems to know. There used to be an airfield beyond Church Farm next to the church that was a base for Mosquito and Lancaster bombers during World War II, commemorated by plaques in the church and a Mosquito and propeller on the village sign.

The gloss put on the area by its religious connections makes it easy to overlook the loveliness of the valley of the River Stiffkey hereabouts. From the Slipper Chapel in Walsingham, you can cross a ford to reach tiny Houghton St Giles and then continue up what seems like a surprisingly steep hill to reach Great Snoring. Stop halfway along just before Canister Hall Farm and you'll be rewarded by what I think is one of the choicest views in north Norfolk, looking west over the valley and the folded hills beyond – a scene that presents perfect counter-evidence for use in any 'it's all flat' debate. Returning on foot to Walsingham from Great Snoring the most scenic route to follow is the leafy, ancient **Greenway**, which has served as a pilgrimage route for at least half a millennium. With all those pious feet tramping the way before you it may come as no surprise that this route can become extremely muddy at times but, in the spirit of pilgrimage, surely it's a matter of 'no pain, no gain'?

5 CREAKE ABBEY

🏠 **The Fox Hat** in South Creake (page 257)

Northwest of Fakenham towards Burnham Market and the coast beyond are the villages of **South Creake** and **North Creake**, both quiet, pleasant villages with greens, duck ponds and neat flint cottages. Just beyond North Creake you'll find the ruins of Creake Abbey, originally an almshouse founded by the Augustinian order which attained abbey status in 1231. Fire and the Black Death in the 15th century, and Henry VIII in the 16th, all contributed to the abbey's downfall and what remains is an evocative ruin in the keep of English Heritage.

FOOD & DRINK

Creake Abbey Café and Food Hall North Creake ✆ 01328 730399 🖰 creakeabbeycafe. com, creakeabbey.co.uk. Next door to Creake Abbey is this craft and arts centre with galleries and a popular café and food hall in a set of converted farm buildings. The food hall stocks locally sourced meat and charcuterie as well as Norfolk cheeses, beers and wines. A farmers' market said to be the largest in Norfolk is held here on the morning of the first Saturday of each month except January, and there's an apple fair in October.

6 FAKENHAM

🏠 **Garden Cottage** Wellingham (page 257)

A medium-sized market town on the River Wensum, Fakenham is more of a place to shop and do business than go out of your way to see. I feel a bit sorry for poor Fakenham as the town seems never to have fully recovered from being described in the *Daily Telegraph* as 'one of the most boring places on earth' a decade or so ago – a wholly unfair slight. The quote was actually taken out of context as it related to a scurrilous comment made in a guidebook about Fakenham on Wednesday afternoons when it is early closing day in the town. As any local will tell you, Thursdays – market day – are quite a different matter. While it's not the most dynamic of towns, I could think of many more places where I would rather not be. Its centre has a modestly attractive Georgian

A NORFOLK CYCLING ODYSSEY

Sheila Rattray is a rare woman – in the very best sense. Having retired from her hospital job, Sheila, a mother of five grown-up children, decided that she needed to keep herself fit now that she would no longer be cycling the seven miles a day between her Norwich home and place of work. She resolved to make up the missing miles by making forays into the Norfolk countryside on her bike. The long-term aim was to visit all the villages marked on her road map – effectively, all of them. Insistent that she should start and finish at her Norwich home, those villages in the Fens of the far west of the county would prove to be the most problematic as they required 140-mile round trips. Sensibly, she chose long midsummer days to attempt these, pedalling off at first light.

Although she had previously cycled as far as her home town of Montrose in Scotland on one occasion, Sheila thoroughly enjoyed her freewheeling day trips in Norfolk. 'I really like those wee roads that don't have white lines down them,' she enthused. 'I like all the wee flowers at the wayside too. Last year, I saw the biggest bank of cowslips I'd ever seen in my life. I enjoy looking at the stock in the fields; it reminds me of growing up on a cattle farm in Aberdeenshire. I love to see the rivers too – especially when they flood – and the wee thatched houses in the villages.'

Sheila's preparation for an excursion was minimal to say the least. 'I don't take food – I'll maybe get something from a farm shop and I like an ice cream sometimes too.' She didn't take a map either. 'I'll follow the signposts and ask for directions. Talking to people, that's the thing – they're usually really friendly when they find out what I'm up to. I do like getting a bit lost too.'

Sheila completed her Norfolk odyssey in August 2013. Her last village was West Beckham where she met family and friends for a celebratory meal and drink. A friend had made her a T-shirt bearing the legend 'Sheila Rattray – I've cycled to every Norfolk village from my home', which she donned for a photograph before cycling back to Norwich. I asked her what she was planning to do next. 'Och, I don't know. Maybe I'll stop for a wee ice cream on the way home.'

square that hosts a very lively weekly market on Thursday mornings and a **farmers' market** on the fourth Saturday morning of each month. The Thursday market really does seem to attract crowds to the town, especially representatives of the county's more senior demographic who dust off their bus passes for a good day out. There's also a town racecourse, the only other one in the county besides Great Yarmouth. Above all though, you also really have to warm to a town that has taken the trouble of opening its very own **Museum of Gas and Local History** (01328 863507 fakenhamgasmuseum.com), which is housed in the former gas works – a designated Scheduled Ancient Monument – that produced the town's gas supply between 1846 and 1965.

Fakenham Market

Fakenham's Thursday market has an air of perpetuity about it, as well it might. The town was originally granted a charter to hold a market in 1250, and the square beneath St Peter and St Paul Church where the market was first held is still busy on Thursdays. The market has long outgrown its designated territory in the square next to the church and now spills over into a large car park towards Cattlemarket Street some distance beyond. Here you can find anything from pot plants to plastic potties, scented candles to smoked sausages. The main market square is crowded with stalls selling fresh fruit and veg, paperback thrillers, sunglasses, army surplus clothing and suspiciously cheap vacuum-packed meat. The Cattlemarket Street extension tends to be a bit more 'fringe' and, as well as having an excellent local cheese stall and a man selling artisan bread from a table by a van, there is also a lot of old green bottles, cigarette card albums and unloved crockery. If you are looking for brass horses, china plates with dogs' faces or a 1966 *Blue Peter Annual* then this is the place. Admittedly, it is mostly retired people that come these days but Fakenham Thursday market remains an important weekly event on the north Norfolk social calendar: a chance to catch up with friends, have a mardle ('chat') and do a bit of shopping at the same time.

FOOD & DRINK

Wisteria Tea Room Newmans Yard, Norwich Rd 01328 851247 wisteriatearoom.co.uk. A pleasant tea room with, as its name suggests, an ancient wisteria draping its entrance, this serves the usual range of scones, sandwiches and light meals, with cream teas in the afternoon. All cakes are homemade and ingredients locally sourced wherever possible.

17 PENSTHORPE NATURAL PARK

Pensthorpe Rd, Fakenham NR21 0LN ℘ 01328 851465 ℘ pensthorpe.com ☺ daily

Just outside Fakenham on the Norwich road, this is the biggest local draw, a nature reserve with a large collection of waterfowl in natural surroundings. With a wide range of habitats, plenty of wild birds turn up too – 171 species recorded in total. The BBC television natural history programme *Springwatch* used to broadcast from here, which is quite a feather in the cap for the place if you'll pardon the (bird) pun. As well as gardens, duck-filled lakes and wildflower meadows for adults to enjoy, there are plenty of activities for children too. WildRootz, a two-acre adventure activity centre for children close to the entrance, opened for business in summer 2013 and has since become a great success with children of all ages. The idea is to re-connect children with the natural world by means of imaginative play equipment and a network of artificial hills, tunnels and burrows. As well as a giant slide tower called 'The Worm', there are trees to climb, zipwires to zip along and shallow streams to wade through – a kind of eco funfair. Beyond the confines of the WildRootz area youngsters can participate in more traditional pursuits like pond dipping and bug walks, while the red squirrel sanctuary seems capable of charming visitors of all ages. The Pensthorpe Explorer, which operates between the end of March and end of September, is a draw for children and adults alike: a specially designed Land Rover and trailer that weaves through the remoter parts of the reserve.

FOLLOWING THE WENSUM WAY ALONG THE WENSUM VALLEY

The Wensum Way, which stretches from Gressenhall Farm and Workhouse (page 130) to Lenwade, on the A1067 south of Reepham, is well worth considering if you fancy a long day-walk through quiet pastoral countryside. The snag is that although there is adequate public transport at Lenwade, the route's eastern end, there is little transport available to Gressenhall at the other, although a few buses do run daily from Dereham. Buses also run to Swanton Morley from Dereham, so walking just part of the route is an option too. The 12-mile Wensum Way passes through some delightful pastoral countryside, alongside or close to the River Wensum for much of the way. *En route* to Lenwade, it passes through the villages of Swanton Morley, Elsing and Lyng, each one charmingly picturesque in its own right. Perhaps more importantly, if you are walking, the first two villages have decent pubs too, as does Lenwade at the end, although Elsing's closed recently.

SCULTHORPE MOOR NATURE RESERVE

Turf Moor Rd, Fakenham NR21 9GN ⏀ 01328 856788 ⏀ hawkandowl.org ⏀ every day except Christmas Day

A little way west of Fakenham, just off the King's Lynn road, this 45-acre nature reserve managed by the Hawk and Owl Trust is a fine example of unimproved fen habitat. With over a mile of walkways threading through woodland and marshes there are plenty of hides and viewing platforms from which to observe the reserve's rich birdlife. As well as birds, the fen flora here is a treat in spring and early summer with a plethora of yellow flag, ragged robin and the like. Having easy access and wooden boardwalks running all the way around it, this reserve must be one of the best wildlife reserves in the country for those with restricted mobility.

SWANTON MORLEY

⌂ **Carrick's at Castle Farm** (page 257)

Swanton Morley has the large imposing 14th-century **All Saints' Church**, a landmark for miles around. There are also two pubs, one of which, The Angel, was once home to Richard Lincoln, an ancestor of President Abraham Lincoln. The village also has one of the best butchers in these parts.

FOOD & DRINK

The Angel 66 Greengate ⏀ 01362 637407 ⏀ theangelpub.co.uk. This handsome brick building dating back to 1610 was built by Richard Lincoln, a distant ancestor of Abraham Lincoln. Woodforde's Wherry and other guest real ales. Traditional pub grub lunchtimes and evenings, Sunday roasts and themed food nights.

Darby's Elsing Rd ⏀ 01362 637647 ⏀ darbysfreehouse.com. This freehouse in the centre of Swanton Morley offers a wide range of food using locally sourced seasonal ingredients and a good range of local real ales.

ELSING

Elsing, the next village on the Wensum Way, is reached by following a footpath alongside the Wensum bank for much of the way.

You'll probably be in the company of wide-horned White Park cattle that tend to sprawl themselves across the track in places but this ancient rare breed, descended from Britain's original wild white cattle (actually feral in forests after the Romans evacuated Britain) with a lineage of more than two millennia, are gentle beasts it would seem. King James I is said to have knighted a joint of White Park beef after a particularly good lunch in Lancashire in 1617. This is claimed by some to be the origin of the term 'sirloin' but sadly its etymology is more prosaic: it comes from the Middle French *surlogne*. The king may well have punned on this occasion but to claim it as the name's originator is clearly a 'mis-steak'.

Walking along the riverbank here in high summer you can enjoy hungry swallows gleefully skimming the water and flood meadows in perfect symbiosis with the fly-luring cattle – an evocatively bucolic scene. Of course, you could always spurn the river and drive or cycle instead – the roads in this part of the county are generally pretty quiet.

St Mary's Church is notable for its pillar-free nave, the widest of any parish church in the region, and its splendid brass commemorating Sir Hugh Hastings, the church's founder. T E Lawrence ('of Arabia' fame) is said to have visited the church on a cycling tour back in 1905 – perhaps he was an enthusiastic brass-rubber? The village really has not changed much since then. No doubt Lawrence would have supped a pint in the Mermaid Inn immediately opposite the church, a welcoming hostelry that has stood here since the 16th century.

¶¶ FOOD & DRINK

Mermaid Inn Church St ✆ 01362 637640 ⌂ elsingmermaidinn.co.uk. Tucked away, this cosy 15th-century country inn has good home-cooked food and a choice of local real ales.

21 LYNG

This village has a charming millhouse next to a river and weir. Curiously, there are also large anti-tank blocks next to the bridge that date from World War II – but if invading Germans had managed to penetrate this far inland then surely the game would have been up anyway? After Lyng, the Wensum Way winds past Sparham Pools, a group of wildlife-rich flooded gravel pits leased to Norfolk Wildlife Trust, before reaching Lenwade on the main A1067. From here, the Marriott's Way leads to Norwich if you are game for more foot-slogging; otherwise, there is a regular bus service, the X29 from Fakenham.

EAST DEREHAM & AROUND
EAST DEREHAM
🏠 **Greenbanks Hotel** (page 257)

> Pretty, quiet Dereham, thou pattern of an English town.
>
> George Borrow, *Lavengro*

So where is *West* Dereham, you might ask? Out in the Fens in the middle of nowhere is the answer, so just plain 'Dereham' will do. If you made a cardboard cut-out of Norfolk and looked for the central point from which to suspend it, you would probably find it passes close to Dereham (although nearby Hoe is also a contender) – it doesn't get much more mid-Norfolk than this.

Although it is not immediately obvious, East Dereham's quite an ancient place. The churchyard of St Nicholas has **Withburga's Well** named after a daughter of the 7th-century Saxon monarch King Anna (yes, king!) who founded a convent here. Withburga's shrine became famous for its miracles until AD984 when the Abbot and monks from the monastery at Ely came trophy hunting and made off with her remains into the mists of the Fens.

The well is said to be filled from a spring that erupted from beneath Withburga's empty grave. You can find it by looking behind the church on its south side. The sunken well has hart's tongue ferns growing on its walls and, less evocatively, is flanked by geraniums in plastic plant pots. The town has a few literary connections too: George Borrow was born at the outskirts of the town at Dumpling Green, just a few years after William Cowper died here; there's a shrine to the latter in the church.

There's nothing to see of Dereham's Saxon past, and little of the medieval other than the church. What greets the eye is mostly the rebuild that followed post-Tudor fires, although there is a row of 16th-century cottages near the church known as **Bonner's Cottages** that have elaborate Suffolk-style pargetting. The buildings, which now serve as a cottage museum (🖉 01362 853453 🖉 derehamhistory.com), take their name from Bishop Bonner, who lived here as a curate before his stint as Bishop of London. Bonner was anything but a kind and gentle soul: as an enthusiastic foot soldier of 'Bloody' Queen Mary's excesses, he sent many a Protestant heretic to a fiery death.

The most enjoyable way to arrive is by train on the **Mid-Norfolk Railway** from Wymondham (page 203). You could buy a return ticket from Wymondham or, alternatively, just a single to here, continuing your journey by bus – there are frequent services east and west to Norwich, Swaffham and King's Lynn. Dereham station is something of a throwback to the 1950s and has quite a nice café, so if you don't want to bother going into town and you could easily while away half an hour or so here whilst waiting for the return train.

23 GRESSENHALL

For a thorough exposition of Norfolk social and agricultural history, visit the village of Gressenhall a few miles north of Dereham, where **Gressenhall Farm and Workhouse** (⌀ 01362 860563 ⌀ museums. norfolk.gov.uk) is a combined museum and farm set in 50 acres of countryside. The approach is hands-on: while the 18th-century workhouse seems to ooze despair from the very fabric of the building, much of the history is told through the recorded lives of inmates. The collections gallery has all manner of fascinating artefacts including a hurdy-gurdy and a portable Turkish bath. Despite the gloomy atmosphere of the workhouse itself, this is a surprisingly good place to visit with small children. The punishment cell may be rather sobering but there are fun activities too – for children, at least – like dressing up in Victorian clothes and cart rides around the farm with enormous shire horses. There is also a very well equipped adventure playground next to an outdoor picnic area. As well as family events during school holidays, the museum stages special events days such as a Norfolk History Fair and Apple Day in October. For walkers, the Nar Valley Way begins (or ends) at the museum, as does the Wensum Way that links Gressenhall museum with Lenwade on the Marriott's Way (pages 106–7).

24 HOE ROUGH NATURE RESERVE

A little way east of Gressenhall, next to the village of Beetley, you'll find Hoe Rough, a Norfolk Wildlife Trust nature reserve of ancient grazing meadows and 300-year-old oaks alongside the River Whitewater, a tributary of the Wensum. If you take a stroll here you might well see basking adders in spring and, if you are really lucky, otters in the river. The reserve has its own small car park, just off the main road east of the bridge.

Immediately opposite the car park entrance, over the road in a small triangle of grass next to Chapel Mill, you'll find a large stone that does not look as if it comes from these parts. It doesn't: this is one of many large glacial erratics found in Norfolk – lumps of alien (as in 'non-indigenous', not from Mars!) rock dragged here by ice during the last glacial period. Whether or not this particular stone was deposited precisely on this very spot is open to debate, as a previous owner of Mill House in the late 19th century

"This is one of many large glacial erratics found in Norfolk rock dragged here by ice during the last glacial period."

was an antiquarian dealer who may well have had it placed here in front of his house. Nevertheless, it is unlikely that the stone could have been transported very far by horse and cart so it's probably local enough – 10,000 years or so is just about long enough to be awarded 'local' status around these parts. The stone is also rumoured to mark the dead centre of Norfolk, although this same geographical distinction is also claimed by a supermarket car park in nearby Dereham.

5 NORTH ELMHAM

A little way north of Gressenhall, you come to North Elmham, a large, rather sprawling village that was once connected to Dereham and Fakenham by the mid-Norfolk Railway. Plans are afoot to extend the Wymondham to Dereham Mid-Norfolk line as far as North Elmham, or rather reinstate it; for the time being, the village has The Railway pub, a station road and even a station building, but no railway.

North Elmham was the site of the Bishopric of East Anglia until 1075, but of the Saxon cathedral that stood here, virtually no trace remains. Instead are the flinty remains of a Norman church built by Herbert de Losinga alongside the earthworks of a 14th-century castle built by Henry le Despenser, a later Bishop of Norwich. The ruins occupy a pretty spot at the edge of the village surrounded by old chestnut trees.

6 FOXLEY WOOD & 27 HONEYPOT WOOD

Norfolk has some wonderful tracts of ancient woodland and two of these lie quite close to Dereham. The Norfolk Wildlife Trust manages Foxley and Honeypot woods, which are fine reminders of what much of central Norfolk must once have been like before widespread agriculture took hold. It is tempting to think of woods like these as truly wild places left over from the last ice age but, really, they are not. They have been rigorously managed over the centuries, albeit in a sustainable way. These days, of course, there is little demand for woodland products like hazel wands but the ancient art of coppicing is still practised, creating the dappled conditions needed for what have become quite scarce plants like primroses, cowslips and early purple orchids.

These woodlands are all habitats for butterflies and birds and, in springtime especially, for idyllic walks along the grassy rides. Northeast of East Dereham, just beyond Foxley and Bawdeswell (which are on the A1067), **Foxley Wood** is Norfolk's largest remaining ancient woodland. It was intensively coppiced in medieval times and, as well as hazel, it yielded other woodland products such as tree bark used in the tanning industry. The bluebells are so well known locally that the woodland rides can get almost busy at bluebell time (late April–early May). Several waymarked trails penetrate the heart of the wood. Their margins are sometimes boggy following prolonged wet weather but if you stick to the central part of the ride it's usually not too wet underfoot.

Four miles west of East Dereham and just north of Wendling, **Honeypot Wood** is smaller and takes its name from a nearby medieval sewage dump or 'honey pit' – a euphemism if ever there was one. Like Foxley Wood, it is at its very best in spring when enough light filters through the canopy to allow woodland plants like twayblades, wood anemones and, of course, bluebells to flourish.

NORFOLK ONLINE

For additional online content, articles, photos and more on Norfolk, why not visit ⊘ bradtguides.com/norfolk.

FOLLOW US

Use #norfolk to share your adventures using this guide with us – we'd love to hear from you.

- Bradt Travel Guides
- @bradtguides (#norfolk)
- @BradtGuides & @SlowNorfolk (#norfolk)
- pinterest.com/bradtguides

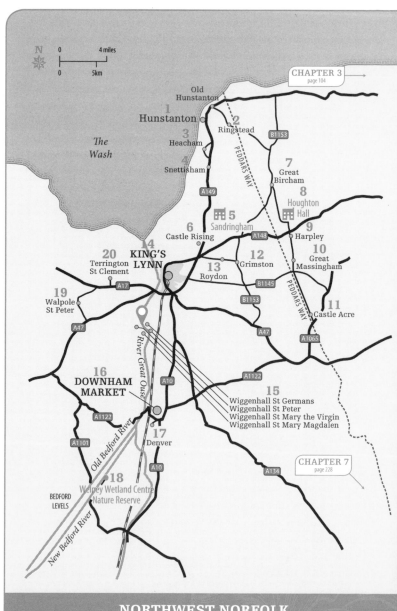

CHAPTER 7
page 228

The
Wash

Old
Hunstanton

1
Hunstanton

2
Ringstead

B1153

3
Heacham

7
Great
Bircham

4
Snettisham

A149

8
Houghton
Hall

5
Sandringham

A148

9
Harpley

6
Castle Rising

10
Great
Massingham

14
KING'S
LYNN

12
Grimston

20
Terrington
St Clement

13
Roydon

B1145

A17

B1153

11
Castle Acre

19
Walpole
St Peter

PEDDARS WAY

A47

A1065

A47

A1122

16
DOWNHAM
MARKET

River Great Ouse

15
Wiggenhall St Germans
Wiggenhall St Peter
Wiggenhall St Mary the Virgin
Wiggenhall St Mary Magdalen

A10

A1122

A1101

17
Denver

Old Bedford River

A10

A134

18
Welney Wetland Centre
Nature Reserve

BEDFORD
LEVELS

New Bedford River

PEDDARS WAY

NORTHWEST NORFOLK
& THE WASH

4
NORTHWEST NORFOLK
& THE WASH

As you head west along the north Norfolk coast, it turns south just before the resort of **Hunstanton** and with a change of direction, comes a change of character. Instead of vast expanses of salt marshes, pebble cottages and silted medieval harbours we find ourselves in a zone of sandy beaches and low dunes, stone-banded cliffs and low chalk ridges inland. The coast runs down as far as **King's Lynn**, which once had a far more important place in the scheme of things than it has today but, there again, so did Norfolk as a whole.

It may seem strange to witness the sun setting out to sea – this is East Anglia after all. But the realisation that **the Wash** is just a rather wide inlet will come when, in fine weather, you see the wind turbines on the far Lincolnshire shore, or, on a very clear day, catch a glimpse of the 'Boston Stump', the improbably tall tower of Boston's St Botolph's Church. The Wash's beaches attract both holiday makers and wildfowl, with buckets, spades and suntan oil out in force at Snettisham in the summer months, and geese, ducks and waders feasting on the tidal mudflats and sandbanks offshore in winter.

Inland from the coast it is a different picture, with low chalk hills, quietly attractive carrstone and chalk-built villages like **Ringstead** and lush pasture with scattered patches of woodland. Further inland still and you edge into the light soils of what's sometimes termed as High Norfolk – the agricultural landscape of north Norfolk enclosure, with its hedgerows and woodland copses.

The slow pace of life here quickens only marginally in its urban centres, old-fashioned market towns like Swaffham and Downham Market that lie on the edge of this region and give way to the Brecks and the Fens respectively. On the whole though, smaller villages like Great Bircham and Great Massingham, both far from 'great', are generally more typical of this ultra-rural corner of the county. This is estate country too, with **Sandringham**, the Royal family's country retreat, being the prime example. The hall at **Houghton** is even more impressive and one of the finest country houses in East Anglia.

King's Lynn, once a thriving port, is central to the area and although it may seem unprepossessing on arrival, has a concentration of intriguing distractions centred around its historic core. South and west of here lie the spectacularly contour-free, drained arable region of **the Fens**, often associated with Norfolk but really far more typical of Cambridgeshire and south Lincolnshire than Norfolk as a whole. The Fens are not to everyone's taste, but have huge wide skies and distant horizons that are unsullied by anything as presumptuous as a hill or even a contour. Lines of straight poplars stretch into the distance like a French impressionist painting; pylons recede to vanishing point – you can almost sense the curvature of the earth.

The **Peddars Way** runs arrow-straight across this area, beginning uncertainly – or rather, ill-defined – in the heathland at Knettishall near Thetford but gaining confidence, and a more obvious surface, as it progresses through **Castle Acre** across the heathland and chalk ridges of west Norfolk to terminate at Holme-next-the-Sea. Such a linear, determined route suggests a Roman origin, and it was constructed as a military thoroughfare in their campaign to pacify Norfolk's warring Iceni tribes. When the Romans finally removed their sandals from these shores and high-tailed it back to Rome in time for the fall of their empire, the route came into its own as a thoroughfare for peddlers, thieves, drovers and pilgrims. There again, the route may well be even older – an extension of the undeniably ancient Icknield Way that was remodelled by road-mad Romans shortly after they arrived.

GETTING AROUND

PUBLIC TRANSPORT

Geographically west Norfolk is somewhat out on a limb and this isolation is reflected in its **train** connections. Rail services connect King's Lynn with Cambridge and London but there's no direct service to Norwich.

By **bus**, the situation is slightly better but by no means marvellous. The exemplary Coasthopper service along Norfolk's north coast runs as far west as Hunstanton, from where good connections south to King's Lynn call at villages along the A149 – Heacham, Snettisham, Dersingham and ℹ **TOURIST INFORMATION**

Downham Market The Priory Centre, 78 Priory Rd ☎ 01553 763044 (King's Lynn TIC)
Fens Tourism ⌨ visitthefens.com
Hunstanton town hall The Green ☎ 01485 532610 ⌨ visithunstanton.info
King's Lynn The Customs House, Purfleet Quay ☎ 01553 763044
Visit West Norfolk website ⌨ visitwestnorfolk.com

Castle Rising. The X1, a direct, and reasonably quick, bus service runs between Norwich and King's Lynn calling at East Dereham and Swaffham *en route*. **Stagecoach Norfolk** (⌨ stagecoachbus.com), the same company that runs the Coasthopper route, has services running from King's Lynn to the north coast and east to Fakenham via larger villages like Great Massingham but unfortunately some of the smaller villages, especially those in the Fens, are harder to reach.

WALKING

Some of the best walking in the county is along stretches of the valley of the **River Nar**, a lovely chalk stream that has been designated an SSSI along its entire length. The river flows through Castle Acre, West Acre and Narborough, which all make good starting points for a circular walk.

The **Nar Valley Way** runs 33 miles from the Gressenhall Farm and Workhouse (page 130) all the way to King's Lynn. This links with both the Peddars Way at Castle Acre and the Wash Coast Path at King's Lynn. The Nar Valley Group of Parishes have produced a useful leaflet, *Footsteps through Time: Walks in the Nar Valley*, which outlines five circular walks starting in Narborough, Castle Acre or West Acre. You should be able to find the leaflet at tourist centres. Norfolk County Council also has useful information and suggestions for circular and short and long linear walks online at ⌨ www.norfolk.gov.uk/narvalleyway.

Close to King's Lynn, **Roydon Common** offers a bracing walk well away from habitation, and **Ringstead Downs** near Hunstanton is another good choice for short, leisurely strolls. To get close up to **the Wash**, explore the **Peter Scott Walk**, which runs a very tranquil ten miles along the sea bank from King's Lynn to the mouth of the Nene at Sutton Bridge in Lincolnshire (the great naturalist after which it's named lived in a lighthouse on the east bank of the Nene), with choice coastal and fenland views and some excellent bird watching opportunities.

CYCLING

Cycling is enjoyable in much of this region, if you keep off major roads like the A149, and avoid the A47, A10 and A17 trunk roads at all costs. The terrain is varied and rewarding, and the hills are gentle. Best of all, is to take advantage of those sections of the **Peddars Way** which, doubling as a bridleway, can be used by mountain or hybrid bikes. The track is fine for mountain and touring bikes but sleek racers with tyres the width of a coin will not do well here.

THE NORTHWEST CORNER: HUNSTANTON TO CASTLE RISING

1 HUNSTANTON

The Lodge (page 257)

Rather like a smaller version of Cromer, Hunstanton – 'Hunston' if you live there, 'Sunny Hunny' if you take to the beach – is a seaside resort that came to prominence during the Victorian railway age. It has a somewhat different appearance and atmosphere to its north Norfolk competitors though, as among the mock Tudor of its seafront hotels are some built of **carrstone**, the tough gingery-red sandstone that gives character to this part of the county. Living in east Norfolk, I am so used to seeing only flint or brick used for domestic architecture that this corner of the county can almost seem like alien territory. But no, this is still Norfolk: the air, the accents, the pace of things – these are all constants. Norfolk is a wide county and Norwich and Great Yarmouth lie so far to the east that many people who live around here hardly ever travel there; instead, they look to King's Lynn or Cambridge for their ration of big city lights.

There are traces of Neolithic settlement in the area, but the town you see today is the result of planned development by Henry Styleman Le Strange of Hunstanton Hall in the mid 1840s, who encouraged investment in the railway line between the town and King's Lynn in an attempt to attract visitors to its fine sandy beaches. The venture was a success and well-to-do Victorians came in droves, even the Prince of Wales, later to be Edward VII, who stayed here while recovering from typhoid (perhaps his other favourite, Cromer, was considered a bit too fast-paced for this purpose).

"Buildings feature carrstone, the gingery-red sandstone typical of this part of the county."

LE STRANGE GOINGS-ON
AT HUNSTANTON BEACH

St Edmund's Point on the coast at Old Hunstanton makes reference to Edmund, the future King of East Anglia who is said to have been shipwrecked here, a mere 14-year-old boy, in AD855. Edmund would go on to become a religious cult hero and England's first patron saint after his matyrdom at the hands of Danes in 869 or 870. In the 13th century, the monks of Bury St Edmunds built a chapel on the cliffs above the spot where Edmund landed in gratitude for his safe deliverance. The ruins of the chapel lie close to an attractive white early 19th-century lighthouse, now a holiday let, whose light was extinguished at the outbreak of World War I never to be rekindled.

The beach at Hunstanton is one of the few places in Britain where the foreshore is privately owned. The Le Strange family, who have been lords of the manor here since shortly after the Norman Conquest, have in their possession a charter that states that as well as the beach itself they own 'everything in the sea as far as a man riding a horse can throw a javelin from the low-tide mark'. The hereditary title of Lord High Admiral of the Wash is also retained by the family. So the seaweed-covered rocks belong, technically at least, to the Le Strange Estate. If St Edmund had pitched up here a couple of centuries later perhaps he would have become the property of the Le Strange Estate too?

Hunstanton is pleasant enough, with a promenade, beach and sloping central green, but for my money, its greatest attraction lies north of the modern town centre in Old Hunstanton, where the gorgeous **banded cliffs** are made of layers of rusty ginger sandstone ('carrstone'), red limestone ('red chalk') with a white chalk layer on top. The cliffs – a perfect geology textbook illustration – are framed by a foreground of chalky sand and green, seaweed-covered rocks. With the setting sun lighting up the cliffs as it lowers across the Wash, and a painterly combination of red, white, green and blue, this is the sort of place that landscape photographers get excited about. The picturesque remains of a wrecked boat, the steam trawler Sheraton, on the tide-line beneath St Edmund's Point provide the final ingredient for a picture perfect scene.

You can take a **boat trip** from the promenade. Searles Sea Tours (✆ 01485 534444 ⬦ seatours.co.uk) run a variety of trips to view seal colonies on sandbanks in the Wash, and they also do trips along the shoreline past the red and white cliffs and St Edmund's Point. Another option is to take a ride in a World War II amphibious DUKW to visit the wreck of the *Sheraton*.

Old Hunstanton, which is really just an estate village that has become a suburb of the larger town, has the remains – little more than an arch – of **St Edmund's Chapel**. This dates from 1272 and is reputed to have been built on the very spot where the saint landed when he arrived from Germany to become King of East Anglia. It's pleasant to stroll along the top of cliffs here, past the pitch and putt course, the ruined chapel and a converted white lighthouse towards the glitzier side of town. Better still though is to go one way along the beach, admiring the candy-striped cliffs, and return via the cliff top walk.

¶¶ FOOD & DRINK

Hunstanton seems to have a dearth of decent, traditional pubs. Your best bet is probably The Lodge Inn in Old Hunstanton or you could make your way out to the Gin Trap in Ringstead (page 142). Many visitors tend to buy fish and chips from Fishers and eat them on the nearby green overlooking the sea.

Fishers of Hunstanton 2–4 Greevegate ✆ 01485 524205 ⊘ fishersofhunstanton.com. This traditional and conveniently placed fish and chip shop has been in business for over 40 years. Indeed, Fishers is so well known in the town that the queue can be very long here in summer.

The Lodge Inn Old Hunstanton Rd ✆ 01485 532896 ⊘ thelodgehunstanton.co.uk. On the coast road next to the post office, the restaurant here serves imaginatively prepared food with an international flavour sourced mostly from Norfolk-grown ingredients. For a slightly less formal atmosphere you can also eat in the large airy bar. See also *Accommodation*, page 257.

Norfolk Deli 16 Greevegate, Hunstanton ✆ 01485 535540 ⊘ norfolk-deli.co.uk. This delicatessen specialises in local produce, especially cheese, of which there are 70 varieties, a dozen from Norfolk. It's also very good for breads, charcuterie, local beers and made-to-order sandwiches.

2 RINGSTEAD

A small, attractive village of whitewashed cottages just inland from the coast, and on the route of the Peddars Way, Ringstead is chocolate-box pretty, has a lovely pub and is a good starting point for leisurely walks along the valley of the Ringstead Downs immediately west of the village. The village's original church, St Peter's, is now long gone as a place of worship but its Norman round tower still remains a little to the south of the village.

Ringstead Downs

These are hardly the South Downs, but there are some similarities. Unimproved chalk grassland such as this is rare in Norfolk. Ringstead Downs is a short stretch of dry glacial valley, a far northern extension of the same chalk strata that make up the Chilterns and Cambridgeshire's Gog Magog Hills. The chalky soil ensures plenty of wildflowers that are rarely found elsewhere in the region, as well as a good show of butterfly species like Brown Argus and warblers in summer. On a sunny day, the gentle slopes here provide an ideal setting for a leisurely picnic, with butterflies fluttering by, the contented buzz of bees and the scent of thyme creating as much a sense of bucolic well-being as a 1970s shampoo advert.

Courtyard Farm

Ringstead PE36 5LQ ✐ 01485 525251 ☝ courtyardfarm.co.uk

Courtyard Farm, just east of Ringstead village, which Lord Peter Melchett, former executive director of Greenpeace and tireless champion of ramblers' rights, farms according to organic principles, is welcoming to walkers and to walkers with dogs on leads too. There are two way-marked circular routes of around two miles and one of six miles on public footpaths around the farm, and more routes on permissive paths – a map can be downloaded from the farm website. Not surprisingly, given its organic credentials, Courtyard Farm is replete with wildlife, with plenty of typical farmland birds like skylarks and a thriving population of hares. Even driving past by car you can't help but notice the kaleidoscopic colour of the native annual wildflowers that grow in the field margins here, an all-too-rare sight elsewhere in arable Norfolk.

"You can't help but notice the kaleidoscopic colour of the native annual wildflowers that grow in the field margins here."

Courtyard Farm Trust also owns 90 acres of grazing marshes managed by Norfolk Wildlife Trust at nearby Holme-next-the–Sea (pages 59–61), a haven for waders and wildfowl. Not wishing to turn its back on material culture in favour of wildlife, the farm has also commissioned works of art in two of its disused marl pits. Both use materials that reflect the local environment: *Carrstone Shale Wall and Boulder* by John Sands, which can be found in an old marl pit northwest of North Wood, and *Chalky Void (absence and presence)* by Martha Winter in North Wood itself.

¶ FOOD & DRINK

Gin Trap Inn High St ✆ 01485 525264 ⏁ thegintrapinn.co.uk. The oak-beamed bar has real ales such as Adnams and Woodforde's and a crackling fire, while the comforting food on offer is mostly locally sourced, with beef and pork from nearby Courtyard Farm and oysters from Thornham.

3 HEACHAM

⌂ The Summerhouse (page 258)

Heacham, just south of Hunstanton on the coast, has a beach but is best known for **lavender**. In summer, coach-loads come from afar to view the bushes in their mauve, serried ranks. On a warm sunny day, the aromatic oils released from the plants permeate the air so much that the whole area is redolent of a National Trust gift shop. Lavender garden and distillery tours are available at **Caley Mill Farm**, headquarters of Norfolk Lavender Ltd (✆ 01485 570384 ⏁ norfolk-lavender.co.uk), where a tea room and gift shop sell all manner of lavender products. The company was founded in 1932 and lavender has been grown around Caley Mill since 1936. Henry Head, who has worked here for over 30 years, told me a little about the company. 'Here at Norfolk Lavender we've kept alive the great tradition of English lavender growing – for 60 years we were the only significant growers in the country. Caley Mill was a Victorian watermill built in 1837 but now it's our headquarters and we've got shops, a tea room and plant centre here, as well as our new Rare Breeds Animal Centre.' I asked him why this part of west Norfolk is so suitable for lavender growing. It is, after all, a plant that has its natural home on sun-baked Mediterranean hillsides. 'With one exception, all the varieties that we grow here were developed by us for their suitability for the local conditions. The locality is ideal: there's plenty of sunshine, free-draining soils and not too much rain.'

"The village sign depicts Pocohontas thanks to a historical association."

The village also has a curious association with **Pocahontas** and the village sign depicts the celebrated Powhatan Indian princess. Pocahontas married an English Virginian settler, John Rolfe, in 1614 and the two of them travelled to England together in 1616. At first, the couple spent some time in the capital, delighting the London set, but later moved on to live at Rolfe's country house at **Heacham Hall** for a while. The pair attempted to return to Virginia in 1617 but Pocahontas fell ill with

KING'S LYNN TO HUNSTANTON – A BETJEMAN TRAIN JOURNEY

There's a charming old film in the East Anglian Film Archive (⊘ eafa.org.uk/catalogue/76) of John Betjeman travelling from King's Lynn to Hunstanton on the former Great Eastern Railway, stopping to admire the Edwardian splendour of Wolferton station along the way, a station so well-appointed for its royal passengers that it sports crowns atop its lamp posts. The film ends at the promenade at Hunstanton, Betjeman hamming it up delightfully as he inhales the bracing sea air in front of the pier.

Much has gone since the film was made in 1961 – the railway line, the poet himself and much else besides. The spectacularly long pier that appears in the documentary was washed away in a storm in 1978. The Sandringham Hotel seen in front of Hunstanton station is long gone too – demolished in 1967 – and the site of the former railway station now serves as a car park. Only half a century ago, this was a very different world – a black and white one in which poet laureates made unhurried documentaries about humble branch lines (now we have unseated Tory politicians in lurid jackets doing the same), schoolboys wore caps and short trousers, and almost everyone who could afford it holidayed at a British coastal resort.

smallpox before they had even left English waters. She was taken ashore before she died, to be buried at Gravesend. Many descendants of the Rolfe family lie buried at **Heacham Church**, a 12th-century building of Norman origin that is said to have the oldest church bell in East Anglia.

Now converted to holiday accommodation, Heacham's erstwhile **railway station** used to serve the now defunct King's Lynn to Hunstanton line, which operated for just over a hundred years between 1866 and 1969, when Norfolk was much better connected by rail than it is today.

SNETTISHAM

🏠 **Rose and Crown** (page 258)

The beach here is enormous – wide and spacious – but the village is just as well known for its RSPB reserve. Both lie away from the village, around two miles to the west. There has been an important carrstone quarry here for centuries and much of the stone that you see in walls around this part of the county probably originates from here.

The Snettisham area has clearly been settled for millennia: a great hoard of treasure trove was discovered close to the village – 75 complete golden torcs (solid gold neck rings, which must have been almost too heavy to wear) and even more fragmentary ones that date from the 1st century AD, as well as a great deal of Romano-British jewellery, all now at the British Museum.

Snettisham's **St Mary's Church**, with its tall 14th-century spire, has been raved about by architectural writers Nikolaus Pevsner and Simon Jenkins for its west window, with its complex, lace-like tracery. The east and south windows were replaced after having been bombed by a Zeppelin in 1915 – the very first air attack on an English church, a unique honour of sorts. Compared to churches in Lincolnshire, St Mary's seems perfectly normal, as spires are not at all unusual in that part of the world. Coming from Norfolk though, it does look a bit odd, as if some sort of boundary has been crossed – an architectural aperitif for the world beyond the Wash.

At the shoreline, the tide can go out for miles here, leaving a vast area of mud and sand, ideal for feeding birds and games of cricket. Naturally, birds have the advantage of being able to fly away if cut off by rapidly incoming tides; strolling humans do not have this facility. The **RSPB reserve** (✆ 01485 542689) here really comes into its own during the autumn and winter months when high tides push tens of thousands of waders up on to the shoreline. The higher the tide, the easier it is to see the birds. Low tides require telescopes and an aptitude for identifying indeterminate blobs in the distant mud. Be aware that it is a fairly long walk from the RSPB car park to the reserve, but there's plenty to look for in the reeds along the way. The nearest bus stop for both beach and reserve is on the A149 at the Beach Road junction.

Snettisham Park Farm (✆ 01485 542425 ⊘ snettishampark.co.uk), with its entrance close to the church on the Bircham road, is a working farm that offers hands-on activities likely to appeal to children. Animals include what you would normally expect on a farm, plus deer and, even more exotically, llamas. Deer safaris feature a 45-minute commentated tractor and trailer ride, and there are a number of farm trails.

¶¶ FOOD & DRINK

Rose and Crown Old Church Rd, Snettisham ✆ 01485 541382 ⊘ roseandcrownsnettisham. co.uk. This whitewashed 14th-century inn has an imaginative menu that uses local produce where possible: all meat is outdoor-reared in Norfolk; mussels, crabs and lobsters come from Brancaster, and vegetables are sourced from a local allotment. See also *Accommodation*, page 258.

SANDRINGHAM HOUSE & ESTATE

Sandringham PE35 6EN ✆ 01485 545408 ⟀ sandringhamestate.co.uk ⊙ house, museum & gardens Easter–early Nov except for last week in Jul, country park open every day; discounted admission to the estate for those who arrive by public transport; free entry & parking for the country park

Adjacent to the village of Dersingham is the Sandringham Estate, with Sandringham House set in 60 acres of landscaped, wooded gardens, and best known as the place where the Queen eats her Christmas turkey before watching herself on TV. Queen Victoria's son, Edward the Prince of Wales, first came across the country house and estate here in 1861 and snapped them up them forthwith (he rejected Houghton Hall, which was also offered for purchase). The Prince rebuilt the main residence to his own tastes in 1870 and landscaped the grounds, adding a ballroom later on, which sees use today as the venue for estate workers' Christmas parties. The author John Seymour describes the house as 'very ugly – like a huge and grandiose Victorian seaside hotel', but he does have a point as, scaled down in size, it wouldn't look too out of place sitting above the promenade in Cromer. Anyway, you can make up your own mind if you choose to visit.

The wooded grounds are, indisputably, quite lovely. For devotees of local vernacular style, the 16th-century **church of St Mary Magdalene** is widely considered to be one of the very finest carrstone buildings in existence. This is, of course, where the Royal Family comes to worship at Christmas and so you have probably glimpsed it already on television. The estate's **museum** has a large and rather bizarre collection of royal vehicles and some of the gifts given to the Royal Family over the years. The gift shop sells all manner of royal memorabilia but the **estate farm shop** is perhaps more appealing, with wares including local cheese, estate-produced rare-breed organic meat and a large selection of jams and chutneys.

Sandringham Country Park, which extends north from the visitor centre and car park to cover an area of nearly 600 acres, has open access and is free to visit. The park dates from 1968 when 350 acres of the Queen's estate was designated as a Country Park. It has been enlarged since then to create a large wooded area with free access to the public. The park has two waymarked nature trails and a sculpture trail as well as numerous woodland paths through stands of mixed evergreen and deciduous trees.

The Coasthopper bus provides a regular service to the visitor centre, as does the Coastliner service from King's Lynn. The Sustrans National Cycle Route 1 passes nearby.

6 CASTLE RISING

Between Dersingham and King's Lynn, Castle Rising village is attractive in its own right. There's **St Lawrence's Church** with its Norman and Early-English features and the Hospital of the Holy and Undivided Trinity opposite, but what most come to see is the village's mighty **Norman castle** (✆ 01553 631330; ☉ closed Mon and Tue in winter; English Heritage). This impressive and seemingly impregnable ruin, owned by English Heritage, has a typical Norman square keep similar to Norwich Castle's; it peeps over the top of the huge oval defensive earthworks that surround it and are believed to be Roman or earlier. Ruins of a Saxon and Norman chapel lie partly buried in the earthworks' north side.

"The village's castle is a seemingly impregnable ruin."

Edward III made use of the castle to banish his mother Isabella, the 'She-wolf of France', after she had colluded with her lover in the death of her husband, Edward II, reputedly by a grisly method that required the unorthodox use of fire-stoking equipment. The means of this brutal murder is most likely pure myth, however, and some accounts even suggest that Edward II escaped to live in exile. For Isabella, it was a relatively liberal banishment, more a kind of voluntary house arrest, as she continued to move around the country relatively freely and did not go mad in her confinement as is sometimes alleged. Later occupants of the castle included the Black Prince and Richard II, and later still, Henry VIII, who sold it to the Howard family.

Opposite the church, the red-brick **Hospital of the Holy and Undivided Trinity**, also known as the Howard Bede House, is effectively an almshouse founded by Henry Howard, the Earl of Northampton, in 1614. It continues to house a dozen elderly ladies to this day who, following the statute set down by Henry Howard, must be 'able to read, single, 56 at least, no common beggar, harlot, scold, drunkard, haunter of taverns, inns or alehouses' – tough conditions indeed, especially the alehouse requirement. Once a year, in thanksgiving to their founder, the Howard Bede women march to church as a group wearing Jacobean costume and conical headgear. Who said tradition was dead?

EAST FROM SANDRINGHAM & CASTLE RISING

GREAT BIRCHAM

East of Dersingham, just beyond the route of the Peddars Way, and south of the village of Docking, lies Great Bircham, which is hime to one of the best-preserved windmills in Norfolk. Like the village of Docking, this sits on a hill. Great Bircham is one of three villages that lie within the parish of Bircham: just north is Bircham Newton and to the east is Bircham Tofts.

Great Bircham Windmill

Great Bircham PE31 6SJ ✐ 01485 578393 ✐ birchamwindmill.co.uk ☉ Mar–Sep daily

Just west of Great Bircham village, this mill has changed hands quite a number of times since it was built in 1846. Originally located on land belonging to the Houghton Estate, it was purchased in a derelict state by the Royal Sandringham Estate in 1939 before being sold on to a private owner in 1976. A thorough restoration project began in 1977, and by 1981 its four sails were back in place. The fully restored mill stands an impressive five storeys tall and has a cottage and long-established bakery attached, where bread is still baked today.

Special events are put on from time to time, with regular courses that teach arcane crafts like walking-stick carving and wool-spinning. The tea rooms on the site of the old granary specialise in cream teas, so after

"Regular courses teach arcane crafts like walking-stick carving and wool-spinning."

indulging in one of these you might need the mill's cycle hire facility. Accommodation features a choice of a campsite, a holiday cottage and a shepherd's hut.

HOUGHTON HALL

PE31 6UE ✐ 01485 528569 ✐ www.houghtonhall.com ☉ end Apr–end Oct, Wed–Sun & bank holiday Mon

Minor roads south and southwest of Great Bircham lead to the south entrance of Houghton Hall at New Houghton where you enter the estate's vast array of woodland and the deer park with an unusual herd of white fallow deer. This part of west Norfolk has been the seat of the Walpole family since the 14th century and the present incumbents, Lord and Lady Cholmondeley, are direct descendants of this long line.

Built in early 18th-century Palladian style, Houghton Hall is Norfolk's largest country house, and both house and estate reflect the flamboyant tastes of Norfolk 'new money' some three centuries ago. Planning regulations were less proscriptive in those days, and **Sir Robert Walpole**, England's first Prime Minister, who built the house in the 1720s, saw fit to pull down the nearby village of Houghton on purely aesthetic grounds as he claimed it spoiled his view. Houghton's Early-English 13th-century village church of St Martin, however, was left well alone. So the unsightly villagers were moved to a new village, New Houghton, immediately south of the estate.

No expense was spared with the new hall: rather than use Norfolk brick, Walpole opted to build in Yorkshire stone, and the interior was sumptuously furnished and decorated with Old Masters. These are no longer at Houghton Hall as its paintings were sold to Catherine the Great, the Czarina of Russia, by Sir Robert's dissolute grandson, George, the third Earl of Orford, in order to pay off debts. His collection ended up in the Hermitage in St Petersburg, where it remains to this day. In light of this, the present incumbents were delighted when a large number of the masterpieces were returned to their home of 200 years ago, albeit temporarily, for a major exhibition in 2013 – a remarkable achievement given that, even today, Russia is not always the easiest country to do business with. *Houghton Revisited* proved so popular that there is always a chance that something similar may happen again one day.

"The lush surrounding parkland is home to a herd of around 600 white fallow deer."

Aside from the house, the lush parkland surrounding the hall is well worth a visit if only for the spectacle of seeing a herd of around 600 white fallow deer. There is a permanent display of sculpture and landscape art in the grounds and walled garden too, featuring the work of renowned artists like Rachel Whiteread, Zhan Wang and Stephen Cox. Most impressive of these is probably *Skyspace* by James Turrell, a natural light installation with its own building tucked away in the woods. There's also a Richard Long piece, *Moon Circle*, located close to the ha-ha. The permanent work is supplemented by a summer exhibition most years, often in tandem with the start of the Norwich & Norfolk Festival – in 2015 this featured a light show by James Turrell, and in 2017 additional commissioned works by Richard Long.

HARPLEY

South of the Houghton Estate, the pleasant but unremarkable village of Harpley has a decent pub and a highly atmospheric church. **St Lawrence's Church** is a curious musty place of decorated Gothic. The ridge of the roof is studded with angels with folded wings and the benches inside have carvings of all manner of wild animals – monkeys, bears and even mythical creatures – in addition to a pleasing carving of St James the pilgrim with his staff, satchel and shell. The village is also one of the highest in Norfolk but not the highest – that honour goes to Docking a few miles to the north.

Close to Harpley, to the northwest clustered alongside the route of the Peddars Way at Harpley Common, is a group of **Bronze Age barrows**. Although the tumuli look impressive marked on the OS map there is not much to see on the ground other than low grassy mounds. Nevertheless, they serve as a worthy reminder that this region has been populated for millennia – the proximity of the Peddars Way suggesting that parts of this ancient route might well date back to before Roman times.

FOOD & DRINK

Rose and Crown Nethergate St ✆ 01485 521807. An intimate village pub with well-kept ale and good, unpretentious food.

GREAT MASSINGHAM

Not far from Houghton Hall and the village of Harpley, and just south of its sister community of Little Massingham, Great Massingham is a very pretty village of 18th- and 19th-century cottages set against an impressively large and carefully mown green studded with daisies. The village has several ponds that originally were probably fish ponds for the village's former 11th-century Augustinian priory that today lies in ruins. It is possible that the village is actually much older than this and dates from as far back as the 5th century when the area was settled by a group of Angles and Saxons in the wake of the Roman withdrawal. The leader of this group may have been Maesron and the settlers known as Maersings, hence the village becoming Maersingham and later, Massingham.

Mad Dog Lane, which leads from the village past council houses to the Peddars Way, does not appear to have any dogs – mad or otherwise – prowling along it but it would be interesting to know how this name came about. Perhaps the deranged animal escaped from nearby Kennel Farm? Given its sizeable ponds, ducks rather than dogs tend to sum up the character of the village – a detail that has not gone unnoticed by the local hostelry.

A small, private airfield just east of the village saw service as an RAF bomber base during World War II. Robert Walpole, the first English Prime Minister, was educated in the village and he appears on the village sign alongside a monk, an RAF bomber, a sheep and a tractor. Curiously, no ducks are represented.

⊪ FOOD & DRINK

Dabbling Duck 11 Abbey Rd ☏ 01485 520827 ⬙ thedabblingduck.co.uk. Sitting comfortably alongside the village green as if it has always been there, the Dabbling Duck is known throughout west Norfolk for the quality of its food.

11 CASTLE ACRE

Conveniently straddling the route of both the Peddars Way and the Nar Valley Way, Castle Acre makes a welcome stopover for hikers, but is well worth a visit even for those not inexorably striding towards Holme-next-the-Sea (where the Peddars Way ends). The village does contain, of course, a castle – an early Norman one in this case – but not that much survives other than its sprawling earthworks and a gateway. Far more impressive are the Norman ruins of **Castle Acre Priory**, founded just after the conquest in 1090, a highly atmospheric place to wander, especially late in the day with the sun low in the western sky. It may seem just like any other picture-perfect Norfolk village today – albeit a bit hillier than most – but, left to your own devices, it is still possible to get an inkling as to just how important Castle Acre was back in the Norman period.

The village sits on a low chalk hill above the River Nar, a compact place of flint and brick houses that take up the space of what would have been the outer bailey of the castle on the hill. The village's flint 16th-century gatehouse would have been the bailey gate. The priory is a little lower down to the east, in fields beside the River Nar's north bank. Down here there is a ford that you need to cross if arriving in the village by means of the Peddars Way. A raised footpath to the left of the road offers a route over the water as well as a fine view of the priory ruins to the left. But even this gets flooded sometimes – coming this way in

SAXON CHURCHES IN WEST NORFOLK

The area immediately east of Castle Acre in west Norfolk is home to several small churches of Saxon origin. All Saints' Church at **Newton by Castle Acre** is one of the oldest in the county and has several surviving Saxon features such as a short central tower and a rounded chancel arch. The Church of St Nicholas at nearby **West Lexham** has a late Saxon tower, while St Andrew's Church at neighbouring **East Lexham** has a round tower with bell windows that is almost entirely Saxon. Immediately south at

Great Dunham, St Andrew's is almost entirely Saxon in structure with a short square central tower with bell windows and nave that are clearly pre-Conquest.

This compact rectangle of sleepy west Norfolk contains more surviving pre-Conquest churches than any other part of the county. Given such a concentration of ancient buildings, it seems a little strange that they all exist so close to Castle Acre, a place that with its huge motte and bailey castle and Cluniac monastery seems so resolutely Norman.

the wet autumn of 2012 I found that the footpath was barely visible beneath a torrent of fast-moving floodwater. My own fault really, as the 'No Access – Flood' sign at the top of the road should have given me some idea of what to expect.

Castle Acre Priory

Castle Acre PE32 2XD ✎ 01760 755394 ☺ Apr–Oct daily, weekends only rest of year; English Heritage

Founded by William de Warenne, son-in-law of William the Conqueror, the abbey was set up as a daughter priory of St Pancras at Lewes in Sussex, which in turn reported to the Cluniac Priory in Burgundy. The original priory was built within the walls of the castle but this proved too small and the monastery was soon moved to its current location. As is often the way with medieval religious orders, the priory went on to have a colourful and sometimes notorious life, with considerable friction between the Cluniac motherhouse and various English kings, notably the early Edwards, resulting in the priory being considered 'alien' and therefore heavily taxed. Not all medieval monks led blameless lives: in 1351, some of those at the priory were accused of 'living as vagabonds in secular habit' and the king felt it necessary to send his Serjeant-at-Arms to make arrests. Castle Acre Priory eventually became naturalised in 1373 and subsequently lost its connection with its French motherhouse.

Lying close to the route of pilgrimage to Walsingham, the priory set itself up in competition by selling indulgences to penitents on the first two days of August each year. The priory already had its very own relic, the arm of St Philip, but this did not turn out to be a particularly big crowd-puller; in fact, it only earned ten shillings from its exhibition during the whole of 1533. With the advent of the Dissolution, the priory changed ownership swiftly several times over, passing through the hands of Thomas Howard the Duke of Norfolk, Elizabeth I, Thomas Gresham and eventually, the Coke family. It is now owned by English Heritage.

¶¶ FOOD & DRINK

In Castle Acre village itself, **The Ostrich Inn** (𝒮 01760 755398 𝒶 ostrichcastleacre.com), a 16th-century former coaching inn, is a decent enough place for a drink or a meal. It has a sunny outdoor beer garden. **Church Gate Tearooms** (𝒮 01760 755551) and **Barnfield's Tearooms** (𝒮 01760 755577), also on Stocks Green, are convenient places for coffee and snacks.

KING'S LYNN & AROUND
12 GRIMSTON HEATH & 13 ROYDON COMMON
🏠 **Congham Hall Hotel** (page 257)

The road (Lynn Lane) that leads from Great Massingham to King's Lynn via Grimston and Roydon is vastly more pleasurable than the frenetic, speed-crazed A47 trunk road further to the south. It is wider than it appears on the map and surprisingly quiet, striking west across the lonely country of Grimston Heath. The road ranges relatively high for Norfolk but seems higher, almost as if it were upland country somewhere else in Britain. Grimston is a carrstone village without any great incentive for travellers to stop, as is Roydon, but shortly after the village is an off-road parking place to the left from where you can make an exploration of Roydon Common.

Roydon Common is a large area of heathland, looked after by the Norfolk Wildlife Trust, where heather thrives and sheep safely graze. The sheep, along with some ponies, are a fairly recent introduction as part of a management scheme to keep the habitat intact. A rough path leads towards an odd-looking isolated tower on a low hill. The tower is marked on the OS map as being among the conifers of Grimston Warren but the trees shown on the map have since been felled. 'Warren' is certainly right, as there is plenty of evidence of rabbits here. Occasional lapwings and curlews fly up from the heather, and hen harriers are not uncommon in winter. What is odd about this large area of heathland, just a stone's throw from the Wash, is how alien it seems to most of the rest of Norfolk. The view is impressive, with gentle valleys and plantations stretching into the distance and barely a village or church tower in sight. It might even be Exmoor or one of the flatter parts of the Pennines but just over the brow of the hill to the west is industrial King's Lynn, Norfolk's third largest town.

Much of the terrain around here, like Snettisham to the north, is one of old and new carrstone quarries, the disused quarries returning to heathland if left to their own devices long enough. A little south of here, just across the B1145, you'll find evidence of another type of mineral extraction – sand – although not just any old sand but the finest and purest variety used for glassmaking. If you head into King's Lynn from here, along the B1145, you'll pass a swanky country park with sailing club and golf course at the smart dormitory village of **Leziate**. South of Leziate, just across the disused railway line, a large neo-Gothic castellated mansion hides behind high walls. This is **Middleton Towers**, a moated medieval house that is pure Gormenghast and looks unlikely to welcome strangers. The house was originally a 14th-century fortified manor house, founded by the Scales family on a large, moated platform. Not much remains of the original today but a bridleway leads off the road into woods just south of the complex to give you a closer look. In the early post-war years, Middleton Towers hosted speedway races and celebrities like George Formby were invited to open the proceedings. These days, it is clear that whatever goes on there is very much a private affair.

4 KING'S LYNN

Everyone driving into Norfolk from the Midlands or the North catches a glimpse of King's Lynn's outer reaches as they negotiate the huge roundabout on the A47. To be honest, it is not a wholly prepossessing sight: an industrial landscape of grain mills and pylons. Just west of the roundabout is a vast paper-recycling plant built of low, square blocks that themselves could even be made up of lofty blocks of old newspapers. With food processing still the biggest employer here, King's Lynn can, at first glance, appear to be a frozen-fish-finger wasteland – the natural domain of Captain Birdseye.

Having said that, it is best that you put all your prejudices to one side until you reach the town centre, as King's Lynn really does have quite a lot to offer, especially for those with an interest in maritime history. Still Norfolk's third largest town, King's Lynn has an important place in both Norfolk and English history. Its rich architectural heritage hints at its hugely eminent status as a port in former times and it still has the scent of distant shores in its nostrils and the dirt of sea trade under its fingernails.

"It still has the scent of distant shores in its nostrils and the dirt of sea trade under its fingernails."

Historic Lynn

King's Lynn was England's third biggest port in the 14th century, the medieval period's equivalent of what Liverpool was in Victorian times, and as a member of the Hanseatic League between the 14th and 17th centuries, it looked east to trading partners in northern Europe and the Baltic as far as modern-day Estonia. Plain old 'Lynn' became King's Lynn (or Lynn Regis) when the town became royal property following Henry VIII's dissolution of the monasteries and it was a royalist stronghold during the civil war a century later. In the aftermath of Norfolk's wool production years, grain exports became increasingly important from the 17th century onwards.

The railway came to the town in 1847, providing an easy London connection and with Sandringham coming to prominence in the later years of the 19th century the town regained some of the prosperity lost during the previous one. The modern town underwent considerable decline in the 1980s and in 1987 became, somewhat notoriously, the first place in the UK to introduce CCTV as a means of monitoring the activity of town centre ne'er-do wells. Despite its position in the far west of the county, the language on the street remains firmly Norfolk, with none of the East Midlands cadences found a little further west in the Lincolnshire Fens. Portuguese and Polish are also widely spoken.

The beauty of King's Lynn as a place to visit is that its historic core is small and easy to walk around. In a half-day you could see most of the major sights and get a feel for the place; a full day is a better option though. The town's most photographed building is its elegant square Custom House, built in 1683 by the local architect Henry Bell and which now serves as the town's tourist office. The helpful staff here can suggest a walking route that takes in all the main places of interest.

The customs house is on **Purfleet Dock**, the original harbour inlet along South Quay. Standing at the Custom House, you should notice immediately the figure of a sailor in tricorn hat clutching a sea chart and looking out across the River Ouse. This being Norfolk, it is reasonable to assume that it's a likeness of Nelson but no, this honours the town's own son, George Vancouver, a sea captain credited with the discovery of the long-searched-for North West Passage and who went on to give his name to Canada's Pacific coast city. A decorative brass compass set into the concrete at the end of the dock associates various maritime aspirations with compass points – northwest is whaling, northeast is trade (and so on) – and has a roll-call of Norfolk mariners around it including Captain Vancouver, Captain John Smith and, of course, Admiral Nelson.

Old King's Lynn certainly has plenty to see: the arcaded terrace of Hanseatic buildings with their distinctive narrow windows and jettied upper storey – the only ones in the country – and plenty of cobbled lanes and handsome Georgian merchants' houses. Town centre life revolves chiefly around two squares, **Saturday Market Place** and **Tuesday Market Place**, which both do exactly what they say on the tin. Tuesday Market Place is the more northerly of the two, just a block in from

"There are plenty of cobbled lanes and handsome Georgian merchants' houses."

the Great Ouse River, and serves as a large car park much of the time. Dominating the market place is the impressive powder blue façade of the Duke's Head Hotel. The **Corn Exchange** here also has an impressive front to it. King Street running south has the **Arts Centre**, a restored 15th-century **guildhall**, and just beyond it a narrow alleyway, Ferry Lane, which leads to the dock for the pedestrian **ferry** across the river to West Lynn.

South of the Customs House is a warren of narrow streets filled with an impressive array of Tudor, Jacobean and Flemish houses, courtyards, warehouses and cottages. Most notable are **St Margaret's House**, a row of restored Hanseatic warehouses that date from 1475 and now house a café and a number of craft shops, but there's plenty of interest at every corner.

Saturday Market Place has the enormous **St Margaret's Church**, which dates from 1101 and dominates the small square. It has twin towers, one of them much rebuilt after it crashed dramatically on to the nave during a storm in 1741. The south tower sports an odd-looking clock. Odd-looking that is until you realise that it gives you the time of the high tide and the phase of the moon. I am no expert on high tides but currently it does not seem to be very accurate.

Directly opposite, the chequerboard stone and flint **Town Hall**, or Guildhall of the Holy Trinity, which stands next to the Old Gaol House, looks at first to be of a single build but the original building, dating back to Tudor times, was enlarged considerably by the town's fathers in the Georgian period. I was lucky enough to be given a tour by a friendly curator, who, very keen to show someone around, explained the development of the building to me in detail. He walked me through to the paintings in the Georgian annex where there was a portrait of Nelson looking boyish and approachable, despite the sea battle raging in the background. 'This was painted six months after his death,'

WHALE BONES ON THE RIVER NAR

King's Lynn was once an important port for the whaling industry. Heavy investments in the trade were made in the late 18th and early 19th centuries and an act of 1771 encouraged the industry by withdrawing the obligation to pay duty on catches for whale ships and also by protecting the whaling crews from Royal Navy press gangs during the whaling season. Whale products found many uses: whalebone was used to make chair backs and brush handles and for use as stiffening in dressmaking (hence a 'whalebone corset'); whale grease was used to lubricate machinery and oil was used to make soap and also for street lighting – St Margaret's Church in King's Lynn was illuminated with whale-oil lamps until the mid 19th century. Whale bone was also ground down to make fertilizer. King's Lynn still has a few reminders of this trade today – the Greenland Fishery Inn and Blubberhouse Creek to the south of the town being most conspicuous, although the blubber houses that once stood here are long gone.

The whale trade made its mark inland too. Follow the Nar Valley Way along the bank of the River Nar a mile or so west of Narborough and you'll come across a very large cast iron waterwheel on the opposite bank. I was surprised to find this the first time I walked this route but thankfully two helpful women, Annie and Chris from the local Ramblers group, just happened to be on the spot to explain its significance to me. 'That belonged to a bone mill that used to be here. They used to transport whale carcasses the curator informed me. 'He looks well, doesn't he, all things considered?' It was apparently a copy of a popular portrait around at the time. We moved on to a portrait of George Vancouver, King's Lynn's own son. 'You know, you used to be able to see his old house in the town centre. There was a plaque and everything. Well, that was until the 1960s when the planners knocked the old buildings down to put up a shopping precinct. They've knocked that down too now.'

Just east of the town hall is a small park that has an isolated tower with an arch beneath – **Greyfriars Tower** – all that remains of a friary established in the 13th century by Fransciscan monks. The southeast corner of the park has the **town library**, an Edwardian gothic fantasy in brick and carrstone. Further east again is a much larger park with a Georgian Walk and the Red Mount Chapel, which, along with **South Gate** on London Road, dates from the time of the 15th-century fortifications of the town. Thanks to a bit of inspired, prescient design, the arch of South Gate is sufficiently large to allow modern-day double-decker bus to pass through it.

here all the way up the river from Lynn. This was about as far as the barges could go, and once they'd removed the blubber at Blubberhouse Creek they would bring the bones here for grinding. They would have to boil them down first though – to remove the fat.' I reflected on how such a process would probably not smell that good as Annie continued, 'I heard that they sometimes brought human bones here for grinding but I don't know if that's true or not.'

A little research showed that Annie was quite right – human bones had indeed been ground down for fertiliser here at Narborough. The whale trade had declined dramatically by 1820 and as a consequence bone mills such as this one had to depend far more on local farms and slaughterhouses for raw materials. Supplies also came to King's Lynn by ship from north Germany; these would sometimes include exhumations from Hamburg burial grounds. No-one seemed to mind that much as it was said that 'One ton of German bone-dust saves the importation of ten tons of German corn'. It was all 'grist to the mill', in a manner of speaking. The old waterwheel from Narborough Bone Mill also makes an appearance on the Narborough village sign although there is no indication of its former use.

In 2015 a restored railway carriage was set up on the site to serve as a visitor centre, although currently this only has limited opening days. Volunteers meet here every Thursday to assist with research and further explore the site.

Lynn's museums

I find the most rewarding activity in King's Lynn is to take a leisurely amble along South Quay and try to rekindle the atmosphere at the height of its maritime trade, but there are some decent museums to investigate too. The recently expanded **True's Yard Fisherfolk Museum** (North St ℘ 01553 770479 ⊘ truesyard.co.uk) explores the town's maritime past. Pride of place must go, however, to **Lynn Museum** (Market St ℘ 01553 775001), in a converted Union Baptist chapel next to the bus station, and which has the reconstructed display of Seahenge (page 60). You'll also find displays on the town's past and oddities, like a Victorian cabinet of curiosities and slightly sinister souvenirs from the colonial era such as a demon mask from Persia and a skull from a West African fetish house. There is also a fair amount of hands-on stuff for children.

The Peter Scott Walk

If you're hankering after a long coastal hike along the Wash, consider the Peter Scott Walk that leads west into Lincolnshire from King's Lynn. The walk begins at West Lynn, easily reached by regular passenger ferry from South Quay. The path leads north along the River Great Ouse as far as the Wash before skirting the south shore as far as the River Nene, where the lighthouse that Peter Scott lived in between 1933 and 1939 lies on the east bank. Sutton Bridge, in Lincolnshire, lies about three miles inland from here. The walk is a little over ten miles in total but if you are depending on public transport you still have to get to and from the end/start point at the mouth of the Nene. One solution might be to take a bus to Sutton and then a taxi to the lighthouse and picnic place at East Bank, which is the furthest point the road goes northwards towards the Wash from Sutton Bank. You could then walk east to West Lynn, taking the ferry to King's Lynn at the end of your walk.

⊪ FOOD & DRINK

Market Bistro 11 Saturday Market Pl ℘ 01553 771483 ⊘ marketbistro.co.uk. This smart, family-run restaurant in the town centre makes excellent use of local produce. With a three-star rating for sustainability, the bistro has a working relationship with local suppliers.
Marriott's Warehouse South Quay ℘ 01553 818500 ⊘ marriottswarehouse.co.uk. Formerly Green Quay, this converted 16th-century warehouse next to the river at South Quay has a daytime café menu offering sharing platters and sandwiches and an evening restaurant menu. Both offer a reasonable amount of local seasonal produce.

WEST INTO FENLAND

Heading west from King's Lynn, you experience a sudden and quite dramatic change of scenery. Instead of leafy hedgerows, scattered woodland and softly undulating valleys, there are wide expanses of black soil, scattered rambling farmsteads with ugly modern barns and occasional villages that have a more insular feel than further east.

Newcomers to East Anglia may assume that all Norfolk looks like this. It doesn't, of course – it is a misleading preface to what comes later with the slightly more undulating charms of High Norfolk – but at least a quarter of the county does consist of the Fens, even if a quarter of Norfolk's population most certainly does not live here. This is definitely the most overlooked part of the county (for good reason, you might say). But despite its relentless flatness and uncompromising scenery, Norfolk's Fenland has more to offer than just celery, fertile soil and easy cycling: there are a couple of quite extraordinary churches, spectacular winter assemblies of swans and wildfowl at places like Welney, and the comfortable market town of **Downham Market**.

5 THE WIGGENHALLS

South of King's Lynn, strung along the course of the Great Ouse River, are four villages prefixed Wiggenhall, each differentiated from the others by the name of its church: Wiggenhall St Mary Magdalen, Wiggenhall St Mary the Virgin, Wiggenhall St Peter and Wiggenhall St Germans. Strictly speaking, these are not of the Fens but in the Norfolk Marshlands – slightly higher land that has been inhabited for millennia. All four villages are pre-Norman, Saxon settlements with a timeless charm about them that is hard to find in the Fens proper. They also have some quite remarkable churches.

Of the four Wiggenhalls, **Wiggenhall St Mary Magdalen** has for me the most distinguished church. This lofty 15th-century building is a fine exemplar of medieval balance and proportion, with a *"This lofty 15th-century building is a fine exemplar of medieval balance and proportion."* plethora of medieval stained glass and fine carved benches. Earnest hagiographers may be interested to note that the church has a gallery featuring some obscure saints who have spectacularly failed to become household names: St Leger, St Callistus, St Britus … the list goes on.

Two river walks around the Wiggenhalls

Three-mile walk ✳ OS Landranger 131; start: west side of Magdalen Bridge, Wiggenhall St Mary Magdalen, ♀ TF599113; easy **Eight-mile walk** ✳ OS Landranger 132; start: Watlington train station, ♀ TF612110; moderate

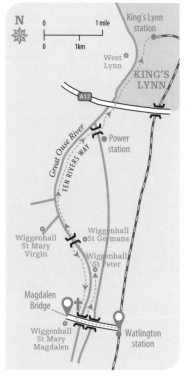

A recommended and easy **three-mile walk from Wiggenhall St Mary Magdalen** crosses **Magdalen Bridge** (note this is the Magdalen Bridge by the village, not to be confused with another of the same name near Lordsbridge a mile or so northwest) and heads north along the east bank of the Great Ouse River, past tiny **Wiggenhall St Peter** and its handsome roofless church to **Wiggenhall St Germans**, probably the most picturesque of all the four villages. The river has always been the life-blood of the village and, for centuries, this has been a favoured mooring place for Fen boatmen on their way to King's Lynn – a factor that explains why such a small place used to have three thriving pubs. Today it just has the Crown & Anchor. Return along the west bank.

You can take an enjoyable **eight-mile walk** by approaching the Wiggenhalls by **train** from King's Lynn. The starting point in this case would be **Watlington station**, which lies at the halfway point on the train line between King's Lynn and Downham Market. From the station, head west to the metal bridge over the Relief Channel and then cross Magdalen Bridge just beyond it.

After crossing the Great Ouse to have a look at St Mary Magdalen Church, re-cross the river and follow the signposted Fen Rivers Way north all the way to King's Lynn, passing Wiggenhall St Peter, Wiggenhall St Germans and the power station at Eau Brink Cut along the way. The Fen Rivers Way terminates at South Quay where you'll find a very welcome café at Marriott's Warehouse.

St Germaine's Church at **Wiggenhall St Germans** has an altogether different appeal. Here it is the woodwork that attracts attention, with resplendent poppies carved in the bench-ends along with a variety of animated human figures that include musicians, drunks, various sinners and courting couples. All of the Seven Deadly Sins are represented: Avarice clutches bags of money; Anger wields a sword; Lust, my favourite (carving that is, not necessarily the sin), is represented by a loving couple standing in the jaws of a giant fish, presumably the mouth of Hell.

FOOD & DRINK

Crown & Anchor 16 Lynn Rd, Wiggenhall St Germans ✆ 01553 617340. A former Greene King pub close to the church, with wood-panelled lounge and outside tables by the river.

6 DOWNHAM MARKET

Downham Market stands at the eastern edge of the Fens, with the Great Ouse River and manmade New Bedford Drain running alongside each other west of the town centre. As with many other places in west Norfolk, the predominant building material here is carrstone, which gives the buildings a warm and mellow look. The town's most memorable sight is probably its **clock tower**, a fancy Victorian cast-iron structure that is central to the marketplace. In medieval times, the town was well known for its butter market and horse fair. It has had a handful of famous visitors over the centuries: Nelson came here to go to school and Charles I stayed (or rather, hid dressed as a clergyman) for a night after fleeing the Battle of Naseby during the civil war. The town was once a busy river port but the arrival of the railway soon took away much of this trade following the construction of the Riley Channel, which succeeded in carrying the waters of the Cut-Off Channel to the main channel of the Great Ouse at King's Lynn.

7 DENVER

Just a couple of miles south of Downham Market, Denver is a relatively new village that dates from the time of the construction of the first **Denver Sluice** in 1651. The brains behind this project was Cornelius Vermuyden, a Dutch engineer commissioned to drain some of vast acreage of wetlands owned by the Duke of Bedford. The original drainage cut is no longer there but the so-called Old Sluice, which serves the same function as the original, dates from 1834, while the newer

LITERARY NORFOLK

In 2013 an article appeared in the *Guardian* newspaper that posed the question: Is Norfolk England's most secretive and strange literary county? It turned out that the author, Ian Sansom, was plugging his own book to some extent but he cited the large number of authors who have used Norfolk as inspiration for their storytelling. Crime novelists in particular seem to favour the county as a setting, and the names Ruth Galloway, P D James and Hilary Mantel were all mentioned as having chosen Norfolk as a literary backdrop. It appears that there is even now a genre called 'Norfolk Gothic'.

Norfolk in literature is nothing new. Charles Dickens famously used Great Yarmouth beach as the setting for the Barkis family's upturned boat-house in *David Copperfield*, L P Hartley's *The Go-Between* paints a picture of rural Norfolk at the turn of the 20th century, while Arthur Ransome celebrates the watery landscape of the Broads in *Swallows and Amazons* and *Coot Club*. It is also likely that Arthur Conan Doyle used Cromer Hall as the inspiration for the hall in his *The Hound of the Baskervilles*; no doubt he would have made use of the local Black Shuck legend (page 72) for inspiration too. The county is also the subject for much affectionate poetry by former Poet Laureate Sir John Betjeman (page 210).

However much the Norfolk landscape has served as a muse to writers from beyond its borders, the county has produced more

---

🍴 FOOD & DRINK

Jenyns Arms 1 Sluice Bank ✆ 01366 383366 ⏍ jenynsarms.com. With a large dining conservatory, outdoor tables by the water, reasonable pub fare and Sunday roasts, this is handily placed for a visit to the area.

18 WELNEY WETLAND CENTRE

Welney, a small village sitting on the Norfolk bank of Hundred Foot Bank, one of the Fens' prime manmade water courses, is home to the splendid Welney Wetland Centre (✆ 01353 860711 ⏍ wwt.org.uk/welney) run by the Wildfowl and Wetlands Trust. This nature reserve has plenty of interest throughout the seasons but really comes into its own in the winter months when vast numbers of wild swans – both whooper and Bewick's – gather on the **Ouse Marshes** here to feed and avoid the far harsher conditions in Siberia and Iceland. One of the joys of watching wild swans here is the centre's heated observatory, which gives visitors a birder's eye view of proceedings while they languish in relative comfort – a far cry from shivering with a telescope outside at the mercy of the elements. The **swan feeds**, in particular, are quite than its fair share of its own writers too. The first of these was Julian of Norwich, whose *Revelations of Divine Love* was the first book written by a woman to be published in English. Later Norfolk-based authors include Anna Sewell of *Black Beauty* fame, who was born in Great Yarmouth and spent her later life just outside Norwich; George Borrow (*The Bible in Spain, Wild Wales, Lavengro*), born in East Dereham; H Rider Haggard (*She, King Solomon's Mines*), who lived at Ditchingham in the Waveney Valley; Henry Williamson, who farmed near Stiffkey for several years and wrote *The Story of a Norfolk Farm* while there. In more recent years, we have the author D J Taylor, and also Malcolm Bradbury, who set up the famous postgraduate Creative Course at UEA that attracted the likes of Ian McEwan and Kazuo Ishiguro. This list is by no means exhaustive.

Then there are the 'new nature writers' – both Mark Cocker and Richard Mabey reside in Norfolk while the late, great Roger Deakin lived just over the Suffolk border close to Diss. Patrick Barker, author of *The Butterfly Isles and Badgerlands*, is another Norfolk-based nature writer. One of Norfolk's most famous writers in recent years is W G Sebald, who died in 2001 – a German native who lived near Norwich and taught at UEA. His best known work, *The Rings of Saturn*, which has attracted something approaching a cult following, is primarily focused on Suffolk but begins and ends in Norfolk.

spectacular, with the birds gracefully thrashing about for grain right beneath your comfortably warm nose. Children and adults tend to love this, even those not normally bowled over by natural history close up in the flesh. Feeds take place between the end of October and the middle of March around midday and just before sunset. Another feed takes place at around 18.30 by floodlight and this is usually the best attended, in bird terms, as many swans fly in to the lagoon to roost after dusk. For all the feeding times, it is best to arrive half an hour before.

The **eco visitor centre** has all the right-on credentials: loos that flush with rainwater, solar power electricity, geothermal heating and reed bed wastewater cleansing – plus a decent café, a gift shop and a pond room with giant models of creatures found on the reserve. In the warmer months, there are walks around the reserve and children can try pond-dipping.

9 WALPOLE ST PETER

The Walpoles – there are three of them – are unexciting dormitory villages filled with modern bungalow estates: here in deepest Fenland, it seems that even houses do not dare raise their heads above the parapet of what most of us regard as sea-level. How odd then that one of Norfolk's very finest churches can be found here, way out west in the agribusiness shabbiness of the Fens, far from the action and as close to Leicester as it is to Norwich. **St Peter's Church** in Walpole St Peter (obviously) is a worthy rival to that of Terrington St Clement; it's a magnificent and very large parish church that is sometimes referred to as the 'Queen of the Marshland'.

20 TERRINGTON ST CLEMENT

The A17 west of King's Lynn is not a road one drives along for pleasure, and **Terrington St Clement** itself, a large and not particularly attractive village, has little to warrant a detour were it not for its magnificent parish church often dubbed 'the Cathedral of the Marshland'. **St Clement's Church** is a massive 14th-century masterpiece with impressive buttresses and a detached tower.

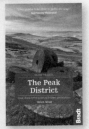

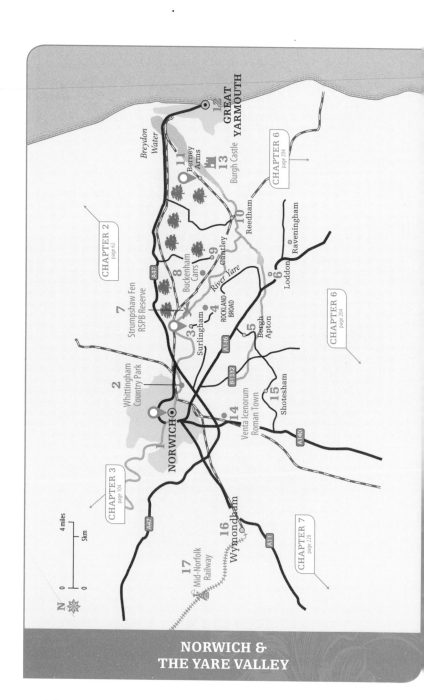

**NORWICH &
THE YARE VALLEY**

5
NORWICH &
THE YARE VALLEY

This area comes as something of a catch-all, a means of including parts of east and south Norfolk that don't conveniently fit in elsewhere. The River Yare that flows from central Norfolk to Great Yarmouth is perhaps an obvious point of focus: a natural conduit for river trade between Norwich and the coast. This same river also connects with the Broads at Breydon Water, and even has a couple of important minor broads of its own at Surlingham and Rockland. If the Yare Valley is a convenient means of incorporating uncooperative slices of east Norfolk, then the valley of the River Tas can be brought in to do the same for south Norfolk. The modest River Tas, which joins the Yare just south of Norwich (having quietly meandered up from south Norfolk), has nothing of the importance of the Yare, but it does link a number of villages that are worth a visit south of Norwich.

Norwich is a place of such importance that in a book like this it is almost tempting to ignore it in case it takes over the text completely. I will aim for the middle way of brevity. It is probably true to say that Slow philosophy has its heart in the villages and market towns rather than the cities, but Norwich is hardly your average city. At the other end of the River Yare stands Great Yarmouth, a large, slightly threadbare sort of place that some might prefer to avoid. It, too, has its own story to tell. The River Tas has no such urban centres, just a few likeable villages strung along minor roads in pretty rolling south Norfolk countryside. There's some interesting history and unsung places half-hidden away here in what is effectively Norwich's commuter belt.

As Norfolk's broadest river the River Yare was a vital waterway for trade until quite recently and remains an important area for wildlife, with the whole of its floodplain, as far as Norwich itself, lying under the aegis of the Broads Authority. It's a formidable barrier too that, strikingly, has only one crossing place between Norwich and Yarmouth.

The nature writer Mark Cocker, himself a resident of the Yare Valley, points out in his fascinating book *Crow Country* that communities that can quite clearly see each other on either side of the river usually have absolutely no contact with each other, as such contact would require a massive detour. How different from the situation along the River Waveney (see *Chapter 6*) where villages on both the Norfolk and Suffolk banks visit each other's marketplaces (and supermarkets) without a second thought. It would make more sense in a way if Norfolk north of the Yare were deemed a different county to that south of the river. Those living in Langley Green south of the Yare tend to be more interested in getting into Norwich at weekends than they are curious about what happens in Cantley, north of the river, whose lights they can see at night.

GETTING AROUND

Travelling along the Yare Valley is easy enough, as long as you don't want to cross the river. The A47 runs between Norwich and Great Yarmouth, north of the River Yare, a dual carriageway for part of the way. This continues as the southern bypass at Norwich and links to the A11 south before continuing west to East Dereham and King's Lynn. The section between Acle and Great Yarmouth is a straight-as-a-die single carriageway across a wind-blown, windmill-studded marshland, and notorious for speed merchants and accidents. Heading south, the A140, an old Roman road, runs more or less parallel to the spidery course of the River Tas, to eventually cross the River Waveney near Diss.

PUBLIC TRANSPORT

This is better than average. A fast, regular **bus service** connects Norwich with Great Yarmouth, while the services that link Norwich with Thetford, Diss and Beccles also pass through south Norfolk towns and villages like Loddon, Long Stratton, Wymondham and Attleborough. The fastest east–west service is the ever-useful X1 that plies between Lowestoft and King's Lynn via Great Yarmouth, Norwich and Swaffham. There are more local services too, like the Anglian Bus 85 Norwich to Surlingham service and the 86 Norwich to Beccles route that goes via Loddon and Bergh Apton.

ℹ TOURIST INFORMATION

Great Yarmouth Maritime House 25 Marine Parade ✆ 01493 846346 🖰 great-yarmouth.
co.uk
Loddon The Old Town Hall, 1 Bridge St ✆ 01508 521028 🖰 south-norfolk.gov.uk (seasonal)
Norwich The Forum, Millennium Plain ✆ 01603 213999 🖰 visitnorwich.co.uk
Wymondham Market Cross, Market Pl ✆ 01953 604721 (winter, Fri & Sat only)

For **train travel**, the invaluable Wherry Line (✆ 03457 114141 🖰 wherrylines.org.uk) has regular trains between Norwich, Great Yarmouth and Lowestoft that usefully stop at places like Buckenham, Acle, Reedham and Berney Arms, which are ideal starting points for walks. Some of the stations, like Berney Arms, are request stops only, and only a limited number of trains will stop at them, so it is best to study the timetable closely. The Greater Anglias Norwich to Cambridge train service has stops at Wymondham and Attleborough.

WALKING

There's plenty of scope for enjoyable waterside walking, particularly east of Rockland Broad from where a riverside path goes all the way to Breydon Water. There's the same on the opposite bank from Buckenham eastwards and the northern bank has the distinct advantage that there are a couple of useful railway stations along the way that avoid the necessity of doubling back. With a car, circular walks are feasible if you are willing to combine stretches of riverside with paths across marshes and some road walking. The Wherry Line website (🖰 wherrylines.org.uk) also has some good suggestions for walks using its stations, and even downloadable audio walks.

The area's long-distance trails deserve a look, if only in part, as they lead through some of the most attractive stretches of the river valleys. The **Wherryman's Way** follows the River Yare from Norwich to Great Yarmouth by way of a 35-mile route that takes in historic sites and wildlife areas. The route – in theory at least – follows the south bank of the River Yare to Hardley, loops around the River Chet to Loddon then, crossing the river at its only ferry point at Reedham, continues along the north bank of the river to Breydon Water and Great Yarmouth. Unfortunately, the section between Loddon and Hardley Flood has been closed for years now because of problems with footpath erosion.

Doubly unfortunately, this used to be one of the way's most picturesque sections. A booklet, available free from tourist information centres or direct from Norfolk County Council (☏ 01603 223317), details a dozen circular walks along the way. The same walks can also be downloaded from ⌨ www.wherrymansway.net. The website is also worth consulting to check if there have been any further temporary path closures due to improvement work.

The last stretch of the Wherryman's Way between Reedham and Great Yarmouth lies conveniently close to the Wherry Line stations of Reedham and Berney Arms, and so lends itself easily to combined rail and foot outings. A good option is to take the train to the Berney Arms request stop then walk either west to Reedham or east to Great Yarmouth and pick up a return train.

Other long-distance trails are the **Boudicca Way**, a 40-mile route connecting Diss to Norwich that meanders through a number of south Norfolk villages along the way, and the **Tas Valley Way**, a 25-mile walk from Eaton, just southwest of Norwich to Attleborough. A further route developed in recent years by South Norfolk Council is **Kett's Country**, a 21-mile walk between Cringleford and Wymondham. Details and maps of all of these can be obtained from South Norfolk Council at their Swan Lane, Long Stratton office (☏ 01508 533945) or downloaded from ⌨ south-norfolk.gov.uk. Norfolk County Council's Norfolk Trails website (⌨ www.norfolk.gov.uk/out-and-about-in-norfolk/norfolk-trails) also has plenty of information on suggested walking routes in the area as well as an interactive map.

CYCLING

As elsewhere in the region, cycling is fine as long as you keep well away from the main roads. Fortunately, there are sufficient minor roads that getting around is reasonable. Some of the narrow lanes close to the river on either bank are a real pleasure, although you need to be ever vigilant of absent-minded locals and Norwich commuters speeding home in their 4x4s.

Sustrans National Cycle Network Route 1 (Harwich to Hull; ⌨ sustrans.org.uk) passes through this area, coming up from the Waveney Valley to Loddon and then following minor roads through villages south of the Yare on its way into Norwich. Part of the Wherryman's Way (see above) is also suitable for cyclists.

NORWICH

A fine old city, perhaps the most curious specimen at present extant
of the genuine old English town.

George Borrow, *Lavengro*

As the city sign tells you as you drive in, Norwich is a fine city. Former
Norwich City goalkeeper Robert Green once dubbed Norwich 'a city
the size of a town with a village mentality', which was probably intended
as a criticism but could also be interpreted as praise depending on your
viewpoint. Despite recent plaudits in 'Best place to live' features by some
newspapers, the general image is that of a city out on a limb that is out of
step with modern times; a place of gauche, unfashionable attitudes and a
plucky, if sometimes unpredictable football team; Alan Partridge, Delia
Smith, parochialism, mustard, banking and insurance.

Naturally enough, the reality is somewhat different: Alan Partridge
is a fictitious character (although there really is a Radio Norwich these
days), Delia Smith lives in Suffolk despite her regular outings to Carrow
Road to watch football, and Norwich Union have re-branded as Aviva
and outsourced to Sheffield and India. Contrary to expectations, the city
is increasingly cosmopolitan, has a thriving university and is one of the
fastest growing cities in England. Simply put, Norwich punches well
above its weight.

Norwich is a very liveable sort of place. Where I live, close to the city
wall, just south of the centre but well outside the fashionable 'Golden
Triangle' beloved of university lecturers and media folk, is a case in
point. Within five minutes' walk from my house are two independent
cafés and half-a-dozen decent pubs, including a couple of really good
ones. It's a five-minute walk to the bus station, and ten minutes to one of
the oldest permanent food markets in the country; 15 minutes' walk to
a thriving arts centre and 20 to a fantastic independent cinema. There's
a 'real meat' butcher's just up the road too, and on Friday mornings
a mobile fish van comes from Lowestoft with fish so fresh that it is
almost still twitching. The fishmonger gives me the news from the coast
– what the fishing's like at Lowestoft, whether the boats are going out
to sea or not. It is good to have this sort of connectedness in an urban
environment, as Norwich is just about big enough to forget sometimes
that you are living in the middle of a mainly rural region. If this sounds
a little smug, then there are a few pitfalls too: traffic noise and fumes,

and the perception by metropolitan types that you reside in some dull and decidedly unfashionable backwater.

The story goes that Norwich has a pub for every day of the year and a church for every week. Not quite right – there were actually 700 pubs in the city in medieval times, 363 in 1905 (within the city walls) and around 140 in the whole of Norwich today – but it does give a ball-park figure. As elsewhere in the country, pubs seem to be closing for business almost every week and of the city's surviving 32 medieval churches, two-thirds lie empty or find modern use as puppet theatres, art studios, or even pregnancy crisis centres. That is still a lot of churches for a city of just 140,000 … and plenty of pubs.

In recent years Norwich has undoubtedly become a far more fashionable place to live. The **Norfolk & Norwich Festival** (⊘ nnfestival.org.uk) has been established as an annual event for many years (it can be traced back to 1772) and goes from strength to strength, featuring international names in the classical, folk and jazz world as well as staging a broad range of theatrical, dance and arts events. The festival, which takes place in the second half of May each year, also includes plenty of free events like street theatre and special activities for children.

A recent feather in the cap for the city was to be on the shortlist for the 2013 UK City of Culture. Norwich was pipped at the post by Derry/Londonderry. Despite disappointment, no-one seemed to mind that much as being one of just four finalists – the other two were Sheffield and Birmingham – raised the city's cultural profile considerably. In 2012 Norwich became England's first **UNESCO City of Literature**, one of only six worldwide joining an elite network along with Edinburgh, Melbourne, Dublin, Reykjavik and Iowa City. Strong associations with the University of East Anglia's MA course in Creative Writing (first student, Ian McEwan, no less) certainly did no harm here. Nor did the fact that the city's literary tradition went back more than 600 years to the time of Julian of Norwich, whose Revelations of Divine Love was not only the first book published in English but also the first to be written in English by a woman.

Around the same time that Norwich earned its UNESCO status, a travel feature about 'Norwich, England' appeared in the *New York Times* that gave the impression of a 'charming medieval town' populated by bookworms and bohemian literary types tapping away at laptops in quaint tea rooms – a somewhat hyperbolic portrait to say the least.

On a less cerebral note, the city was also heavily promoted as **Norwich City of Ale** in 2011, an inaugural 10-day beer and brewing event that was successfully followed up in 2012 and has now become become an annual occurrence.

So: City of Literature, City of Ale, City of Culture (… well, almost). If the term 'Slow' were to be applied to cities as well as to market towns then no doubt Norwich would be one of the first to bear the title.

A POTTED HISTORY

Back in the late 11th century, Norwich was England's second largest city. It had existed as a large Saxon town before the conquest but the arrival of the Normans brought the cathedral, castle and a large increase in population. As it was an important weaving centre, Flemish and Walloon migrants came from across the North Sea in the 16th century to join the throng, to be followed later by French Huguenots. Weaving was of sufficient importance in the city for Daniel Defoe to observe in 1723 that 'if a stranger was only to ride through or view the city of Norwich for a day, he would have much more reason to think there was a town without inhabitants . . . on the contrary, if he was to view the city either on a Sabbath day, or on any public occasion, he would wonder where all these people could dwell'. Norwich's Flemish immigrants brought with them the pet canaries that would later become the emblem of Norwich City Football Club and appear on its crest. It is worth noting that, with the exception of the city's Jews who were persecuted here and elsewhere in England in the 12th century because of blood libel suspicions, Norwich has generally welcomed its newcomers. Indeed, the city has always been demonstrably tolerant of 'strangers' and even sometimes radical in outlook, with a strong working-class tradition.

To see Norwich simply as a quaint cathedral city is misleading; as well as medieval streets and cosy Anglo-Saxon provincialism there are also the usual urban problems. Beyond the centre with its cobbled streets, 12th-century walls and Tudor buildings, lie grids of Victorian terraces, large council estates (some of Britain's very first council estates – Mile Cross and Larkman – were constructed here in the late 1920s) and sprawling suburbs. The city was bombed quite badly during World War II, especially in April 1942 as part of the so-called Baedeker Raids, in which the popular tourist guide was used to select targets of cultural rather than strategic importance.

THE CITY CENTRE

Plenty of guidebooks will give you the nitty-gritty background – the churches, historic buildings, etc. Instead I've picked a few favourite places. All the buildings mentioned below are open throughout the year. If you want to gain access to some of those that are normally closed to the public then a good time to come to the city is during **Norwich Heritage Open Days** (⌀ heritageopendays.org.uk) in September. The Tourist Information Centre puts on a number of walking tours of the historic city centre in spring and summer. Most of these start outside The Forum and can be booked at the TIC or online at ⌀ thenorwichshop.co.uk.

The castle & museums

The first places that most guidebooks mention are the castle and cathedral, both Norman in origin and both worthy of your time. **Norwich Castle** stands on a hill above the city centre, its Norman keep a serious square building that serves as the city's historical museum these days: **Norwich Castle Museum and Art Gallery** (✆ 01603 493625 ⌀ museums.norfolk. gov.uk). A sign at the entrance tells the story of Robert Kett, a yeoman farmer who led a peasants' revolt in 1549 and, after camping out on Mousehold Heath with thousands of followers, was finally defeated by government troops. It is probably significant that it took 400 years before he attained local hero status and received a plaque to his memory. As the sign tells you, Kett was hanged at the castle, although it does not mention that he was hanged alive in chains to suffer a slow, cruel death. Norwich Castle once featured in *Monty Python's Flying Circus* as the setting for a particularly silly sketch in which medieval soldiers hurled themselves from battlements, but whenever I see the castle walls, I just think of poor Robert Kett.

"As well as displays of Iceni bling, there is a virtual Roman chariot ride to delight children."

Inside the Castle Museum, there's the usual dungeon display to frighten sensitive souls, as well as galleries devoted to archaeology and natural history. An interesting room dedicated to the Iceni-Roman conflict in East Anglia has, as well as displays of Iceni bling – huge gold torcs – from the Snettisham Treasure, a virtual Roman chariot ride to delight children. Probably most distinctive though, is the museum's fine art collection. Several rooms are devoted to works of the Norwich School, with a wealth of paintings by artists such as John Crome, Joseph Stannard and John Sell Cotman. My personal favourites are the watercolours by John Sell Cotman that make use of an exquisite blue and gold palette. **St Benet's Abbey** (1831) looks as if it is almost floating on the water. Give or take a few Broads cruisers, the scene looks much the same today (page 96). The Castle Museum has a very sensible 'Twilight Ticket' policy, which allows visits during the hour before closing for just £2.

On the subject of museums, there are a couple of others that are worth an hour of anyone's time. **Strangers' Hall** (✆ 01603 667229), at Charing Cross in the shadow of St Gregory's Church, is an interesting social history museum in a delightful Tudor building. Just above it, on Colegate, is St John Maddermarket, another recycled medieval church that has long functioned as a tiny independent theatre. There's a good small museum dedicated to Norwich trade and shopping since 1700 at **The Bridewell** (✆ 01603 629127) in Bridewell Alley, a building that once served as a prison and a house of correction. St Andrew's Church next door is second only to St Peter Mancroft in size and has a 15th-century window that shows the Devil dancing with a bishop on a chessboard.

The cathedral

Any decent guidebook will tell you that work started on Norwich Cathedral in 1086 at the behest of Bishop Herbert Losinga, so I won't elaborate. It is a magnificent Gothic building, with the second-highest spire and second largest cloisters in Britain, but I like the small details best. Take a peek at the intricately carved wooden bosses in the cloisters and you'll find some that go well beyond the usual themes of the Life of Christ and the Apocalypse, and some which are downright rude. There's an impressive and quite fearsome Green Man too, if you look hard enough. In fact, there are several.

Over the past few years the cathedral's lofty spire has been gazed at for reasons other than its impressive architecture: it has become home to a pair of breeding peregrine falcons. The falcons first appeared at the cathedral in 2009 when a male took up residence to be soon followed by a female. A nesting platform fitted with a webcam was set up by the Hawk and Owl Trust in 2011 and in the following year two healthy chicks were produced, a first for the cathedral. The adults returned in 2013 to produce four chicks this time, one died but three successfully fledged, and peregrines have continued to return to the cathedral to breed every year since. The birds are quite easy to see – from April and June the Hawk and Owl Trust usually have a telescope set up for interested visitors in the cathedral cloister square; there's also a live webcam feed to the cathedral's Refectory Restaurant.

From the castle to the river

Another part of the inner city frequently included on city tours, and for good reason, is **King Street**, southeast of the castle mound, which has a number of Tudor buildings, tiny courtyards and, best of all, **Dragon Hall** (✐ 01603 877177 ✐ writerscentrenorwich.org.uk), an impressive medieval merchant's hall that is now used as a base for the Norwich Writers Centre. Dragon Hall will be transformed into the National Centre for Writing in 2018, when it will re-open for guided tours and an extensive programme of literary events.

There are plenty of interesting nooks and crannies around here, so simply delving and wandering at will is probably the best policy. Further on from Dragon Hall there's Wensum Lodge, an adult education centre. The bar here, **Jurnet's Bar**, is worth a look – and a drink if it's open – as it is in the crypt-like basement of a medieval Jewish merchant's house. Immediately over the river is **Riverside**, a stretch of new entertainment development that, to put it mildly, is 'lively' at weekends. Prince of Wales Road, the thoroughfare that leads down across the river to the railway station, sees a great deal of pre-nightclub carousing on Friday and Saturday nights. All cities have similar areas, of course, but Prince of Wales Road is best avoided on weekend nights unless you are under 25 and full of cheap booze. A taxi driver once remarked 'It's like Beirut out there', as we drove slowly along it trying to avoid the lurching bodies. I felt it necessary to mention that I had been to Beirut and compared with this it was actually rather peaceful.

The Lanes & market

Norwich Lanes is an effective re-branding of the city centre's narrow medieval streets. This complex of streets, lanes and alleyways, designated 'the independent shopping and lifestyle quarter' (✐ norwichlanes.co.uk), connect three parallel streets north of Norwich Market and Guildhall: St Giles Street, Pottergate and St Benedict's Street, with Norwich Castle, St Andrew's Hall, St Benedict's Church (just a tower since 1944) and

St Giles Church all standing as corner pieces. There are plenty of independent shops, cafés and yet more churches within, as well as Jarrold's elegant department store and the pedestrian thoroughfare of London Street with its shops, buskers and Big Issue sellers.

Connecting Castle Street and Gentleman's Walk in front of the market, **Royal Arcade** is the delightful Edwardian passageway with a charming Art Nouveau entrance and lamps. Alongside a Jamie Oliver's, a decent café and jewellery, toy and fudge shops there is rumoured to also be a 'ghost shop' down here, one that mysteriously appears and disappears from time to time. The arcade was designed in 1899 by George Skipper, a local architect who was also responsible for Jarrold's department store and the Norwich Union headquarters on Surrey Street near the bus station, which has a hugely impressive marble hall inside. John Betjeman, an admirer of Skipper's Art and Craft designs, said that the architect 'is to Norwich rather what Gaudi was to Barcelona'. Skipper also designed the sunflower wrought iron railings at Chapelfield Park and many of the grander hotels along the seafront in Cromer.

Norwich Market has operated continuously in the same spot since Norman times (the earlier Saxon market was down at Tombland but was moved when the Normans began to build the cathedral). It's a six-day-a-week affair (closed Sunday) – the largest daily open market in Britain – selling all manner of local food products as well as books, records, clothes, household goods and takeaway meals. There's a place to get keys cut and shoes mended while you wait, and a chip stall that comes highly rated by Norwich residents judging by its never-ending queue. The mushy-pea stall here has been in business for 60 years, with the same family running it all that time. A few years ago the market complex was expensively revamped after much deliberation and not a little controversy. The old market had uneven floors and narrow alleyways but the new stalls are a little smaller than those that stood before and haven't gone down too well with some stallholders and shoppers – a textbook example of a committee coming up with a compromise that, ultimately, nobody really seems to like.

City Hall looms above the market, a long, brick 1930s building with rampant lions at its steps that look decidedly Babylonian. The design was apparently based upon that of Stockholm Town Hall but the large square clock tower, seen from all over the city, always puts me in mind of a Marrakech minaret. I am more taken with the two buildings that stand opposite each other just to the south. **St Peter Mancroft Church** has dominated the marketplace since the mid 15th-century, a wonderful Perpendicular building with a hammerbeam roof that is filled with light – my favourite Norwich church, and I am sure I am not alone in this. The church contains the grave of Sir Thomas Browne (1605–82), a Norwich-based medical man and all-round polymath famous for the books *Urn Burial* and *Religio Medici* (W G Sebald devotes half a chapter to him in Rings of Saturn). A statue of him contemplating a piece of urn is just across the way in front of Next. There is also a large modernist

A city river stroll

❋ OS Landranger 134; start: St Benedict's Street, St Lawrence's Church; ♀ TG227088; 2.5 miles; easy

This walk begins on St Benedict's Street at **St Lawrence's Church**. Descend the steps to cross Westwick Street and pass the apartment block that used to be the Anchor Brewery, before crossing Coslany Bridge to follow the pedestrian access along the River Wensum's north bank. Across the water is a disused warehouse where the entire text of Thomas More's *Utopia* has been scrawled in white across the brickwork as if it were the work of a 16th-century graffiti artist with a taste for political philosophy. It was actually done by local artist Rory Macbeth in 2006 – the building was scheduled for demolition in the following year yet, perhaps as a result of its utopian graffiti, it still stands today.

Crossing Duke Street by means of **Duke's Palace Bridge**, a brief detour along Colegate is necessary to reach **Blackfriars Bridge** by the Norwich School of Art from where a path continues beside the river to reach Fye Bridge and Fishergate. Whitefriars Bridge comes next and the eponymous friary once stood on the site of the large edifice that looms ahead: the Jarrold's Printing Works, built in 1834 and formerly a mill owned by the Norwich Yarn Company.

Beyond the printing works you'll come to a *renga* – a word map created by means of an ancient Japanese tradition of shared writing – stringing a snake of words and phrases along hoardings beside the river. A Renga for St James, which utilises the local Norwich vernacular, was created here on site in 2009.

Continuing east, you soon see **Peter's Bridge**, a footbridge opened in 2012 and named after a former Jarrold's chairman. Most of the Wensum's bridges are so ancient that they are firmly embedded in the city's psyche but there have been three new footbridges so far this millennium: this one, the 2009 Lady Julian Bridge close to the railway station, and the Novi Sad Friendship Bridge, opened in 2001, near Carrow Bridge and Norwich City FC football ground.

'brain' sculpture – in the spirit of Browne's intellectual pursuits, perhaps, but not without its critics. Browne once lived just across the way on the other side of Gentleman's Walk, where Pret a Manger now stands. St Peter Mancroft really comes into its own during the Norfolk & Norwich Festival in May when the church serves as a medieval backdrop to modern (and usually French or Catalan) street theatre. The church interior is made use of too, and candle-lit it is hugely atmospheric. I have fond memories of seeing the great jazz bassist Charlie Haden perform here a few years back – medieval architecture and modern jazz is such a heady mix.

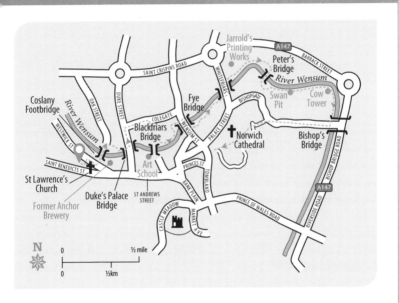

Crossing this graceful, J (for Jarrold's)-shaped footbridge, the riverside walk continues towards **Cow Tower**, a 14th-century defensive tower that was badly damaged in Kett's Rebellion of 1549. Just before Cow Tower you will pass what looks like a sluice leading into the river. This is, in fact, a rare 18th-century example of a swan pit, a pool in which wild cygnets were kept and fattened for the table after having their wings clipped and beaks marked by their owners. From Cow Tower walk a little further on to reach **Bishops Bridge**, then turn right to leave the river behind as you head for Cathedral Close and Tombland.

A car park and lacklustre library used to stand opposite St Peter Mancroft but this burned down in 1994 – public records and hardback thrillers are highly combustible. The void has been filled by **The Forum** (*∂* theforumnorwich.co.uk), a bold Millennium Commission project that has been an enormous success. The Forum is a large glass-fronted complex in the shape of a horseshoe that contains the Norfolk and Norwich Millennium Library, one of the most visited libraries in the country, the regional BBC studios, Fusion – a digital gallery – a café, a restaurant and tourist information. There's a large internal foyer area for exhibitions and performances, and regular craft markets. How a building made of glass, tubular steel and brick can fit so well into such a tight space in a medieval city is remarkable. Part of this may be down to the longer-than-standard handmade bricks used in the horseshoe walls, the same as in the city hall opposite. Between The Forum and St Peter Mancroft is a paved plaza with amphitheatre-like steps that provide a ready venue for street theatre events and for an ice skating rink in winter. It's always busy and, whether by accident or design, seems to provide what the Italians term 'a convivial space', a natural relaxed focus for the city centre.

In addition to the castle and cathedral, the place most often mentioned on tourist trawls through the city is Elm Hill, a cobbled street that descends down to Wensum Street from behind St Andrew's Hall. There's no longer an elm but I do remember the one that used to stand here and the valiant efforts made to save it once it had become infected with that arboreal plague, Dutch elm disease. Elm Hill has galleries, a café or two and a couple of quirky shops, and by the time you reach the bottom you are very close to Fye Bridge and the River Wensum – once across the bridge you are in the part of Norwich that locals refer to as 'Norwich over the Water'. There are fine walks to be had along the river in either direction from here. Head west from Fye Bridge and you'll soon come to Blackfriars Bridge and the impressive Victorian buildings that make up the Norwich School of Art to the south of the bridge, with Norwich Playhouse just to the north. Venture east and you'll come to Whitefriars Bridge with the elegantly tall Jarrold's Printing Works building – formerly a mill – a little way beyond on the north bank.

The building is home to one of the city's lesser known museums, the **John Jarrold Printing Museum** (*∂* 01603 677183 *∂* johnjarroldprintingmuseum.org.uk; ☉ Wed 09.30–12.30). If you

ROUND TOWER CHURCHES

Norfolk has a total of 124 round tower churches, far more than any other county in England. Although they are found largely in East Anglia – Suffolk also has 38 and Essex six – there are also church towers of similar design in Germany. Most, but not all, round tower churches tend to be of Saxon origin but the reason for their construction is still open to debate. It is likely that they were built because of a lack of suitable building materials for constructing square towers in a region where the only stone available was flint. Corners are hard to build using flint and so round towers may have simply been a pragmatic solution to the problem given the cheap and plentiful supply of building material that was available locally. There are even those who think that round towers may have originally been defensive structures but this seems unlikely.

manage to get here within its somewhat exacting timeslot then you will more than likely be given a personal tour as I was. No sooner had I entered the building when a genial retired compositor collared me to explain the painstaking work that went on in the hand-composing room. 'They used to keep the capital letters in the top part of the letter case and the others in the lower part, hence upper and lower case', he explained before going into detail about the difference between serif and sans serif fonts. 'Serif is much easier to read because they are curved and draw the eye along. For some reason a lot of women's magazines use sans serif – they're pretty well unreadable in my opinion.' We went on to look at the actual printing process. The skill involved was quite daunting as were the tight deadlines that were imposed. 'We went to print at 11.45 in the morning and if the first copies of that day's paper weren't on sale on the street outside Jarrold's at 12.15 then questions would be asked'. After just half an hour in his company I not only learned a lot – and forgot a great more – about the printing industry of yore but I also gained renewed respect for the skill and hard work involved.

Norwich churches

Norwich has so many medieval churches – 32 in fact – that it is easy to overdo it and see too many in too short a time. Ecclesiastical architecture needs plenty of time for digestion. A personal choice would be the aforementioned St Peter Mancroft, Norwich Cathedral, naturally, and perhaps the tiny **shrine church of St Julian**, just off King Street. St Julian's is actually a reconstruction – the original was bombed during

UNGODLY NORWICH

Curiously, given so many places of worship, nonconformist or otherwise, Norwich came top in a 2011 survey as the ungodliest city in England, with 42.5% of its citizens saying they have no religion compared to a national average of 25.1%. This is nothing new: Norwich was, in fact, excommunicated by the Pope following anti-clerical riots in the city way back in the late 13th century, the only English city ever having to suffer a spiritual snub of this nature. Norwich has always been true to its motto of 'Do Different': who knows – if a similar survey were to be done on paganism or New Age beliefs rather than orthodox religion then Norwich might actually score rather well?

World War II – but it still has a story to tell. This was the site where Julian of Norwich, a 14th-century mystic anchoress, built a cell for herself and turned her back on the world to write *Revelations of Divine Love*, the first work to be written by a woman in English. I'm fond too of **St Benedict's Street** with its five decommissioned churches strung along its length like ports of call on a spiritual pub crawl. Closest to Grapes Hill with its flinty scraps of city wall is **St Benedict's Church**, now just a freestanding round tower thanks to a World War II bombing raid, one of the Baedeker Raids that took place in 1942. A little further on, opposite the Ten Bells pub, is St Swithin's, which has long served as the venue for the **Norwich Arts Centre**, a wonderful institution that puts on a broad range of concerts and events.

"St Benedict's Street has five decommissioned churches strung along its length like ports of call on a spiritual pub crawl."

A little further still is **St Margaret's** and then my namesake **St Laurence's**, which in medieval times would have had direct access via steps to the River Wensum below. If you take a close look at its western wall from the delightfully named St Lawrence Little Steps (note the spelling; people get my name wrong too), you should be able to make out a stone carving showing St Laurence's martyrdom on a hot iron grill. Reportedly crying out to his tormentors, 'Turn me over I'm done on this side', he has become the patron saint of both cooks and comedians. Although empty now, the church has served as a craft market in recent years. One of the stallholders told me that some of those who use the place sense a none-too-pleasant atmosphere in the western end of the church. 'There's a very strange feel to it – really quite evil. We all think it. There's a door there and I was thinking of having a look to see what was behind it. Then I just thought to myself, "No, I really don't think so"'. Further on at Charing Cross, the junction of St Benedict's with Westlegate, stands **St Gregory's Church**. All this – five redundant churches – within a five-minute, 400-yard walk.

Nonconformist Norwich

Norwich has more than just medieval churches, of course; and the churches built in more recent centuries have not been solely Anglican either. Roman Catholics have their own **pro-cathedral of St John the Baptist**, a massive Victorian Gothic edifice, at the top of Earlham Road, with The Tuns, a genuine (rather than faux-Paddy) Irish pub, conveniently opposite. As a centre of nonconformity, there have been all sorts of congregations worshipping in the city. The 18th-century **Octagon Chapel** on Colegate, built by Thomas Ivory, the same architect who built the splendid Georgian Assembly Rooms on Rampant Horse Street, is highly unusual and indeed octagonal. Originally built by Presbyterians, it became Unitarian in the 19th century. The chapel with its wonderful wooden acoustic is now regularly used for musical events organised by the Bicycle Shop.

There's also a marvellous curio in the form of the nonconformist **Rosary Road Cemetery** just east of Thorpe railway station, where the same nonconformist worshippers often ended up, as well as quite a few railway workers from the nearby station. This is a delightful place to wander in peace and quiet, listening to birdsong and examining gravestones. Surprisingly, this is the earliest nonconformist cemetery in England, and older than any of the larger London equivalents. In earlier times, resolute nonconformists often met grisly deaths at the hands of the orthodoxy. The site of the **Lollards Pit** just across Riverside Road from Bishop's Bridge is testament to this, although only a commemorative plate remains today. As George Borrow remarks in *Lavengro*, 'It has had its martyrs, the venerable old town'.

SAINSBURY CENTRE FOR VISUAL ARTS

If modern architecture floats your boat, you might want to make a pilgrimage west of the city to my alma mater, the University of East Anglia, where you'll find the Sainsbury Centre for Visual Arts, an aircraft hangar of a building designed by Sir Norman Foster when he was still relatively unknown. Whatever your view is of the building's aesthetic appeal – I doubt if Prince Charles is an admirer – it certainly works well as a gallery for the arts and, as well as the permanent collection, hosts frequent special exhibitions by prestigious artists. The Sainsbury Centre and 'ziggurats' of the university buildings look down on a tree-lined manmade lake, usually referred to as UEA Broad, which has matured nicely since it was first created out of a gravel pit in the mid 1970s and now has a wealth of wildlife in and around its waters. It's a favourite spot for anglers, local joggers and dog walkers.

North of UEA Broad, behind woodland and parallel to Bluebell Lane, a footpath takes you past a series of meadows filled with rescue horses of all shapes and sizes: tiny Shetland ponies, standard-size horses, donkeys, even a mule. The kind chap who rescues and nurtures these unfortunate beasts told me: 'We get a lot of them from the continent, Italy especially. It costs a lot to ship them over here but it's worth it.' On regular walks here, it is heart-warming to see what were once sorry animals slowly regain their fettle with time. The place made the local news a while ago when a Shetland pony shared the same field as an old mare. To everyone's surprise, the pair produced a foal together in defiance of the assumption that the stallion was too short and the mare, too old.

GREEN NORWICH

⌂ **38 St Giles** (page 258)

Norwich is by any standards a green city, and I'm not referring to its many parks and open spaces like Chapelfield Gardens within the city walls and Mousehold Heath, beyond. In 2006, the city was voted England's greenest city, having the highest concentration of eco-friendly businesses in the country. This is probably not unconnected to the fact that the Green Party generally do well here, holding a considerable number of seats in both city and county councils. The first **Norwich and Norfolk Sustainable Living Festival** was held in the city in 2009, with all manner of exhibitions and events taking place at The Forum and the University of East Anglia. The festival continues to be held each May with two days of free events and activities for all ages. The Forum is also the location for regular farmers' markets.

As you might expect, the city has a decent number of outlets for locally produced organic produce. **The Green Grocers** (2 Earlham House, Earlham Rd ✆ 01603 250000) sells food and drink that is 90% organic and/or locally produced and also has a carbon-neutral project to offset its emissions. This is also the location for the **Golden Triangle Farmers' Market**, which takes place from 10.00 to 15.00 every second Sunday of the month. For meat eaters, **Harvey's Pure Meat** (63 Grove Rd ✎ 01603 621908 ✐ puremeat.org.uk) specialises in organic meat and seasonal game. **Anna's Farm Store** (30 Magdalen Rd ✎ 01603 665982) in the north of the city has all kinds of local organic produce. The best bread in the city can be found at **Dozen Artisan Bakery** (107 Gloucester St ✎ 01603 764798 ✐ dozenbakery.co.uk) and also at **Timberhill Bakery** (27–9 Timberhill ✎ 01603 613172 ✐ timberhillbakery.com) in the city centre, which produces a wide variety of delicious sourdough loaves. There is also the excellent **Norwich Providore** (✎ 07597 746089) artisan bread stall in **Norwich Market**, which should not be overlooked either for its wealth of local produce – cheese, meat, vegetables and fruit – its excellent wet fish stalls and its wide choice of takeaway food.

Returning to the sense of green meaning 'foliage', several city gardens are worth a visit. My first choice would be The **Plantation Garden** (4 Earlham Rd ✎ 07504 545810 ✐ plantationgarden.co.uk), right beside St John's RC Church. This was created a century and a half ago in an abandoned chalk quarry but lay completely forgotten until its rediscovery 30 years ago. Its Gothic fountain, Italianate terrace and woodland walkways have all been lovingly restored, although it is still very much a work in progress. It is open year-round but there's the bonus of tea and cake on some Sunday afternoons in summer. There are also occasional outdoor film screenings in summer too. **The Bishop's Garden** (✐ dioceseofnorwich.org), open a dozen or so times in summer, is a delightful swathe of perennial borders hidden away behind 700-year-old walls in the cloistered enclave of Cathedral Close.

FOOD & DRINK

Like Aylsham, the 'Slow' market town in north Norfolk, Norwich has its own Slow Food convivium (✐ slowfoodnorwich.org.uk), which works on forging links with local organic producers and promoting Slow Food events in the city and beyond. The city also hosts an annual Food and Drink Festival weekend as part of the Norfolk Food and Drink Festival (✐ norfolkfoodanddrink.com) sponsored by the Eastern Daily Press and Adnams brewery.

Even without any special events taking place, Norwich is blessed with a large and varied selection of places to eat and drink – from pubs, cafés and tea rooms to gastro pubs and smart restaurants. There's also a lot of talk about good coffee these days – central Norwich has quite a few places where the barista is king (or queen). Listed overleaf are some of my favourites.

Cafés & restaurants

Assembly House Theatre St ✆ 01603 626402 🖥 assemblyhousenorwich.co.uk. Offering elevenses and cake, traditional afternoon tea and pre-theatre dinner (17.00–18.45), this is the place to come for a meal or a snack in elegant Georgian surroundings. The cakes, scones and classic afternoon tea, available noon–16.30, are especially highly rated.

The Bicycle Shop 17 St Benedict's St ✆ 01603 625777 🖥 thebicycleshopcafe.com. A quirky, cosy café on three floors that, as its name suggests, was formerly a bicycle shop. This place has a bohemian, laid back atmosphere and decent food made with mostly locally sourced ingredients. Good for breakfasts, tapas and crêpes. Also regular evening performances by acoustic artists in the cellar bar.

Café Britannia Britannia Rd ✆ 01603 708770 🖥 cafebritannia.co.uk. Based at Britannia Barracks next to St James Hill, with superb views over the city, this worthy social enterprise employs low-risk prison inmates among its staff. As a result, the re-offending rate is said to be reassuringly low. Always busy but large enough to cope, the Britannia serves wholesome good-value food throughout the day and evening, although the best bet here are probably the excellent cooked breakfasts, which also offer a vegetarian option.

Farmyard 23 St Benedict's St ✆ 01603 733188 🖥 farmyardrestaurant.com. With a produce-driven menu that sources ingredients from across Norfolk, this modern-style bistro has a short but inspired 'mix and match' menu of starters, mains and extras. Farmyard defines its approach as 'bistronomy' – a bistro atmosphere coupled with no-fuss fine dining.

Frank's Bar 19 Bedford St ✆ 01603 618902 🖥 franksbar.co.uk. A quirky, relaxed café-bar in the Norwich Lanes serving imaginative food that is free-range, locally sourced, fair trade and organic wherever possible.

Grosvenor Fish Bar 28 Lower Goat Lane ✆ 01603 625855 🖥 fshshop.com. The Grosvenor is a 90-year-old fish and chip shop that in recent years has been remodelled as a hip fish and chip grotto. There's extensive downstairs seating but a better idea is to order your food and have it delivered to the Birdcage pub across the road where you can enjoy a beer with your food. Apart from the standard choices there are also sea bass, mackerel, and squid options as well as sandwiches and fish burgers. Be aware that the Grosvenor closes fairly early in the evening – around 19.30.

Little Red Roaster 1 St Andrews Hill ✆ 01603 624886. A friendly café in the city centre, just off London St close to the Book Hive, with excellent coffee as well as all manner of delicious cakes and snacks. There's another branch with a small outside table area south of the city centre at 81B Grove Rd, near the Trafford Arms pub. The Roaster's sister branch at Norwich market once achieved national fame when its proprietor put up a notice refusing service to anyone ordering while using a mobile phone.

Moorish Falafel Bar 17 Lower Goat Lane ✆ 01603 622250. This good-value place has an excellent range of falafels in pitta bread, which are made to order while you wait;

delicious homemade lemonade too. Very popular at lunchtime when there is usually a long queue leading out of the door. There's seating available upstairs or you can take away.

No 33 33 Exchange St ℘ 01603 626097. Good value, with tasty sandwiches and huge portions of cake. This often gets so busy that it is hard to find a table.

North 7–9 Fye Bridge St ℘ 01603 620805 ⌂ norwichnorth.co.uk. Formerly known as the King of Hearts but now managed by the same people as Frank's Bar, this café, located in a Tudor merchant's house by the river, has an imaginative Mediterranean and Middle Eastern menu that makes good use of locally sourced ingredients.

Strangers Coffee House 21 Pottergate ⌂ strangerscoffee.com. This small coffee shop in the heart of The Lanes is the base for the Strangers Coffee company and serves excellent fair trade coffee, paninis, homemade cakes and sausage rolls.

The Tea House 5 Wrights Court, Elm Hill ℘ 01603 631888 ⌂ theteahousenorwich.co.uk. Halfway down Elm Hill and tucked away in a courtyard, this has a good selection of cakes, sandwiches and a choice of over 40 different loose-leaf teas.

Timberhill Bakery 27–9 Timberhill ℘ 01603 613172 ⌂ timberhillbakery.com. As well as selling all manner of sourdough bakery products this bright modern place at the top of Timberhill is also an excellent café that serves delicious toasted sandwiches and cakes and excellent coffee. There's outdoor seating for watching the world go by on Timberhill.

Pubs

Norwich is one of the best places in the country for good, unadulterated pubs serving good, unadulterated real ale. These are just some of my favourite places for a drink in the city:

Adam and Eve Bishopsgate ℘ 01603 667423. Splendidly ancient and character-laden hostelry, resplendent with floral tubs and hanging baskets. This place is worth visiting if only for the fact that it is the city's oldest pub. It is said that builders working on the nearby cathedral once used it (they were paid in bread and ale) – this may or may not be true but, either way, the Adam and Eve is at least 750 years old. Naturally, the pub is rumoured to be haunted.

Alexandra Tavern 16 Stafford St ℘ 01603 627772 ⌂ alexandratavern.co.uk. West of the city centre, on the edge of the 'Golden Triangle', the 'Alex' is a friendly street-corner pub that has real ales from Norwich's Chalk Hill Brewery and a decent variety of pub snacks and nibbles. The pub's landlord, Tiny Little, once rowed across the Atlantic for charity.

Duke of Wellington 91–93 Waterloo Rd ℘ 01603 441182 ⌂ dukeofwellingtonnorwich. co.uk. North of the city centre, this pub has no food but at least 17 real ales to choose from including Wolf. There are also traditional pub games and folk music on Tuesdays.

Fat Cat 49 West End St ℘ 01603 624364 ⌂ fatcatpub.co.uk. A Victorian corner pub that is real ale heaven, with around 30 real ales on offer at any given time. Strictly booze and no food, this traditional pub of the old school is austere, crowded, noisy and very good fun.

Fat Cat Brewery Tap 98–100 Lawson Rd ✆ 01603 413153 ⌖ fatcattap.co.uk. Better known as 'The Shed' to many, this has all the Fat Cat real ales and many more beers, wines and ciders besides. A lively place that can sometimes get very full, there is live music on some nights.

Kings Head 42 Magdalen St ✆ 01603 620468. A traditional city pub north of the river, run by the same people who own the Humpty Dumpty Brewery. No frills, just bare floorboards, bar billiards and well-kept real ale.

Trafford Arms 61 Grove Rd ✆ 01603 628466 ⌖ traffordarms.co.uk. This local, which has a strong community feel, lies just south of the centre. Well-kept real ales include Woodforde's, Adnams and a steady rotation of guest beers, and there are decent-value bar meals to be had.

Wig and Pen 6 St Martin's Plain ✆ 01603 625891 ⌖ thewigandpen.com. In a 17th-century building opposite Norwich Cathedral, 'The Wig' has good food prepared from locally sourced ingredients and a more than reasonable choice of real ales and wines. There's also a nice outdoor seating area for warm summer nights.

ALONG THE YARE – SOUTH BANK

2 WHITLINGHAM COUNTRY PARK

Across the River Yare a little way southeast of Norwich city centre is Whitlingham Country Park, centred on a manmade body of water that, like UEA Broad west of the city, was once a gravel pit. There's a very active canoeing centre here and a pleasant two-mile track around the lake that is often busy with dog walkers and joggers at weekends. Both lake and woods are a good place for birdwatching, especially in spring. A large converted flint barn at the main car park serves as a café and information centre for the Broads Authority.

Camping is available nearby at Whitlingham Broad Campsite (⌖ whitlinghambroadcampsite.com).

3 SURLINGHAM

A few miles east of Norwich, on the south bank of the River Yare, lies the village of Surlingham. The riverside Ferry Boat pub is busy in summer with boat customers but the ferry no longer operates, which is a pity. Most people arriving by boat tend just to call in at the pub, or perhaps moor in the broad further on, but there's plenty to see on foot around the village.

Surlingham parish is a large one that extends east of the village to Surlingham Marsh, Surlingham Wood and **Wheatfen Nature Reserve**

FINE WINE FROM THE YARE VALLEY

In 2017 Norfolk took an unexpected bow in the heady world of viniculture when a Yare Valley vineyard won an award for the world's best single varietal white wine. This was the first time an English vineyard had won such an award for a still wine. Winbirri Vineyards at Surlingham had already received eight awards in the previous three years, including East Anglian Wine of the Year, for the same wine. The wine in question ('very elegant' with a 'complex, oily nose with spice, elderflower and citrus') was the vineyard's Bacchus 2015, bottles of which became impossible to find in any of the county's supermarkets and wine stores soon after it won the prestigious award. The Bacchus grape, according to head winemaker Lee Dyer, was perfectly suited to the Norfolk climate, favouring the dry autumnal conditions found at the Surlingham vineyard. Not resting on its laurels and looking to the future, Winbirri hopes to broaden its output and aims to be producing sparkling wines and pinot noir vintages of comparable quality in the near future.

(✆ 01508 538036 🖑 wheatfen.org), first established by the naturalist Ted Ellis (see walk box, pages 190–1), who lived in a cottage here for 40 years before his death in 1986. Visitors to the reserve are welcome and there are several trails across marshes and woodland, where you are likely to see (or, more likely, hear) sedge and reed warblers, and perhaps witness marsh harriers gliding overhead. In late May and early June, you might even come across that Broadland speciality, the swallowtail butterfly.

Surlingham is also home to Winbirri Vineyards (✆ 07595 894841 🖑 winbirri.com), a small vineyard with a growing reputation for fine wines (see box, above). Occasional tours and tasting days are hosted throughout the year.

ROCKLAND BROAD

This sheltered body of water lies just south of Wheatfen Nature Reserve, and is connected to the Yare by a dyke. The New Inn pub is on the road next to a footpath that leads around the west side of the broad.

From Claxton, the road more or less follows the course of the river through Langley Green and Langley Street to Hardley Street, all tiny hamlets surrounded by vast marshes. The floodplain of the river is very wide, flat and low here and the marshes extensive. The very mention of Hardley Street puts me in mind of a time 25 years or so ago when I found myself out on the marshes here during a violent thunderstorm.

A walk around Surlingham

✳ OS Explorer map OL40; start: St Mary's Church, ♥ TG304065; 2 miles; easy

If you have your own transport, St Mary's Church just west of the village is the best place to park up as you can make an interesting two-mile circular walk from here that takes in a good variety of scenery within a relatively short distance.

A footpath leads down past ponds and dykes to the river. There are dragonflies aplenty and all those other things that tend to characterise Norfolk's slow-moving waterways – yellow flag irises, reed-mace, ragged robin, the sweet smell of water mint and the occasional splash of a frog. Arriving at the river, you come to a path that leads to the right, eastwards along the river shaded by willows, that continues past reed beds and a bird hide as far as the Ferry House pub. Blackthorn grows plentifully along the path here, which is one of my favourite places to collect sloes (for making sloe gin) on a bright, late autumn's day when there's a nip in the air.

A concrete road leads inland from the pub through a swampy alder carr, at the end of which is a track to the right next to a house with a dovecote. The path leads along the edge of a field and past a rifle range until it passes beneath the remains of St Saviour's, an evocative ruined church, and continues along a track to St Mary's where you started.

In a vast wet area where everything is at sea level and with no trees, a soggy man makes a rather good lightning conductor – or so I thought, as I ran back to my car with jagged shafts of electricity fizzing around me. Fortunately, it did not turn out to be the electrifying experience that it might have been and I escaped unscathed. I tend to listen more closely to weather forecasts these days.

5 BERGH APTON

Bergh Apton – that's *Ber*-apton not *Bergh*-apton – is a large, sprawling village south of Rockland St Mary, just the other side of the A146. The village was originally two separate settlements, Apton to the northwest and Bergh to the southeast, which explains its considerable size. Apton's church disappeared long ago and the two parishes were combined so that Bergh's church of St Peter and St Paul might serve both. There used to be an enjoyable sculpture trail held here every three years in late May and June, which offered the opportunity not only to see works by local sculptors but also to snoop around some rather wonderful village gardens. Unfortunately, this eventually

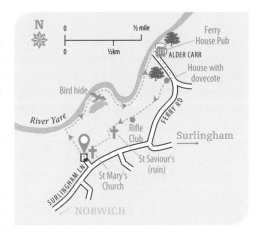

If you make a short detour to the ruins of St Saviour's you'll come across the graves of local naturalist and writer Ted Ellis (1909–86) and his wife, Phyllis. The graves are simple, austere even, but it is undeniably a lovely spot for any lifelong lover of nature to rest his bones.

Continuing up the track towards St Mary's, the house on the left, just before the church, usually has jars of honey for sale and an honesty box at its gate – this is the home of Orchid Apiaries, which produces several tons of honey annually from Surlingham hives.

became a victim of its own success, with several thousand attending the final three events, the last of which was in 2011. The village still stages occasional arts events and has hosted a specially commissioned cycle of mystery plays in recent years.

LODDON

Continuing southeast along the A146 from the Bergh Apton turn-off, you come to the small market town of Loddon, which lies immediately south of the River Chet, a tributary of the Yare. On the north side of the river is the neighbouring village of **Chedgrave** but it is Loddon that is the more interesting – a tidy, self-sufficient sort of place with a parish church, a couple of pubs, a boat-lined staithe and all the requisite services strewn along its High Street. The Norwich bus to Beccles diverts off the main road to pass through the village and it always seems a bit of a squeeze for a double-decker to negotiate its way along the narrow High Street before returning to the unfettered and broad A146. Because the River Chet is part of the Broads system the town lies just within the bounds of the Broads National Park. The town's 15th-century

Holy Trinity Church is certainly attractive in its own right but really Loddon is more of an ensemble piece – an unspoiled array of fine Georgian and Victorian buildings, pretty cottages and an old mill complex. The mill complex now serves as **Loddon Mill Arts**, which organises arts events and even stages a regular comedy club in its converted steam engine room and grain barn.

A good **walk** to be had from Chedgrave is to follow the country lane east from the crossroads towards Hardley Street and after about a mile take the footpath that leads off to the right past Hardley Hall down to the edge of the River Chet. The riverbank can then be followed left to reach the River Yare. At the confluence of the two rivers you'll come across **Hardley Cross**, which dates from 1543. This historic cross marks the boundary between the City of Norwich and the Borough of Great Yarmouth, and also the end of Norwich's jurisdiction over the river and the beginning of Yarmouth's. In past times the mayors of both Norwich and Great Yarmouth would travel here each year by wherry for the annual inquest on river liberties. Coming back, you can either retrace your steps, or better, follow the bank of the River Yare a mile or so west to reach Hardley Staithe near the church. From here, follow the minor lane that leads southwest all the way back to Chedgrave. Please note: the footpath shown on maps that leads along Hardley Flood is no longer open because of flood damage.

ᵞ⏧ FOOD & DRINK

Rosy Lee's Tea Room 37a Bridge St, Loddon ✆ 01508 520204. A small, cosy tea room opposite Loddon Staithe, this is a local institution and deserves its far-flung reputation. Caroline, the ever-accommodating and friendly proprietor, serves up large pots of tea and very good sandwiches, soup and light dishes made with local produce, as well as cakes made by the local WI.

White Horse 5 Norwich Rd, Chedgrave ✆ 01508 520250 🖉 whitehorsechedgrave.co.uk. Just across the river in Chedgrave, this village pub offers up to five real ales and decent bar meals.

ALONG THE YARE – NORTH BANK

The north bank of the River Yare has the railway line to Great Yarmouth and so is far more accessible if you want to use public transport. A couple of stops along the line are worth heading for if you are looking for a quiet walk or are at all interested in birds and other wildlife.

A TASTE OF NORFOLK

Norfolk has much to offer the discerning foodie. There's the freshest of fish from the coast, rare-breed meat from the farms and local specialities like marsh samphire to savour. The coastal waters also provide excellent crab, lobster and shellfish.

1 Cley Smokehouse takes full advantage of the bounty the Norfolk coast has to offer. **2** The Norfolk Food & Drink Festival in Norwich is just one of several food festivals held annually in the county. **3** As a primarily agricultural county, Norfolk has an abundance of fresh, seasonal produce throughout the year. **4** Marsh samphire, a wild plant that thrives in the north Norfolk mud flats, is a regional delicacy best eaten with fish.

SACRED BUILDINGS

Norfolk is well known for its remarkable churches. As well as the hundreds of large medieval churches built in the county during the height of the wool trade, Norfolk also has more round tower churches than anywhere else in Europe, some of which date back to the Saxon period.

1 The ruins of St Benet's Abbey (founded 1020) beside the River Bure in the Broads. **2** St Peter Mancroft in Norwich is a 15th-century Perpendicular-style church with a fine hammerbeam roof. **3** Twin-towered Wymondham Abbey started life as a Benedictine priory. **4** St Mary's Church, Surlingham, one of 124 round tower churches in the county. **5** Norwich Cathedral, dating from 1086, has the second-highest spire and second-largest cloisters in England.

STRUMPSHAW FEN RSPB RESERVE

NR13 4HS *01603 715191* rspb.org.uk/strumpshawfen; free entry for RSPB members

The village of Strumpshaw lies midway between Brundall and Lingwood but Strumpshaw Fen Nature Reserve, an extensive wetland reserve run by the RSPB, is actually closer to Brundall.

The reserve, which lies just across the river from Wheatfen Reserve and Surlingham Marshes, has all the wetland birds that you might expect plus some others that you might not, with bitterns, harriers, warblers, woodpeckers and numerous waders and ducks all lining up to be seen. It is also a reliable place to see swallowtail butterflies, which in my experience are easiest to spot in late May when they are still a tad sluggish.

"The reserve has bitterns, harriers, warblers, woodpeckers and numerous waders and ducks all lining up to be seen."

The main entrance and visitor centre are a little over a mile from Buckenham station and so this is a possibility if you are arriving by train. You should bear in mind though that only a limited number of trains stop at Buckenham as it is a request stop – four on Saturdays and Sundays but none in the week.

On a Sunday, you could combine a visit to Strumpshaw with one to Berney Arms and Breydon Water. The rest of the week, you'll have to use Brundall station instead, which requires a slightly longer walk to reach the reserve entrance. Bus 15a (First in Suffolk & Norfolk) also runs hourly between Norwich and Strumpshaw; get off at the stop at the junction of Long Lane and Stone Road, from where it's a ten-minute walk.

BUCKENHAM CARRS

A large wooded area just east of Buckenham station, Buckenham Carrs is home to an enormous rook and jackdaw roost mentioned in the Domesday Book. It's thought there may be as many as 80,000 birds. The roost is the central motif of Mark Cocker's *Crow Country*, which celebrates both crows and the Yare Valley where he lives.

The Buckenham roost, which takes place in the winter months, roughly between late October and March, is quite a spectacle to behold, a natural phenomenon that has been taking place long before the fields were ploughed here and the church at Buckenham constructed. Ideally, you'll want a crisp winter's evening with a clear sky and a full moon.

The best vantage point is to walk up the narrow road from Buckenham station until you reach a copse on the left with a small ruined brick shelter. You'll see it all from here.

The performance – if you can call it that – is a slow burn. Just after sunset, groups of rooks, and some jackdaws, fly in to gather on the large ploughed area immediately to the west; others land in the trees that surround it. Some have come quite a long way to be sociable but the crow conversation taking place sounds rather tetchy, all guttural complaining caws.

Momentum slowly builds as more and more groups of birds fly in to land in the field. As the light fades, the noise from the congregation

A walk from Berney Arms

✿ OS Outdoor Leisure map 40 or Landranger map 134; start: Berney Arms station,
♀ TG468052; 6 miles; moderate

With just two trains a day and four on Sundays, walking is the only thing to do here, unless you want to spend hours waiting on the platform. Fortunately, the walking is very good: the Wherryman's Way runs nearby and you have the choice of going west to Reedham, northwest along the Weavers' Way to Halvergate or east to Great Yarmouth along the shore of Breydon Water. My preferred choice would be the third.

From the station follow the footpath, part of the Weavers' Way, to the river, where there is a drainage windmill. Then head east along the Wherryman's Way to reach the **Berney Arms** (✆ 01493 700303), surely Norfolk's most isolated pub. At the time of updating this edition, the pub was closed for renovation but the café next door was open for business. It should be said that this pub is notoriously phoenix-like in terms of being open (or not) for business but as a rule it is usually open daily in the summer and sometimes at weekends in the winter (but do check first). The trade these days is almost entirely walkers, birdwatchers or boaters – there are several moorings here – but in the past this isolated pub would have had a colourful clientele of wherrymen, wildfowlers, poachers and fishermen.

Just after the pub, you arrive at the confluence of the Yare and Waveney and the start of **Breydon Water**. Look south along the Waveney River and you should be able to make out the outline of **Gariannonum/Burgh Castle** (pages 200–1). From here, the Wherryman's Way continues all the way along the north shore of Breydon Water until it reaches **Great Yarmouth**, where it narrows to a channel to flow south into the sea at Gorleston. Great Yarmouth railway station is right by Breydon Bridge at the start of the town.

builds louder and eerily expectant: something is clearly about to happen. Eventually, when the darkness is almost complete some sort of signal spurs the birds airborne and the sky blackens with rooks that swirl noisily east to settle in the woods of Buckenham Carrs where they will spend the night together.

"The noise of the birds is eerily expectant: something is clearly about the happen."

It's an astonishing, almost primal, event. One that almost laughs in the face of man's perceived dominion over nature. No collective noun can adequately describe it: a building of rooks, a train of jackdaws. It's less a murder of crows, more a mass execution.

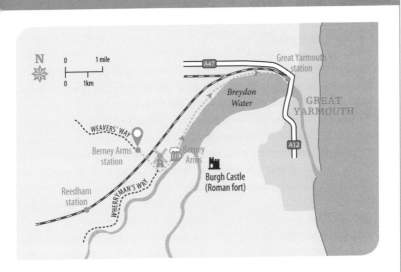

Breydon Water is a large tidal estuary, a wonderful place for birdwatchers and a great place to walk, although it is quite an austere landscape, especially at low tide when glistening grey mud stretches to the skyline. The sky is often grey too, or that is how it seems to me, as whenever I come here it always seems to be overcast as if there were a perpetual cloud hanging over the place.

Winter is peak season here, for birds at least, with tens of thousands of waders, ducks and swans feeding in the mud.

9 CANTLEY & 10 REEDHAM

Working eastwards, the next village along the river is **Cantley**, best known for its **sugar beet factory** that belches out sickly-smelling smoke in the winter months. Cantley's sugar-beet factory, seen from far and wide, is as much an icon of the River Yare as a Norfolk wherry, and is the magnet for all the lumbering lorries that trundle these roads in winter brimful of knobbly roots.

Reedham, further east, has the only surviving **car and passenger ferry** along the river and consequently is the only point between Norwich and Great Yarmouth where it is possible to cross. The cable ferry, which takes up to three cars at a time, operates year-round. If this service seems a quaint throwback of value only to tourists then consider that crossing the river here can save a round-trip of around 30 miles, so there may be queues in summer. The village, listed as Redaham in the Domesday Book, is thought to have been a Roman military station – there are fragments of Roman brick in the village's St John the Baptist Church. As well as having a popular riverside pub, the village is also home to the **Humpty Dumpty Brewery** (✆ 01493 701818 ⌂ humptydumptybrewery.co.uk), which uses locally produced malt and whose Broadland Surprise has been voted Champion Beer of Norfolk. Some of the other Humpty Dumpty brews – Reedcutter, Swallowtail, Swingbridge Stout – also take their name from local features. It's a 3½ mile walk along the riverbank to Berney Arms from here, a worthwhile outing from which you could return by train if you got your timing right. Otherwise, there are easy circular road walks around the village.

¶¶ FOOD & DRINK

Lord Nelson 38 Riverside, Reedham ✆ 01493 700367 ⌂ lordnelson-reedham.co.uk. Now a little more upmarket than it used to be, with a restaurant and outside dining area and a choice of four real ales, this pub by the water and the swing bridge is a convenient stop.

11 BERNEY ARMS

Berney Arms must be the oddest railway stop in the country. I use the word 'stop' advisedly, rather than station, as that is all there is to it: a sign and small platform to get off or on the few trains that stop here. It takes its name from a local landowner, Thomas Trench Berney, who in 1844 sold land to the railway company on condition that they built a station and kept it open for perpetuity. The station is unstaffed, of course, and as you might imagine, 3½ miles from the nearest road and right in the heart of the vast spread of Halvergate Marshes, rather isolated.

2 GREAT YARMOUTH

Yarmouth is an ancient town, much older than Norwich. And at present, though not standing on so much ground, yet better built, much more complete; for number of inhabitants, not much inferior, and for wealth, trade and advantage of its situation, infinitely superior to Norwich.

Daniel Defoe, *A Tour Thro' The Whole Island of Great Britain, divided into Circuits or Journies*, 1724

Not so great these days, some might say. Great Yarmouth is hardly an obvious Slow destination but it would be wrong to dismiss it completely. There was once a thriving herring fishing industry here. This faded out in the early years of the 20th century, by which time the town had found new fortune as a seaside resort. The 1970s heralded an era of cheap Mediterranean holidays and many of the town's former devotees started to look further afield to destinations like the Costa Brava instead. Once again, the town's diminishing fortunes were bailed out by a new source of income; this time, it was North Sea oil and gas.

Great Yarmouth is a town of two halves: an isthmus that shows its seafaring side along South Quay to the west, and its holiday resort face along the promenade to the east. Neither half is doing particularly well these days but both will provide a degree of culture shock if you travel here direct from somewhere like Southwold, a very different sort of place although just 20 miles away. Great Yarmouth, the resort, is as you might expect: an East Anglian Blackpool with a pier, sandy beach, deckchairs, buckets and spades – it's traditional in the sense of being a place where you can still buy sticks of rock, see a waxworks museum and even have a 'gypsy' woman tell your fortune. The accents are northern, Midlands or Norfolk, although move a few streets in from the promenade and you'll hear plenty of Polish and Portuguese instead.

There's still something quintessentially English about Great Yarmouth seafront, and it's refreshing to discover that not everyone who can afford it has upped sticks to Benidorm or Corfu. Next to the pier, you might see a large extended family of Birmingham Indians, as I did one bright August day: mothers and aunties in glorious saris chatting and devouring chips on the sea wall; teenage girls texting their friends and giggling; boys playing serious cricket on the sand with proper stumps and a hard ball. Observing this heart-warming scene from posters above Britannia Pier are Jim Davidson and Roy 'Chubby' Brown, comedians not known for their love of liberal inclusivity – it all struck a wonderful chord.

Heritage Quarter

The fishiest town in all England
Charles Dickens

Yarmouth's other side can be found in its Heritage Quarter along South Quay, which begins at the bridge and Victorian Town Hall and stretches south along the River Yare. There will also be the 1930 herring boat *Lydia Eva*, the very last of the steam drifters, moored at the top of the quay unless it has been moved to pastures new since I was last there. **Elizabethan House** (4 South Quay ✎ 01493 855746 ⊘ museums. norfolk.gov.uk) was the home of a Tudor merchant, while **The Tollhouse** (✎ 01493 858900), a little further south and just inland, dates from the 12th century and was used as a gaol. Some surviving row houses (✎ 01493 857900 ⊘ English Heritage) are open to visitors just south of here, while back on South Quay is **Nelson Museum** (26 South Quay ✎ 01493 850698 ⊘ nelson-museum.co.uk), which is precisely that, a museum dedicated to the life and times of the Norfolk naval hero. You'll encounter more Row Houses along Nottingham Way near the museum. Not all Yarmouth's architectural heritage is Victorian or older. The town also has a sprinkling of noteworthy buildings of more recent pedigree too, like the lovely art deco **Hippodrome** (⊘ hippodromecircus.co.uk) on St George's Road, dating from 1903, one of only two surviving purpose-built circus buildings in Britain that likes to describe itself as 'East Anglia's mini Albert Hall'. Both Houdini and Chaplin once performed here and shows and summer spectaculars are still staged here today. Regular guided heritage walks are run by the borough council (✎ 01493 846346 ⊘ great-yarmouth.co.uk).

If you're not heading straight from the Nelson Museum to the Time and Tide Museum (page 199), wander further along South Quay towards the 169-foot high **Nelson Monument** that overlooks the mouth of the river. This is not vintage Norfolk scenery, but interestingly grim, with enormous heaps of metal scrap in yards, closed warehouses, rough-looking pubs and a few dodgy-looking characters. There's a semi-abandoned air to the streets here that reminds me a little of Sheffield's Don Valley in the late 1980s – the ghost of unemployment and vanished industry. You can usually ascend the Nelson Monument on Sundays in summer for a small charge – arrangements can be made through the Nelson Museum. It is best to book ahead (✆ 01493 850698) as only two people at a time are permitted to climb the 217 steps up the slim spiral staircase to the top. Guides are available to explain the monument's history. Needless to say, small children and visitors with heart, lung or mobility problems are not allowed to ascend – it is a tough climb.

The **Time and Tide Museum** (✆ 01493 743930 ⌂ museums.norfolk. gov.uk) on Blackfriars Road, opposite a large chunk of the medieval Town Wall, is rather wonderful and it's worth visiting Yarmouth for this alone. Giving a wonderful account of Great Yarmouth life through the ages, particularly its seafaring tradition, it's a hands-on place that children really enjoy and there's plenty of archive film and taped interviews to make the history come alive. 'We're a bit Tardis-like here,' the guide explained. 'But we manage to pack a lot into a small space. The building used to be a herring curing works and a lot of people ask if we pump the smell in for atmosphere. We don't: it's in the fabric of the building itself.' The building really does smell strongly of herrings, which gives you a clue as to the sort of social stigma that the itinerant Scots fisher girls who came 'tae Yarmooth' must have suffered, given that their working days were spent elbow-deep in briny fish. As well as plenty of great displays and nostalgic newsreels of the joys of the herring fishing life ('There's nothing statelier than a shoal of herring

TALL SHIPS IN YARMOUTH

Great Yarmouth's **Maritime Festival** (⌂ maritimefestival.co.uk), which takes place every September, is a fine reminder of East Anglia's once-glorious seafaring tradition. With majestic tall ships moored on South Quay alongside numerous tents and stalls with a general maritime theme, it draws large crowds of local families, old sailors and curious landlubbers. It's a rare opportunity to poke around a tall ship, talk to experts and hang around with sailors. You can even go on a 2½- or 3½-hour cruise on one of the tall ships if you book ahead. The sailing times depend on the tide. As well as ships to explore, there are craft stalls, information stands and even displays by Newfoundland rescue dogs, with fried herrings for sale, and salty sea shanties sung by crusty men with pewter tankards in the real ale tent. If you want to buy a ship in a bottle, a piece of seashell sculpture or a Caister Lifeboat sweatshirt, this is definitely the place to be.

coming over the side'), there's a reconstructed 'row' of cottages with tiny, tidy front rooms and piped voices. It is all rather moving, which is surely what any top-notch museum should aspire to be. The Silver Darlings café (see below) across the courtyard from the entrance is excellent too – a great place for a fish platter lunch if all this talk of herrings has given you an appetite.

▌❚ FOOD & DRINK

Mariners Tavern 60 Howard St South ☎ 01493 332299. One of the few real ale pubs in town (it won Norfolk CAMRA Branch Pub of the Year in 2010), this has a cosy feel and is reasonably close to the railway station.

Quayside Plaza 9 South Quay ☎ 01493 331777 ⟁ quaysideplaza.com. Convenient for the Rows and the Nelson Museum, this small restaurant is tucked away in the remains of Greyfriars cloisters. Good-value and eclectic Mediterranean-style meals, also cakes, salads and sandwiches, all made using organic locally sourced produce wherever possible.

Silver Darlings Café 16 Blackfriars Rd ☎ 01493 743932. Hidden away in the courtyard of the Time and Tide Museum, this is an excellent place for lunch, with a good range of reasonably priced sandwiches, quiches, smoked fish platters and other dishes to choose from.

St John's Head 58 North Quay ☎ 01493 843443 ⟁ stjohnsheadrealalepub.co.uk. This long-established pub has an excellent choice of real ales that include Elgood Cambridge Bitter and at least four guest ales.

13 BURGH CASTLE

Heading west along the south bank of Breydon Water brings you to the village of Burgh Castle where, as well as a boatyard, a couple of pubs and a small round tower church idyllically set among trees, the impressive Roman ruins of Burgh Castle (originally known as Gariannonum) loom above the confluence of the Yare and Waveney. With massive 3rd-century walls sloping at a precarious angle above the river and reed beds, it's certainly an impressive spot (free access) and well worth the effort of walking to along the estuary bank from Yarmouth. This route is actually the first (or last) section of the Angles Way and so is signposted fairly clearly for the most part. Besides, once you are at the estuary it is impossible to go wrong – just follow the path west until you see the ruins rising to your left. If you are not feeling quite so energetic, you could always catch one of the regular buses to the village from Yarmouth's Market Gates bus station instead, or perhaps take the bus one way and then walk back.

The castle's crucial strategic position is self-evident; these massive brick and flint fortifications were abandoned at the beginning of the 5th century when the Romans finally thought better of occupying such intractable northern territory. It is possible that Burgh Castle also marks the location of Cnobheresburg, a 7th-century monastery founded by Saint Fursa, the first Irish missionary in southern England. Whether or not the monastery's actual site was within these walls or elsewhere on this coast is open to debate; either way, subsequent attacks by Danish raiders soon encouraged Fursa to decamp to the relative safety of France.

AWAY FROM THE YARE

14 VENTA ICENORUM & 15 SHOTESHAM

The River Tas wiggles its way up from south Norfolk to its confluence with the Yare just outside Norwich. There's a Bronze Age henge marked on maps close to this point, beneath pylons next to the railway tracks and the Norwich inner ring road, but I have never been able to make out more than a few vague bumps in a field – evidently it's a job for a photographer in a helicopter.

TWO HISTORIC TREES

A little way northeast of Wymondham, beside the B1172, the old road to Hethersett and Norwich, stands **Kett's Oak**, the tree that Robert Kett is said to have mustered supporters beneath prior to the 1549 rebellion. Another tale relates that this was actually the tree from which nine of the rebels were hanged. Whether or not this is the original tree in question or a later replacement is open to debate. Either way, the tree is surrounded by railings and much propped-up these days.

There's another historic tree fairly close by. At Hethel, close to Mulbarton to the east of Wymondham, there's an ancient hawthorn. The **Hethel Old Thorn** is a 700-year-old hawthorn, the oldest of its kind in Norfolk and possibly the UK. This once measured 12 feet in circumference but is now much reduced. The tree is protected as a Norfolk Wildlife Trust nature reserve, which at just 0.06 acres is the smallest in the country. Not to be outdone by Kett's Oak's historical pedigree, this ancient hawthorn is supposedly where rebels met in the time of King John, while another legend has it that the tree grew from the staff of Joseph of Aramathea brought here by pilgrims from the Holy Land. All Saints' Church that stands nearby is even more ancient, with parts of it nearly a thousand years old and of Saxon origin.

Venture a little further south, past Caistor St Edmund, and there's more impressive archaeology in the form of **Venta Icenorum Roman Town** (sometimes referred to as Caistor Roman Town), a rectangle of raised walls and fortifications with traces of Roman brick that once served as the *Civitas* of the Iceni tribe and the most important Roman centre in northern East Anglia. The **Boudicca Way**, a long-distance footpath, passes right by it, although the evidence suggests that the streets and buildings of the town were not constructed until well after Boudica's bloody revolt against Roman rule in AD61.

Away from the river, **Shotesham** is an attractive village set among lush bucolic meadows. A good circular walk from here would be to follow the Boudicca Way south to Saxlingham Nethergate, then return to the village via Shotesham Lane and Roger's Lane. On the return leg, you will pass the evocatively ruined church of St Martin alongside its replacement next to Shotesham Old Hall.

16 WYMONDHAM

Wedged in between the course of the Yare and Tas rivers southwest of Norwich, just off the A11 dual carriageway, stands the market town of Wymondham, a prosperous sort of place that is just far enough away from Norwich to have a life of its own. Wymondham is both well to do and well connected, having a major road running past it, a good bus service and regular train connections to Norwich and Cambridge.

The first thing you need to know is that it's pronounced 'Wind-am' – to say 'Wy-mond-ham' will just induce hilarity among the natives. If you take the B1172 via Hethersett to reach the town, as the bus does, you'll pass **Kett's Oak** (see box, page 201) by the roadside a mile short of the town's outskirts. The tree is reputed to be that under which Robert Kett, a Wymondham native, gathered supporters and made a rousing speech that set in motion his uprising against the enclosure of common land in 1549. The tree is partially supported by props these days but it still seems to be flourishing enough to produce acorns.

Like many other market towns, much of medieval Wymondham went up in smoke, and, in 1615, a fire gutted many of the town's buildings. Much of the historic town centre is a 17th-century rebuild, and it is thanks to the town remaining rather a backwater in the Victorian era that so many old buildings still stand today. The prominent 1617 **market cross** doubles as the tourist information centre and is raised on stilts to protect valuable documents from floodwater and rats. Live rats used to be nailed to it in order to set an example to fellow vermin but the practice was discontinued in 1902 when a child died as the result of a rat bite.

The two towers make **Wymondham Abbey**, or to give it its full name, the abbey church of St Mary and St Thomas of Canterbury, a distinctive local landmark. It started life as a Benedictine priory, its monastic buildings being demolished following the Dissolution when the church was partially destroyed. A visit by Elizabeth I in 1573 ensured that some repairs were made. The eastern octagonal tower is the older, part of the original Norman abbey church, while the square western tower dates from 1448 and once had Robert Kett's brother, William, hung in chains from it and left to rot. Looking at the interior, it is hard to imagine such cruel events ever taking place here, as the hammerbeam roof bristles with benign wooden angels beaming goodwill down onto the congregation.

FOOD & DRINK

Bird in Hand Church Rd, Wreningham ✆ 01508 489438 ⟨ birdinhandwreningham.com. In Wreningham, close to Hethel Old Thorn, this country freehouse has a relaxed atmosphere, an excellent selection of local ales, good bar meals and Sunday roasts using locally sourced meat.

Green Dragon 6 Church St, Wymondham ✆ 01953 607907 ⟨ greendragonnorfolk.co.uk. A 14th-century inn serving home-cooked English food with an emphasis on local produce. Cask-conditioned ales, an extensive wine list and choice of over 50 different whiskies.

Station Bistro Wymondham Station ✆ 01953 606433 ⟨ station-bistro-wymondham. co.uk. At Wymondham's 'proper' station, on the main network. All-day breakfasts, snacks, light lunches and Sunday roasts that use locally supplied meat and vegetables.

7 THE MID-NORFOLK RAILWAY

✆ 01362 851723 ⟨ mnr.org.uk ⊙ two or three trains a day in either direction between Wymondham and East Dereham

Walk towards the River Tiffey from Wymondham Abbey and cross it and you'll arrive at a railway line and the station – well, platform – of the Mid-Norfolk Railway. Enthusiastic volunteers ensure that the trains always run on time and it's a highly enjoyable excursion, especially if you manage to get on one of the steam trains. *En route*, you'll pass through some forgotten little outposts of central Norfolk like Thuxton and Yaxham, where you can get off if you like and have a walk. East Dereham is the terminus for the time being, but plans are afoot for the line to be restored as far as North Elmham.

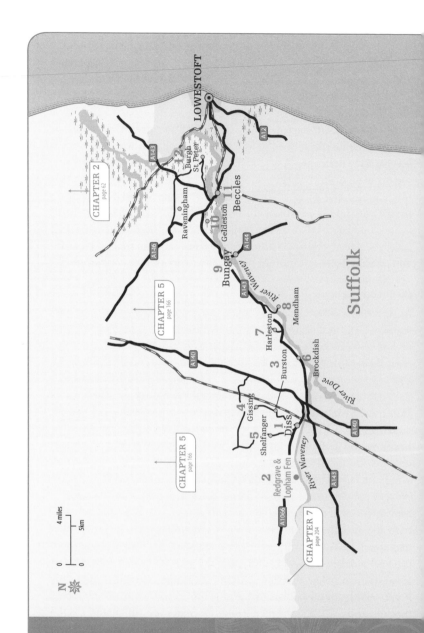

THE WAVENEY VALLEY

6
THE WAVENEY VALLEY

Were I in my castle upon the River Waveney
I wouldne give a button For the King of Cockney.
Hugh 'the Bold' Bigod, 1173

Just as the Little Ouse River forms a natural boundary between Norfolk
and Suffolk in the west of the region, the River Waveney performs the
same function in the centre and east. The Waveney's source lies between
the villages of Redgrave in Suffolk and South Lopham in Norfolk, close
to where the Little Ouse also rises. The sources of the two rivers are
actually so close that Norfolk is almost an island – a heavy downpour
and a flooded road or two and the separation is complete.

From its humble origins in Redgrave Fen, the Waveney flows east
through the small towns of Diss (Norfolk), Bungay and Beccles (Suffolk)
before looping north around Lowestoft to join the River Yare at Breydon
Water and eventually go to sea at Great Yarmouth. East of Bungay, the
river lies within the boundary of the Broads Authority and the river
is connected to Oulton Broad just west of Lowestoft by a manmade
channel, Oulton Dyke.

All this talk of rivers and county boundaries might suggest that the
Waveney forms some sort of impenetrable barrier. Far from it: the
river is more of a conduit than anything, a far cry from the situation
with the Yare to the north where the river represents a real physical
obstacle. The Waveney, in contrast, has plenty of bridges spanning it,
especially in its western reaches. The Waveney Valley may not be much
of a valley in physical terms – it's hardly Kashmir – but it does have
a personality all of its own that seems quite separate from the rest of
Norfolk and Suffolk. Teenagers along the Waveney Valley may display
keen allegiances to either Norwich City or Ipswich Town but that is
about as far as it goes. The birdsong in the hedgerows sounds pretty
much the same on either bank. Because of this singular character it

is will occasionally be necessary to cross the county boundary here and there in this chapter, and so both Bungay and Beccles are included despite belonging to Suffolk.

So what characterises the Waveney Valley? It's a sense of cosy isolation, where south Norfolk eases into the clay country of north Suffolk, where there are fewer big estates, and more commons, ancient hedgerows and moated farmhouses; more meandering tracks that seem to follow every field boundary before ending up nowhere in particular. There has probably been less change over the past half century in this region than anywhere else in southern England. While the attractions of north Norfolk have undoubtedly lured numerous outsiders, downsizers and weekenders over the years, the Waveney Valley has a different kind of draw. Those that have settled here have tended to become more integrated into the existing community. It has long attracted artists, writers and craftsmen and there was a noticeable, if small-scale, invasion of folk escaping the city for something simpler and more wholesome back in the 1970s – they are mostly still here.

THE ARTY SIDE

A surprising number of artists work from the towns and villages of the valley: for three weekends in late June and early July of the annual **Harleston and Waveney Arts Trail** (⊘ hwat.org.uk) you can visit them in their studios. Constable and Gainsborough may have immortalised the Stour Valley on the Suffolk/Essex border but that just happened to be where they lived. It might just as easily have been the Waveney Valley. To quote author and pioneer of sustainable living John Seymour: 'If John Constable had been born at Harleston, instead of at East Bergholt, we would have processions of motor coaches along the Waveney instead of along the Stour'. As for present-day local artists, perhaps the recently deceased Mary Newcomb (1922–2008) is the most representative for her innocent, yet evocative, vignettes of country life – not exclusively featuring the Waveney Valley but certainly evoking its spirit.

Several well-known writers are or have been based in the valley too. Roger Deakin, who used to live just south of Diss, chronicled the changes of the season in *Notes from Walnut Tree Farm* and to a lesser extent in *Wildwood*, while nature writer Richard Mabey moved to the area some years ago and his Waveney Valley home features prominently in his book *Nature Cure*. Louis '*Captain Corelli's Mandolin*' de Bernières has settled near Bungay, and W G Sebald in *The Rings of Saturn*, his meandering introspective walk through a rather sombre Suffolk, spent enough time in the Waveney Valley to be quite spectacularly rude about a small hotel in Harleston.

It's easy to get carried away of course. Like everywhere else, there's an element of reactionary nimbyism here on occasion – the greatest fears seemingly being the provision of caravan sites for travellers and wind-farms – but overall it's pretty welcoming and lacking the self-satisfaction sometimes found in more high-profile parts of the region. The key words here are probably 'self-contained' and 'authentic': real places with real shops serving real people. I begin by looking at Diss, the urban centre for the west of the valley, which exemplifies this outlook perfectly. As Britain's third appointed **Cittaslow** (Slow Town), it is a town that perfectly encapsulates the Waveney Valley's distinctive atmosphere and human pace of life. Diss and Beccles are about as urban as it gets here, which may give you some idea as to what to expect.

GETTING AROUND

Making your way along the Waveney Valley is easy enough. The main towns and villages are linked by the A143 that runs from Bury St Edmunds to Great Yarmouth. From its Suffolk beginning, the road crosses the county boundary at Diss and continues along the Norfolk side of the river as it heads towards the coast, apart from a brief detour into Bungay on the Suffolk bank. For those on four wheels, this makes a convenient way of speeding east or west, but it has to be said that the minor roads that thread through the valley are infinitely more enjoyable. Thankfully – and sensibly – the buses that run along the valley avoid the A143 for the most part, preferring to detour through the villages where most of their passengers live.

TOURIST INFORMATION

Beccles The Quay, Fen Lane ✐ 01502 713196
Broads website ✐ broads-authority.gov.uk
Diss Mere's Mouth Mere St ✐ 01379 650523
Harleston Tourist information Point 8 Exchange St ✐ 01379 851917

PUBLIC TRANSPORT

This could be better; there again, it could be worse. Diss has a regular **train** service to Norwich, as it lies on the main Norwich–London line. Regular trains also run between Norwich and Lowestoft, which has a branch line to Beccles. **Bus** transport is reasonable enough in daylight hours, with buses running along most of the length of the valley. The Anglian Bus (☎ 01502 711109 ⬚ anglianbus.co.uk) 60H service runs several times a day between Beccles and Harleston during working hours, Monday to Saturday (excluding bank holidays), while the Borderbus 580 between Beccles and Great Yarmouth runs more or less hourly. The Anglian Bus service 88/X88 connects Norwich to Bungay with hourly buses during working hours, Monday to Saturday, and with a two-hourly service on Sundays and bank holidays. Simonds Bus services 1 and 2 also connect Norwich and Diss several times a day, but not on Sundays.

RIVER CRAFT & CANOEING

Transport by boat is an option east of Geldeston, which is the limit of navigation for motor boats. Day boats are for hire at Beccles,

FAMILY CANOEING CAPERS

Poppy Mathews

We are Poppy, John, Jamie (15) and Izzy (12) and we all enjoy canoeing.

The Broads are very busy with cruisers throughout the summer and we were keen to see if it was possible to hire Canadian canoes from the commercial boatyards and still find quiet places to paddle. In early June, John and I caught the train to Wroxham then walked through the moored yachts, gleaming in the early summer sunshine, until we found a little wooden shed that advertised canoe hire.

After paying our £20 for three hours, we set off, paddling rather nervously past the shiny hulls towering over us in the marina until we got out into the river. We went under a couple of bridges thronging with shoppers and cars, then upstream into what quickly became an oasis of quiet and calmness. For half of our allotted time we paddled quite steadily, interested in how far we could go without killing ourselves, but also wanting to appreciate the glorious day around us. After a quick stop for lunch, we turned around and headed back, noticing that it was quite a bit harder going back against the wind – or maybe we were just getting tired! In total, we paddled about five miles in three hours.

It was a lovely afternoon and we decided that we should do it again sometime, next time with the kids. Fast forward to the summer hols and, with packed lunch and swimming things,

Burgh St Peter and Oulton Broad and there is scope for **canoeing** too, although the river is noticeably tidal east of Beccles. A stretch for canoeing recommended by the Upper Waveney Valley Project is the 20-mile section of the river between Brockdish, west of Harleston, and Ellingham Weir, east of Bungay. **Canoe hire** is possible at Bungay at Outney Meadow Caravan Park (𝒥 01986 892338 𝄐 outneymeadow. co.uk), Geldeston at Rowan Craft (𝒥 01508 518208 𝄐 rowancraft.co.uk) and Burgh St Peter at the Waveney River Centre. Contact the Waveney Valley Canoe Club (𝄐 waveneyvalleycanoeclub.org.uk) for further advice. A guide to canoeing the Waveney is available for download from 𝄐 outneymeadow.co.uk.

WALKING

Some absolutely lovely walking is to be had, particularly by the river. Most villages lie close enough to one another for decent circular walks to be possible and with such quiet back roads even road walking is a pleasure. The Angles Way long-distance route threads its way along the valley between Breckland and Lowestoft; eastwards from Beccles it

we caught the bus from Norwich to Bungay on the River Waveney. We had phoned ahead and booked two canoes, so knew we had a great day ahead of us. After a quick chat about who was going with whom, we were off on our second canoe adventure of the summer. Jamie and Izzy led the way downstream, negotiating a couple of low bridges before we got out into open countryside where the river meandered elegantly through meadows with grazing cows.

The river is quite shallow and we played a game of trying to hit patches of reed growing in the water with the canoe. Much enjoyment was had with lots of shrieking and laughing; not so good if any of your party was trying to spot water voles as John was.

There was a spot of portaging to do before reaching a mill pool overhung by willows, where we had a sandwich and a swim before heading back.

We paddled upstream past the launching place, with the river becoming much narrower and windy with overhanging branches. This was exciting and we felt as if we were paddling through mangroves. Early morning or evening canoeists have often seen otters in this stretch. We weren't lucky in this respect but were compensated with fine views of kingfishers flashing along the river and diving to catch fish.

Canoeing as a family was less tranquil than being on our own but it was more fun and we will certainly be doing it again.

follows the riverbank – the best option is to walk the nine miles from there to Oulton Broad South station and get the train back to Beccles.

CYCLING

If you want to make use of muscle power alone, there is plenty of potential for cycling in the Waveney Valley, although you will want to avoid the A143 wherever possible. Otherwise, there are lots of quiet country roads and tracks to explore. If needs be, you can **hire a bike** at Bungay at Outney Meadow Caravan Park and at Burgh St Peter in the Waveney River Centre (✆ 01502 677343 ⌂ waveneyrivercentre.co.uk).

DISS & AROUND

1 DISS

Dear Mary, yes, it will be bliss, to go with you by train to Diss.

John Betjeman in a letter to Mary Wilson

Diss is very much a town of two halves. The modern part of the town, east of the centre close to the A140, with its supermarkets, swimming pool, fitness centre and railway station, is pretty undistinguished and could be almost anywhere: passing through it on the way to the bus station by the park does not prepare you for what is to come. The bus station – just a small bus park with a shelter – lies on Park Road, a busy thoroughfare that has lorries thundering along it shaking the leaves from the trees. But cross the road into the park and walk past a pavilion down to the water and historic Diss will suddenly unveil itself in front of you – a far more appealing prospect.

Old Diss centres around a body of water, **The Mere**, a six-acre, spring-fed lake that gives the town its name, as *dice* in Anglo-Saxon means 'standing water' or words to that effect. Diss folk claim that this glacial remnant is at least 60 feet deep, with about 20 feet of water and 40 feet of mud, so it is not a place to drop your keys. The common theory is that it was formed when the underlying chalk bedrock collapsed, an altogether more plausible theory than it being the mouth of an extinct volcano, as a few Diss residents still believe. The Mere was badly polluted in the 19th century, with high mercury levels brought about by local hatters and dyers making use of its water. Bizarrely, it was also around this time that The Mere was stocked with eels, which, according to some

SLOW DISS

Diss, along with Aylsham, bears the distinction of being one of two Norfolk towns that belong to the **Cittaslow** movement. Diss became a Cittaslow in 2006 and its sense of community is actively promoted by **Diss Community Partnership**. Having helped Diss gain its Cittaslow status, the partnership has gone on to establish a film festival and a local history and art festival in the town, as well as setting up **Taste of Diss**, a festival of local food held in July, and **Dissit**, a literature festival. Taste of Diss has since been superseded by the **Diss & Harleston Food Festival**, which takes place in October.

Fair Green is set apart from the rest of the old town but worth a detour. You can reach it by walking west along Park Road from the bus station and turning left at the roundabout. Once you round the corner, the contrast is extreme. Gone are the noisy lorries thundering along Park Road; you suddenly find yourself next to an idyllic village green with a café, a pub and a restaurant clustered around its eastern end. The trestle tables on the green itself are certainly inviting, the perfect place to sit whilst enjoying an early evening pint at The Cock, but if you keep going, you'll soon reach the bridge across the River Waveney, little more than a weed-strewn stream at this point. The green, which is surrounded by highly attractive 16th- and 17th-century houses, was granted a charter for a fair in 1185 and must have presented quite a sight back in the days when bear baiting and cock fighting were regarded as quite ordinary pursuits. The Cock Inn no doubt gets its name from such activities, as do many other 'Cock' pubs in the region. The fair was finally closed by Parliament in 1872, ostensibly because of its reputation for 'disorderly behaviour'.

accounts, threw themselves from the water at every opportunity such was the level of pollution. Thankfully, it's clean enough to swim in these days, although this is expressly forbidden. Global warming being what it is, it is unlikely that there will ever be a repeat of the winter cricket matches and ice carnivals that were held on its frozen waters in the early 19th century.

A waterside path leads from the southern shore to what is usually referred to as **The Mere's Mouth**, where there is an information centre and the Diss Publishers Bookshop and Café, which as well as a selection of local books has café tables by the water. Quite likely, there will also be someone selling ice creams from the back of a Morris Traveller next to the town sign. It's a place to feed the ducks, lick an ice cream and have a 'mardle' (Norfolk-speak for leisurely chat) on market days. Formerly, this was the only part of The Mere that provided open access to the public, although now there is access to all of the southern side from the park where Diss's rebellious youth flaunt authority by riding their bikes in a no-cycling area – that's about as lawless as it gets. These days, there's an electric fountain in the middle of The Mere that spouts like a miniature version of Lake Geneva's Jet d'Eau.

Mere Street leads north from The Mere's Mouth up towards the **marketplace** past a few pubs, cafés and independent shops. There's a good showing of Tudor timber-framed buildings in addition to some fine red-brick Georgian and Victorian houses. Friday – market day – is definitely the day to be here, when the street is filled with locals shopping and socialising, and there is an almost Mediterranean feel of savoured conviviality. The market itself may be small but, unlike in much of clone-town Britain, it's still an important weekly event. It's all very traditional, with stallholders pitching their produce while the market-day chip van does good business, with an ever-lengthening queue of hungry locals queuing for a large portion served in recycled squares of the *Daily Express*. As well as the weekly event, there's a **farmers' market** held here on the second Saturday of each month.

"The street is filled with locals shopping and socialising, and there is an almost Mediterranean feel of savoured conviviality."

Diss Museum (✆ 01379 650618 ⬦ dissmuseum.co.uk), located in a small building right at the top of the marketplace, is a community museum run by enthusiastic volunteers. As well as archive photos of the town and a 19th-century doll's house it has changing exhibitions about Diss and the surrounding villages, which in the past has featured Thomas Paine and John Betjeman, who both had connections with the town. There's a decent selection of secondhand books too: for 50p, I came away clutching a history of Diss Town FC and subsequently discovered that 7 May 1994 was the club's greatest hour: they beat Taunton FC 2–1 in extra time at Wembley to win the FA Vase – real 'Roy of the Rovers' stuff. Chatting with the volunteer on duty, I learned a little about local rivalries in this border town. 'They're a funny lot over there in Suffolk but it's mostly good-natured banter between us,' she said. 'Mind you, there's some old boys at The Cock at Fair Green who'll tell you about how they used to keep a close eye on those that came over the Palgrave bridge. There are all sorts of stories about how some used to lie in wait to attack Suffolk men coming over.'

We got talking about Fair Green itself – the meadow on the edge of town that was once the setting for medieval fairs and which is still used today for special events. 'If there is one thing that would make Diss people revolt it would be to try to develop Fair Green for new housing. It's an absolute no-no – the people would be up in arms.'

St Mary's Church dominates the marketplace, a fine 13th-century building in the Decorated style with a peaceful churchyard that has benches for market-day chip-eaters, town philosophers and courting couples. The unusual thing about this church is the processional archway through the base of the tower that allow religious processions to remain within the confines of the churchyard. If you have an interest in folklore, you might like to seek out the rather owl-like Green Man grimacing above the south porch. The church's most famous rector was John Skelton, who held the position here from 1504 until his death in 1529. Skelton, who had earlier served as tutor to the young Henry VIII and had been Poet Laureate of both Oxford and Cambridge universities, remains firmly in the number one place of the town's most illustrious citizens. A later Poet Laureate, John Betjeman, another admirer of the town, would become president of the Diss Society, a position of which he was immensely proud. The church puts on free monthly lunchtime concerts in summer and has a few stalls selling local produce at its church hall on Friday mornings.

Opposite the church stands the 16th-century **Dolphin House**, a striking black and white timbered building that has seen life as a wool merchant's house and a pub in the past. These days it houses various small businesses. If you continue north along Mount Street from St Mary's you'll find more handsome Georgian houses lining a quiet street. If, instead, you head west along St Nicholas Street then you'll come to the **Corn Hall**, which like most such buildings in these parts is in the

BLOOMING BRESSINGHAM

If you're a steam-engine fanatic, you might be interested in the collection at Bressingham Steam and Gardens (☎ 01379 686900 ⬧ bressingham.co.uk) on the road to Diss, which has endless rainbow beds of hardy perennials as well as a large collection of steam engines, a fire museum and a half-mile-long light railway. Alan Bloom, who must have felt a calling given his surname, created the gardens in 1961, and grandson Jason, who manages the nursery over the road, has kept up the family tradition.

mid 19th-century neoclassical style. The days of cereal wheeling and dealing may be past but it is still an active place, with regular concerts, films and plays.

🍴 FOOD & DRINK

Cobb's Yard and **Norfolk House Yard** in St Nicholas Street have a number of tempting independent shops and cafés that include Frederick's Fine Foods delicatessen and an old-fashioned sweet shop, appropriately called The Sweetie Shop, that has numerous jars of sticky confections and, rather improbably, sugar-free chocolate. (Walking through the marketplace I had heard two teenage girls say, 'Let's go straight to the Sweetie Shop' before putting a spurt on up the hill.) There's also a wholefood shop, Natural Foodstore, as well as Amandines, a vegetarian and vegan café.

For those looking for a regular local supplier, **Organics For All** (✆ 03330 444192 ⟡ organicsforall.co.uk) can provide boxes packed full of organic fruit and vegetables, delivered free to addresses in Suffolk and the Norwich area.

If you are just looking for a coffee and a snack, there are several options along Mere Road. **Diss Publishers Bookshop and Café** (✆ 01379 644612 ⟡ disspublishing.co.uk) at number 41 has some tables outside overlooking The Mere, as does **Mere Moments** (✆ 07790 695056) at number 44, and Café Culture at the marketplace further up. **The Saracens Head** (75 Mount St ✆ 01379 652853 ⟡ saracensheaddiss.co.uk), just behind the church, has standard pub grub and steaks. The options listed below are a little further away from the centre but really not that far.

Angel Café 1 Fair Green ✆ 07502 285957. Rustic, friendly and low key, the Angel Café serves up organic meals and snacks, with plenty of vegetarian options. It's also good for espresso coffee, homemade cakes and desserts.

Cock Inn Lower Denmark St, Fair Green ✆ 01379 643633 ⟡ cockinndiss.co.uk. With a decent selection of real ales and a great view over the green, this is a sound choice. Live music events on some Saturday nights.

2 REDGRAVE & LOPHAM FEN

West of Diss, the Waveney begins as a tiny trickle at Redgrave and Lopham Fen, very close to where the Little Ouse also rises. Dig a ditch between them and you have an island – Norfolk! The Fen, which covers 300 acres and is the largest surviving area of river valley fen in England, has been managed by the Suffolk Wildlife Trust (⟡ suffolkwildlifetrust. org/redgrave) for the past 50 years (although the reserve straddles both counties and the visitor centre is actually in Norfolk) and has an impressive cluster of designations as a wetland of national and international importance. It is also one of only two sites in the country that has native **fen raft spiders**, as well as being a prime habitat for dragonflies and butterflies, mammals like otters and pipistrelle bats, and a recorded 96 bird species.

Like the Norfolk Broads, the fen was traditionally used for reed and sedge cutting for thatching, as well as cattle grazing at its drier margins. Part of the Suffolk Wildlife Trust's management strategy is to use Hebridean sheep and Polish Konik ponies to control the vegetation. The black Hebridean sheep look strangely at home grazing here, as do the small grey ponies that thrive in the

"Arachnophobes should probably be aware that the fen raft spider is one of Britain's largest."

wet conditions. These all add to its atmosphere as quite a primeval place and the presence of the semi-aquatic raft spiders certainly fits in with this image. Arachnophobes should probably be aware that the fen raft spider is one of Britain's largest, although even here they are pretty scarce. I once spent a long time looking for them to no avail at one of the designated viewing pits but you may be luckier. There's a visitor centre (Low Common Rd, South Lopham ✆ 01379 687618) run by the Suffolk Wildlife Trust, and three dedicated nature trails. Be warned, the mosquitoes can be vicious here in summer, especially in the woodland areas – either lather up with 'Jungle Formula' or similar, or wear long sleeves and trousers.

If you come here, you can take a look at either or both of **South Lopham** and **Redgrave** villages. Both are pleasant places that have exactly what you expect: a pub, a church and (for the time being, anyway) a post office, and a green. Take your pick – Norfolk or Suffolk. Redgrave is slightly closer; South Lopham has the larger, older church with what Simon Jenkins describes as Norfolk's best Norman tower.

BURSTON

The village of Burston, a couple of miles north of Diss, is famous for its **Burston Strike School** and its teachers, Tom and Kitty Higdon, who kept the school going from 1914 until just after Tom Higdon's death in 1939 (see box, pages 216–17). This was the longest strike in British history and a textbook case of Norfolk's radical tradition that often has the working man standing up to overbearing authority. Today, the school is a museum and a rallying point for the old guard of the political

THE BURSTON STRIKE SCHOOL

The labourer must henceforth take his place
industrially, socially and politically with the best
and foremost of the land.

Tom Higdon, 1917

In brief, the story goes that Tom and Kitty Higdon were appointed as teachers at Burston School in 1911 after previously working for nine years at Wood Dalling in north Norfolk. The Higdons, who were Christian socialists, had complained about the poor conditions at the Dalling school and the frequent interruption of the children's education when recruited for farm work. Many of the farmers employing the children were also school managers and tensions mounted as a result of this, particularly as the Higdons had also encouraged local farm labourers to join trade unions. When matters came to a head, the Higdons were given the simple choice of dismissal or removal to a different school.

The couple were transferred to Burston, where they found conditions much the same: their complaints to the school managers, the chairman of whom was the local rector, created tensions here too. The pair were dismissed on fabricated charges of pupil abuse on April Fool's Day 1914 and, following

Left on the first weekend in September. The strike school **museum** (✆ 07810 301398) on the green has a fascinating photographic display and selection of newspaper cuttings, and an information booklet that has the picture of a Norfolk pig with the words: 'You may push me, You may shuv, But I'm hanged if I'll be druv, From Burston', which says all there is to say.

The **annual rally** takes place on the first Sunday in September. It's a colourful, upbeat affair with bunting and trades union banners alongside stalls selling snacks and the collected works of V I Lenin. Proceedings get fully under way after a march 'around the candlestick' that replicates the route taken by the schoolchildren on 1 April 1914. Then there are a few speeches and music. I have been here a few times but individual rallies tend to blur into each another. I clearly remember seeing Dennis Skinner with shirt unbuttoned to his waist making a stirring, and very funny, speech on one occasion, and Tony Benn recounting the famous words of Thomas Paine from *Rights of Man*: 'My country is the world, my religion is to do good.' Billy Bragg did a short acoustic set on this occasion too, although I am sure that he has played here several times.

their dismissal, 66 of the school's 72 pupils marched along Burston's 'candlestick' (a circular route around the village) carrying placards that bore messages like 'We Want Our Teachers Back'. Many parents refused to send their children to the official council school and, as a result, a separate 'strike' school was established.

The Burston Strike School began as little more than a tent on the village green but later moved to a carpenter's shop. There was considerable intimidation by local employers against the rebel parents and many workers were sacked or evicted from their tied cottages. The village rector, the Reverend Charles Tucker Eland, who believed that labourers should know their place in the social order, went as far as evicting poor families from church land. Fortunately, the labour shortage created by the onset of World War I worked to the advantage of the labourers. Money was raised by labour organisations such as the Agricultural Labourers' Union and the Railwaymen and, by 1917, there were sufficient funds to build a new schoolhouse. Both Sylvia Pankhurst and George Lansbury attended the opening ceremony in that same year. The school ran until 1939 when Tom Higdon died and the same modest building serves today as a museum of the strike school's history. There has been a rally organised by the TGWU held annually in the village since 1984, the 70th anniversary of the school's founding.

The Higdons lie buried side by side in the churchyard of **St Mary's**, which lost its tower back in the 18th century and was unceremoniously patched up with red brick. Now the church functions partially as a sort of school hall and is usually kept locked. It would be interesting to know what the Reverend Eland, the Higdons' nemesis, would make of this were he alive.

GISSING & **5** SHELFANGER

Heading north from Burston, the next village is **Gissing**, which also has a **St Mary's Church**, this one with a round tower and Norman doorway. There's an old hall with a medieval moat here, now a hotel and events centre, and a modern water tower too – both south Norfolk specialities. To the west, **Shelfanger** has its **Lammas Meadows**, which stand on the side of the road to Diss forming a tract of land attached to several farms. These are a relic of a medieval open field system of farming and, according to tradition, cannot be cropped, although the various owners are permitted to cut hay after Lammas Day (1 August). I recall seeing them carpeted with wild orchids in early summer 25 or so years ago.

DISS TO BUNGAY

Take the A143 east of Diss and you'll soon end up in Harleston. It's better to take your time though, and explore the villages and footpaths that lead down to the water meadows. Even the local bus has the good sense to avoid the main road where it can and make a tour through the villages along the way.

There's something very ancient about the landscape in this part of the Waveney Valley and, beyond the moated medieval halls, thousand-year-old churches and ancient commons that dot the landscape, there is an underlying sense that the land has been cultivated here for millennia. This is more than an instinct: it has been demonstrated by Professor Tom Williamson from the University of East Anglia that the field system between Scole and Dickleburgh, a few miles north, is older than the Roman road that cuts diagonally across it and probably dates from the late Iron Age.

6 BROCKDISH

Brockdish is a lovely little place in the valley just a few miles shy of Harleston. There's not much here other than a decent pub and a small antiques shop that seems to keep irregular hours. As part of a pattern that seems typical of small regional communities such as this, the village's highly regarded primary school closed down in 2016 due to low pupil numbers.

There are some good walks hereabouts: you could follow the Angles Way down to the river and cross to the south bank here, or follow it in the opposite direction where it climbs above the village before leading west towards Diss. The valley here, on the East Anglian scale of things at least, is impressive and the briefest of climbs up out of the village is rewarded by a view of the water meadows in the valley bottom that stretch east from here along the Waveney's northern bank. Across the river in Suffolk, there's another short but sharp incline and it's hard to think of anywhere else in the region where you are more aware of actually being in a valley. Granted, it's hardly south Wales but it's impressive after Broadland or the Fens.

"The briefest of climbs up out of the village is rewarded by a view of the water meadows in the valley."

7 HARLESTON

Harleston is the urban magnet for this stretch of the valley, although 'urban' is perhaps too big a word for a pleasant little market town. As with many places of this size, medieval fires saw to it that most of the town's earlier thatch and timber frames went up in flames so what remains today is mostly solid Georgian red brick with the odd Tudor survivor. Market day, still important to the town, is on Wednesdays. Although it might seem quite a traditional, old-fashioned sort of place, the town has an arty side too and serves as host to the **Harleston and Waveney Art Trail** (⊘ hwat.org.uk) that takes place over three weekends in June and July and opens up the studios of dozens of local artists to visitors. Most of the studios are within an eight-mile radius of Harleston and can be visited by bike, car or on foot. A guide to the current year's artists and a map can be downloaded from the HWAT website.

Harleston's most conspicuous landmark is the almost minaret-like **clock tower** on the marketplace that used to belong to St John's Chapel of Ease. The chapel was founded in the 14th century but was in a ruinous state by the 18th. A new church was built on Broad Street to replace it and the old chapel was demolished and replaced with a grocer's shop, which remains there today. Conspicuous by its absence, there is no medieval parish church to be seen in the town. The simple reason for this is that Harleston is part of the combined parish of Redenhall with Harleston and the parish church, St Mary's, a splendid 14th-century edifice with what seems an inordinately tall tower, lies in – or rather, towers over – **Redenhall**, the neighbouring village.

As with many agricultural towns in the region, there's a conspicuous Victorian **corn exchange**: a stark white neoclassical building that was opened for commerce in 1849 but which served as a local court in later years. Since its early days, when its walls must have resounded to the bargaining cries of Norfolk farmers, the building has seen use as a skating rink, furniture market, dance hall and even a delicatessen and restaurant. At the time of writing it had just been sold after being on the market for seven years and plans were afoot to reopen it as an antique centre with a 1940s-style tea room and a museum.

The marketplace, which tends to be on the sleepy side apart from Wednesday mornings, has another town landmark: the J D Young Hotel, originally known as **The Magpie Inn** – the original distinctive sign can still be seen – which has served as a coaching inn for centuries.

Churchill and Eisenhower are reputed to have met here during World War II, presumably not over a pint. Just across from the hotel is a large Georgian house with two enormous sequoias that look as if they will burst out of the garden like slow-growing triffids in the next century or two. The town's other coaching inn is **The Swan** in The Thoroughfare, which was built by Robert Green, a conspirator in Kett's Rebellion who may have been rewarded with this property for snitching on his colleague – hardly the noblest of ways to get a start in the pub trade.

The Old Market Place, which no longer has a market, has Harleston's oldest building at number 18, an Elizabethan hall house that originally would have been jettied.

FOOD & DRINK

The Farmers Kitchen Station Rd, Alburgh IP20 0EP ✆ 01986 788315 ✎ farmers-kitchen.co.uk. A few miles from Harleston in the tiny village of Alburgh, this combined farm shop and eatery at what used to be known as The Dove serves excellent breakfast and lunches that feature quality local meat and home-grown vegetables.

Parlour Tea Rooms at the Harleston Cornucopia The Corn Exchange, 5 Exchange St, Harleston ✆ 01379 854500 ✎ harlestoncornucopia.co.uk. Located within the town's Victorian corn exchange, this quirky place is part bric-a-brac emporium and part vintage tea room that serves teas, coffees, cakes, lunchtime light bites and afternoon tea.

Yakety Yak Tea Room 7B Bullock Fair Close, Harleston ✆ 01379 855484 ✎ yaketyyaktearooms.co.uk. A converted furniture shop that now serves as a 40s- and 50s-themed tea room with a choice of 18 different varieties of loose leaf tea and homemade cakes and scones.

8 MENDHAM (SUFFOLK)

Just across the Waveney from Harleston, in Suffolk, is the small village of Mendham. This was the birthplace of **Sir Alfred Munnings**, the East Anglian painter of horses and rural scenes and one-time president of the Royal Academy, whose father owned the mill just outside the village. Mendham is set in the river's flood valley amid lush water meadows and lines of poplars, and the village feels quite remote despite its proximity to Harleston. It's a quiet, dreamy place, with a church and a single pub that is called, appropriately, The Sir Alfred Munnings. The Angles Way passes through the village as it crosses into Norfolk and there's a footpath that leads across Mendham Marshes past the ruins of a Cluniac priory.

BUNGAY (SUFFOLK)

Your school geography lessons may have taught you that the ideal defensive site is either at the top of a hill or in the meander of a river. This is East Anglia, so the first of these requirements is rather wishful thinking; the second, however, is provided for perfectly at Bungay where the River Waveney coils like a flexing eel. It does have a hill of sorts too, and this is the site Hugh Bigod, the 1st Earl of Norfolk, chose for his castle in 1173, on high ground overlooking a meander. Hugh 'the Bold' Bigod was a fierce rival of Henry II but was forced to surrender his Bungay fortress to the king as a penalty for aligning himself with an insurrection led by Henry's rebellious sons. If it had succeeded he would have gained custody of Norwich Castle; the words at the start of this chapter record his regrets.

I can't quite make my mind up about which Waveney Valley town I like the best – Diss or Bungay. Some days – especially on market days – Diss seems to be firm favourite, but at other times it's the latter that steals the show. Either way, Bungay is certainly a self-contained, likeable place that, with a castle, an independent theatre and a distinctive eccentric character, seems to punch well above its weight for somewhere so small. Over the years, it's been a centre for leather working, boat building and more recently printing but it has always also been an important market town for the region.

As with most small towns in East Anglia, Bungay's heart is its marketplace. Central to this is the octagonal **Butter Cross** that has a lead figure of Justice with her scales on top of its cupola. Like many other settlements where medieval wood and thatch predominated, a serious fire spread through the old town in the late 17th century and Bungay's plentiful Georgian buildings reflect a post-1688 rebuild. There's a pleasing mix of architecture spread throughout the centre but **Bridge Street**, with its colourfully painted houses sloping steeply down towards the river, is particularly attractive. This is a street that seems to happily harbour some of Bungay's undeniable eccentricities too: take a look at the anarchic bric-a-brac shop with its back-yard chicken coops opposite the Chequers pub for a taste of what indifference to convention can do.

Most of what you see now of **Bungay Castle** was actually constructed by Hugh's ancestor Roger Bigod at the end of the 13th century. Today, there are two crumbling towers of the original gatehouse and some outer walls that you can visit, and with a bit of luck they will have removed the scaffolding by the time you get here. There's a visitor centre at the entrance, which has a café and tourist information in season. To get a good view across to Earsham on the other side of the Waveney Valley you can climb up **Castle Hills** from the visitor centre. In celebration of its founder, the **Bigod Way** is a ten-mile loop around the town that starts and ends at the castle. It's a lengthy walk that takes four or five hours but there's plenty of historical and wildlife interest along the way.

Although there were said to be five churches in the town in the 11th century, just two survive today: **Holy Trinity** with its Saxon round tower, the oldest complete building in town, and **St Mary's**. St Mary's, now deconsecrated, is famous in these parts for its role in the **Black Shuck legend** (see box, page 72), when the legendary black dog with fiery eyes ran amuck in the church and killed two worshippers having already caused untold damage at far-off Blythburgh church that same morning of 4 August 1577. This fanciful tale has long passed into local folklore, although versions of it differ quite widely. According to one account, a woman who went to school in Bungay in the late 19th century remembers Black Shuck as being a cat and recalls children singing the song:

Scratch cat of Bungay
Hanging on the door
Take a stick and knock it down
And it won't come anymore.

Whatever his form, puss or pooch, Black Shuck did not leave any evidence of his visit at St Mary's, although he does put in an appearance on the town's coat of arms. There's also a rather attractive tapestry of Bungay's history hanging in the church with a panel detailing the rampaging dog with the legend, '1577: Black Dog entered during a fearful storm and two men died.'

Bungay is not all about castles and churches. With the River Waveney just a shadow of what it used to be, it is easy to overlook the importance that the river once held for the town. Once the lock at Geldeston was established in the late 17th century, and the river canalised, wherries were able to ship goods up here from the coast. Upper Olland Street in the town centre probably gets its name from a derivation of 'oak lands' and locally plentiful oak would have been used to build wherries in the Staithe area of the town. Indeed, William Brighton, builder of the *Albion* (page 90), used to work here, while the boat itself used to ply its trade between Bungay Staithe and the coast at Lowestoft. These days, Geldeston is as far as navigation goes for anything larger than a canoe.

For cycling, the **Godric Way** is a 24-mile route around Bungay that starts and ends at Butter Cross and passes through Ellingham, Broome, Ditchingham, Earsham, Denton, Alburgh, Homersfield, Mettingham and The Saints – all places in which a slow cycle through is worth a dozen drive-bys.

FOOD & DRINK

Several cafés and tea rooms are dotted around the town centre.

Buttercross Tearooms 6 Cross St ✆ 01986 893002. Just down from the Buttercross on Cross Street, this is an unfussy but perfectly pleasant place for a snack, coffee or all-day breakfast. There's also a hidden garden with a pond for fine weather.

Castle Inn 35 Earsham St ✆ 01986 892283 ⌂ thecastleinn.net. With an imaginative menu that makes good use of locally sourced food, this is probably Bungay's nicest place to eat.

Earsham Street Café 11–13 Earsham St ✆ 01986 893103 ⌂ earshamstreetcafe.co.uk. Located in an attractive 17th-century building, this is a little more upmarket than the Buttercross Tearooms and has a more adventurous menu. At the back is a courtyard garden where a cock-fighting pit once stood. Good for cakes and light meals as well as brunches at the weekend.

BECCLES & THE LOWER WAVENEY VALLEY

GELDESTON

Halfway between Bungay and Beccles, just south of the main road on the Norfolk side of the border, Geldeston is a small attractive village with two pubs. One of these, the **Wherry Inn**, is in the village itself next to the green. The other, **Geldeston Locks Inn**, lies at the end of a narrow track right beside the River Waveney. This pub is closely linked to the historic navigation of the river, which was privately owned by coal, grain and malt merchants between the 16th and 18th century. Wherries would pass through here as they hauled goods between Great Yarmouth, Lowestoft and Bungay.

The building that is now the Geldeston Locks Inn started life as a mill-keeper's cottage and later served as a dwelling for the lockkeeper before becoming an inn in the 17th century.

Given its isolated location on the Norfolk–Suffolk border, the inn became a popular haunt for cross-border smugglers and an ideal setting for illegal prize fights. These days, **Geldeston Locks** marks the limit of navigation for boats. There is a footbridge across the river to the Suffolk bank here from where the Angles Way may be joined. A footpath runs along the north bank to Geldeston from Beccles – a lovely walk – and there's even a regular boat service from Beccles Lido (page 225).

The river around Geldeston Locks makes for near-perfect **canoeing**, especially west of the bridge in the Bungay direction – kingfishers and otters are distinctly possible sightings. For details of canoe hire, see pages 208–9. It is a paddle of three hours or more to and from Beccles and one hour or less from Geldeston village to the Locks.

East of Geldeston, the river is wide enough for navigation as it meanders north to merge with the River Yare at Breydon Water, although the low bridge at Beccles deters many hire boats and larger craft from sailing west of the town. This, of course, has considerable effect on the river's character, which morphs from sleepy tranquil backwater to busy thoroughfare – in summer at least – within a matter of miles. The county line itself follows the river faithfully until it branches off to the coast near Herringfleet towards a point more or less midway between Great Yarmouth and Lowestoft.

¶¶ FOOD & DRINK

Geldeston Locks Inn Locks Lane ✆ 01508 518414 ⬧ geldestonlocks.co.uk. An isolated, traditional pub with a sunny garden right by the River Waveney. Good locally sourced food, Green Jack ales from Lowestoft, regular musical events and a beer festival in September.
Wherry Inn 7 The Street ✆ 01508 518371 ⬧ wherryinn.co.uk. A traditional village pub with a range of Adnams beers and a seasonal menu of light bites, burgers and pub grub favourites.

11 BECCLES (SUFFOLK)

The largest town in the valley, Beccles is pleasant enough but a place that most tend to pass through rather than stay in. The town is solidly Georgian as its timbered Tudor core was destroyed by a succession of ravaging fires. The river used to have far more significance to town life than it does now, but this was once a flourishing port with many wherries passing by. Herrings from the coast used to be an important commodity here and, in the medieval period, Beccles annually provided tens of thousands of the fish to the monks at Bury St Edmunds.

Boats still have a part to play, as Beccles is the most southerly point on the Broads system. The river here is not quite as hectic in summer as the Bure and Thurne but it's busy enough. There's some good walking on the Beccles Marshes close to the town and also along the north bank of the River Waveney to Geldeston Locks where there is a pub (page 224). There is also a regular **boat service** to Geldeston Locks, the Big Dog Ferry (07532 072761 bigdogferry.co.uk), which runs from Beccles Lido between Easter and October. The ferry also drops off at Geldeston Marina with access to the Wherry Inn. Short **boat trips** can also be made on the Edwardian-style electric launch *Liana*. You can book this at the Broads Information Centre at The Quay (01502 713196).

FOOD & DRINK

Beccles Farmers' Market Beccles Old Heliport becclesfarmersmarket.co.uk. Has around 30 stalls on the first and third Saturday of the month.

Garden Tea Rooms 4 The Walk 01502 712631. Go through a discount shop to arrive at a bright pink dining room and a garden beyond. This small café has the usual cakes, scones, snacks and breakfasts.

Waveney House Hotel Puddingmoor 01502 712270 waveneyhousehotel.co.uk. With a pleasant terrace right next to the river, the Riverside Bar offers a good varied menu for lunch and dinner.

2 'THE TRIANGLE' & BURGH ST PETER

Waveney River Centre (page 258)

The Waveney turns back on itself at Oulton Dyke, where there is a channel leading through to Oulton Broad and Lowestoft. To the west of the river, tucked away inland almost equidistant between the Waveney and the Yare, are the somewhat isolated villages of **Wheatacre**, **Aldeby**, where there is a priory, and **Burgh St Peter**.

The parishes of these three villages make up an area known locally as '**The Triangle**' – as they are bound on two sides by a bend of the River Waveney and on the third side by the now defunct Beccles to Great Yarmouth railway. This triangle of land has something of the feel of an island about it, with a genuine sense of isolation despite its crow's-flight proximity to Beccles and Lowestoft. There is no through road here nor any bridge across the river, just a single-track road that links the farmsteads that lie on the higher ground above a large area of marshland and the river beyond.

Lovely views extend over the marshes but otherwise there's not so much to see other than the odd-looking **church of St Mary the Virgin** in Burgh St Peter, which has a strange five-section tower shaped like a ziggurat or, as some have fancied, even a collapsible square telescope. The body of the church dates from the 13th century but the tower is a late 18th-century replacement for an earlier one; its curious form is supposed to have been based on a Mesopotamian ziggurat seen by William Boycott, the rector's son, on his travels.

There was, in fact, a whole dynasty of Boycotts serving as rectors at the church for a continuous period of 135 years. It was Captain Charles Cunningham Boycott, the son of the second Boycott rector, who, serving as an Irish estate agent, first introduced the word 'boycott' into the English language when he suffered social ostracism for refusing to reduce rents.

Close to the church is the **Waveney River Centre** (✆ 01502 677343 ⌂ waveneyrivercentre.co.uk), which has canoes for hire and a ferry across the river to Carlton Marshes Nature Reserve on the Suffolk bank, where there's a circular walk to be had as well as access to the Angles Way long distance path. Lowestoft is really not that far away but you would never guess it given the tranquillity of the marshes here. See also *Accommodation*, page 258.

13 RAVENINGHAM

Between Beccles and Loddon, just south of the B1136 that leads off the A146 towards Haddiscoe, is the 5,500-acre Raveningham Estate. The main attraction here is **Raveningham Gardens** (⌂ raveningham. com/garden), which contain a walled kitchen garden, late 19th-century glasshouses and an arboretum established in the wake of the 1987 gale. There's also a herb garden, a rose garden and a 'Time Garden' whose design is influenced by the essays on the passage of time by Sir Francis Bacon. The Bacon family have owned the estate since 1735. The Raveningham Centre, close to Raveningham Park, is a range of converted Victorian farm buildings that contain various craft outlets and a café.

In 2017 the centre took over as the base for the annual summer **Waveney Valley Sculpture Trail** organised by Waveney & Blyth Arts. The trail features site-specific work from a number of established artists and includes bronze sculpture, textiles, ceramics and sound installations.

SEND US YOUR SNAPS!

We'd love to follow your adventures using our **Slow Travel Norfolk** guide — why not send us your photos and stories via Twitter (@BradtGuides) and Instagram (@bradtguides) using the hashtag #Norfolk? Alternatively, you can upload photos directly to the gallery on the Norfolk destination page via our website (bradtguides.com/norfolk).

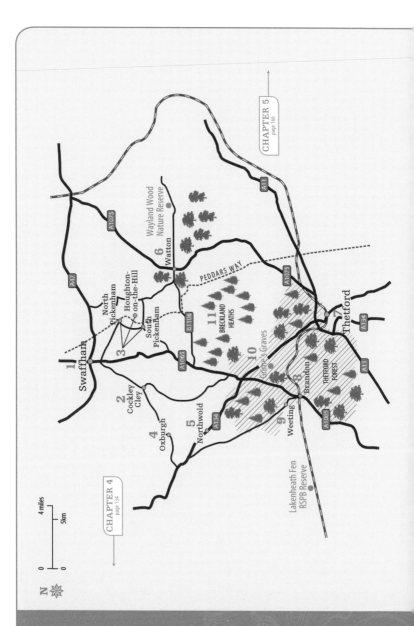

THE BRECKS

7

THE BRECKS

This chapter covers the region known as the Brecks, the western part of Norfolk that lies between Swaffham in the north and Thetford in the south. Both towns have historical interest well beyond what one might expect. Thetford was home to the monarchs of East Anglia and the seat of a bishopric; it was also the birthplace of that staunch anti-monarchist Thomas Paine. Swaffham is an old-fashioned market town with a futuristic and heartwarmingly eco-friendly Green Britain Centre. As a discrete region, the Brecks reaches well into Suffolk across the border. Of the five market towns that belong to the Brecks area – Swaffham, Watton, Thetford, Mildenhall and Brandon, the last two are in Suffolk. Although this chapter will deal mostly with the Norfolk part of the Brecks there are occasional detours across the county boundary.

THE BRECKS & THETFORD FOREST

Although the Brecks borders the pancake-flat region of the Fens, it really could not be more different. The Brecks, in contrast to the fertile black soil found in the Fens, has light, sandy soil that is far less ideal for intensive farming. The word 'breck' comes from a word that means land that becomes quickly exhausted. It's the closest thing that Britain has to a desert, as the rainfall is the lowest in the country, summer temperatures can be among the highest, and winter frosts the hardest. The sand that covers the chalk was originally wind-blown, but trees have since been planted to stabilise the soil. Back in the days before such enlightened ideas, when large estates sought to maximise their profits by introducing sheep, the sand blew freely around causing untold damage, depleting thin topsoil in one place and covering up fertile land in another.

Naturally, what is a shortcoming today was actually a boon in the distant past. In Neolithic times, Britain's very first farmers were drawn to the region because its light soil was easy to work with their limited stone tools, and because there was no dense forest needing to be cleared with nothing other than brute strength and a hand axe. The region had a plentiful supply of flint too, the machine steel of the Stone Age.

With careful farming, the Brecks became reasonably prosperous and **Thetford**, its capital, became an important regional capital in the Anglo-Saxon period. It was later, in the medieval period, when the real damage was done. Sheep were introduced to the land in large numbers and allowed to roam freely, overgrazing and damaging the soil with their hooves. In north Norfolk, sheep may have brought fortune but here they just heralded disaster. The Brecks became increasingly depopulated as a result – the area is still sparsely populated today – and rabbits and pheasants became the land's only bounty.

The vast **Thetford Forest**, flanking the A11 around Thetford itself, is a recent innovation, planted by the Forestry Commission after World War I to provide a strategic reserve of timber. Much of what is not forest goes to make up the **Stanford Battle Area**, established in 1942, where the Army practise manoeuvres and test ordnance. Vast stands of Scots and Corsican pine may be what most people immediately associate with the Brecks these days but it is a very recent trend. Step back just a hundred years in time and you would see only sandy heathland, gorse and rabbits – lots of rabbits. It almost goes without saying that this is a part of East Anglia that many speed through without stopping. Consequently, it is not as well known as perhaps it deserves to be. Outside the few towns, the Brecks distinctive habitat is a prized haven for wildlife: it is home to several species of plant, insect, bird and mammal that are found almost nowhere else in the country.

GETTING AROUND
PUBLIC TRANSPORT
This is far from wonderful. Swaffham no longer has a functioning railway, but Thetford stands on the Norwich to Cambridge rail line and has a regular **rail service** to both cities – almost hourly during the day. Trains to Ely link with national services north and south.

Bus services run from Norwich to Swaffham and Thetford. There's the useful X1 service run by First in Suffolk & Norfolk, half-hourly through most of the day, which connects Swaffham with King's Lynn and

Peterborough to the west and Norwich, Great Yarmouth and Lowestoft to the east. Local services also run from all three main towns to outlying villages. Although regular buses run between Thetford and Bury St Edmunds there are none between Thetford and Swaffham; for this, you will need to travel via Norwich, Watton or King's Lynn, a long detour.

WALKING

Most will probably want to rely on their own two legs though, and there's some excellent walking to be had. The obvious choice for long-distance hikers is, of course, the **Peddars Way**, an ancient route that is now a designated National Trail. It begins at Knettishall Heath near the Norfolk–Suffolk border close to Thetford and strides irrepressibly north–northwest until it reaches the Wash at Holme-next-the-Sea. It is perfectly feasible to do short sections of this, and some of its most interesting stretches actually lie within the Brecks. The route is waymarked with acorn motifs and very easy to follow, though its sheer straightness can make the going a tad monotonous at times.

Other long-distance routes are **Angles Way** (Thetford to Great Yarmouth via the Waveney valley; 93 miles), **Iceni Way** (Knettishall Heath to Holme-next-the-Sea via Brandon and the Fens; 83 miles), **Hereward Way** (Thetford to Rutland via Peterborough, Ely and Brandon; 110 miles) and the **Little Ouse Path**, a ten-mile meander along the Little Ouse valley.

You can walk anywhere you like on Forestry Commission land and numerous circular walks are waymarked from all the main parking areas. A good choice of short forest trails begin at High Lodge Forestry Centre. **Harling Drove** between Roudham Heath and Bromehill at Weeting is a good option for a longer, ten-mile walk right through the heart of the forest. Further suggestions for shorter walks are made in the appropriate places in this chapter.

ℹ TOURIST INFORMATION

Brecks Tourism Partnership website ⬠ www.brecks.org
Swaffham Town Museum, 4 London St ✐ 01760 722255 ⬠ aroundswaffham.co.uk
Thetford Belmont House, 20 King St ✐ 01842 751975 ⬠ leapinghare.org
Watton Wayland Visitor Centre, Wayland House, High St ✐ 01953 880212 ⬠ visitwayland.co.uk

HORSERIDING

Horseriders have free access on all Forestry Commission freehold land. The Peddars Way is bridleway for most of its course, and other possibilities include the Swaffham Bridle Route and the ten-mile-long Hockwold-cum-Wilton Bridle Route.

CYCLING

Given a general lack of traffic and quiet roads, the Brecks have plenty of potential for cycling. Thetford Forest has lots of off-road choices too. For those who want to go further afield, Sustrans National Cycle Route 13 (✆ 0845 1130065 ⌂ sustrans.org.uk) connects Thetford and Watton with National Cycle Route 1.

The Brecks Cycling Discovery Route is an interesting 20-mile circular route (with a possible ten-mile short cut), centred on Swaffham, that links the Ecotech wind turbine, Cockley Cley Nature Reserve, Oxburgh Hall, Beachamwell and Gooderstone Water Gardens; a guide to the route can be downloaded from ⌂ www.brecks.org. There is also a 21-mile **Swaffham Bridle Route** around the town that makes use of tracks and minor roads.

You can buy a cycling pack that details five **easy routes** in the Brecks suitable for family cycling from tourist information centres and elsewhere. These routes tend to be theme-based, for instance a Pingoland Explorer Trail and a Flint-Hunters' Explorer Trail.

Thetford Forest Park has three waymarked forest trails of varying difficulty that start from the High Lodge Forest Centre, where bike hire is also available at Bike Art (✆ 01842 810090 ⌂ bikeartthetford.co.uk). A map of these routes can also be downloaded from ⌂ forestry.gov.uk. Harling Drove is a fairly long easy route through the heart of Thetford Forest and is suitable for both cyclists and walkers.

For more suggestions in the area, the useful website ⌂ peacefulbyways. co.uk shows a 24-mile ride that starts in **Swaffham** (plus another 11 that start within a 15-mile radius of Swaffham). This route is an interesting southwestern circuit that takes in Drymere, Beachamwell, Barton Bendish, Boughton, Oxburgh Hall, Gooderstone and Cockley Cley. With so many things to see *en route* and a couple of decent pubs too, this deserves a slow cycle and savouring it all in full. There's scope to abandon two wheels for four legs in the region too and the potential for riding is probably the best in East Anglia.

SWAFFHAM & AROUND

1 SWAFFHAM

⌂ Strattons Hotel (page 258)

Swaffham is something of a perfect example of an old-fashioned market town, with all the necessary ingredients: a market square, handsome Georgian houses, a leisurely rhythm and little evidence of the more boorish trappings of modern life. Having said that, Swaffham has its rough edges too and there is certainly more to it than a just a quaint country town frozen in time. Sitting midway between King's Lynn and East Dereham, Fakenham and Thetford, the town has long served as the regional centre for the farming country hereabouts. It lies within the Brecks but only just, located at that region's northern edge. In the 18th and early 19th century the town became a fashionable social centre for the gentry and even became known as the 'Montpelier of England', such was its elegance and the reputation of its healthy, dry air. Wealthy farmers would come here with their families in season for dancing and racing. At some stage in its history, hare-coursing was invented here. William E Johns of Biggles fame lived here before World War I.

Swaffham life centres on its **marketplace** where a market is held each Saturday. Author and self-sufficiency pioneer John Seymour claimed it to be 'one of the excellent surviving old markets where you can buy a secondhand washing machine, a dozen white rabbits, or a goat'. He was writing back in the late 1960s, and things have changed a little, but not that much – it's still thriving. You might have trouble finding a goat these days but rabbits should not prove too difficult. There's a handsome array of Regency buildings neatly arranged around this commercial wedge with its central **Butter Cross**, a neoclassical dome mounted on pillars, with a statue of the Roman grain goddess Ceres on top, an apposite choice for this arable region. Facing the marketplace, the Italianate red-brick 1858 **Cornhall** – now the location for a well-known coffee chain – has more arable allusions, with a round panel containing a wheat sheaf on its gable. Many of the surrounding buildings are Georgian, the most noteworthy being the 1817 **Assembly Rooms**, home to an indoor market on Fridays with stalls selling all manner of wholesome homemade goods.

"Butter Cross has a statue of the Roman grain goddess Ceres on top, an apposite choice for this arable region."

Among other less grand but cheerfully quirky buildings are the old post office, just off the marketplace on Lynn Street, with its tiny conical tower that serves no obvious useful purpose and handsome Victorian brick lettering above its door.

Swaffham's appeal lies in its detail and mix. Although several of the major supermarkets have a base here there are still an encouraging number of independent shops selling household goods, groceries, hardware and haircuts, while a gent's hairdresser on the square advertises itself with a traditional barber pole and a large wooden sign that takes up half the window stating 'The Town Barber'. Swaffham's more cosmopolitan than first appears and boasts a Lithuanian shop, Indian and Chinese takeaways and even a Russian restaurant called 'Rasputin's' – 'the first in Norfolk' – a strange name for a place to eat perhaps (but then I do recall seeing a 'Lady Di' restaurant in Azerbaijan).

A short distance from the marketplace you'll find the 15th-century **church of St Peter and St Paul** with a splendid hammerbeam roof adorned with 88 carved angels flying in formation. The churchyard itself is a peaceful green haven that seems as if it should belong to a tiny village rather than the centre of a market town. It's worth the teeniest of detours to take a look at the wooden angels inside and perhaps wonder what an untutored medieval peasant might have made of them as he sat there on a Sunday. For a congregation mostly made up of farm workers that rarely travelled far beyond the parish of their birth the local church would almost inevitably be the most remarkable sight they would ever witness. The church's wooden benches have medieval carvings that include the so-called **'Swaffham Pedlar'** – the merchant John Chapman, who also features on the well-known Swaffham town sign. The story behind this is that Chapman, following an impulse to seek his fortune in London, is told by a stranger on London Bridge that he should return home and look under a tree there to find his treasure. Eventually he returns home to find a pot of gold in his own garden. Whatever the truth behind this tale, John Chapman was certainly a generous benefactor of the church, most likely just a wealthy merchant who made his money in the time-honoured way.

'The Pedlar of Swaffham' town sign is the handiwork of Harry Carter, former art teacher at Hammond's High School, who is also the talent behind many other north Norfolk carved village signs. Harry Carter's uncle was Howard Carter, the eminent Egyptologist who discovered the tomb of Tutankhamun and, rather fancifully, is rumoured to have died as the result of the boy-king's 'curse'. Harry Carter's sign is at a corner of the marketplace in a flower bed opposite the old school gates, while an exhibition of Howard Carter's quest in Egypt's Valley of the Kings can be seen in **Swaffham Museum** (✆ 01760 721230 ⌑ swaffhammuseum.co.uk), which also has a gift shop and doubles as the tourist information centre.

Standing outside the door of the museum and looking towards the marketplace you may suddenly become aware of a large white rotor blade slicing up the air above Ceres on the Butter Cross, an astonishing juxtaposition of classical tradition, medieval commerce and the modern green technology of the **Green Britain Centre** (✆ 01760 726100 ⌑ greenbritaincentre.co.uk ⊙ summer daily, autumn–spring Mon–Fri only). Modern credibility came to the town with the establishment of this back in 1998, its enormous wind turbine looming next to the A47 giving the impression of blowing speeding King's Lynn-bound motorists further westwards. (There's a local joke that the wind turbines in the Wash do their bit to dissipate global warming by cooling the land with their fanning action.) Turbine tours can be pre-booked or you can take your chances and just turn up. They say this is the only wind turbine in the world that is open to the public. It's a climb of 300 steps up a spiral staircase to the top, where there is a Norman Foster-designed observation deck and a panoramic view. A ticket also includes free entrance to the gardens, café (both organic) and Ecotopia shop in which everything is fair trade, local, organic or sustainably sourced and the motto is 'Shopping your principles'. The centre is also home to Greenbird, the fastest wind-powered vehicle on the planet, and one of Britain's largest solar trackers.

FOOD & DRINK

A **farmers' market** is held in Swaffham marketplace on the third Sunday of each month (⊙ 09.00–14.00). The town is also host to the **Brecks Food & Drink Festival** (⌑ www. brecks.org/food-and-drink) in early September, a celebration of local food and drink that showcases everything from local cheeses to garden produce and which aims to re-connect local people to the Brecks countryside they live in.

Swaffham's marketplace has several cafés and pubs, although most of the latter seem to cater for aficionados of widescreen TV. The **Peddars Hall Café** may well be half-timbered but its interior might best be described as 'down to earth'. By the Butter Cross itself is the

Market Cross Coffee Bar (🕿 01760 33671) with outdoor tables, while through the arch at the pedestrianised thoroughfare of Plowright Place you'll find the **The Teapot Café** (🕿 07926 952295), again with both inside and outside tables.

Ceres Book and Coffee Shop 20 London St 🕿 01760 722504 🖥 ceresbookshopswaffham. co.uk ⊙ bookshop open Mon–Sat, coffee shop open Tue–Sat. This excellent independent bookshop selling new and secondhand books, maps and guides also serves coffee and homemade cakes in its charming three-table backroom café.

CoCoes Ash Close 🕿 01760 725605 🖥 strattonshotel.com. Tucked away off the marketplace in the alley that leads to Strattons Hotel, this café-deli has coffee, homemade cakes, fresh baked bread, light bites and imaginative daily specials all made using quality produce. As with the hotel restaurant, care has been taken to provide a strong regional identity, sourcing from the Brecks area. CoCoes's Brecks sausage roll has been commended by comedian Al Murray, no less.

The Station Station Rd 🕿 01760 722300. A traditional no-frills pub, popular with locals, that is a good choice for a Sunday lunch roast.

Strattons Hotel Ash Close 🕿 01760 723845 🖥 strattonshotel.com. Just off the marketplace, this luxurious eco-friendly hotel serves wonderful locally sourced food in its semi-basement, an area known as 'The Rustic' (⊙ from 18.30 daily). The food is Modern British, organic wherever possible, and includes herbs and vegetables from the hotel's own gardens, with meat and dairy supplied by a large number of local small producers. See also page 258.

2 COCKLEY CLEY & AROUND

As you leave Swaffham to the southwest through bungalow-filled outskirts, the Breckland scenery starts quickly to become apparent, with twisted stands of Scots pine shading the verges and large open fields of barley and sugar beet before the forest beyond. The first village you reach is Cockley Cley, a small place which is home to a reconstructed Iceni Village (more low-budget theme park than museum).

Just west of Cockley Cley, **Beachamwell** has the lovely thatched church of St Mary's with its Saxon round tower topped by an octagonal belfry. The church, which has pride of place on a large village green, is the last survivor of four churches that used to serve the area in more populous medieval times when there were two parishes here – Bicham and Wella. If you take a walk from the village armed with the appropriate OS map (Landranger 143) you can see the visible remains of some of the others. Just south of Beachamwell, All Saints' Church was abandoned in the 17th century and all that remains today are fragments of flint walls.

More complete is St John's Church northwest of the village, which still has a standing square tower – an evocative sight in a field full of horses.

When I visited Beachamwell, I parked my car in the lay-by in front of the village hall. No sooner had I switched the engine off when an elderly woman with a concerned look on her face approached me. 'Excuse me. Are you going to park there? The thing is, the post office van will be coming soon and he'll need to park here as it's the only place in the village he can get a signal.' Sure enough, the post office van arrived a minute or two later and I nudged forwards so it could squeeze in behind me. It turned out that the van was doing the rounds of the north Brecks villages and being pension day a mobile signal was necessary to work the computer so that the villagers could get their allowance. An interesting juxtaposition of modern technology and old-fashioned community spirit, I thought.

An earthwork just north of Beachamwell – the Devil's Dyke – is believed to be a Saxon territorial boundary. Other earthworks of this type turn up elsewhere in southwest Norfolk, such as west of Garboldisham between Thetford and Diss, as well as in the northeast of the county near Horning. **Barton Bendish**, a little further west, has two churches, St Mary's and St Andrew's. The parish used to have three, but the church of All Saints' was pulled down in the 18th century for material to patch up St Mary's Church and for repairing roads. There seems to be a plethora of St Mary's churches in this part of the county.

FOOD & DRINK

Twenty Churchwardens Cockley Cley ✆ 01760 721439. Close to All Saints' Church in the village; the name refers to a type of clay pipe rather than the pub's clientele. This used to be a school and it has only been a pub since 1968. Adnams and other real ales are served alongside straightforward, homemade food that includes some tasty pies. Cash only.

THE PICKENHAMS & HOUGHTON-ON-THE-HILL

Just east of Swaffham, on the route of the Peddars Way and next to the banks of the River Wissey, are North and South Pickenham. **South Pickenham** has All Saints, a lovely little round tower church with a very rural feel to it. You can find five round towers within a nine-mile radius of here: at South Pickenham, Merton, Watton, Threxton and Rockland. Pickenham Hall is central to the village, a large turn-of-the-century edifice that stands out very much as the local squire's abode.

The restored **St Mary's Church** (⊘ houghtonstmarys.co.uk) at nearby **Houghton-on-the-Hill** is little more than a five-minute detour for Peddars Way walkers and a worthy expedition in its own right too. The church has become quite well known for its wall murals but is equally famous for its remarkable restoration story, the work for the most part of just one man. The church has been painstakingly restored thanks to the efforts of Bob Davey, a retired engineer from North Pickenham. He first began work on what was an ivy-covered, semi-derelict ruin back in 1987, when it had been abandoned since the 1930s. By 1993, thanks to Bob's interest and hard work, it had attained Grade 1 listed status. This involved far more than simply physical renovation. When he first discovered the church, it was being used for black magic rituals and the Satanist congregation were none too keen on Bob's renewed interest in their ceremonial centre (Satanists had been reported here back in 1968 by

A VISIT TO ST MARY'S, HOUGHTON-ON-THE-HILL

I walked up here on a hot summer's afternoon to be greeted by Pam, one of Bob Davey's enthusiastic helpers, who showed me around and explained the murals using an artist's impression of what they may have looked like in their original, complete form. Pam pointed out the details on *The Last Judgement*, in which the virtuous rose to heaven while sinners had to undergo torment by little red devils.

'The idea was to scare the locals into leading good lives.' The drawings are cartoon-like, not especially skilled but endearing, with figures that have the moonish faces and big eyes of Byzantine frescoes. *Adam and Eve in the Garden of Eden* portrays Eve as a much larger figure than Adam, which leads me to mutter something about this being a pre-Renaissance lack of understanding about perspective. 'Yes possibly, but Bob thinks this just may be the way that women were

revered back in those times. Most men got killed one way or another when they were still young. Women generally lived longer and were more important than we might give credit for.'

Bob himself came over to speak, a twinkle-eyed octogenarian in a bright yellow shirt with a flowing snowy beard. He handed me some leaflets on the church before telling me, 'We haven't had chance to print it yet but this all needs updating a bit I'm afraid. We've got some new dates now and everything's a bit earlier than it says in the booklet.' He went on: 'Originally there was a Roman spa up here – it's a natural aquifer – and there's quite a lot of recycled Roman brick in the nave. There was a wooden church here first that was dedicated to St Felix and we've found some evidence of that. Then they added a flint chancel in the 7th century and a round tower in the 13th century a frightened walker who had accidentally stumbled upon them). Almost single-handedly, Bob stood up to what he considered a desecration of the church and continually tried to bar the Satanists entry, despite death threats and curses that were hurled his way. Pragmatically, he did go on to recruit a burly Territorial Army unit to lie in wait for the Satanists one night, and this surprise ambush seemed to drive them away for good, although the threats continued for a while. Since then, the church has been re-blessed and used for occasional non-denominational services – it had never actually been deconsecrated. There's no doubt that St Mary's has had more than its fair share of problems over the years. During World War I, a returning Zeppelin dumped its bombs in the churchyard damaging the building and in the 1930s it lost all of its parishioners when the neighbouring village of Houghton was finally deserted. The indignity of Satanistic worship came with the second half of the

but that fell down, so they put up one of those fashionable square towers instead.'

Since interest in St Mary's, and especially the wall paintings, has taken off, there has been a constant stream of experts coming to offer their opinions about the church's history. With so many axes to grind, it is hardly surprising that sparks have flown on occasions. Opinions vary but the nave that stands today may be anything between late Saxon to early Norman in origin. As for the murals, estimates favour the 11th century or, as Bob himself thinks, perhaps even earlier. It is undoubtedly a complex sequence, but a church in some form or other has stood here since Anglo-Saxon times. The murals are faded and partial but, having been buried beneath later medieval wall paintings and Victorian plaster for centuries, it is quite remarkable that they have survived at all,

especially as they were exposed without a roof for many years. Spend a little time contemplating the paintings and savouring the atmosphere of this remote place and you may feel that you are getting some rare insight into what the world would have looked like to Anglo-Saxons at the dawn of the second millennium. It is certainly a special place. After being ticked off by Pam for standing too long, and being told to sit down, Bob went on to tell me something of his television appearances – he has become quite a celebrity in the world of church restoration. The BBC had wanted to do a re-enactment of the time when a Satanist tried to run him over with a car. 'They had to do about six takes for that one,' he tells me, chuckling mischievously. 'I had to keep jumping out of the way of this car until they got the camera angles right.'

20th century, and to cap all of this, thieves stole lead from the newly replaced roof in 2007. For good measure, it is also supposed to be haunted by a couple of Carmelite monks.

Bob – now Bob Davey MBE – is still devoted to the church despite his advanced years. A dedicated support group, the Friends of St Mary's, is now responsible for the work and activities here. There is now also a beautiful garden in what was once an overgrown churchyard. If you want to pay a visit, you can view the interior of the church between 14.00 and 16.00 daily (✆ 01760 440470 for group visits or tours at other times). The hamlet that once stood near here was known as **Houghton Town**, but the church and a few farm buildings are all that now remain. The last villagers left in 1936, evicted by a squire who wanted to turn his arable land over to the more profitable use of shooting for game. The last of the surviving cottages were bulldozed in 1994. Look carefully and you may be able to make out a few bumps in the fields to the north – the ghostly remnants of what was once a community.

North Pickenham, the village to the north, has St Andrew's as its parish church, a much grander affair than little St Mary's. Just west of the village is an old airfield that used to be RAF North Pickenham, which served as an American B-24 Liberator bomber base during World War II. This became a base for nuclear missiles in the late 1950s and 60s and a focus for early CND (Campaign for Nuclear Disarmament) protests. The planes and missiles are long gone now and these days the airbase provides the site for a karting circuit, a wind farm and a Bernard Matthews turkey farm, which according to the *Guinness Book of Records* is the world's largest, producing one million birds annually.

4 OXBURGH

Oxburgh is only a tiny village but it is also the location of **Oxburgh Hall**, a splendid Tudor country house. Even without the Tudor hall, the village is interesting for the **church of St John the Evangelist**, with its adjoining Tudor Bedingfield Chapel, endowed by Sir Edmund Bedingfield and containing the terracotta tombs of Sir Edmund and his wife. This was no exercise in humility: terracotta may be commonplace today but it was considered ultra chic in Tudor times. The main church building, just outside the walls of the house, has a ruinous demeanour thanks to its spire collapsing in 1948. The nave was ruined by the incident but the chancel, south chapel and north aisle managed to escape damage.

Oxburgh Hall

Oxburgh PE33 9PS ✐ 01366 328258 ☺ April–Oct daily, weekends only in winter;
National Trust

This is an undeniably lovely building. Its location is very special too,
in fertile farmland on the edge of both the Fens and the Brecks. With
turrets and crenellations, intricate brickwork, tall chimneypots and a
surrounding moat, it is pretty much the ideal of the perfect stately home.
The Bedingfelds built the place in 1482, obtaining a charter for a fortified
building from Edward IV, but despite its turrets and crenellations, it
has always served as an ancestral home and never as a castle. As both
Catholics and Royalists in Protestant East Anglia, the Bedingfelds
tended to find themselves caught between two stones: Rome and the
English crown. Their position was precarious, but they managed to
survive and even became prosperous once more during the Restoration.
The hall passed into the hands of the National Trust in 1952.

Just up the road from Oxburgh is the neighbouring village of
Gooderstone with its Gooderstone Water Gardens (✐ 01603 712913
⌀ gooderstonewatergardens.co.uk), with six acres of ponds, waterways
and nature trails connected by footbridges.

FOOD & DRINK

Bedingfeld Arms Oxburgh ✐ 01366 328300 ⌀ bedingfeldarms.co.uk. Originally an estate
coach house, this pub close to the entrance and car park for Oxburgh Hall has a beer garden
for summer drinking and a log fire for cold winter days. The emphasis is on seasonal, locally
sourced food with lamb and venison from nearby Foulden Latimer Estates, and fish from
Coles of King's Lynn. There's also a choice of cask ales and a comprehensive wine list.

THE BRECK–FEN BORDER COUNTRY,
& INTO THE BRECKS PROPER

Continuing due south from Oxburgh you enter a borderland where the
Brecks meets the Fens. Some have gone so far as to describe this as a
coastline, which is not so fanciful when you ponder that not so very long
ago most of the Fens were underwater. It's a marvellous area, explored
by few outsiders, that has all the wide horizons and enormous skies you
might expect. Although it's a long way from the traditional notion of
'hilly', it can almost seem as if you can see halfway across England as
the land dips down west into Fenland and lays out a tapestry of fields

filled with corn, barley and beet. Among a clutch of notable villages here, Northwold is one of the finest.

5 NORTHWOLD

This long linear village comes as an unexpected delight when you first stumble across it after a long, confusing meander south from Oxburgh. With bee-buzzing gardens of hollyhocks and roses lining the road, and walls sporting a diverse array of brick, carrstone, chalk and flint, it's a place that might genuinely fit into the clichéd category of 'best-kept secret'. If this were on the north coast it would be full of holiday homes, with a delicatessen and a stream of motorists passing by. Thankfully, it's refreshingly ungentrified – there's just an active pub and a post office/shop – and the road is mercifully quiet.

There's a lovely church here too. **St Andrew's Church** is best known for its Easter Sepulchre in the chancel, largely made from chalk, which has a relief of Roman soldiers skulking in an olive grove. Being chalk, it's soft and was easily damaged by marauding Puritans who came this way in the mid 17th century; nevertheless, it's easy enough to make out the detail. The hammerbeam roof is likely to draw your eyes upwards before you even reach the chancel as it's painted sky blue, as are the pipes of the organ – the same colour as the bunches of delphiniums that filled the church when I visited. There had just been a flower festival to celebrate 900 years of the Ely diocese and the air was redolent with the cloying scent of lilies. 'That'll be quite a job clearing up that lot,' the cheery churchwarden told me. 'There's a wedding coming up so we'll be getting in some fresh blooms.' They do like their flowers in Northwold.

Methwold, the neighbouring Breck–Fen border village, is quite a bit bigger, almost a small town, and has a church with a steeple that can be seen from afar. Head west from here to Methwold Hythe and then climb up the road south towards Feltwell and you really get off the beaten track with vast views west across the Methwold Dens and south to the giant satellite-tracking 'golf-ball' domes at RAF Feltwell.

6 WAYLAND WOOD & WATTON

Just south of the workaday market town of Watton, **Wayland Wood** is where the nursery tale of Babes in the Wood has its origins, based upon a 16th-century legend in which a pair of orphaned children were taken to the wood to be killed by two men in the pay of a wicked uncle who

ENGLISH WHISKY FROM ST GEORGE'S

St George's Distillery, Harling Rd, Roudham, nr East Harling NR16 2QW 📞 01953 717939
🖰 englishwhisky.co.uk

'English Whisky' might sound almost oxymoronic to some ears, particularly Scottish ones, but in the distant past whisky was widely distilled on both sides of Hadrian's Wall. Although the practice lapsed south of the border a long time ago, St George's Distillery at Roudham near East Harling has turned history on its head by becoming the first place to brew whisky in England for over a century.

The location, a little way east of Thetford on the edge of the Brecks, might at first seem an odd choice, but it does makes sense geographically. Whisky requires two principal ingredients – barley and water – and the first of these is available in profusion in grain-growing south Norfolk. The second ingredient is perhaps less plentiful – this is, after all, one of the driest parts of Great Britain. Fortunately there is a ready supply of pure, clean water available from deep below the ground in an underground aquifer.

At St George's the operation is small enough in scale for both cask-filling and bottling to be done individually by hand. Small-scale or not, since the original distillation back in 2006 nearly 3,000 casks have been produced. The first release, limited to 2,694 bottles, was made in 2009, and several different peated and non-peated bottles have been released since then. In addition to fine single malts, fruit-flavoured liqueurs like Norfolk Bramble, Sloe Liqueur and Norfolk Nog are also made.

Tours (£10) of the distillery are available hourly between 10.00 and 16.00 every day of the week.

lived at Griston Hall. With a twinge of conscience, one of the hired men decided to kill his accomplice instead and, instead of killing them, left the children to their fate in the wood. The legend has it that the brother and sister perished and that they still haunt the wood to this day. Fortunately, the printed version, first published as the ballad *The Norfolk Tragedy* by Thomas Millington in Norwich in 1595, has an altogether happier ending in which the siblings find their way home. The village signs of both Watton and nearby Griston contain representations of the 'babes'.

The wood's name seemingly refers to the 'Babes in the Wood' legend, as Wayland is most likely a corruption of 'wailing'. However, rather than the ghostly moans of abandoned children, you are far more likely to be soothed by the contented buzzing of bees and chirruping of birds. Wayland Wood is in the hands of the Norfolk Wildlife Trust these days and is a gorgeous place in late spring when the bird cherry is in bloom and the ground is carpeted with bluebells and early purple orchids.

This is a real live chunk of rare ancient woodland and the spirit of the wildwood looms large here. Wayland Wood has probably stood since the last ice age; it's a dappled, mysterious place but, unlike some woods that have a slightly dark and foreboding atmosphere, this one feels light and benevolent. Nevertheless, there used to be a large oak tree here, struck by lightning in 1879, that was rumoured to have been the place where the abandoned children died. The wood is far from completely wild but has been carefully managed since time immemorial to yield hazel rods

SOME HISTORY

As a strategic crossing point where the Icknield Way crosses the Little Ouse River, Thetford takes its name from the Anglo-Saxon *Theod* ford – people's ford. Whether or not it was the royal seat of Boudica, the Iceni queen, is highly uncertain but it was certainly an important centre during the late Iron Age and early Roman period. In Anglo-Saxon times, when it was sacked on several occasions by invading Danes, Thetford became the home of the East Anglian monarchs and seat of a bishopric. A more peaceful Dane, Canute, made the town his capital too in 1015, half a century before the Norman Conquest, when Bishop Herbert de Losinga's building of a cathedral in Norwich brought about a slight downsizing of what had become the sixth largest city in England. Despite the religious focus being transferred to Norwich, a Cluniac priory was established here in the 12th century that lasted until the Reformation.

Like much of the Brecks, Thetford saw a decline in its fortunes in the medieval period when the bulk of the wool trade shifted to north Norfolk where there was better land and closer ports. The town came back into favour in the 1960s when an influx of people from London moved here to work in the newly opened factories. These days, Thetford has a surprisingly large Portuguese population, estimated to constitute around 30% of the town's total. There has been a slow trickle of foreign workers here since the late 1990s when Portuguese migrants started to come to the town to take up low-paid jobs in the agricultural sector. An unpleasant incident occurred in 2004 following the England versus Portugal football match in which England were defeated and between 100 and 200 drunken England fans rioted and hurled missiles at the town's Portuguese-run Red Lion pub, trapping terrified Portugal supporters inside. Generally though, relations are far more cordial and many Portuguese have chosen to settle here long-term, hence the number of Portuguese-language signs on shops, cafés and even hairdressers. It is a similar situation in King's Lynn, Great Yarmouth and, to a lesser extent, East Dereham. Polish is another language you will hear widely spoken around town and keen linguists might detect Russian, Lithuanian and Spanish too.

by coppicing. Indeed, it is the long-term practice of coppicing that has enabled such wonderful ground flora to thrive.

As well as Griston Hall, where the wicked uncle is said to have resided, the nearby village of **Griston** is home to Wayland Prison, a category-C establishment that has included Jeffrey Archer and Reggie Kray among its inmates, although not at the same time.

Watton was host to a large RAF base for many years, which both stimulated the local economy and created a distinct atmosphere in the town. These days it seems somewhat gloomy and the constant parade of thundering goods lorries along the High Street make the town a little hard to love. Nevertheless, its traffic-ravaged main thoroughfare is home to a really good second-hand bookshop – J C Books (✆ 01953 883488) at number 55 – and the friendliest of cafés – Adem's (✆ 01953 884838) at number 37. The town's most prominent 17th-century clock tower, also on the High Street, was put up in 1679 to house a fire warning bell (there had been a serious fire here a few years earlier). The lower part of the clock tower was also once used as a lock-up for prisoners, which gives new meaning to the expression 'doing time'. The Wednesday market has been taking place in the same spot since the 13th century.

THETFORD

Raced past by motorists on their way up the A11 to Norwich and the coast, and frequently dismissed as a 'London overspill town', Thetford tends to get overlooked. Like King's Lynn and Great Yarmouth, it can seem a bit run down compared with the rest of the county and, true, it does have some large and unlovely housing and industrial estates that were built for an influx of workers from the south in the 1960s. This is just part of the picture though. Thetford was hugely important before the Norman invasion and even held the bishopric of East Anglia before Norwich did. In historical terms, Norwich is still the young pretender. Ignore the lacklustre outskirts and head straight to the centre and you will find some lovely medieval architecture and absorbing history.

Beyond the humdrum shopping precinct just across the river from Thetford Grammar School, the town centre has a good assortment of medieval and Georgian buildings in timber and flint. The best of these is the **Ancient House**, now the Museum of Thetford Life (✆ 01842 752599), in White Hart Street, a 15th-century timber-framed building that is also the base for the town's **tourist information centre**.

As well as exhibitions on Thomas Paine and Maharajah Duleep Singh, the museum has 4th-century gold and silver jewellery from the so-called Thetford Treasure hoard discovered in 1979: an object lesson to those who think that putting in long hours with a metal detector is inevitably a waste of time.

The stonework of the town's Norman **castle** is long gone but the motte remains to provide a satisfying mound to climb up and get a view over the town. There is rather more to see at the site of the **Cluniac priory** west of the centre by the river. This was founded in 1103–04 by Richard Bigod to become one of the largest and richest priories in East Anglia. The priory was torn down after the Dissolution but there are still some impressive flinty remains and even bits of original tile flooring in places. The towering remains of the arch of the massive Presbytery window are particularly striking.

Nearby, **Thetford Grammar School** dates back to Saxon times, was re-founded in 1566 and is still active today. Its most famous ex-pupil is **Thomas Paine** (1737–1809), who had the distinction of being involved in both the French Revolution (where he only escaped execution by a whisker) and the American War of Independence; he was one of the original signatories to the Declaration of Independence and invented the term 'United States of America'. Born in the town, he attended the school between 1744 and 1749 before going on to be apprenticed to his father as a corset maker. The part of the school that Paine would have attended serves as the school library today and, although you cannot enter, you can get a look at this through its wrought-iron gate on Bridge Street.

Paine's gilt **statue** by Sir Charles Wheeler, President of the Royal Academy, stands outside the King's House, with the radical thinker clutching a copy of his revolutionary book *Rights of Man* upside down. Why he holds the book upside down is open to some speculation, although it is generally believed that Wheeler did this as a means of stimulating debate. The statue was erected by an American benefactor, Joseph Lewis, who was shocked to discover that the birthplace of one of the great supporters of American independence did not have a monument to his memory. Naturally, there was some controversy regarding the erection of the statue as Paine was a freethinker and deeply republican. To their credit though, most natives of Thetford have since taken Paine to their hearts and seem happy to celebrate their connection with this extraordinary man. The statue, which may

THOMAS PAINE:
CORSET MAKER & REVOLUTIONARY

My country is the world, my religion is to do good.
Rights of Man

Chad Goodwin of the Thomas Paine Society, a font of knowledge regarding all things relating to the man, led walking tours of Paine's Thetford during the bicentennial celebrations of 2009. Standing by the statue in front of the Town Council building, he filled us in on details of his early life before we moved around the corner to White Hart Street where the Ancient House is. 'This used to be the main London to Norwich road and anyone and everyone who came through Thetford would pass this way. Thetford assizes used to be held here each year and this was the next best thing to a public holiday, with all sorts of entertainment going on and, naturally, public hangings. They used to hang somebody for simply stealing a sheep in those days and it was probably partly from seeing the goings on here that Paine started to develop his social conscience and sense of injustice. Thetford was a classic rotten borough and I am sure that later on when Paine wrote about the corruption of the political class he was probably thinking of Thetford. Reading between the lines, I get the impression that he couldn't wait to leave.'

We walked uphill to the Thomas Paine Hotel, where a plaque commemorates Paine. 'This used to be a private residence known as Grey Gables. There are those who think that it is where Paine was born but there's nothing certain about this. It could have been here, or perhaps it was a place called the Wilderness next to St Andrew's Church. Unfortunately, there is no record of his birth at all.' Paine spent just a fraction of his early life in Thetford, and returned to the town only on rare occasions to see his mother once he moved south. 'It's worth noting that Paine left Thetford with its River Ouse, Cluniac monastery and round-tower church to go and settle in Lewes in Sussex, which coincidentally also has a River Ouse, a Cluniac monastery and a round-tower church. You could say this was just coincidence but Paine must have felt quite at home there.'

After receiving an invitation from Benjamin Franklin, Paine crossed the sea to America but he was rarely still for long, frequently flitting across the Channel to France and even crossing the Atlantic a total of five times in his lifetime. He died and was buried at New Rochelle in New York State in 1809. One of his former adversaries, William Cobbett, who had been gradually converted, partially at least, to Paine's cause, turned up ten years later to dig up his bones and bring them back to Britain for a heroic burial that never happened. 'Cobbett carried the bones around with him when he was fighting a by-election at Coventry. This may not have been considered bizarre in those days, but it was certainly unusual.' By all accounts, Cobbett kept Paine's mortal remains in a box underneath his bed but following his death they disappeared completely, never to be found again.

not be to everyone's taste, stands on a plinth that bears the legend: *World Citizen – Englishman by Birth, French Citizen by Decree, American by Adoption*. Tourist information at the Ancient House can give details of a **Tom Paine Trail** through the town and the occasional guided tours.

Tom Paine aside, Thetford's other associations include the TV series *Dad's Army*, much of which was recorded in and around the town. A **Dad's Army tourist trail** highlights spots that became the fictitious Sussex town of Walmington-on-Sea. In 2010 the Thetford Society erected a bronze statue of Captain Mainwaring (the Arthur Lowe character) seated on a bench next to the River Ouse by the bus station. There's a Dad's Army museum (✆ 07562 688641 🖉 dadsarmythetford.org.uk) at the back of the Guildhall on Cage Lane, and you can see Jones's butcher's van from the series at the nearby **Charles Burrell Museum** (✆ 01842 751166 🖉 thecharlesburrellmuseum.com) on Minstergate.

Nearby, and reached by means of a footbridge, **Maharajah Duleep Singh**, the former squire of the nearby Elveden Estate a little further down the A11 in Suffolk, has a very fine equestrian statue set among the shady willows of **Butten Island** in the midst of the Little Ouse River. This is a popular pilgrimage place for Sikhs from all over Britain and beyond and you may well find yourself becoming involved in a friendly photo session here. The town's three statues – 18th-century revolutionary pamphleteer, 19th-century Anglophile maharajah and 20th-century pompous sitcom character – make for a strange juxtaposition: one wonders what the characters would have made of each other.

A Little Ouse walk

Outside the town, some good **walks** are to be had around Thetford. The most obvious route is along the **Little Ouse Path** that links Thetford with Brandon, most of which follows an old towpath. It's about ten miles of easy walking in total and if you are up to this you could walk all the way then catch a bus or train back from Brandon. A slightly shorter, circular option is to walk west and north along the Little Ouse from Thetford, past a tempting picnic spot at Abbey Heath Weir, and through waterside woodland as far as a large factory. Soon after a footbridge over the river you can zigzag south through forest until you reach a waymarked path to the left, leading you back to the river and a footbridge at Abbey Heath Weir from where you can retrace your steps to Thetford.

Even if you walk just a short distance along the river path past the abbey ruins you get a sense of being in open countryside despite the proximity of the town's council estates. A group of otters caused quite a stir down here in 2013 when they displayed themselves freely to visitors and even posed for photographs in a most un-otter-like way.

FOOD & DRINK

Bell Hotel King St ✆ 01842 754455. This 15th-century inn, right in the heart of town, was where the *Dad's Army* cast and crew used to stay. The hotel, now part of a national chain, tends to make the most of this association as well as its reputation for being haunted but serves decent enough pub food and Greene King ales.

The Mulberry 11 Raymond St ✆ 01842 824122 🔗 mulberrythetford.co.uk. A cut – actually, several cuts – above all of the town's other dining options, this tastefully decorated restaurant offers a sumptuous Mediterranean and English menu that makes excellent use of locally sourced ingredients.

Tall Orders 22–24 King St. This conveniently located café in the town centre has seating on several levels including tables outside – a decent enough choice for coffee, cakes, breakfasts and sandwiches.

BRANDON (SUFFOLK)

Just over the border into Suffolk, and west of Thetford on the southern bank of the Little Ouse, is Brandon. If the presence of nearby Grimes Graves is not enough to attest that the town was once central to an important **flint industry**, then just take a look at the buildings. The flint trade was big business here as far back as the Neolithic period and returned to prominence with the invention of the musket and the need for gun flints. It is interesting to reflect that, given the area's USAF and RAF bases, the war industry has long played a part in the region.

Brandon's flintknappers had their work cut out back in Napoleonic times when the town grew quite prosperous through supplying the

"The flint trade was big business here as far back as the Neolithic period."

essential parts for the British Army's muzzle-loaders. Virtually all the shots fired at Waterloo would have involved Brandon flint to spark them off. The invention of the percussion cap saw the demise of this trade but, according to John Seymour, flintknappers were still active in the town in the 1960s, when he witnessed men in leather aprons chipping away in the back yard of the Flintknappers Arms pub – where else indeed?

BRANDON'S BREWS

Not to be outdone by the **Iceni Brewery** (☎ 01842 878922; tours available by appointment) just up the road at Ickburgh, there's a brewery in Brandon too – **The Brandon Brewery** (☎ 07876 234689 🖱 brandonbrewery.com) – where you can sample the produce.

What's more, the brewery is doing its bit for the environment in providing a herd of Breckland highland cattle with spent malted barley for an occasional special treat. It is widely repeated that the cattle, which it would seem are far more conservation-conscious grazers than sheep, are very fond of the grain – who can blame them? – and can always be tempted back from wild, overgrown areas with generous helpings of the stuff.

You can get a good idea of the town's flintknapping past by visiting the **Brandon Heritage Centre** (☎ 07882 891022 brandonheritage.org.uk) in George Street.

The Little Ouse River used to be of far more importance here back in the days when Brandon served as the port for nearby Thetford. These days, forestry rules supreme and it is articulated lorries and the A11, not boats and water, that privide the means of transportation amd distribution for Brandon's produce.

Brandon Country Park, a mile or so south of the town, has forest walks, a tree and history trail, an orienteering course and a visitor centre (☎ 01842 810185 🖱 brandoncountrypark.org.uk). About the same distance to the east, along the B1107 to Thetford, is the **Thetford Forest and High Lodge Forest Centre** (☎ 01842 815434 🖱 forestry.gov.uk/highlodge), which offers free entrance to cyclists and walkers arriving without a car. Four waymarked walks of varying length explore the forest area from the visitor centre, and the four cycling routes include a family route as well as more challenging mountain-bike rides. **Cycle hire** is available from Bike Art (page 232). The centre also organises special summer events such as dusk nightjar rambles and moth expeditions.

9 WEETING

Weeting is a village just north of Brandon back over the Norfolk border. A Norfolk Wildlife Trust **nature reserve** here, just west of the village, is home to a summer population of **stone curlews**, which might be described as the signature bird of the Brecks – a stocky wader that doesn't wade, with thick strong legs and a large, yellow gimlet eye. It looks the kind of exotic thing that you might expect to come across on parched African plains and, indeed, the Senegal thicknee is a very close relation. The Brecks are, after all, the closest thing we have to African savanna, and birds like stone curlews just emphasise this exoticism. The NWT reserve has a visitor centre (℘ 01842 827615) and hides with wheelchair access open between April and September, the breeding season of the stone curlew. You might also see woodlarks here, another Breckland speciality, as well as wheatears, hobbies and plenty of butterflies. Interestingly rabbits, often vilified for the damage they do to crops, are actually encouraged here to keep the heathland habitat in check and accordingly are fenced in. The prisoners seem content enough – more *Watership Down* than *Colditz*.

The village itself has a round tower church, **St Mary's**, alongside an evocatively ruined **Norman castle**. It is also home to what is considered to be the longest terrace of **thatched-roof cottages** in England – I counted eight chimney pots in total. Unfortunately, many of the roofs were damaged in a fire in 2007 but they seem to have been neatly repaired to their former reedy glory now. The castle, owned by English Heritage and with free access, is not, in fact, a castle at all but a 12th-century fortified **manor house** with a 14th-century moat. On one corner of the moat stands a domed ice-house, previously used to store ice broken from the frozen moat in winter.

▶ GRIME'S GRAVES
Near Lynford IP26 5DE ℘ 01842 810656 ○ Apr–end Sep 10.00–18.00 daily; English Heritage

Grime's Graves can be found a little way east of Weeting, just off the Mundford road. If the Peddars Way can be described as being a Roman period M1, then Grime's Graves might be seen as being the equivalent of a Neolithic Sheffield. The 'graves' referred to are actually mine shafts and they belong not to Grime but to Grim, a pagan god. Anglo-Saxons probably knew the site as 'the Devil's holes' because any earlier human working of the landscape was usually viewed to be the work of dark forces.

The product here was that Neolithic equivalent of steel – **flint** – the hard, sharp-edge fracturing stone that litters the fields around here. The site consists of a large complex of flint mineshafts that were worked for at least a millennium from around 3000BC – and probably for much longer, as flint was always inexpensive by comparison with metal. Even after hand axes had long disappeared from the craftsman's and farmer's toolkit, they were still in demand for building and later for the firing mechanism for muskets (page 249).

The complex is certainly impressive on the ground but aerial photographs give an even more compelling view of this dimpled landscape of over 400 filled-in shafts covering an area of over 90 acres. Thirty or so pits have been excavated to date and you can actually go down one of them, the only place in the country where you can do this. By descending the ladder and peering into the extremely low-roofed galleries you really get a feel for what life must have been like working on the Neolithic flint-face. Bear in mind that Neolithic miners had only red-deer antlers available for picks. Excavation has revealed that, for each pit examined to date, an average of 142 antler picks has been found. Interestingly, about 10% of these were left-handed. A herd of at least a hundred red deer would have been necessary to provide an adequate supply of antlers for excavation.

11 THE BRECKLAND HEATHS

Just north of Thetford is the vast expanse of heathland occupied by the **Stanford Military Training Area** marked on OS maps somewhat alarmingly as 'Danger Area'. For obvious reasons, you are not allowed to go here, although limited access is permitted for walkers passing through on the Peddars Way that runs across its eastern edge. It is a shame in a way because, apart from the odd tank and artillery unit, this is mostly unspoiled heathland with all its usual attendant wildlife. Naturally, the very fact that the public are not permitted to trample across the area means that it is pretty good for wildlife anyway, at least those species that are able to tolerate the odd exploding shell and spurt of mortar fire.

In my capacity as a surveyor of historic farm buildings 30 years or so ago, I did manage to visit the area once with a military escort. There used to be a number of farms dotting the area and we were interested in taking a look. Unfortunately, the army had used most of the buildings for target practice and so there wasn't very much to see, but it was good at least to witness what a wild and unspoiled area this was. The area continues to be used for military training of all sorts and in recent years a facsimile Afghan village has been constructed for training purposes.

This comes complete with flat-roofed adobe houses, a mosque and a street market. The roles of Afghan villagers, friend and foe alike, are played by injured Gurkhas. How much useful preparation this gives for subsequent operations in Helmand Province is uncertain. As civilians, we will never get to know just how authentic this faux Afghan enclave is but it's certainly a surreal notion to think that the equivalent of a Taliban theme park lies hidden out here in the Brecks.

With all this talk of where you cannot go, it is important to identify where you can. A couple of places on the fringes of the battle area give an authentic flavour of true Breckland heath. **East Wretham Heath,** off the A1075 and belonging to the Norfolk Wildlife Trust, has old pine woodland and grass heathland on what used to be an airfield. It also has a couple of meres (small lakes) that fluctuate depending on groundwater levels and recent rainfall. **Brettenham Heath**, nearby, has acid heath but no public access although you can view it from the Peddars Way. Of more interest to most and a great place for walking is **Thompson Common** on the eastern fringe of the battle area.

This NWT wetland area is best known for its three hundred or so pingo ponds that were created during the last glacial period. Pingos are mounds of earth-covered ice that collapse to form shallow depressions when the ice eventually melts. The pingo ponds, which provide habitat for rare water plants, dragonflies and damselflies, were formed here around 10,000 years ago. At least, that is the theory: I know of one geologist who maintains that they are more probably the result of ordnance testing on the battle area. For walkers, the **Great Eastern Pingo Trail** is a circular route that follows the route of a disused railway as well as part of the Peddars Way. It runs for around eight miles in total, taking in both Thompson and Stow Bedon commons and heathland at Great Hockham and Breckles. With

"These ponds provide habitat for dragonflies, and were formed around 10,000 years ago."

luck, you'll see roe deer in the woodland rides. The route also passes through wet woodland at Cranberry Rough, which was once a large lake, the product of retreating glaciers of the last ice age. The former lake, known as Hockham Mere, was an important source of fish and wildfowl as recently as Tudor times but it eventually silted up to create the large swampy area that remains today. Now it is a designated Site of Special Scientific Interest with many species of plant, bird and insect –

TURNING THE STONE AT GREAT HOCKHAM

Lying just east of the A1075, close to the expanse of Breckland heaths north of Thetford, is Great Hockham, a pleasant village with little to recommend it other than the unusual stone that has pride of place on its village green. The large sandstone boulder, an erratic mass from the Lower Cretaceous that was deposited in the Brecks during the last glacial period, was actually discovered in a pit close to the village in the 1800s before it was transported to its current resting place.

It soon became village practice to turn the stone over on special occasions – no mean feat given its bulk and weight, an estimated 3 or 4 tons. The first recorded turning was to celebrate Queen Victoria's Golden Jubilee in 1887. In more recent times it was turned over for the Queen Elizabeth's Silver Jubilee in 1977, and again in 1995 to celebrate the half-century anniversary of the end of World War II. The millennium was another occasion that was celebrated appropriately with some community heavy lifting, as was the Queen's Golden Jubilee in 2002 and Diamond Jubilee in 2012. The stone has been turned to celebrate more local events too: in 2008 it was turned to celebrate the saving of nearby Holkham Woods from quarrying.

there are certainly plenty of mosquitoes here in summer. Access to the trail is from a car park on the A1075 Watton to Great Hockham road. There's a shorter alternative route too that cuts through woodland at Stow Heath and a short 'access for all' trail from the car park. The Peddars Way stretch of the trail goes right past **Thompson Water**, a shallow manmade lake created by damming the River Wissey in the 19th century, which is an excellent place to see grebes and reed warblers in summer and wildfowl in winter. As it's the only sizeable piece of water for miles around, even ospreys sometimes turn up here on passage.

FOOD & DRINK

Chequers Inn Griston Rd, Thompson ✆ 01953 483360 ⌂ thompsonchequers.co.uk. This attractive 17th-century thatched inn opposite the village cricket pitch has seen service as a manor court, doctor's surgery and meeting room in the past. Today it's a village pub convenient for the Great Eastern Pingo Trail. There's decent pub grub and a reasonable range of real ales.

NORFOLK ONLINE

For additional online content, articles, photos and more on Norfolk, why not visit ⌂ bradtguides.com/norfolk.

ACCOMMODATION

The places to stay listed below have been selected for their location and because they embrace the Slow mindset, either in terms of their overall feel or because they embody a 'green' approach. Prices for hotels vary, but two people sharing a room in a B&B can expect to spend around £70–90 per night. Holiday cottage prices also cover a wide range, depending on capacity, season and location. Of course, school holidays mean peak prices. There is plenty to be said for visiting out of season in order to save money. Campsites run the gamut from no-frills to luxurious 'glamping' options.

The hotels, B&Bs and self-catering options featured in this section are indicated by 🏠 under the heading for the town or village in which they are located. Campsites are indicated by ⛺. For complete listings, go to ⊘ bradtguides.com/norfolksleeps.

1 THE NORTH NORFOLK COAST

Hotels
Gunton Arms Cromer Rd, Thorpe Market NR11 8TZ ✆ 01263 832101 ⊘ theguntonarms.co.uk
Titchwell Manor Titchwell, near Brancaster PE31 8BB ✆ 01485 472027 ⊘ titchwellmanor.com
The White Horse Brancaster Staithe PE31 8BY ✆ 01485 210262 ⊘ whitehorsebrancaster.co.uk

B&Bs
Cley Windmill The Quay, Cley-next-the-Sea NR25 7RP ✆ 01263 740209 ⊘ cleywindmill.co.uk. Self-catering is also available in the converted stable building.
The Merchant's House 47 Freeman St, Wells-next-the-Sea NR23 1BQ ✆ 01328 711877 ⊘ the-merchants-house.co.uk
Pirate House 16 Priory Rd, Sheringham NR26 8EW ✆ 01263 825943 ⊘ piratehousebandb.co.uk

Self-catering (see box opposite for websites)
Albert's Cottage Wells-next-the-Sea
Bagthorpe Treehouse Bagthorpe Hall near Burnham Market ✆ 0117 2047830 ⊘ canopyandstars.co.uk
Little Orchard Cley-next-the-Sea
The Maltings Brancaster Staithe
The Music Room Thornham
Rhu Sila Church Lane, Cley-next-the-Sea ✆ 01263 740304 ⊘ cleyannexeblog.wordpress.com
Sea View Barn Titchwell

Campsites
Deepdale Backpackers & Camping Deepdale Farm, Burnham Deepdale PE31 8DD ✆ 01485 210256 ⊘ deepdalebackpackers.co.uk. See also pages 54–5.

Kelling Heath Holiday Park Weybourne, Holt NR25 7HW ✆ 01263 588181 🖰 kellingheath.co.uk

Scaldbeck Cottage Stiffkey Rd, Morston NR25 7BJ ✆ 01263 740188

Wild Luxury ✆ 01485 750850 🖰 wildluxury.co.uk

THE NORTHEAST NORFOLK COAST & THE BROADS

Hotel

Norfolk Mead Hotel Coltishall NR12 7DJ ✆ 01603 737531 🖰 norfolkmead.co.uk

B&B

The Green House Cromer Rd, Thorpe Market ✆ 01263 834701 🖰 greenhousenorfolk.co.uk

Campsite

Clippesby Hall Touring and Camping Park Clippesby NR29 3BL ✆ 01493 367800 🖰 clippesbyhall.com

NORTH CENTRAL NORFOLK

Hotel

Greenbanks Main Rd, Great Fransham NR19 2DA ✆ 01362 687742 🖰 greenbankshotel.co.uk

B&Bs

Byfords Posh B&B 1–3 Shirehall Plain, Holt NR25 6BG ✆ 01263 711400 🖰 byfords.org.uk/posh-bb

Carrick's at Castle Farm Swanton Morley, Dereham NR20 4JT ✆ 01362 638302 🖰 carricksatcastlefarm.co.uk

White Horse Farm Sharrington Rd, Holt NR24 2PB ✆ 01263 860693 🖰 white-horse-farm.co.uk

Self-catering (see box below for websites)

The Fox Hat South Creake

Garden Cottage Manor House Farm, Wellingham, King's Lynn PE32 2TH ✆ 01328 838348 🖰 manor-house-farm.co.uk

The Gamekeeper's Hut Westfield Fram, Foxley Rd, Foulsham NR20 5RH ✆ 01275 395447 🖰 canopyandstars.co.uk

4 NORTHWEST NORFOLK & THE WASH

Hotels

Congham Hall Hotel Lynn Rd, Grimston PE32 1AH ✆ 01485 600250 🖰 conghamhallhotel.co.uk

The Lodge Old Hunstanton Rd, Old Hunstanton PE36 6HX ✆ 01485 532896 🖰 thelodgehunstanton.co.uk

SELF-CATERING

Norfolk Bed and Breakfasts 🖰 norfolk-bed-and-breakfast.co.uk. More than 250 properties that can be searched for online according to location and facilities.

Self-catering

All of the self-catering accommodation listed in this appendix may be booked through one or more of the companies listed below.

Glaven Valley 🖰 glavenvalley.co.uk. Company with a large range of cottages in north Norfolk.

Heritage Hideaways ✆ 01502 322405 🖰 heritagehideaways.com. A number of options. Also covers Suffolk.

Norfolk Country Cottages ✆ 01263 715779 🖰 norfolkcottages.co.uk. Hundreds of Norfolk cottages.

Norfolk Hideaways ✆ 01485 558547 🖰 norfolkhideaways.co.uk. Over 300 coastal cottages to rent.

Sowerby's Holiday Cottages ✆ 01328 730880 🖰 sowerbysholidaycottages.co.uk. A large selection in north Norfolk.

Rose and Crown Old Church Rd, Snettisham PE31 7LX ✆ 01485 543172 ⏱ roseandcrownsnettisham. co.uk

Self-catering (see box, page 257, for websites)
The Summerhouse Heacham

5 NORWICH & THE YARE VALLEY

B&B
38 St Giles St Giles St, Norwich NR2 1LL ✆ 01603 662944 ⏱ 38stgiles.co.uk

6 THE WAVENEY VALLEY

Campsite
Waveney River Centre Burgh St Peter NR34 0BT ✆ 01502 677343 ⏱ waveneyrivercentre.co.uk

7 THE BRECKS

Hotel
Strattons Hotel 4 Ash Close, Swaffham PE37 7NH ✆ 01760 723845 ⏱ strattonshotel.com

FEEDBACK REQUEST & UPDATES WEBSITE

There are only so many special places and aspects of Norfolk life that you can focus on when limited by word counts and book length. Much as we'd like to include them all, it simply isn't possible. We've done our best to include a good mix and to check facts but there are bound to be errors (phone numbers and websites change with alarming frequency) as well as inevitable omissions of really special places. You can post your comments and recommendations, and read the latest feedback from other readers online at ⌀ bradtupdates.com/norfolk. Alternatively, email us at ✉ info@bradtguides.com.

INDEX

Page numbers in **bold** refer to main entries; *italics* refer to walk maps.

INDEX OF ADVERTISERS